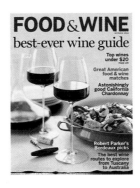

FOOD & WINE

an entire year of recipes

FOOD & WINE ANNUAL COOKBOOK 2007

EDITOR **Kate Heddings**
ART DIRECTOR **Patricia Sanchez**
DESIGNER **Nancy Blumberg**
SENIOR EDITOR **Andrea Glick**
ASSISTANT FOOD EDITOR **Melissa Rubel**
COPY EDITOR **Kathy Antrim**
EDITORIAL ASSISTANT **Melissa Denchak**
PRODUCTION **Carl Hesler**
PHOTO COORDINATOR **Lisa S. Kim**

SENIOR VICE PRESIDENT, CHIEF MARKETING OFFICER **Mark V. Stanich**
VICE PRESIDENT, BOOKS AND PRODUCTS **Marshall Corey**
SENIOR MARKETING MANAGER **Bruce Spanier**
ASSISTANT MARKETING MANAGER **Sarah H. Ross**
CORPORATE PRODUCTION MANAGER **Stuart Handelman**
DIRECTOR OF FULFILLMENT AND PREMIUM VALUE **Phil Black**
ASSISTANT FULFILLMENT AND OPERATIONS MANAGER **Rene O'Connell**
BUSINESS MANAGER **Tom Noonan**
BUSINESS ANALYST **Angela Fong**

FRONT COVER

Braised Chicken Legs with Green Olives, p. 95
PHOTOGRAPH BY Tina Rupp
FOOD STYLING BY Jee Levin

BACK COVER

PHOTOGRAPHS (BURGER, PAPPARDELLE) BY Tina Rupp
FOOD STYLING (BURGER, PAPPARDELLE) BY Jee Levin
PHOTOGRAPH (SWEET POTATO TART) BY Anna Williams
FOOD STYLING (SWEET POTATO TART) BY Alison Attenborough

FLAP PHOTOGRAPHS

DANA COWIN PORTRAIT BY Andrew French
KATE HEDDINGS PORTRAIT BY Andrew French

AMERICAN EXPRESS PUBLISHING CORPORATION

ISBN 1-932624-18-X
ISSN 1097-1564

Published by American Express Publishing Corporation
1120 Avenue of the Americas, New York, New York 10036

Manufactured in the United States of America

FOOD & WINE MAGAZINE

VICE PRESIDENT/EDITOR IN CHIEF **Dana Cowin**
CREATIVE DIRECTOR **Stephen Scoble**
MANAGING EDITOR **Mary Ellen Ward**
EXECUTIVE EDITOR **Pamela Kaufman**
EXECUTIVE FOOD EDITOR **Tina Ujlaki**
EXECUTIVE WINE EDITOR **Lettie Teague**

FEATURES

FEATURES EDITOR **Michelle Shih**
TRAVEL EDITOR **Salma Abdelnour**
SENIOR EDITORS **Ray Isle, Kate Krader**
ASSISTANT EDITORS **Jen Murphy, Ratha Tep**
ASSISTANT HOME & STYLE EDITOR **Dani Fisher**
EDITORIAL ASSISTANTS **Megan Krigbaum, Jessica Tzerman**

FOOD

SENIOR EDITOR **Kate Heddings**
SENIOR ASSOCIATE EDITOR **Nick Fauchald**
TEST KITCHEN SUPERVISOR **Marcia Kiesel**
SENIOR TEST KITCHEN ASSOCIATE **Grace Parisi**
TEST KITCHEN ASSOCIATE **Melissa Rubel**
EDITORIAL ASSISTANT **Kristin Donnelly**
KITCHEN ASSISTANT **Natalya Buleyev**

ART

ART DIRECTOR **Patricia Sanchez**
SENIOR DESIGNER **Courtney Waddell**
DESIGNER **Michael Patti**
DESIGNER (BOOKS) **Nancy Blumberg**

PHOTO

DIRECTOR OF PHOTOGRAPHY **Fredrika Stjärne**
DEPUTY PHOTO EDITOR **Lucy Schaeffer**
ASSISTANT PHOTO EDITOR **Lisa S. Kim**
PHOTO ASSISTANT **Molly Ryder**

PRODUCTION

ASSISTANT MANAGING EDITOR **Christine Quinlan**
PRODUCTION MANAGER **Matt Carson**
DESIGN/PRODUCTION ASSISTANT **Carl Hesler**

COPY & RESEARCH

COPY EDITOR **Ann Lien**
RESEARCH EDITOR **Stacey Nield**
ASSISTANT RESEARCH EDITORS **Kelly Snowden, Emery Van Hook**

EDITORIAL BUSINESS ASSISTANT **Kalina Mazur**

FOOD & WINE

an entire year of recipes
2007

American Express Publishing Corporation, New York

FOOD & WINE
BOOKS

American actress Jeri Ryan and her French fiancé, chef Christophe Emé, prepare roasted red pepper sandwiches (p. 294) and a corn salad (p. 50).

contents

Miami chef Michelle Bernstein at a floating party on Biscayne Bay.

foreword

At FOOD & WINE we're committed to one-upping ourselves every year. In 2006, we published a record-breaking 700 recipes, both in the magazine and on our Web site, foodandwine.com. As always, these dishes represent the newest ideas from the world's most outstanding cooks, all meticulously perfected by our diligent test kitchen staff.

A highlight of 2006 was the debut of two innovative columns in the magazine. For "Chef Recipes Made Easy," our test kitchen transforms a chef's brilliant, often complex creations into accessible, delicious dishes any home cook can make. For instance, the 20-ingredient meatballs that Andrew Carmellini serves at his New York City restaurant, A Voce, morphed into a simple Pork Meat Loaf with Chickpeas (p. 170), an incredible recipe that requires only a half an hour of hands-on prep. Our other new column, "Tasting & Testing," also showcases our test kitchen's talents, as Grace Parisi, F&W's senior test kitchen associate, shares her favorite riffs on iconic dishes like roast turkey and glazed ham.

One of the major food trends of '06 was the rise of the celebrity pastry chef with his or her own dessert restaurant. The result for F&W: pages and pages of imaginative sweets like Kate Neumann's Nutty Toffee-Date Cake (p. 351), spiced with cinnamon and ginger and topped with a gooey toffee sauce. Karen Hatfield's Devil's Food Cupcakes with Espresso Meringue (p. 345) were also fabulous—rich and chocolaty, with a delightfully fluffy topping.

At FOOD & WINE we're well aware that great dishes can taste even better when they're accompanied by terrific wines. That's why you'll see wine pairings throughout the book, plus a wonderful glossary that clearly explains what makes each wine distinctive and names the best and easiest-to-find labels.

We hope you enjoy this bigger-than-ever compendium of a year's worth of recipes from FOOD & WINE.

Dana Cowin
Editor in Chief
FOOD & WINE Magazine

Kate Heddings
Editor
FOOD & WINE Cookbooks

MINI ROASTED TOMATO TATINS (P. 18)

starters

"Artisanal cheesemakers combine science with art. All over the world, without scientific instruments, people make cheeses the way their grandparents did."

–Ricki Carroll, artisanal cheesemaker, Ashfield, Massachusetts

MARINATED GOAT CHEESE, OLIVES, ARTICHOKES AND TOMATOES

GOAT CHEESE—STUFFED ROASTED FIGS

Marinated Goat Cheese, Olives, Artichokes and Tomatoes

TOTAL: 30 MIN PLUS 24 HR MARINATING
12 SERVINGS ● ●

Chef and co-owner Christophe Emé of Ortolan in Los Angeles spices up goat cheese with fresh herbs and the piquant ground red pepper *piment d'Espelette,* then forms it into balls. He likes to serve them in a spectacular way, by packing them with olive oil, artichokes, olives and tomatoes in a giant jar that he sets on the table with a big spoon for scooping.

½ **cup pine nuts**
1½ **pounds fresh goat cheese, softened**
2 **teaspoons chopped rosemary**
2 **teaspoons chopped thyme**
½ **teaspoon *piment d'Espelette* pepper (see Note) or hot paprika**
Salt
1 **quart extra-virgin olive oil**
20 **cooked baby artichoke hearts, from the deli counter**
1 **cup red cherry tomatoes or grape tomatoes**
1 **cup Niçoise olives**
Toasted baguette slices, for serving

1. Preheat the oven to 350°. Spread the pine nuts in a pie plate; bake for 10 minutes, or until fragrant and lightly toasted. Transfer to a plate and let cool.

2. In a standing mixer, using the paddle, blend the cheese with the pine nuts, rosemary, thyme and pepper. Season with salt. Shape rounded tablespoons of the cheese into balls.

3. Pour 1 inch of oil into a tall 1-gallon glass container. Layer the cheese, artichoke hearts, tomatoes and olives in the container with olive oil to cover. Let marinate at room temperature for 24 hours. Serve with the toasted baguette slices.
—*Christophe Emé*

NOTE The mildly spicy *piment d'Espelette* from France's Pays Basque region is available from L'Epicerie (866-350-7575) or lepicerie.com.

MAKE AHEAD The recipe can be assembled, minus the tomatoes, and refrigerated for up to 3 days. Add the tomatoes shortly before serving.

Goat Cheese—Stuffed Roasted Figs

ACTIVE: 20 MIN; TOTAL: 30 MIN
MAKES 12 FIGS ● ●

12 **figs**
¼ **cup fresh goat cheese, softened**
Warmed honey, for drizzling

Preheat the oven to 425°. Quarter the figs, cutting three-quarters of the way down. Stuff the figs with goat cheese. Roast in an oiled pan at for 12 minutes, until softened. Serve drizzled with warmed honey.
—*Marco Pasanella*

Chickpea Panelle with Goat Cheese and Salsa Rustica

ACTIVE: 1 HR; TOTAL: 1 HR PLUS OVERNIGHT RESTING

6 SERVINGS ●

Panelle is a classic Sicilian chickpea fritter that is typically deep-fried. In this healthy version, it's simply pan-fried until crisp.

PANELLE

5 ounces chickpea flour (1⅓ cups)
2 cups water
½ teaspoon salt
Freshly ground pepper
3 tablespoons extra-virgin olive oil, plus more for frying
3 tablespoons snipped chives
1½ tablespoons minced flat-leaf parsley
1 teaspoon minced rosemary
¾ cup crumbled fresh goat cheese

SALSA RUSTICA

1¾ pounds tomatoes, halved crosswise and seeded
1 small red onion, quartered
1 poblano chile, quartered
¼ cup extra-virgin olive oil
2 garlic cloves, minced
2 tablespoons capers, chopped
2 tablespoons chopped oil-cured black olives
4 anchovy fillets, minced
3 tablespoons red wine vinegar
1½ tablespoons shredded basil leaves
Salt and freshly ground pepper

1. MAKE THE PANELLE: In a medium bowl, whisk the chickpea flour with the water until smooth. Add the salt and pepper, cover and refrigerate overnight.

2. Preheat the oven to 475°. Heat a 13-by-9-inch rimmed baking sheet in the oven for 5 minutes. Add the 3 tablespoons of olive oil to the sheet and tilt to coat. Stir the chickpea batter. Add the chives, parsley and rosemary and pour onto the sheet. Bake for 2 minutes. Sprinkle the goat cheese on top and bake for 20 minutes, until golden and firm. Let cool slightly.

3. MEANWHILE, MAKE THE SALSA: Heat a large cast-iron griddle or grill pan. Toss the tomatoes, red onion and poblano with 1 tablespoon of the oil. Add the vegetables to the griddle and cook over high heat until charred all over, about 5 minutes. Coarsely chop the tomatoes and finely chop the onion and poblano. Transfer the vegetables to a large bowl and add the garlic, capers, olives, anchovies, vinegar, basil and the remaining 3 tablespoons of oil. Season the salsa with salt and pepper.

4. Cut the *panelle* into 12 rectangles. Heat ⅛ inch of oil in a large nonstick skillet. Cook the *panelle* over high heat until crisp on the bottom, about 3 minutes. Drain the *panelle* and serve with the salsa.
—*Melissa Kelly*

Persimmon–Goat Cheese Wedges

ACTIVE: 30 MIN; TOTAL: 40 MIN

12 SERVINGS ● ● ●

½ cup salted roasted almonds, very finely chopped
1½ teaspoons chopped flat-leaf parsley
4 ounces fresh goat cheese, softened
4 Fuyu persimmons, sliced crosswise ¼ inch thick
Aged balsamic vinegar, for serving

1. In a small bowl, mix 3 tablespoons of the chopped almonds and the chopped parsley with the softened goat cheese. Divide the mixture into 6 equal pieces and roll each into a ball. Using a 2-inch round biscuit cutter, stamp out 12 rounds from the persimmon slices.

2. Put each goat cheese ball between 2 persimmon slices, pressing to flatten slightly. Roll the edges in the remaining almonds and refrigerate until firm, at least 10 minutes or overnight. Cut each round into quarters and transfer to a plate. Drizzle lightly with balsamic vinegar and serve. —*Maria Helm Sinskey*

Lemon Mascarpone-Stuffed Dates

TOTAL: 25 MIN

4 SERVINGS ● ●

Here Medjool dates are stuffed with silky lemon-spiked mascarpone cheese, then wrapped in salty cured ham before being cooked until they're crisp.

2 tablespoons mascarpone cheese or cream cheese
Pinch of finely grated lemon zest
1 teaspoon fresh lemon juice
½ teaspoon honey
Salt and freshly ground black pepper
12 large Medjool dates (about ½ pound)
6 paper-thin slices of *speck* or prosciutto (1½ ounces total), cut In half crosswise
1 tablespoon extra-virgin olive oil
2 teaspoons chopped parsley

1. Preheat the oven to 400°. In a small bowl, combine the mascarpone with the lemon zest, lemon juice and honey and season the filling with salt and pepper. Make a slit in each Medjool date and remove the pit. Carefully fill each date with 1½ teaspoons of the mascarpone mixture. Wrap a slice of *speck* around each date and secure it with a toothpick.

2. In a nonstick, ovenproof skillet, heat the olive oil. Add the dates and cook over high heat until the *speck* is crisp on the bottom, about 30 seconds. Turn the dates over. Transfer the skillet to the oven and bake the dates for about 2 minutes, or until they are heated through and the centers are slightly runny. Discard the toothpicks and transfer the dates to a serving plate. Sprinkle the dates with the chopped parsley and serve immediately.
—*Jennifer Jasinski*

MAKE AHEAD The dates can be stuffed, wrapped and refrigerated overnight. Bring the dates back to room temperature before cooking them.

starters

Argentine Grilled Provolone
TOTAL: 15 MIN
6 SERVINGS ●

Provolone is the perfect cheese for the grill, because it's compact and firm so it won't become too gooey. Be careful not to overcook the cheese or you will have fondue. Remove the cheese from the grill when it's just beginning to melt in the center.

One ½-pound piece of young
    provolone cheese
Extra-virgin olive oil, for rubbing
  2 teaspoons dried oregano
  ½ teaspoon crushed red pepper
Grilled bread, for serving

Light a grill. Rub the provolone all over with olive oil. Grill the cheese over moderately high heat for about 2 minutes per side or until it starts to melt and grill marks appear. Transfer the provolone to a metal baking dish, sprinkle the oregano and crushed red pepper over the cheese and set the dish over the grill. Cook until the cheese has just started to melt and is browned on the bottom, about 5 minutes. Serve immediately with grilled bread. —*Michelle Bernstein*

Peppery Ricotta Cheese Crostini
TOTAL: 20 MIN
8 SERVINGS ●

  1 pound fresh ricotta cheese,
     preferably goat's milk (2 cups)
  3 garlic cloves, 2 minced, 1 whole
  3 tablespoons minced oregano
Salt and freshly ground pepper
  1 baguette, cut diagonally into
     24 slices (½ inch thick)
24 anchovy fillets, drained
Extra-virgin olive oil, for drizzling

1. Light a grill. In a bowl, blend the ricotta cheese with the minced garlic and oregano; season with salt and pepper.
2. Grill the baguette slices over a medium-hot fire without turning until golden brown, about 20 seconds. Lightly rub the grilled side of each toast with the whole garlic clove and top with the ricotta mixture and an anchovy fillet.
3. Return the crostini to the grill, anchovy side up. Cover and cook the crostini until the ricotta is hot, about 2 minutes. Transfer the crostini to a platter, drizzle with olive oil and serve. —*Mario Batali*
MAKE AHEAD The ricotta spread can be refrigerated overnight.

Fresh Ricotta and Radish Crostini
ACTIVE: 30 MIN; TOTAL: 1 HR 30 MIN
8 SERVINGS ●

Homemade ricotta cheese is delicious and unbelievably easy to prepare—all it takes is milk, lemon juice and a little heat.

  2 quarts whole milk
  ¼ cup fresh lemon juice
Salt
Eight ¾-inch-thick slices of ciabatta
    or Tuscan bread
  2 tablespoons extra-virgin olive oil,
     plus more for brushing
Freshly ground black pepper
  6 large radishes, very thinly
     sliced
  1 small bunch arugula, thick
     stems discarded

1. Line a colander with moistened cheesecloth and set it over a large bowl. In a large saucepan, bring the whole milk to a gentle boil. Add 3 tablespoons of the lemon juice to the milk and cook over low heat, stirring gently, until curds form and rise to the surface, about 3 minutes. Remove the cooked milk from the heat, cover the pan and let stand for 5 minutes; the curds will firm up slightly.

ingredients
fresh cheeses

Mascarpone Made from cow's cream. Sweet, buttery and faintly nutty. **Best Uses** Savory sauces, dessert sauces and fillings. Topping for fresh fruit. **Substitutions** Devonshire or clotted cream, whipped ricotta.

Ricotta Made from sheep's or cow's whey. Sweet, with a faint vanilla aroma. **Best Uses** Fillings for dumplings, pasta and pastries. **Substitutions** *Fromage blanc*, quark, small-curd cottage cheese.

Fromage Blanc Made from cow's milk. Sweet, with a faint vanilla aroma. **Best Uses** Sauces, custards, dips and dressings. **Substitutions** Quark, ricotta.

Crème Fraîche Made from cow's cream. Creamy and spoonable. Slightly sweet and tangy. **Best Uses** Sauces, custards, dips and dressings. **Substitutions** Devonshire or clotted cream, sour cream.

Quark Made from cow's milk. Ranges from spoonable to dense and spreadable. Mild, faintly tangy. **Best Uses** Spread for breads. **Substitutions** *Fromage blanc*, *lebneh*, small-curd cottage cheese.

Queso Fresco Made from cow's or goat's milk. Mild with pleasantly salty, milky flavor. **Best Uses** Topping for soups, tamales and salads. **Substitutions** Small-curd cottage cheese, farmer cheese.

Lebneh Made from goat's, sheep's or cow's milk. Creamy and thick enough to hold up a spoon. **Best Uses** Dips, sauces and pastry fillings. **Substitutions** Greek yogurt, quark.

Goat Cheese Made from goat's milk. Soft, smooth, slightly grainy and spoonable. **Best Uses** Dressings, sauces, spreads or melted in savory foods. **Substitutions** *Fromage blanc*, quark, ricotta.

2. Using a slotted spoon with small holes, gently scoop the curds into the colander; discard the remaining liquid. Let the ricotta drain for 15 minutes, then gently lift the cheesecloth to flip the curd and let drain for 15 minutes longer. Transfer the ricotta to a bowl and season with salt.

3. Preheat the broiler. Arrange the bread on a baking sheet; brush with olive oil. Broil 8 inches from the heat for 4 minutes, turning once, until golden and crisp.

4. In a bowl, whisk the remaining 1 tablespoon of lemon juice with the 2 tablespoons of oil; season with salt and pepper. Add the radishes and arugula and toss.

5. Spread the ricotta generously on the toasts and top with the radishes and arugula. Garnish with pepper and serve. —*Paul Kahan*

MAKE AHEAD The ricotta can be refrigerated for up to 3 days.

Aged Gouda Fondue with Caraway Croutons

TOTAL: 30 MIN

10 SERVINGS ● ●

- 1 tablespoon caraway seeds
- 1 stick unsalted butter
- 1 baguette (about 12 ounces), cut into 1-inch cubes

Salt

- 3 cups heavy cream
- 1 pound medium-aged Gouda cheese, coarsely shredded

Freshly ground white pepper

1. Preheat the oven to 350°. In a small skillet, toast the caraway seeds over moderate heat for 1 minute, shaking the pan frequently. Add the butter and let melt. In a large bowl, toss the bread cubes with the caraway butter until evenly coated; season lightly with salt. Spread the bread on a large rimmed baking sheet and toast, turning once, until lightly browned and crisp, 10 minutes. Transfer to a basket, reserving 1 teaspoon of the caraway seeds left behind on the baking sheet.

2. In a saucepan, simmer the cream over moderate heat until reduced to 2 cups, about 15 minutes. Whisk in the Gouda until melted. Strain the sauce through a fine sieve over a heatproof bowl or fondue pot; season lightly with white pepper. Sprinkle with the reserved caraway seeds, then serve hot with the croutons and either toothpicks or skewers. —*Barbara Lynch*

MAKE AHEAD The croutons can be stored in an airtight container overnight. Recrisp in the oven if necessary.

Bayless's Queso Fundido al Tequila

TOTAL: 20 MIN

6 SERVINGS ●

With *Mexican Everyday,* chef Rick Bayless has finally published a cookbook for fast weeknight cooking. This simple, 20-minute dip of melted cheese flavored with tomatoes, chiles, onion and a hit of tequila is just the thing to satisfy a sudden craving for something warm, salty and gooey.

- 1 tablespoon extra-virgin olive oil
- 2 medium tomatoes—cored, seeded and cut into ¼-inch dice
- 2 jalapeños, seeded and minced
- 1 small onion, cut into ¼-inch dice

Kosher salt

- 3 tablespoons tequila
- ½ pound Monterey Jack cheese, shredded (3 cups)
- ¼ cup coarsely chopped cilantro

Warm corn tortillas or corn chips

1. In a large nonstick skillet, heat the olive oil. Add the tomatoes, jalapeños, onion and a large pinch of salt and cook over moderately high heat, stirring often, until softened, about 5 minutes. Pour in the tequila and cook, stirring frequently, until the skillet looks nearly dry, about 2 minutes.

2. Reduce the heat to low. Add the cheese and cook, stirring constantly, until fully melted, about 30 seconds. Quickly transfer the *queso fundido* to a serving bowl. Sprinkle with the cilantro and serve with tortillas or chips. —*Rick Bayless*

Fried Scallion Dip with Lebneh

TOTAL: 15 MIN

MAKES ABOUT 2 CUPS ● ●

French onion soup mix combined with sour cream is the quintessential '70s dip. This luxurious upgrade eschews the powdered stuff in favor of crunchy fried scallions. Replacing the sour cream with the Lebanese cheese *lebneh* creates a dip that's fairly low in fat; substituting nonfat *fromage blanc* or drained Greek yogurt will make the dip more virtuous yet.

- 6 large scallions, thinly sliced crosswise
- ¼ cup all-purpose flour
- ¼ cup plus 2 tablespoons extra-virgin olive oil
- ½ teaspoon chile powder
- ¼ teaspoon ground coriander
- ¼ teaspoon ground cumin
- 1 garlic clove, very finely chopped
- 1 jalapeño, seeded and minced
- 2 cups *lebneh* (see Note)

Salt and freshly ground black pepper

1. In a bowl, toss the scallions with the flour. Transfer to a colander and tap out any excess flour.

2. In a medium skillet, heat the olive oil until shimmering. Add the scallions and fry over high heat, stirring frequently, until golden and crisp, about 4 minutes. Drain the scallions in a colander set over a heatproof bowl; reserve 2 tablespoons of the scallion oil. Wipe out the skillet.

3. Return the reserved scallion oil to the skillet. Add the chile powder, coriander, cumin, garlic and jalapeño and cook over high heat, stirring, for 1 minute. Transfer to a bowl and stir in the *lebneh*. Season with salt and pepper and stir in the fried scallions. —*Grace Parisi*

SERVE WITH Pita chips, potato chips or crudités.

NOTE *Lebneh* is available at specialty and health food stores.

WARM CAMEMBERT WITH
WILD MUSHROOM FRICASSEE

Warm Camembert with Wild Mushroom Fricassee

TOTAL: 30 MIN

4 SERVINGS ●

½ cup walnut pieces

One 8-ounce wheel of ripe
    Camembert cheese in its wooden
    box, at room temperature

1 tablespoon walnut oil

¾ pound wild mushrooms,
    trimmed, caps thinly sliced

Salt and freshly ground black pepper

1 shallot, minced

2 tablespoons chopped flat-leaf
    parsley

2 large sage leaves, minced

Sourdough toasts, for serving

1. Preheat the oven to 350°. Spread the walnuts on a baking sheet; toast in the oven for 7 minutes, or until lightly browned. Lower the oven temperature to 300°.

2. Remove the Camembert from the box and unwrap it. Put the cheese back in the bottom half of the box and set on a baking sheet. Bake for 10 minutes, or until soft.

3. Meanwhile, in a large skillet, heat the walnut oil. Add the mushrooms and season with salt and pepper. Cover and cook over moderate heat, stirring occasionally, until softened, about 5 minutes. Uncover and cook, stirring, until lightly browned, 3 minutes longer. Add the shallot and cook until softened, 2 minutes. Stir in the parsley and sage; season with salt and pepper.

4. Invert the Camembert onto a platter. Stir the walnuts into the mushrooms and spoon over the cheese. Serve with the toasts.—*Daniel Boulud*

Crispy Arepitas with Mozzarella and Chorizo

ACTIVE: 30 MIN; TOTAL: 1 HR

MAKES 2 DOZEN AREPITAS

Arepas, fried or baked skillet breads made from corn flour, are eaten night and day in Venezuela (usually stuffed) and Colombia (usually not).

3 ounces fresh Mexican chorizo,
    casings removed

4 tablespoons unsalted butter

1½ cups milk

1½ cups instant masa (see Note)

1 tablespoon sugar

1 teaspoon salt

1 cup grated mozzarella cheese

1 tablespoon vegetable oil

1. In a medium skillet, cook the chorizo over moderate heat, breaking it up with a wooden spoon, until fully cooked, 5 minutes. Drain on paper towels; let cool.

2. In a small saucepan, melt the butter in the milk over moderately high heat. In a large bowl, mix the instant masa with the sugar, salt, mozzarella and cooked chorizo. Add the milk and stir until a smooth dough forms. Cover and let rest for 5 minutes; it should be slightly tacky to the touch.

3. Roll out the dough between 2 sheets of wax paper to a ½-inch thickness; transfer in the wax paper to a baking sheet. Refrigerate for at least 30 minutes, until firm.

4. Preheat the oven to 300°. Peel off the wax paper. Using a lightly greased 2-inch round cookie cutter, stamp out arepitas as close together as possible and transfer them to a baking sheet. Gather up the scraps, roll them between two sheets of wax paper and stamp out more arepitas.

5. In a large cast-iron skillet, heat 1 teaspoon of the oil. Add one-third of the arepitas. Cook over moderate heat until golden outside and moist within, 3 minutes per side. Transfer to another baking sheet; keep warm in the oven. Repeat with the remaining oil and arepitas. Arrange on a platter; serve hot. —*Michelle Bernstein*

NOTE Instant masa, like masa harina, is made from corn treated with limewater. It can be found in the Latin section of most supermarkets or at Latin markets. Do not substitute other types of cornmeal.

MAKE AHEAD The arepitas can be made through Step 3; cover and refrigerate them for up to 6 hours.

Mini Arepas with Melted Cheese and Serrano Ham

TOTAL: 1 HR

MAKES 3 DOZEN MINI AREPAS ●

2½ cups arepa meal (see Note)

1 tablespoon kosher salt

Pinch of sugar

2⅔ cups warm water

Vegetable oil, for frying

½ pound Oaxaca cheese or
    whole milk mozzarella cheese,
    cut into 36 thin 2-inch squares

½ pound thinly sliced serrano
    ham, each slice cut into
    4-inch pieces

Hot sauce, for serving

1. Preheat the oven to 350°. In a large bowl, mix the arepa meal with the salt and sugar. Stir in the warm water. Press out any lumps in the dough. Cover the bowl and let the dough stand for 10 minutes, until firm.

2. Using moistened hands, divide the dough into 4 pieces. Roll each piece into a 12-inch rope. Cut each rope into 9 pieces and keep covered with a damp towel. Using moistened hands, roll each piece into a ball and flatten into a 2½-inch round, a scant ½ inch thick. Keep covered.

3. Heat ¼ cup of oil in each of 2 large nonstick skillets. Working in batches, fry the arepas over moderate heat, turning occasionally, until golden and crisp, about 7 minutes. Add more oil to the skillet as necessary. Drain the arepas on paper towels and transfer to a large baking sheet.

4. Using a small serrated knife, split the arepas horizontally. Fill them with the cheese and ham and return to the baking sheet. Bake for about 5 minutes, until the cheese is melted. Transfer the arepas to a platter and serve warm, with hot sauce. —*Carolina Buia*

NOTE When buying arepa meal, look for P.A.N. or Goya brand at supermarkets.

MAKE AHEAD The filled arepas can be kept at room temperature for up to 2 hours; keep them loosely covered.

starters

Corn Bread Tartlets with Ricotta and Green Zebra Tomatoes

ACTIVE: 45 MIN; TOTAL: 1 HR

MAKES 3 DOZEN TARTLETS ●

Tangy Green Zebra tomatoes are especially good with creamy fresh ricotta cheese and a sweet corn bread crust.

- ½ cup stone-ground yellow cornmeal
- ½ cup all-purpose flour
- 3 tablespoons sugar
- 1 teaspoon baking powder
- ½ teaspoon salt
- ½ cup milk
- 1 large egg
- 2 tablespoons unsalted butter, melted, plus more for coating
- 4 Green Zebra or other heirloom tomatoes (10 ounces)—halved, seeded and finely chopped
- 1 garlic clove, minced
- 1 tablespoon freshly grated Parmesan cheese
- 1 tablespoon chopped basil
- 1 tablespoon extra-virgin olive oil

Kosher salt and freshly ground pepper

- ¾ cup ricotta cheese, preferably fresh

1. Preheat the oven to 375°. Generously butter three 12-cup mini-muffin pans. In a bowl, whisk the cornmeal, flour, sugar, baking powder and salt. In another bowl, whisk the milk and egg. Pour the milk into the dry ingredients, add the butter and stir to combine; don't overmix. Fill the muffin cups halfway with the batter. Bake for 10 to 12 minutes, or until golden. Transfer to a rack and let cool for 10 minutes, then turn out to cool completely.

2. In a medium bowl, toss the tomatoes, garlic, Parmesan, basil and olive oil; season with salt and pepper. In a bowl, season the ricotta with salt and pepper, Mix well.

3. Using a small knife, slice off the domed muffin tops. Top the muffins with the ricotta and tomatoes. Serve. —*Joe Vitale*

MAKE AHEAD The cooled muffins can be stored in an airtight container overnight.

Fried Green Tomatoes with Bacon Vinaigrette and Warm Frisée

TOTAL: 1 HR 10 MIN

12 SERVINGS

- 4 large green (unripe) tomatoes, sliced crosswise ½ inch thick
- 1 garlic clove, minced
- 1 tablespoon extra-virgin olive oil

Salt and freshly ground pepper

- 6 slices thickly sliced bacon (6 ounces), cut crosswise into ½-inch strips
- 1 tablespoon cider vinegar
- 1¼ cups all-purpose flour

Cayenne pepper

- 2 large eggs
- 1 tablespoon water
- 1 cup yellow cornmeal
- 1 teaspoon dried thyme

Canola oil, for frying

- 1 large head of frisée lettuce (½ pound), torn into pieces

1. In a large bowl, gently toss the tomatoes with the garlic and olive oil. Season with salt and pepper and let stand for 10 minutes.

2. In a medium skillet, cook the bacon over moderately high heat until crisp, 6 minutes. Drain on paper towels. Pour off all but 2 tablespoons of the fat; stir in the vinegar.

3. In a pie plate, season ¾ cup of the flour with salt, pepper and cayenne. In another pie plate, whisk the eggs with the water. In a third pie plate, mix the cornmeal with the remaining flour and the thyme and season with salt, pepper and cayenne. Line a baking sheet with wax paper. Drain the tomatoes. Working with 1 slice at a time, dip the tomatoes in the flour, tapping off any excess, then dip them in the beaten egg, then in the cornmeal; press to help it adhere. Transfer to the prepared baking sheet.

4. In a large skillet, heat ¼ inch of canola oil until shimmering. Fry the tomatoes in batches over moderately high heat, turning once, until golden, 5 to 6 minutes per batch. Transfer to a rack lined with paper towels to drain. Sprinkle with salt.

5. Rewarm the bacon fat and vinegar in the skillet over low heat. Add the frisée and season with salt and pepper; toss until slightly wilted, 1 minute. Transfer the tomatoes to plates. Top with the frisée. Garnish with the bacon and serve. —*Joe Vitale*

Tomatillo-Poblano Guacamole

TOTAL: 30 MIN

6 SERVINGS ● ●

This healthy incarnation of guacamole deserves the best homemade, oven-baked tortilla chips: Cut stacked corn tortillas into wedges, brush them lightly with oil and bake at 375° until curled and crisp.

- 1 large poblano chile
- 4 medium tomatillos, husked
- 1 small onion, minced
- 1 garlic clove, minced
- ¼ cup chopped cilantro, plus 1 tablespoon leaves for garnish
- 1 tablespoon fresh lime juice
- 3 Hass avocados, diced

Salt and freshly ground pepper

Baked tortilla chips, for serving

1. Preheat the broiler. Put the poblano chile on a baking sheet and broil as close to the heat source as possible, turning once, until charred all over, 4 minutes. Transfer to a small bowl, cover tightly with plastic and let stand for 5 minutes. Rub the skin off the chile with a paper towel; discard the stem and seeds. Cut the chile into ¼-inch dice. Transfer all but 1 tablespoon to a bowl.

2. In a metal baking pan, broil the tomatillos, turning once, until lightly browned, about 3 minutes. Transfer the tomatillos to a food processor and puree.

3. Add the tomatillo puree to the poblano in the bowl with the onion, garlic, chopped cilantro, lime juice and half the avocados; mash well with a fork. Add the remaining avocados; mash lightly. Season with salt and pepper. Transfer to a bowl and top the guacamole with the reserved tablespoon of diced chile and the cilantro leaves. Serve with tortilla chips. —*Susan Spungen*

TOMATILLO-POBLANO GUACAMOLE

starters

Mini Roasted Tomato Tatins

ACTIVE: 50 MIN; TOTAL: 1 HR 10 MIN
MAKES 2 DOZEN TATINS ● ● ○

- 2 tablespoons unsalted butter, softened
- 12 Black Cherry or other small tomatoes
- 2 tablespoons extra-virgin olive oil
- 6 large shallots, thinly sliced
- 2 garlic cloves, minced
- ¼ cup sherry vinegar
- 2 tablespoons honey
- Salt and freshly ground black pepper
- All-purpose flour, for dusting
- 1 pound all-butter puff pastry
- 1 tablespoon snipped chives

1. Preheat the oven to 375°. Generously butter two 12-cup mini-muffin pans. Fold a 12-inch square of wax paper or parchment paper into quarters. Trace six 1¼-inch circles close together on the top of the quartered paper. Cut out the 6 circles, cutting through the layers of paper to make 24 small disks. Line the bottom of each muffin cup with one of the paper liners. Butter the paper liners.

2. Bring a medium pot of water to a boil. Meanwhile, fill a large bowl with ice water. Using a sharp knife, make a shallow X in the bottom of each tomato. Add the tomatoes to the boiling water and blanch just until the skins begin to pull away, about 20 seconds. Using a slotted spoon, immediately transfer the tomatoes to the ice water. Drain and peel the tomatoes. Halve the tomatoes crosswise.

3. In a medium skillet, heat the olive oil until shimmering. Add the shallots and cook over moderate heat, stirring frequently, until lightly browned, about 8 minutes. Add the garlic and cook for 2 to 3 minutes. Add the sherry vinegar and honey, season with salt and pepper and cook over low heat until the liquid has evaporated and the shallots are jamlike, about 5 minutes. Transfer to a bowl and let cool.

4. On a lightly floured surface, roll out the puff pastry ⅛ inch thick. Using a 1¾-inch biscuit cutter, stamp out 24 rounds.

5. Set a tomato half, cut side down, in each muffin cup. Top each with a scant teaspoon of the shallot marmalade and a puff pastry round. Bake for about 20 minutes, or until the puff pastry is golden brown.

6. Run a knife around the edge of each tomato tatin. Set a baking sheet over the muffin tins and then invert them, giving the pans a firm tap to release the tatins. Replace any tomatoes and shallots stuck to the muffin pans. Discard the paper disks, sprinkle the tomato tatins with the chives and serve at once. —*Joe Vitale*

MAKE AHEAD The tatins can be made a day ahead and kept at room temperature in an airtight container. Reheat in a 325° oven for 5 minutes.

Roasted Grape Tomatoes and Garlic in Olive Oil

ACTIVE: 10 MIN; TOTAL: 1 HR
8 SERVINGS ● ●

Pressed and released in time for the winter holidays, "new oil" olive oil—called *olio novello* or *olio nuovo* in Italian—is vibrantly green and fresh tasting. Its pronounced flavors transform this simple recipe, which can be served on toast as bruschetta or as a sauce with fish or chicken.

- 2 pints grape tomatoes
- 6 garlic cloves, smashed
- ¼ teaspoon crushed red pepper
- ⅔ cup plus 1 tablespoon extra-virgin olive oil, preferably *olio novello* or *olio nuovo*
- Kosher salt and freshly ground black pepper
- 1 sprig fresh rosemary
- 1 sprig fresh oregano
- Eight ¾-inch slices of ciabatta

1. Preheat the oven to 400°. On a large rimmed baking sheet, toss the grape tomatoes with the garlic, crushed pepper and 1 tablespoon of the olive oil and season with salt and pepper. Roast the tomatoes for about 20 minutes, until they burst and their skins begin to shrivel, stirring once halfway through roasting.

2. Pour the remaining ⅔ cup of olive oil into a medium bowl. Crush the rosemary and oregano sprigs between your fingers and submerge them in the oil. Add the

ingredient
heirloom tomatoes

Copia Discovered at Napa's COPIA museum of wine, food and the arts. A large sweet salad tomato with a yellow background and red striping.

Amish Paste A deep red tomato with a thick outside layer and robust flavor from a high-yielding plant. Ideal in salads and sauces.

Earl of Edgecombe A medium-size orange-colored New Zealand salad tomato with firm flesh.

Moonglow Six- to eight-ounce yellow globes with a meaty texture and fruity flavor. Great for salads.

Paul Robeson A large beefsteak tomato with an earthy, smoky flavor.

ROASTED GRAPE TOMATOES AND GARLIC IN OLIVE OIL

SPICY TOMATO GRANITA

tomatoes and their juices, stir gently and let stand for 30 minutes.

3. Reduce the oven temperature to 350°. Arrange the ciabatta on a baking sheet and toast for 10 minutes, or until crisp. Spoon the tomatoes and some of the infused oil over the ciabatta, sprinkle with salt and serve. —*Melissa Rubel*

MAKE AHEAD The tomato-and-herb-infused oil can be stored in the refrigerator for up to 3 days. Bring to room temperature before serving.

Spicy Tomato Granita
ACTIVE: 30 MIN; TOTAL: 3 HR 20 MIN
12 SERVINGS ●

This icy, savory palate cleanser resembles a frozen gazpacho. Like all granitas, it is easy to prepare without an ice cream machine. Simply freeze the mixture in a shallow dish, stirring it occasionally as it hardens to form flaky crystals.

4½ pounds juicy, ripe tomatoes
½ cup cilantro leaves
3 tablespoons fresh lime juice
1 serrano chile, seeded and chopped
Salt
12 tarragon sprigs (optional)

1. Bring a large pot of water to a boil. Fill a large bowl with ice water. Using a sharp knife, make a small, shallow X in the bottom of each tomato. Add the tomatoes to the boiling water and blanch them just until the skins begin to pull away, about 20 seconds. Using a slotted spoon, immediately transfer the tomatoes to the ice water to stop the cooking. Drain and peel the tomatoes.

2. Halve the tomatoes crosswise. Squeeze the seeds into a fine-mesh sieve set over a bowl. Press on the seeds to extract the tomato juice; discard the seeds. Cut the seeded tomatoes into large chunks. In a food processor, puree the tomato chunks with the tomato juice, the cilantro leaves, the lime juice and the serrano chile until the mixture is smooth. Season the pureed tomato mixture with salt.

3. Spread the tomato mixture in a shallow 13-by-9-inch glass baking dish and transfer to the freezer. Freeze until the granita is set around the edges, about 1 hour. Using a fork, scrape the ice crystals into the center of the dish and freeze the granita again. Repeat the scraping every 30 minutes until the entire mixture has turned into ice flakes, about 2 hours longer. Spoon the spicy tomato granita into glasses, then garnish each granita with a tarragon sprig.
—*Joe Vitale*

MAKE AHEAD The spicy tomato granita can be transferred to a plastic container and frozen, covered, overnight. Stir the granita before serving.

● FAST ● HEALTHY ● MAKE AHEAD ● STAFF FAVORITE

starters

Mini Potato Cakes with Smoked Sturgeon and Herbed Cream

TOTAL: 30 MIN

8 SERVINGS ● ●

To ensure that these delectable little fried cakes are crisp, squeeze as much liquid as possible from the shredded potatoes.

- ¼ cup crème fraîche
- 1½ teaspoons fresh lemon juice
- ½ teaspoon each of chopped dill, tarragon, chives and celery leaves
- Salt and freshly ground pepper
- 1 pound Yukon Gold potatoes, peeled and coarsely shredded
- 2½ tablespoons all-purpose flour
- 2 tablespoons unsalted butter
- 2 tablespoons canola oil
- 4 ounces sliced smoked sturgeon or other smoked fish, torn in pieces
- Radish sprouts, for garnish

1. In a small bowl, whisk the crème fraîche with the lemon juice and chopped herbs and season with salt and pepper.

2. Squeeze small handfuls of the shredded potatoes over a colander to remove as much liquid as possible. Transfer the potatoes to a medium bowl and toss with the flour; season with salt and pepper.

3. In a very large nonstick skillet, melt the butter in the oil. Add rounded tablespoons of the potato mixture to the skillet, about 2 inches apart; you should have 16 mounds. Flatten the mounds slightly into cakes ½ inch thick and 1½ inches wide. Cook them over moderate heat, turning once, until golden and crisp, about 6 minutes. Drain on paper towels.

4. Arrange the potato cakes on a platter. Top each cake with a small dollop of the herbed cream, a few pieces of sturgeon and a few radish sprouts and serve.
—*Colin Devlin*

MAKE AHEAD The herbed cream can be refrigerated overnight. The potato cakes can be pan-fried 8 hours ahead and kept at room temperature. Reheat them in a 325° oven before serving.

Two Cheese–Shiitake Beignets

TOTAL: 30 MIN

MAKES ABOUT 4 DOZEN

BEIGNETS ● ●

- 9 tablespoons unsalted butter
- 6 ounces shiitake mushrooms, stemmed, caps thinly sliced
- Kosher salt and freshly ground black pepper
- 1 cup milk
- ¼ teaspoon cayenne pepper
- 1 cup all-purpose flour
- 4 large eggs
- 1 packed cup shredded Gruyère cheese (4 ounces)
- ½ cup freshly grated Parmesan cheese
- 1 tablespoon chopped parsley
- 1 quart vegetable oil, for frying

1. In a medium skillet, melt 1 tablespoon of the butter. Add the shiitakes, season with salt and pepper and cook over high heat, stirring, until tender and golden, 8 minutes. Finely chop the mushrooms.

2. In a saucepan, bring 8 tablespoons of butter, milk, cayenne and 2½ teaspoons of salt to a boil. Remove from the heat and add the flour, stirring vigorously until combined. Cook the dough over moderate heat, stirring constantly, until it comes away from the sides of the pan, about 2 minutes. Remove from the heat. Using a handheld electric mixer, beat in the eggs, one at a time, beating well between additions, until a soft, silky dough forms. Stir in the shiitakes, Gruyère, Parmesan and parsley.

3. In a large saucepan, heat the oil to 375°. Using a small ice cream scoop or teaspoon and working in batches, add 12 level scoops of the batter to the hot oil. Fry until the beignets are golden brown and cooked through, about 4 minutes. Using a slotted spoon, transfer them to a paper towel–lined rack to drain. Serve hot.
—*Maria Helm Sinskey*

MAKE AHEAD The beignets can be rewarmed in a hot oven until crisp.

Baby Artichokes Stuffed with Crab Salad

ACTIVE: 40 MIN; TOTAL: 1 HR 30 MIN

10 SERVINGS ● ●

- 1 lemon, halved, plus 2 teaspoons lemon juice
- 20 baby artichokes
- ¼ cup extra-virgin olive oil
- 1 large carrot, finely diced
- 1 large celery rib, finely diced
- ¼ cup finely diced onion
- Salt and freshly ground pepper
- 1 cup dry white wine
- ¼ cup white wine vinegar
- ½ teaspoon black peppercorns
- ½ teaspoon coriander seeds
- 2 bay leaves
- 8 thyme sprigs
- 3 tablespoons crème fraîche
- 1 tablespoon snipped chives
- ½ pound jumbo lump crabmeat

1. Squeeze the lemon halves into a large bowl of water. Working with 1 artichoke at a time, snap off all of the outer leaves and trim the stem so the artichoke will stand upright. With a small, sharp knife, cut ½ inch off the top and peel the base. With a melon baller, scoop out some of the choke to form a cup with a ¼-inch rim. Drop the artichoke into the lemon water.

2. Drain the artichokes and pat dry. Heat the oil in a large, deep skillet. Add the artichokes and cook over moderately high heat, turning occasionally, until lightly browned, about 4 minutes. Add the carrot, celery and onion, season with salt and pepper and cook for 1 minute longer. Add the wine, vinegar, peppercorns, coriander seeds, bay leaves and thyme. Cover with parchment paper and a tight-fitting lid and simmer over moderately low heat, turning once or twice, until the artichokes are tender and the liquid has reduced slightly, about 30 minutes. Transfer the artichokes to a large platter to cool. Remove the bay leaves and thyme sprigs; season the liquid with salt and pepper and reserve.

BABY ARTICHOKES STUFFED WITH CRAB SALAD

SAUSAGE POTATO PUFFS

3. In a small bowl, mix the crème fraîche with the lemon juice and chives. Fold in the crabmeat and season the crab mixture lightly with salt and pepper. Using a small spoon, fill the cooled artichokes with the crab salad. Arrange the stuffed artichokes on a platter. Drizzle with the reserved cooking liquid and serve right away.
—*Barbara Lynch*

MAKE AHEAD The cooked artichokes and the crab mixture can be refrigerated separately overnight.

Sausage Potato Puffs
ACTIVE: 30; TOTAL: 1 HR
MAKES 4 DOZEN PUFFS ●
Vegetable oil cooking spray
- ¾ pound medium Yukon Gold potatoes
- 1 pound sweet Italian sausages, casings removed
- ¾ cup water
- 6 tablespoons unsalted butter
- 1½ teaspoons kosher salt
- ¾ cup all-purpose flour
- 4 large eggs
- ½ cup shredded Gruyère cheese
- ¼ cup freshly grated Parmesan cheese
- 1 teaspoon chopped thyme
- ½ teaspoon chopped rosemary

Freshly ground pepper
- 1 large egg yolk mixed with 2 tablespoons water

1. Preheat the oven to 425°. Coat four 12-cup mini-muffin pans with vegetable oil cooking spray. In a saucepan, simmer the potatoes in water over moderate heat until tender, 20 minutes. Let cool slightly, then peel and coarsely mash the potatoes.

2. Meanwhile, in a medium skillet, cook the sausage over high heat until browned, 8 minutes; coarsely crumble.

3. In a medium saucepan, bring the water, butter and salt to a boil. Remove from the heat and add the flour, stirring vigorously with a wooden spoon, until combined. Set the pan over moderately high heat and cook the dough, stirring, until it comes away from the sides of the pan, 2 to 3 minutes; remove from the heat.

4. Using a handheld electric mixer, beat the dough at low speed for 1 minute. Beat in the eggs one at a time at medium speed; beat in the Gruyère, Parmesan, thyme, rosemary and a pinch of pepper. Stir in the mashed potatoes and sausage.

5. Fill the muffin cups with the dough. Brush the tops with the egg wash and bake for 20 minutes, or until puffed and golden. Let cool slightly then transfer the puffs to a platter and serve right away.
—*Maria Helm Sinskey*

MAKE AHEAD The puffs can be refrigerated overnight; rewarm them in a hot oven.

starters

Sweet Potato Bruschetta

ACTIVE: 15 MIN; TOTAL: 1 HR 20 MIN

6 SERVINGS ● ●

- 2 medium sweet potatoes (18 ounces)
- 1 cup cottage cheese
- 3 tablespoons finely chopped chives
- 1 small garlic clove, minced
- 1 tablespoon plus 1 teaspoon fresh lemon juice
- 1 tablespoon extra-virgin olive oil
- 1½ teaspoons balsamic vinegar

Kosher salt and freshly ground pepper

Twelve ¾-inch-thick slices of rustic Italian bread

1. Preheat the oven to 425°. Put the sweet potatoes on a baking sheet and roast for 50 minutes, or until tender when pierced. Remove from the oven and let cool slightly. Reduce the oven temperature to 375°.

2. Halve the sweet potatoes lengthwise and scrape the flesh into a medium bowl; discard the skins. Mash the sweet potatoes until smooth. Stir in the cottage cheese, chives, garlic, lemon juice, olive oil and vinegar and season with salt and pepper.

3. Toast the bread slices on a baking sheet for 10 minutes, or until crisp. Top each slice with the sweet potato mixture and serve.
—*Jake Tilson*

MAKE AHEAD The sweet potato topping can be made up to 3 days ahead without the chives. Bring to room temperature and stir in the chives before serving.

Potato–Smoked Salmon Crostini

ACTIVE: 20 MIN; TOTAL: 40 MIN

8 SERVINGS ●

- 1 pound small fingerling potatoes, scrubbed and halved lengthwise
- 2 tablespoons vegetable oil

Kosher salt and freshly ground pepper

- ½ cup crème fraîche or sour cream
- 2 tablespoons chopped dill
- 1 tablespoon capers, chopped
- 1 tablespoon drained prepared horseradish
- 6 ounces thinly sliced smoked salmon, cut into 1½-inch strips

1. Preheat the oven to 450°. On a rimmed baking sheet, toss the potatoes with the oil. Season with salt and pepper and roast, cut side down, for 15 minutes. Using a spatula, turn the potatoes and roast them for about 15 minutes longer, or until golden and crisp. Drain the potatoes on paper towels.

2. Meanwhile, in a small bowl, blend the crème fraîche with the dill, capers and horseradish; season with salt and pepper.

3. To assemble the crostini, top each potato half with a smoked salmon strip and a dollop of sauce. Arrange the crostini on a platter and serve.
—*Mary Ellen Carroll and Donna Wingate*

MAKE AHEAD The crème fraîche sauce can be refrigerated overnight. Let warm to room temperature before serving

African-Spiced Lentil Dip

ACTIVE: 15 MIN; TOTAL: 1 HR

12 SERVINGS ● ●

- 2 cups brown lentils
- 1 carrot, cut into 1-inch pieces
- 1 medium red onion, chopped
- 1 quart water
- 4 tablespoons unsalted butter
- 1 teaspoon ground cumin
- 1 teaspoon ground coriander
- 1 teaspoon ground ginger
- ½ teaspoon freshly grated nutmeg
- ½ teaspoon ground allspice
- ¼ teaspoon cayenne pepper

Salt and freshly ground black pepper

- 1 tablespoon fresh lemon juice
- 2 tablespoons chopped cilantro

Toasted pita triangles, for serving

1. In a large saucepan, cover the lentils, carrot and onion with the water and bring to a boil. Simmer until the lentils are tender and almost all the liquid has evaporated, 35 minutes. In a food processor, puree the lentils and vegetables.

2. In the same saucepan, melt the butter. Add the cumin, coriander, ginger, nutmeg, allspice and cayenne and cook over low heat, stirring a few times, until fragrant, about 3 minutes. Add the lentil puree and cook, stirring, for 5 minutes. Season with salt and black pepper and stir in the lemon juice. Transfer to a serving bowl and sprinkle with the cilantro. Serve warm or at room temperature with the pita toasts.
—*Marcus Samuelsson*

Yellow Split Pea Dip

TOTAL: 30 MIN

MAKES 4 CUPS ● ● ●

This hearty and slightly tangy spread is served as a meze in Greece.

- ½ pound yellow split peas
- 1 small onion, chopped
- 1 bay leaf
- 6 oil-packed sun-dried tomato halves, drained
- 2 tablespoons red wine vinegar
- 3 large garlic cloves
- 2 shallots, chopped
- 3 large basil leaves
- 1½ teaspoons dried Greek oregano
- ½ teaspoon fresh thyme
- ½ cup extra-virgin olive oil, plus more for drizzling

Kosher salt and freshly ground pepper

Toasted pita triangles, for serving

1. In a large saucepan, combine the split peas with the onion, bay leaf and 4 cups of water and bring to a simmer. Cover and cook over moderate heat until the split peas are tender, about 25 minutes. Drain the split peas and discard the bay leaf.

2. In a food processor, pulse the sun-dried tomatoes with the vinegar, garlic, shallots, basil, oregano and thyme until minced. Add the split peas. With the machine on, slowly pour in the ½ cup of olive oil and process until a smooth paste forms. Season with salt and pepper. Transfer the dip to a bowl, drizzle with olive oil and serve with toasted pita. —*Michael Psilakis*

Salt Cod Fritters with Garlicky Skordalia

ACTIVE: 30 MIN; TOTAL: 50 MIN

6 SERVINGS

Kosher salt
1   tablespoon sugar
1½ pounds skinless center-cut cod fillet, cut into 4 pieces
1   pound baking potatoes, peeled and cut into 2-inch pieces
2   medium garlic cloves, minced
½   cup extra-virgin olive oil
½   cup plain Greek yogurt
3   tablespoons white wine vinegar
1   tablespoon minced oregano
Freshly ground pepper
Vegetable oil, for frying
1   cup all-purpose flour
¾   cup light ale
2   large eggs, beaten
¼   teaspoon anise seeds

1. In a bowl, mix 6 tablespoons of salt with the sugar. Spread half of the mixture on a large plate. Set the cod pieces on the plate and sprinkle the remaining mixture on top. Cover the cod with another large plate and weight it down with a heavy can. Let stand at room temperature for 30 minutes.
2. In a medium saucepan of boiling water, cook the potatoes until tender, 15 minutes. Drain, reserving ¾ cup of cooking water. Pass the potatoes through a ricer into a large bowl. Using the flat side of a chef's knife, mash the garlic with a generous pinch of salt until a paste forms. Using an electric mixer, beat the potatoes, garlic paste, olive oil, yogurt and 2 tablespoons of vinegar. Gradually beat in about ½ cup of the reserved cooking water at low speed until a smooth, loose sauce forms; use more water if needed. Add the oregano; season lightly with salt and pepper.
3. Rinse the salt cod and pat dry. Cut the cod into 1½-inch pieces. In a large saucepan, heat 1½ inches of vegetable oil to 350°. In a medium bowl, whisk the flour, ale, eggs, anise seeds and remaining 1 tablespoon of vinegar until smooth. Add the cod and turn to coat thoroughly with batter. Fry the cod in 3 batches over high heat until golden and puffed, 3 to 4 minutes. Using a slotted spoon, transfer the fritters as they are done to paper towels to drain. Serve hot, with the skordalia.
—*Dionisis Papanikolauo*

Mini Smoked-Salmon Croque-Monsieur

TOTAL: 1 HR

20 SERVINGS ●

1   stick unsalted butter
3   tablespoons all-purpose flour
2   cups milk
10 ounces thinly sliced smoked salmon, coarsely chopped
1½ cups shredded Gruyère cheese (6 ounces)
1   cup minced chives
½   teaspoon freshly grated nutmeg
Salt and freshly ground pepper
40 slices of cocktail rye bread
40 slices of cocktail pumpernickel
6   large eggs

1. In a medium saucepan, melt 3 tablespoons of the butter. Stir in the flour until completely blended, then cook over moderately high heat, stirring constantly, until golden brown, 3 minutes. Gradually whisk in the milk until smooth. Bring the sauce to a boil, whisking constantly. Reduce the heat to moderately low and simmer, whisking often, until no floury taste remains, 5 minutes. Remove the saucepan from the heat and let the sauce cool, stirring, until lukewarm. Stir in the salmon, cheese, chives and nutmeg. Season with salt and pepper. Let the sauce cool completely.
2. Spread half of the rye slices with a rounded tablespoon of the salmon and close the sandwiches. Repeat with the pumpernickel and remaining filling.
3. Preheat the oven to 400°. In a pie plate, beat the eggs. Stack 2 large rimmed baking sheets on one side of the stove.
4. In a large skillet, melt 1 tablespoon of the butter over moderate heat. Dip 8 sandwiches in the beaten eggs to coat completely; cook the sandwiches over moderately high heat, turning once, until browned, 1 minute per side. Transfer to a baking sheet; leaving a little space between each one. Repeat with the remaining sandwiches and eggs, using 1 tablespoon of butter per batch.
5. Reheat the sandwiches for about 8 minutes, until piping hot. Cut the sandwiches in half on the diagonal, skewer with small wooden forks and serve hot.
—*Alison Attenborough and Jamie Kimm*
MAKE AHEAD The sandwiches can be prepared earlier in the day and reheated.

Smoked Salmon Involtini

TOTAL: 30 MIN

MAKES 24 ROLLS ● ●

1   small carrot, cut into julienne
½   medium fennel bulb—halved, cored and cut into julienne
1   medium shallot, thinly sliced
1   teaspoon fresh lemon juice
Salt and freshly ground pepper
¼   cup mayonnaise
½ to ¾ teaspoon chipotle hot sauce or adobo sauce from canned chipotles
¼   teaspoon finely grated lemon zest
14 ounces thinly sliced smoked salmon

1. In a bowl, toss the carrot, fennel, shallot and lemon juice; season with salt and pepper. In a small bowl, blend the mayonnaise, hot sauce and zest; season with salt.
2. Cut the salmon into 12 pieces, each about 3½-by-3 inches. Spoon the vegetable salad across one end of each piece of salmon (some of the salad can stick out of each end). Tightly roll the salmon around the salad. Cut each roll in half crosswise and transfer to a platter, cut side down. Top each roll with a dollop of the chipotle mayonnaise and serve. —*Marcia Kiesel*

starters

Crab Salad with Avocado and Mango

ACTIVE: 20 MIN; TOTAL: 1 HR 10 MIN

4 SERVINGS

- 2 large eggs

Salt and freshly ground pepper

- 1 shallot, minced
- 1 tablespoon chopped fresh ginger
- 3 tablespoons fresh lime juice
- 2 teaspoons Asian fish sauce
- ¾ cup plus 2 tablespoons canola oil
- 1 pound jumbo lump crabmeat
- 1 large mango, finely diced
- 1 Hass avocado, finely diced
- 2 tablespoons snipped chives

Peppercress or watercress sprigs, for garnish

1. In a medium bowl, vigorously beat the eggs; season with salt and pepper. Refrigerate for 1 hour.

2. In a blender, combine the shallot, ginger, lime juice and fish sauce and puree. With the machine on, add ¼ cup plus 2 tablespoons of the oil in a thin stream and blend until emulsified. Transfer the dressing to a medium bowl. Add the crab, mango, avocado and chives to the dressing and season with salt and pepper. Fold gently until it is mixed and evenly dressed. Refrigerate the crab salad.

3. In a large nonstick skillet, heat the remaining ½ cup of oil until shimmering. Using your fingertips, drizzle half of the beaten eggs into the hot oil in a lacy pattern; spoon some of the hot oil over the eggs so they puff and sizzle. Cook until set and golden, about 1 minute. Carefully transfer the lacy eggs to a paper towel–lined plate. Repeat with the remaining beaten eggs.

4. On a small plate, pack one-fourth of the crab salad into a 4-inch ring mold; lift off the ring. Repeat for the remaining 3 servings. Drape some of the lacy eggs over the crab and garnish with the peppercress. —*Harold Dieterle*

Open-Faced Crab Empanadas

ACTIVE: 40 MIN; TOTAL: 1 HR 15 MIN

12 SERVINGS

All-purpose flour, for dusting

One 14-ounce package frozen all-butter puff pastry, thawed

- 3 tablespoons extra-virgin olive oil
- 2 garlic cloves, minced
- 1 small onion, minced
- 1 small red bell pepper, cut into ¼-inch dice
- 1 small green bell pepper, cut into ¼-inch dice
- 1 teaspoon sweet pimentón de la Vera (smoked Spanish paprika)
- ½ pound lump crabmeat, picked over

Salt

1. Preheat the oven to 375°. Line a large rimmed baking sheet with parchment paper. On a large, lightly floured work surface, roll out the pastry to ⅛ inch thick. Using a pizza cutter or knife, cut out two 12-by-3-inch rectangles and brush off any excess flour. Transfer the rectangles to the prepared baking sheet. From the remaining puff pastry, cut four 12-by-¼-inch strips and four 3-by-¼-inch strips. Moisten the border of the rectangles with water. Lay the long strips on the long edges of each rectangle and the short strips on the short edges; press lightly to seal. With a fork, prick the bottom of the pastry all over. Freeze the pastry shells for 15 minutes.

2. Bake the pastry shells for about 30 minutes, until browned and crisp and the borders have risen nicely. If the centers start to puff up, gently tamp them down with a fork during baking.

3. In a large skillet, heat the olive oil. Add the garlic and cook over moderate heat for 30 seconds. Add the onion and cook until softened, about 7 minutes. Add the bell peppers, cover and cook, stirring a few times, until tender, about 8 minutes. Uncover and stir in the pimentón. Cook, stirring, for 3 minutes. Add the crab and cook, tossing gently, until heated through, about 3 minutes. Season with salt.

4. Spread the crab filling into the center of each pastry shell. With a serrated knife, cut the pastry shells crosswise into 12 slices each. Arrange the slices on a platter and serve. —*José Andrés*

MAKE AHEAD The baked, unfilled pastry shells can be wrapped in aluminum foil and kept at room temperature overnight. Reheat the pastry shells in a 350° oven for 3 minutes before filling.

Mixed Seafood Seviche

ACTIVE: 25 MIN; TOTAL: 2 HR 45 MIN

6 SERVINGS ● ●

- 1 tablespoon Old Bay seasoning
- ¼ pound medium shrimp, shelled and deveined
- ½ pound large sea scallops (about 6)
- ¼ pound small squid, bodies cut crosswise into ½-inch rings, tentacles left whole
- 1 dozen littleneck clams, scrubbed
- ½ pound skinless red snapper fillet, cut into ½-inch pieces
- 1 tablespoon kosher salt
- 1 tablespoon finely chopped fresh ginger
- 1 celery rib, minced
- ½ habanero chile, minced
- ¾ cup fresh lime juice (5 limes)
- ¼ cup chopped cilantro
- 1 medium red onion, thinly sliced

Freshly ground pepper

1. Bring a saucepan of water to a boil. Prepare a bowl of ice water. Add the Old Bay seasoning and the shrimp and scallops to the boiling water and cook for 1 minute. With a slotted spoon, transfer the shrimp and scallops to the ice water bath. Cook the squid in the boiling water for 5 seconds, then transfer to the ice water bath. Add the clams to the saucepan and boil until they open, then transfer to a separate bowl; discard any that don't open.

MIXED SEAFOOD SEVICHE

SHRIMP AND SQUID COCKTAILS WITH AVOCADO AND TOMATO

2. Remove the clams from their shells. Drain the shrimp, scallops and squid and pat dry. In a large, shallow dish, combine the shrimp, scallops, squid, clams and snapper. Sprinkle with the salt, ginger, celery and habanero and toss. Refrigerate for 30 minutes.

3. Add the lime juice, cilantro and onion to the seviche. Season with pepper and toss well. Refrigerate for 2 hours, stirring twice. Spoon the seviche into martini glasses and serve. —*Michelle Bernstein*

Shrimp and Squid Cocktails with Avocado and Tomato

ACTIVE: 30 MIN; TOTAL: 1 HR 30 MIN
PLUS OVERNIGHT MARINATING
12 SERVINGS ● ● ●
½ cup fresh lime juice
¼ cup fresh orange juice
¼ cup tomato juice
1 tablespoon tomato paste

Salt and freshly ground black
    pepper
Hot sauce
2 pounds shelled and deveined
    large shrimp
½ pound cleaned squid, cut into
    ½-inch rings, tentacles halved
2 pounds tomatoes—halved,
    seeded and finely diced
2 Hass avocados, diced
4 scallions, white and tender
    green parts only, thinly sliced
1 small red onion, finely diced
2 tablespoons chopped cilantro
1 tablespoon chopped flat-leaf
    parsley
Plantain chips, for serving
1. Bring a large pot of salted water to a boil. Fill a large bowl with ice water. In another large bowl, whisk the lime, orange and tomato juices with the tomato paste. Season with salt, pepper and hot sauce.

2. Cook the shrimp in the boiling water until curled and pink, about 1 minute. Using a slotted spoon, transfer the shrimp to the ice water. Return the water to a boil and add the squid. Cook the squid for 30 seconds, until firm but tender. Drain the squid immediately and add it to the ice water.

3. Drain the cool shrimp and squid and pat dry. Add the seafood to the juices in the large bowl and toss to coat. Transfer the contents of the large bowl to a large resealable plastic bag. Close the bag, pressing out the air. Refrigerate overnight, turning the bag occasionally.

4. Transfer the seafood salad to a bowl. Stir in the tomatoes, avocados, scallions, onion, cilantro and parsley. Season the seafood cocktail with salt, pepper and hot sauce. Refrigerate for at least 30 minutes or for up to 2 hours. Scoop into martini glasses and serve with plantain chips.
—*Carolina Buia*

● FAST ● HEALTHY ● MAKE AHEAD ● STAFF FAVORITE

SHRIMP AND WATER CHESTNUT TOASTS

CRAB BALLS WITH GRAPEFRUIT SALAD

Shrimp and Water Chestnut Toasts

TOTAL: 40 MIN

6 SERVINGS ● ○

- ¾ pound medium shrimp—shelled, deveined and coarsely chopped
- 4 tablespoons unsalted butter, softened
- 6 canned whole water chestnuts, drained and cut into ⅛-inch dice
- 2 large scallions, sliced crosswise
- ¼ cup Shao-Hsing cooking wine or dry sherry
- 1 tablespoon plus 1 teaspoon low-sodium soy sauce
- 1 tablespoon Asian sesame oil
- 1 teaspoon salt
- 1 teaspoon sugar
- 1 baguette, sliced ⅓ inch thick on the diagonal (24 slices)

Vegetable oil, for frying

- ¼ cup sesame seeds

1. Preheat the oven to 450°. In a food processor, combine half of the shrimp with the butter and process until pureed.

2. In a bowl, toss the rest of the shrimp, water chestnuts, scallions, wine, soy sauce, sesame oil, salt and sugar. Blend in the shrimp butter. Spread 1½ tablespoons of the mixture on each bread slice.

3. In a large skillet, heat ⅛ inch of vegetable oil until shimmering. Put the sesame seeds in a small bowl. Dip each shrimp toast in the sesame seeds to coat the shrimp mixture. Fry about 8 of the toasts at a time over moderately high heat, shrimp side down, until the shrimp salad turns pink, about 25 seconds. Using tongs, transfer the toasts to a large rimmed baking sheet, shrimp side up. Repeat with the remaining toasts, adding oil as needed. Bake the toasts for about 5 minutes, or until the shrimp mixture is cooked through. Serve at once.

—Jean-Georges Vongerichten

Crab Balls with Grapefruit Salad

TOTAL: 45 MIN PLUS 2 HR 20 MIN

FREEZING AND THAWING TIME

4 SERVINGS

CRAB BALLS

- 1 tablespoon unsalted butter
- 2 tablespoons finely chopped onion
- 2 tablespoons cornstarch
- ½ cup unsweetened coconut milk
- ½ pound lump or peekytoe crabmeat, picked over and lightly shredded

Salt

- 1 cup *panko* (Japanese bread crumbs)
- 1½ tablespoons mixed white and black sesame seeds
- 2 large egg whites, lightly beaten

Vegetable oil, for frying

GRAPEFRUIT SALAD

- ¼ cup plus 2 tablespoons sugar
- 2 tablespoons fresh lemon juice

2 tablespoons finely grated
   fresh ginger
2 pink grapefruit
1 green Thai chile, minced
1 tablespoon soy sauce

1. MAKE THE CRAB BALLS: In a saucepan, melt the butter. Add the onion. Cook over moderately low heat until softened, 4 minutes. In a small bowl, whisk 1 tablespoon of cornstarch into the coconut milk until smooth. Add to the onion. Cook over moderately high heat, whisking, until bubbling and thick, 2 minutes. Remove from the heat. Let cool to room temperature. Stir in the crab; season with salt. Roll rounded tablespoons of the mixture into 20 small balls. Transfer to a parchment-lined baking sheet, cover and freeze until firm, 1 hour.
2. In a large bowl, toss the *panko* with the sesame seeds. In another large bowl, whisk the egg whites and remaining cornstarch until smooth. Dip the frozen crab balls into the egg mixture, letting any excess drip off. Dredge the balls in the *panko* mixture to coat thoroughly. Return them to the baking sheet; let stand at room temperature until thawed but not too soft.
3. MAKE THE GRAPEFRUIT SALAD: In a small saucepan, bring the sugar, lemon juice and ginger to a boil over moderately high heat, stirring, until the sugar dissolves. Strain into a small bowl. Peel the grapefruit with a sharp knife, removing all of the bitter white pith. Cut in between the membranes to release the sections. Transfer to a fine strainer set over a bowl; let stand for 15 minutes to drain. Transfer the grapefruit to a medium bowl; gently toss with 3 tablespoons of ginger syrup and the chile. Let stand for 5 minutes. In another small bowl, mix the remaining ginger syrup and the soy sauce.
4. In a medium saucepan, heat 1½ inches of oil to 300°. Set a rack over a baking sheet. Fry the crab balls, about 4 at a time, until golden brown, about 1 minute; transfer to the rack to drain while you fry the rest.

5. Mound the grapefruit salad in shallow bowls or plates. Arrange the crab balls next to the grapefruit. Pour a puddle of soy syrup on the other side of the crab balls and serve. —*Jean-Georges Vongerichten*

Warm Piquillo and Crab Dip
TOTAL: 25 MIN
4 SERVINGS ● ● ●
1 pound lump crab, picked over
¼ cup mayonnaise
¼ cup crème fraîche
2 tablespoons chopped parsley
2 tablespoons snipped chives
1 tablespoon Dijon mustard
2 teaspoons fresh lemon juice
¼ pound Manchego cheese,
   shredded (1 cup)
One 9-ounce jar piquillo peppers,
   drained and cut into strips

Preheat the broiler. In a bowl, combine the crab, mayonnaise, crème fraîche, parsley, chives, mustard, lemon juice and ¾ cup of the Manchego. Spread in an 11-by-8-inch baking dish. Top with the piquillos and sprinkle with the remaining Manchego. Broil for 5 minutes, or until the cheese is melted and the dip is heated through. Serve hot. —*Jose Garces*
SERVE WITH Crusty bread or crostini.

Pork Dumplings with Aged Black Vinegar
TOTAL: 1 HR
MAKES ABOUT 42 DUMPLINGS ●
½ pound fatty ground pork
1 tablespoon Chinese rice wine
   or sake
1 teaspoon sugar
½ teaspoon salt
¼ teaspoon freshly ground pepper
Cornstarch, for dusting
1 package gyoza wrappers
¼ cup vegetable oil
1 cup water
2 tablespoons Chinese aged black
   vinegar or balsamic vinegar

2 tablespoons light soy sauce
42 paper-thin slices of red apple
   (Optional), for serving

1. In a bowl, mix the pork, wine, sugar, salt and pepper. Dust a rimmed baking sheet with cornstarch. Moisten the edge of a gyoza wrapper with water. Place 1 teaspoon of the filling in the center. Bring the sides up and over, pleating the wrapper; twist the top and set on the baking sheet. Repeat with the remaining filling and wrappers.
2. In each of 2 large skillets, warm 2 tablespoons of oil over low heat. Add the dumplings, increase the heat to high and fry until browned on the bottom, 2 minutes. Pour ½ cup of the water into each skillet, cover and reduce the heat to moderate. Cook until the water has evaporated and the dumplings are tender on top and sizzling and crisp on the bottom, 7 minutes.
3. In a bowl, mix the vinegar and soy sauce. Pour into individual dipping bowls. Arrange the apples on a platter or plates. Set the dumplings on the apple slices. Serve with the dipping sauce. —*Han Feng*

Edamame Tossed with Smoky Salt
TOTAL: 10 MIN
6 SERVINGS ● ●
Any leftover flavored salt is excellent sprinkled on steamed fish or vegetables.
1½ teaspoons Lapsang souchong
   tea leaves
1½ teaspoons kosher salt
One 14-ounce package frozen
   unshelled edamame
1½ teaspoons extra-virgin olive oil

1. In a spice grinder or mini processor, grind the tea and salt to a fine powder.
2. Put the edamame in a microwave-safe bowl and cover with plastic wrap. Microwave at high power until heated through, 5 minutes. Let stand covered for 1 minute.
3. Drain any excess water from the edamame. Transfer to a serving bowl. Toss with the oil, then season with the smoky flavored salt. Serve hot. —*Jonnatan Leiva*

BRIOCHE CRAB MELTS

Brioche Crab Melts

TOTAL: 30 MIN
8 SERVINGS ●

8 small, round brioche or buttery dinner rolls, split crosswise
6 tablespoons truffle butter or unsalted butter, softened (see Note)
½ cup mayonnaise
¼ cup minced red onion
¼ cup chopped flat-leaf parsley
1 tablespoon fresh lime juice
½ Granny Smith apple—quartered lengthwise, cored and thinly sliced crosswise
Several dashes of hot sauce
Salt and freshly ground pepper
1 pound lump crabmeat, picked over
1½ cups shredded Gruyère cheese

1. Preheat the broiler. Spread the cut sides of the brioche with truffle butter and set on a baking sheet, cut sides up. Broil the rolls 6 inches from the heat, until toasted. Reduce the oven temperature to 400°.
2. In a large bowl, mix the mayonnaise, red onion, parsley, lime juice, apple and hot sauce and season with salt and pepper. Fold in the crabmeat.
3. Set the tops of the rolls aside. Top the bottoms with the crab salad; sprinkle with the Gruyère. Bake in the upper third of the oven until the cheese is melted. Close the crab melts and serve. —*Vitaly Paley*
NOTE Urbani Truffles (215-699-8780) sells both white and black truffle butters.
MAKE AHEAD The crab salad can be refrigerated overnight.

Banh Cuon

TOTAL: 1 HR 30 MIN
MAKES 18 CRÊPES ●

Vietnamese *banh cuon* ("rolling cake") is a tender rice-flour crêpe filled with a luscious mix of pork and mushrooms and topped with fried shallots. Here, the crêpes are steamed on a baking sheet in the oven to get them on the table more quickly.

RICE CRÊPES AND FILLING
½ cup rice flour
½ cup cornstarch
¼ cup tapioca flour (see Note)
½ teaspoon salt
3 cups water
2 tablespoons plus 2 teaspoons vegetable oil, plus more for brushing
2 tablespoons dried tree ear mushroom pieces
¾ pound ground pork
1 small onion, finely chopped
1 tablespoon Asian fish sauce
Salt and freshly ground pepper
Nuoc Cham Sauce (recipe follows)
GARNISHES
1 large cucumber, peeled and thinly sliced
½ cup fried shallots (see Note)
½ cup mung bean sprouts

1. **MAKE THE RICE CRÊPES AND FILLING:** In a large bowl, whisk the rice flour with the cornstarch, tapioca flour and salt. Whisk the water and 2 teaspoons of the vegetable oil into the dry ingredients until they are blended.
2. In a small bowl, cover the tree ear mushrooms with warm water and let stand until they are softened, about 5 minutes. Drain and chop the mushrooms.
3. In a small skillet, heat the remaining 2 tablespoons of vegetable oil. Add the ground pork and the chopped onion and cook over moderate heat, breaking up the meat until no pink remains, for about 4 minutes. Stir in the chopped tree ear mushrooms and the fish sauce and season the filling with salt and pepper.
4. Preheat the oven to 425°. Oil 3 large baking sheets. Heat an 8-inch nonstick skillet and brush it with vegetable oil. Whisk the rice-flour batter well. When the vegetable oil is hot, pour 2 tablespoons of the batter into the skillet; tilt and shake

the pan to evenly coat the bottom with batter. Cover the skillet and cook over moderate heat until the crêpe is firm, about 2 minutes. With a spatula, flip the crêpe and cook for 30 seconds longer. Flip the crêpe out flat onto one of the prepared baking sheets. Repeat with the remaining batter to make a total of 18 crêpes; don't let the crêpes overlap on the baking sheets or they will stick together.
5. Spoon about 2 tablespoons of the pork filling into the center of each crêpe and fold in the sides to enclose the filling and form a neat square. Cover the crêpes with foil and bake them until they are heated through, about 5 minutes.
6. Arrange the rice crêpe packets on a platter. Spoon the Nuoc Cham Sauce over them. Scatter the cucumber slices, fried shallots and bean sprouts all over the crêpe packets and serve right away.
—*Marcia Kiesel*
NOTE Tapioca flour is available at specialty food stores. Fried shallots are available at Asian markets.
MAKE AHEAD The pork filling can be refrigerated overnight. The crêpe packets can stand at room temperature, covered, for up to 2 hours before reheating.

NUOC CHAM SAUCE

TOTAL: 10 MIN
MAKES ABOUT ⅓ CUP ● ●

2 red Thai chiles or 1 medium jalapeño, thickly sliced
2 medium garlic cloves, thickly sliced
2 tablespoons sugar
2 tablespoons Asian fish sauce
2 tablespoons fresh lime juice
2 tablespoons water

In a mortar, pound the sliced red Thai chiles, sliced garlic and sugar to a paste. Stir in the Asian fish sauce, lime juice and water and serve. —*M.K.*
MAKE AHEAD The nuoc cham sauce can be refrigerated overnight.

starters

Sprouted Mung Bean Chaat

TOTAL: 20 MIN

4 SERVINGS ● ● ●

Chaat are small plates of delectable snacks eaten in India and South Asia.

- 3 cups chilled sprouted mung or other beans
- 1 large vine-ripe tomato, cut into ⅓-inch dice
- 1 medium red onion, cut into ¼-inch dice
- ⅓ cup chopped cilantro
- 1 jalapeño, seeded and minced
- 1 teaspoon dried mint
- 3 tablespoons fresh lemon juice
- ½ teaspoon ground cumin
- ½ teaspoon sugar
- ⅛ teaspoon cayenne pepper
- ¼ teaspoon freshly ground black pepper

Kosher salt

Rinse the mung beans under cold running water, drain well. In a large bowl, toss the mung beans with all of the other ingredients. —*Suvir Saran*

SERVE WITH Pappadams or pita chips.

MAKE AHEAD The chaat can be refrigerated for up to 4 hours.

Mushroom Spring Rolls with Creamy Ginger Sauce

TOTAL: 50 MIN

MAKES 10 SPRING ROLLS

- 3 tablespoons unsalted butter
- ½ pound oyster mushrooms, cut into ½-inch pieces
- ½ pound shiitake mushrooms, stems discarded, caps sliced ¼ inch thick
- ½ pound cremini mushrooms, sliced ¼ inch thick
- 2 tablespoons Shaoxing wine or dry sherry
- 2 tablespoons soy sauce

Salt and freshly ground black pepper

- 2 tablespoons extra-virgin olive oil

- 2 garlic cloves, thinly sliced
- 1 plump lemongrass stalk, tender white inner bulb only, minced
- 1 red Thai chile, minced
- 1 medium shallot, minced
- 1 tablespoon plus 1½ teaspoons minced fresh ginger
- ½ teaspoon finely grated lemon zest
- 10 thin egg roll or spring roll wrappers
- 1 large egg, beaten
- ¼ cup mayonnaise
- ¼ cup vegetable oil, plus more for frying
- 1 tablespoon chopped tarragon
- 1 tablespoon fresh lime juice
- 1 tablespoon rice vinegar
- 10 Boston lettuce leaves, halved

1. In a very large skillet, melt the butter. Add all of the mushrooms, the wine and soy sauce and season with salt and pepper. Cook over high heat, stirring, for 1 minute. Cover and cook over moderately low heat, stirring a few times, until the mushrooms have released their liquid and are tender, about 8 minutes. Uncover and cook over moderate heat, stirring occasionally, until browned, about 4 minutes longer.

2. In a small skillet, heat the olive oil. Add the garlic, lemongrass, chile, shallot and 1 tablespoon of ginger. Cook over low heat, stirring occasionally, until golden brown, about 7 minutes. Add the lemon zest, then stir into the mushrooms.

3. On a work surface, lightly brush an egg roll wrapper with the beaten egg. Spread ¼ cup of the mushrooms on the lower third of the wrapper; bring the lower edge up and over the filling and roll up, folding in the sides as you go. Lightly flatten the roll and brush it with the beaten egg. Repeat with the remaining wrappers and filling.

4. In a blender, puree the mayonnaise with the ¼ cup of vegetable oil, the tarragon, lime juice, vinegar and the remaining 1½ teaspoons of ginger until smooth. Season with salt and pepper.

5. Line a baking sheet with paper towels. In a medium skillet, heat 1 inch of vegetable oil to 250°. Add 3 or 4 spring rolls and fry gently until nicely browned, about 1 minute per side. Drain on the prepared baking sheet. Repeat with the remaining spring rolls.

6. Cut the rolls in half on the diagonal, wrap in lettuce leaves and serve with the ginger sauce. —*Jean-Georges Vongerichten*

MAKE AHEAD The spring rolls can be assembled and refrigerated for up to 4 hours. Bring them to room temperature before frying, about 30 minutes.

Grilled Prosciutto and Fontina Rolls with Mostarda

TOTAL: 30 MIN

4 SERVINGS ●

- 24 thin slices of prosciutto (¾ pound)
- 12 thin slices of Fontina cheese (6 ounces)
- 1¼ cups Dried Apricot and Cherry Mostarda (recipe follows)
- ½ large baguette, halved lengthwise and cut crosswise into eight 1-inch slices, for a total of 16

Extra-virgin olive oil, for brushing

1. Light a grill. Arrange the prosciutto slices on a work surface in pairs, forming twelve 8-by-4-inch rectangles. Top the prosciutto with the cheese, being sure not to let the cheese hang over the prosciutto. Spoon 1 teaspoon of the mostarda on top of the cheese and roll up the prosciutto to form short cylinders.

2. Double-skewer 3 of the prosciutto rolls between 4 alternating slices of baguette. Push the skewers through the cut sides of the bread. Repeat with the remaining prosciutto rolls and bread. Brush the skewers with olive oil and grill over high heat, turning occasionally, until lightly browned and sizzling, 2 to 3 minutes. Serve the rolls and toasted bread with the remaining mostarda. —*Grace Parisi*

DRIED APRICOT AND CHERRY MOSTARDA

TOTAL: 20 MIN

MAKES 1¼ CUPS ● ● ●

- ¼ pound dried apricots, cut into ¼ inch pieces
- ¼ cup dried cherries, coarsely chopped
- 1 shallot, minced
- ½ teaspoons minced crystallized ginger
- ½ cup dry white wine
- 3 tablespoons white wine vinegar
- 3 tablespoons water
- 3 tablespoons sugar
- 1 teaspoon dry mustard
- 1 teaspoon Dijon mustard
- 1 tablespoon unsalted butter

In a small saucepan, combine the apricots, cherries, shallot, ginger, wine, vinegar, water and sugar and bring to a boil. Cover and cook over moderate heat until the liquid is absorbed and the fruit is softened, 10 minutes. Stir in the mustards and butter. Simmer until the mostarda is jamlike, 2 to 3 minutes longer. Serve the mostarda warm or at room temperature. —*G.P.*

OTHER USES Serve the mostarda alongside charcuterie or cheese, or spread on a sandwich. It's also delicious with grilled chicken, steak, pork, lamb and sausages.

MAKE AHEAD The mostarda can be refrigerated for up to 1 week.

Daikon-Papaya Summer Rolls with Minted Yogurt Sauce

ACTIVE: 1 HR; TOTAL: 2 HR 30 MIN

4 SERVINGS ● ●

- One 4-inch piece of daikon, peeled and julienned
- 2 medium carrots, peeled and julienned
- 1 European seedless cucumber— peeled, seeded and julienned
- ½ small green papaya—peeled, seeded and julienned
- 1 tablespoon kosher salt

- 2½ tablespoons sugar
- 3 ounces rice vermicelli
- 2 tablespoons chopped mint
- 2 tablespoons chopped basil
- 2 tablespoons chopped cilantro
- ¼ cup plus 2 tablespoons fresh lime juice
- 3 tablespoons Asian fish sauce
- 1 tablespoon rice vinegar
- 1 tablespoon mirin
- 1 tablespoon minced fresh ginger
- 1 tablespoon minced shallot
- 1 tablespoon whole-milk Greek yogurt
- 1 tablespoon mayonnaise

Eight 8-inch-round rice paper wrappers, plus extra in case of breakage

1. In a large bowl, toss the daikon, carrots, cucumber and papaya with the salt and ½ tablespoon of the sugar. Let stand, stirring occasionally, until the vegetables are wilted and have released a good amount of liquid, about 1 hour. Drain and squeeze out as much liquid as possible. Wipe out the bowl and return the vegetables to it.

2. Meanwhile, bring a large saucepan of water to a boil. Add the vermicelli, cover and remove from the heat; let stand until softened, 3 to 4 minutes. Drain and cool under cold water. Drain again, pressing out the excess water. Using scissors, cut the vermicelli into 4-inch lengths. Add to the vegetables, along with the chopped mint, basil and cilantro.

3. In a small bowl, combine the lime juice, fish sauce, vinegar and mirin with the remaining 2 tablespoons of sugar; stir to dissolve the sugar. Add the ginger and shallot and pour all but 2 teaspoons of the dressing over the vermicelli and vegetables. Let stand for 1 hour.

4. Drain the mixture, pressing to squeeze out as much liquid as possible. Add the yogurt and mayonnaise to the reserved 2 teaspoons of dressing and refrigerate.

5. Fill a large pie plate halfway with warm water. Working with 1 or 2 rice papers at a time, soak the wrappers in the water until pliable, about 2 minutes. Lay the wrappers on a work surface and blot any excess water. Spoon about ½ cup of the vegetables and vermicelli onto the bottom third of a wrapper and tightly roll into a 5-inch log, tucking in the ends as you roll. Transfer to a cutting board. Cover the summer roll with a damp paper towel and a sheet of plastic wrap. Repeat with the remaining wrappers and filling.

6. Cut each roll into 4 pieces and stand them cut side up on a platter. Spoon about ½ teaspoon of the creamy sauce onto each roll and serve. —*Douglas Keane*

Olives Stuffed with Almonds, Anchovies and Peppers

ACTIVE: 40 MIN; TOTAL: 1 HR 10 MIN

12 SERVINGS ● ●

- 36 large Sicilian olives (about 1 pound)
- 36 salted roasted whole almonds
- 9 oil-packed anchovy fillets, each cut lengthwise into 4 thin strips
- 4 large piquillo peppers from a jar, drained, each cut lengthwise into 9 thin strips
- 3 tablespoons extra-virgin olive oil
- 1 tablespoon sherry vinegar
- 1 garlic clove, minced
- 1½ teaspoons finely grated orange zest

1. With the side of a large chef's knife, lightly crush each of the olives and remove the pits, keeping the olives as intact as possible. Stuff 1 almond, 1 anchovy strip and 1 piquillo strip into each olive. Place the stuffed olives on a platter.

2. In a bowl, stir together the olive oil, vinegar, garlic and orange zest. Pour over the olives and marinate at room temperature for at least 30 minutes or up to 2 hours. —*José Andrés*

starters

Roman-Style Chopped Chicken Liver Crostini

TOTAL: 30 MIN

8 SERVINGS ● ● ●

- 1 large baguette, sliced on the diagonal ¼ inch thick
- 3 tablespoons extra-virgin olive oil, plus more for brushing
- ½ pound chicken livers, trimmed

Salt and freshly ground pepper

- 4 large sage leaves, chopped
- 2 medium shallots, minced
- 2 garlic cloves, minced
- 2 anchovy fillets, chopped
- ⅓ cup vin santo or dry Marsala
- 2 tablespoons drained capers, 1 tablespoon chopped
- 1 hard-cooked egg, coarsely grated

1. Preheat the oven to 350°. Brush both sides of the baguette slices with olive oil and arrange them on a large rimmed baking sheet. Bake the crostini for 12 minutes, or until crisp and golden. Let cool.

2. In a large skillet, heat the 3 tablespoons of olive oil. Add the chicken livers, season with salt and pepper and cook over moderately high heat until browned on the bottom, 1 minute. Turn the livers. Add the sage, shallots, garlic and anchovies. Cook over moderate heat, stirring occasionally, until the shallots are softened, 3 minutes. Add the vin santo and the 1 tablespoon of whole capers and cook until the wine has reduced by half, 3 minutes.

3. Transfer the liver mixture to a food processor and pulse until coarsely chopped. Scrape the liver into a crock or serving bowl. Fold in the egg and season with salt and pepper. Sprinkle the chopped capers on top and serve at room temperature with the crostini. —*Vitaly Paley*

MAKE AHEAD The chopped liver can be tightly covered with plastic wrap pressed to the surface and refrigerated overnight. Let return to room temperature before serving. The crostini can be stored in an airtight container for up to 2 days.

Pastrami-Spiced Gravlax

ACTIVE: 30 MIN; TOTAL: 30 MIN
PLUS 3 DAYS CURING

4 SERVINGS ● ●

GRAVLAX

- 1½ pounds center-cut salmon fillet with skin
- 1½ tablespoons fresh lemon juice
- ½ cup kosher salt
- 3 tablespoons raw sugar, such as turbinado or demerara
- 1½ tablespoons coarsely cracked black pepper
- 1 cup coarsely chopped cilantro leaves and stems
- 1 cup coarsely chopped parsley leaves and stems
- 2 shallots, minced

PASTRAMI GLAZE

- 2 tablespoons molasses
- 2 bay leaves, torn into large pieces
- ¼ teaspoon cayenne pepper
- 1 teaspoon caraway seeds
- 1 teaspoon coriander seeds
- 1 teaspoon sweet paprika
- 1 teaspoon freshly ground pepper

1. MAKE THE GRAVLAX: Rub the salmon fillet all over with the lemon juice; place skin side down, in a glass dish. In a bowl, mix the salt, raw sugar, black pepper, cilantro, parsley and shallots and rub all over the fish. Cover the salmon loosely with plastic wrap; refrigerate for 2 days.

2. MAKE THE PASTRAMI GLAZE: In a small saucepan, combine the molasses, bay leaves and cayenne and bring to a simmer. Let cool to room temperature.

3. In a skillet, lightly toast the caraway and coriander seeds over moderate heat, shaking the pan, until fragrant, 1 minute. Transfer to a mortar and let cool completely; crush as finely as possible with a pestle. Stir in the paprika and ground pepper.

4. Gently scrape the seasonings off the gravlax. Set the gravlax on a plate, skin side down. Brush the gravlax with the molasses; pick off the bay leaves. Sprinkle

the ground spices evenly over the fillet. Refrigerate the gravlax, uncovered, for at least 12 hours or overnight.

5. Using a long, sharp knife, cut the gravlax crosswise into very thin slices. Arrange the slices on plates. Serve. —*Nicki Reiss*

SERVE WITH Toasted brown or black bread and *moutarde violette* (grainy mustard with grape must) or Dijon mustard.

MAKE AHEAD The pastrami-cured gravlax can be tightly wrapped in plastic and refrigerated for up to 1 week.

Crudités with Wasabi Dip

TOTAL: 20 MIN

4 SERVINGS ● ● ●

- 2 teaspoons wasabi powder
- 2 teaspoons water
- 1 cup plain, nonfat Greek or Greek-style yogurt
- 3 ounces fresh goat cheese, at room temperature

Pinch of sugar

Salt

- 1 medium head of broccoflower or cauliflower, cut into 1½-inch florets
- 4 celery ribs, cut into 4-by-½-inch sticks
- 1 fennel bulb, halved lengthwise and cut into ½-inch wedges
- 1 large seedless cucumber, peeled and cut into 3-by-½-inch sticks
- ⅓ cup radish sprouts (optional)

1. In a medium bowl, whisk the wasabi powder with the water until a smooth paste forms; let stand for 5 minutes. Whisk in the yogurt, goat cheese and sugar. Season with salt. Transfer the dip to a serving bowl and refrigerate until chilled.

2. In a large pot of boiling salted water, cook the broccoflower until al dente, 3 minutes. Drain and rinse under cold water until cool. Drain well and pat dry.

3. Arrange the broccoflower, celery, fennel and cucumber on a platter. Top the dip with the sprouts and serve. —*Susan Spungen*

starters

Three-Pepper Spiced Pepitas

ACTIVE: 5 MIN; TOTAL: 20 MIN

6 SERVINGS ● ● ●

These salty, smoky toasted pumpkin seeds are utterly addictive and great with cocktails.

- ½ pound raw *pepitas* (pumpkin seeds)
- 2 teaspoons extra-virgin olive oil
- 1½ teaspoons Spanish pimentón de la Vera or other smoked paprika
- ½ teaspoon hot paprika

Large pinch of cayenne pepper

Kosher salt

Preheat the oven to 350°. Spread the *pepitas* in a single layer on a rimmed baking sheet. Bake in the oven for about 12 minutes, stirring once, until the pepitas are lightly toasted. Transfer the toasted pepitas to a large, shallow bowl. Add the olive oil and toss to coat. Add the pimentón, hot paprika, cayenne and salt and toss the pepitas again. Let the spiced pepitas cool completely, then serve.
—*Matthew Hamilton*

MAKE AHEAD The *pepitas* can be kept in an airtight container for up to 3 days.

Truffled Popcorn

TOTAL: 10 MIN

6 SERVINGS ● ●

This luxe popcorn is flavored with both truffle oil and minced black truffles.

- 6 tablespoons unsalted butter
- 1 tablespoon minced black truffle (optional), see Note
- 1 teaspoon white truffle oil

Salt

- 3 tablespoons vegetable oil
- 7 ounces popcorn kernels (1 cup)

Freshly ground pepper

1. In a small saucepan, melt the butter over low heat. Stir in the truffles, truffle oil and a pinch of salt; keep warm.

2. In a large, heavy pot, heat the vegetable oil. Add the popcorn kernels, cover and cook over moderate heat until the popcorn starts popping. Continue cooking, shaking the pan continuously, until the popping has almost stopped. Carefully pour the popcorn into a very large bowl, add the truffled butter and toss well. Season with salt and pepper and serve right away.
—*Bruce Dillon*

NOTE Jarred truffle shavings are available at specialty food stores.

Natchitoches Meat Pies with Pepper Dipping Sauce

ACTIVE: 50 MIN; TOTAL: 1 HR 10 MIN

PLUS 6 HR CHILLING

8 SERVINGS

These crusty little meat pies, filled with seared chile-spiked beef and pork, are a staple of Louisiana cooking; in fact, the town of Natchitoches (pronounced "NAK-uh-tush") hosts a festival in their honor each fall.

- 1½ cups sour cream
- ⅓ cup buttermilk
- 1½ teaspoons dried thyme
- 1 teaspoon freshly cracked black pepper
- 1 scant teaspoon granulated garlic

Tabasco sauce

Kosher salt

- 1 tablespoon extra-virgin olive oil
- 2 tablespoons diced onion
- 2 tablespoons diced celery
- 2 tablespoons diced green bell pepper
- 1 jalapeño, seeded and minced
- 2 large garlic cloves, minced
- ½ pound ground pork

ingredients
cured meats

DRY-CURED MEAT

Jambon de Bayonne, the most well-known French dry-cured ham, is traditionally made in the southwest, near the Pyrenees. Italy's **prosciutto** is probably the most famous cured ham in the world; **coppa,** made from pork shoulder, is equally tasty. In Spain, dry-cured hams like **jamón serrano** are rubbed with sea salt, then aged a year or more; **lomo embuchado** is cured pork loin. Real **Black Forest ham** is an air-dried, salt-cured, smoked German ham.

DRY-CURED SAUSAGE

French **saucisson sec** is made from pork and seasoned with spices that vary by region. **Soppressata** is a sweet-tasting, coarsely ground sausage from Italy; other classic Italian sausages include **finocchiona** and **cacciatorini. Chorizo,** from Spain, gets its characteristic tangy flavor from paprika. **Fuet,** is a long, thin Spanish pork sausage.

COOKED SAUSAGE

French garlic sausage, or **saucisson à l'ail,** is delicious by itself, but it's also a key ingredient in cassoulet. Italian **mortadella** is flavored with pistachios, black pepper, wine and

sugar, then steamed. Spanish **butifarra negra,** made with pig's blood, is popular in Barcelona; **butifarra blanca** is pork seasoned with nutmeg and white pepper. Germany's **frankfurter,** the original hot dog, is made from pork and beef. Spreadable **liverwurst,** also German, is made with pork and pork liver.

½ pound ground beef
Freshly ground black pepper
16 frozen empanada wrappers
(see Note), thawed
All-purpose flour, for dusting
Vegetable oil, for frying

1. In a medium bowl, whisk the sour cream with the buttermilk, thyme, cracked black pepper and granulated garlic. Season the sauce with Tabasco and salt. Cover the bowl and refrigerate the sauce for at least 6 hours or overnight.

2. In a large skillet, heat the olive oil. Add the diced onion, celery and bell pepper, the minced jalapeño and garlic and cook over moderate heat until the onion is translucent, about 5 minutes.

3. Raise the heat to moderately high, add the ground pork and beef and cook until no trace of pink remains, about 5 minutes. Season the meat with salt and freshly ground pepper. Transfer the meat to a baking sheet and refrigerate until chilled, at least 20 minutes.

4. Arrange the empanada wrappers on a very lightly floured work surface. Spoon 2 tablespoons of the meat filling onto the lower half of each wrapper. Lightly moisten the edge of each wrapper with water, fold it over the meat filling and press the edges together to seal the meat pie. Crimp decoratively with a fork.

5. In a large, deep skillet, heat 1½ inches of vegetable oil to 375°. Line a baking sheet with paper towels. Working in batches, fry the meat pies, turning them once, until they are golden, about 2 minutes. Transfer the cooked meat pies to the prepared baking sheet to drain, then serve them hot with the black pepper dipping sauce. —*Jeff Tunks*

NOTE Empanada wrappers, also called *discos*, are available at Latin American food stores and in the freezer section of most supermarkets; Goya makes a good variety. If you can't find them, substitute wonton wrappers.

Avocado-Caviar Mousse
TOTAL: 15 MIN
MAKES 1⅓ CUPS ● ●

This delicately creamy and briny mousse is a clever combination of F&W's Grace Parisi's two favorite dips—guacamole and taramasalata (the salty, tangy, roe-rich Greek recipe).

2 ripe Hass avocados—halved, pitted and flesh scooped out
4 ounces fresh goat cheese, at room temperature
2 tablespoons heavy cream or whole milk
½ teaspoon finely grated lemon zest
1 tablespoon fresh lemon juice
1½ ounces sturgeon-style caviar, such as paddlefish, hackleback, or California osetra (3 tablespoons)
2 tablespoons snipped chives
Salt and freshly ground black pepper

In a food processor, puree the avocados with the goat cheese, cream, lemon zest and lemon juice. Transfer to a bowl. Fold in the caviar and chives and season with salt and pepper. —*Grace Parisi*

SERVE WITH Brioche toasts, grissini, pita crisps, steamed shrimp or cut-up raw vegetables such as celery sticks, endive spears and cucumber batons.

MAKE AHEAD Cover the mousse directly with plastic wrap and refrigerate for up to 2 hours. Let stand at room temperature for 15 minutes before serving.

Cauliflower Fritters
TOTAL: 45 MIN
MAKES ABOUT 3 DOZEN FRITTERS ● ●

The batter for these wonderful tapas contains crunchy nubs of chopped cauliflower florets. Spoonfuls of the batter are fried in a skillet and then the fritters are topped with both a yogurt sauce and a dollop of salmon caviar.

½ large head of cauliflower, florets finely chopped (2 cups)
Salt
½ teaspoon baking powder
¼ teaspoon ground cumin
¼ teaspoon ground coriander
¼ teaspoon freshly ground black pepper
⅛ teaspoon ground allspice
3 large egg whites
1½ teaspoons extra-virgin olive oil, plus more for frying
6 tablespoons whole milk yogurt
Salmon caviar, for garnish

1. Preheat the oven to 350°. Bring a medium saucepan of salted water to a boil. Add the cauliflower and cook for 2 minutes. Drain well; spread it out on a paper towel–lined baking sheet to cool; pat dry.

2. In a small bowl, combine ½ teaspoon of salt with the baking powder, ground cumin, coriander, black pepper and allspice. In a large bowl, using an electric mixer, beat the egg whites with a pinch of salt at high speed until firm peaks form. Fold the cauliflower and the spice mixture into the beaten egg whites.

3. Heat a large nonstick skillet. Very lightly oil the skillet. Drop tablespoons of the fritter batter into the skillet and cook over moderately high heat until the fritters are browned on the bottom, about 2 minutes. Reduce the heat to moderate and cook the fritters until browned on the other side, about 2 minutes. Transfer the fritters to a large rimmed baking sheet. Repeat with the remaining batter, coating the skillet with oil as needed.

4. In a bowl, blend the yogurt with the 1½ teaspoons of olive oil and season with salt. Reheat the fritters in the oven, about 2 minutes. Garnish each fritter with ½ teaspoon of yogurt sauce and some caviar and serve. —*José Andrés*

MAKE AHEAD The fritters can made 3 hours in advance. Reheat the fritters in a 350° oven for 5 minutes.

HEARTS OF PALM SALAD WITH
CILANTRO VINAIGRETTE (P. 43)

salads

"It's great when I can do a sunchoke and arugula salad at the restaurant and say 'The arugula is from my garden.'"

—**Brian Bistrong,** chef, The Harrison, New York City

ARUGULA SALAD WITH GRILLED MUSHROOMS AND GOAT CHEESE

CHOPPED GREEK SALAD

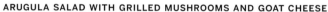

Arugula Salad with Grilled Mushrooms and Goat Cheese

ACTIVE: 25 MIN; TOTAL: 50 MIN

4 SERVINGS ●

Dr. Andrew Weil, the famed holistic healer and author, crumbles just a little fresh goat cheese over the mushrooms in this peppery salad.

- ½ cup dry white vermouth
- ½ cup extra-virgin olive oil
- Salt and freshly ground black pepper
- 1 pound mixed mushrooms— oyster, shiitake, portobello and cremini
- 1 tablespoon white wine vinegar
- 1 tablespoon very finely chopped shallot
- 4 ounces baby arugula
- ¼ cup coarsely chopped walnuts
- 1½ ounces fresh goat cheese, crumbled (scant ¼ cup)

1. In a large bowl, whisk the vermouth and olive oil; season with salt and pepper. Trim the root ends of the oyster mushrooms, leaving them attached in small bunches. Discard the shiitake stems and leave the caps whole. Stem the portobellos. Wipe off the cremini. Add all of the mushrooms to the marinade; toss and let stand for 20 minutes, stirring occasionally.

2. Light a grill or preheat a broiler. Drain the mushrooms; reserve 1 tablespoon of the marinade. Grill the mushrooms or broil them over high heat until browned and tender, about 15 minutes. Thickly slice the grilled mushrooms.

3. Add the vinegar and shallot to the large bowl and whisk in the reserved marinade to taste. Add the arugula and walnuts, season with salt and pepper and toss to coat. Transfer the salad to four plates, top with the mushrooms and goat cheese and serve.—*Dr. Andrew Weil*

Chopped Greek Salad

TOTAL: 25 MIN

4 SERVINGS ● ●

Use dried Greek oregano in this vinegary salad. Found at specialty food markets, it has a lovely floral aroma.

- ½ pound green beans, halved crosswise
- 3 tablespoons red wine vinegar
- 1 garlic clove
- ½ small shallot, chopped
- ½ teaspoon Dijon mustard
- ½ teaspoon dried Greek oregano
- ½ teaspoon fresh thyme
- 1 large basil leaf
- ¼ cup extra-virgin olive oil
- Kosher salt and freshly ground pepper
- 1 pound grape tomatoes, halved
- ½ small red onion, halved lengthwise and very thinly sliced crosswise
- ¼ pound Greek feta cheese, crumbled (1 cup)

1. In a medium pot of boiling salted water, cook the green beans until they are just tender, about 4 minutes. Drain the green beans and rinse them under cold water; pat the beans dry.

2. In a blender, combine the red wine vinegar with the garlic clove, shallot, Dijon mustard, oregano, thyme and basil and puree until smooth. With the machine on, slowly add the olive oil. Season the vinaigrette with salt and pepper.

3. In a large bowl, combine the blanched green beans with the halved grape tomatoes, sliced red onion and crumbled feta cheese. Toss the salad with the vinaigrette and serve immediately.
—*Michael Psilakis*

Greek Salad with Shallot Vinaigrette

TOTAL: 30 MIN

8 SERVINGS ●

For this clever riff on Greek salad, traditional ingredients like feta cheese and black olives get chopped into smallpieces, then tossed with a shallot dressing.

- 2 **tablespoons white balsamic vinegar**
- 1 **teaspoon fresh lemon juice**
- 1 **small shallot, halved**
- 2 **tablespoons extra-virgin olive oil**
- 2 **tablespoons canola oil**

Salt and freshly ground pepper

- 10 **ounces mixed baby greens, coarsely chopped**
- 4 **Belgian endives—halved, cored and coarsely chopped**
- 1 **English cucumber—peeled, halved, seeded and cut into ½-inch dice**
- 1 **pint grape tomatoes, halved**
- ¼ **cup coarsely chopped dill**
- 5 **ounces pitted kalamata olives (¾ cup), halved**
- ½ **pound feta cheese, crumbled (2 cups)**

1. In a blender, combine the vinegar, lemon juice and shallot and puree. With the machine on, add the olive oil and canola oil and puree until emulsified. Season the dressing with salt and pepper.

2. In a bowl, toss the greens, endives, cucumber, tomatoes, dill, olives and feta. Add half of the dressing, season with salt and pepper and toss. Add the remaining dressing, toss and serve. —*Colin Devlin*

MAKE AHEAD The dressing can be refrigerated overnight.

Chopped Salad with Beets, Beans, Goat Cheese and Hazelnuts

ACTIVE: 30 MIN; TOTAL: 1 HR

6 SERVINGS ●

Chef Hugo Matheson of The Kitchen in Boulder, Colorado, suggests reserving the beet greens to use as a bed for grilled fish: Clean them, then wilt in a saucepan with a bit of water, olive oil and salt.

- 1 **large beet (6 ounces), quartered**

Water

- ¼ **cup skinned hazelnuts**
- ¼ **pound green beans**
- 2 **tablespoons plain low-fat yogurt**
- 1½ **tablespoons fresh lemon juice**
- 1 **teaspoon honey**
- 2 **tablespoons extra-virgin olive oil**

Salt and freshly ground pepper

- ½ **pound mixed salad greens, such as baby romaine, butter lettuce, radicchio and endives, coarsely chopped**
- 1 **carrot, finely diced**
- 1 **celery rib, finely diced**
- 1 **plum tomato, seeded and chopped**
- 1 **tablespoon chopped mint leaves**
- 2½ **ounces soft, fresh goat cheese, crumbled**

1. Preheat the oven to 375°. Place the beet in a small baking dish with ¼ cup of water. Cover with foil and roast the beet for 45 minutes, until tender. Let cool slightly, then peel and finely dice.

2. Meanwhile, spread the hazelnuts in a pie plate and toast them in the oven for about 10 minutes, until they are golden. Let cool, then coarsely chop the nuts.

3. In a small saucepan of boiling salted water, blanch the green beans until crisp-tender, about 5 minutes. Drain and cool under running water. Pat the beans dry and cut them into ¼-inch pieces.

4. In a large bowl, whisk the yogurt with the lemon juice, honey and olive oil and season the dressing with salt and pepper. Add the diced beet, hazelnuts, green beans, salad greens, carrot, celery, tomato, mint and goat cheese and toss gently. Serve the salad right away.
—*Hugo Matheson and Kimbal Musk*

MAKE AHEAD The recipe can be prepared through Step 3 and refrigerated overnight. Store the toasted hazelnuts in an airtight container.

Arugula and Endive Salad with Pine Nuts and Parmesan

TOTAL: 20 MIN

4 SERVINGS ● ●

- 3 **tablespoons pine nuts**
- 2 **tablespoons extra-virgin olive oil**
- 1 **tablespoon fresh lemon juice**

Salt and freshly ground pepper

- 2 **Belgian endives, thinly sliced crosswise**

One 6-ounce bunch of arugula, thick stems discarded

- 1 **cup cherry or grape tomatoes, halved**
- ¼ **cup Parmesan cheese shavings**

1. In a small skillet, toast the pine nuts over moderately low heat, shaking the skillet occasionally, until golden, about 4 minutes. Transfer the pine nuts to a plate to cool.

2. In a large bowl, combine the olive oil with the lemon juice and season with salt and pepper. Add the endives, arugula, tomatoes, Parmesan cheese shavings and the toasted pine nuts and toss thoroughly. Serve right away. —*Steven Raichlen*

salads

Baby Leaf Lettuce with Olives and Watermelon

TOTAL: 30 MIN

6 SERVINGS ● ● ●

Chef Brian Bistrong of The Harrison in New York City loves adding crisp and juicy watermelon chunks to salads. He takes the idea one step further here by mixing watermelon juice into the dressing, for a sweet-tangy vinaigrette.

- 2 cups seedless watermelon chunks (¾ inch thick)
- 2 tablespoons extra-virgin olive oil
- 1 tablespoon Champagne or white wine vinegar

Salt and freshly ground pepper

- 12 loose cups baby leaf lettuce or 3 heads Bibb lettuce, torn
- ½ small red onion, thinly sliced
- ½ cup snipped chives
- ¼ cup flat-leaf parsley leaves
- 3 ounces pitted Picholine olives, halved (½ cup)

1. In a blender or food processor, puree ½ cup of the watermelon chunks. Strain the juice through a fine sieve into a large bowl. You should have about 2 tablespoons. Discard the solids.

ingredient

nut oils

Pistachio and pecan oils from **La Tourangelle** are pressed from nuts roasted in cast-iron kettles. **Details** $25 for 250 ml; latourangelle.com.

2. Whisk the olive oil and Champagne vinegar into the watermelon juice and season with salt and pepper. Add the lettuce, onion, chives, parsley, olives and the remaining 1½ cups of watermelon chunks and toss gently. Transfer the salad to a large platter and serve right away.
—*Brian Bistrong*

Watercress and Orange Salad with Black Olive Vinaigrette

TOTAL: 30 MIN

8 SERVINGS ● ●

- ½ cup pitted kalamata olives
- 1 small garlic clove, chopped
- ½ teaspoon chopped rosemary
- 3 tablespoons red wine vinegar
- 5 tablespoons extra-virgin olive oil

Kosher salt and freshly ground pepper

- 3 navel oranges
- 2 large bunches of watercress, thick stems discarded
- 2 Belgian endives—halved, cored and thinly sliced lengthwise
- 1 cup flat-leaf parsley leaves
- 1 small red onion, halved and thinly sliced

1. Coarsely chop ¼ cup of the olives and transfer them to a small bowl. In a mini processor, pulse the remaining ¼ cup of olives with the garlic and rosemary until the olives are chopped. Add the vinegar and pulse twice to combine; add to the chopped olives in the bowl. Whisk in the olive oil and season with salt and pepper.
2. Using a sharp knife, peel the oranges, removing all of the bitter white pith. Working over a bowl, cut in between the membranes to release the orange sections into the bowl; drain the juice and reserve for another use. Add the watercress, endives, parsley and onion. Pour the dressing over the salad and toss well. Season with salt and pepper and serve at once.
—*Melissa Rubel*

MAKE AHEAD The dressing can be refrigerated for up to 2 days.

Spinach Salad with Bacon and Buttermilk–Blue Cheese Dressing

TOTAL: 25 MIN

8 SERVINGS ●

Vitaly Paley, chef and owner of Paley's Place in Portland, Oregon, uses crinkly spinach leaves instead of traditional shredded iceberg lettuce in his satisfying version of the classic Cobb salad because he thinks spinach adds more flavor. For the dressing, he favors a pungent, creamy blue cheese like Roquefort, Point Reyes Original Blue, Rogue River or Maytag.

- ¼ cup buttermilk
- ¼ cup sour cream
- 1 small shallot, minced
- 2 teaspoons cider vinegar
- 3 ounces Roquefort or other blue cheese, crumbled (¾ cup)

Salt and freshly ground pepper

- ½ pound lean slab bacon, sliced ¼ inch thick and cut crosswise into thin strips
- ¾ pound spinach, large stems discarded
- 1 small red onion, halved lengthwise and thinly sliced
- 2 hard-cooked eggs, quartered

1. In a medium bowl, whisk the buttermilk with the sour cream, shallot and cider vinegar. Stir in the blue cheese. Season the dressing with salt and pepper.
2. In a large nonstick skillet, cook the bacon over moderate heat until it is crisp, about 6 minutes. Using a slotted spoon, transfer the cooked bacon to paper towels to drain.
3. In a very large bowl, toss the spinach with the red onion slices and bacon and then toss the spinach salad with the blue cheese dressing. Mound the spinach salad on plates, top with the hard-cooked egg quarters and serve.
—*Vitaly Paley*

MAKE AHEAD The dressing can be refrigerated for up to 3 days.

SPINACH SALAD WITH WARM BACON VINAIGRETTE

MIXED GREENS WITH PLUMS AND PARMESAN CHEESE

Spinach Salad with Warm Bacon Vinaigrette

TOTAL: 25 MIN

4 SERVINGS ●

- 3 strips thickly sliced lean bacon, cut into ¼-inch strips
- 2 tablespoons extra-virgin olive oil
- 1 shallot, minced
- 2 tablespoons sherry vinegar
- 1 tablespoon whole-grain mustard
- 1 teaspoon chopped thyme
- 2 small plums, cut into thin wedges, or 4 fresh purple figs, quartered

One 5-ounce bag of baby spinach

Salt and freshly ground pepper

- ¼ cup marcona or other salted roasted almonds, coarsely chopped
- 2 ounces crumbled blue cheese, such as Cabrales
- ¼ pound thinly sliced serrano ham or prosciutto (8 slices)

1. In a large skillet, cook the bacon in the olive oil over moderately high heat until browned and crisp, about 6 minutes. Remove from the heat and stir in the shallot, vinegar, mustard and thyme.

2. Scrape the dressing into a large bowl. Add the plums and spinach, season with salt and pepper and toss. Add the nuts and crumbled blue cheese and toss again. Transfer the salad to plates, top with the sliced ham and serve. —*Jose Garces*

Mixed Greens with Plums and Parmesan Cheese

TOTAL: 20 MIN

6 SERVINGS ● ●

This salad features sweet Elephant Heart plums, known for their brownish skin and extremely juicy ruby-red flesh. Cut the plums into wedges over a bowl to catch the juices that drip out; whisk them into the salad dressing.

- 2 tablespoons fresh lemon juice
- ¼ cup extra-virgin olive oil

Salt and freshly ground pepper

- 6 ripe plums, preferably Elephant Heart plums, cut into thin wedges, juices reserved
- ½ pound mixed salad greens
- 2 ounces Parmesan cheese, shaved (1 cup)

In a large salad bowl, whisk the lemon juice with the olive oil and season the dressing with salt and pepper. Add the plum wedges and any reserved plum juices to the salad dressing and let stand for 5 minutes. Add the mixed salad greens and Parmesan cheese to the salad bowl and season the salad gently with salt and pepper if needed. Toss the salad gently to coat the greens with dressing and serve right away. —*Hugo Matheson and Kimbal Musk*

GREENS WITH CHÈVRE DRESSING

MÂCHE SALAD WITH GOAT CHEESE

Greens with Chèvre Dressing

TOTAL: 20 MIN

4 TO 6 SERVINGS ● ●

The combination of chèvre (goat cheese) and walnut oil in this salad pays homage to the south of France. But the transformation into a creamy ranch-style dressing? Pure American. Crème fraîche, *fromage blanc, lebneh,* mascarpone or quark may be used in place of the chèvre.

- ¾ cup walnut halves
- 1 small garlic clove, smashed

Kosher salt

- 3 ounces creamy fresh chèvre (goat cheese), at room temperature, mixed with 1 tablespoon of water
- 1½ teaspoons white wine vinegar
- 1½ teaspoons water
- 1 tablespoon extra-virgin olive oil
- 1 tablespoon walnut oil
- ½ teaspoon chopped thyme leaves

Freshly ground pepper

- 2 heads of Belgian endive, cored and leaves halved lengthwise

One 4-ounce head of frisée, torn into bite-size pieces

- 1 cup baby arugula
- 1 Granny Smith apple—halved, cored and thinly sliced

1. Preheat the oven to 350°. Spread the walnuts in a pie plate and bake them for 8 minutes, until they are toasted. Transfer them to a plate and let cool.

2. Meanwhile, on a work surface, sprinkle the garlic with a pinch of salt and mash it into a paste with the side of a large, heavy knife. Transfer the garlic paste to a bowl and whisk in the goat cheese, and then the vinegar and water. Add the olive oil and walnut oil and the thyme to the dressing and season with pepper to taste. Whisk the salad dressing until it is blended.

3. In a large salad bowl, toss the endive, frisée, arugula, apple slices and toasted walnuts with the goat cheese dressing and serve the salad at once. —*Grace Parisi*

Mâche Salad with Goat Cheese and Fennel-Mustard Vinaigrette

TOTAL: 15 MIN

8 SERVINGS ●

- 1 teaspoon fennel seeds
- 2 tablespoons rice vinegar
- 1 tablespoon lemon juice
- 1 tablespoon Dijon mustard
- 1 garlic clove, minced
- 6 tablespoons extra-virgin olive oil

Salt and freshly ground pepper

- 10 ounces mâche or other baby greens (16 loosely packed cups)
- ½ pound fresh goat cheese

1. In a small skillet, toast the fennel seeds over moderately high heat until fragrant. Let them cool completely, then transfer to a spice grinder; grind to a powder.
2. In a large bowl, whisk the ground fennel with the vinegar, lemon juice, mustard and garlic. Whisk in the oil and season the dressing with salt and pepper. Add the mâche and toss gently. Scatter the goat cheese on top and serve. —*Jim Clendenen*

Hearts of Palm Salad with Cilantro Vinaigrette

TOTAL: 30 MIN

12 SERVINGS ● ●

The citrusy dressing on this Caribbean-inspired hearts of palm salad is marvelously dense with fresh cilantro, shallots, lemon juice and honey. The oranges here release juice as they sit, so be sure to serve the salad right after you make it.

- ⅔ cup cilantro leaves
- 1 tablespoon finely chopped shallot
- 3 tablespoons fresh lemon juice
- 1 tablespoon red wine vinegar
- 2 teaspoons honey
- ½ cup extra-virgin olive oil

Salt and freshly ground pepper

- 3 navel oranges

Two 14-ounce cans or jars of hearts of palm, drained and cut on the diagonal into ½-inch slices

- 3 bunches of watercress, cut into 2-inch lengths, thick stems discarded
- 4 cups grape tomatoes (1¼ pounds), halved lengthwise

1. In a blender, combine the cilantro, shallot, lemon juice, vinegar and honey and pulse until the cilantro is finely chopped. With the machine on, add the olive oil in a steady stream and blend until smooth. Season with salt and pepper.
2. Using a sharp knife, peel the oranges, removing all of the bitter white pith. Working over a very large bowl, cut in between the membranes, releasing the sections into the bowl. Add the hearts of palm, watercress and tomatoes and toss gently. Add the vinaigrette, toss to coat and serve. —*Carolina Buia and Isabel González*

Chicory Salad with Warm Fig Dressing

TOTAL: 20 MIN

4 SERVINGS ● ●

This salad from chef Dennis Leary of San Francisco's Canteen shows his interest in historical ingredients and cooking. "Bitter greens and nuts have been foraged for thousands of years," he says. Leary likes to wilt the greens, but in a summer salad, they're equally delicious when left crisp.

- ½ cup hazelnuts
- 3 tablespoons red wine vinegar
- 3 tablespoons water
- 6 dried Calimyrna figs, 4 cut into ¼-inch dice and 2 quartered

One 10-ounce head of chicory, torn into bite-size pieces (10 cups)

- ¼ cup flat-leaf parsley leaves
- ¼ cup extra-virgin olive oil

Salt and freshly ground pepper

2 ounces aged pecorino cheese, preferably Sardinian

1. Preheat the oven to 350°. In a pie pan, toast the hazelnuts in the oven until browned, about 10 minutes. Transfer to a

kitchen towel and rub well to remove the skins. Coarsely chop the nuts.
2. In a medium skillet, combine the vinegar, water and diced figs and bring to a boil. Cover and simmer over low heat until 1 tablespoon of liquid remains, 3 minutes.
3. Meanwhile, in a large bowl, toss the chicory with the hazelnuts, parsley leaves and quartered figs.
4. Whisk the olive oil into the fig mixture in the skillet and bring to a simmer. Season with salt and pepper. Pour the hot dressing over the salad and toss well. Shave the pecorino on top, toss again and serve. —*Dennis Leary*

Claudine's Mixed Greens with Zucchini and Pecorino

TOTAL: 20 MIN

4 SERVINGS ● ●

One of the best lessons Claudine Pépin ever learned from her father, Jacques, is that a simple vinaigrette and very fresh, crisp greens are all you need to make a great salad. The zucchini, pecorino and cherry tomatoes here are all optional. If you don't have a mandoline for slicing the zucchini and shaving the pecorino, thinly slice them with a sharp knife or a sturdy vegetable peeler.

- 1 tablespoon red wine vinegar
- 2 teaspoons Dijon mustard
- 1 garlic clove, minced
- 3 tablespoons extra-virgin olive oil

Kosher salt and freshly ground pepper

- 6 ounces mixed greens
- 1 cup cherry or grape tomatoes
- 1 small very firm zucchini, very thinly sliced lengthwise

Pecorino shavings

In a large bowl, whisk together the vinegar, mustard and garlic, then whisk in the olive oil. Season the dressing with salt and pepper. Add the mixed greens, tomatoes and zucchini and toss well. Garnish the salad with pecorino shavings and serve. —*Claudine Pépin*

salads

Asparagus, Greens and Beans with Tapenade Toasts

ACTIVE: 40 MIN; TOTAL: 1 HR PLUS OVERNIGHT SOAKING

4 SERVINGS ●

5½ ounces dried flageolet beans (¾ cup), soaked overnight in cold water and drained

 1 small onion, halved

 1 bay leaf

 1 thyme sprig, plus ½ teaspoon thyme leaves

 2 tablespoons white wine vinegar

 1 tablespoon minced shallot

 1 teaspoon Dijon mustard

 ½ cup extra-virgin olive oil

Salt and freshly ground pepper

 25 pitted green olives

 1 tablespoon capers, rinsed

1¼ pounds asparagus

Eight ½-inch-thick slices of baguette, cut on the diagonal and lightly toasted

One 5-ounce bunch of arugula, thick stems discarded and large leaves torn in half

One 4-ounce bunch of watercress, thick stems discarded

1. Preheat the oven to 350°. In a large saucepan, combine the flageolets, onion, bay leaf and thyme sprig. Add cold water to cover by 2 inches and bring to a boil. Reduce the heat and simmer the beans until tender, 30 minutes. Remove from the heat and let the beans cool in their liquid for at least 30 minutes; drain. Discard the onion, bay leaf and thyme.

2. In a medium bowl, mix the vinegar with the minced shallot and the thyme leaves. Whisk in the mustard, then gradually whisk in 6 tablespoons of the olive oil. Season the dressing with salt and pepper.

3. In a mini food processor, combine the olives with the capers and the remaining 2 tablespoons of olive oil and pulse until the olives are finely chopped. Season the tapenade with salt and pepper.

4. In a large skillet of boiling salted water, cook the asparagus until tender, 5 minutes. Drain and rinse the asparagus under cold running water, then pat thoroughly dry.

5. Toss the beans with 3 tablespoons of the dressing and season with salt and pepper. Spread the green-olive tapenade on the baguette toasts. Arrange the arugula and watercress in the center of four plates. Top with the beans and asparagus spears. Drizzle the remaining dressing over the greens and asparagus and serve with the tapenade toasts. —*Susan Spungen*

MAKE AHEAD The cooked beans and tapenade can be refrigerated separately overnight; drain the beans before chilling. Bring the beans to room temperature before assembling the salad.

Haricot Vert Salad with Quail Eggs and Shrimp

TOTAL: 45 MIN

12 SERVINGS ● ●

Chef Christophe Emé of Ortolan in Los Angeles says this is the kind of food his mother, Maryvonne, used to make when he was growing up in the Loire valley. Everything came from their backyard: the beans, shallots, *laitue* (similar to Boston lettuce), and eggs. His mother even made vinegar for the dressing. Emé refines and updates the recipe by using quail eggs instead of hen eggs and substituting arugula for the lettuce. Maryvonne used peanut oil in the dressing, as is traditional in the Loire valley, but Emé opts for olive oil.

 2 tablespoons white wine vinegar

 2 dozen quail eggs (see Note)

 6 cups water

Three 3-inch strips of lemon zest

 1 tablespoon cracked black pepper

 2 bay leaves

 1 teaspoon fennel seeds

 1 star anise pod

Kosher salt

 1 pound medium shrimp, shelled down to the tails, and deveined

 2 pounds haricots verts

 2 tablespoons sherry vinegar

 2 tablespoons Dijon mustard

 ¼ cup plus 2 tablespoons extra-virgin olive oil

Freshly ground pepper

 1 bunch of arugula (6 ounces), large stems discarded

 2 medium shallots, minced

1. Bring a medium saucepan of water to a simmer and add the white wine vinegar. Add the eggs and simmer over moderate heat until hard cooked, about 7 minutes. Drain the eggs and crack the shells against the side of the pan. Fill the pan with cold water; let stand until the eggs are cool.

2. In a medium saucepan, combine the water, lemon zest, pepper, bay leaves, fennel seeds, star anise and 1 teaspoon of salt. Simmer the court bouillon (seasoned water) for 5 minutes. Add the shrimp and simmer just until cooked, about 2 minutes. Drain the shrimp in a colander; let cool. Pick out and discard any bits of seasoning.

3. In a large pot of boiling salted water, cook the haricots verts until crisp-tender, about 4 minutes. Drain well and spread the beans out on a baking sheet to cool.

4. In a small bowl, whisk the sherry vinegar with the mustard. Whisk in the olive oil and season with salt and pepper.

5. Peel the quail eggs and halve them lengthwise. In a large bowl, toss the arugula with 1 tablespoon of the dressing and spread on a platter. In the same bowl, gently toss the haricots verts, shallots, eggs and all but 1 tablespoon of the remaining dressing. Mound the haricot vert salad on the arugula. Add the shrimp to the bowl and toss with the remaining dressing. Top the salad with the shrimp and serve. —*Christophe Emé*

NOTE Instead of quail eggs, you can use 6 large chicken eggs; boil for 10 minutes and halve lengthwise.

MAKE AHEAD The recipe can be prepared through Step 4 up to 1 day in advance. Refrigerate the ingredients separately.

salads

Celery Root with Apples, Walnuts and Blue Cheese

TOTAL: 45 MIN

12 SERVINGS ● ●

½ cup walnut halves
¼ cup cider vinegar
2 tablespoons minced shallot
1 tablespoon Dijon mustard
Sea salt and freshly ground pepper
6 tablespoons extra-virgin olive oil
1 cup crumbled blue cheese
2 celery roots (¾ pound each), peeled and cut into ¼-inch dice
3 large Granny Smith apples— peeled, cored and cut into ¼-inch dice

1. Preheat the oven to 350°. Toast the walnuts for 8 to 10 minutes, or until golden. Let cool, then coarsely chop them.
2. In a large bowl, whisk the vinegar, shallot, mustard and a generous pinch each of salt and pepper; let stand for 10 minutes. Whisk in the olive oil and ¼ cup of the blue cheese. Just before serving, add the celery root and apples, season with salt and pepper and toss well. Add the chopped nuts and the remaining ¾ cup of blue cheese and serve. —*Maria Helm Sinskey*

Chickpea and Grilled Scallion Salad

TOTAL: 20 MIN

6 SERVINGS ● ● ●

This simple salad is a great accompaniment to grilled or stewed meats such as lamb or beef.

¼ cup sweet sherry
6 scallions
¼ cup extra-virgin olive oil, plus more for brushing
Salt and freshly ground pepper
1 garlic clove, minced
1 tablespoon fresh lemon juice
Two 19-ounce cans chickpeas, rinsed and drained
1 tablespoon chopped flat-leaf parsley

1. Light a grill or preheat a grill pan. In a small saucepan, bring the sweet sherry to a boil. Reduce the heat to moderate and simmer until the sherry is syrupy, about 5 minutes. Brush the scallions with olive oil and season with salt and pepper. Grill the scallions over a hot fire until nicely charred, about 3 minutes. Let cool slightly, then cut the scallions on the bias into ½-inch lengths.
2. In a large bowl, mix the ¼ cup of olive oil with the garlic and lemon juice; season with salt and pepper. Add the chickpeas, parsley and scallions. Toss to coat. Season with salt and pepper and drizzle with the sherry syrup. Serve at room temperature or slightly chilled. —*Tommy Habetz*
MAKE AHEAD The finished salad can be refrigerated overnight.

Warm Chanterelle and Frisée Salad

TOTAL: 20 MIN

8 TO 10 SERVINGS ● ●

¼ cup plus 2 tablespoons extra-virgin olive oil
1 large shallot, thinly sliced
5 large garlic cloves, very thinly sliced
1½ pounds chanterelles, thickly sliced
½ cup chicken stock or low-sodium broth
1 tablespoon soy sauce
Salt and freshly ground pepper
3 heads of frisée (1¾ pounds), coarsely chopped
2 tablespoons fresh lemon juice
¼ pound dry Jack cheese or fresh pecorino cheese, shaved with a vegetable peeler (about 1½ cups)

1. In a large, deep skillet, heat ¼ cup of oil until shimmering. Add the shallot and garlic. Cook over moderately high heat, stirring, until softened, 1 minute. Add the chanterelles and cook over high heat, stirring occasionally, until they begin to brown and the liquid is evaporated, 10 minutes. Add the stock and soy sauce, season with salt and pepper and cook until almost dry, about 2 minutes. Remove from the heat.
2. Add the remaining olive oil and the frisée to the skillet and season with salt and pepper. Toss well. Add the lemon juice and toss just until the frisée is lightly wilted, about 1 minute. Transfer the warm salad to a platter, scatter the cheese on top and serve. —*Mateo Granados*

taste test
supermarket cheese

We tasted dozens of cheeses to find the best blue, Brie and goat.

ROQUEFORT SOCIÉTÉ
This ewe's-milk cheese, made in southern France, is creamy and salty, with a hint of sweetness; roquefort-societe.com.

ILE DE FRANCE LE BRIE
This buttery, mild cheese is named after the first ship to transport Brie from France to the U.S.; iledefrancecheese.com.

VERMONT BUTTER & CHEESE COMPANY CHÈVRE
Cheesemaker Allison Hooper gets milk for her nicely tangy goat cheese from 20 family farms in the New England area; vtbutterandcheeseco.com.

Celery Salad with Pecorino

TOTAL: 30 MIN

4 SERVINGS ●

A rich and peppery olive oil will help to highlight the tastes of this tart and crunchy celery salad. To ensure that the celery in the salad pops with crispness, soak it in ice water for at least 10 minutes before combining it with the other ingredients.

- 12 celery ribs, thinly sliced crosswise
- ½ cup extra-virgin olive oil
- ¼ cup fresh lemon juice
- 1 shallot, finely chopped

Kosher salt and freshly ground black pepper

- 1 small head of red leaf lettuce, leaves torn into bite-size pieces

One 4-ounce piece of pecorino cheese

1. Fill a medium bowl with cold water and add about 2 cups of small ice cubes. Add the sliced celery to the bowl and let it soak in the ice water bath for at least 10 minutes or for up to 30 minutes, until the celery is very crisp.

2. Meanwhile, in a small bowl, whisk the olive oil with the lemon juice. Stir in the finely chopped shallot. Season the dressing with salt and pepper.

3. In a large salad bowl, toss the leaf lettuce with 3 tablespoons of the citrus and olive oil dressing. Transfer the lettuce to a platter or plates.

4. Drain the sliced celery and pat dry thoroughly with paper towels. Add the celery to the salad bowl and toss it with the remaining dressing. Season the dressed celery with salt and pepper. Using a slotted spoon, scatter the sliced celery over the red leaf lettuce, leaving some of the dressing behind. Using a very sharp vegetable peeler, shave long strips of the pecorino cheese over the salad. Drizzle the salad lightly with some of the remaining dressing. Season the celery salad with pepper and serve right away.
—*Gerald Gass*

Cremini Mushroom and Fennel Salad with Truffle Oil

TOTAL: 25 MIN

8 SERVINGS ● ●

Since the cremini mushrooms used for this recipe need to be sliced paper-thin, it is important to choose fresh, firm ones that won't fall apart when sliced on a mandoline. If you feel like splurging on a fresh white truffle, you can shave it right on the salad and skip the truffle oil called for here.

- 3 medium fennel bulbs, halved lengthwise and cored
- 5 very fresh large cremini mushrooms
- 5 tablespoons extra-virgin olive oil
- 2 tablespoons fresh lemon juice

Kosher salt and freshly ground black pepper

Parmesan cheese, for shaving

- 1 tablespoon white truffle oil (see Note)

1. Using a mandoline, thinly slice the fennel bulb and transfer the slices to a large bowl. Again, using a mandoline if possible, thinly slice the cremini mushrooms into another bowl and set them aside.

2. In a small bowl, whisk the olive oil with the lemon juice. Season the salad dressing generously with kosher salt and black pepper. Pour all but 1 tablespoon of the dressing over the sliced fennel, then season the fennel with salt and pepper and toss to coat with the dressing.

3. Mound the sliced fennel on salad plates and top the fennel with the sliced cremini mushrooms. Using a vegetable peeler, shave some Parmesan cheese over each of the salads. Drizzle the salads with the remaining 1 tablespoon of dressing, and then with the truffle oil. Serve the cremini mushroom and fennel salads right away.
—*Mary Ellen Carroll and Donna Wingate*
NOTE White truffle oil is available at most specialty food stores.

Roasted Beet and Fennel Salad

ACTIVE: 20 MIN; TOTAL: 1 HR 15 MIN

4 SERVINGS ●

Beets are a good vegetable to prepare for a dinner party because they can be cooked ahead of time. Roasting beets brings out their sweetness.

- 4 beets, peeled and cut into ½-inch wedges (1½ pounds)
- 2 thyme sprigs
- 2 tablespoons water
- 2 tablespoons extra-virgin olive oil

Salt and freshly ground black pepper

- 1 large fennel bulb with fronds, bulb cut into ½-inch wedges, 1 tablespoon chopped fronds
- 1 teaspoon sherry vinegar

1. Preheat the oven to 400°. In a medium baking dish, toss the beet wedges with the thyme sprigs, the water and 1 tablespoon of the olive oil. Season the beets with salt and pepper. Cover the baking dish with aluminum foil and cook the beets for about 40 minutes, or until they are tender. Let the beets cool slightly. Discard the thyme sprigs.

2. In a small baking dish, drizzle the fennel wedges with the remaining 1 tablespoon of olive oil and season them with salt and pepper. Cover the small baking dish with aluminum foil and bake the fennel for 15 minutes. Uncover the baking dish and bake the fennel for 15 minutes longer, or until it's tender and lightly browned.

3. Pour the beet juices from the baking dish into a bowl and whisk in the sherry vinegar. Add the roasted beet wedges, the fennel wedges and the fennel fronds and season the salad with salt and pepper. Serve the beet and fennel salad warm or at room temperature.
—*Matthew Malin and Andrew Goetz*
MAKE AHEAD The beets can be roasted up to 1 day ahead and stored in an airtight container in the refrigerator.

● FAST   ● HEALTHY   ● MAKE AHEAD   ● STAFF FAVORITE

salads

Roasted Beet and Poached Apple Salad with Curry Vinaigrette

ACTIVE: 25 MIN; TOTAL: 1 HR 10 MIN

4 SERVINGS ●

This elegant salad with plump golden raisins and thin slices of beet and apple is dressed with an exotic curry vinaigrette.

- 1 **pound beets (4 medium)**
- 1 **cup unsweetened apple juice**
- 1 **cup dry white wine**
- 1 **tablespoon sugar**

Pinch of saffron threads, crumbled

Salt

- 2 **Granny Smith apples—peeled, cored and sliced ¼ inch thick**
- 6 **tablespoons vegetable oil**
- 1 **teaspoon curry powder**
- 3 **tablespoons white balsamic vinegar**
- 1 **tablespoon toasted pine nuts**
- 2 **tablespoons golden raisins**
- 2 **tablespoons flat-leaf parsley**

1. Preheat the oven to 350°. Put the unpeeled beets in a small roasting pan, cover the pan with aluminum foil and bake for about 1 hour, or until tender. Peel the beets, then slice them ¼ inch thick.

2. Meanwhile, in a large saucepan, combine the unsweetened apple juice with the white wine and the sugar, saffron threads and a pinch of salt. Bring the dressing to a boil. Strain the dressing through a fine strainer and return it to the saucepan. Bring the dressing back to a boil and add the sliced apples. Simmer over moderate heat for 3 minutes, or until the apples are crisp-tender. Drain the apples and discard the liquid.

3. In a small skillet, heat 3 tablespoons of the vegetable oil. Add the curry powder, remove the skillet from the heat and let stand for 10 minutes. Stir in the remaining 3 tablespoons of vegetable oil, along with the balsamic vinegar, toasted pine nuts and golden raisins; season the dressing with salt.

4. In a medium bowl, toss the apple slices with half of the dressing and arrange on a serving platter. Put the beets in the bowl and toss with the remaining dressing. Arrange the beets on the platter, garnish with the parsley and serve right away.
—*Daniel Humm*

MAKE AHEAD The whole roasted beets can be refrigerated for up to 2 days.

Thai Vegetable and Eggplant Salad in Parmesan Cups

TOTAL: 50 MIN

4 SERVINGS

Parmesan cheese cups not only hold the hearty eggplant salad here but also add a delicious salty crunch. To make the cheese cups, spread small mounds of grated cheese on a baking sheet and melt them in the oven until they are golden, then drape each over an inverted glass or ceramic bowl. As they cool, they will harden into a cup shape.

- ½ **cup extra-virgin olive oil, plus more for brushing**
- One **1¼-pound eggplant, cut into 1½-inch cubes**
- **Salt and freshly ground black pepper**
- 1 **cup freshly grated Parmesan cheese**
- 1 **tablespoon balsamic vinegar**
- 2 **ounces mesclun greens (4 cups)**
- 3 **scallions, thinly sliced crosswise**
- 1 **cup red and yellow cherry tomatoes, halved**

technique
making red wine vinegar

1. Buy an earthenware crock (see Box p. 208 for Paula Wolfert's favorites) with a top-quality wood or plastic spigot. Add water to the crock to check for leaks; drain the crock.

2. Buy an 8-ounce bottle of commercial mother from a wine- and beer-making supply shop.

3. Add 2 cups of good-quality red wine and 1 cup of filtered water to the crock, then add the mother.

Cover the crock with a double layer of cheesecloth and fasten with a rubber band.

4. Set the crock in a warm (70 to 90 degrees), dark spot and let it stand for 1½ weeks.

5. Add more good-quality red wine to the crock in three 2½-cup installments over the next 1½ weeks. Once a thin veil has formed on the surface, add the wine through a bulb baster tucked under the edge of the veil. Let the crock stand for a total of 10 weeks. Check it periodically: If the vinegar ever begins to smell like furniture polish, discard it, wash out the crock and start the process over.

6. Bottle the vinegar when it smells sharp and crisp: Carefully strain it into sterile bottles through a plastic funnel lined with a paper coffee filter. The vinegar will continue to mellow in the bottles and the flavor will improve with age, but if you plan to keep it for more than four months you will need to pasteurize it: Heat the vinegar to 155 degrees in a large stainless steel saucepan and hold it there for 30 minutes. Store the pasteurized vinegar in sterilized, well-sealed bottles in a cool, dry place. Use homemade vinegar for dressings and sauces, but it should never be used for pickling. —*Paula Wolfert*

1. Preheat the oven to 350°. In a large skillet, heat 2 tablespoons of the olive oil over moderately high heat until shimmering. Add half of the eggplant cubes in a single layer, season with salt and pepper and cook over moderate heat, undisturbed, until the eggplant cubes are browned on the bottom, about 3 minutes. Stir, cover and cook until the eggplant is tender, about 5 minutes longer. Scrape the eggplant onto a large plate and repeat with 2 more tablespoons of the olive oil and the remaining eggplant cubes.

2. Lightly oil a large rimmed nonstick baking sheet. Sprinkle ¼ cup of the Parmesan cheese into a 6-inch round on each half of the baking sheet. Bake the grated Parmesan cheese rounds for about 3 minutes, until the Parmesan has melted into a flat cake and turned golden brown. Let the Parmesan cheese rounds cool for about 30 seconds to firm up partway; do not let them harden. With a spatula, carefully lift each Parmesan round off the baking sheet and drape it over an inverted 4-inch-wide glass or ceramic bowl. Let the cheese stand until cooled and crisp, about 2 minutes, before carefully removing the cups from the bowls. Repeat with the remaining Parmesan to make 2 more cheese cups.

3. In a small bowl, whisk the remaining ¼ cup of olive oil with the balsamic vinegar. Season the dressing with salt and pepper. In a large bowl, toss the mesclun greens, sliced scallions, halved tomatoes and cooked eggplant cubes with the balsamic dressing. Carefully spoon the eggplant salad into the crisp cheese cups and serve at once. —*Nick Nairn*

MAKE AHEAD The recipe can be prepared through Step 2 up to 4 hours ahead and kept at room temperature. At the same time, the scallions can be sliced and the cherry tomatoes washed. Place the scallions and tomatoes in separate bowls, cover the bowls with plastic wrap and keep them in the refrigerator.

Smoky Eggplant Salad
TOTAL: 1 HR
4 SERVINGS ● ●

British cookbook author Celia Brooks Brown balances the freshness and crunch of raw carrot and cucumber and the sweetness of cherry tomatoes with soft, smoky eggplant that is seasoned lime juice, soy and chile dressing.

- 2 long purple eggplants (1½ pounds each)
- 8 fresh kaffir lime leaves, minced, or 1 teaspoon finely grated lime zest
- ½ cup fresh lime juice
- ¼ cup soy sauce
- 1 red Thai chile, minced
- 1 tablespoon light brown sugar
- 1 small garlic clove, minced
- 1 teaspoon finely grated lemon zest
- 1 Hass avocado—halved, pitted and thinly sliced
- 1 large carrot, cut into thin julienne strips
- 1 medium English cucumber, thinly sliced crosswise
- ½ pound cherry tomatoes, halved
- ½ medium red onion, halved and thinly sliced

Snipped chives, for garnishing
- 3 tablespoons finely chopped mint
- ½ cup roasted cashews, coarsely chopped

1. Light a grill. Using a fork, prick the eggplants in a few places. Grill over very high heat, turning occasionally, until the eggplants are very soft and blackened all over, about 35 minutes. Transfer them to a baking sheet and let cool slightly. Cut the stems off the eggplants and scrape off the charred skin. Tear the eggplants into long strips and discard the seeds. Transfer to a bowl.

2. In a small bowl, mix the kaffir lime leaves with the lime juice, soy sauce, Thai chile, light brown sugar, minced garlic and lemon zest to make a dressing. Stir 3 tablespoons of the dressing into the grilled eggplant.

3. Arrange the dressed eggplant in a neat mound on a serving platter and then arrange the other ingredients: the sliced avocado, carrot strips, cucumber slices, halved cherry tomatoes and red onion slices in separate sections to show off their colors and shapes. Drizzle the remaining dressing over the salad and sprinkle with the chives, mint and cashews. Serve right away. —*Celia Brooks Brown*

MAKE AHEAD The smoky eggplant salad can be prepared through Step 1 and refrigerated overnight.

Triple-Fennel Salad with Pink Grapefruit and Black Olives
TOTAL: 30 MIN
6 SERVINGS ● ●

- 3 large pink grapefruit
- 2 medium shallots, minced
- 6 tablespoons extra-virgin olive oil
- 1 teaspoon honey

Salt and freshly ground pepper
- 3 fennel bulbs (1½ pounds)— halved, cored and sliced paper-thin crosswise, fronds chopped
- ⅔ cup black oil-cured olives—pitted, rinsed and coarsely chopped

Fennel pollen or ground fennel seeds

1. Using a sharp knife, peel the grapefruit, removing the bitter white pith. Working over a bowl, cut in between the membranes to release the sections. Squeeze the juice from the membranes into the bowl.

2. Transfer ½ cup of the juice to a large bowl. Add the shallots and let soak for 10 minutes. Stir in the olive oil and honey; season with salt and pepper. Add the fennel and toss. Arrange on a platter. Scatter the olives, grapefruit sections and fennel fronds on top. Dust lightly with fennel pollen and serve. —*Morgan Brownlow*

salads

Corn and Tomato Salad with Shrimp and Watercress

TOTAL: 30 MIN

6 SERVINGS ● ●

- ¼ cup plus 1 tablespoon extra-virgin olive oil
- 5 ears of corn, kernels cut from the cob (2½ cups)
- 1 pint grape tomatoes, halved lengthwise
- ½ small red onion, thinly sliced lengthwise
- 1 tablespoon chopped flat-leaf parsley
- 1 tablespoon snipped chives
- 1½ teaspoons coarsely chopped tarragon
- 2 tablespoons white wine vinegar
- Salt and freshly ground pepper
- 1 pound shelled and deveined large shrimp
- ½ teaspoon finely grated lemon zest
- 1 tablespoon fresh lemon juice
- 1 bunch watercress, thick stems discarded

1. Light a grill. In a large skillet, heat 1 tablespoon of the olive oil. Add the corn and cook over high heat, stirring, until softened, about 4 minutes. Transfer the corn to a bowl and let cool. Add the tomatoes, onion, parsley, chives, tarragon, vinegar and 2 tablespoons of olive oil and season the salad with salt and pepper.

2. In a bowl, toss the shrimp with 1 tablespoon of the olive oil and season with salt and pepper. Grill the shrimp over high heat, turning once, until pink and curled, about 3 minutes. Transfer to a bowl and stir in the lemon zest.

3. In a large mixing bowl, stir the remaining 1 tablespoon of olive oil with the lemon juice and season generously with salt and pepper. Add the watercress and toss to coat. Transfer the watercress to a large serving platter. Top with the corn and tomato salad and the grilled shrimp and serve right away. —*Brian Bistrong*

Zucchini Salad with Almonds and Taleggio

TOTAL: 20 MIN

4 SERVINGS ●

- 1 large shallot, thinly sliced, plus 1 teaspoon minced shallot
- ¼ cup vegetable oil
- 1 teaspoon fresh lemon juice
- Salt and freshly ground pepper
- 3 very fresh 4-ounce zucchini, cut into 2-by-⅓-inch sticks
- 1 tablespoon minced parsley
- ½ cup roasted, salted almonds, preferably marcona, coarsely chopped
- ¾ pound Taleggio cheese, at room temperature, cut into 4 wedges

1. Separate the sliced shallot into rings. In a small skillet, heat 2 tablespoons of the oil. Add the shallot rings in an even layer and cook over moderate heat until lightly browned, about 5 minutes. With a slotted spoon, transfer to paper towels.

2. In a medium bowl, combine the remaining 2 tablespoons of oil, minced shallot and lemon juice. Season with salt and pepper. Add the zucchini and toss to coat. Mound the salad on plates. Sprinkle with the parsley, almonds and shallots. Serve the Taleggio on the side.—*Marcia Kiesel*

Corn and Tomato Salad with Thyme and Roasted Poblanos

TOTAL: 50 MIN

12 SERVINGS ●

- 2 large poblano chiles
- 12 ears of corn, kernels cut from the cob (6 cups)
- 3 tablespoons extra-virgin olive oil
- Two 6-ounce zucchini, diced (½ inch)
- 3 scallions, thinly sliced crosswise
- 2 garlic cloves, minced
- 1 large shallot, minced
- 2 teaspoons chopped thyme or lemon thyme
- 1½ pints cherry tomatoes, halved
- 3 tablespoons chopped cilantro
- Salt and freshly ground pepper

1. Roast the poblanos over a gas flame until charred all over. Transfer to a plate and let cool. Discard the skin and seeds and cut the poblanos into ½-inch dice.

2. In a large saucepan of boiling salted water, cook the corn until tender, about 3 minutes. Drain well.

3. In a large, deep skillet, heat the oil and cook the corn and zucchini over moderately high heat until browned on the bottom. Reduce the heat to moderate and add the poblanos, scallions, garlic, shallot and thyme. Cook, stirring, for 2 minutes. Transfer to a bowl; cool to room temperature. Stir in the tomatoes and cilantro, season with salt and pepper. Serve. —*Jeri Ryan*

Citrus Salad with Saffron Dressing

TOTAL: 40 MIN

12 SERVINGS ● ●

- 2 tablespoons extra-virgin olive oil
- Pinch of saffron threads
- ½ cup fresh orange juice
- 6 pink grapefruit
- 6 navel oranges
- 3 clementines, peeled
- 2 teaspoons finely grated lemon zest

1. In a saucepan, heat the olive oil. Transfer to a bowl and crumble in the saffron. Let stand for 10 minutes. Add the orange juice to the pan and boil over moderately high heat until reduced to ¼ cup, 7 minutes. Add the juice to the oil; let cool.

2. Using a sharp knife, peel the grapefruit and oranges, cutting off all of the bitter white pith; cut the pith from the clementines. Finely chop the clementines and add to the saffron oil with the lemon zest.

3. Working over a large, shallow bowl with the oranges and grapefruit, cut in between the membranes to release the sections. Pour the dressing over the citrus sections and stir gently. Serve the salad at once. —*José Andrés*

CITRUS SALAD WITH
SAFFRON DRESSING

CHILLED CELERY SOUP WITH
BAY SCALLOPS (P. 57)

soups

"People put their trust in me to cook wholesome food that actually tastes like food."

—**Nicki Reiss,** personal chef, Hollywood, California

FROTHY LETTUCE SOUP WITH ONION CUSTARD

WHITE GAZPACHO WITH PICKLED SHRIMP

Frothy Lettuce Soup with Onion Custard

ACTIVE: 50 MIN; TOTAL: 1 HR 10 MIN

4 SERVINGS

This recipe calls for a head of Boston lettuce per person, resulting in a soup with pure, intense flavors that is then poured over delicate custard. It's a riff on *petits pois à la française,* the classic French dish of peas, lettuce and spring onions braised in butter and chicken stock.

Salt

Four 6-ounce heads of Boston lettuce, trimmed, 2 medium lettuce leaves reserved

2 ounces lean slab bacon, sliced ¼ inch thick and cut into ¼-inch dice (⅓ cup)

5 tablespoons cold unsalted butter

One ½-pound white onion, thinly sliced

1¼ cups chicken stock or low-sodium broth

1 large egg

½ cup milk

Freshly ground pepper

Pinch of freshly grated nutmeg

3 tablespoons crème fraîche

1. Bring a large saucepan of water to a boil. Add 2 tablespoons of salt and blanch the lettuce, stirring gently with a wire skimmer, for 3 minutes. Drain and rinse under cold water; lightly squeeze out excess water. Transfer still wet to a blender and puree until smooth. Scrape into a bowl.

2. In a skillet, cook the bacon over moderate heat until lightly browned, 4 minutes.

3. In a large skillet, combine 2 tablespoons of the butter with the onion. Cover and cook over low heat, stirring often, until softened, about 15 minutes.

4. Transfer the onion to a blender. Add ¼ cup of the chicken stock and puree. In a medium bowl, whisk the egg, then whisk in the milk and onion puree. Season with ½ teaspoon of salt, ⅛ teaspoon of pepper and the nutmeg. Butter four 8-ounce coffee mugs or ramekins. Pour the mixture into the mugs; cover with plastic wrap.

5. Set a round rack in a large, wide pot. Add enough water to reach just under the rack without touching it and bring to a boil. Set the mugs on the rack. Cover and steam over low heat until the onion custards are barely set, about 22 minutes.

6. In a saucepan, bring the remaining stock to a boil. Whisk in the lettuce puree and simmer over moderate heat for 3 minutes. Whisk in the crème fraîche and simmer for 3 minutes. Remove from the heat and gradually whisk in the remaining butter. Season with salt and pepper.

7. Finely shred the reserved lettuce leaves. When the custards are done, discard the plastic. Scatter the bacon and lettuce over the top. Serve the custards and pour in the soup at the table. —*Joël Robuchon*

White Gazpacho with Pickled Shrimp

ACTIVE: 45 MIN; TOTAL: 2 HR

4 SERVINGS ●

White gazpacho, a classic Spanish soup made with cucumbers, almonds, garlic, olive oil, sherry vinegar and day-old bread soaked in water, is common all over the Spanish region of Andalucía, especially in summer. Jonathan Benno of Manhattan's Per Se prepares his version with delectable marcona almonds, the skinned, roasted Spanish nuts sold at specialty markets. Instead of the traditional green grapes used in Spain, this intensely nutty white gazpacho is topped with pickled shrimp, adding another level of sweet-tart flavor.

2¼ cups sherry vinegar
1 cup sugar
1 large jalapeño, halved lengthwise
½ teaspoon black peppercorns
½ teaspoon coriander seeds
½ teaspoon cumin seeds
3 mint sprigs, plus 1 teaspoon chopped mint
3 cilantro sprigs, plus 1 teaspoon chopped cilantro
½ pound large shrimp in their shells
4 garlic cloves, thickly sliced
½ cup vegetable oil
1½ cups crustless 1-inch cubes of peasant bread
1 cup Greek whole milk yogurt
4 ounces marcona almonds (¾ cup)
½ pound seedless green grapes
½ large seedless cucumber— peeled, seeded and coarsely chopped
¼ cup plus 1 tablespoon extra-virgin olive oil, plus more for drizzling
½ teaspoon sweet smoked paprika (pimentón de la Vera)
Salt and freshly ground white pepper

1. In a medium saucepan, combine 2 cups of the sherry vinegar with the sugar, halved jalapeño, peppercorns, coriander seeds, cumin seeds and 1 cup of water and bring the mixture to a rapid boil, stirring to dissolve the sugar. Add the mint sprigs and the cilantro sprigs. Remove the pickling liquid from the heat and add the shrimp. Cover the shrimp with a lid or a heatproof plate to keep them submerged and let the shrimp stand for 1 hour to pickle them.

2. Meanwhile, in a small saucepan, simmer the garlic in the vegetable oil over moderate heat until very soft but not browned, about 10 minutes. Using a slotted spoon, transfer the garlic to a blender. Reserve the garlic oil for another use.

3. In a small bowl, soak the bread in cold water until softened. Squeeze out the excess water and transfer the bread to the blender. Add the whole milk yogurt, marcona almonds, seedless grapes, chopped cucumber, 3 tablespoons of the sherry vinegar and 2 tablespoons of water and puree until smooth. With the machine on, add ¼ cup of the olive oil in a thin stream. Set a fine strainer over a medium bowl and strain the soup, pressing hard on the solids. Season the soup with the smoked paprika, salt and white pepper and refrigerate until cold.

4. Drain the shrimp and discard the pickling liquid. Shell and devein the shrimp. In a medium bowl, toss the shrimp with the remaining 1 tablespoon each of sherry vinegar and olive oil. Add the 1 teaspoon each of chopped mint and cilantro and season the shrimp with salt and white pepper. Ladle the soup into shallow bowls and mound the shrimp in the center. Drizzle the soup with olive oil. Serve right away. —*Jonathan Benno*

MAKE AHEAD The undressed, pickled shrimp and finished white gazpacho can be refrigerated separately overnight. Season and garnish the shrimp just before serving.

Gazpacho Gelées with Avocado Cream

ACTIVE: 25 MIN; TOTAL: 1 HR 25 MIN

4 SERVINGS ● ● ●

Philippe Braun, who created this soft, slightly spicy tomato jelly topped with an unctuous avocado cream, is the extremely talented executive chef at L'Atelier de Joël Robuchon in Paris. One of Joël Robuchon's closest associates, Braun travels with the master to keep standards high at outposts in Las Vegas, Tokyo and New York City.

½ cup drained canned tomatoes, chopped
½ cup peeled, seeded and chopped cucumber
½ cup peeled and chopped red pepper
1 tablespoon red wine vinegar
¼ teaspoon minced garlic
Dash of Tabasco
Pinch of ground cumin
Salt
¾ teaspoon powdered unflavored gelatin
1 Hass avocado—seeded, peeled and chopped
¼ cup water
1 tablespoon fresh lime juice
2 teaspoons extra-virgin olive oil

1. In a blender, puree the tomatoes, cucumber, pepper, vinegar, garlic, Tabasco and cumin. Pass through a fine strainer into a glass measuring cup. Season with salt. Transfer half of the mixture to a small saucepan. Sprinkle the gelatin evenly over the top. Let stand for 5 minutes; cook over moderate heat until melted, about 1 minute. Stir in the remaining tomato mixture. Pour into 4 small glass bowls and refrigerate until firm, about 1 hour.

2. Clean the blender, then puree the avocado, water, lime juice and olive oil. Season with salt. Spoon the avocado cream over each gelée and serve. —*Philippe Braun*

MAKE AHEAD The gelées and puree can be refrigerated separately overnight.

soups

Gazpacho Shooters

TOTAL: 35 MIN

12 SERVINGS ● ● ●

- 2½ pounds Brandywine or other flavorful beefsteak tomatoes
- 1 garlic clove, smashed
- ½ small jalapeño, seeded
- 2 tablespoons cider vinegar
- ½ small red onion, finely diced
- 1 large celery rib, finely diced
- ½ medium European cucumber—peeled, seeded and finely diced

Salt and freshly ground pepper
Extra-virgin olive oil, for drizzling

1. Bring a large pot of water to a boil. Meanwhile, fill a large bowl with ice water. Using a sharp knife, make a shallow X in the bottom of each tomato. Add the tomatoes to the boiling water and blanch just until the skins begin to pull away, about 20 seconds. Using a slotted spoon, immediately transfer the tomatoes to the ice water. Drain and peel.

2. Halve the tomatoes crosswise. Squeeze the seeds into a sieve set over a bowl. Press on the seeds to extract the juice; discard the seeds. Cut the tomatoes into large chunks. In a food processor or blender, puree the tomatoes with ½ cup of the strained juice. Add the garlic, jalapeño, vinegar and half each of the diced red onion, celery and cucumber and process until smooth. Transfer the gazpacho to a bowl. Stir in the remaining diced red onion, celery and cucumber and season with salt and pepper. Pour into small glasses, drizzle with olive oil and serve. —*Joe Vitale*

MAKE AHEAD The gazpacho can be refrigerated overnight.

ingredient
3 great olive oils

Pianogrillo Robust and spicy olive oil from Sicily. **Details** $27 for 500 ml; chefshop.com.

McEvoy Ranch California organic oil made in a Tuscan style. **Details** $38 for 750 ml; mcevoyranch.com.

Grati Italy's Grati family produces three excellent *cru* oils in Tuscany. **Details** $23 for 500 ml; rarewineco.com.

Chilled Cucumber-Avocado Soup with Spicy Glazed Shrimp

ACTIVE: 45 MIN; TOTAL: 1 HR 30 MIN

6 SERVINGS ●

Chef Douglas Keane of Cyrus in Healdsburg, California, is such a fan of chilled soups that he puts at least one on his menu every season including winter. The combination of cucumber and red wine vinegar in this recipe reminds Keane of the wonderful Greek salads he ate growing up outside Detroit, Michigan, home to a huge Greek community.

- 1 large European cucumber, seeded and coarsely chopped
- 2 Hass avocados—pitted, peeled and quartered
- 1½ cups buttermilk
- 2 tablespoons red wine vinegar
- 1 teaspoon sugar
- 1½ tablespoons fresh lime juice

Kosher salt

- 3 tablespoons extra-virgin olive oil
- ¾ pound large shrimp, shelled and deveined, shells reserved
- 3 garlic cloves, thinly sliced
- 1 shallot, thinly sliced
- 1 small carrot, thinly sliced crosswise
- 1 teaspoon black peppercorns
- 1 teaspoon coriander seeds
- 1 teaspoon crushed red pepper
- ½ teaspoon cumin seeds
- 1 teaspoon tomato paste
- 2 cups water
- 1 tablespoon honey

Freshly ground pepper

- 1 tablespoon unsalted butter
- 6 mint leaves, chopped

1. In a blender, combine the cucumber with the avocados, buttermilk, red wine vinegar, sugar, ½ tablespoon of the lime juice and a pinch of salt. Blend the soup until smooth. Strain through a fine sieve into a medium bowl, cover the bowl with plastic wrap and refrigerate until chilled, about 40 minutes.

2. In a large saucepan, heat 2 tablespoons of the olive oil. Add the shrimp shells, garlic, shallot and carrot and cook over moderate heat, stirring until the shrimp shells are lightly browned and the vegetables are softened, about 8 minutes. Add the peppercorns, coriander seeds, crushed red pepper and cumin seeds and cook, stirring, for 1 minute. Add the tomato paste and cook, stirring, for 1 minute. Add the water, honey and remaining 1 tablespoon of lime juice and bring to a boil. Simmer the shrimp sauce over moderate heat until it is reduced to ½ cup, about 15 minutes. Strain the shrimp sauce into a heatproof bowl and set aside.

3. In a medium skillet, heat the remaining 1 tablespoon of olive oil until shimmering. Add the shrimp, season with salt and pepper and cook over high heat for 1 minute. Turn over, add the shrimp sauce and simmer just until the shrimp are cooked through, about 2 minutes. Swirl the butter into them.

4. Using a slotted spoon, place the glazed shrimp in soup bowls, spoon the chilled cucumber soup all around them and drizzle the shrimp sauce on top. Sprinkle the servings with the mint and serve right away. —*Douglas Keane*

MAKE AHEAD The cucumber soup and the shrimp sauce can be refrigerated overnight separately. Reheat the shrimp sauce gently before using.

Green Grape and Marcona Almond Gazpacho

TOTAL: 30 MIN PLUS 2 HR CHILLING

4 SERVINGS ● ●

Most people think tomato when they hear the word *gazpacho*, but there's no tomato in sight here. This version of Spain's classic white gazpacho features cucumbers and green grapes, and it's thickened with a few luscious marcona almonds into a silky creaminess.

- 1 large garlic clove
- 2½ large seedless cucumbers, peeled and cut into 1-inch dice (5 cups), plus ¼ cup finely diced peeled cucumber, for garnish
- 1¼ cups whole green grapes, plus ¼ cup diced grapes, for garnish
- ¾ cup marcona almonds
- 3 cups crustless ½-inch cubes of good white bread
- 4 scallions, white and tender green parts, cut into 1-inch lengths
- 1 cup packed watercress leaves
- ½ cup cold water
- ¼ cup extra-virgin olive oil
- 2 tablespoons sherry vinegar

Salt and freshly ground pepper

1. In a small saucepan of boiling water, cook the garlic clove for 10 minutes; drain.

2. In a blender, working in batches, puree the garlic with the 5 cups of diced cucumber, the 1¼ cups of whole green grapes, ½ cup of the almonds and the bread cubes, scallions, watercress, water, olive oil and sherry vinegar until very smooth. Transfer the soup to a large pitcher and season with salt and pepper. Refrigerate until chilled, about 2 hours.

3. To serve, chop the remaining ¼ cup of almonds. Stir the gazpacho, then pour it into shallow bowls. Garnish with the cucumber, grapes and almonds and serve at once. —*Susan Spungen*

MAKE AHEAD The gazpacho can be refrigerated overnight.

Chilled Celery Soup with Nantucket Bay Scallops

TOTAL: 30 MIN

10 SERVINGS ● ●

- 6 tablespoons unsalted butter
- 4 large shallots, thinly sliced (1 cup)
- 8 celery ribs, thinly sliced, plus 2 tablespoons shredded celery leaves, for garnish
- 4 cups water
- ½ cup flat-leaf parsley leaves
- 1⅓ cups crème fraîche

Salt and freshly ground white pepper

- 2 tablespoons grapeseed oil
- 1¼ pounds Nantucket bay scallops (see Note)

1. In a large saucepan, melt the butter over moderate heat. Add the shallots; cook until softened, about 3 minutes. Add the sliced celery and cook, stirring occasionally, until crisp-tender and still bright green, 4 to 5 minutes. Add the water and bring to a boil. Simmer over moderate heat until the celery is tender, about 8 minutes.

2. Working in batches, puree the soup with the parsley. Strain into a bowl, pressing on the solids. Whisk in the crème fraîche and refrigerate until chilled. Season the soup with salt and white pepper.

3. Just before serving, heat 1 tablespoon of the oil in a large skillet until smoking. In a bowl, season the scallops with salt and pepper and toss with the remaining 1 tablespoon of oil. Add the scallops to the pan; cook over high heat, turning, until golden and cooked through, about 3 minutes.

4. Ladle the soup into bowls and mound the scallops in the center. Sprinkle with the celery leaves and serve immediately. —*Barbara Lynch*

NOTE If you can't find Nantucket bay scallops, larger scallops can be used instead; quarter them before cooking.

MAKE AHEAD The celery soup can be refrigerated overnight.

No-Cook Tomato Buttermilk Soup

ACTIVE: 30 MIN; TOTAL: 1 HR 35 MIN

4 SERVINGS ● ●

Using market-fresh ingredients, chef Dennis Leary serves four-star cuisine diner style at Canteen in San Francisco. For this recipe, he drains fresh tomato puree slowly through cheesecloth to get clear tomato water, which he blends with buttermilk to create a pure-white chilled soup. In this more rustic version of that soup, the tomato puree is drained through a coarser strainer, giving the soup a lovely pink hue.

- 3 pounds red tomatoes, coarsely chopped

Kosher salt

- ¾ cup buttermilk

Freshly ground pepper

- 1 pound red and yellow cherry tomatoes, halved
- 2 tablespoons chopped basil
- 1 tablespoon chopped parsley
- 1 scallion, minced
- 1 tablespoon extra-virgin olive oil
- 1 teaspoon fresh lemon juice

1. Season the chopped tomatoes with 2 teaspoons of kosher salt and let them stand at room temperature for 1 hour.

2. In a blender, puree the tomatoes. Strain the tomato puree through a coarse sieve set over a large bowl. Stir the buttermilk into the tomato puree. Season the tomato buttermilk soup with salt and pepper and refrigerate the soup until it is chilled, at least 30 minutes.

3. In a medium bowl, toss the cherry tomatoes with the chopped basil and parsley, the minced scallion, olive oil and lemon juice. Season the cherry tomatoes with salt and pepper.

4. Ladle the tomato buttermilk soup into shallow soup bowls. Spoon the cherry tomato salad in the center of each serving of soup and serve at once. —*Dennis Leary*

TEA-SCENTED PUMPKIN SOUP

Tea-Scented Pumpkin Soup

ACTIVE: 30 MIN; TOTAL: 1 HR 10 MIN

8 SERVINGS ● ●

Fashion designer Han Feng, a celebrated Shanghai hostess, lightly flavors this silky, creamy soup with Ceylon tea, then garnishes each serving with a drizzle of roasted pumpkin seed oil. She restocks her supply of the lovely, nutty oil whenever she's in New York City.

One 3-pound sweet pumpkin or kabocha squash—quartered, seeded, peeled and cut into 2-inch pieces

6 cups chicken stock

1 teaspoon Ceylon tea

½ cup boiling water

Salt and freshly ground pepper

2 teaspoons vegetable oil

2 scallions, green part only, thinly sliced crosswise

Roasted pumpkin seed oil, for drizzling

1. In a large enameled cast-iron casserole, cover the pumpkin pieces with the chicken stock and bring to a boil. Simmer over moderate heat until the pumpkin is tender, about 35 minutes.

2. In a cup, steep the Ceylon tea in the boiling water for 5 minutes. Strain the tea and reserve.

3. Working in batches, puree the pumpkin soup in a blender and return it to the casserole. Add the tea and bring the soup to a simmer. Season the soup with salt and pepper.

4. In a small skillet, heat the vegetable oil. Add the scallion greens and cook over high heat until softened, about 30 seconds. Season the scallions with salt.

5. Ladle the pumpkin soup into 8 small bowls and drizzle it lightly with roasted pumpkin seed oil. Garnish the soup with the scallions and serve immediately.

—*Han Feng*

MAKE AHEAD The soup can be refrigerated overnight. Reheat gently.

Big Heart Artichoke and Parmesan Soup

ACTIVE: 30 MIN; TOTAL: 1 HR

4 SERVINGS ●

Chef David Myers of Sona in Los Angeles makes the most of California's exemplary Big Heart artichokes in this simple soup. Big Hearts have thicker leaves and larger hearts than almost any other artichoke, so the effort of cooking and eating them is much more rewarding. The artichoke soup is also a great way to use up leftover Parmesan cheese rind: Myers tosses the rind into the simmering soup, then discards it before pureeing.

½ lemon

4 Big Heart or globe artichokes (1 pound each)

2 tablespoons extra-virgin olive oil

¾ pound Yukon Gold potatoes, peeled and cut into ½-inch pieces

4 large shallots, halved

3 large garlic cloves, halved

Salt

1 cup dry white wine

4 cups chicken stock or low-sodium broth

One 4-ounce Parmesan rind, plus ½ cup of shavings, for garnish

12 thyme sprigs and 1 tablespoon whole black peppercorns, tied in cheesecloth

½ cup heavy cream

1 cup pure olive oil

1. Fill a large bowl with cold water and squeeze the juice from the lemon half into the water. Working with 1 artichoke at a time, snap off the outer leaves. Using a sharp knife, trim the stem and base of the artichoke and cut off the top two-thirds of the leaves. With a spoon or melon baller, scrape out the furry choke. Rub the remaining artichoke heart all over with the lemon half and add the artichoke

to the water. Repeat with the remaining 3 artichokes. Cut 3 of the artichoke hearts into 1-inch pieces and return them to the water; return the lemon half to the water. Leave the fourth artichoke heart whole to use in making the crispy garnish.

2. In a large saucepan, heat the extra-virgin olive oil until it is shimmering. Drain the artichoke pieces and pat dry. Add the artichoke pieces to the saucepan along with the potato pieces and the halved shallots and garlic. Season the vegetables with salt. Cook over moderate heat, stirring occasionally, until the vegetables are lightly browned and barely tender, about 20 minutes. Add the white wine to the soup and cook until it is nearly evaporated, about 7 minutes. Add the chicken stock, Parmesan rind and thyme bundle to the soup and bring to a boil. Partially cover the soup and cook over moderately low heat until the vegetables are tender, about 30 minutes. Pick out and discard the thyme bundle and Parmesan rind.

3. Working in batches, puree the soup in a blender or food processor until smooth. Return the soup to the saucepan. Add the heavy cream to the saucepan and season the soup with salt. Keep the soup warm while you finish making the crispy fried artichoke garnish.

4. Drain the reserved whole artichoke heart and pat thoroughly dry. Thinly slice it on a mandoline. In a medium skillet, heat the pure olive oil until it is shimmering. Add the slices of artichoke heart and fry them over high heat, stirring occasionally, until golden, about 1½ minutes. Using a slotted spoon, transfer the fried artichoke slices to paper towels to drain; sprinkle lightly with salt.

5. Ladle the artichoke and cheese soup into shallow soup bowls. Mound some of the Parmesan shavings in the center of each bowl, then top with the crispy fried artichoke slices and serve right away.

—*David Myers*

soups

Smoky Potato Soup with Bacon Croutons

TOTAL: 45 MIN
4 SERVINGS ●

This ultrasmooth potato soup gets a smoky kick from the addition of bacon puree, a homemade riff on the Italian pork-fat delicacy *lardo*.

- 4 tablespoons unsalted butter
- 2 medium shallots, thinly sliced
- 1½ pounds baking potatoes, peeled and sliced ⅓ inch thick
- 6 cups chicken stock or low-sodium broth
- ½ cup heavy cream
- Salt and freshly ground white pepper
- 4 ounces fatty slab bacon, cut into ½-inch cubes
- 2 garlic cloves, chopped
- Eight ⅓-inch-thick baguette slices

1. Preheat the oven to 375°. In a saucepan, melt the butter. Add the sliced shallots and cook over low heat, stirring, until softened, about 4 minutes. Add the potato slices and stock to the pan and bring to a boil. Simmer the soup over low heat until the potatoes are tender, about 15 minutes. Working in batches, puree the soup in a blender. Return the soup to the saucepan, add the heavy cream and season with salt and white pepper; keep the soup hot.

2. Meanwhile, in a small saucepan, cover the slab bacon with ½ inch of water. Simmer over low heat until the bacon is very tender, about 15 minutes. Using a slotted spoon, transfer the bacon to a mini food processor, then add the garlic and puree until smooth.

3. Arrange the baguette slices on a baking sheet and spread with half of the bacon puree. Bake for about 8 minutes, or until lightly browned and crisp. Ladle the soup into bowls and stir 1 generous tablespoon of bacon puree into each bowl. Serve at once with the croutons. —*Marcia Kiesel*

MAKE AHEAD The soup and bacon puree can be refrigerated separately overnight.

Cauliflower Soup with Pecans and Rye Croutons

ACTIVE: 35 MIN; TOTAL: 1 HR 20 MIN
6 SERVINGS ● ● ●

- 3 tablespoons light olive oil
- 2 leeks, white and pale green parts only, cut into 2-inch pieces
- 4 garlic cloves, smashed
- Two 2-pound heads of cauliflower, cored and cut into 2-inch florets, ½ cup of tiny florets reserved for garnish
- 1 Granny Smith apple—peeled, cored and cut into 2-inch pieces
- 6 cups low-sodium chicken broth
- 5 thyme sprigs
- 1 slice crustless rye bread, cut into ½-inch dice (1 cup)
- ½ cup pecan pieces
- Salt and freshly ground pepper

1. Preheat the oven to 350°. In a large, heavy pot, heat 2 tablespoons of the olive oil. Add the leeks and garlic and cook over moderate heat until softened, about 5 minutes. Add the large cauliflower florets and the apple and cook, stirring, for 2 minutes. Add the broth and thyme sprigs and bring to a boil. Cover and simmer over low heat for 45 minutes.

2. Spread the diced rye bread, pecan pieces and tiny cauliflower florets on a large rimmed baking sheet. Drizzle with the remaining 1 tablespoon of olive oil and toss to coat. Season generously with salt and pepper and bake, stirring once, for about 10 minutes, or until the rye bread croutons are crisp.

3. Discard the thyme sprigs. Working in batches, puree the soup in a blender. Return the soup to the pot and season with salt and pepper. Ladle into bowls, scatter the croutons, pecans and cauliflower on top and serve. —*Mary Ellen Diaz*

MAKE AHEAD The soup can be refrigerated overnight. Reheat gently before serving. Add more chicken broth to thin the soup to the desired consistency, if needed.

Butternut Squash Soup

ACTIVE: 45 MIN; TOTAL: 1 HR 30 MIN
6 SERVINGS ● ●

- 6 cups low-sodium chicken broth
- One 2-pound butternut squash—quartered, seeded, peeled and cut into 2-inch pieces
- 5 thyme sprigs
- 2 garlic cloves, halved
- 2 medium leeks, white and pale green parts only, cut into 2-inch pieces
- 1 celery rib, cut into 2-inch pieces
- 1 tablespoon vegetable oil
- 2 thick slices of bacon, cut crosswise into ½-inch-thick pieces
- 2 packed cups coarsely chopped collards or kale
- One 15-ounce can pinto or Roman beans, drained and rinsed
- 1 medium carrot, finely diced
- 1 red bell pepper, finely diced
- 1 cup corn kernels
- Salt and freshly ground pepper

1. In a large, heavy pot, combine the chicken broth, squash pieces, thyme sprigs, garlic, leeks and celery and bring to a boil. Cover and simmer over low heat for 45 minutes.

2. In a medium skillet, heat the vegetable oil. Add the bacon strips and cook over moderately high heat, turning once, until crisp, about 7 minutes.

3. Remove the thyme sprigs from the soup and discard. Working in batches, puree the soup in a blender. Return the soup to the pot. Add the bacon, collards, pinto beans, carrot, bell pepper and corn and bring to a boil. Simmer over moderately low heat, stirring occasionally, until the vegetables are tender, about 7 minutes. Season the soup with salt and pepper and serve. —*Mary Ellen Diaz*

MAKE AHEAD The soup can be refrigerated overnight. Reheat gently.

BUTTERNUT SQUASH SOUP

SPICY GRAIN SOUP

Spicy Grain Soup

ACTIVE: 40 MIN; TOTAL: 1 HR 40 MIN
8 SERVINGS ● ●

Based on a brothy tortilla soup, this fiery, substantial soup is full of nutty-tasting barley, brown rice and bulgur.

½ cup pearl barley
Water
½ cup short-grain brown rice
½ cup bulgur
1 tablespoon light olive oil
3 ancho or dried mulato chiles—stemmed, seeded and broken into 2-inch pieces
1 large onion, thinly sliced
2 garlic cloves, halved
2 quarts low-sodium chicken or vegetable broth
1½ cups canned diced tomatoes
6 cilantro sprigs, plus ¼ cup chopped cilantro
1 teaspoon ground allspice
Kosher salt and freshly ground pepper
½ pound shiitake mushrooms, stems discarded, caps thinly sliced
One 15-ounce can black beans, drained and rinsed
1 medium carrot, finely diced
1 medium zucchini, finely diced
1 medium parsnip, finely diced
½ cup salted roasted pumpkin seeds

1. In a medium saucepan, cover the barley with 4 cups of water and bring to a boil. Cover and simmer over low heat until tender, about 35 minutes; drain. Return the barley to the pan and cover. In another medium saucepan, cover the brown rice with 2 cups of water and bring to a boil. Cover and simmer over low heat until tender, about 35 minutes. Drain the brown rice and add to the barley.

2. In a medium bowl, cover the bulgur with 1 cup of hot water. Cover and let stand until the water is absorbed, 10 minutes.

3. In a large, heavy pot, heat the light olive oil. Add the ancho chiles, onion and garlic and cook over moderately high heat, stirring occasionally, until the onion is lightly browned, about 5 minutes. Add the chicken broth, tomatoes, cilantro sprigs and allspice and season the soup with 1 tablespoon of salt and a pinch of pepper. Bring to a boil, then cover the soup and simmer over low heat for 45 minutes. Let cool slightly. Puree the soup in a blender and return to the pan.

4. Add the shiitake mushrooms, black beans, diced carrot, zucchini and parsnip to the pureed soup and bring to a boil. Cover the soup and simmer over low heat for 20 minutes. Add the barley, brown rice and bulgur and season with salt and pepper. Ladle the spicy grain soup into bowls, sprinkle with the pumpkin seeds and chopped cilantro and serve at once.
—*Mary Ellen Diaz*

● FAST ● HEALTHY ● MAKE AHEAD ● STAFF FAVORITE

soups

White Bean and Ham Soup

TOTAL: 30 MIN

6 SERVINGS ●

When F&W's Grace Parisi was growing up, her mother made white bean and escarole soup every Friday. To transform the soup into a main course, Parisi substitutes ham and spiced croutons for the greens.

- 1 tablespoon unsalted butter
- 1 large white onion, chopped
- 1 carrot, coarsely shredded
- 1 garlic clove, peeled and smashed
- 3 thyme sprigs
- ½ teaspoon ground coriander
- 4 cups chicken stock or broth
- Three 15-ounce cans cannellini beans, drained
- 1 pound smoked ham in 1 piece
- 1½ cups cubed (1-inch) baguette
- 2 tablespoons extra-virgin olive oil
- 1 teaspoon sweet paprika
- Salt and freshly ground pepper
- 1 scallion, thinly sliced crosswise

1. Preheat the oven to 350°. In a soup pot, melt the butter. Add the onion, carrot, garlic, thyme and coriander. Cook over moderately high heat, stirring, until softened. Add the stock, beans and ham and bring to a boil. Cover partially and cook over moderate heat for 20 minutes.

2. Toss the baguette cubes with the olive oil and paprika. Season with salt. Spread on a baking sheet and bake for 10 minutes, stirring occasionally, until toasted.

3. Remove the ham from the soup and cut it into ½-inch pieces. Discard the thyme sprigs. Working in 2 batches, transfer the soup to a blender or food processor and puree until smooth. Return the soup to the pot and stir in the diced ham. Season the soup with salt and pepper and ladle into warmed shallow bowls. Top with the croutons and scallion and serve.
—*Grace Parisi*

MAKE AHEAD The soup can be refrigerated for up to 3 days. Store the croutons in an airtight container for up to 3 days.

Garlic and Pasilla Chile Soup

ACTIVE: 30 MIN; TOTAL: 50 MIN

4 SERVINGS ●

- 3 large dried pasilla chiles
- 1 quart hot water
- 3 tablespoons olive oil
- 1 medium onion, coarsely chopped
- 1 head garlic, cloves peeled and coarsely chopped
- 1 large tomato, cut into 1-inch dice
- ½ teaspoon dried oregano, preferably Mexican
- Salt
- 1 cup ½-inch dice of country bread or baguette
- ¼ cup crème fraîche or sour cream
- 1 Hass avocado, cut into ½-inch dice
- ¼ cup cilantro leaves

1. In a large bowl, cover the chiles with the hot water; set a small plate over the chiles to keep them submerged. Let soak until softened, about 20 minutes. Strain and reserve the soaking liquid. Stem, seed and coarsely chop the chiles.

2. Preheat the oven to 400°. In a large saucepan, heat 2 tablespoons of the olive oil. Add the onion and garlic and cook over moderate heat until softened, about 5 minutes. Add the chopped chiles and cook, stirring, for 1 minute. Add the tomato, oregano, a pinch of salt and the strained chile soaking liquid and bring to a boil. Cover the soup and simmer gently over low heat for 20 minutes.

3. Meanwhile, in a cake pan, toss the diced bread with the remaining 1 tablespoon of olive oil and spread in an even layer. Bake until golden brown, about 8 minutes.

4. Working in batches, puree the soup in a blender. Return the soup to the saucepan, bring to a simmer and season with salt. Ladle into bowls, top with the crème fraîche, avocado, cilantro and croutons and serve. —*Jean-Claude Szurdak*

Roasted Red Pepper Soup with Seared Scallops

ACTIVE: 30 MIN; TOTAL: 1 HR 20 MIN

6 SERVINGS ● ●

- 4 large red bell peppers (2¼ pounds), stems removed
- 3 tablespoons extra-virgin olive oil
- 2 garlic cloves, minced
- 1 medium onion, finely chopped
- 1 teaspoon ground cumin
- ¼ teaspoon crushed red pepper
- 1 quart low-sodium chicken broth
- ½ cup fresh orange juice
- ¼ teaspoon grated orange zest
- 2 tablespoons chopped cilantro
- Salt and freshly ground pepper
- 6 sea scallops

1. Preheat the oven to 425°. Put the red bell peppers on a cookie sheet, stemmed side down, and bake for 45 minutes, or until the skins are black. When cool enough to handle, remove and discard the skins, cores and seeds. Finely dice 2 of the peppers.

2. In a large saucepan, heat 2 tablespoons of the olive oil. Add the garlic, onion, cumin and crushed red pepper and cook over moderately low heat, stirring occasionally, until the onion is softened, about 10 minutes. Add the whole roasted peppers and the chicken broth and bring to a boil over high heat. Reduce the heat to low and simmer for 20 minutes. Add the orange juice, orange zest and cilantro.

3. In a blender, puree the soup in batches. Return the soup to the saucepan and season with salt and pepper; keep hot.

4. In a medium skillet, heat the remaining 1 tablespoon of olive oil until shimmering. Season the scallops with salt and pepper. Add the scallops to the skillet and cook over high heat until richly browned on the bottom, about 2 minutes. Turn the scallops and cook on the second side for 1 minute. Ladle the soup into bowls, garnish with the scallops and diced peppers and serve.
—*Annabel Langbein*

ROASTED RED PEPPER SOUP
WITH SEARED SCALLOPS

soups

Pistou de Marseille

**ACTIVE: 1 HR 15 MIN; TOTAL: 3 HR
15 MIN PLUS OVERNIGHT SOAKING
10 SERVINGS** ● ●

- 1 small eggplant (½ pound), peeled and cut into ½-inch dice

Kosher salt

- ¼ cup extra-virgin olive oil
- 2 medium onions, diced (¼ inch)
- 3 garlic cloves, minced
- 1 Italian frying pepper, cut into ½-inch dice
- 1 pound medium zucchini, cut into ½-inch dice
- 7 Roma or plum tomatoes— peeled, seeded and cut into ¼-inch dice (2½ cups)
- 3 quarts boiling water
- ½ pound dried cannellini beans (1¼ cups), soaked in cold water overnight and drained

Bouquet garni made with 3 large basil leaves, 2 parsley sprigs, 1 thyme sprig and 1 bay leaf

- 2 carrots, cut into ½-inch dice
- ½ pound mixed green beans and yellow wax beans, cut into 1-inch lengths (2 cups)

technique
classic pistou

Paula Wolfert says there's only one true way to make pistou—by hand. In a large mortar, pound 1 teaspoon kosher salt with 1 tablespoon crushed garlic to a paste. Tear 4½ cups basil leaves into pieces, add by the handful and grind against mortar side until almost smooth. Stir in ¼ cup grated plum tomatoes; gradually stir in ¼ cup extra-virgin olive oil. Stir in 1 cup finely grated aged Gouda cheese.

- ¼ teaspoon freshly grated nutmeg

Freshly ground black pepper

- 1 pound Yukon Gold potatoes, peeled and cut into ⅓-inch dice
- 1 cup elbow macaroni
- 1 cup Classic Pistou (see Box at left)

Finely grated Mimolette or lightly aged Gouda, for serving

1. In a colander, toss the eggplant with 2 teaspoons of salt; let drain for 20 minutes. Rinse the eggplant well and squeeze out as much water as possible.

2. Heat the oil in a soup pot. Add the onions. Cook over moderate heat, stirring occasionally, until very soft but not browned, 10 minutes. Add the garlic and cook for 2 minutes, stirring. Add the eggplant, frying pepper and half of the zucchini. Cook until the vegetables begin to soften, 5 minutes. Stir in the tomatoes. Cover and cook over moderately low heat for 30 minutes, stirring occasionally, until very soft.

3. Pour the boiling water into the pot and add the drained beans. Cover and simmer gently over moderately low heat until the beans are tender, 1 hour and 15 minutes.

4. Add the bouquet garni, carrots, mixed beans and nutmeg to the soup and cook until the beans are tender. Season generously with salt and pepper. Stir in the remaining zucchini, the potatoes and the macaroni and cook until tender, 10 minutes. Remove from the heat and stir in the Classic Pistou. Ladle the soup into bowls and sprinkle with grated Mimolette; pass additional grated cheese at the table.
—*Paula Wolfert*

Soupe au Pistou

**ACTIVE: 1 HR; TOTAL: 2 HR
6 TO 8 SERVINGS** ● ● ●

Soupe au pistou is like a Provençal version of minestrone. The *pistou*, Provence's answer to pesto, gets stirred into the soup at the end. Unlike other soups, this is delicious served hot or room temperature.

- 1 cup dried white beans such as navy or cannellini, soaked in cold water overnight and drained

One 1-ounce slice of pancetta

- 1 small onion, halved, plus 1 medium onion, coarsely chopped
- 4 garlic cloves, 2 whole and 2 smashed
- 1 bay leaf
- 2 quarts plus 3 cups water
- 1 tablespoon extra-virgin olive oil
- 1 small fennel bulb, cored and coarsely chopped
- 2 red potatoes (10 ounces), peeled and halved
- 4 small zucchini (1 pound), cut into ½-inch pieces
- ¾ pound green beans or Romano beans, cut into ½-inch pieces
- 3 medium tomatoes—peeled, seeded and cut into ½-inch dice
- 1 tablespoon unsalted butter
- 1 cup small-shaped pasta, such as elbows or ditalini

Salt and freshly ground pepper

- 1 cup Classic Pistou (see Box at left)

Basil sprigs, for garnish

1. Put the drained white beans, pancetta, halved onion, whole garlic cloves and bay leaf in a medium saucepan. Add the 3 cups of water and bring to a boil over high heat. Reduce the heat to low, cover the saucepan and simmer until the beans are tender, about 1½ hours. Discard the pancetta, onion, garlic and bay leaf.

2. Meanwhile, in a large, heavy pot, heat the olive oil. Add the fennel, potatoes, chopped onion and smashed garlic. Cover the pot and cook the vegetables over moderately low heat, stirring occasionally, until the fennel and onion are softened, about 10 minutes. Add the 2 quarts of water and gradually bring to a boil. Reduce the heat and simmer for 30 minutes.

3. Add the zucchini and green beans to the pot and simmer for 20 minutes. Mash the potatoes against the side of the pot using a large fork; the potatoes will thicken the soup. Add the diced tomatoes and the white beans and their cooking liquid and simmer the soup over moderately low heat for 5 to 10 minutes.

4. In a small skillet, melt the butter. Add the pasta and cook over moderate heat until golden brown and toasty, about 4 minutes. Stir the pasta into the soup and simmer for 1 minute. Cover, remove from the heat and let stand until the pasta is tender, about 25 minutes. Season with salt and pepper.

5. Put the Classic Pistou in a large soup tureen. Gradually stir in some of the liquid from the soup, then pour in the rest of the soup and stir well. Ladle the soup into bowls, garnish with basil sprigs and serve hot or at room temperature.
—*Paula Wolfert*

MAKE AHEAD The soup can be prepared through Step 4 and refrigerated overnight. Reheat gently before adding it to the Classic Pistou.

Ham, Escarole and Bean Stew
TOTAL: 45 MIN
4 SERVINGS ● ● ●

- 6 ounces lean slab bacon, sliced ¼ inch thick and cut into ¼-inch dice
- 1 tablespoon extra-virgin olive oil, plus more for drizzling
- 1 small onion, chopped
- 2 garlic cloves, minced
- 1 Yukon Gold potato (8 ounces), cut into ½-inch dice
- 3 cups chicken or beef stock or low-sodium broth
- 6 ounces smoked ham, shredded (1 cup)
- One 15-ounce can cannellini beans, drained
- ½ small head of escarole, cut into ½-inch ribbons (2 packed cups)
- Freshly ground pepper

1. In a saucepan, fry the bacon in the 1 tablespoon of olive oil over moderately high heat until browned, about 6 minutes. Spoon off all but 1 tablespoon of the fat. Add the onion and garlic and cook over moderate heat, stirring, until softened, about 5 minutes. Add the potato and cook, stirring, for 1 minute. Add the stock and boil over high heat. Reduce the heat to moderate and cook until the potato is tender, about 15 minutes.

2. Add the ham, beans and escarole and season with pepper. Cook over moderately high heat until the escarole is tender, about 5 minutes. Transfer to bowls, drizzle with olive oil and serve. —*Jose Garces*

Smoky Clam Chowder
TOTAL: 1 HR
4 SERVINGS ● ●

Los Angeles personal chef Nicki Reiss set out to develop this hearty, tomato-packed clam chowder based on flavors she enjoyed on a trip to Spain. As an alternative to smoky (and fatty) chorizo, Reiss turned to soyrizo (available at melissas.com), her favorite soy-based vegetarian sausage.

- 3 tablespoons extra-virgin olive oil
- 4 garlic cloves, minced
- 1½ tablespoons fresh lemon juice
- 2½ cups water
- ½ cup dry white wine
- 4 dozen littleneck clams, scrubbed
- One 28-ounce can whole tomatoes, drained
- 1 small onion, thinly sliced
- 1 medium shallot, thinly sliced
- 2 celery ribs, thinly sliced crosswise
- 3 tablespoons soyrizo (optional)
- ½ to 1 teaspoon crushed red pepper
- 2 thyme sprigs
- ¼ cup finely chopped flat-leaf parsley
- Salt and freshly ground pepper
- 1 teaspoon pimentón de la Vera (smoked Spanish paprika) or other smoky paprika

1. In a large saucepan, heat 1 tablespoon of the olive oil. Add half of the garlic and the lemon juice and cook over moderate heat until the garlic is fragrant, about 2 minutes. Add the water and wine and bring to a boil over high heat. Add half of the clams, cover the saucepan and boil until the clams start to open, about 3 minutes. Using tongs, transfer the open clams to a heatproof bowl. Cover and continue boiling until all of the clams in the saucepan have opened; discard any clams that do not open. Carefully pour the clam broth into a heatproof bowl, stopping before you reach the grit at the bottom. Remove the clams from their shells and coarsely chop them. Rinse out and dry the saucepan.

2. In a food processor, puree the drained tomatoes until smooth.

3. Heat 1 tablespoon of the olive oil in the saucepan. Stir in the onion, shallot, celery, soyrizo, crushed red pepper and the remaining garlic. Cover and cook over low heat, stirring occasionally, until the vegetables are softened, about 6 minutes. Add the thyme sprigs, reserved clam broth, chopped clams, pureed tomatoes and half of the parsley. Simmer over low heat until the clams are tender, about 25 minutes. Discard the thyme sprigs and season the chowder with salt and pepper.

4. Meanwhile, in a small saucepan, heat the remaining 1 tablespoon of olive oil over moderately high heat. When the olive oil is hot, add the paprika and, as soon as it sizzles, scrape it into a small bowl.

5. Bring the chowder to a boil over moderately high heat and add the remaining clams. Cover and simmer until the clams open, about 4 minutes. Using tongs, transfer the open clams to a bowl. When all of the clams have opened, season the chowder with salt and pepper. Ladle the chowder into large, shallow bowls and arrange 6 clams in each bowl. Sprinkle with the remaining parsley. Drizzle the paprika oil over the chowder; serve. —*Nicki Reiss*

soups

Pasta e Fagioli

TOTAL: 45 MIN

6 SERVINGS ● ●

For his version of the Italian classic *pasta e fagioli*, chef Andrew Carmellini of New York City's A Voce simmers Tuscan corona beans in pork belly stock, then adds goat cheese ravioli and farro. For an easier recipe, we used canned beans, prosciutto, fresh goat cheese and orzo.

- **6 cups chicken stock or broth**
- **One 4-ounce slice of prosciutto**
- **½ cup orzo**
- **1 tablespoon extra-virgin olive oil**
- **1 medium onion, thinly sliced**

equipment

3 great pans

In an F&W survey, chefs selected the following pans as the best:

All-Clad Chef Felicia Willett of Felicia Suzanne's in Memphis likes their durability; allclad.com.

Le Creuset "They're wonderful for braising," says chef Cory Schreiber of Wildwood in Portland, Oregon; lecreuset.com.

Old-Fashioned Cast-Iron Chef Tom Douglas of Seattle's Dahlia Lounge uses his grandmother's pan; staubusa.com.

- **1 carrot, thinly sliced**
- **1 celery rib, thinly sliced**
- **2 garlic cloves, thinly sliced**
- **1 rosemary sprig**
- **½ teaspoon crushed red pepper**
- **1 tablespoon tomato paste**
- **Two 19-ounce cans cannellini beans, drained**
- **Salt and freshly ground pepper**
- **¼ pound fresh goat cheese, crumbled**

1. In a large saucepan, bring the stock to a boil with the prosciutto. Add the orzo, cover partially and cook until al dente, about 6 minutes. Strain into a heatproof bowl. Pick out the prosciutto and dice it. Reserve the orzo separately.

2. Wipe out the saucepan and heat the olive oil in it. Add the onion, carrot, celery, garlic, rosemary, crushed pepper and prosciutto. Cook the vegetables over moderately high heat, stirring occasionally, until lightly browned, 6 minutes. Add the tomato paste and broth, cover partially and simmer until the prosciutto and vegetables are tender, 8 minutes. Discard the rosemary.

3. Add half of the beans to the soup. Puree in a blender and return to the pan. Add the remaining beans and reserved orzo. Cook until heated through. Season with salt and pepper. Stir in the goat cheese and serve.
—*Andrew Carmellini*

White Bean and Broccoli Rabe Soup

ACTIVE: 30 MIN; TOTAL: 1 HR 15 MIN

4 SERVINGS ● ●

- **4 slices hearty whole wheat bread, cut into 1-inch cubes**
- **¼ cup extra-virgin olive oil**
- **1 large Spanish onion, thinly sliced**
- **2 tablespoons dry white vermouth**
- **2 carrots, coarsely chopped**
- **2 celery ribs, coarsely chopped**
- **2 thyme sprigs**
- **1 rosemary sprig**
- **1 bay leaf**

- **4 garlic cloves, minced**
- **1 quart low-sodium chicken stock**
- **Two 19-ounce cans white cannellini beans, drained and rinsed**
- **Salt and freshly ground black pepper**
- **¼ teaspoon crushed red pepper**
- **2 pounds broccoli rabe, large stems discarded, the rest coarsely chopped**
- **1 tablespoon fresh lemon juice**

1. Preheat the oven to 350°. On a large rimmed baking sheet, toss the bread cubes with 1 tablespoon of the olive oil and spread in an even layer. Bake until browned and crisp, about 10 minutes.

2. In a medium casserole, heat 1 tablespoon of the olive oil. Add the onion and cook over moderate heat, stirring occasionally, until softened and golden, about 10 minutes. Add the vermouth and stir, scraping up any browned bits from the bottom of the casserole. Add the carrots, celery, thyme, rosemary, bay leaf and half the garlic and cook, stirring occasionally, until the vegetables are softened, about 5 minutes. Add the chicken stock, beans and a large pinch each of salt and black pepper and bring to a boil. Simmer the soup over low heat for 30 minutes, until the vegetables are very tender.

3. Meanwhile, heat the remaining 2 tablespoons of olive oil in a large skillet. Add the remaining garlic and the crushed red pepper and cook over moderately high heat, stirring, until fragrant, about 1 minute. Stir in the broccoli rabe. Cover and cook over moderate heat, stirring occasionally, until the broccoli rabe is tender, about 5 minutes. Season the broccoli rabe with salt and pepper.

4. Remove the thyme, rosemary and bay leaf from the soup. Puree the soup, using an immersion blender, or in batches in a regular blender. Return the pureed soup to the casserole and bring to a simmer. Add the lemon juice and season the soup with salt and pepper. Ladle the soup into

shallow bowls, top with the broccoli rabe and croutons and serve. —*Melissa Clark*
MAKE AHEAD The croutons, soup and broccoli rabe can be prepared 1 day in advance. Store the croutons in an airtight container at room temperature. Refrigerate the soup and broccoli rabe separately.

Sherried Black Bean Soup with Shrimp

ACTIVE: 30 MIN; TOTAL: 2 HR 20 MIN PLUS OVERNIGHT SOAKING
6 SERVINGS ●

- ½ pound dried black beans, soaked overnight in water and drained
- ¼ cup extra-virgin olive oil
- 1 medium onion, minced
- 3 garlic cloves, minced
- ½ green bell pepper, minced
- 1 teaspoon ground cumin
- 1 teaspoon dried oregano
- ½ cup heavy cream
- 1 tablespoon dry sherry
- 2 teaspoons sherry vinegar
- 1 tablespoon plus 1 teaspoon chopped cilantro
- Salt and freshly ground pepper
- 6 medium shrimp, shelled and deveined
- 1 teaspoon chopped mint

1. Cover six 4-inch skewers with water and soak for 2 hours. Put the beans in a medium saucepan, add enough water to cover by 2 inches and bring to a boil. Reduce the heat to low and simmer the beans until tender, about 2 hours; add water as needed to keep the beans submerged. Pour off all but 2½ cups of the cooking liquid.
2. Meanwhile, in a medium skillet, heat 3 tablespoons of the olive oil. Add the onion, garlic and green pepper and cook over moderate heat until the vegetables are softened, about 6 minutes. Add the cumin and oregano and cook, stirring, until fragrant, about 2 minutes.
3. Scrape the vegetables into the beans.

Add the cream, sherry, vinegar and 1 tablespoon of the cilantro. Working in batches, puree the beans in a blender until very smooth. Return the soup to the pan and season with salt and pepper; keep warm.
4. Light a grill. In a small bowl, toss the shrimp with the remaining 1 tablespoon of olive oil and 1 teaspoon of cilantro and the mint. Thread 1 shrimp onto each skewer and season with salt and pepper. Grill the shrimp over a hot fire until curled and lightly charred, about 1 minute per side. Pour the soup into tall shot glasses and garnish each glass with a grilled shrimp skewer. —*Michelle Bernstein*
MAKE AHEAD The sherried black bean soup can be refrigerated for up to 3 days and reheated gently.

Minted Pea Soup with Smoked Salmon

TOTAL: 30 MIN
4 SERVINGS ● ●

- 3 tablespoons unsalted butter
- 1 onion, coarsely chopped
- 1 pound frozen peas, thawed
- 2 tablespoons coarsely chopped mint
- 3 cups chicken stock or broth
- Kosher salt
- ½ pound Scottish smoked salmon in one piece, skinned and cut into ½-inch dice
- 2 tablespoons crème fraîche

1. In a large saucepan, melt the butter. Add the onion and cook over moderate heat until softened, about 8 minutes. Add all but 2 tablespoons of the peas. Add the mint and cook for 1 minute. Add the stock and simmer for 5 minutes.
2. Working in batches, puree the soup in a blender until silky smooth. Return the soup to the saucepan and season with salt. Gently rewarm the soup and ladle it into 4 shallow bowls. Garnish with the reserved peas, the smoked salmon and a dollop of crème fraîche and serve. —*Nick Nairn*

Prosciutto Consommé with Arugula and Melon

ACTIVE: 1 HR; TOTAL: 3 HR PLUS CHILLING
4 SERVINGS ● ●

- 1 pound lean prosciutto in 1 piece, plus 4 thin slices, cut into ribbons
- 1 medium carrot, finely chopped
- 1 medium onion, finely chopped
- 1 garlic clove, minced
- ½ teaspoon fennel seeds
- 2 small rosemary sprigs
- ¾ pound lean ground pork
- 6 large egg whites
- 1½ tablespoons fresh lemon juice
- Salt
- ½ cantaloupe, scooped into balls
- 1 cup baby arugula

1. With a sharp knife, remove the prosciutto skin and cut into 1-inch pieces. Cut the meat and fat into 1-inch pieces and coarsely grind in a meat grinder or food processor; pulsing several times. Transfer with the skin to a soup pot. Add the carrot, onion, garlic, fennel and rosemary. Cook over moderate heat, stirring, until the fat is rendered, 10 minutes. Add 12 cups of cold water and bring to a boil. Simmer over moderately low heat until the broth is flavorful and reduced to 10 cups, 1½ hours. Strain into a clean soup pot and refrigerate until chilled. Discard the solids.
2. Skim off the fat. In a medium bowl, knead the pork, egg whites and lemon juice. Stir into the broth and slowly bring to a simmer, stirring, until the pork rises completely to the top. Stir gently to dislodge any pork from the bottom. Simmer over moderately low heat, undisturbed, for 15 minutes. Gently skim the "raft."
3. Strain the soup through a sieve lined with cheesecloth into a saucepan. Skim any remaining fat from the surface. Season the consommé with salt and keep warm.
4. Place the melon and prosciutto in soup bowls, top with arugula and ladle in 1 cup of consommé. Serve. —*Michael Carlson*

soups

Chicken-and-Garlic Chowder

ACTIVE: 15 MIN; TOTAL: 60 MIN

6 SERVINGS ● ●

To make this recipe incredibly quickly, use prepared ingredients from the supermarket: pre-peeled garlic, precut butternut squash, rotisserie chicken and frozen *sofrito* (the Spanish green-pepper-and-onion seasoning paste). Poaching the garlic cloves in milk helps bring out their flavor.

- 5 peeled garlic cloves
- 1½ cups milk
- 6 cups chicken stock or low-sodium broth
- 12 ounces peeled butternut squash, cut into 1-inch cubes
- ¼ cup *sofrito* (see Note)
- One 3½-pound rotisserie chicken—juices reserved, skin and bones discarded, meat shredded (about 4 cups)
- ¼ cup frozen peas
- Salt and freshly ground black pepper

1. In a small saucepan, combine the pre-peeled garlic cloves with the milk and bring to a simmer. Cook over moderately low heat until the garlic is soft and the milk has reduced to 1 cup, about 40 minutes. Transfer the mixture to a blender and puree until smooth.

2. Meanwhile, in a large soup pot, combine the chicken stock, butternut squash and *sofrito* and bring to a boil. Cover the pot and cook the soup over moderate heat until the squash is just tender, about 20 minutes. Add the shredded chicken and its juices, the frozen peas and the creamy garlic puree. Season the chicken-and-garlic chowder with salt and pepper. Simmer the soup for 5 minutes longer and serve right away. —*Grace Parisi*

NOTE *Sofrito* is available in tubs in the freezer section of many supermarkets.

MAKE AHEAD The chowder can be refrigerated overnight.

Light and Creamy Oyster Chowder with Salsify

ACTIVE: 35 MIN; TOTAL: 50 MIN

MAKES 6½ CUPS ●

Salsify is a root vegetable shaped like a thin parsnip; it tastes a little like an artichoke heart. If you have trouble finding it, use sunchokes or the pedestrian potato.

- Juice of 1 lemon
- ¾ pound salsify or Jerusalem artichokes (sunchokes) or potatoes
- ¼ pound sliced bacon, cut crosswise into ¼-inch strips
- 1 large white onion chopped
- Kosher salt and freshly ground pepper
- ½ cup dry white wine
- 2 cups clam juice
- 1 cup water
- 4 thyme sprigs
- 1 cup heavy cream
- 2 dozen freshly shucked oysters, oyster liquor reserved
- Pinch of cayenne pepper
- 1 tablespoon chopped parsley

1. Fill a medium bowl with cold water and add the lemon juice. Peel the salsify, cut into ¼-inch dice and add to the water.

2. In a saucepan, cook the bacon over moderate heat until crisp. Drain on paper towels; reserve 2 tablespoons of the fat.

3. Add the onion and cook over moderate heat until softened. Drain the salsify, add to the pan and season with salt and black pepper. Cover and cook over moderately low heat, stirring occasionally, until almost tender, 10 minutes. Add the wine and bring to a boil. Add the clam juice, water and thyme. Cover and simmer over moderately low heat until the salsify is tender, 10 minutes. Add the cream, oysters and liquor and cayenne and simmer for 5 minutes, or until the oysters are just cooked through. Discard the thyme. Season with salt and pepper and ladle into warmed bowls. Serve topped with the bacon and parsley. —*Mary Ellen Carroll and Donna Wingate*

Spiced Beef Pho with Sesame-Chile Oil

ACTIVE: 1 HR; TOTAL: 3 HR PLUS OVERNIGHT CHILLING

6 SERVINGS ●

The rice vermicelli soup *pho* is a staple all over Vietnam; this spicy beef version is the specialty of Hanoi. At home in Connecticut, F&W's Marcia Kiesel often eats it for breakfast, as the Vietnamese do. "It's a perfect meal and an invigorating way to start the day," she says. She's tried innumerable *phos* but considers the recipe from Binh Duong, her co-author on the book *Simple Art of Vietnamese Cooking*, to be the best. This *pho* tweaks Duong's recipe by adding an escarole garnish.

BEEF BROTH

- 4 pounds oxtails or beef short ribs
- 18 cups water
- 1 teaspoon vegetable oil
- 1 medium onion, halved
- One 3-inch piece unpeeled fresh ginger, halved lengthwise
- 2 bay leaves
- Two 3-inch cinnamon sticks, broken into pieces
- One 2-inch piece of rock sugar or 6 sugar cubes (see Note)
- Kosher salt
- 4 whole cloves
- 4 star anise pods, broken up
- 2 teaspoons fennel seeds

SESAME-CHILE OIL

- ¼ cup vegetable oil
- 3 large garlic cloves, chopped
- 2 tablespoons crushed red pepper
- 1½ teaspoons sesame seeds
- ½ teaspoon Asian sesame oil
- Kosher salt

SOUP GARNISHES

- 1 pound rice vermicelli
- 1 pound beef round, partially frozen and very thinly sliced across the grain

LIGHT AND CREAMY OYSTER CHOWDER WITH SALSIFY

SPICED BEEF PHO WITH SESAME-CHILE OIL

Asian fish sauce

Asian sesame oil

Sriracha chile sauce

Lime wedges

Cilantro sprigs

Basil leaves

Onion slices

Chile slices

Escarole leaves

Mung bean sprouts

1. MAKE THE BEEF BROTH: In a large soup pot, cover the oxtails with cold water and bring to a boil over high heat; drain. Add the 18 cups of water and bring to a boil.

2. Meanwhile, heat the vegetable oil in a small nonstick skillet. Add the onion halves and the ginger, cut sides down, and cook over moderately high heat until richly browned, about 5 minutes, Transfer the onion and ginger to the oxtail pot with the bay leaves, cinnamon sticks, rock sugar and 1 tablespoon of salt.

3. Put the cloves, star anise and fennel seeds in a tea ball or tie them up in a piece of cheesecloth. Add them to the oxtail pot and simmer, skimming occasionally, until the oxtails are tender, about 2 hours. Strain the broth in a large sieve set over a large heatproof bowl. Remove the meat from the oxtails. Refrigerate the beef broth and the oxtail meat separately overnight.

4. MAKE THE SESAME-CHILE OIL: Heat the vegetable oil in a small saucepan. Add the garlic and cook over moderate heat until golden, about 2 minutes. Add the crushed red pepper and sesame seeds and cook for 1 minute; transfer to a bowl. Stir in the sesame oil and a pinch of salt.

5. ASSEMBLE THE SOUP: Put the rice vermicelli in a large bowl and cover with cold water. Let the vermicelli soak until pliable, about 20 minutes.

6. Skim the fat from the broth; discard. Simmer the broth over moderately high heat. Boil a large saucepan of water.

7. Place the raw beef in a large strainer and lower into the simmering broth for 4 seconds; transfer to soup bowls. Drain the vermicelli. Working in 6 batches, lower the vermicelli in the strainer into the boiling water for 30 seconds, or until barely tender; drain. Transfer to the bowls. Ladle about 1½ cups of the broth into each bowl and add the chilled oxtail meat.

8. Put the remaining ingredients in separate bowls or arrange on a platter. Serve the soup with the condiments and the sesame-chile oil. Serve right away.

—Marcia Kiesel

NOTE Rock sugar, available at Asian markets, comes in large amber crystals.

MAKE AHEAD The broth and oxtail meat can be refrigerated for up to 3 days. The sesame-chile oil can be refrigerated overnight. Let return to room temperature before serving.

PAPPARDELLE WITH LAMB RAGÙ (P. 73)

pasta

"At the end of the day, the stuff people come back for isn't the veal head cooked three different ways. It's the ravioli."

—**Andrew Carmellini,** chef, A Voce, New York City

SAGE FETTUCCINE

FRASCATELLI CARBONARA

Sage Fettuccine

ACTIVE: 30 MIN; TOTAL: 1 HR

4 SERVINGS

- 2¼ cups all-purpose flour
- 2 tablespoons minced sage
- 2 large eggs beaten with
  ⅓ cup water
- 2 tablespoons unsalted butter
- 2 tablespoons extra-virgin olive oil

Salt and freshly ground pepper

- 6 tablespoons freshly grated
  Parmigiano-Reggiano

1. On a work surface, toss the flour with the minced sage. Make a well in the center of the flour and pour in the egg-and-water mixture. Stir the dough with a fork, gradually incorporating all of the flour. Once the dough is too stiff to stir, knead it to work in as much of the remaining flour as possible. Divide the dough into 2 pieces, wrap them in plastic and let rest at room temperature for 30 minutes.

2. Lightly flour the pasta dough and, working with one piece at a time, run it through a pasta machine set on successively narrower notches, ending at the second-to-thinnest setting. Cut the pasta sheet into 4 pieces and drape them over a rack to dry for a few minutes. Repeat with the remaining half of the dough. Run the pasta sheets through the fettuccine cutter, lightly dusting with flour. Spread the fettuccine out on a baking sheet and let stand for 15 minutes.

3. Cook the fettuccine in boiling salted water until al dente, about 5 minutes. Drain well, reserving ¾ cup of the cooking water. Return the water to the pot and stir in the butter, olive oil and a pinch of salt and pepper. Add the fettuccine and cook over moderate heat for 2 minutes. Add the cheese, toss and serve right away.
—*Marco Pasanella*

WINE Fresh, lively Soave.

Frascatelli Carbonara

TOTAL: 45 MIN

4 SERVINGS ● ●

At Union Square Cafe in New York City, chef Michael Romano tops homemade *frascatelli*, a dense spaetzle-like pasta, with a combination of pancetta, cheese and cream.

- 1 tablespoon extra-virgin olive oil
- 6 ounces pancetta, sliced ¼ inch thick and cut into 1-inch strips
- 1 cup heavy cream

Freshly ground black pepper

- ½ cup freshly grated Parmesan cheese
- ½ cup freshly grated pecorino cheese, plus more for serving
- 1 large egg yolk

Cold water

- 2 tablespoons kosher salt
- 1 pound semolina flour
  (2½ cups)

1. In a large skillet, heat the olive oil. Add the pancetta strips to the skillet and cook over moderate heat until the pancetta is crisp, about 7 minutes. Drain the pancetta in a strainer over a bowl; reserve 2 tablespoons of the fat.

2. Add the heavy cream to the skillet and bring it to a simmer over moderate heat. Grind black pepper into the cream, then add in the freshly grated Parmesan and pecorino cheeses, stirring until they are blended into the cream, about 2 minutes. Scrape the cream-and-cheese mixture into a bowl and let cool. Whisk in the egg yolk, pancetta and the reserved pancetta fat and refrigerate the cream sauce.

3. Bring 4 quarts of cold water to a boil; add the kosher salt. Spread the semolina flour on a large, rimmed baking sheet. Put 1 cup of cold water in a bowl. Dip your fingertips in the water and scatter drops all over the surface of the semolina. Keep scattering water until the entire surface is covered with drops. With a rubber spatula, turn the moistened semolina over on itself, tossing to form small lumps. Shake the baking sheet to spread the loose semolina in an even layer. Repeat with more water until just about all of the semolina has been formed into irregular lumps about the size of small peas. Transfer the *frascatelli* to a colander and shake to remove any loose semolina flour.

4. Pour the *frascatelli* into the boiling water and cook, stirring a few times, until the pasta is al dente, about 4 minutes.

5. Meanwhile, in a large, deep skillet, reheat the sauce gently over moderately low heat, stirring constantly. Drain the *frascatelli,* add it to the carbonara sauce and bring to a simmer, stirring. Transfer the *frascatelli* to shallow bowls and serve, passing grated pecorino at the table. —*Michael Romano*

MAKE AHEAD The carbonara sauce can be refrigerated overnight.

WINE Cherry-inflected, earthy Sangiovese.

Spaghetti Carbonara with Green Peas
TOTAL: 30 MIN
4 SERVINGS ●

- 1 tablespoon extra-virgin olive oil
- 2 large garlic cloves, lightly crushed
- 6 ounces pancetta, sliced ⅓ inch thick and cut into 1-inch matchsticks
- ¾ cup heavy cream
- 3 large egg yolks
- ⅓ cup freshly grated Parmesan cheese, plus more for serving

Salt
- ¾ cup fresh or thawed frozen baby peas
- ¾ pound spaghetti

Freshly ground pepper

1. Bring a large pot of water to a boil. In a large, deep skillet, heat the olive oil. Add the garlic and cook over moderate heat until golden, about 3 minutes. Discard the garlic. Add the pancetta and cook over moderately high heat, stirring occasionally, until golden and crisp and the fat has been rendered, about 5 minutes. Using a slotted spoon, transfer the pancetta to a bowl.

2. Pour off all but 2 tablespoons of the fat from the skillet. Add the heavy cream and scrape up any browned bits from the bottom of the skillet, then pour the cream into a medium bowl. Whisk in the egg yolks and ⅓ cup of the Parmesan cheese.

3. Add salt to the pot of boiling water. Add the baby peas and cook just until tender, about 1 minute. Using a slotted spoon, transfer the cooked peas to a bowl.

4. Add the spaghetti to the boiling water and cook until al dente; drain. Return the spaghetti to the pot and add the cream mixture, pancetta and peas. Season with salt and pepper and toss until the sauce coats the spaghetti. Transfer the spaghetti to bowls and serve immediately with the remaining grated Parmesan cheese. —*Elia Aboumrad and Sam Talbot*

WINE Dry, fruity sparkling wine.

Pappardelle with Lamb Ragù
ACTIVE: 30 MIN; TOTAL: 1 HR
6 SERVINGS ●

- 3 tablespoons extra-virgin olive oil
- 1 carrot, finely diced
- 1 onion, finely diced
- 1 celery rib, finely diced
- 1½ pounds ground lamb
- 2 teaspoons ground coriander
- 1 teaspoon ground fennel seeds
- ½ teaspoon ground cumin
- 1 teaspoon chopped rosemary
- 1 teaspoon chopped thyme

Salt and freshly ground pepper
- 1 tablespoon tomato paste
- ½ cup dry red wine

One 28-ounce can diced tomatoes
- 1¼ cups chicken stock or low-sodium broth
- ¾ pound pappardelle
- 1 tablespoon unsalted butter
- ¾ cup fresh ricotta cheese
- 2 tablespoons chopped mint

1. In a large cast-iron casserole, heat 2 tablespoons of the olive oil. Add the carrot, onion and celery and cook over high heat, stirring occasionally, until slightly softened, about 5 minutes. Add the ground lamb, coriander, fennel, cumin, rosemary and thyme; season with salt and pepper. Cook, stirring, until the liquid evaporates, about 5 minutes. Stir in the tomato paste. Add the wine and cook until evaporated, about 5 minutes. Add the tomatoes and their juices, along with the stock, and bring to a boil. Cover partially and cook over moderately low heat until the liquid is slightly reduced, 25 to 30 minutes.

2. In a large pot of boiling salted water, cook the pasta until al dente. Drain, shaking well. Add the pasta to the sauce. Add the butter and the remaining 1 tablespoon of olive oil and toss over low heat. Serve the pasta in bowls, topped with the ricotta and mint. —*Andrew Carmellini*

WINE Bright, tart Barbera.

pasta

Pappardelle with Zucchini and Mint-Parsley Pesto

TOTAL: 20 MIN

6 SERVINGS ● ● ●

Lots of mint and earthy walnuts make this pesto a nice change from the standard basil. Here, the pesto and just a little Parmesan get tossed with pappardelle and zucchini ribbons. If you're using shorter, squatter pasta, like shells, slice the zucchini into chunks to match.

- 1 cup packed flat-leaf parsley leaves
- 1 cup packed mint leaves, plus mint sprigs for garnish
- 2 garlic cloves, coarsely chopped
- ¼ cup walnuts
- ½ cup extra-virgin olive oil
- ¼ cup freshly grated Parmesan cheese, plus more for serving

Kosher salt and freshly ground pepper

- 2 medium zucchini (1 pound)
- 1 pound dried pappardelle

1. In a food processor, combine the parsley, mint, garlic and walnuts and pulse until coarsely chopped. Pour in the olive oil and add the ¼ cup of grated Parmesan; process to a puree. Season the pesto generously with salt and pepper.

2. Trim ends from zucchini. Using a sturdy vegetable peeler, cut each zucchini lengthwise into long, paper-thin ribbons; discard the central core of seeds.

3. In a large pot of boiling salted water, cook the pappardelle noodles until they are al dente. Add the zucchini ribbons to the pot of boiling water, stir once and drain; reserve ¼ cup of the pasta water. Return the pappardelle and zucchini to the pot. Add the pesto and the reserved pasta water and toss the pasta and zucchini to coat with the pesto. Season the pasta with salt and pepper. Transfer the pappardelle to a large bowl, garnish with mint sprigs and serve. Pass the remaining grated Parmesan cheese at the table.
—*Susan Spungen*

WINE Fresh, lively Soave.

Pasta with Robiola and Truffles

TOTAL: 25 MIN

4 FIRST-COURSE SERVINGS ● ●

This indulgent first course marries three of Italy's best ingredients: egg pasta, winter truffles and Robiola Rocchetta, a creamy cheese from northern Italy that forms the base for an incredibly rich sauce.

- 4 tablespoons salted butter
- 8 ounces dried egg fettuccine or tagliatelle
- 8 ounces Robiola Rocchetta cheese, at room temperature, cut into 1-inch pieces

Salt and freshly ground pepper

- 1 medium fresh white or black truffle, peeled and sliced, or one 2-ounce jar sliced truffles

1. Bring a large pot of salted water to a boil. In a small saucepan, melt the butter. Cook the butter over moderate heat until the milk solids turn a rich brown and the butter smells nutty, about 6 minutes. Pour the butter into a bowl and set aside.

2. Cook the fettuccine in the boiling water until al dente. Drain the cooked pasta, reserving ½ cup of the cooking water. Return the pasta to the pot. Add the reserved water and the browned butter and toss the pasta with 2 forks. Add the cheese and toss until it begins to melt; season with salt and pepper. Transfer the pasta to warmed bowls, shave the truffle on top and serve right away.
—*Marcia Kiesel*

WINE Complex, aromatic Nebbiolo.

taste test

top pasta & robiola

GIOVANNI PERNA
Egg Fettuccine A delicate pasta made with stone-ground durum wheat. **Details** $9 for 500 g; formaggiokitchen.com.

RUSTICHELLA D'ABRUZZO
Egg Tagliatelle The dense pasta's rough texture helps each strand hold on to sauces. **Details** $6 for 8.8 oz; markethallfoods.com.

SPINOSI
Egg Fettuccine A quick-cooking dried pasta from Campofilone, said to be the birthplace of Italian egg pasta. **Details** $9 for 8.8 oz; agferrari.com.

CASEIFICIO DELL'ALTA LANGA
Robiola Rocchetta A fresh and tangy blend of cow's, sheep's and goat's milk. **Details** $15 for 9 oz; artisanalcheese.com.

GIANNI CORA
Robiola Castagna An earthy mixed-milk cheese from Piedmont aged in chestnut leaves. **Details** $24 for 12 oz; formaggiokitchen.com.

CASEIFICIO DELL'ALTA LANGA
Robiola Bosina A mild, creamy robiola made from cow's and sheep's milk, with balanced salty and sweet flavors. **Details** $11 for 8 oz; murrayscheese.com.

pasta

Spaghetti with Cauliflower

TOTAL: 30 MIN

4 TO 6 SERVINGS ● ●

    5   tablespoons extra-virgin olive oil
    ¼   cup *panko* (Japanese bread
        crumbs)
    1   medium onion, halved and
        thinly sliced
    1   head of cauliflower (1½ pounds),
        cut into 1-inch florets
    2   large garlic cloves, minced
    1   teaspoon cinnamon
    3   cups chicken stock or
        low-sodium broth
    2   tablespoons white vinegar
    ½   cup prepared tomato sauce
    1   tablespoon tomato paste
    ¼   cup golden raisins
    1   pound spaghetti
Salt and freshly ground pepper
    ¼   cup pine nuts, toasted

1. Bring a large pot of water to a boil. In a large, deep skillet, heat 2 tablespoons of the olive oil. Add the *panko* and toast until golden, about 1 minute. Transfer to a plate. Wipe out the skillet and heat the remaining 3 tablespoons of olive oil. Add the onion and cook until it is translucent, about

superfast
pasta sauce

CREAMY TOMATO-BASIL SAUCE
Heat 2 tablespoons of extra-virgin olive oil in a skillet. Add 1 chopped garlic clove and 1 cup of grape tomatoes, halved, and cook over high heat, stirring, until the tomatoes are softened, about 5 minutes. Add ¾ cup of mascarpone and cook over moderately high heat, stirring, until hot. Season with salt and freshly ground pepper, stir in 1 teaspoon of sherry vinegar and 2 tablespoons of finely shredded basil leaves and serve. —*Grace Parisi*

3 minutes. Add the cauliflower, garlic and cinnamon and cook for 1 minute. Add the stock, vinegar, tomato sauce, tomato paste and raisins and bring to a simmer. Cover partially and cook until the cauliflower is just tender, about 10 minutes.
2. Salt the boiling water, add the spaghetti and cook until al dente; drain.
3. Add the spaghetti to the cauliflower and toss to coat. Season with salt and pepper and cook over moderate heat, tossing, until the sauce thickens, about 3 minutes. Transfer the spaghetti to bowls, garnish with the pine nuts and *panko* and serve. —*Michael Psilakis*
WINE Fresh, fruity rosé.

Whole Wheat Spaghetti with Pancetta, Chestnuts and Vin Santo

ACTIVE: 25 MIN; TOTAL: 40 MIN

6 SERVINGS ●

    2   tablespoons unsalted butter
   10   ounces lean pancetta, sliced
        ¼ inch thick and cut into
        ½-inch squares
    3   large shallots, thinly sliced
    2   tablespoons chopped sage
    ½   cup vin santo
   20   vacuum-packed roasted chestnuts
        (from a 14-ounce jar), chopped
    ¾   pound whole wheat spaghetti
Salt and freshly ground pepper

1. Bring a large pot of salted water to a boil. In a large, deep skillet, melt 1 tablespoon of the butter. Add the pancetta and cook over moderately low heat until most of the pancetta fat has been rendered, about 12 minutes. Increase the heat to moderate and cook, stirring occasionally, until the pancetta is golden brown, about 8 minutes. Add the shallots and sage and cook over low heat, stirring occasionally, until the shallots are softened, about 8 minutes. Add the vin santo and simmer over moderate heat for 4 minutes, then stir in the chopped chestnuts and the remaining 1 tablespoon of butter.

2. Meanwhile, cook the spaghetti until al dente. Drain the pasta, reserving 1 cup of the cooking water. Add the spaghetti and the reserved cooking water to the sauce, season with salt and pepper and toss over low heat. Serve. —*Morgan Brownlow*
MAKE AHEAD The recipe can be prepared through Step 1 earlier in the day and refrigerated. Let return to room temperature before proceeding.
WINE Fruity, low-oak Chardonnay.

Lemony Broccoli and Chickpea Rigatoni

TOTAL: 30 MIN

4 TO 6 SERVINGS ● ●

This quick and healthy pasta with chickpeas in a piquant lemon–Parmesan cheese sauce epitomizes the unfussy, ingredient-centric style of Manhattan chef Marc Meyer, whose first book, *Brunch*, offers outrageously good recipes from his first restaurant, Five Points.

One 19-ounce can chickpeas,
        drained and rinsed
    ⅓   cup fresh lemon juice
    ¾   cup extra-virgin olive oil
Kosher salt and freshly ground black
        pepper
  1½   pounds broccoli, cut into
        florets
    1   pound rigatoni
    5   large garlic cloves, thinly sliced
    ½   teaspoon crushed red pepper
    1   cup freshly grated Parmesan
        cheese

1. In a medium bowl, toss the chickpeas with the lemon juice and ½ cup of the olive oil. Season the chickpeas with salt and pepper.
2. In a large pot of boiling salted water, cook the broccoli florets until they are crisp-tender, about 4 minutes. Using a slotted spoon, transfer the broccoli to a colander and rinse under cold water until cool. Add the rigatoni to the boiling water and cook until al dente.

LEMONY BROCCOLI AND CHICKPEA RIGATONI

SPAGHETTI WITH LEMON, CHILE AND CREAMY SPINACH

3. Meanwhile, in a large, deep skillet, heat the remaining ¼ cup of olive oil. Add the sliced garlic and crushed red pepper and cook over moderate heat until the garlic is golden, about 3 minutes. Add the blanched broccoli and cook until it is tender, about 5 minutes. Add the chickpea mixture and cook until the vegetables are warmed through, about 1 minute longer.

4. Drain the rigatoni, reserving ¼ cup of the pasta cooking water. Add the rigatoni to the broccoli and chickpeas along with the reserved pasta cooking water and season the pasta with salt and pepper. Cook over moderate heat, stirring, until the rigatoni is coated with sauce. Remove the pasta from the heat and stir in ½ cup of the Parmesan cheese. Transfer the pasta to a large serving bowl, sprinkle with the remaining Parmesan and serve right away. —*Marc Meyer*

WINE Zippy, fresh Pinot Bianco.

Spaghetti with Lemon, Chile and Creamy Spinach

TOTAL: 20 MIN

4 SERVINGS ● ●

Instead of using heavy cream, this tangy, spicy dish calls for low-fat yogurt, which is packed with protein and calcium. Stirring a little flour into the yogurt prevents curdling as it simmers and creates a thick, rich and satisfying sauce.

½ **pound whole wheat spaghetti**
1½ **cups plain low-fat yogurt**
 1 **tablespoon all-purpose flour**
 1 **tablespoon extra-virgin olive oil**
 4 **garlic cloves, minced**
 1 **red Thai chile, minced**
10 **ounces baby spinach**
**Finely grated zest of 2 lemons, plus
    1 tablespoon fresh lemon juice**
Salt and freshly ground pepper
 ¼ **cup freshly grated
    Parmesan cheese**

1. In a large saucepan of boiling salted water, cook the whole wheat spaghetti until it is al dente. Drain the spaghetti and return it to the saucepan.

2. Meanwhile, in a bowl, whisk the low-fat yogurt with the flour until the mixture is smooth. In a large skillet, heat the olive oil. Add the minced garlic and chile and cook over moderately low heat, stirring occasionally, until fragrant, about 2 minutes. Add the yogurt and bring to a simmer over moderate heat, stirring. Add the baby spinach by the handful and cook, stirring, until it is wilted. When all of the spinach has been added, stir in the lemon zest and the lemon juice and season the sauce with salt and pepper.

3. Add the sauce to the spaghetti and toss well to coat. Mound in bowls, sprinkle with the Parmesan and serve right away. —*Celia Brooks Brown*

WINE Light, fresh Pinot Grigio.

pasta

Cauliflower and Crab Ravioli

ACTIVE: 45 MIN; TOTAL: 1 HR 15 MIN

4 SERVINGS

These impressive supersized ravioli are constructed with rectangles of homemade pasta that are dotted with parsley leaves and filled with the unexpectedly alluring combination of crab and cauliflower.

- 1½ teaspoons unsalted butter
- 1 tablespoon plus 2 teaspoons extra-virgin olive oil, plus more for drizzling
- 2 garlic cloves, minced
- 1 small head of cauliflower (1 pound), cut into 1-inch florets
- 2 tablespoons water
- 1 cup heavy cream
- ½ pound lump crabmeat, picked over

Salt and freshly ground white pepper
- 8 Fresh Pasta Sheets with Parsley (recipe follows)
- ½ cup freshly grated Parmesan cheese

1. Bring a large pot of water to a boil. In a large, deep skillet, melt the butter in 2 teaspoons of the olive oil. Add the garlic. Cook over moderate heat until fragrant, 2 minutes. Add the cauliflower florets and cook over moderately high heat, stirring, just until lightly browned, 3 minutes. Add the water, cover and cook until the cauliflower is tender, 4 minutes.

2. Add the heavy cream and simmer until slightly thickened, about 6 minutes. Add the crab and stir gently to heat through. Season with salt and pepper; keep warm.

3. Add salt and the remaining 1 tablespoon of oil to the boiling water and cook the pasta sheets until just tender, about 1 minute. Drain and return to the pot. Lightly drizzle the sheets with olive oil and, using 2 large spoons, toss lightly to coat.

4. Place 1 pasta sheet on each of 4 warmed plates. Spoon the creamed crab and cauliflower onto the pasta sheets and sprinkle with half of the Parmesan cheese. Cover with the remaining pasta sheets and sprinkle with the remaining Parmesan. Serve right away. —*Susan Spungen*

MAKE AHEAD The pasta sheets can be cooked, tossed with oil and refrigerated overnight. The creamed cauliflower can be made earlier in the day; add the crab just before serving.

WINE Light, crisp white Burgundy.

FRESH PASTA SHEETS WITH PARSLEY

ACTIVE: 25 MIN; TOTAL: 55 MIN

MAKES EIGHT 8-BY-6-INCH SHEETS

- 1¾ cups all-purpose flour, plus more for dusting
- ½ teaspoon kosher salt
- 2 large eggs
- 1½ tablespoons water

Cornmeal or semolina, for dusting
- 36 medium flat-leaf parsley leaves

1. In a food processor, pulse the flour and salt to blend. With the machine on, add the eggs, one at a time, and the water. Process until the dough forms a ball. Transfer the dough to a work surface and knead into a smooth ball. Cover the dough with plastic wrap and let stand at room temperature for 30 minutes.

2. Sprinkle 2 large cookie sheets with cornmeal. Lightly flour a work surface. Cut the dough into 2 equal pieces. Working with one piece at a time, flatten the dough with your hand and run it through a pasta machine: Begin at the thickest setting and work your way through consecutively thin-

---

taste test
top domestic caviar

Caviarteria sells large, natural-colored salmon eggs from Alaskan chum with a clean flavor and excellent pop. **Details** $15 for 3.5 oz; caviarteria.com.

Seattle Caviar has natural paddlefish (a sturgeon cousin) caviar that resembles steel-gray Caspian sevruga and has a delicate earthy taste and silky texture. **Details** $25 per oz; caviar.com.

Tsar Nicoulai sustainably farms its white sturgeon California Estate Osetra, then sells its nutty, creamy roe to superstar chefs like Wolfgang Puck. **Details** $59 per oz; tsarnicoulai.com.

Sunburst Trout, a company based in North Carolina, has small, juicy orange trout caviar with a subtle trout flavor. **Details** $28 for 2 oz; sunbursttrout.com.

Petrovich Caviar offers a sweet and buttery onyx-colored roe from hackleback sturgeon in the Missouri and Mississippi rivers. **Details** $16 per oz; surfasonline.com.

CAULIFLOWER AND CRAB RAVIOLI

PASTA WITH SALMON CAVIAR

ner settings until you reach the thinnest one. Spread the pasta sheet on the prepared cookie sheet, brushing away any excess flour.

3. With a moistened finger, make 18 dots of water on the left half of each pasta sheet randomly or in rows; they should be 2 inches apart. Set a parsley leaf on each dot and press down lightly. Fold the other half of the pasta sheet over to cover the parsley leaves. Run the folded sheet through the pasta machine on the next-to-thinnest setting. You may need to cut the pasta dough in half, partway through rolling out.

4. Cut the parsley-flecked sheets into 8-by-6-inch rectangles of dough. Repeat with the second piece of dough and the remaining parsley leaves.—*S.S.*

MAKE AHEAD The pasta dough can be prepared through Step 1 and refrigerated overnight or frozen for up to 1 month.

Pasta with Salmon Caviar

TOTAL: 30 MIN

4 MAIN- OR 6 FIRST-COURSE SERVINGS ● ●

Salmon eggs add a delicate crunch to this luxurious pasta dressed with smoked salmon. If you prefer a more subtle flavor, substitute trout roe and smoked trout.

Salt

- ½ **pound dry tagliarini or fettuccine**
- 2 **tablespoons unsalted butter**
- 1 **shallot, minced**
- ¼ **cup plus 2 tablespoons crème fraîche or sour cream**
- 1 **tablespoon finely chopped flat-leaf parsley**
- 1 **teaspoon chopped tarragon**

Freshly ground pepper

- 2 **ounces thinly sliced smoked salmon, cut into ½-inch ribbons (½ cup)**
- 4 **ounces salmon caviar**

1. Bring a large pot of water to a boil and add a large pinch of salt. Add the tagliarini and cook until the pasta is al dente. Drain the pasta, reserving about ½ cup of the cooking water.

2. In a large, deep skillet, melt the butter over moderate heat. When the foam subsides, add the minced shallot and cook it over moderately low heat for 2 minutes, stirring frequently. Add the crème fraîche and the chopped parsley and tarragon. Stir in about ¼ cup of the reserved pasta cooking water and season with pepper. Add the cooked pasta and the smoked salmon ribbons and toss well. Add up to 2 more tablespoons of the reserved cooking water if the pasta seems too dry. Remove from the heat. Add three-fourths of the caviar; toss gently. Serve in shallow bowls, garnished with the remaining caviar. —*Grace Parisi*

WINE Rich, complex white Burgundy.

PASTA SHELLS WITH PEAS AND HAM

Pasta Shells with Peas and Ham

TOTAL: 30 MIN

4 SERVINGS ● ●

Country ham—rubbed with salt and sugar and smoked for weeks then hung to cure for at least six months—is a quintessential Southern delicacy. Because it's so salty, it's ideal as an accent in dishes like this homey pasta.

- 1 pound small pasta shells or elbow macaroni
- 2 tablespoons plus 1 teaspoon extra-virgin olive oil
- 5 garlic cloves, thinly sliced
- One 10-ounce package frozen peas
- ¼ pound thinly sliced country ham or prosciutto, coarsely chopped
- 1¼ cups heavy cream
- 1 cup chicken stock or low-sodium broth
- ¼ cup freshly grated Parmesan cheese
- ⅓ cup chopped dill
- Salt and freshly ground pepper

1. In a large pot of boiling salted water, cook the pasta shells until al dente. Drain the shells, return them to the pot and toss with 1 teaspoon of the olive oil to prevent the shells from sticking together.

2. Meanwhile, in a large skillet, heat the remaining 2 tablespoons of olive oil. Add the sliced garlic cloves and cook over moderate heat until the garlic is golden, about 4 minutes. Add the frozen peas and the country ham and cook until the peas are hot and the ham is lightly browned, about 5 minutes. Add the heavy cream and the chicken stock and simmer over moderate heat until the cream has slightly thickened, about 5 minutes.

3. Stir the cream sauce into the cooked shells. Add the Parmesan cheese and the chopped dill to the pasta and season with salt and pepper. Transfer the pasta to bowls and serve right away.
—*Amy Tornquist*

WINE Dry, fruity sparkling wine.

Orzo Risotto with Buttery Shrimp

TOTAL: 30 MIN

4 SERVINGS ●

- 16 thin asparagus (6 ounces)
- 12 ounces orzo (1¾ cups)
- 6 tablespoons unsalted butter, at room temperature
- ½ pound shelled and deveined medium shrimp
- Salt and freshly ground pepper
- 1 cup chicken stock or low-sodium broth
- 2 tablespoons chopped flat-leaf parsley
- ½ cup grated Parmesan cheese, plus more for serving

1. Bring a large saucepan of salted water to a boil. Add the asparagus; cook over high heat until tender. With a slotted spoon, transfer to a plate. Add the orzo to the boiling water; cook, stirring occasionally, until al dente, 10 minutes.

2. Meanwhile, cut the asparagus into 1-inch lengths. In a medium skillet, melt the butter over moderately high heat. Reduce the heat to moderate and cook until the butter begins to brown. Add the shrimp, season with salt and pepper and cook over moderate heat until pink and curled, about 1 minute per side. With a slotted spoon, add the shrimp to the asparagus. Reserve the skillet.

3. Drain the orzo, reserving ¼ cup of the cooking water, then return to the saucepan and stir in the brown butter. Set the skillet over high heat and add the stock, scraping up any browned bits stuck to the bottom of the pan. Pour the stock and the reserved cooking water into the orzo; cook over moderate heat, stirring, until creamy, 2 minutes. Stir in the asparagus and shrimp and cook until heated through. Remove from the heat. Stir in the parsley and the ½ cup of Parmesan. Season with salt and pepper. Transfer the risotto to bowls and serve with more Parmesan. —*Ryan Poli*

WINE Light, fresh Pinot Grigio.

Crab and Artichoke Orzo Salad

TOTAL: 25 MIN

4 TO 6 SERVINGS ● ●

Marinated-artichoke lovers will adore this unusual take on cold pasta salad. Pureed artichokes flavor the tangy vinaigrette; chopped ones get tossed with the orzo and crab.

- 1 pound orzo
- One 6-ounce jar marinated artichoke-heart quarters, drained, 4 reserved and the rest coarsely chopped
- 2 garlic cloves
- 1 shallot, chopped
- 1 teaspoon Dijon mustard
- 1 teaspoon dried Greek oregano
- 2 large basil leaves
- ½ cup white wine vinegar
- ¾ cup extra-virgin olive oil
- Salt and freshly ground pepper
- 10 oil-packed sun-dried tomato halves, drained and sliced into ¼-inch strips
- 5 scallions, thinly sliced crosswise
- 1 pound jumbo lump crabmeat, picked over
- 2 tablespoons chopped flat-leaf parsley

1. In a pot of boiling salted water, cook the orzo until al dente. Drain the pasta and rinse under cold water, then drain again; transfer the orzo to a large bowl.

2. Meanwhile, in a blender, puree the 4 reserved artichoke quarters with the garlic, shallot, mustard, oregano, basil and vinegar. With the machine on, pour in the olive oil; season the with salt and pepper.

3. Stir 1 cup of the vinaigrette into the bowl of orzo. Add the chopped artichokes, the sun-dried tomatoes, scallions, crabmeat and parsley to the orzo; season the pasta with salt and pepper. Spoon the orzo into shallow bowls and serve, passing the remaining vinaigrette at the table.
—*Michael Psilakis*

WINE Fresh, minerally Vermentino.

● FAST ● HEALTHY ● MAKE AHEAD ● STAFF FAVORITE

pasta

Baked Cheese-Stuffed Shells
ACTIVE: 1 HR; TOTAL: 2 HR 30 MIN

12 SERVINGS

Two 12-ounce boxes large shells
 2 tablespoons extra-virgin olive oil
 2 shallots, minced
 2 garlic cloves, minced
One 10-ounce package frozen chopped
  spinach or Swiss chard, thawed
  and squeezed dry
 2 pounds fresh ricotta (4 cups)
 1 pound fresh mozzarella, cut into
  ½-inch cubes
 ½ cup freshly grated Parmesan
  cheese
 2 tablespoons chopped parsley
 ¼ teaspoon freshly grated nutmeg
Salt and freshly ground pepper
 1 large egg, lightly beaten
Spicy Tomato Sauce (recipe follows)
 ½ cup pitted, sliced kalamata olives

1. In a very large pot of boiling salted water, cook the shells until al dente; drain. Rinse under cold water and pat dry thoroughly.
2. In a skillet, heat the olive oil. Add the shallots and garlic; cook over moderately high heat until softened and starting to brown, 1 minute. Add the spinach and cook, stirring, for 1 minute. Transfer to a bowl and let cool. Add the ricotta and half each of the mozzarella and Parmesan. Stir in the parsley and nutmeg. Season with salt and pepper. Stir in the beaten egg.
3. Preheat the oven to 375°. Spoon ½ cup of the tomato sauce into each of two 13-by-9-inch baking dishes. Stuff each pasta shell with a heaping tablespoon of the filling. Arrange the stuffed shells in neat rows in the baking dishes. Spoon 2 cups of the sauce over the shells in each dish. Sprinkle the olives and the remaining mozzarella and Parmesan on top of the pasta and bake for 50 minutes, or until golden and bubbling. Let rest for 15 minutes. Serve the baked shells with the remaining sauce on the side. —*Maria Helm Sinskey*
WINE Cherry-inflected, earthy Sangiovese.

SPICY TOMATO SAUCE
ACTIVE: 10 MIN; TOTAL: 1 HR

MAKES ABOUT 6½ CUPS

 2 tablespoons extra-virgin olive oil
 8 large garlic cloves, sliced
Two 28-ounce cans diced tomatoes
  with their liquid
 2 cups water
 3 bay leaves
 ¼ teaspoon crushed red pepper
 1 teaspoon sugar
Kosher salt and freshly ground pepper

In a saucepan, heat the oil. Add the garlic and cook over moderate heat, stirring, until golden. Add the tomatoes and their liquid, the water, bay leaves, crushed pepper and sugar. Season with salt and bring to a boil. Reduce the heat to low and simmer, stirring occasionally, until slightly thickened, 45 minutes. Discard the bay leaves. Working in batches, puree the sauce in a blender. Transfer to a bowl; season with salt and pepper. —*M.H.S.*

Fresh Cheese Spaetzle
TOTAL: 25 MIN

4 SERVINGS ● ●

 2 large eggs, lightly beaten
 ¼ cup plus 1 tablespoon milk
 ¼ cup small-curd cottage cheese
Kosher salt and freshly ground pepper
 1 cup all-purpose flour
 2 tablespoons unsalted butter
 ½ cup quark
1½ tablespoons snipped chives

1. Bring a large pot of salted water to a boil. In a medium bowl, beat the eggs, milk, cottage cheese, ½ teaspoon of salt and ¼ teaspoon of pepper. Stir in the flour to form a smooth, thick, sticky batter.
2. Spoon the batter into a small colander with ¼-inch holes; set or hold 1 inch above the boiling water and scrape the batter through the holes, using a spatula. Stir the spaetzle once or twice to separate. As they rise to the surface, use a slotted spoon to transfer to a clean colander; drain well.

3. In a large nonstick skillet, melt the butter. Cook the spaetzle over moderately high heat, stirring and shaking the pan occasionally, until browned and crisp in spots, 5 minutes. Add the quark and chives, reduce the heat to moderately low and cook, stirring, until creamy. Season with salt and pepper. Serve. —*Grace Parisi*
WINE Tart, citrusy Riesling.

Grant's Mac and Cheese
ACTIVE: 30 MIN; TOTAL: 2 HR

8 SERVINGS ●

 1 tablespoon unsalted butter
 6 thick slices of bacon, diced
 1 medium onion, minced
 2 bay leaves
 1 tablespoon sweet paprika
 ½ teaspoon cayenne pepper
 ⅓ cup all-purpose flour
 6 cups whole milk
 1 pound elbow macaroni
 1 pound extra-sharp cheddar
  cheese, shredded (5 cups)
Salt

1. Preheat the oven to 350°. Butter a 13-by-9-by-2-inch baking dish. In a large saucepan, melt the butter. Add the bacon and cook over moderate heat until crisp, about 7 minutes. Transfer to a plate.
2. Add the onion and bay leaves. Cook over moderate heat, stirring, until softened. Add the paprika and cayenne and cook, stirring, until fragrant. Blend in the flour. Gradually whisk in the milk until smooth. Boil over high heat, whisking until thickened. Reduce the heat to low. Simmer gently for 30 minutes, whisking. Discard the bay leaves.
3. In a large pot of salted water, boil the pasta until pliable, 4 minutes. Drain and return to the pot. Stir 4 cups of cheddar into the sauce, add the bacon and season with salt. Mix the sauce with the pasta and spread in the dish. Scatter on the remaining cheese. Bake until golden, 30 minutes. Cool for 10 minutes. —*Grant Achatz*
WINE Fruity, low-oak Chardonnay.

GRANT'S MAC AND CHEESE

pasta

Orecchiette Bolognese with Chestnuts

ACTIVE: 40 MIN; TOTAL: 1 HR 20 MIN
6 SERVINGS ●

1¼ pounds thickly sliced smoked ham, torn into small pieces
2 tablespoons extra-virgin olive oil
1¼ pounds ground beef chuck
Pinch of ground cloves
1 celery rib, finely chopped
1 carrot, finely chopped
1 onion, finely chopped
2 garlic cloves, finely chopped
1 tablespoon finely chopped sage
1 tablespoon minced rosemary
¼ teaspoon crushed red pepper
1½ cups dry red wine
One 28-ounce can tomato puree
2 cups chicken stock or broth
Pinch of sugar
Freshly ground pepper
1 pound orecchiette pasta
½ cup heavy cream
1 cup vacuum-packed chestnuts, coarsely chopped (4 ounces)
2 tablespoons minced parsley
Salt
Freshly grated Parmesan, for serving

1. Pulse the ham in a food processor until it is coarsely chopped. In a large, deep casserole or Dutch oven, heat the olive oil. Add the ham, ground beef and the cloves and cook over high heat, stirring once or twice, until the meat begins to brown, about 10 minutes.
2. Add the celery, carrot, onion and garlic to the casserole and cook, stirring, until they are barely softened, about 3 minutes. Stir in the sage, rosemary and crushed pepper and cook until fragrant, 2 to 3 minutes. Add the red wine and cook until it is nearly evaporated, about 10 minutes. Add the tomato puree, stock and sugar, season with pepper and bring to a boil over moderately high heat. Simmer uncovered over low heat, stirring occasionally, until thick and reduced by half, about 45 minutes.
3. In a large pot of boiling salted water, cook the orecchiette until al dente.
4. Stir the cream into the sauce and simmer for 5 minutes. Stir in the chestnuts and parsley; season lightly with salt. Drain the pasta and transfer to a large bowl. Spoon the sauce over the pasta and serve, passing the cheese. —*Daniel Boulud*
WINE Bright, tart Barbera.

Pierogi Choucroute

ACTIVE: 30 MIN; TOTAL: 1 HR 20 MIN
8 SERVINGS ●

Two 14-ounce packages of fresh potato-and-cheese pierogi
4 slices of bacon, cut into 1-inch pieces
½ pound kielbasa, halved lengthwise and thinly sliced crosswise
2 tablespoons unsalted butter
1 large white onion, thinly sliced
1 pound sauerkraut, drained and squeezed dry (1½ cups)
8 juniper berries (optional)
Salt and freshly ground pepper
1 tablespoon all-purpose flour
2 cups chicken stock or broth
⅓ cup sour cream
⅓ cup whole-grain mustard

1. In a large pot of boiling salted water, cook the pierogi until just done, about 3 minutes. Drain and gently shake off any excess water. Arrange the pierogi in a 3-quart baking dish in an even layer.
2. In a large skillet, cook the bacon and kielbasa over moderately high heat, stirring occasionally, until lightly browned, about 5 minutes. Transfer to a plate.
3. Melt the butter in the skillet. Add the onion and cook over moderate heat, stirring occasionally, until softened, about 6 minutes. Add a few tablespoons of water if the onion seems dry. Add the sauerkraut and juniper berries, season with salt and pepper and cook, stirring, for 2 minutes. Add the flour and cook for 1 minute, stirring. Add the stock and bring to a boil. Stir in the bacon and kielbasa and spoon over the pierogi. Cover the pierogi with foil and bake for 30 minutes, or until they are heated through. Uncover the pierogi and bake for 10 minutes longer. Let the choucroute stand for 10 minutes.
4. In a small bowl, mix the sour cream with the whole-grain mustard. Serve with the pierogi choucroute. —*Grace Parisi*
WINE Rich Alsace Gewürztraminer.

tools

pasta machine

Typhoon's Italian Job Pasta Machine Set, a durable enamel-on-steel machine, is available in chrome or red. It can create four different pasta widths: pasta sheets (for ravioli and lasagna), pappardelle, linguine and tagliatelle. It comes with a pastry brush for cleaning cutting surfaces and a beechwood drying rack.
Details $60 for set; $40 for basic machine at typhoonus.com.

Spinach and Ricotta Gnudi with Tomato-Butter Sauce

ACTIVE: 45 MIN; TOTAL: 1 HR 40 MIN

6 SERVINGS ●

Chef Tommy Habetz describes *gnudi* as "ravioli filling without the pasta." He learned how to make his light and creamy version while working at Mario Batali's former New York City restaurant Pó.

- 1 stick unsalted butter
- 2 garlic cloves, smashed
- 1 small onion, halved
- 1 bay leaf

Pinch of crushed red pepper

One 28-ounce can diced
  Italian plum tomatoes,
  juices reserved

Salt

- 2 cups spinach, stems discarded
- 2 pounds fresh ricotta
- 4 large eggs, lightly beaten

Pinch of freshly grated nutmeg

Freshly grated Parmesan cheese

- 2 cups all-purpose flour

1. In a large, deep skillet, melt the butter. Add the garlic, onion, bay leaf and crushed red pepper and cook over moderate heat until the garlic is fragrant. Add the tomatoes and their juices and bring to a boil. Simmer the sauce over low heat, stirring occasionally, until thickened and reduced to 2½ cups, about 1½ hours. Discard the garlic, onion and bay leaf. Season the sauce with salt and keep warm.

2. Meanwhile, heat a medium skillet. Add the spinach, a handful at a time, and stir over moderately high heat until wilted; transfer to a colander and let cool slightly. Squeeze the spinach dry and finely chop it.

3. Bring a large pot of salted water to a boil. In a food processor, combine the spinach, ricotta, eggs, nutmeg and ¼ cup of Parmesan until blended. Add the flour in 3 batches, pulsing between additions, until almost incorporated. Scrape the dough onto a lightly floured work surface. Knead 5 to 10 times, until smooth.

4. Add one-fourth of the *gnudi* dough to a large, resealable plastic bag; with scissors, cut off a ½-inch corner. Working over the boiling water, squeeze the dough through the corner opening and use a knife to cut it into 1-inch pieces. Cook the *gnudi* over moderately high heat until firm, about 3 minutes. With a slotted spoon or wire skimmer, transfer the *gnudi* to a baking sheet; repeat with the remaining dough.

5. Carefully transfer the *gnudi* to the sauce and stir lightly to heat through. Spoon into shallow bowls. Serve at once, passing more Parmesan at the table. —*Tommy Habetz*

WINE Cherry-inflected, earthy Sangiovese.

Three-Cheese Baked Pasta

ACTIVE: 20 MIN; TOTAL: 45 MIN

8 SERVINGS ● ●

- 5 tablespoons unsalted butter
- ¼ cup all-purpose flour
- 3 cups whole milk

One 10½-ounce log fresh goat cheese

- 3 ounces freshly grated Parmesan cheese (1 cup)
- 2 teaspoons salt
- ¼ teaspoon freshly grated nutmeg
- 1 pound dried penne or garganelli
- ½ pound Taleggio cheese, rind discarded, cut into 1-inch pieces

1. Preheat the oven to 350°. In a saucepan, melt the butter. Stir in the flour until smooth. Cook over moderate heat, stirring, until pale brown, 4 minutes. Slowly whisk in the milk until smooth and bubbling. Cook over moderately low heat, whisking, until very thick, 10 minutes. Stir in the goat cheese, Parmesan, salt and nutmeg.

2. In a pot of boiling salted water, cook the penne until al dente; drain and return to the pot. Stir in the sauce. Spoon into eight 2-cup ovenproof dishes or a 13-by-9-inch baking dish. Tuck the Taleggio into the pasta and scatter a few pieces on top. Bake until heated through and nicely browned, 25 minutes; serve. —*Susan Spungen*

WINE Cherry-inflected, earthy Sangiovese.

Vegetable-and-Ravioli Lasagna

ACTIVE: 30 MIN; TOTAL: 1 HR 30 MIN

8 SERVINGS ●

This recipe is especially fast to make using roasted or grilled vegetables from the prepared food section of most supermarkets.

- 1 tablespoon extra-virgin olive oil
- 4 sweet Italian pork or turkey sausages (12 ounces), casings removed

One 24-ounce jar marinara sauce

- ½ cup water

Two 14-ounce packages fresh cheese ravioli

One 14-ounce package fresh spinach-and-cheese ravioli

- 12 ounces shredded mozzarella cheese (3 cups)
- 3 tablespoons freshly grated Parmesan cheese
- 1½ pounds mixed roasted or grilled vegetables, cut into 1-inch pieces

1. Preheat the oven to 375°. Bring a large pot of salted water to a boil. In a saucepan, heat the oil until shimmering. Add the sausage and cook over moderately high heat, stirring and breaking up the lumps, until no longer pink, 5 minutes. Add the sauce and water; simmer for 5 minutes.

2. Add the ravioli to the boiling water; cook until al dente. Drain and return to the pot. Add the sauce and toss gently to coat.

3. Spoon one-third of the ravioli and sauce into a 3-quart baking dish. Sprinkle with 1 cup of mozzarella and 1 tablespoon of Parmesan. Layer on another third of the ravioli, followed by the vegetables, 1 cup of mozzarella and 1 tablespoon of Parmesan. Top with the remaining ravioli and any remaining sauce and sausage. Sprinkle on the remaining mozzarella and 1 tablespoon of Parmesan; cover with foil.

4. Bake the lasagna for 30 minutes, until bubbling. Uncover and bake for 25 minutes, until browned and bubbling. Let stand for 10 minutes and serve. —*Grace Parisi*

WINE Juicy, fresh Dolcetto.

ROASTED BLUE FOOT CHICKENS WITH
GLAZED PARSNIPS AND CARROTS (P. 98)

poultry

"I was in Singpore trying satay for the first time, and it was like eating in Technicolor."

—**Nick Nairn,** chef and cooking school owner, Port of Menteith, Scotland

CHICKEN BREAST WITH ROSEMARY AND THYME

GRILLED CHINESE CHICKEN SALAD

Chicken Breasts with Rosemary and Thyme

TOTAL: 30 MIN

4 SERVINGS ● ●

- 4 large rosemary sprigs
- 4 large thyme sprigs
- 4 skinless bone-in chicken breast halves, (about ¾ pound each)
- ½ teaspoon crushed red pepper

Salt

Freshly ground black pepper

- 2 tablespoons extra-virgin olive oil
- ½ cup chicken stock or low-sodium broth
- 1 teaspoon all-purpose flour mixed with 2 teaspoons water

1. Preheat the oven to 375°. Press a rosemary sprig and a thyme sprig on each chicken breast. Sprinkle the chicken breasts with the crushed red pepper and season with salt and black pepper.

2. In a large nonstick, ovenproof skillet, heat the olive oil until shimmering. Add the chicken breasts, herb side down, and cook over moderately high heat until lightly browned, about 5 minutes. Season the chicken with salt and black pepper, turn and cook until lightly browned, 2 to 3 minutes longer. Transfer the skillet to the oven and roast the chicken for 20 minutes, or until the juices run clear when the breast is pierced near the wing joint.

3. Transfer the chicken breasts to a platter, cover and keep warm. Pour off any fat in the skillet and set the skillet over a burner. Add the stock and cook over high heat, scraping up any bits stuck to the bottom. Whisk the flour and water mixture into the skillet and boil until slightly thickened, about 1 minute. Pour the sauce into a bowl and serve with the chicken.

—*Matthew Malin and Andrew Goetz*

WINE Ripe, juicy Pinot Noir.

Grilled Chinese Chicken Salad

TOTAL: 30 MIN

4 SERVINGS ●

- 1 pound skinless, boneless chicken thighs
- ¼ cup Ginger-Miso Spice Paste (recipe follows)
- ¼ cup vegetable oil

Salt

- ¼ pound snow peas
- 1½ tablespoons fresh lime juice
- 2 scallions, cut into thin 1-inch julienne strips
- 10 ounces shredded coleslaw mix (4 cups)

1. Light a grill. Make ¼-inch-deep slashes in the chicken thighs. In a bowl, combine 2 tablespoons of the spice paste with 2 tablespoons of the oil and spread all over the chicken. Grill over high heat until cooked through, 7 to 8 minutes. Let cool, then cut the chicken into thin strips.

2. Meanwhile, bring a small saucepan of salted water to a boil. Add the snow peas and blanch for 1 minute. Drain and rinse under cold water; pat dry. Slice in half lengthwise. In a large bowl, whisk the remaining 2 tablespoons of paste with the lime juice and the remaining 2 tablespoons of oil. Season with salt. Add the snow peas, scallions, coleslaw mix and chicken, toss well and serve. —*Grace Parisi*

WINE Full-bodied, minerally Riesling.

GINGER-MISO SPICE PASTE

TOTAL: 10 MIN
MAKES ¼ CUP ● ● ●

- 1 tablespoon finely grated fresh ginger
- 1 tablespoon miso paste
- 2 garlic cloves, smashed
- 1 teaspoon Chinese chile-garlic sauce
- 1 teaspoon light brown sugar
- 1 teaspoon Asian sesame oil
- 1½ teaspoons fresh lime juice

Combine all of the ingredients in a bowl and mash to a paste. —*G.P.*

OTHER USES Rub the paste on skirt steak, shrimp, spareribs, chicken and pork before grilling, or stir into broth or noodle soup.

Chicken with Morels and Tarragon Cream Sauce

ACTIVE: 40 MIN; TOTAL: 1 HR
4 SERVINGS

- 1 ounce dried morels
- ¾ cup hot water
- 1 tablespoon vegetable oil
- Four 6-ounce boneless chicken breast halves with skin
- Salt and freshly ground pepper
- 2 tablespoons unsalted butter
- ½ pound cremini mushrooms, caps quartered
- ½ cup dry white wine
- ½ cup chicken stock or low-sodium broth
- ½ cup heavy cream
- 1 tablespoon coarsely chopped tarragon
- 1 teaspoon fresh lemon juice

1. Preheat the oven to 425°. Put the morels in a bowl and pour the hot water over them. Invert a small dish over the morels to keep them submerged and let stand until softened, about 20 minutes. Lift the morels from the soaking liquid and rinse them to get rid of any grit. Chop any large ones. Reserve the soaking liquid.

2. In a large, deep, ovenproof skillet, heat the oil until shimmering. Season the chicken with salt and pepper. Add to the skillet, skin side down, and cook over moderately high heat until browned on the bottom, 6 minutes. Turn the breasts and cook until browned on the bottom, 3 minutes. Add 1 tablespoon of the butter to the skillet; swirl to melt. Put the skillet in the oven and roast the chicken for about 8 minutes, until just cooked through. Transfer to a plate and keep warm.

3. Melt the remaining 1 tablespoon of butter in the skillet. Add the creminis, season with salt and pepper and cook over moderate heat until browned, about 5 minutes. Add the morels and cook, stirring, until they start to darken, about 3 minutes. Add the wine and simmer over moderately high heat until reduced to 3 tablespoons, about 3 minutes. Add the stock and slowly pour in the reserved soaking liquid, stopping before you reach the grit at the bottom. Simmer until reduced by two-thirds, about 6 minutes. Add the cream and tarragon and simmer until thickened, about 4 minutes. Add the lemon juice and season the sauce with salt and pepper. Add the chicken breasts to the skillet, skin side up, along with any accumulated juices, and simmer over low heat until hot, about 3 minutes. Transfer the chicken to plates and serve with the sauce. —*Nick Nairn*

SERVE WITH Boiled potatoes.

WINE Complex, elegant Pinot Noir.

Chicken with Potatoes and Fried Eggs

TOTAL: 45 MIN
4 SERVINGS ●

- ¾ pound small fingerling potatoes, halved lengthwise
- ¼ cup plus 2 tablespoons extra-virgin olive oil
- Salt and freshly ground pepper
- 2 cups chicken stock or low-sodium broth
- 1 tablespoon unsalted butter
- 1 teaspoon truffle oil
- Four 6-ounce boneless chicken breast halves with skin
- 4 large eggs

1. Preheat the oven to 375°. In a medium roasting pan, toss the potatoes with 2 tablespoons of the olive oil. Season the potatoes with salt and pepper and roast for about 25 minutes, or until they are golden and tender.

2. Meanwhile, in a small saucepan, boil the chicken stock until reduced to ½ cup, 8 to 10 minutes. Remove from the heat and add the butter and truffle oil. Keep the chicken stock warm.

3. In a large nonstick skillet, heat 1 tablespoon of the olive oil until shimmering. Season the chicken breast halves with salt and pepper and add them to the skillet, skin side down. Cook the chicken breasts over moderately high heat, turning once, until browned and cooked through, about 16 minutes. Transfer the chicken to plates and keep warm. Wipe out the skillet.

4. Add the remaining 3 tablespoons of olive oil to the skillet. Crack the eggs into the skillet and cook over moderate heat until the whites are set, about 1½ minutes. Turn the eggs and cook for 20 seconds longer. Using a spatula, transfer the eggs and the potatoes to the chicken breasts. Drizzle the chicken breasts with the truffle sauce and serve right away. —*Jose Garces*

WINE Dry, earthy sparkling wine.

poultry

Honey-Mustard Chicken

ACTIVE: 20 MIN; TOTAL: 1 HR

6 SERVINGS

You haven't really had an authentic Southern restaurant experience until you've had meat-and-three: a choice of meat plus three vegetable side dishes. Here, TV chef Bobby Flay bakes chicken—the centerpiece of many a meat-and-three—with a sticky sweet-and-spicy honey glaze inspired by the Savannah Bee Company's tupelo honey.

Two 4-pound chickens, each cut into 8 pieces
¼ cup extra-virgin olive oil
Kosher salt
1 cup honey
2 tablespoons Dijon mustard
1 teaspoon coarsely ground pepper

1. Preheat the oven to 400°. On 2 large rimmed baking sheets, toss the chicken pieces with the olive oil and season with salt. Roast the chicken until nearly cooked through, about 20 minutes for the breasts and 25 minutes for the legs, thighs and wings. Pour off the fat on the baking sheets. Preheat the broiler and position a rack just below center.

2. In a small saucepan, bring the honey, Dijon mustard, pepper and a pinch of salt to a boil.

3. On 1 of the baking sheets, toss all of chicken pieces with the honey mixture. Lay the chicken skin side down and broil for about 5 minutes, basting with the honey and shifting the baking sheet, as necessary, until the pieces are browned. Turn the chicken skin side up and broil for 5 minutes longer, basting occasionally. The chicken is done when it's cooked through and the skin is deeply glazed but not blackened. Transfer the chicken pieces to a platter. Pour the juices from the baking sheet into a heatproof bowl and skim off the fat. Serve the chicken right away, passing the juices on the side. —*Bobby Flay*
WINE Intense, fruity Zinfandel.

Honey-and-Spice-Glazed Chicken

TOTAL: 30 MIN

4 SERVINGS ●

¼ cup honey
2 garlic cloves, minced
2 tablespoons fresh lemon juice
2 teaspoons Dijon mustard
1 teaspoon sweet paprika
¼ teaspoon cayenne pepper
Four 10-ounce bone-in chicken breast halves with skin
Salt and freshly ground pepper

1. Preheat the oven to 425°. In a small bowl, stir together the honey, garlic, lemon juice, mustard, paprika and cayenne.

2. Put the chicken breasts on a rimmed baking sheet. Using a sharp knife, make 2 deep slashes in each chicken breast. Season the breasts with salt and black pepper, then brush most of the honey glaze over them. Bake the chicken for 15 minutes. Brush the remaining honey glaze over the chicken breasts and bake for about 10 minutes, until they are just cooked through.

3. Remove the chicken breasts from the oven, then preheat the broiler. Brush the juices from the baking sheet onto the chicken and broil for about 1 minute, or until the skin is crisp. Serve the honey-and-spice-glazed chicken right away.
—*Amy Tornquist*
WINE Round, deep-flavored Syrah.

Chicken Curry with Potatoes and Squash

ACTIVE: 30 MIN; TOTAL: 1 HR

4 SERVINGS

Kerala, a region on the southwestern coast of India, bases its cuisine on the culinary traditions of the Christian, Hindu and Muslim communities, and each group puts its own imprint on every recipe. This mildly sweet chicken curry (*nadan kozhi*) is in the style of Syrian Christian Keralites; cooks from other communities may omit the potato and squash.

2 tablespoons ground coriander
1 tablespoon plus 1 teaspoon pure chile powder, such as pasilla
¼ teaspoon turmeric
3 tablespoons water
½ cup vegetable oil
3 onions, halved and thinly sliced
8 garlic cloves, thinly sliced
One 1-inch piece of fresh ginger, peeled and thinly sliced
12 curry leaves
2 teaspoons garam masala
1 teaspoon freshly ground pepper
One 3½-pound chicken, cut into 8 pieces, wing tips removed
Kosher salt
1 large baking potato, peeled and cut into 1-inch dice
¾ pound butternut squash—peeled, seeded and cut into ½-inch dice
One 14-ounce can unsweetened coconut milk
1 cup chicken stock or broth
Steamed white rice, for serving

1. In a small skillet, toast the coriander, chile powder and turmeric over moderate heat until fragrant, about 1 minute. Stir in the water to form a paste.

2. In a very large, deep skillet, heat the oil. Add the onions, garlic, ginger and curry leaves. Cook over moderately high heat, stirring occasionally, until the onions are translucent, 5 minutes. Add the spice paste, garam masala and pepper and cook over moderate heat, stirring, until the oil separates from the paste, 2 minutes.

3. Lightly season the chicken with salt and add with the potato and squash to the skillet; stir to coat. Stir in the coconut milk and stock. Bring to a simmer. Cover and cook over moderately low heat until the chicken is cooked through and the potato and squash are tender, 25 minutes. Transfer the chicken to a large bowl. Season the sauce with salt, pour over the chicken and serve with rice. —*Aniamma Philip*
WINE Fruity, soft Chenin Blanc.

CHICKEN CURRY WITH POTATOES AND SQUASH

poultry

Chicken with Mulato Chile Sauce

ACTIVE: 40 MIN; TOTAL: 1 HR 20 MIN

4 SERVINGS ● ●

- 2 large dried mulato or ancho chiles
- 3 cups hot water
- 4 chicken drumsticks
- 4 chicken thighs
- Salt and freshly ground pepper
- 3 large scallions, coarsely chopped
- 2 large garlic cloves, coarsely chopped
- 1 medium onion, coarsely chopped
- 1 ounce firm chorizo, cut into ½-inch dice (¼ cup)
- ¼ cup dry white wine
- 1 large tomato, cut into 1-inch dice (1¼ cups)
- 1 teaspoon dried Mexican oregano
- 2 small chayote—peeled, quartered lengthwise and pitted
- Achiote Rice (recipe follows), for serving

1. Put the mulato chiles in a medium bowl and cover with the hot water; cover them with an inverted small plate to keep them submerged. Let the chiles soak until softened, about 30 minutes. Drain the chiles, reserving ½ cup of the soaking liquid. Stem, seed and coarsely chop them.

2. Heat a very large nonstick skillet. Season the chicken with salt and pepper and add to the skillet, skin side down. Cover partially and cook over moderately high heat until well browned on both sides, about 15 minutes. Transfer to a plate. Pour off all but 1 tablespoon of fat from the skillet and reserve for cooking the rice.

3. Add the scallions, garlic, onion and chorizo to the remaining fat in the skillet and cook, stirring, until softened, about 4 minutes. Add the chopped chiles, wine, tomato, oregano and the reserved ½ cup of chile soaking liquid and simmer for 1 minute. Arrange the chicken in the skillet, skin side up. Tuck the chayote in between the pieces of chicken. Cover and cook over low heat until the chayote is tender and the chicken is cooked through, about 30 minutes.

4. Transfer to plates and boil the sauce over high heat until reduced, about 4 minutes. Season with salt and pepper. Spoon the sauce around the chicken and serve with Achiote Rice. —*Jacques Pépin*

MAKE AHEAD The recipe can be prepared through Step 3 and refrigerated overnight.

WINE Fruity, light-bodied Beaujolais.

ACHIOTE RICE

ACTIVE: 10 MIN; TOTAL: 35 MIN

4 SERVINGS ●

- 2 teaspoons achiote paste (see Note)
- 2 cups water
- 2 tablespoons reserved chicken fat or vegetable oil
- 1 medium onion, coarsely chopped (1 cup)
- 1 cup short grain rice
- 1 teaspoon kosher salt

In a bowl, dissolve the achiote paste in the water. In a medium saucepan, heat the chicken fat. Add the onion and cook over low heat until softened, 5 minutes. Add the rice and stir well. Add the achiote water and the salt and bring to a boil. Cover the saucepan and cook over low heat until the water has been absorbed and the rice is tender, 20 minutes. Remove from the heat and let steam, covered, for 5 minutes. Fluff the rice and serve. —*J. P.*

NOTE Achiote or annatto seed paste (*recado rojo*) is available at Latin markets and at specialty food shops.

Roasted Chicken with Garlic-Thyme Butter

ACTIVE: 30 MIN; TOTAL: 2 HR 10 MIN

4 SERVINGS

Nothing says comfort food more than a simple roasted chicken. For extra flavor, garlicky butter is rubbed under the breast skin and the cavity is packed with garlic, thyme sprigs and lemon quarters.

- 1 stick unsalted butter, softened
- 6 garlic cloves—2 cloves minced, 4 cloves crushed
- 1½ teaspoons chopped thyme, plus 2 thyme sprigs
- Salt and freshly ground pepper
- One 4¼-pound chicken
- 1 lemon, quartered
- ¼ cup water
- Mustardy Potato Pierogies (recipe follows), for serving

1. Preheat the oven to 375°. In a bowl, blend the butter with the minced garlic and chopped thyme and season with salt and pepper. Carefully loosen the breast skin of the chicken. Spread the butter evenly over the breast meat, then smooth out the skin. Rub any extra garlic-thyme butter all over the outside of the chicken.

2. Stuff the crushed garlic, thyme sprigs and lemon quarters into the cavity and tie the legs together with twine. Season the chicken with salt and pepper and set in a small, flameproof roasting pan. Roast the chicken for about 1½ hours, or until the juices run clear when an inner thigh is pierced. Transfer to a carving board and let rest for 10 minutes.

3. Pour the pan juices into a saucepan. Add the water to the roasting pan and bring to a boil over moderately high heat; scrape up the browned bits from the bottom of the pan. Simmer for 2 minutes, then pour the liquid into the saucepan. Season the jus with salt and pepper. Carve the chicken and serve with the jus and Mustardy Potato Pierogies. —*Grant Achatz*

WINE Dry, rich Champagne.

MUSTARDY POTATO PIEROGIES

ACTIVE: 1 HR; TOTAL: 1 HR 30 MIN

4 SERVINGS ● ●

PIEROGI DOUGH

- 2½ cups all-purpose flour
- 1 cup sour cream
- 1 large egg, beaten
- 1 large egg yolk, beaten

4 tablespoons unsalted butter,
melted

½ teaspoon salt

FILLING

¾ pound medium Yukon Gold
potatoes

3 tablespoons sour cream

1½ tablespoons Dijon mustard

4 tablespoons unsalted butter,
softened

Salt and freshly ground pepper

Vegetable oil, for coating

1 tablespoon finely chopped
parsley

1. MAKE THE PIEROGI DOUGH: In a large bowl, mix the flour, sour cream, egg, egg yolk, butter and salt. On a lightly floured work surface, knead the dough briefly until smooth. Cover with plastic and let rest at room temperature for 15 minutes.

2. MAKE THE FILLING: In a medium saucepan, cover the potatoes with water and boil until tender, 12 minutes. Drain and peel the potatoes as soon as possible. In a bowl, mash them with the sour cream, mustard and 2½ tablespoons of the butter until smooth. Season with salt and pepper.

3. Boil a large pot of salted water. On a floured work surface, roll the dough ⅛ inch thick. With a 3½-inch biscuit cutter, stamp out 20 rounds. Brush off excess flour and moisten the edges with water. Place a level tablespoon of filling on one side of each round, leaving a ¼-inch border. Fold the dough over the filling to form half-moons; press the edges firmly to seal.

4. Cook the pierogies in the boiling water until tender, about 5 minutes. Drain well and transfer to a large, shallow dish. Add a little oil and toss to coat lightly.

5. In a large skillet, melt the remaining 1½ tablespoons of butter. Add the pierogies and cook over moderate heat, turning once, until browned, about 3 minutes per side. Transfer the pierogies to a platter. Season with salt and pepper, sprinkle with the parsley and serve. —G.A.

Braised Chicken with Peppers

ACTIVE: 30 MIN; TOTAL: 1 HR 15 MIN

6 SERVINGS ●

2 tablespoons extra-virgin olive oil

6 whole chicken legs

Salt and freshly ground pepper

¼ pound thickly sliced pancetta,
cut into ½-inch pieces

1 onion, finely chopped

1 carrot, finely chopped

1 celery rib, finely chopped

2 garlic cloves, minced

1 cup roasted red peppers from
a jar, cut into strips

¼ cup sliced Peppadew peppers
or sweet cherry peppers

1 tablespoon tomato paste

¾ cup dry white wine

2 thyme sprigs

1 rosemary sprig

¼ cup sliced pitted kalamata olives

1 cup chicken stock or broth

1½ tablespoons red wine vinegar

1. Preheat the oven to 350°. Heat the olive oil in a deep, 12-inch ovenproof sauté pan. Season the chicken with salt and pepper and cook over high heat, turning once, until the chicken is browned, about 12 minutes. Transfer the chicken to a platter.

2. Add the pancetta to the pan. Lightly brown over moderate heat, about 5 minutes. Add the onion, carrot, celery, garlic and peppers and cook over high heat, stirring, until the carrot is softened, about 5 minutes. Add the tomato paste and wine. Cook until the wine is nearly evaporated. Add the herbs and olives and season with salt and pepper. Nestle the chicken in the vegetables, add the stock and bring to a boil. Cover tightly, transfer to the oven and braise until cooked through, 30 minutes.

3. Return the pan to the stove. Boil over moderate heat, uncovered, until the sauce is thickened slightly, 10 minutes. Discard the herb sprigs, stir in the vinegar and serve. —Andrew Carmellini

WINE Bright, tart Barbera.

Bacon-Wrapped Chicken Breasts

TOTAL: 45 MIN

4 SERVINGS ●

4 skinless, boneless chicken
breast halves

Salt and freshly ground pepper

4 thyme sprigs, plus 1 teaspoon
chopped thyme

½ pound thick-cut bacon (8 slices)

3 tablespoons unsalted butter

2 tablespoons plus 2 teaspoons
extra-virgin olive oil

½ pound chicken livers, trimmed

1 medium shallot, minced

1 garlic clove, minced

2 tablespoons plus 1 teaspoon
sherry vinegar

1 cup chicken stock or broth

1. Preheat the oven to 400°. Season the chicken with salt and pepper. Place a thyme sprig on each breast and wrap in 2 slices of bacon; secure with toothpicks.

2. Heat an ovenproof skillet. Add the bacon-wrapped chicken and cook over high heat until the bacon is browned. Turn and roast in the oven for 10 minutes, or until cooked through. Add 1 tablespoon of butter and the chopped thyme to the pan; baste the chicken. Let rest for 5 minutes.

3. In a small skillet, heat 2 tablespoons of the oil. Season the livers with salt and pepper. Cook over moderately high heat until golden, 4 minutes. Add the shallot and garlic and cook until softened. Add 2 tablespoons of the vinegar and cook for 2 minutes. Add the stock and the remaining butter. Simmer over low heat until the livers are firm. Puree in a blender and strain through a very fine sieve set over a saucepan. Stir in the remaining oil and vinegar; season with salt and pepper.

4. Discard the toothpicks; thickly slice the chicken. Spoon the sauce onto plates and top with the chicken. —John Schaefer

SERVE WITH Roasted fingerling potatoes and sautéed Swiss chard.

WINE Peppery, refreshing Grüner Veltliner.

MALAYSIAN GLAZED CHICKEN WINGS

Malaysian Glazed Chicken Wings

ACTIVE: 20 MIN; TOTAL: 1 HR PLUS 4 HR CHILLING

6 TO 8 SERVINGS

At New York's Fatty Crab, chef Zak Pelaccio pays tribute to the street food he loved when living in Kuala Lumpur. Here, he recreates his favorite chicken wings, using ginger, fish sauce and molasses for a richly pungent sauce.

- 12 small dried red chiles
- 3 tablespoons coriander seeds
- 1½ tablespoons fennel seeds
- 1 tablespoon cumin seeds
- ½ cup sugar
- ⅔ cup molasses
- ½ cup Asian fish sauce
- ½ cup low-sodium soy sauce
- ⅓ cup soy sauce
- 8 garlic cloves, smashed and peeled
- One 4-inch piece of fresh ginger, thinly sliced
- 5½ pounds chicken wings

1. In a skillet, toast the chiles and coriander, fennel and cumin seeds over moderate heat until fragrant, 3 minutes. Transfer to a spice grinder or mortar and grind to a fine powder. Transfer to a medium bowl and whisk in the sugar, molasses, fish sauce, soy sauces, garlic and ginger. Divide the wings among 2 or 3 resealable plastic bags and pour in the marinade. Refrigerate for 4 hours, turning occasionally.

2. Preheat the oven to 425°. Remove the wings from the marinade and pat dry with paper towels; reserve the marinade. Arrange the wings on 2 wire racks set over a foil-covered baking sheet. Roast for about 40 minutes, or until well browned and cooked through.

3. Strain the marinade into a saucepan and bring to a boil. Cook over moderately high heat until thick and sticky, 20 minutes. Transfer to a large bowl. When the wings are done, add to the bowl and toss to coat. Pile on plates and serve. —*Zak Pelaccio*

WINE Lush, fragrant Viognier.

Braised Chicken Legs with Green Olives

ACTIVE: 30 MIN; TOTAL: 1 HR 45 MIN

6 SERVINGS ● ●

- 2 tablespoons extra-virgin olive oil
- 6 whole chicken legs
- Salt and freshly ground pepper
- 4 ounces thickly sliced lean bacon, cut into ¼-inch dice
- 1 medium onion, chopped
- 3 carrots, quartered lengthwise and cut into 1-inch pieces
- 4 small turnips, peeled and cut into 1-inch pieces
- 1 cup pitted green olives, preferably Picholine
- 2 large thyme sprigs
- 1 bay leaf
- 2 cups chicken stock or low-sodium broth

1. Preheat the oven to 350°. In a large cast-iron casserole, heat the olive oil until shimmering. Season the chicken with salt and pepper. Add 3 legs to the casserole and cook over moderately high heat, turning once, until browned, 10 minutes. Transfer to a plate and brown the remaining 3 legs over moderate heat. Pour off the fat.

2. Add the bacon, onion, carrots and turnips and cook over moderately high heat, stirring, until barely softened, 2 to 3 minutes. Add the olives, thyme, bay leaf and stock. Nestle the chicken in the pot, partially submerged, and bring to a boil. Cover with a tight-fitting lid; transfer to the oven and cook for 45 minutes, or until the chicken and vegetables are tender.

3. Transfer the chicken and vegetables to a platter; cover and keep warm. Strain the broth into a large measuring cup and skim off as much fat as possible. Return the broth to the pot; boil until reduced by half, 5 minutes. Season with salt and pepper. Return the chicken and vegetables to the pot, cover and cook for 5 minutes to heat through and then serve. —*Daniel Boulud*

WINE Earthy, medium-bodied Tempranillo.

Chicken and Okra Fricassee

ACTIVE: 40 MIN; TOTAL: 1 HR 30 MIN

4 SERVINGS ●

- One 4-pound chicken, cut into 8 pieces
- Salt and freshly ground pepper
- 1 tablespoon minced oregano
- 2 tablespoons vegetable oil
- 2 tablespoons minced fresh ginger
- 1 small onion, finely chopped
- 1 garlic clove, minced
- 1 teaspoon all-purpose flour
- 1½ cups low-sodium chicken broth
- 1 cup unsweetened coconut milk
- 2 large stalks of lemongrass, lower half cut into 3-inch lengths and lightly smashed
- ¾ pound baby okra

1. Put the chicken pieces in a large shallow dish and season them with salt, pepper and the oregano. Cover the chicken and refrigerate for 1 hour.

2. Heat the oil in a large enameled cast-iron casserole. Add half of the chicken pieces and cook over moderately high heat until browned, about 4 minutes per side. Transfer the chicken to a large plate; repeat with the remaining chicken.

3. Add the ginger, onion and garlic to the casserole and cook over low heat, stirring, until softened, about 4 minutes. Stir in the flour until blended, then stir in the chicken broth, coconut milk and lemongrass and bring to a boil. Add the chicken and its juices and simmer over low heat, turning the pieces once, until the breasts are cooked through, about 20 minutes. Transfer the breasts to a plate. Cook the dark meat for about 10 minutes longer.

4. Meanwhile, in a medium saucepan of boiling salted water, cook the okra until bright green, about 2 minutes. Drain well. Return the chicken to the stew and stir in the okra. Season with salt and pepper and simmer for 3 minutes. —*Eric Ripert*

SERVE WITH Rice and lime wedges.

WINE Juicy, spicy Grenache.

poultry

Wine-Baked Chicken Legs with Marjoram

ACTIVE: 20 MIN; TOTAL: 1 HR 35 MIN

4 SERVINGS ●

The creamy, rich sauce for this crisp-skinned chicken is deliciously balanced by pungent marjoram.

- 2 large shallots, thinly sliced
- 1 bay leaf
- 6 whole chicken legs
- 2 cups dry white wine
- Salt and freshly ground pepper
- ¼ cup heavy cream
- 4 tablespoons cold unsalted butter, cut into tablespoons
- 2 tablespoons chopped marjoram, plus 1 tablespoon marjoram leaves, for garnish

1. Preheat the oven to 425°. Spread the sliced shallots and bay leaf in a 14-by-12-inch baking dish or roasting pan. Arrange the chicken legs in the pan, skin side up, and pour the dry white wine over the legs. Season the chicken with salt and pepper and bake in the upper third of the oven for about 50 minutes, or until the skin is crisp and the chicken is cooked through. Reduce the oven temperature to 300°.

2. Transfer the chicken legs to a heatproof platter. Discard the bay leaf. Pour the pan juices into a small saucepan and boil over high heat until reduced to 2 cups, about 10 minutes. Add the heavy cream to the pan juices and boil until reduced by one-third, about 5 minutes. Pour the sauce into a large glass measuring cup and let stand for 5 minutes.

3. Meanwhile, reheat the chicken legs in the oven, about 5 minutes.

4. Whisk the butter into the sauce, 1 table-spoon at a time, until thoroughly blended. Season the sauce with salt and stir in the chopped marjoram. Spoon the sauce over the chicken legs. Sprinkle the chicken with the marjoram leaves and serve right away. —*Marcia Kiesel*

WINE Fruity, low-oak Chardonnay.

Tunisian Spice-Roasted Chicken

ACTIVE: 30 MIN; TOTAL: 1½ HR

4 SERVINGS

- 1½ pounds red potatoes, cut into 2-inch pieces
- One 4-pound chicken, cut into 8 pieces
- ¼ cup extra-virgin olive oil
- 2 teaspoons ground coriander
- 1 teaspoon ground cumin
- ½ teaspoon ground cinnamon
- ½ teaspoon freshly ground pepper
- 1½ teaspoons Harous (recipe follows)
- Large pinch of saffron threads, crushed in 2 tablespoons water
- Salt
- 1 pound green bell peppers, cut into ½-inch strips
- 2 pounds plum tomatoes, quartered lengthwise
- 1 lemon, thinly sliced

1. Preheat the oven to 400°. In a medium saucepan of boiling water, cook the potatoes until barely tender, about 8 minutes. Drain and pat dry.

2. In a large bowl, toss the chicken pieces with the olive oil, coriander, cumin, cinnamon, pepper, Harous, saffron water and a pinch of salt. Add the potatoes and toss. Transfer to a roasting pan and roast until the chicken is cooked through and the potatoes are tender, about 45 minutes. Transfer the roasted chicken to a platter and keep warm.

3. Mix the green bell pepper strips, quartered tomatoes and lemon slices into the potatoes. Roast the vegetables, stirring occasionally, until the peppers are tender, about 20 minutes.

4. Preheat the broiler. Arrange the chicken pieces on the vegetables, skin side up, and broil 4 inches from the heat until the chicken skin is browned and crisp, about 1 minute. Transfer the chicken and vegetables to the platter, drizzle with the pan juices and serve. —*Abderrazak Haouari*

WINE Intense, fruity Zinfandel.

HAROUS

ACTIVE 20 MIN; TOTAL: 20 MIN PLUS OVERNIGHT MACERATING

MAKES ½ CUP

This southern Tunisian sauce has a deep, husky red pepper flavor that's excellent with soups, meat, poultry, fish and couscous dishes.

- 1 medium onion, very thinly sliced
- Pinch of turmeric
- 2 tablespoons kosher salt
- 4 ancho chiles, stemmed and seeded
- 3 dried chipotle chiles, stemmed and seeded
- ½ teaspoon ground coriander
- ½ teaspoon ground caraway seeds
- ½ teaspoon freshly ground pepper
- Pinch of cinnamon
- 3 tablespoons extra-virgin olive oil

1. In a shallow bowl, toss the onion slices with the turmeric and salt. Cover the onion with plastic wrap and let stand overnight at room temperature.

2. Meanwhile, heat a cast-iron skillet until hot to the touch. Add the ancho chiles and chipotle chiles and toast over moderate heat, pressing lightly with a spatula until the chiles are very pliable and fragrant, about 1 minute. Transfer the chiles to a work surface and let cool completely, then tear them into 1-inch pieces. In a spice grinder, coarsely grind them.

3. Drain the macerated onion slices in a strainer, pressing hard to extract as much liquid as possible. Transfer the onions to a food processor and pulse until they are pureed. Add the ground chiles, ground coriander, ground caraway seeds, pepper and cinnamon and process to a paste. With the machine on, gradually add the olive oil and puree until the sauce is fairly smooth.—*A.H.*

MAKE AHEAD The *harous* can be kept, covered, in the refrigerator for up to 6 months.

TUNISIAN SPICE-ROASTED CHICKEN

ROASTED CHICKEN WITH HERB JUS

Roasted Chicken with Herb Jus

ACTIVE: 45 MIN; TOTAL: 2 HR

4 SERVINGS

Jing Tio, owner of LA's Le Sanctuaire cookware and design shop, makes a supremely juicy roasted chicken adapted from a recipe by chef Mohammad Islam, formerly at Hollywood's famed Chateau Marmont.

  1 medium onion, sliced ¼ inch thick
  1 large carrot, sliced ¼ inch thick
One 4½-pound chicken
Salt and freshly ground pepper
  2 thyme sprigs, plus 1 teaspoon finely chopped thyme
  2 rosemary sprigs, plus 1 teaspoon finely chopped rosemary
  2 teaspoons dried lavender buds
  2 tablespoons unsalted butter—
     1 tablespoon softened,
     1 tablespoon chilled
  ½ cup chicken stock or broth
  ½ cup dry red wine

1. Preheat the oven to 450°. In a medium roasting pan, spread the onion and carrot slices evenly. Set a rack in the pan. Season the cavity of the chicken with salt and pepper and stuff with the thyme and rosemary sprigs and 1 teaspoon of the lavender. Tie the legs together with kitchen string. Rub the softened butter all over the chicken and season with salt and pepper. Set the chicken on the rack, breast side up. Sprinkle the chopped thyme and rosemary and the remaining 1 teaspoon of lavender buds over the chicken. Roast for 15 minutes.

2. In a glass measuring cup, combine the stock and wine. Baste the chicken with 2 tablespoons of the liquid. Turn the chicken on its side and roast for 10 minutes. Baste again, turn to the other side and roast for another 10 minutes. Reduce the oven temperature to 350° and baste, then roast the chicken for 15 minutes. Turn the chicken breast side down, baste and roast for 15 minutes. Turn the chicken breast side up and baste. Roast the chicken for about 25 minutes longer, basting once. The chicken is done when the juices run clear and an instant-read thermometer inserted in the inner thigh registers 165°.

3. Transfer the chicken to a carving board and let rest in a warm place for 10 minutes. Remove the rack from the roasting pan. Set the pan over 2 burners on moderate heat. Pour the remaining ¼ cup of basting mixture into the pan and simmer for 2 minutes, scraping up the browned bits from the bottom of the pan. Strain the pan juices into a small saucepan, pressing on the solids. Skim off the fat and bring the jus to a simmer. Remove the saucepan from the heat and whisk in the 1 tablespoon of chilled butter until blended. Season with salt and pepper. Carve the chicken and serve with the herb jus. —*Jing Tio*

WINE Fruity, low-oak Chardonnay.

● FAST   ● HEALTHY   ● MAKE AHEAD   ● STAFF FAVORITE

poultry

Garam Masala–Crusted Chicken with Fig Jus

ACTIVE: 30 MIN; TOTAL: 2 HR
4 SERVINGS

At DeWolf Tavern in tiny Bristol, Rhode Island, Indian-born chef Sai Viswanath prepares everything from cauliflower to lobster in his wood-fired tandoor oven, which imparts a slightly smoky flavor to foods. For American home cooks, Viswanath developed this crispy cumin-and-coriander-spiced chicken, roasted in a Western-style oven. In another departure from typical Indian practice, Viswanath cooks the bird whole instead of cutting it into pieces and removing the skin.

- ¼ cup plus 1 tablespoon Garam Masala (recipe follows)
- 3 tablespoons vegetable oil
- Two 3½-pound chickens
- Salt
- 2 cups chicken stock or low-sodium broth
- 8 garlic cloves
- 1 teaspoon tamarind paste (see Note)
- 4 dried black Mission figs, stemmed and quartered
- ¼ cup honey
- Freshly ground pepper

1. Preheat the oven to 450°. In a small bowl, mix the Garam Masala with the oil. In a roasting pan, rub the chickens all over with the spiced oil and season them with salt. Roast the chickens for 15 minutes. Reduce the oven temperature to 350° and continue roasting for 1 hour and 15 minutes, basting twice. Return the oven temperature to 450° and roast the chickens for about 15 minutes longer, or until they are browned and crisp. Transfer the chickens to a carving board and let them rest for about 10 minutes.

2. While the chickens roast, in a medium saucepan, combine the chicken stock with the garlic cloves and tamarind paste and bring to a boil over high heat. Reduce the heat to low and simmer the stock until the garlic is very soft, about 40 minutes. Strain the stock through a coarse sieve into a small saucepan and then press the softened garlic through the sieve. Stir the quartered dried black Mission figs and the honey into the chicken stock, cover and let steep until the figs are tender, about 10 minutes. Set the fig jus aside while the chickens finish roasting.

3. Carve the chickens. Reheat the fig jus, season with salt and pepper and serve with the chicken. —*Sai Viswanath*

NOTE Tamarind paste is available at Latin, Asian and Indian markets and specialty food shops.

WINE Juicy, spicy Grenache.

GARAM MASALA

TOTAL TIME: 20 MIN
MAKES ABOUT 1 CUP ● ● ○

- ½ cup plus 2 tablespoons cumin seeds
- ¼ cup coriander seeds
- ¼ cup cardamom pods, seeds removed
- 1 bay leaf
- Two 3-inch cinnamon sticks, broken in pieces
- 1½ tablespoons whole cloves
- ⅛ teaspoon ground mace
- 2½ tablespoons ground ginger
- ⅛ teaspoon freshly grated nutmeg

1. Finely grind the cumin seeds, coriander seeds, cardamom pods, bay leaf, cinnamon sticks and whole cloves in batches in a spice grinder.

2. Transfer each batch of ground spices to a coarse strainer set over a bowl. Sift the ground spices into the bowl and add the ground mace and ginger and the grated nutmeg.

3. Whisk the spices to combine them and set aside until ready to use. —*S. V.*

NOTE The garam masala can be stored in a tightly sealed jar in a cool, dry place for up to 6 months or frozen in a plastic bag for up to 1 year.

Roasted Blue Foot Chickens with Glazed Parsnips and Carrots

ACTIVE: 30 MIN; TOTAL: 2 HR
4 SERVINGS

Chef David Myers of Sona in Los Angeles puts brown butter to ingenious use in this showcase for California's succulent Blue Foot chickens (America's version of France's famed Poulets de Bresse, prized for their moistness, firm texture and excellent flavor). For this recipe, Myers first drizzles the supermoist birds with brown butter, then sautés baby carrots, parsnips and radishes in additional brown butter until the root vegetables are glazed. Blue Foots are available by mail order through D'Artagnan (dartagnan.com).

- 1 stick unsalted butter
- Two 2½- to 3-pound Blue Foot chickens
- Salt and freshly ground pepper
- 2 tablespoons grapeseed or vegetable oil

ingredients
spices

Gourmet Sleuth's *masala dabba*, a traditional Indian spice box, has two lids to keep its contents super fresh. **Details** $44; gourmetsleuth.com.

6 unpeeled garlic cloves
12 thyme sprigs
¼ cup plus 2 tablespoons fresh
    orange juice
3 tablespoons sherry vinegar
½ pound baby carrots
½ pound parsnips, peeled and
    cut into thick batons
¼ pound small radishes, trimmed

1. Preheat the oven to 375°. In a small skillet, cook the butter over moderately low heat until golden brown, about 7 minutes. Pour the brown butter into a bowl.
2. Season the chickens with salt and pepper. In a large, flameproof roasting pan, heat the grapeseed oil. Add the chickens and cook over moderately high heat, turning occasionally, until lightly browned all over, about 7 minutes. Turn the chickens breast side up and scatter the garlic cloves and thyme sprigs all around them. Drizzle 2 tablespoons of the brown butter over the chicken breasts. Roast the chickens for about 1 hour and 10 minutes, or until an instant-read thermometer inserted into an inner thigh registers 165°. Let the chickens rest for 10 minutes. Pour the pan drippings into a bowl and skim off the fat. Discard the garlic and thyme.
3. Meanwhile, in a small saucepan, combine the orange juice and sherry vinegar and boil over moderately high heat until the liquid is reduced to 2 tablespoons, about 7 minutes.
4. In a large skillet, heat the remaining brown butter. Add the carrots, parsnips and radishes and cook the vegetables over moderately high heat, stirring until they are tender, about 12 minutes. Add the orange glaze and the drippings and cook, stirring, until the vegetables are coated, about 1 minute; season the vegetables with salt and pepper.
5. Carve the chickens and transfer to plates. Serve the chicken at once with the vegetables. —David Myers
WINE Complex, elegant Pinot Noir.

Chicken in Red Wine Vinegar
ACTIVE: 25 MIN; TOTAL: 1 HR 5 MIN
4 SERVINGS ● ●
For master cook Paula Wolfert, an F&W contributor and the author of many cookbooks, this rustic Lyonnais dish defines comfort food. Slow cooking transforms red wine vinegar, tomato paste, shallots, garlic and a touch of honey into a perfectly balanced sauce for chicken.

¾ cup plus 2 tablespoons red wine
    vinegar
½ cup low-sodium chicken broth
1 tablespoon honey
1 tablespoon tomato paste
2 tablespoons unsalted butter
8 large chicken thighs, trimmed
Salt and freshly ground pepper
4 garlic cloves, thinly sliced
3 large shallots, thinly sliced
¾ cup dry white wine
2 tablespoons crème fraîche
3 tablespoons chopped tarragon

1. In a medium saucepan, boil the vinegar with the broth, honey and tomato paste, stirring well. Simmer until reduced to ½ cup, about 8 minutes.
2. Heat the butter in a large skillet. Season the thighs with salt and pepper and add half of them to the skillet, skin side down. Cook them over moderate heat, turning once, until browned. Transfer the cooked thighs to a plate; repeat with the rest
3. Add the garlic and shallots to the skillet and cook over low heat for 5 minutes. Add the dry white wine and boil until reduced to ¼ cup. Add the sauce; bring to a simmer.
4. Return the chicken thighs to the skillet, skin side up. Cover and simmer over low heat until cooked through, about 20 minutes. Transfer the chicken to plates.
5. Add the crème fraîche to the skillet and boil for 3 minutes. Add the tarragon and season with salt and pepper. Pour the sauce over the chicken and serve right away. —Paula Wolfert
WINE Fruity, light-bodied Beaujolais.

Goat Cheese–Stuffed Chicken
TOTAL: 30 MIN
4 SERVINGS ● ●
¼ cup walnut halves
¼ cup fresh goat cheese, softened
½ teaspoon finely grated
    lemon zest
1 garlic clove, minced
Salt and freshly ground pepper
Four 6-ounce skinless, boneless
    chicken breast halves
1 tablespoon extra-virgin
    olive oil
3 tablespoons fresh lemon juice
¼ cup chicken stock or low-sodium
    broth
2 tablespoons walnut oil
¼ cup chopped flat-leaf parsley

1. Preheat the oven to 400°. Spread the walnuts in a pie plate and toast for 6 minutes, until fragrant. Let cool, then chop.
2. In a small bowl, mash the goat cheese with the lemon zest, garlic and half of the walnuts; season with salt and pepper. Using a small knife, cut a pocket in the side of each chicken breast; keep the pocket opening as small as possible. Stuff the chicken breasts with the mixture and gently press to flatten them.
3. In a large ovenproof skillet, heat the olive oil until shimmering. Season the chicken with salt and pepper and cook over moderately high heat, turning once, until browned, about 6 minutes. Transfer the skillet to the oven and roast the chicken for 5 minutes. Transfer the chicken breasts to a platter and keep warm.
4. Add the lemon juice and stock to the skillet and cook over moderately high heat, scraping up any browned bits stuck to the pan. Simmer for 3 minutes. Stir in the walnut oil, parsley and the remaining chopped walnuts. Transfer the chicken breasts to plates, spoon the walnut sauce on top and serve. —Annie Wayte
SERVE WITH Steamed rice or couscous.
WINE Fruity, soft Chenin Blanc.

poultry

Chicken with Zucchini Salad

TOTAL: 35 MIN

4 SERVINGS ● ●

- ¼ cup fresh lemon juice
- 1 large garlic clove
- 1 small shallot, chopped
- 1½ teaspoons chopped dill
- 1 teaspoon Dijon mustard
- ½ cup extra-virgin olive oil
- 2 tablespoons chopped mint

Kosher salt and freshly ground pepper

- 4 boneless chicken breast halves with skin
- 2 medium yellow squash (1 pound), sliced crosswise on the diagonal ⅓ inch thick
- 2 medium zucchini (1 pound), sliced crosswise on the diagonal ⅓ inch thick
- ¼ pound feta cheese, crumbled (1 cup)

1. In a blender, combine the lemon juice with the garlic, shallot, dill and mustard and puree until smooth. With the machine on, slowly pour in 6 tablespoons of the olive oil. Stir in the mint and season the vinaigrette with salt and pepper.

2. Light a grill or preheat a grill pan. In a bowl, coat the chicken with ½ cup of the vinaigrette. Let stand for 5 minutes.

3. Meanwhile, in a large bowl, toss the yellow squash and zucchini with the remaining 2 tablespoons of olive oil and season with salt and pepper. Grill the squash and zucchini, turning once, until tender and slightly charred, about 3 minutes total. Transfer the vegetables to a platter and keep warm.

4. Season the chicken breasts with salt and pepper and grill over moderately high heat, turning once, until cooked through, about 10 minutes. Transfer the chicken to the platter and sprinkle with the feta cheese. Drizzle with the remaining vinaigrette and serve. —*Michael Psilakis*

WINE Zippy, fresh Pinot Bianco.

Jasmine Rice, Chicken and Almond Stir-Fry

ACTIVE: 55 MIN; TOTAL: 55 MIN PLUS 4 HR CHILLING

4 SERVINGS

There are two kinds of rice in this chicken stir-fry: fragrant jasmine rice and oval Korean rice cakes, which look like sliced scallops and have a deliciously chewy texture. Lightly toasted sliced almonds and slivers of daikon add an appealing crunch.

- 1 large egg white
- 1 tablespoon cornstarch
- 3 tablespoons dry sherry

Kosher salt

- 1 pound skinless, boneless chicken breasts, cut into 1-inch cubes
- ½ pound jasmine rice (1¼ cups), rinsed
- 2 ounces sliced blanched almonds (½ cup)
- 20 fresh or frozen Asian thin rice cakes (see Note)
- ¼ cup vegetable oil
- 4 ounces small white mushrooms, stems discarded, caps thinly sliced
- 1 tablespoon fresh lemon juice
- 1 medium white onion, finely chopped
- 2 large garlic cloves, minced
- 1½ tablespoons minced fresh ginger

Freshly ground white pepper

- 4 ounces daikon radish, peeled and cut into 2-by-¼-inch sticks
- ½ cup unsweetened coconut milk

Asian sesame oil, for drizzling

1. In a medium bowl, whisk the egg white until frothy. Whisk in the cornstarch, 1 tablespoon of the sherry and 1 teaspoon of salt. Add the chicken breasts and toss to coat. Refrigerate for at least 4 hours or overnight.

2. Preheat the oven to 350°. In a medium saucepan, cover the jasmine rice with 2 cups of water and bring to a boil. Cover the saucepan and cook over low heat for 12 minutes. Turn off the heat and let the rice stand, covered, for 5 minutes. Fluff the rice and transfer to a large rimmed baking sheet; spread it out in an even layer. Let cool to room temperature, then cover and refrigerate until chilled.

3. Spread the sliced almonds in a pie pan and bake for about 4 minutes, or until pale golden. Let them cool.

4. In a medium saucepan of boiling salted water, cook the rice cakes until tender but still chewy, about 7 minutes. Drain the rice cakes and spread them out on a large plate. Add 4 cups of water and 1 tablespoon of oil to the saucepan and bring to a boil. Add the chicken breasts and simmer over low heat, stirring once or twice, until the outside of the chicken turns white, about 25 seconds; drain. In a bowl, mix the mushrooms with the lemon juice.

5. In a wok, heat the remaining 3 tablespoons of oil until shimmering. Add the onion and cook over moderate heat until translucent, 5 minutes. Add the garlic and ginger and stir-fry until fragrant, 4 minutes. Add the mushrooms and cook over moderately high heat until softened, 3 minutes. Add the chicken and rice cakes, season with salt and pepper and stir-fry for 1 minute. Add the remaining 2 tablespoons of sherry and simmer for 10 seconds. Add the rice and heat through. Add the almonds and daikon and toss again. Stir in the coconut milk. Off the heat, season with salt and pepper and a drizzle of sesame oil. Serve at once.

—*Marcia Kiesel*

NOTE Korean rice cakes are available at many Asian markets. Although they're most often sold frozen, you can sometimes find bags of fresh rice cakes in the refrigerated section.

WINE Spicy American Gewürztraminer.

Chicken–Black Bean Quesadillas

TOTAL: 30 MIN

4 SERVINGS ● ●

Chef Annie Wayte is spreading delicious and healthy ideas at fashion designer Nicole Fahri's namesake restaurants in New York City and London. She has also published a book, *Keep it Seasonal*. The recipe below is one of her best and fastest.

1½ tablespoons canola oil
1 small red onion, coarsely chopped
1 garlic clove, minced
1 teaspoon ground cumin
Cayenne pepper
One 15-ounce can black beans, drained
Salt and freshly ground pepper
½ cup coarsely chopped cilantro
1 mango, peeled and cut into large chunks
1 scallion, cut into ½-inch lengths
2 tablespoons fresh lime juice
Four 8-inch fat-free flour tortillas
1½ cups shredded skinless roasted chicken breast
¼ cup crumbled feta cheese
¾ cup shredded part-skim mozzarella cheese

1. In a saucepan, heat ½ tablespoon of the oil. Add the onion, garlic, cumin and a pinch of cayenne and cook over moderate heat, stirring, for 5 minutes. Add the beans and ⅓ cup of water and simmer for 5 minutes. Season with salt and pepper. Stir in ¼ cup of the cilantro.

2. Meanwhile, in a food processor, pulse the mango, scallion, lime juice and the remaining cilantro until finely chopped. Season with salt, pepper and cayenne.

3. Heat ½ tablespoon of oil in each of 2 large skillets. Top the tortillas with the beans, chicken, feta and mozzarella and fold in half. Add 2 quesadillas to each skillet and cook over moderate heat, turning until golden and the cheese is melted, 5 minutes. Transfer to plates and serve with the mango salsa. —*Annie Wayte*

WINE Fruity, light-bodied Beaujolais.

Chicken with Red Curry–Peanut Glaze

TOTAL: 30 MIN

4 SERVINGS ●

F&W's Grace Parisi published 500 recipes in her book *Get Saucy*, which was nominated for a James Beard Foundation award. And the ideas still keep coming—for rubs, pastes and sauces. The Red Curry–Peanut Sauce here is one of her smartest, speediest ways to add flavor to a variety of foods before, during or after grilling. A bit of the sauce brushed onto the chicken and mango skewers help them caramelize while they are cooking on the grill.

1 large mango, peeled and cut into 2-inch squares, about ¼ inch thick
1½ pounds skinless, boneless chicken thighs, cut into 1-inch pieces
1½ cups Red Curry–Peanut Sauce (recipe follows)
Salt and freshly ground black pepper
Vegetable oil, for brushing
Lime wedges, for serving

Light a grill. In a large bowl, toss the mango with the chicken and 3 tablespoons of the Red Curry–Peanut Sauce and season lightly with salt and pepper. Loosely thread the mango and chicken onto 8 skewers, alternating the mango with the chicken. Brush the skewers with oil and grill over high heat, turning occasionally, until the chicken is lightly charred in spots and nearly cooked through, 8 to 10 minutes. Brush 2 more tablespoons of the sauce on the skewers and grill, turning, until the chicken is lightly browned, about 2 minutes. If the sauce becomes too thick to brush, thin it slightly with water. Transfer the chicken-and-mango skewers to a platter or plates and serve with lime wedges; pass the remaining Red Curry–Peanut Sauce at the table. —*Grace Parisi*

WINE Lush, fragrant Viognier.

RED CURRY–PEANUT SAUCE

TOTAL: 15 MIN

MAKES 1½ CUPS ● ●

When F&W senior test kitchen associate Grace Parisi makes this red curry–peanut sauce for her kids, she adds less of the spicy Thai red curry paste; when she makes it for her husband and herself, she adds more.

1 tablespoon peanut oil
1 shallot, very finely chopped
1 garlic clove, very finely chopped
1 tablespoon Thai red curry paste
1 tablespoon light brown sugar
6 tablespoons unsweetened peanut butter
¾ cup unsweetened coconut milk
2½ tablespoons fresh lime juice
1 tablespoon Asian fish sauce

1. In a medium saucepan, heat the peanut oil. Add the chopped shallot and garlic to the saucepan and cook them over moderate heat, stirring, until the shallot is softened, about 2 minutes. Add the Thai red curry paste and whisk it into the shallot and garlic for 1 minute. Add the brown sugar to the pan and cook until the sugar is melted. Whisk the peanut butter into the sauce, then slowly whisk in the coconut milk. Simmer the sauce for 2 minutes.

2. Remove the sauce from the heat and whisk in the lime juice and the Asian fish sauce. Serve sauce warm or at room temperature. —*G.P*

OTHER USES Serve the red curry–peanut sauce as a condiment with grilled beef, chicken, spareribs, shrimp or pork. Use it as a dipping sauce with crudités. The sauce is also good mixed into rice noodles or stir-fries.

MAKE AHEAD The red curry–peanut sauce can be refrigerated for up to 1 week. Bring to room temperature before serving.

poultry

Thai-Style Chicken Legs

ACTIVE: 30 MIN; TOTAL: 1 HR PLUS
OVERNIGHT MARINATING
4 SERVINGS

- 5 garlic cloves, coarsely chopped
- ¼ cup chopped cilantro
- ¼ cup Asian fish sauce
- ¼ cup vegetable oil
- 2 tablespoons hoisin sauce
- 1½ teaspoons ground coriander
- 1 teaspoon kosher salt
- 1 teaspoon freshly ground white pepper
- 8 whole chicken legs, split, or 8 drumsticks and 8 thighs (about 5 pounds total)

Thai sweet chile sauce, for serving (see Note)

1. In a blender, combine the chopped garlic with the chopped cilantro, fish sauce, vegetable oil, hoisin sauce, ground coriander, kosher salt and white pepper; blend until smooth. Arrange the pieces of chicken in a large, shallow glass or ceramic dish. Pour the marinade over the chicken and turn to coat the pieces thoroughly. Cover and refrigerate the chicken overnight.

2. Light a grill. When the coals are covered with a light gray ash, push them to opposite sides of the grill and set a disposable drip pan in the center. If using a gas grill, turn off the center burners.

3. Arrange the chicken on the hot grate above the drip pan and away from the coals, skin side down. Cover and grill the chicken thighs and drumsticks for 40 minutes or until the skin is crisp and the meat is cooked through. Transfer the chicken to plates and serve with Thai chile sauce. —*Steven Raichlen*

NOTE Thai chili sauce is available at large supermarkets and at Asian markets. Two of the top brands are Mae Ploy and A Taste of Thai.

MAKE AHEAD The marinade can be refrigerated overnight.

WINE Creamy, supple Pinot Blanc.

Sesame Chicken Salad with Ginger-Lime Dressing

ACTIVE: 30 MIN; TOTAL: 1 HR 15 MIN
4 SERVINGS ●

- ¼ cup Ginger-Lime Syrup (p. 373)
- 2 tablespoons Champagne vinegar or white wine vinegar
- 2 tablespoons soy sauce
- 1 Hass avocado—halved, seeded and diced
- 2 teaspoons fresh lime juice
- 3 tablespoons plus 2 teaspoons extra-virgin olive oil

Salt

- 6 radishes, thinly sliced

Four 6-ounce skinless, boneless chicken breast halves

Freshly ground white pepper

- ⅓ cup sesame seeds
- 1 bunch of watercress (6 ounces), thick stems discarded

1. Preheat the oven to 350°. In a bowl, mix the syrup, vinegar and soy sauce.

2. In a bowl, lightly mash the avocado with a fork. Fold in the lime juice and 1 teaspoon of the olive oil. Season lightly with salt.

3. In a bowl, toss the radishes with 1 teaspoon of oil; season with salt. Refrigerate.

4. Season the chicken with salt and white pepper. Spread the sesame seeds in a shallow dish and press the skinned side of the breasts into the seeds to coat.

5. Set a large, ovenproof skillet over high heat until very hot. Add the remaining olive oil and heat until smoking. Add the chicken breasts, seed side down, and cook over high heat until the seeds are golden, 3 minutes. Turn the breasts. Transfer the skillet to the oven and bake the chicken for 5 minutes, until just cooked through.

6. Dollop the mashed avocado on plates and top with half of the radish slices. Set the chicken on top and garnish with the remaining radish slices and watercress sprigs. Drizzle the dressing on top and serve. —*Jean-Georges Vongerichten*

WINE Tart, citrusy Riesling.

Vietnamese Chicken Meatballs in Lettuce Wraps

ACTIVE: 25 MIN; TOTAL: 45 MIN
4 SERVINGS ● ● ●

- 1 pound skinless, boneless chicken thighs, trimmed of visible fat and cut into 1½-inch pieces
- 3 tablespoons Asian fish sauce
- 3 small shallots, finely chopped
- 3 garlic cloves, minced
- 1 stalk of fresh lemongrass, tender white inner bulb only, minced
- 3 tablespoons chopped cilantro, plus ⅓ cup leaves for serving
- 1 tablespoon finely chopped mint, plus ⅓ cup leaves for serving
- 1½ teaspoons cornstarch
- ½ teaspoon kosher salt
- ½ teaspoon freshly ground pepper
- ½ cup sugar
- 1 head Boston or red leaf lettuce, leaves separated
- 1 small seedless cucumber—peeled, halved lengthwise and thinly sliced crosswise
- 1 small red onion, halved and sliced

Asian chili sauce, for serving

1. Preheat the oven to 400°. Position a rack in the top third of the oven. In a food processor, pulse the chicken until coarsely ground; transfer to a bowl. Add the fish sauce, shallots, garlic, lemongrass, chopped cilantro and mint, cornstarch, salt and pepper and mix with your hands.

2. Line a large rimmed baking sheet with parchment. Spread the sugar on a plate. Using slightly moistened hands, roll the chicken mixture into 1½-inch balls. Roll the meatballs in the sugar until evenly coated. Transfer to the prepared baking sheet and bake for 15 minutes, until lightly browned and cooked through.

3. Arrange the lettuce, cilantro and mint leaves, cucumber and onion on a platter. Transfer the meatballs to the platter and serve with chili sauce. —*Jennifer Joyce*

WINE Zesty, fresh Albariño.

poultry

Lentils with Chicken Sausage

TOTAL: 30 MIN

4 SERVINGS ● ● ●

This recipe is chef Annie Wayte's healthy rendition of the classic British dish of bangers and mash. Instead of pork sausages, she uses chicken sausages, and she replaces mashed potatoes with fiber-rich lentils.

> 7 ounces French green lentils (1 cup)
> 4 cups chicken stock or low-sodium broth
> 1 carrot, cut into 1-inch pieces
> 1 celery rib, cut into 1-inch pieces
> 1 small onion, quartered, plus 1 large onion, cut through the root end into 8 wedges
> 1 garlic clove
> 2 tablespoons canola oil
> 4 thyme sprigs
> 1 cup baby spinach leaves, coarsely chopped
>
> Salt and freshly ground black pepper
> 4 precooked chicken sausages (¾ pound), thickly sliced
> 1½ tablespoons balsamic vinegar

1. In a heavy medium soup pot, combine the French green lentils with the chicken stock. Cover the pot and bring the chicken stock and lentils to a boil.

2. In a food processor, pulse the carrot with the celery, quartered onion and garlic until they are all very finely chopped. In a large skillet, heat 1 tablespoon of the canola oil. Add the vegetables and thyme sprigs and cook over moderately high heat until the vegetables are softened, about 3 minutes; scrape the vegetables into the lentils and chicken stock, cover and cook over moderate heat until the lentils are tender, about 20 minutes. Stir the baby spinach into the lentils; season with salt and pepper.

3. Meanwhile, heat the remaining 1 tablespoon of canola oil in the large skillet. Add the onion wedges and the chicken sausages and cook over moderate heat, turning the sausages occasionally, until the onion is softened, 8 to 10 minutes. Add the balsamic vinegar to the skillet and cook the lentils and sausages for 1 minute. Discard the thyme sprigs. Spoon the lentils into a large serving bowl and top with the chicken sausages. Serve right away. —*Annie Wayte*

MAKE AHEAD The cooked lentils can be refrigerated overnight. Reheat them gently and then add the baby spinach while cooking the sausages.

WINE Bright, tart Barbera.

Beer-Braised Chicken Stew with Fava Beans and Peas

ACTIVE: 1 HR; TOTAL: 2 HR

8 SERVINGS ●

Chef Paul Kahan of Chicago's Blackbird restaurant is a big fan of chicken thighs because they have so much flavor and are so inexpensive—the best of both worlds. Here, he braises the thighs in a dark, malty Belgian-style beer to make an excellent chicken stew with spring vegetables.

> 2 tablespoons anise seeds
> 4 garlic cloves, coarsely chopped
> ½ teaspoon loosely packed saffron threads
> 2 teaspoons sweet paprika
> ½ teaspoon cayenne pepper
> ¼ cup fresh lemon juice
> ½ cup plus 2 tablespoons pure olive oil
> 8 skinless chicken thighs
>
> Salt
> 1 cup shelled fava beans
> ½ cup fresh peas, preferably English peas
>
> Freshly ground black pepper
> 2 tablespoons unsalted butter
> 1 pound button mushrooms, halved
> 8 scallions, thinly sliced
> 2 thyme sprigs
> 1 tablespoon all-purpose flour
>
> One 12-ounce bottle Belgian beer
> ½ cup heavy cream
> ¼ cup chopped flat-leaf parsley

1. In a small skillet, toast the anise seeds over moderate heat, shaking the skillet, until the seeds are fragrant, about 3 minutes. Let the anise seeds cool slightly, then crush them with the side of a knife.

2. In a mini food processor, combine the toasted anise seeds with the chopped garlic, the saffron threads, the sweet paprika and the cayenne pepper. Add the lemon juice and puree the mixture. Transfer the marinade to a large, shallow bowl and stir in ½ cup of the olive oil. Add the chicken thighs and turn to coat them with the marinade. Refrigerate the chicken thighs in the marinade for 1 hour.

3. Meanwhile, bring a medium saucepan of water to a boil. Generously salt the water and add the fava beans to the saucepan. Cook the fava beans for 1 minute. Using a slotted spoon, transfer the cooked fava beans to a small bowl and let cool slightly.

Add the peas to the boiling water and cook until they are tender, 5 to 6 minutes; drain the peas and transfer them to a small bowl. Peel the fava beans and add them to the bowl with the peas.

4. Heat the remaining 2 tablespoons of olive oil in a large enameled cast-iron casserole. Remove the chicken thighs from the marinade, scraping off the excess. Season the chicken thighs with salt and black pepper and cook over moderately high heat, turning occasionally, until the chicken thighs are browned, about 10 minutes. Transfer the cooked chicken thighs to a platter.

5. Wipe out the casserole, add the butter and heat until the butter is melted. Add the halved mushrooms, the sliced scallions and the thyme and cook over moderate heat, stirring occasionally, until any liquid has evaporated and the mushrooms are browned, about 8 minutes. Sprinkle the flour over the mushrooms and cook, stirring, for 1 minute. Slowly stir the beer into the stew and bring it to a boil, scraping up any browned bits from the bottom of the casserole.

6. Return the chicken thighs to the casserole and season them with salt and black pepper. Cover the casserole and simmer the stew over low heat until the chicken thighs are tender and cooked through, about 25 minutes. Add the heavy cream to the stew along with the fava beans and peas. Increase the heat to moderate and cook the stew uncovered until the sauce has reduced slightly, about 5 minutes. Remove the thyme sprigs from the stew and discard. Serve the braised chicken stew right away in shallow soup bowls, sprinkled with the chopped parsley.
—*Paul Kahan*

MAKE AHEAD The chicken stew can be refrigerated overnight. Reheat the gently and garnish with the chopped parsley before serving.

WINE Juicy, fresh Dolcetto.

LENTILS WITH CHICKEN SAUSAGE

BEER-BRAISED CHICKEN STEW WITH FAVA BEANS AND PEAS

poultry

Mustard-and-Herb Chicken

TOTAL: 30 MIN

2 SERVINGS ● ●

Two 1-inch slices of country bread,
  crusts removed, bread torn
  2 garlic cloves, minced
  1 teaspoon minced rosemary
  ¼ cup finely grated Parmesan cheese
Salt and freshly ground pepper
  ¼ cup extra-virgin olive oil
  4 boneless chicken thighs with skin
  (about 6 ounces each)
  2 tablespoons Dijon mustard
  2 tablespoons unsalted butter
  1 small onion, thinly sliced
  lengthwise
Pinch of sugar
  1 tablespoon fresh lemon juice

1. Preheat the oven to 400°. In a food processor, pulse the bread until finely shredded. Add the garlic, rosemary and cheese, season with salt and pepper and pulse until combined. Add 2 tablespoons of the olive oil; pulse just until the crumbs are evenly moistened. Transfer to a bowl.
2. In a medium, ovenproof skillet, heat the remaining 2 tablespoons of olive oil until shimmering. Season the chicken with salt and pepper and add to the skillet, skin side down. Cook over moderately high heat until golden, about 6 minutes. Turn the chicken and spread the skin with the mustard. Carefully spoon the bread crumbs onto the chicken, patting them on with the back of the spoon. Transfer the skillet to the oven and roast the chicken for about 15 minutes, until the crumbs are golden and crisp and the chicken is cooked through.
3. Meanwhile, in a medium saucepan, melt the butter. Add the onion and sugar, season with salt and pepper and cook over moderate heat until softened, 6 to 7 minutes. Add the lemon juice and cook until the liquid has evaporated, 2 minutes. Spoon the onions onto 2 plates, top with the chicken and serve. —*Stuart Brioza*
WINE Peppery, refreshing Grüner Veltliner.

Grilled Chicken Thighs

ACTIVE: 30 MIN; TOTAL: 3 HR

4 SERVINGS ●

Tandoori chicken, with its smoky flavor and shocking red color, is as popular in India as fried chicken is in America. Cookbook writer and chef Suvir Saran is a fan too, especially of the version he tried at Delhi's Sahara Chicken Palace, with its tangy yogurt marinade seasoned with ginger, garlic and cumin. Saran dislikes food dye, which is why this chicken is a lovely golden brown instead of red.

  8 skinless, bone-in chicken thighs
  1 teaspoon ground cumin
  4 garlic cloves, crushed
  2 tablespoons grated fresh ginger
Kosher salt
  2 tablespoons fresh lemon juice
  1 teaspoon finely grated lemon zest
  ½ cup plain Greek yogurt
  ½ teaspoon cayenne pepper
  ¼ teaspoon Garam Masala (p. 98)
Melted unsalted butter, for basting

1. With a sharp paring knife, make several shallow slashes in each chicken thigh; transfer to a large baking dish. Sprinkle the thighs with the cumin, garlic, ginger and 1 teaspoon of salt. Rub the seasonings into the meat. Refrigerate for 1 hour.
2. In a small bowl, combine the lemon juice and lemon zest with the yogurt, cayenne and Garam Masala to make a marinade. Pour the marinade over the chicken thighs and turn to coat them. Let them stand in the marinade at room temperature for 1 hour.
3. Light a grill. Remove the thighs from the marinade, scraping some of it off. Lightly brush the chicken with the butter and transfer to the grill, buttered side down. Grill over moderate heat for 22 to 25 minutes, turning and brushing occasionally, until charred in spots and cooked through. Serve right away.
—*Suvir Saran*
WINE Intense, fruity Zinfandel.

Pancetta-Wrapped Roasted Turkey

ACTIVE: 1 HR; TOTAL: 6 HR PLUS

12 HR BRINING

12 SERVINGS

BRINE
  1 cup kosher salt
  ½ cup crushed red pepper
  2 garlic cloves, mashed
  2 jalapeños, sliced
  2 quarts hot water
One 13-pound turkey
  6 quarts cold water
RUB
  1 tablespoon chile powder
  1 tablespoon kosher salt
  2 teaspoons ground cumin
  1 teaspoon chopped rosemary
  1 teaspoon chopped thyme
  1 teaspoon garlic powder
  1 teaspoon dark brown sugar
  2 teaspoons ground black pepper
  1 pound sliced pancetta

1. MAKE THE BRINE: In a large bucket or pot, stir the salt, red pepper, garlic and jalapeños into the water until the salt is dissolved. Fully submerge the turkey, breast side down. Cover and refrigerate for 12 hours.
2. Preheat the oven to 325°. Drain, rinse and pat the turkey dry. **MAKE THE RUB:** In a bowl, mix the chile powder, salt, cumin, rosemary, thyme, garlic powder, brown sugar and pepper. Rub all over the turkey; place in a large roasting pan. Overlap three-quarters of the pancetta over the breast; wrap the legs and thighs with the remaining pancetta. Secure it in several spots with toothpicks.
3. Roast the turkey for 4½ hours, or until an instant-read thermometer inserted in the thigh registers 165°. After 1½ hours of cooking, cover the turkey loosely with foil. When the turkey is done, transfer to a carving board; let rest for 30 minutes. Discard the toothpicks and carve. Serve the crispy pancetta on the side. —*Tim Love*
WINE Ripe, juicy Pinot Noir.

PANCETTA-WRAPPED ROASTED TURKEY

TURKEY KIBBE KEBABS WITH TWO SAUCES

Turkey Kibbe Kebabs with Two Sauces

ACTIVE: 45 MIN; TOTAL: 1 HR 30 MIN

6 SERVINGS ● ● ○

PARSLEY, LEMON, WALNUT SAUCE

2 lemons
¾ cup chopped flat-leaf parsley
⅓ cup coarsely chopped fresh mint
⅓ cup coarsely chopped walnuts
1 garlic clove, finely chopped
2 tablespoons extra-virgin olive oil
2 tablespoons water
¼ teaspoon kosher salt
Pinch each of freshly ground black pepper and Aleppo pepper

YOGURT-GARLIC SAUCE

2 cups plain low-fat Greek yogurt
½ cup water
½ cup minced flat-leaf parsley
2 garlic cloves, finely chopped
¼ teaspoon kosher salt

TURKEY KEBABS

1 pound skinless, boneless turkey thigh meat, trimmed and cut into 1-inch pieces
2 tablespoons extra-virgin olive oil, plus more for brushing
1 cup medium-grain bulgur, rinsed
1 small onion, coarsely chopped
1½ tablespoons all-purpose flour
2 teaspoons kosher salt
½ teaspoon freshly ground black pepper
½ teaspoon ground allspice
½ teaspoon ground cumin
¼ teaspoon Aleppo pepper
Warm pita bread, for serving

1. MAKE THE PARSLEY, LEMON, WALNUT SAUCE: Cut the lemons into eighths. Cut the flesh from the peel and coarsely chop the flesh. Transfer to a bowl. Add the parsley, mint, walnuts, garlic, oil, water, salt and peppers. Set aside for 1 hour.

2. MAKE THE YOGURT-GARLIC SAUCE: In a bowl, whisk together the yogurt and water. Stir in the parsley, garlic and salt. Let stand for 1 hour.

3. MAKE THE TURKEY KEBABS: Light a grill or preheat the broiler. In a food processor, pulse the turkey until finely ground. Add the olive oil, bulgur, onion, flour, salt and spices; process to a paste, 30 seconds. Form the mixture into six 7-by-1½-inch logs on metal skewers.

4. Brush the kebabs with oil; grill for 5 minutes over moderately high heat, turning once, until golden and cooked through. Alternatively, broil the kebabs for 5 minutes, turning once, until golden and cooked through. Serve the kebabs with warm pita bread and the 2 sauces. —*Paula Wolfert*
MAKE AHEAD The parsley sauce can be made 2 hours ahead. The yogurt sauce and kebabs can be refrigerated overnight.
WINE Fresh, fruity rosé.

ROASTED STUFFED TURKEY
WITH GIBLET GRAVY

Roasted Stuffed Turkey with Giblet Gravy

ACTIVE: 2 HR; TOTAL: 6 HR

10 SERVINGS

One 17-pound turkey—heart, gizzard and liver reserved

Wild Mushroom Whole Wheat Stuffing with Tarragon (p. 296)

6 tablespoons plus 1 teaspoon unsalted butter, softened

Salt and freshly ground pepper

Water

6 cups Turkey Stock (recipe at right)

¼ cup all-purpose flour

1. Preheat the oven to 375°. Set the turkey on a rack in a roasting pan and pat dry. Loosely fill the cavity with 5 cups of the Wild Mushroom Stuffing and the neck cavity with 1 cup of stuffing. Rub the skin with 2 tablespoons of the butter and season generously with salt and pepper. Loosely tie the legs together with kitchen string. Add 2 cups of water to the pan.

2. Roast the turkey in the center of the oven until the skin begins to brown, about 45 minutes. Loosely cover the turkey with a large sheet of foil. Lower the oven temperature to 325° and roast the turkey for about 4½ hours longer, until an instant-read thermometer inserted in the inner thigh registers 165°. Add water to the pan throughout roasting as necessary to keep the pan moistened. Transfer the turkey to a platter, cover loosely with foil and let rest for at least 30 minutes.

3. Meanwhile, in a medium saucepan, simmer the heart and gizzard in the Turkey Stock over moderately low heat until tender and the stock is reduced to 4 cups, about 45 minutes. Strain the reduced stock into a heatproof bowl. Finely chop the heart and gizzard.

4. In a small skillet, melt 1 teaspoon of the butter. Add the turkey liver and cook over moderately high heat, turning once, until lightly browned outside and light pink within, about 4 minutes. Transfer the turkey liver to a plate and let cool, then finely chop and add it to the heart and gizzard.

5. In a skillet, melt the remaining 4 tablespoons of butter. Add the flour and whisk over moderate heat until the roux is the color of peanut butter and has a nutty aroma, about 8 minutes. Scrape the roux into a bowl.

6. Set a fine strainer over a medium bowl. Pour the drippings from the roasting pan (there should be about 1 cup) into the strainer and spoon off the fat. Set the roasting pan over 2 burners. Add the reduced turkey stock and simmer over moderately high heat, scraping up any browned bits from the bottom and side of the pan. Strain the stock into a medium saucepan and add the reserved pan juices from the bowl. Whisk in the roux and bring to a boil. Simmer the gravy over moderate heat until thickened, about 7 minutes. Stir in the reserved giblets and season with salt and pepper.

7. Spoon the stuffing from the turkey into a bowl. Carve the turkey and serve with the stuffing and gravy. —*Barbara Lynch*

SERVE WITH Cranberry-Grapefruit Conserve (recipe follows).

WINE Ripe, luxurious Chardonnay.

Cranberry-Grapefruit Conserve

ACTIVE: 25 MIN; TOTAL: 2 HR 35 MIN

MAKES 3 CUPS ● ●

One 1¼-pound red grapefruit

Water

1 pound fresh or frozen cranberries

2½ cups sugar

1. Cut the peel from the grapefruit in large strips, including about ¼ inch of the white pith. Reserve the grapefruit. Put the grapefruit peels in a medium saucepan and cover with cold water. Bring to a boil over moderately high heat, drain and repeat 3 more times. Cut the blanched peels into ¼-inch dice and reserve.

2. Meanwhile, juice the grapefruit. In a large saucepan, combine the grapefruit juice, cranberries, 1¼ cups plus 2 tablespoons of the sugar and 1½ cups of water and bring to a boil. Simmer over low heat, stirring occasionally, until the liquid has reduced by half and the cranberries are cooked down, about 1½ hours.

3. In a medium saucepan, combine the reserved grapefruit peel with the remaining sugar and 1 cup of water; bring to a boil. Simmer over moderate heat, stirring occasionally, until the peel is translucent, about 40 minutes. Add the peel and syrup to the cranberry mixture; simmer over moderate heat, stirring occasionally, until reduced to 3 cups, about 25 minutes. Serve the conserve at room temperature or slightly chilled. —*B.L.*

TURKEY STOCK

ACTIVE: 20 MIN; TOTAL: 4 HR 30 MIN

MAKES ABOUT 3 QUARTS ● ●

7 pounds turkey parts, such as wings, thighs and drumsticks

4 quarts water

1 large onion, thickly sliced

1 large carrot, thickly sliced

1 large celery rib, thickly sliced

2 garlic cloves, smashed

1 teaspoon kosher salt

½ teaspoon freshly ground pepper

1. Preheat the oven to 400°. In a large sturdy roasting pan, roast the turkey parts for 1½ hours, or until well browned; transfer to a large stockpot.

2. Set the roasting pan over 2 burners. Add 1 quart of the water and bring to a boil, scraping up the browned bits from the bottom of the pan. Add the pan liquid to the stockpot.

3. Add the onion, carrot, celery, garlic, salt and pepper to the pot with the remaining water and bring to a boil. Reduce the heat to moderately low, partially cover and simmer for 2½ hours. Strain the stock and skim off any fat from the surface before using or freezing. —*B.L.*

poultry

Classic Roasted Turkey

ACTIVE: 45 MIN; TOTAL: 3 HR 15 MIN

12 SERVINGS ●

One 16-pound turkey, legs tied and
**   giblets reserved**
** 1 celery rib, thinly sliced**
** 1 carrot, thinly sliced**
** 1 onion, thinly sliced**
** 6 garlic cloves, thinly sliced**
** 8 thyme sprigs**
** 2 rosemary sprigs**
Kosher salt and freshly ground pepper
** 4 cups water**
4½ cups Turkey Stock (p. 109)
**   or low-sodium chicken broth**
** ¼ cup plus 2 tablespoons**
**   all-purpose flour**

1. Preheat the oven to 350°. Set the turkey on a rack in a large roasting pan. Scatter the heart, gizzard, neck, celery, carrot, onion, garlic and herbs all around. Season with salt and pepper. Add 2 cups of water to the pan; roast the turkey for 1 hour and 15 minutes. Add the remaining water. Cover the turkey with foil and roast for 1 hour and 15 minutes, or until an instant-read thermometer inserted into the thickest part of an inner thigh registers 165°.

tools

basters

Fed up with basters that spatter scalding liquids, we found a better option: the **Cuisipro Dual Baster.** One nozzle gently sprays juices; a second pointy one injects flavor right into meat. **Details** $12; cuisipro.com.

2. Transfer the turkey to a cutting board and let rest for 30 minutes. Strain the pan juices into a large heatproof measuring cup, pressing on the solids. Skim the fat. 3. Pour the juices into a saucepan. Add 4 cups of stock. Boil until reduced to 5 cups. In a bowl, whisk the flour with the remaining stock, then whisk into the stock. Boil, whisking, until thickened. Carve the turkey. Serve with the gravy. —*Grace Parisi*
WINE Rich, complex white Burgundy.

Roasted Turkey with Lemon-Garlic Gravy

ACTIVE: 45 MIN; TOTAL: 3 HR 15 MIN

12 SERVINGS ● ●

** 2 garlic cloves, minced, plus 2**
**   heads of garlic, halved crosswise**
** 1 teaspoon finely grated lemon**
**   zest, plus 2 lemons, quartered**
** 1 teaspoon minced thyme**
** 1 teaspoon minced rosemary**
Kosher salt and freshly ground pepper

Follow the Classic Roasted Turkey recipe at left: In Step 1, mix the minced garlic, lemon zest, thyme, rosemary, 1 tablespoon of salt and 1 teaspoon of pepper. Loosen the skin over the breast and legs; rub the mixture evenly under the skin. Add the garlic heads and lemons to the pan. In Step 2, remove the garlic before straining the juices. Mash the cloves from 3 halves to a puree; stir into the gravy. Serve the remaining garlic on the side. —*Grace Parisi*
WINE Dry, rich Champagne.

Roasted Turkey with Muscat and Dried-Fruit Gravy

ACTIVE: 45 MIN; TOTAL: 3 HR 15 MIN
PLUS OVERNIGHT SOAKING

12 SERVINGS ●

** 1 cup dried apricots, diced**
** ½ cup dried cranberries**
** ½ cup pitted prunes, diced**
** 1 cup Orange Muscat wine**
** ½ pound sliced bacon**
Kosher salt and freshly ground pepper

In a bowl, cover the fruits and wine and let stand overnight at room temperature. Follow the Classic Roasted Turkey recipe at left: In Step 1, before roasting, loosen the breast skin; tuck the bacon under the skin to cover the breast. In Step 3, add the fruits and soaking liquid to the gravy; season with salt and pepper and simmer for 3 minutes before serving. —*Grace Parisi*
WINE Lush, fragrant Viognier.

Spicy Turkey Posole

ACTIVE: 1 HR; TOTAL: 3 HR 30 MIN

4 TO 6 SERVINGS ● ● ●

Carcass from one 13-pound turkey,
**   plus 6 cups shredded turkey**
**   (see p. 106)**
** 1 medium yellow onion, quartered**
** 1 carrot, chopped**
** 1 celery rib, chopped**
** 1 bay leaf**
Two 15-ounce cans yellow hominy,
**   drained**
** 3 tomatoes, seeded and diced**
** 4 garlic cloves, minced**
** 1 large jalapeño, thinly sliced**
**   crosswise**
** ¼ cup chopped cilantro leaves**
Salt
Avocado chunks, shredded Monterey
**   Jack cheese and warm corn**
**   tortillas, for serving**

In a stockpot, cover the turkey carcass, onion, carrot, celery and bay leaf with 16 cups of water and bring to a boil over moderately high heat. Simmer over moderate heat until the broth is flavorful, about 2 hours. Strain through a coarse sieve into a heatproof bowl and return to the pot. Add the hominy, tomatoes, garlic and jalapeño and cook over moderately high heat until reduced to 6 cups, about 30 minutes. Add the shredded turkey and the cilantro. Simmer until heated through. Season with salt, ladle into bowls and serve with the avocado, cheese and tortillas. —*Tim Love*
WINE Fresh, fruity rosé.

SPICY TURKEY POSOLE

poultry

Duck Breasts with Tamarind Sauce and Pickled Daikon Salad

ACTIVE: 45 MIN; TOTAL: 1 HR 30 MIN

6 SERVINGS ●

- 1 cup water
- ½ cup unseasoned rice vinegar
- ¼ cup mirin (sweet rice wine)
- 2 tablespoons sugar

Kosher salt

- ½ pound daikon, peeled and cut into ¼-inch matchsticks
- 4 ounces pressed tamarind from a 1-pound block, cut into 1-inch pieces
- 2½ cups boiling water
- 3 tablespoons vegetable oil
- 1 shallot, minced
- 1½ tablespoons minced peeled fresh ginger
- 1 lemongrass stalk, thinly sliced
- ½ teaspoon ground cardamom
- 2 tablespoons fresh lime juice
- ¼ cup plus 2 tablespoons honey

Freshly ground pepper

- Four 6- to 7-ounce duck breast halves, skin lightly scored in a crosshatch pattern

equipment

roasting pan

The French company **Mauviel** now sells its sturdy stainless steel roasting pan in the U.S. **Details** From $210; mauviel.com.

- 6 Medjool dates, pitted and thinly sliced lengthwise
- 4 ounces baby spinach or *tatsoi*

1. In a small saucepan, combine the 1 cup of water, rice vinegar, mirin and sugar with 1½ tablespoons of salt and bring to a boil. Add the daikon and remove the saucepan from the heat. Let stand for 1 hour. Drain, reserving 2 tablespoons of the liquid. Refrigerate the daikon just until chilled.
2. Meanwhile, in a medium bowl, combine the tamarind with the 2½ cups of boiling water and let soak for 10 minutes, or until it has broken up into a pulp. Mash the tamarind pulp with a potato masher and push it through a strainer set over a bowl.
3. In a saucepan, heat 2 tablespoons of the oil. Add the shallot, ginger and lemongrass and cook over moderate heat until softened, 3 minutes. Add the tamarind pulp and ground cardamom and bring to a boil. Cook the mixture over moderately high heat until reduced to ¾ cup, 10 minutes. Add the lime juice and honey and bring to a boil. Season with salt and pepper.
4. Heat a large skillet until very hot. Season the duck with salt and pepper and add to the skillet, skin side down. Cook over moderate heat until the skin is deeply golden brown, about 15 minutes; pour off the fat as it accumulates. Turn the duck and cook for 5 minutes longer for medium. Transfer the duck to a cutting board and let rest for 5 minutes. Pour off the fat in the pan, add the tamarind sauce and bring to a boil.
5. In a large bowl, whisk 2 tablespoons of the reserved pickling liquid into the remaining 1 tablespoon of oil and season the dressing lightly with salt and pepper. Add the daikon and the dates and toss to coat. Add the baby spinach and toss again. Mound the salad on plates. Thinly slice the duck breasts on the diagonal and set them next to the salad. Drizzle the duck with some of the tamarind sauce and pass the rest at the table. —*Douglas Keane*
WINE Intense, fruity Zinfandel.

Duck Breast, Lentil and Parsnip Salad

ACTIVE: 25 MIN; TOTAL: 1 HR

4 SERVINGS ● ●

- ½ cup French green lentils
- ¼ cup extra-virgin olive oil
- 2 tablespoons plus 1 teaspoon red wine vinegar

Salt and freshly ground pepper

One medium parsnip, peeled

Vegetable oil, for frying

Four 5- to 6-ounce skinless duck breasts

- 5 ounces mesclun greens (10 loosely packed cups)

1. In a small saucepan, cover the lentils with 1 inch of water; bring to a boil. Simmer over low heat until tender, 20 minutes.
2. In a small bowl, combine the olive oil with the vinegar and season with salt and pepper. Drain the lentils and return to the saucepan. Add 2 tablespoons of the vinaigrette, season with salt and pepper and toss well. Cover and keep warm.
3. Using a mandoline or vegetable peeler, thinly slice the parsnip lengthwise into strips. In a large skillet, heat ½ inch of oil until shimmering. Add one-fourth of the strips at a time to the oil and fry over moderate heat until browned, 1 minute. Carefully transfer to paper towels to drain. Lightly season the parsnips with salt; pour off all but 1 tablespoon of the oil. Heat until shimmering. Season the duck breasts with salt and pepper, add them to the skillet and cook over moderately high heat until nicely browned outside and medium rare within, 4 minutes per side. Transfer to a carving board and let rest for 5 minutes.
4. In a large bowl, toss the mesclun and lentils. Thinly slice the duck crosswise; add to the salad with the remaining vinaigrette and toss well. Add some of the parsnips to the salad and carefully toss again. Transfer to a platter, top with the remaining parsnips and serve. —*Nick Nairn*
WINE Ripe, juicy Pinot Noir.

Balsamic-Glazed Duck Legs with Figs and Onions

ACTIVE: 30 MIN; TOTAL: 2 HR 40 MIN

6 SERVINGS ●

- ½ cup apple juice
- ½ cup plus 1 tablespoon balsamic vinegar
- 12 dried figs
- ½ cup fresh orange juice
- 6 large Pekin duck legs

Salt and freshly ground pepper

- 1 pound medium red onions, each cut into 6 wedges
- 1 tablespoon extra-virgin olive oil
- 1 tablespoon honey
- ½ cup low-sodium chicken broth

1. Preheat the oven to 425°. In a small saucepan, combine the apple juice with ½ cup of the balsamic vinegar and bring to a boil. Simmer over high heat until thickened and reduced to ¼ cup, about 6 minutes. Pour the balsamic glaze into a glass measuring cup and let it cool to room temperature.

2. In a heatproof bowl, combine the dried figs with the orange juice. Cover the figs and microwave at 50 percent power for 8 minutes.

3. Prick the duck legs all over with a fork and season them with salt and pepper. Transfer the legs to a rimmed baking sheet and roast in the upper third of the oven for about 30 minutes, or until most of the fat has been rendered and the skin is crisp. Transfer the duck legs to a platter and pour off the fat from the baking sheet.

4. Reduce the oven temperature to 350°. Arrange the plumped figs and the onion wedges, cut side down, on the baking sheet. Drizzle with the fig cooking liquid, olive oil, honey and the remaining 1 tablespoon of balsamic vinegar. Season with salt and pepper. Set the duck legs on top of the onions and figs, pour the chicken broth around the duck legs and bake in the upper third of the oven for about 1 hour, or until the duck is very tender.

5. Transfer the duck legs to the platter. Continue roasting the onions and figs for 45 minutes longer. Return the duck legs and their juices to the baking sheet and roast for 10 minutes, or until the duck is heated through. Transfer the roasted duck legs to plates. Using tongs, set the onion wedges and figs alongside the duck legs. Pour the pan juices over the red onions, drizzle with the balsamic glaze and serve.
—*Annabel Langbein*

WINE Spicy American Gewürztraminer.

Keralan Duck Curry

TOTAL: 1 HR 30 MIN

6 SERVINGS

- 1 teaspoon turmeric

Kosher salt

- 6 skinless, boneless Pekin duck breast halves (5 ounces each)

Seeds from 6 cardamom pods

- 6 whole cloves
- 1 teaspoon black peppercorns
- ¼ cup plus 2 tablespoons vegetable oil
- 3 medium red potatoes, peeled and sliced ¼ inch thick
- 6 fresh curry leaves
- 6 garlic cloves, smashed
- 4 long hot green chiles, seeded and thinly sliced crosswise

One 1½-inch piece of ginger, peeled and julienned (3 tablespoons)

- 1 medium red onion, thinly sliced

One 14-ounce can unsweetened coconut milk (see Note)

- ½ cup water

1. In a small bowl, mix ½ teaspoon of the turmeric with 2 teaspoons of kosher salt and rub the seasoning over the duck breasts. Cover and refrigerate the duck breasts for 30 minutes.

2. Meanwhile, in a spice grinder, grind the cardamom seeds, cloves and peppercorns to a powder. Transfer to a small bowl and stir in the remaining ½ teaspoon of turmeric.

3. In a large, deep skillet, heat ¼ cup of the vegetable oil until shimmering. Add the potato slices in a single layer and cook over moderate heat until browned, about 4 minutes per side. Drain on paper towels and season with salt.

4. In the same skillet, heat the remaining 2 tablespoons of vegetable oil. Add the duck breasts and cook over high heat until browned, about 2 minutes per side; transfer to a large plate.

5. In the same skillet, cook the curry leaves over moderate heat for 2 minutes. Add the garlic, chiles and ginger and cook until softened, about 3 minutes. Add the onion and cook over moderately low heat, stirring occasionally, until softened, about 5 minutes. Stir in the spice powder and cook, stirring, until fragrant, about 3 minutes. Return the duck to the skillet along with any accumulated juices, cover and cook over low heat for 5 minutes, turning the breasts a few times. Return the duck breasts to the plate.

6. Spoon out ¼ cup of the thickened coconut milk from the top of the can; set aside. Put the rest in a small bowl and stir in the water. Add the thinned coconut milk to the skillet and simmer over moderately high heat for 10 minutes. Reduce the heat to moderate. Add the potato slices and simmer for 1 minute. Add the duck breasts and simmer for 8 minutes, turning once. Stir in the thickened coconut milk and simmer over low heat for 3 minutes. Season with salt. Transfer the duck breasts to plates and spoon the potatoes and sauce around the duck and serve.
—*Aniamma Philip*

SERVE WITH Steamed white rice.

NOTE Don't shake the can of coconut milk before opening it to make sure the thickened milk stays on top. If cooking the curry with homogenized coconut milk, add the entire can plus ½ cup of water at the beginning of Step 6.

WINE Ripe, juicy Pinot Noir.

poultry

Chorizo-Stuffed Capon with Sorrel Brown Butter

ACTIVE: 30 MIN; TOTAL: 3 HR PLUS 6 HR BRINING

8 SERVINGS

Reserve 1¼ pounds (4 cups) of skinless, boneless capon from this recipe to make the Pulled Capon and Watercress Salad with Citrus Dressing (p. 119).

- 4 cups hot water
- ¼ cup crushed red pepper
- 2 large garlic cloves, smashed
- ½ cup kosher salt, plus more for seasoning
- 8 cups cold water

One 11-pound capon

- 6 ounces dry chorizo, thinly sliced
- ½ pound smoked cheddar cheese, shredded
- 4 cups cubed crustless peasant bread (½-inch dice)
- 1 cup chicken stock or low-sodium broth

Extra-virgin olive oil, for rubbing

Freshly ground pepper

- 1 stick unsalted butter
- 2 ounces sorrel, stemmed and finely shredded

1. In a large pot, combine the hot water with the crushed red pepper, garlic and the ½ cup of salt and stir until the salt is dissolved. Add the cold water and the capon. Cover and refrigerate for 6 hours.
2. Preheat the oven to 350°. Drain and rinse the capon, then pat dry. In a medium skillet, cook the chorizo over moderate heat until lightly browned, about 5 minutes. Transfer to a medium bowl. Add the smoked cheddar, bread cubes and stock and stir. Loosely stuff the capon with half of the mixture and transfer the rest to a small baking dish.
3. Transfer the capon to a roasting pan and tie the legs together with kitchen string. Rub the bird with olive oil and season generously with salt and pepper. Roast the capon for about 2 hours until golden

and an instant-read thermometer inserted in the meaty part of the thigh registers 170°; turn the pan occasionally during roasting for even browning. Let the capon rest for 20 minutes.
4. Meanwhile, bake the stuffing in the baking dish for 20 minutes, until heated through and browned and crusty on top.
5. In a medium skillet, cook the butter over moderate heat until nutty and lightly browned, about 5 minutes. Add the sorrel and a pinch of salt and cook, stirring until wilted, about 1 minute.
6. Spoon the stuffing from the cavity of the capon into a serving dish. Carve the capon and transfer to a platter. Spoon the sorrel butter over the capon and serve with the baked stuffing. —*Tim Love*
WINE Earthy, medium-bodied Tempranillo.

Duck Confit Quesadillas

TOTAL: 1 HR

6 SERVINGS

Stuffed with shredded duck confit and cheese and topped with chipotle-honey mayonnaise, these are quite possibly the world's most indulgent quesadillas.

- 2 pieces of duck leg confit, skin discarded and meat coarsely shredded (1½ cups)
- 1 small red onion, finely chopped
- 2 jalapeños—1 seeded and minced, 1 thinly sliced
- 3 tablespoons finely chopped cilantro, plus 2 tablespoons whole leaves

Kosher salt and freshly ground black pepper

- 1 small zucchini, cut into ¼-inch dice
- 1 small yellow squash, cut into ¼-inch dice
- 1 plum tomato—halved, seeded and cut into ¼-inch dice
- 2 tablespoons fresh lime juice
- ¼ cup plus 2 tablespoons extra-virgin olive oil

- ½ cup mayonnaise
- 2 chipotles in adobo sauce, seeded and minced
- 1 tablespoon fresh lemon juice
- 1 teaspoon honey

Six 8-inch flour tortillas

- 4 ounces Monterey Jack cheese, shredded (1 cup)
- 2 scallions, white and tender green parts, thinly sliced

1. Preheat the oven to 350°. In a bowl, combine the duck confit with half of the chopped red onion, the minced jalapeño and 1 tablespoon of the chopped cilantro. Season with salt and black pepper.
2. In another bowl, mix the remaining half of the red onion with 1 tablespoon of chopped cilantro, the diced zucchini, yellow squash and tomato, the lime juice and 2 tablespoons of the olive oil. Season the zucchini salsa with salt and pepper.
3. In a small bowl, whisk the mayonnaise with the chipotles in adobo sauce, the lemon juice, the honey and the remaining 1 tablespoon of chopped cilantro. Season the mayonnaise with salt and pepper.
4. Arrange the tortillas on a work surface. Spoon the duck confit mixture on the bottom half of each tortilla and top with the cheese. Fold the top half of each tortilla over the filling.
5. In a very large skillet, heat 2 tablespoons of the olive oil. Add 3 of the quesadillas and them cook over moderate heat, turning once, until they are crisp on the outside and the cheese has melted, about 5 minutes. Transfer the quesadillas to a baking sheet and keep warm in the preheated oven; cook the remaining 3 quesadillas in the remaining 2 tablespoons of olive oil.
6. To serve, cut each quesadilla into 3 triangles. Top each with a dollop of chipotle mayonnaise and a large spoonful of the zucchini salsa. Garnish the quesadillas with the cilantro leaves, scallions and jalapeño slices and serve. —*Michael Schlow*
WINE Fresh, fruity rosé.

DUCK CONFIT QUESADILLAS

poultry

Buckshot Gumbo

ACTIVE: 35 MIN; TOTAL: 2 HR 10 MIN

6 SERVINGS ●

- 3 tablespoons salted butter
- 5 tablespoons all-purpose flour
- 1 tablespoon vegetable oil
- Two 1½-pound boneless goose breast halves with skin, skin scored in a crosshatch pattern (see Note)
- Two 1½-pound goose legs (see Note)
- 7 ounces diced andouille sausage
- 4 garlic cloves, minced
- 2 celery ribs, finely diced
- 4 jalapeños, finely diced
- 1 large Spanish onion, finely diced
- 1 green bell pepper, finely diced
- 1 bay leaf
- 1 teaspoon each of chopped oregano, thyme and sweet paprika
- ½ teaspoon cayenne pepper
- ½ cup dry Riesling
- 3 cups low-sodium chicken broth
- 3 cups water
- 4 large scallions, thinly sliced
- 2 tablespoons chopped parsley
- Salt and freshly ground black pepper

1. In a small skillet, melt the butter. Stir in the flour and cook over moderately low heat, stirring often, until the mixture turns a rich, dark brown, 1½ hours. Transfer the roux to a bowl and refrigerate until cold.

2. In a large skillet, heat the oil. Add the goose breasts, skin side down, and cook over moderately high heat until browned, 7 minutes. Pour off the fat, reserving 2 tablespoons. Turn the breasts and brown the other side, 3 minutes. Transfer to a rimmed baking sheet. Repeat with the goose legs.

3. In a large enameled cast-iron casserole, heat the reserved fat. Add the sausage, garlic, celery, jalapeños, onion and bell pepper and cook over moderate heat until softened, 10 minutes. Add the bay leaf, oregano, thyme, paprika and cayenne and cook for 4 minutes. Add the wine and boil until reduced by half, 2 minutes. Add the broth, water and goose and simmer over low heat, skimming occasionally, until the goose is tender, 1½ hours. Transfer to the baking sheet and let cool to room temperature. Discard the skin and bones and cut the meat into bite-size pieces.

4. Whisk 1 cup of the hot gumbo liquid into the cold roux, then whisk it back into the gumbo. Bring to a simmer, stirring often. Simmer over low heat for 15 minutes, stirring occasionally. Return the goose to the gumbo. Bring to a simmer, add the scallions and parsley, season with salt and black pepper and serve. —*Bryan Caswell*

NOTE Goose parts are available from Schiltz Foods (roastgoose.com).

WINE Full-bodied, minerally Riesling.

Fennel-Scented Duck Breasts with Pinot Noir Sauce

ACTIVE: 30 MIN; TOTAL: 1 HR PLUS OVERNIGHT BRINING

6 SERVINGS

DUCK

- 1 teaspoon black peppercorns
- 1 teaspoon fennel seeds
- 4 cups cold water
- 1 fennel bulb, thinly sliced, fronds chopped
- ½ cup white balsamic vinegar
- 2 teaspoons honey
- 2 teaspoons salt
- Three 12-ounce duck breasts

SAUCE

- 1 tablespoon unsalted butter
- ½ small white onion, thinly sliced
- 2 tablespoons honey
- ½ cup Pinot Noir
- 1 cup chicken stock or broth
- ½ teaspoon black peppercorns
- 2 thyme sprigs
- 1 small plum tomato, chopped
- Salt and freshly ground pepper
- Celery Root and Potato Puree (p. 270), for serving

1. PREPARE THE DUCK: In a small skillet, toast the peppercorns and fennel seeds over moderate heat until fragrant, 2 minutes. Transfer to a large bowl; add the water, fennel bulb and fronds, vinegar, honey and salt. Whisk to dissolve the salt. Add the duck, cover and refrigerate overnight.

2. MAKE THE SAUCE: Preheat the oven to 325°. In a small saucepan, melt the butter. Add the onion and cook over moderately high heat, stirring, until browned. Add the honey and cook over moderate heat until the onion starts to caramelize, 2 minutes. Add the wine and simmer until reduced by half, 4 minutes. Add the stock, peppercorns, thyme and tomato and cook over moderately high heat until the sauce has thickened enough to coat the back of a spoon, about 10 minutes. Strain the sauce into a bowl and season with salt and pepper.

3. Remove the duck from the marinade and pat dry; season with salt and pepper. In a large, ovenproof skillet, arrange the duck, skin side down, and cook over moderate heat until browned, 12 minutes. Turn the duck skin side up and transfer the skillet to the oven; cook until medium rare, about 7 minutes. Transfer the duck to a cutting board and let rest for 5 minutes. Slice the breasts crosswise ¼ inch thick. Spoon the Celery Root and Potato Puree onto plates, top with the duck and the Pinot Noir sauce. —*Andy Arndt*

WINE Ripe, juicy Pinot Noir.

Crunchy Almond-Crusted Duck Breasts with Chanterelle Salad

TOTAL: 1 HR

4 SERVINGS

Duck is often paired with something sweet, as in *canard à l'orange*. F&W contributing editor and star chef Jean-Georges Vongerichten tops it here with chopped sugar-coated almonds. The sugar burns slightly as the meat is broiled to form a bittersweet crust that pairs beautifully with the juicy richness of the duck.

- ⅔ cup honey wine (see Note) or white port
- ¼ cup plus 2 tablespoons white port

FENNEL-SCENTED DUCK BREAST WITH PINOT NOIR SAUCE

CRUNCHY ALMOND-CRUSTED DUCK BREAST WITH CHANTERELLE SALAD

3 tablespoons duck and veal or veal demiglace (see Note)

2 tablespoons fresh lemon juice

3 tablespoons unsalted butter

½ teaspoon chestnut honey

Salt and freshly ground black pepper

3 magret duck breasts (about 11 ounces each)

¼ cup Jordan almonds or white dragées, finely chopped

½ pound chanterelle mushrooms, thickly sliced if large

1 shallot, minced

1½ tablespoons walnut oil

1 tablespoon grapeseed oil

½ tablespoon hazelnut oil

1 tablespoon sherry vinegar

1 tablespoon chopped parsley

½ pound frisée, pale green and white leaves only, torn into pieces

Cayenne pepper

1. In a saucepan, bring the wine, ¼ cup plus 1 tablespoon of port, demiglace and lemon juice to a boil. Simmer over moderate heat until reduced to ⅓ cup, 10 minutes. Whisk in 1 tablespoon of butter and the honey; season with salt and pepper.
2. Preheat the broiler. Heat a large skillet. Add the duck, skin side down, and cook over moderate heat until the skin is crisp and golden, 15 minutes; spoon off the fat as it accumulates. Season the duck, then turn skin side up and cook for 7 minutes for medium rare. Transfer the duck to a rimmed baking sheet, skin side up, and sprinkle with the almonds, pressing to adhere. Transfer the duck breasts to the center of the oven and broil for about 2 minutes, or until the sugar is caramelized; turn the baking sheet as necessary for even browning. Let the duck breasts rest before slicing them.
3. In a medium skillet, melt the remaining butter. Add the chanterelles; cook over

moderately high heat, stirring occasionally, until their liquid has evaporated and they are lightly browned, 8 minutes. Season with salt and black pepper, add the shallot and cook for 1 minute longer.
4. In a large bowl, whisk the oils with the vinegar and the remaining port. Stir in the parsley. Add the frisée and chanterelles, season with salt and cayenne and toss to coat. Mound the salad on plates. Reheat the sauce. Cut the duck breasts crosswise into ½-inch slices and arrange them next to the salad. Drizzle the sauce all around and serve. —*Jean-Georges Vongerichten*
SERVE WITH Boiled baby turnips or radishes sautéed in butter.
NOTE Honey wine, also called mead, is available at most liquor stores. Duck and veal demiglace and veal demiglace are available at specialty food shops and from D'Artagnan (800-327-8246 or dartagnan.com).
WINE Dry, rich Champagne.

● FAST ● HEALTHY ● MAKE AHEAD ● STAFF FAVORITE

117

poultry

Spiced Squabs with Onion Compote

ACTIVE: 35 MIN; TOTAL: 1 HR 15 MIN

4 SERVINGS

- 6 tablespoons unsalted butter
- 6 medium onions (2 pounds), halved and thinly sliced

Water

- 2 tablespoons fresh lemon juice

Salt and freshly ground pepper

Four 1-pound squabs, butterflied

- ½ teaspoon ground cumin
- ¼ teaspoon ground ginger
- ¼ teaspoon curry powder
- ¼ teaspoon cinnamon
- 1½ tablespoons extra-virgin olive oil
- 4 ounces baby arugula

Golden Corn Cakes (p. 304), for serving

1. In a large, deep skillet, melt the butter. Add the onions and cook over moderate heat, stirring occasionally, until golden, about 35 minutes; add 2 tablespoons of water as necessary during cooking to prevent the onions from drying out. Stir in 1 tablespoon of the lemon juice and season with salt and pepper.

2. Meanwhile, preheat the broiler. On a rimmed baking sheet, season the squabs with salt and pepper. Broil the birds 8 inches from the heat for about 20 minutes, turning the baking sheet occasionally, until the skin is deep golden brown and an instant-read thermometer inserted in the breast registers 145° for medium rare.

3. In a bowl, combine the cumin with the ginger, curry powder and cinnamon. Sprinkle on both sides of the squabs.

4. In a medium bowl, whisk the remaining 1 tablespoon of lemon juice with the olive oil and season with salt and pepper. Add the arugula and toss to coat. Spoon the onion compote onto 4 plates. Arrange the squabs and Golden Corn Cakes on the plates, mound the arugula on the side and serve. —*Jean-Georges Vongerichten*
WINE Complex, elegant Pinot Noir.

Crispy Quails with Chile Jam and Three-Bean Salad

ACTIVE: 1 HR 5 MIN; TOTAL: 1 HR 5 MIN
PLUS 2 HR MARINATING

4 SERVINGS

Bryan Caswell, chef de cuisine at the three-year-old Bank by Jean-Georges in Houston, left Texas for nine years, but there are some things he couldn't shake, like three-bean salad. It gives a Southern touch to his Asian-accented quail, which marinates in ginger, garlic and soy sauce. Casswell also serves the quail with chile jam, which he learned to make in Bangkok; he says Texans love the heat.

QUAILS

- ¼ cup thinly sliced peeled ginger
- 4 garlic cloves, smashed
- 3 shallots, quartered
- ½ cup soy sauce
- 3 tablespoons sugar
- 2 tablespoons rice vinegar
- 1 teaspoon five-spice powder
- ½ teaspoon freshly ground black pepper
- 8 semiboneless quails

CHILE JAM

- ¾ cup water
- 2 ounces tamarind paste (see Note)
- 2 tablespoons grapeseed oil
- 8 garlic cloves, thinly sliced
- 2 shallots, thinly sliced
- 2 large jalapeños, preferably red, seeded and thinly sliced
- 1½ tablespoons granulated sugar
- 1 tablespoon light brown sugar
- 1½ tablespoons Asian fish sauce
- 1 teaspoon ground dried shrimp (optional)
- 2 tablespoons soy sauce
- 3 tablespoons fresh lime juice

BEAN SALAD

- 4 ounces yellow wax beans
- 1 cup frozen butter beans, thawed
- 1 cup frozen black-eyed peas, thawed
- 1 cup grape tomatoes, halved
- 1 shallot, thinly sliced
- 2 tablespoons chopped cilantro
- ¼ teaspoon pure ancho chile powder
- ¼ cup grapeseed oil

1. PREPARE THE QUAILS: In a blender, puree the ginger with the garlic cloves, shallots, soy sauce, sugar, rice vinegar, five-spice powder and black pepper. Transfer the marinade to a resealable plastic bag, add the quails and seal, pressing out the air. Let the quails marinate in the refrigerator for 2 hours.

2. MEANWHILE, MAKE THE CHILE JAM: In a small saucepan, bring the water to a boil. Add the tamarind paste and simmer for 2 minutes, mashing with a wooden spoon to dissolve the paste. Strain the tamarind puree through a coarse sieve into a small bowl, pressing on the solids.

3. In a medium saucepan, heat the grapeseed oil until shimmering. Add the garlic, shallots and jalapeños and cook over moderately high heat, stirring, until the garlic is lightly browned, about 4 minutes. Add the granulated sugar and the brown sugar and cook until melted. Stir in the tamarind puree and simmer until thickened, about 3 minutes. Remove from the heat and stir in the fish sauce and dried shrimp.

4. In a small bowl, whisk 3 tablespoons of the chile jam with the soy sauce and lime juice to make a dressing.

5. MAKE THE BEAN SALAD: In a medium saucepan of boiling salted water, cook the wax beans until they are crisp-tender, about 5 minutes. Using a slotted spoon, transfer the wax beans to a colander and rinse them under cold running water. Pat the beans dry and cut them into 1-inch pieces, then transfer the wax beans to a bowl. Boil the butter beans and the black-eyed peas for 1 minute, then drain. Add the butter beans, black-eyed peas, tomatoes, shallot, cilantro and chile powder to the wax beans. Add three-fourths of the dressing to the bean salad and toss to coat.

6. Heat 2 large skillets until they are very hot. Add 2 tablespoons of the grapeseed oil to each skillet. Drain the quails and pat them dry; add the quails to the skillets, breasts down, and brown over high heat, turning once, until crisp, about 6 minutes.

7. Mound the bean salad on plates. Top with the quails and drizzle with the remaining dressing. Serve the chile jam on the side. —*Bryan Caswell*

NOTE Tamarind paste is available at specialty food shops and at Asian markets.

WINE Full-bodied, rich Pinot Gris.

Herb-Roasted Pheasants with Endives and Horseradish Puree

ACTIVE: 45 MIN; TOTAL: 1 HR 45 MIN

4 SERVINGS ●

Chef Jean-Georges Vongerichten, whose growing empire of 18 restaurants keeps him very busy, recently took a rare vacation in Texas to brush up on his shooting skills. After the hunt, the chef shared his recipes for birds. The lean pheasants in this recipe are roasted with an herb butter spread under the skin—delicious all by itself, but Vongerichten makes the birds even better by serving them with a fiery condiment of pureed fresh horseradish. He places caramelized endives on the plate too, hiding thin slices of apple between the leaves like sweet and tangy petals.

½ **pound fresh horseradish, peeled and sliced crosswise ¼ inch thick**
3 **cups water**
1 **tablespoon sugar**
Salt
2 **tablespoons crème fraîche**
4 **tablespoons unsalted butter, softened**
1 **teaspoon chopped thyme**
1 **teaspoon finely chopped rosemary**
1 **teaspoon finely chopped sage**
Freshly ground pepper

Two 3-pound pheasants
1 **lemon, quartered**
Caramelized Endives with Apples (p. 262), for serving

1. In a covered medium saucepan, simmer the horseradish with 2 cups of the water, the sugar and a large pinch of salt until the horseradish is tender, about 30 minutes. Drain the horseradish well. In a food processor, puree the horseradish with the crème fraîche. Scrape the puree into a small bowl and season with salt.

2. Preheat the oven to 400°. In a small bowl, blend the butter with the thyme, rosemary and sage and season with salt and pepper. Rub 1½ tablespoons of herb butter under the skin of each pheasant. Rub the remaining 1 tablespoon of herb butter all over the outside of the birds and season with salt and pepper. Tuck 2 lemon quarters into each cavity and tie the legs with string.

3. Set the pheasants on an oiled rack in a roasting pan on their sides, and roast for 30 minutes. Carefully turn the birds to their other side and roast them for 30 minutes longer. Turn the pheasants breast side up and roast them for 10 minutes. Pour the cavity juices into the roasting pan, pressing lightly on the lemon to release the juice. Transfer the pheasants to a carving board and let rest for 10 minutes.

4. Place the roasting pan over 2 burners. Add the remaining 1 cup of water and simmer the juices, scraping up the brown bits from the bottom of the pan, until the juices are reduced to ¾ cup, about 3 minutes. Pour the juices into a small saucepan and season with salt and pepper. Keep warm.

5. Carve the pheasants and arrange the slices on serving plates. Using 2 soupspoons, scoop the horseradish puree into neat ovals and set the horseradish beside the sliced pheasant. Pour the pan juices over the pheasant and serve with the Caramelized Endives with Apples. —*Jean-Georges Vongerichten*

WINE Complex, aromatic Chenin Blanc.

Pulled Capon and Watercress Salad with Citrus Dressing

TOTAL: 20 MIN

4 SERVINGS ● ●

This fantastic alternative to the usually mayonnaise-rich, chunky chicken salad uses leftover capon or chicken.

2 **garlic cloves, thickly sliced**
¼ **cup plus 2 tablespoons extra-virgin olive oil**
1 **small shallot, halved**
1 **tablespoon fresh lemon juice, plus ½ teaspoon finely grated lemon zest**
1 **tablespoon fresh lime juice, plus ½ teaspoon finely grated lime zest**
1 **jalapeño, seeded**
1 **tablespoon white wine vinegar**
1 **tablespoon dry white wine**
Salt and freshly ground pepper
1 **head of Bibb lettuce, torn into large pieces**
4 **cups reserved shredded capon (see p. 114) or chicken (1¼ pounds)**
1 **bunch of watercress (6 ounces), thick stems discarded**
½ **small red onion, thinly sliced**
1 **avocado, cut into 1-inch cubes**

1. In a skillet, cook the garlic in the oil over moderately low heat until it is fragrant and soft, about 5 minutes. Transfer to a blender and let cool. Add the shallot, lemon juice and zest, lime juice and zest, jalapeño, vinegar and wine and process until smooth. Season with salt and pepper.

2. Transfer 1 tablespoon of the dressing to a large bowl. Add the lettuce and toss. Arrange the lettuce on a platter. Add the capon and watercress to the bowl along with the onion, avocado and the remaining dressing and toss. Mound the capon salad over the lettuce; serve. —*Tim Love*

MAKE AHEAD The dressing can be refrigerated overnight.

WINE Fruity, soft Chenin Blanc.

STILTON SIRLOIN BURGER WITH
ONION JAM (P. 133) AND SWEET
POTATO FRIES (P. 263)

beef & lamb

"If your dish is straightforward, like braised meat and roasted vegetables, start with amazing ingredients or you won't end up with anything special."

—Troy MacLarty, chef, Lovely Hula Hands, Portland, Oregon

GRILLED BEEF WITH SESAME DRESSING

SKIRT STEAK WITH MOROCCAN SPICE RUB AND YOGURT SAUCE

Grilled Beef with Sesame Dressing

TOTAL: 35 MIN

4 SERVINGS ● ●

- 1 teaspoon *sambal oelek* or Asian chile paste
- 2 small garlic cloves
- 2 tablespoons unseasoned rice vinegar
- 1 tablespoon soy sauce
- 1½ teaspoons sugar
- 1 teaspoon Asian sesame oil
- ¼ cup vegetable oil
- 4 large scallions, white and light green parts

Four 4-ounce beef tenderloin steaks

Salt and freshly ground pepper

- 1½ cups shelled edamame (7 ounces), thawed
- 6 medium radishes, thinly sliced
- 1 bunch of watercress, thick stems discarded

Sesame seeds, for garnish

1. Light a grill. In a blender, combine the *sambal oelek,* garlic, vinegar, soy sauce, sugar with the sesame oil and process until the dressing is smooth. Blend in the vegetable oil until it is incorporated.

2. Brush the scallions and steaks with 1 tablespoon of the dressing and season them with salt and pepper. Grill over moderately high heat, turning occasionally, about 5 minutes for the scallions and 8 minutes for medium-rare steaks. Let the steaks rest for 5 minutes, then slice.

3. Cut the scallions into ½-inch pieces and transfer them to a bowl. Add the edamame, radishes, watercress and about 5 tablespoons of the dressing and toss. Mound the salad on plates and place the sliced steak alongside. Drizzle the remaining dressing over the grilled steak, sprinkle with sesame seeds and serve right away. —*Shawn McClain*

WINE Lively, fruity Merlot.

Skirt Steak with Moroccan Spice Rub and Yogurt Sauce

TOTAL: 30 MIN

4 SERVINGS ●

- 1¼ pounds skirt steak, cut into 6-inch lengths
- 3 tablespoons plus 1½ teaspoons Moroccan Spice Rub (recipe follows)
- ¾ cup plain whole milk yogurt
- 2 scallions, thinly sliced
- 1 garlic clove, smashed
- 1 tablespoon chopped pickled jalapeños
- 1 tablespoon extra-virgin olive oil, plus more for brushing

Salt and freshly ground pepper

- 4 large pita breads, for serving

Romaine lettuce leaves, for serving

1. Light a grill. Rub the steaks all over with 3 tablespoons of the spice rub and let stand for 5 minutes.

2. In a bowl, mix the yogurt, scallions, garlic, jalapeños and the remaining 1½ teaspoons of the spice rub. Stir in the olive oil and season with salt and pepper.

3. Brush the steaks lightly with olive oil and grill over high heat, turning occasionally, for 7 to 8 minutes for medium rare. Brush the pitas with olive oil and grill until lightly toasted, about 30 seconds. Transfer the steaks to a cutting board and let rest for 5 minutes; thinly slice across the grain. Transfer the steaks to a platter and serve with the toasted pita, yogurt sauce and lettuce leaves. —*Grace Parisi*
WINE Juicy, spicy Grenache.

MOROCCAN SPICE RUB
TOTAL: 5 MIN
MAKES ABOUT ⅓ CUP ● ●
- 1 tablespoon ground coriander
- 1 tablespoon ground cumin
- 1 tablespoon ground chile powder
- 1 tablespoon light brown sugar
- 1½ teaspoons kosher salt
- ½ teaspoon cinnamon
- ½ teaspoon caraway seeds, crushed
- ½ teaspoon freshly ground black pepper

In a small bowl, combine all of the ingredients, pressing out any lumps of brown sugar. —*G.P.*
OTHER USES Try the rub on beef, chicken, pork and lamb. It's especially good on skirt steak, chicken thighs and pork ribs.

Strip Steak with Arugula Pesto
TOTAL: 30 MIN
2 SERVINGS ●
The secret to this pesto is adding an ice cube to the blanched arugula while pureeing. This keeps the pesto fresh-tasting and bright green.

- **One 1-pound boneless strip steak, about 2 inches thick**
- ¼ cup plus 2 tablespoons extra-virgin olive oil, plus more for rubbing

- Salt and freshly ground pepper
- 6 garlic cloves, unpeeled
- 2 rosemary sprigs
- 2 thyme sprigs
- 2 tablespoons unsalted butter
- 5 ounces baby arugula (7 loose cups)
- 1 ice cube
- ¼ cup pine nuts
- 2 tablespoons finely grated Parmesan cheese

1. Heat a medium cast-iron skillet until hot. Lightly rub the steak with olive oil and season generously with salt and pepper. Add the steak to the hot skillet and cook over moderate heat until browned on the bottom, about 6 minutes. Add the garlic cloves, herb sprigs and butter to the skillet. Turn the steak and cook for 5 minutes. Using kitchen tongs, turn the steak on each side and cook until browned, about 2 minutes per side. Lay the steak flat, baste it with the butter in the skillet and turn the garlic cloves. Continue to cook the steak for about 5 minutes longer, until an instant-read thermometer inserted in the center registers 125° for medium rare. Transfer the steak and garlic cloves to a cutting board and let rest.
2. Bring a small saucepan of water to a boil. Add all but 1 cup of the arugula and cook for 10 seconds, then drain and cool under running water. Squeeze out the excess water and transfer the arugula to a mini food processor. Add the ice cube, 3 tablespoons of the pine nuts, the Parmesan and the ¼ cup plus 2 tablespoons of olive oil. Process to a fine paste. Season the pesto with salt and pepper.
3. Spoon the pesto onto 2 plates. Thinly slice the steak and arrange on the pesto. Mound the remaining 1 cup of arugula on the steak and drizzle with any steak juices. Garnish with the remaining 1 tablespoon of pine nuts and the garlic cloves and serve. —*Stuart Brioza*
WINE Firm, complex Cabernet Sauvignon.

Hanger Steak with Shallots and Mushrooms
TOTAL: 40 MIN
4 SERVINGS ●
- **One 1½-pound hanger steak**
- 3 tablespoons extra-virgin olive oil, plus more for brushing
- Salt and freshly ground pepper
- 2 tablespoons unsalted butter
- ½ pound shiitake mushrooms, stems discarded, caps thickly sliced
- ½ pound white mushrooms, thickly sliced
- 6 shallots, very thinly sliced (1 cup)
- 2 tablespoons red wine vinegar
- ½ cup dry red wine
- ¼ cup chicken stock or broth
- 2 tablespoons finely chopped flat-leaf parsley

1. Brush the steak with olive oil and season with salt and pepper. Heat a large cast-iron skillet until nearly smoking. Add 1 tablespoon of the olive oil, then add the steak and cook over high heat, turning once, until well browned outside and medium rare within, about 12 minutes. Transfer to a plate, cover loosely with foil and let rest.
2. Meanwhile, in a large skillet, heat the remaining 2 tablespoons of olive oil with 1 tablespoon of the butter. Add the mushrooms, season with salt and pepper and cook over moderate heat, stirring occasionally, until beginning to brown, about 6 minutes. Add the shallots and cook, stirring, until softened but not browned, about 4 minutes longer. Add the vinegar and cook until evaporated. Add the wine and cook until nearly evaporated, about 5 minutes. Stir in the stock and the remaining 1 tablespoon of butter.
3. Halve the steak lengthwise, cutting on either side of the sinew that runs down the center, then thinly slice and transfer to plates. Add the parsley and accumulated juices to the mushrooms. Spoon the sauce over the steak. Serve. —*Daniel Boulud*
WINE Earthy, medium-bodied Tempranillo.

beef & lamb

Smoky Spiced T-Bone Steaks with Chilean Salsa

ACTIVE: 30 MIN; TOTAL: 1 HR

4 SERVINGS

Four 1-inch-thick T-bone steaks
4   teaspoons pure chipotle powder
Salt and freshly ground pepper
1   garlic clove, minced
1   large beefsteak tomato, cut into ¼-inch dice, with seeds and juices
1   small green bell pepper, diced
1   small sweet onion, finely diced
1   large jalapeño, seeded and minced
¼   cup chopped cilantro leaves
Extra-virgin olive oil, for brushing

Light a grill. Sprinkle each steak with 1 teaspoon of chipotle powder; season with salt and pepper. Let stand for at least 5 or up to 20 minutes. In a bowl, mash the garlic with a pinch of salt. Add the tomato, pepper, onion, jalapeño and cilantro; do not stir. Lightly brush both sides of the steaks with oil. Grill over high heat until well-browned and medium rare, 4 minutes per side. Transfer to plates. Let rest for 5 minutes. Stir the salsa. Season with salt and pepper and serve. —*Steven Raichlen*
WINE Fruity, luscious Shiraz.

tools

tongs

Precision Tongs have a finely ridged tip for grasping delicate foods and feature a lock for compact storage. **Details** $10; oxo.com.

Grilled Hickory-Smoked Hanger Steak

ACTIVE: 20 MIN; TOTAL: 1 HR 40 MIN

4 SERVINGS

Kenny Callaghan, chef at New York City's Blue Smoke, makes different types of barbecue complemented by different kinds of sauces—smoky, tangy, sweet, fruity. Cooking food over hickory chips adds another layer of flavor, as in these delicious steaks.

2   cups hickory chips
Four 10- to 12-ounce trimmed hanger steaks
Salt and freshly ground black pepper
Roasted Fall-Vegetable Hash (p. 263), for serving

1. Put the hickory chips in a medium bowl and cover with water. Let the chips stand for 1 hour, then drain.
2. Light a gas grill and turn it to high on one side; remove the grate over that side. Keep the grate over the other side of the grill. Make a foil box with heavy-duty foil, about 4 inches square. Set the foil box directly over the gas flame to heat. Put the drained hickory chips in the box. Close the grill until it fills with smoke, about 3 minutes. Lay the steaks on the grate opposite the smoke box, cover and smoke for 20 minutes. Transfer the smoked steaks to a large platter.
3. Remove the foil smoke box and replace the grate. Light the other side of the grill and turn the heat to high. Season the steaks with salt and pepper and grill until nicely charred outside and medium rare within, 4 to 5 minutes per side. Transfer the steaks to a carving board and let rest for 5 minutes. Thickly slice the steaks across the grain and serve with the Roasted Fall-Vegetable Hash. —*Kenny Callaghan*
MAKE AHEAD The smoked steaks can be refrigerated overnight. Bring to room temperature before grilling.
WINE Round, deep-flavored Syrah.

Grilled Skirt Steak and Peaches

TOTAL: 35 MIN

4 SERVINGS ●

2   garlic cloves
1   small bay leaf
1   small shallot
1   jalapeño, halved and seeded
Finely grated zest and juice of 1 lemon
2   tablespoons soy sauce
½   teaspoon chopped thyme
½   cup plus 1 tablespoon canola oil
Salt and freshly ground pepper
1½ pounds skirt steak, cut into 4 pieces
1   tablespoon Dijon mustard
½   cup very hot water
2   tablespoons honey
½   teaspoon cinnamon
1½ teaspoons finely grated fresh ginger
4   peaches, halved and pitted

1. In a blender, puree the garlic, bay leaf, shallot, jalapeño, lemon zest and juice, soy sauce and thyme. With the blender on, slowly pour in ½ cup of the oil and puree until smooth. Season the marinade with salt and pepper. Pour half of it into a shallow baking dish, add the steak and turn to coat. Let the steak stand for 20 minutes. Add the mustard to the remaining marinade and blend; transfer to a small bowl.
2. Light a grill. In a small saucepan, combine the water, honey, cinnamon and ginger. Let stand for 5 minutes. Transfer the mixture to a bowl with the remaining 1 tablespoon of oil and the peaches.
3. Scrape the marinade off the skirt steak. Generously season with salt and pepper. Grill over high heat, 6 to 7 minutes, turning once, for medium rare. At the same time, grill the peaches, turning frequently, until charred in spots and softened, 8 minutes; cut into wedges. Thinly slice the steaks. Transfer to plates and serve, passing the dressing on the side. —*David Burke*
WINE Ripe, juicy Pinot Noir.

Beef Tenderloin "Dogs" with Corn Relish

ACTIVE: 30 MIN; TOTAL: 45 MIN

4 SERVINGS ● ●

- 1 cup fresh corn kernels (from 2 ears)
- ¼ cup finely diced red bell pepper
- 2 tablespoons finely diced red onion
- 2 tablespoons finely diced celery
- ¼ cup cider vinegar
- 1½ teaspoons sugar
- Salt and freshly ground pepper
- 3 tablespoons canola oil
- ½ teaspoon minced garlic
- ½ teaspoon sweet paprika
- ½ teaspoon dry mustard
- ¼ teaspoon cayenne pepper
- One 1-pound center-cut beef tenderloin in 1 piece
- 1 baguette, halved lengthwise and cut into four 6-inch pieces

1. Light a grill. Bring a small saucepan of water to a boil. Add the corn and cook for 2 minutes. Drain and cool under running water. Shake off the excess water and pat the kernels dry. Transfer to a bowl and add the bell pepper, onion and celery.

2. In the same saucepan, heat the vinegar, sugar and a generous pinch each of salt and pepper just until the sugar dissolves. Pour the vinegar over the vegetables and refrigerate the corn relish until chilled.

3. In a bowl, stir the oil, garlic, paprika, mustard and cayenne; season generously with salt and pepper. Using a very sharp knife, quarter the tenderloin lengthwise to form 4 long "dogs." Rub with half of the seasoned oil. Brush the cut sides of the bread with the remaining seasoned oil.

4. Grill the dogs over high heat, turning occasionally, until lightly charred outside, about 10 minutes for medium rare. Grill the baguette, oiled side down, until lightly toasted. Serve the beef tenderloin dogs on the toasted baguette, topped generously with the corn relish. —*David Burke*
WINE Juicy, fresh Dolcetto.

GRILLED SKIRT STEAK AND PEACHES

BEEF TENDERLOIN "DOGS" WITH CORN RELISH

beef & lamb

Chile-Rubbed Flank Steak with White Polenta

ACTIVE: 50 MIN; TOTAL: 3 HR
4 SERVINGS

One 1¾-pound flank steak
4 garlic cloves, minced
3 Thai bird chiles, minced
¼ cup extra-virgin olive oil
3½ cups chicken stock or
    low-sodium broth
5½ ounces white polenta or stone-
    ground white cornmeal
    (1 cup)
Salt and freshly ground pepper
¼ cup mascarpone cheese
¼ cup freshly grated
    Parmesan cheese
Aged balsamic vinegar, for
    serving

1. In a large, shallow dish, coat the flank steak with the garlic and chiles. Drizzle with 2 tablespoons of the olive oil and set aside at room temperature for 2 hours.

2. In a medium saucepan, bring the chicken stock to a boil over high heat. Gradually whisk in the polenta and bring to a simmer. Cook over moderately low heat, whisking often, until the polenta is thick and no longer gritty, about 45 minutes.

3. Meanwhile, light a grill. Season the steak with salt and pepper and grill over a hot fire until nicely browned on the outside and medium rare within, about 4 minutes per side. Transfer the steak to a carving board and let rest for 5 minutes.

4. When the polenta is tender, stir in the mascarpone, Parmesan and the remaining 2 tablespoons of olive oil. Season the polenta with salt and pepper.

5. Slice the steak against the grain ¼ inch thick. Drizzle it with balsamic vinegar and serve with the polenta.
—*Ron Siegel*

MAKE AHEAD The flank steak can marinate overnight in the refrigerator. Bring to room temperature before grilling.
WINE Juicy, spicy Grenache.

Seared Tri-Tip Steak with Asian Black-Bean Rice Cakes

ACTIVE: 35 MIN; TOTAL: 1 HR 30 MIN
6 SERVINGS

½ cup mirin (sweet rice wine)
1 tablespoon unseasoned
    rice vinegar
1 cup water
Kosher salt
1 cup sushi or other short-grain
    rice, rinsed and drained
1 teaspoon minced peeled
    fresh ginger
3 tablespoons fermented black
    beans, rinsed and finely chopped
4 scallions, thinly sliced crosswise
One 2-pound tri-tip or sirloin steak
    (1½ to 2 inches thick)
Freshly ground pepper
3 tablespoons vegetable oil
Hoisin sauce, for serving

1. In a small saucepan, combine the mirin, vinegar, water and 1 teaspoon of salt; bring to a boil. Add the rice and bring to a boil. Cover and cook over low heat for 22 minutes, or until the liquid is absorbed and the rice is just tender. Stir in the minced ginger, black beans and sliced scallions.

2. Preheat the oven to 400°. Line six ½-cup ramekins or standard muffin cups with plastic. Pack with the warm rice; let cool.

3. Season the steak with salt and pepper. Heat 2 tablespoons of oil in a skillet. Add the steak and cook over moderately high heat for 8 minutes, until well browned on both sides. Transfer to a rimmed baking sheet; roast until an instant-read thermometer inserted in the center registers 130° for medium rare, 20 minutes. Transfer to a cutting board and let rest for 5 minutes. Heat the remaining oil in a large nonstick skillet. Unmold the rice cakes. Fry over moderately high heat until golden and crisp, turning, 2 minutes. Thickly slice the steak against the grain; serve with rice cakes and hoisin sauce. —*Douglas Keane*
WINE Rich, ripe Cabernet Sauvignon.

Garlicky Grilled Beef Tenderloin with Herbs

ACTIVE: 40 MIN; TOTAL: 50 MIN PLUS
2 TO 4 HR MARINATING
12 SERVINGS

Actress Jeri Ryan combines July Fourth and Bastille Day into one celebration with her French fiancé, chef Christophe Emé, at their house in Los Angeles. She prefers to serve a whole grilled beef tenderloin rather than grilled steaks because she finds it more magnificent and the flavor more delicate. When you're selecting a tenderloin, opt for a small one over a big one because it will be firmer.

One 4½-pound trimmed beef
    tenderloin
⅓ cup extra-virgin olive oil
6 garlic cloves, thinly sliced
2 tablespoons coarsely cracked
    black pepper
1 tablespoon chopped thyme
2 teaspoons chopped marjoram
2 teaspoons chopped rosemary
2 teaspoons kosher salt

1. Fold the thin end of the tenderloin roast under to make the meat an even thickness. Tie the beef tenderloin roast at 1-inch intervals with kitchen string and transfer it to a large rimmed baking sheet. In a small bowl, combine the olive oil with the garlic cloves, black pepper, chopped thyme, marjoram and rosemary and season with the kosher salt. Rub the herb oil all over the tenderloin roast and refrigerate it for 2 to 4 hours. Bring the tenderloin roast back to room temperature before putting it on the grill.

2. Light a grill. Grill the tenderloin roast directly over moderately high heat, turning it often, until the outside is nicely charred, about 30 minutes for medium-rare meat. Transfer the tenderloin to a carving board and let rest for 10 minutes. Carve the roast into ½-inch-thick slices and serve immediately. —*Jeri Ryan*
WINE Complex, aromatic Nebbiolo.

GARLICKY GRILLED BEEF
TENDERLOIN WITH HERBS

beef & lamb

Strip Steak and Vegetables with Garlicky Olivada

TOTAL: 30 MIN

4 SERVINGS ●

- 1 small red onion, cut crosswise into 4 thick slices
- ½ medium cauliflower, cut into 2-inch florets
- ¾ pound medium asparagus, trimmed
- 1 large yellow bell pepper, cored and quartered
- ¼ cup extra-virgin olive oil, plus more for brushing

Salt and freshly ground pepper

Four 8- to 10-ounce New York strip steaks, cut 1 inch thick

- 1 cup Garlicky Olivada (recipe follows)

1. Light a grill. Secure each onion slice on a toothpick. In a bowl, toss the onion and vegetables with ¼ cup of oil; season with salt and pepper. Brush the steaks with olive oil; season with salt and pepper. Grill the steaks over high heat, turning occasionally, about 8 minutes for medium rare. Grill the vegetables, turning, until crisp-tender and charred in spots, 8 to 10 minutes.

superfast
main course

LONDON BROIL WITH MUSTARD CRUMBS

Preheat the oven to 400°. Season a London broil on both sides with salt and pepper. Heat a very large sauté pan and sear the steak on both sides until nicely browned. Brush a thin layer of Dijon mustard over the steak and top with dried bread crumbs, patting to adhere. Roast the London broil in the oven until medium rare. Let rest for 5 minutes, then slice thinly to serve.
—Maria Helm Sinskey

2. Remove the toothpicks from the onion slices. In the large bowl, toss the grilled vegetables with ½ cup of the *olivada*. Transfer the vegetables to plates and set the grilled steaks alongside. Spoon the remaining ½ cup of *olivada* over the steaks and serve. *—Grace Parisi*
WINE Rich, ripe Cabernet Sauvignon.

GARLICKY OLIVADA

TOTAL: 10 MIN

MAKES 1 CUP ● ●

- 1 cup mixed pitted brine-cured olives, coarsely chopped
- 1 tablespoon chopped capers
- 2 small garlic cloves, smashed
- ½ teaspoon crushed red pepper
- 3 tablespoons red wine vinegar
- ½ cup extra-virgin olive oil

In a bowl, combine all of the ingredients.
OTHER USES Mix the *olivada* into mayonnaise to create a quick aioli to spread on bruschetta, or to mix into a tuna or chicken salad. Brush on bread, vegetables, fish, chicken, lamb or steak while grilling or serve on the side. *—G. P.*
MAKE AHEAD The *olivada* can be refrigerated for up to 3 days.

Grilled Bison Tenderloin with Black Rice and Shiso-Plum Compote

TOTAL: 1 HR

4 SERVINGS

Grass-fed bison has grown in popularity in California, where chef David Meyers of Sona in Los Angeles says people love its novelty but appreciate its likeness to beef. Meyers, who has a predilection for Asian flavors, serves the meat with nutty-tasting black rice from China and a sweet-tart plum compote flavored with the aromatic Japanese herb shiso.

- 4 tablespoons unsalted butter
- 1 cup Chinese black rice (see Note)
- 1 cup dry red wine
- 2 cups chicken stock or low-sodium broth

Salt

- 1½ pounds red or purple plums, pitted and cut into eighths
- 2½ tablespoons sugar
- 3 shiso leaves, shredded, or 2 tablespoons chopped celery leaves plus ½ tablespoon chopped tarragon

Four 8-ounce bison tenderloin steaks, 1½ inches thick, tied with string (see Note)

- 1 tablespoon pure olive oil

Freshly ground pepper

1. In a medium saucepan, melt 2 tablespoons of the butter. Add the rice and cook over moderate heat, stirring for 3 minutes. Add ½ cup of the wine and cook, stirring, until nearly evaporated, about 5 minutes. Add the stock and a pinch of salt and bring to a boil. Cover and cook over moderately low heat until the liquid is absorbed and the rice is tender, about 35 minutes.

2. In a large skillet, melt the remaining butter. Add the plums and cook over moderately high heat, stirring occasionally, until lightly browned, about 4 minutes. Add the remaining wine and the sugar and bring to a boil. Cover partially and cook over moderate heat until the plums are soft and the liquid is thick, about 4 minutes. Remove from the heat and stir in the shiso.

3. Preheat a grill. Rub the steaks with the olive oil; season generously with salt and pepper. Grill over a hot fire for 15 minutes, turning occasionally, until an instant-read thermometer inserted in the center registers 125° for medium rare. Let the steaks rest for 5 minutes, then snip off the strings. Transfer to plates and serve with the black rice and plum compote. *—David Myers*
NOTE Chinese black rice is available at Asian markets or specialty stores. Bison is available from lindnerbison.com or eastofadinbison.com.
MAKE AHEAD The black rice and plum compote can be refrigerated overnight.
WINE Intense, spicy Syrah.

Beef Tenderloin with Ancho and Fennel Seeds

ACTIVE: 20 MIN; TOTAL: 1 HR 20 MIN

8 SERVINGS

This luscious beef tenderloin won over more than a few skeptical cooks in F&W's test kitchen, who agreed that the seemingly discordant spice combination of ground anchos, fennel seeds and star anise not only works, but works brilliantly.

- 1 tablespoon plus 1 teaspoon fennel seeds
- 1 star anise pod, broken into pieces
- 2 tablespoons pure ancho chile powder

One trimmed 4-pound beef tenderloin roast

Salt and freshly ground pepper

- ¼ cup plus 2 tablespoons vegetable oil
- 1 cup water

1. Preheat the oven to 450°. In a spice grinder, grind the fennel seeds and star anise to a powder. Transfer to a small bowl and stir in the ancho powder.

2. Set the tenderloin on a large rimmed baking sheet and season all over with salt and pepper. Sprinkle the spice mixture all over the beef and evenly drizzle with the oil, then gently pat the spices into the meat. Roast the beef in the upper third of the oven for 35 minutes, turning once with sturdy tongs, until browned all over and an instant-read thermometer inserted in the thickest part registers 135° for medium-rare meat. Transfer to a carving board and let stand for up to 10 minutes.

3. Meanwhile, set the baking sheet over 2 burners and add the water. Simmer over moderate heat, scraping up the browned bits stuck to the bottom of the sheet, until reduced to ¾ cup, about 3 minutes. Season the jus with salt and pepper and transfer into a warmed gravy boat. Carve the tenderloin into ⅓-inch-thick slices and serve with the jus. —*Vitaly Paley*

WINE Ripe, juicy Pinot Noir.

Parmesan and Herb-Crusted Beef Tenderloin

ACTIVE: 40 MIN; TOTAL: 1 HR 45 MIN

12 TO 14 SERVINGS ●

This pepper-rubbed roasted beef tenderloin is coated with herbed bread crumbs mixed with anchovies, which adds a nice pungent accent to the rich meat.

Two 3-pound center-cut beef tenderloin roasts, at room temperature

- 2 tablespoons extra-virgin olive oil, plus more for rubbing

Salt

- 2 teaspoons coarsely cracked peppercorns
- 2 cups fresh bread crumbs
- ½ cup grated Parmesan cheese
- 3 anchovy fillets, minced
- 1 garlic clove, minced
- 1 tablespoon chopped thyme
- 1 tablespoon chopped flat-leaf parsley

Freshly ground black pepper

- 2 cups dry red wine
- 2 cups veal demiglace (see Note)
- 4 tablespoons cold unsalted butter, cut into tablespoons

1. Preheat the oven to 425°. Rub the tenderloins all over with olive oil and season them with salt and the cracked peppercorns. Set the roasts on a large, heavy-gauge rimmed baking sheet, allowing space between them, and roast in the upper third of the oven for 20 minutes.

2. In a medium bowl, mix the crumbs with the Parmesan, anchovies, garlic, thyme and parsley. Blend in the 2 tablespoons of olive oil; season with salt and pepper.

3. Carefully pack the bread crumbs on top of each tenderloin. Lower the oven temperature to 400° and roast the tenderloins for about 20 minutes, or until an instant-read thermometer inserted in the center registers 130° for medium rare. Using 2 long spatulas, transfer the beef to a carving board and let rest for 15 minutes.

4. Meanwhile, place the baking sheet over 2 burners. Add the wine and bring to a simmer over moderately high heat, scraping up any browned bits from the bottom of the sheet. Strain the wine into a medium saucepan and simmer over high heat until reduced to ½ cup. Whisk in the demiglace and bring the sauce to a boil; simmer for 3 minutes. Remove from the heat and let stand for 5 minutes. Whisk in the butter, 1 tablespoon at a time, and season the sauce with salt and pepper.

5. Carve the tenderloins into ½-inch-thick slices and serve, passing the sauce at the table. —*Maria Helm Sinskey*

NOTE Veal demiglace is available at specialty food stores and from D'Artagnan (800-327-8246 or dartagnan.com).

WINE Earthy, medium-bodied Tempranillo.

Tenderloin with Sake-Mirin Butter

TOTAL: 20 MIN

4 SERVINGS ●

- 2 tablespoons plus 1 teaspoon extra-virgin olive oil
- 2 garlic cloves, very finely chopped
- 4 tablespoons unsalted butter
- 2 tablespoons sake or dry sherry
- 1 tablespoon mirin (sweet rice wine)

Salt and freshly ground pepper

Four 6-ounce beef tenderloin steaks (3 inches thick)

1. In a small skillet, heat 1 teaspoon of the olive oil. Add the garlic and cook over low heat until fragrant but not browned, about 1½ minutes. Stir in the butter until melted, then add the sake and mirin. Season the sauce with salt and pepper and remove from the heat.

2. In a large skillet, heat the remaining 2 tablespoons of olive oil. Season the steaks with salt and pepper and cook over moderate heat until browned outside and rare within, about 7 minutes per side. Transfer to plates, drizzle with the sake-mirin butter and serve. —*Doug Stonebreaker*

WINE Deep, velvety Merlot.

beef & lamb

Scottish Beef Stew

ACTIVE: 45 MIN; TOTAL: 2 HR 30 MIN

4 SERVINGS ●

Scottish TV chef and cooking school owner Nick Nairn says that Scottish beef is some of the best in the world: "Our hardy wee beasts spend most of their time outdoors feeding on grass and have the minimum amount of human intervention in their rearing." He strongly advises seeking out well-marbled beef for the most tender and succulent stew.

> 2 tablespoons pure olive oil
>
> All-purpose flour, for dredging
>
> 2½ pounds well-marbled
>   boneless beef chuck,
>   cut into 1½-inch pieces
>
> Salt and freshly ground pepper
>
> 2 tablespoons unsalted butter
>
> 2 medium onions, cut into
>   ½-inch dice
>
> 2 carrots, cut into ½-inch dice
>
> 2 celery ribs, cut into ½-inch dice
>
> 4 ounces rutabaga, peeled and
>   cut into ½-inch dice (1 cup)
>
> 2 tablespoons red currant jelly
>
> 2 cups dry red wine
>
> 2 cups beef stock or
>   low-sodium broth
>
> 2 thyme sprigs
>
> 1 garlic clove, smashed
>
> 1 bay leaf
>
> Skirlie Potato Cakes (p. 269),
>   for serving

1. In an enameled cast-iron casserole, heat 1 tablespoon of the oil until shimmering. Spread the flour in a shallow bowl. Season the beef with salt and pepper and dredge in the flour; shake off any excess. Add half the meat to the casserole and cook over moderately high heat until browned on the bottom, 3 minutes. Reduce the heat to moderate and cook until browned on the other side, 2 minutes longer. With a slotted spoon, transfer the meat to a bowl. Repeat with the remaining tablespoon of oil and floured meat.

2. Melt the butter in the casserole. Add the onions, carrots, celery and rutabaga and cook over moderately low heat, stirring occasionally, until the onion is softened, 7 minutes. Add the jelly and the wine and bring to a boil over high heat, stirring to scrape up any browned bits on the bottom. Add the stock and bring to a boil. Add the browned meat and any accumulated juices along with the thyme, garlic and bay leaf and bring to a simmer. Cover and simmer over low heat until tender, 1½ hours.

3. With a slotted spoon, transfer the meat to a bowl. Boil the sauce over high heat until reduced to 2 cups, about 10 minutes. Return the meat to the casserole and season with salt and pepper. Discard the thyme sprig and bay leaf. Serve the beef stew with the potato cakes.
—Nick Nairn

MAKE AHEAD The stew can be refrigerated for up to 2 days.

WINE Firm, complex Cabernet Sauvignon.

Caesar Salad with Meatballs

TOTAL: 30 MIN

4 SERVINGS ●

This clever riff on a caesar salad includes juicy meatballs in place of the traditional croutons. The silky dressing is mixed in a blender without the typical egg yolks.

> 3 garlic cloves
>
> 2 anchovy fillets
>
> 2 tablespoons fresh lemon juice
>
> 2 tablespoons mayonnaise
>
> 1 teaspoon Worcestershire sauce
>
> 1 cup mild olive oil
>
> ½ cup plus 3 tablespoons freshly
>   grated Parmesan cheese
>
> Salt and freshly ground pepper
>
> 3 romaine hearts, coarsely
>   chopped
>
> 1 cup grape tomatoes, halved
>
> 2 slices of bacon, coarsely
>   chopped
>
> 3 tablespoons dry bread crumbs
>
> 3 tablespoons milk

> 1 large egg
>
> 1 tablespoon chopped basil
>
> ½ teaspoon thyme leaves
>
> ½ teaspoon hot sauce
>
> ¾ pound lean ground sirloin
>
> ¼ cup all-purpose flour

1. In a blender, puree 2 of the garlic cloves with the anchovy fillets, lemon juice, mayonnaise and Worcestershire sauce. With the blender on, add ½ cup of the olive oil in a thin stream and process until incorporated. Add ¼ cup of the Parmesan, season with salt and pepper and blend. Pour 2 tablespoons of the Caesar dressing into a medium bowl. Transfer the remaining dressing to a large bowl and add the lettuce, tomatoes and ¼ cup of the Parmesan; don't toss.

2. In a food processor, pulse the remaining garlic clove with the bacon until chopped. Add the bread crumbs, milk, egg, basil, thyme, hot sauce and the remaining 3 tablespoons of Parmesan; season generously with salt and pepper and process to a paste. Transfer to a bowl and knead in the sirloin. Working with 2 tablespoons of meat at a time, roll it into 18 balls. Dust the meatballs with the flour.

3. In a large skillet, heat the remaining ½ cup of oil until shimmering. Add the meatballs and cook over moderately high heat until golden and cooked through, about 8 minutes. Drain well on paper towels. Add the meatballs to the dressing in the medium bowl and toss gently. Toss the salad and transfer to plates. Top with the meatballs and serve. *—David Burke*

WINE Lively, fruity Merlot.

Spicy Steak Salad with Blue Cheese Dressing

TOTAL: 40 MIN

4 SERVINGS ●

> ¼ cup mild olive oil
>
> 1 serrano or jalapeño chile, halved
>   lengthwise and seeded
>
> 1 tablespoon dill

1 teaspoon chile powder
Salt and freshly ground pepper
1¼ pounds center-cut beef
   tenderloin, sliced ½ inch thick
1 small garlic clove, smashed
½ small shallot, sliced
1 tablespoon red wine vinegar
1 teaspoon Worcestershire sauce
½ teaspoon hot sauce
¼ cup mayonnaise
¼ cup sour cream
2 tablespoons milk
¼ pound crumbled Roquefort or
   Maytag blue cheese
2 romaine lettuce hearts, quartered
1 cup grape tomatoes, halved
1 Kirby cucumber, thinly sliced
½ small red onion, cut into thin rings
2 hard-cooked eggs, halved

1. In a mini food processor, combine the olive oil, serrano chile, dill, chile powder and a generous pinch of salt and pepper; puree. Transfer the marinade to a bowl, add the sliced meat and turn to coat. Let stand for 10 minutes.

2. Meanwhile, rinse out the food processor. Add the smashed garlic, sliced shallot, red wine vinegar, Worcestershire sauce and hot sauce to the food processer and process until the garlic and shallot are finely chopped. Add the mayonnaise, sour cream and milk and process until the mixture is smooth. Add the blue cheese and pulse once or twice to combine. Transfer the blue cheese dressing to a bowl and season with salt and pepper.

3. Preheat a grill pan. Grill the beef tenderloin slices over high heat for 5 to 6 minutes, turning once, for medium-rare meat.

4. Arrange the lettuce hearts, halved tomatoes, cucumber slices, onion rings and hard-cooked egg halves on plates and drizzle with the blue cheese dressing. Arrange the beef tenderloin slices on the plates and serve at once. —*David Burke*
WINE Rustic, peppery Malbec.

CAESAR SALAD WITH MEATBALLS

SPICY STEAK SALAD WITH BLUE CHEESE DRESSING

TAGLIATA WITH ARUGULA

SCALLION-AND-BRIE-STUFFED BURGERS

Tagliata with Arugula

ACTIVE: 20 MIN; TOTAL: 50 MIN

4 SERVINGS

Whether cooking for family or customers, Manhattan wine merchant Marco Pasanella gravitates toward simple Italian flavors as in this Tuscan-inspired steak salad.

- 1 garlic clove, minced
- 1½ teaspoons chopped rosemary
- 1½ teaspoons chopped sage
- Coarse sea salt and freshly ground pepper
- 1 boneless rib eye steak, cut 2 inches thick (2¼ pounds)
- Extra-virgin olive oil
- 1 bunch of arugula
- 1 tablespoon fresh lemon juice
- 1 cup shaved Parmesan cheese

1. Preheat the oven to 350°. Heat a cast-iron skillet. Mix the garlic, rosemary, sage, 1½ teaspoons of salt and ½ teaspoon of pepper in a bowl; rub over the steak.

2. Add 1 tablespoon of olive oil to the skillet. Cook the rib eye steak over moderate heat until it is browned all over. Stand the steak on its side in the skillet and roast in the oven for 20 minutes, or until an instant-read thermometer inserted in the center of the meat registers 135°. Transfer the steak to a cutting board and let rest for 10 minutes, then slice. Spread the arugula on a platter and top with the steak. Drizzle with oil and lemon juice and top with the Parmesan cheese shavings.

—*Marco Pasanella*

WINE Cherry-inflected, earthy Sangiovese.

Scallion-and-Brie-Stuffed Burgers

TOTAL: 30 MIN

4 SERVINGS ●

- 1½ pounds ground beef
- Salt and freshly ground pepper
- 4 ounces Brie, rind removed, cut into 4 slices
- ¼ cup Spicy Scallion Paste (recipe follows)
- Vegetable oil, for brushing
- ¼ cup mayonnaise
- 4 hamburger buns, split
- Tomato slices and lettuce, for serving

1. Light a grill. Season the ground beef with salt and pepper; form eight 4-inch patties that are slightly thicker in the center. Top each of 4 patties with a slice of Brie, a scant tablespoon of scallion paste and 1 of the remaining patties; pinch the edges to seal.

2. Brush the burgers with oil and grill over high heat, turning once or twice, about 8 minutes for medium-rare meat.

3. Mix the mayonnaise and remaining paste. Grill the buns until toasted. Spread mayonnaise on the bottoms; top with the burgers, tomatoes and lettuce. Close the burgers and serve. —*Grace Parisi*

WINE Deep, velvety Merlot.

SPICY SCALLION PASTE

TOTAL: 15 MIN

MAKES ¼ CUP ● ●

- 4 scallions, thinly sliced
- 2 garlic cloves, minced
- 1 fresh hot chile, seeded and minced
- ½ teaspoon finely grated lemon zest
- ¼ teaspoon cayenne pepper
- 2 tablespoons extra-virgin olive oil
- ½ teaspoon salt

In a small bowl, mix the scallions, garlic, chile, lemon zest and cayenne, mashing slightly with the back of a spoon. Stir in the olive oil and salt. —*G.P.*

OTHER USES Lightly brush the paste onto tofu, shrimp, steaks, chicken or pork before grilling.

Gouda Burgers with Grilled Onions and Pickled Peppers

TOTAL: 1 HR 15 MIN PLUS OVERNIGHT PICKLING FOR PEPPERS

4 SERVINGS

- 1½ pounds ground beef chuck
- 1 cup shredded lightly aged Gouda cheese plus 4 slices, cut ¼ inch thick (7 ounces total)
- 1 medium sweet onion, cut crosswise into four ½-inch rounds

Vegetable oil, for brushing

Salt and freshly ground pepper

- 2 tablespoons unsalted butter, softened
- 4 hamburger buns, split
- 1 head Bibb lettuce, separated into leaves
- 1 large tomato, thinly sliced

Pickled Grilled Peppers (recipe follows)

1. Light a grill. In a large bowl, mix the beef with the shredded Gouda. Form into 4 patties. Thread each onion slice onto 2 bamboo or metal skewers. Brush with oil and season with salt and pepper. Grill the onions over a hot fire until nicely charred, about 3 minutes per side.

2. Season the patties on both sides with salt and pepper and grill for 4 minutes per side for medium rare. Top the patties with the sliced Gouda, cover and grill until the cheese is melted, about 2 minutes. Butter the buns and grill them, cut side down, until they are toasted, about 10 seconds.

3. Place a few lettuce leaves and tomato slices on the bottom halves of the buns and set the cheeseburgers on top. Cover with the grilled onions and top with some of the pickled peppers. Close the burgers and serve with the remaining pickled peppers on the side. —*Steven Raichlen*

WINE Fruity, luscious Shiraz.

PICKLED GRILLED PEPPERS

ACTIVE: 40 MIN; TOTAL: 40 MIN PLUS OVERNIGHT PICKLING

4 TO 6 SERVINGS ● ●

- 1 large red bell pepper
- 1 large yellow bell pepper
- 1 large orange bell pepper
- 1 large green bell pepper
- 2 cups distilled white vinegar
- 2 cups water
- ½ cup sugar
- 2½ tablespoons kosher salt
- 5 dill sprigs
- 3 garlic cloves, halved
- 2 dried red chiles, crushed

1. Light a grill. Set the bell peppers over a hot fire and grill, turning as necessary, until charred all over. Transfer the peppers to a large plate and let cool. Peel the peppers and discard the cores and seeds. Cut the peppers into thin strips.

2. In a medium bowl, combine the white vinegar with the water, sugar and salt and stir to dissolve the sugar and salt. Add the dill sprigs, halved garlic, crushed dried red chiles and the grilled pepper strips to the pickling solution and refrigerate overnight. Bring the peppers to room temperature before serving, lifting them from the pickling liquid with a slotted spoon. —*S.R.*

Stilton Sirloin Burgers with Onion Jam

TOTAL: 50 MIN

4 SERVINGS

- 2 tablespoons extra-virgin olive oil
- 1 large red onion, halved and thinly sliced

Kosher salt

- 1 cup dry red wine
- 2 tablespoons red wine vinegar
- 2 teaspoons honey
- 1 thyme sprig

Freshly ground pepper

- 2 pounds ground sirloin
- 4 ounces Stilton cheese, cut into 4 slices
- 4 hamburger buns or kaiser rolls, split
- 1 large tomato, sliced ¼ inch thick
- 4 Boston lettuce leaves

Dill pickles, for serving

1. In a skillet, heat the olive oil. Add the onion and a pinch of salt. Cook over moderately low heat, stirring, until softened but not browned, 10 minutes. Add the wine, vinegar, honey and thyme and simmer over moderately low heat, stirring frequently, until all the liquid has evaporated, 15 minutes. Discard the thyme and season the jam with salt and pepper.

2. Light a grill or preheat the broiler. Generously season the meat with salt and pepper. With your hands, mix gently and shape into four 1-inch-thick patties. Lightly season with salt and pepper.

3. Grill the patties over a hot fire or broil 2 inches from the heat, turning once, until charred on the outside and pink within, 3 minutes per side. Just before they're done, top the burgers with the Stilton and let melt. Transfer to a plate. Lightly grill the buns.

4. Set the burgers on the buns. Top with the onion jam, tomato slices and lettuce and serve with pickles. —*Terry Crandall*

SERVE WITH Sweet Potato Fries (p. 268).

WINE Fruity, luscious Shiraz.

beef & lamb

Baby Burgers with Angry Onions

ACTIVE: 30 MIN; TOTAL: 40 MIN

4 SERVINGS ●

At David Burke at Bloomingdale's, in New York City, chef David Burke serves his adorable mini burgers on homemade rolls with Asiago cheese. In this simplified version, the mini burgers are topped with cheddar and "angry" (spicy) onions.

Vegetable oil
- 1 small onion, thinly sliced
- 1 teaspoon Cajun spice mix
- 6 slices of bacon
- 1½ pounds lean ground beef

Salt and freshly ground black
    pepper
- 12 small dinner rolls or
    biscuits, split horizontally
- 1 large half-sour or dill pickle,
    thinly sliced
- 2 plum tomatoes, thinly sliced

Twelve 2-inch-square slices
    of cheddar cheese
    (about 3 ounces)

1. Preheat the oven to 350°. Oil a parchment paper–lined baking sheet. Arrange the thinly sliced onion rings on the parchment paper in a single layer and sprinkle them all over with the Cajun spice mix. Bake the onion slices for about 30 minutes, until they are slightly dry and browned in spots.

2. Meanwhile, in a medium skillet, cook the bacon slices over moderate heat until they are crisp, about 6 minutes. Drain the bacon slices on paper towels and cut them into 2-inch pieces.

3. Season the ground beef with salt and pepper and form into 12 small hamburger patties. Arrange the dinner rolls on a large baking sheet. Place a pickle slice on the bottom half of each roll, then top the pickle with a tomato slice.

4. Preheat a grill pan or a griddle. Brush the beef patties with vegetable oil and cook them over high heat, turning once, until they are browned, about 3 minutes. Set the baby burgers on the dinner roll bottoms and top each of them with a slice of cheddar cheese, a few onion rings and some of the crisp bacon. Cover the baby burgers with the roll tops and bake them in the oven for 5 minutes for medium-rare meat. Serve the hot burgers immediately.

—David Burke

WINE Intense, fruity Zinfandel.

technique

the perfect burger

Tim Goodell, owner of Hollywood's 25 Degrees, uses organic meat to make fantastic burgers, like his Red Chili Burgers (p. 137). Here are his tips for the perfect burger:

1. For a juicy burger, use a mix of 45 percent beef chuck, 45 percent beef sirloin and 10 percent pork fatback.

2. If you're grinding the beef yourself, don't trim any fat; it adds flavor and moisture.

3. Never mix salt into the ground beef when you're forming the patties, as this will dry out the burgers. Season liberally with salt just before grilling.

4. Prior to cooking, preheat the grill on high for 15 to 20 minutes and make sure the grates are clean.

5. To avoid flame-ups and charring, never grill with high heat.

6. Add cheese during the last minute of grilling and close the lid to melt the cheese.

7. Use the ripest tomatoes seasoned with salt and pepper and place them directly on the burger.

Hamburgers with Chowchow

TOTAL: 30 MIN

4 SERVINGS ●

Chowchow, a vibrant vegetable-and-pickle relish, is rumored to have been introduced to the United States by Chinese railroad workers in the 19th century.

- ½ pound green cabbage, cored and
    coarsely chopped (4 cups)
- ½ pound green or unripe tomatoes,
    cored and coarsely chopped
- 1 red bell pepper, coarsely chopped
- 1 small onion, coarsely chopped
- ½ cup cider vinegar
- ½ cup sugar
- 1½ teaspoons celery seeds
- ½ teaspoon turmeric
- ¼ teaspoon cayenne pepper

Kosher salt
- 1½ pounds ground beef

Freshly ground black pepper
- 4 hamburger buns, split

1. Light a grill or preheat a grill pan. Finely chop the green cabbage in a food processor and transfer it to a large, heavy pot. Put the chopped tomatoes, bell pepper and onion in the processor and finely chop; add to the pot of cabbage. Add the cider vinegar, sugar, celery seeds, turmeric, cayenne and 1½ teaspoons of kosher salt to the pot and bring the pickle relish to a boil over high heat. Cook the chowchow over moderate heat, stirring occasionally, until it's cooked down to about 2 cups, about 10 minutes.

2. Meanwhile, form the ground beef into 4 patties and season with salt and pepper. Grill the burgers until nicely charred outside and medium rare within, about 3 minutes per side. Grill the buns, cut side down, until toasted, about 20 seconds.

3. Set the grilled hamburgers on the bottom halves of the buns. Spoon a thick layer of chowchow on the burgers, top with the toasted buns and serve right away.

—Amy Tornquist

WINE Lively, fruity Merlot.

Green-Chile Burgers with Fried Eggs

TOTAL: 30 MIN

4 SERVINGS ● ●

2¼ pounds ground chuck, preferably organic

Salt and freshly ground pepper

½ pound mild American blue cheese, such as Maytag, cut into 4 thin slices

Vegetable oil

4 large eggs

4 brioche buns, split

4 tablespoons unsalted butter, melted

1 cup Green-Chile Relish (recipe follows), warmed up

Light a grill. Gently form the beef into 4 thick patties; season with salt and pepper. Grill over moderately high heat until lightly charred on the outside and medium rare within, 5 minutes per side. Just before the burgers are done, top each with a slice of cheese and let melt. Heat a large cast-iron skillet and brush lightly with oil. Crack the eggs into the pan and cook sunny-side up over moderate heat, 4 minutes. Spread the cut sides of the buns with butter and toast on the grill. Transfer the burgers to the buns. Top with the Green-Chile Relish and the fried eggs; serve. —*Tim Goodell*

WINE Fruity, light-bodied Beaujolais.

GREEN-CHILE RELISH

TOTAL: 30 MIN

MAKES ABOUT 1 CUP ● ● ●

1 pound long green New Mexico or Anaheim chiles

3 garlic cloves, minced

Salt and freshly ground pepper

Roast the chiles over a gas flame or under a preheated broiler, turning often, until charred all over. Transfer them to a plate and let cool. Discard the skin, seeds and stems. Cut the chiles into ½-inch dice. Transfer to a bowl. Stir in the garlic. Season with salt and pepper. —*T.G.*

Salt-Crusted Prime Rib Roast

ACTIVE: 30 MIN; TOTAL: 5 HR 15 MIN

14 SERVINGS

1½ cups kosher salt

¾ cup coarsely ground black pepper

1 head of garlic, peeled

½ cup rosemary leaves

2 tablespoons chile powder

¾ cup extra-virgin olive oil

One 15- to 16-pound prime rib roast (6 bones) (see Note)

1. In a food processor, process the salt, black pepper, garlic cloves, rosemary and chile powder until fine. Add the olive oil and pulse to form a paste. Place the rib roast on a cutting board, bone side up, and rub with 1 tablespoon of the paste. Transfer the meat to a large roasting pan and pack the salt paste all over the fatty surface, pressing to help it adhere. Let the roast stand at room temperature for 1 hour.

2. Preheat the oven to 450°. Roast the prime rib roast for 1 hour, until the crust is slightly darkened. Lower the oven temperature to 300°. Roast for about 2 hours and 15 minutes longer, until an instant-read thermometer inserted into the center of the roast (not touching the bone) registers 135°. Transfer the roast to a large carving board and let rest for 30 minutes.

3. Carefully lift the salt crust off the prime rib roast and transfer it to a bowl. Brush away any excess salt from the roast. To remove the roast in one piece while keeping the rib rack intact, run a long sharp carving knife along the bones, using them as your guide. Leave ½ inch of meat on the bones, more if reserving for leftovers. Carve the prime rib roast ½ inch thick and serve right away, passing some of the crumbled salt crust as a condiment. —*Tim Love*

NOTE To make the Sticky Barbecue Beef Ribs (recipe at right), reserve the rib bones in Step 3.

WINE Complex, aromatic Nebbiolo.

Sticky Barbecued Beef Ribs

ACTIVE: 30 MIN; TOTAL: 1 HR

MAKES 6 RIBS ●

These beef ribs—leftovers from the Salt-Crusted Prime Rib Roast at left—are incredibly luscious. They're doused in a sweet and tangy homemade barbecue sauce, then cooked on the grill until they're crusty, sizzling and outrageously good.

2 tablespoons extra-virgin olive oil

1 large celery rib, finely chopped

1 carrot, finely chopped

1 small onion, finely chopped

3 ancho chiles—stemmed, seeded and cut into small pieces

2 cups chicken stock or low-sodium broth

1 cup ketchup

¼ cup distilled white vinegar

¼ cup molasses

¼ cup dark brown sugar

¼ teaspoon dry mustard

Salt

Rack of 6 ribs (reserved from the recipe at left), at room temperature

1. In a large saucepan, heat the olive oil until shimmering. Add the celery, carrot and onion and cook over moderate heat, stirring, until lightly browned, 10 minutes. Add the anchos and cook until fragrant, 2 minutes. Add the stock, ketchup, vinegar, molasses, sugar and mustard and simmer over moderate heat until the sauce is reduced to about 3 cups, 30 minutes.

2. In a blender, puree the mixture until smooth. Return the sauce to the saucepan and simmer until thickened and reduced to 2¾ cups, 5 minutes. Season with salt.

3. Light a grill. Cut in between the bones to separate the rack into individual ribs. Grill over moderate heat, turning, until crusty and sizzling, 10 minutes. Brush generously with sauce and grill, turning, until deeply glazed, 5 minutes. Serve with the extra sauce on the side.—*Tim Love*

WINE Intense, fruity Zinfandel.

RED CHILI BURGER

Red Chili Burgers

ACTIVE: 30 MIN; TOTAL: 1 HR 30 MIN

4 SERVINGS ●

2¼ pounds ground chuck,
preferably organic

Salt and freshly ground pepper

½ pound Crescenza Stracchino
or buffalo mozzarella, cut into
4 slices (see Note)

4 tablespoons unsalted butter,
melted

4 brioche buns, split

1 cup prepared sauerkraut, warmed

1 cup Red Chili (recipe follows),
warmed up

1 cup Griddled Onions (recipe
follows), warmed up

1. Light a grill. Gently form 4 thick beef patties and season generously with salt and pepper. Grill over moderately high heat until lightly charred on the outside and medium rare within, about 5 minutes per side. Just before the burgers are done, lay a slice of cheese on each one to melt.

2. Butter the cut sides of the buns and toast on the grill. Set the burgers on the buns. Top with the sauerkraut, chili and onions and serve at once. —*Tim Goodell*

NOTE Crescenza Stracchino is a creamy cow's-milk cheese, similar to fresh mozzarella. We like BelGioioso brand, available at cheese shops or specialty stores.

WINE Intense, fruity Zinfandel.

RED CHILI

ACTIVE: 15 MIN; TOTAL: 1 HR 20 MIN

MAKES ABOUT 4½ CUPS ●

2 tablespoons extra-virgin olive oil

3 garlic cloves, minced

1 small onion, finely chopped

1½ pounds ground chuck

½ pound fresh chorizo, removed
from the casings and crumbled

¼ cup ancho chile powder

½ teaspoon cayenne pepper

One 14½-ounce can chopped tomatoes

Salt and freshly ground pepper

In a saucepan, heat the oil. Add the garlic and onion. Cook over moderate heat until softened, 5 minutes. Add the beef and chorizo. Cook over moderately high heat, stirring, until browned, 5 minutes. Add the chile powder and cayenne and cook over low heat, stirring, until fragrant. Add the tomatoes and their juices and simmer for 1 hour, stirring occasionally. Season with salt and pepper. —*T.G.*

GRIDDLED ONIONS

ACTIVE: 15 MIN; TOTAL: 1 HR 10 MIN

MAKES ABOUT 1½ CUPS ●

3 tablespoons extra-virgin olive oil

4 medium yellow onions,
thinly sliced

Salt and freshly ground pepper

In a skillet, heat the olive oil. Add the onions and cook over moderate heat, stirring occasionally, until almost golden, 15 minutes. Reduce the heat to moderately low. Cook, stirring occasionally, until softened and richly browned, 45 minutes. Season with salt and pepper. —*Sue Moore*

Beef-Stuffed Poblano Chiles

ACTIVE: 45 MIN; TOTAL: 2 HR

10 SERVINGS ●

¼ cup extra-virgin olive oil, plus
more for rubbing

2 medium white onions, coarsely
chopped

6 garlic cloves, finely chopped

Two 28-ounce cans diced tomatoes

10 large poblano chiles (about
6 ounces each)

1 habanero chile

Salt and freshly ground pepper

2 pounds ground sirloin

1 cup pitted green Spanish olives,
sliced

3 tablespoons drained small capers

2 tablespoons dried currants

1 tablespoon ground cumin

¼ cup water

¼ cup chopped cilantro

1. In a large saucepan, heat 2 tablespoons of olive oil until shimmering. Add half each of the onion and garlic and cook over moderate heat until softened, 6 minutes. Add the tomatoes and their juices. Cook over moderate heat for 25 minutes.

2. Light a grill or preheat the broiler. Rub the poblanos and habanero lightly with oil and grill or broil, turning frequently, until charred but still firm, 3 minutes. Transfer the habanero to a plate; set aside. Transfer the poblanos to a bowl, cover with plastic. Let stand for 15 minutes, until cool. Peel the poblanos. Be careful not to rip the flesh. Cut a lengthwise slit down one side of each; carefully remove the core and seeds.

3. Working in batches, puree the sauce until smooth; return it to the pan and add the whole, unpeeled charred habanero. Simmer the sauce over moderate heat, stirring occasionally, until very thick, 40 minutes; be careful not to break the habanero or the sauce will be extremely spicy. Remove the habanero and discard. Season the tomato sauce with salt and pepper.

4. In a large, deep skillet, heat the remaining 2 tablespoons of oil until shimmering. Add the remaining onion and garlic; cook over moderate heat, stirring occasionally, until softened, 6 minutes. Add the ground beef and cook, breaking it up, until no trace of pink remains, 8 minutes. Add the olives, capers, currants, cumin and water and season with salt and pepper. Cook over moderate heat until the liquid is nearly evaporated, 2 to 3 minutes. Let cool.

5. Preheat the oven to 400°. Spoon 1 cup of sauce into a 13-by-9-inch glass baking dish. Stir ¼ cup of tomato sauce into the beef; season with salt and pepper. Stuff each chile with about ⅔ cup of filling; carefully arrange in the dish. Cover with foil and bake for 15 minutes, until heated through. Sprinkle the stuffed poblanos with cilantro and serve, passing the extra sauce at the table. —*Mateo Granados*

WINE Rustic, peppery Malbec.

beef & lamb

Smoky Meat Loaf with Prune Ketchup

ACTIVE: 30 MIN; TOTAL: 1 HR 40 MIN

8 TO 10 SERVINGS ●

- 1 tablespoon celery seeds
- 1 tablespoon fennel seeds
- 1 tablespoon black peppercorns
- 1 star anise pod, broken
- 2 tablespoons vegetable oil
- ¼ cup minced onion
- ¼ cup minced fennel bulb
- 1 small celery rib, minced
- 1 garlic clove, minced
- 2 tablespoons sweet pimentón de la Vera (smoked Spanish paprika)
- 1 pound sliced bacon, chopped
- 3 pounds ground beef chuck
- 3 large eggs, beaten
- ¼ cup pure maple syrup
- 1 cup fresh pumpernickel bread crumbs
- ½ cup shelled unsalted pistachios
- 1 tablespoon plus 1 teaspoon kosher salt or smoked sea salt

Prune Ketchup (recipe follows), for serving

1. Preheat the oven to 350°. Grind the celery and fennel seeds, peppercorns and star anise to a powder in a spice grinder.

2. In a skillet, heat the oil. Add the onion, fennel, celery, garlic, pimentón and ground spices and cook over low heat, stirring occasionally, until softened, 8 minutes. Cool to room temperature.

3. In a food processor, pulse the bacon until fine. In a bowl, mix the bacon with the ground beef. Mix in the eggs and maple syrup, then the vegetable mixture, bread crumbs, pistachios and salt.

4. Pat the meat into two 9-by-4-inch loaves and set on opposite sides of a large rimmed baking sheet. Bake for 1 hour, or until an instant-read thermometer inserted in the center registers 160°. Let rest for 10 minutes. Cut into thick slices and serve with Prune Ketchup. —*Grant Achatz*

WINE Fruity, light-bodied Beaujolais.

PRUNE KETCHUP

ACTIVE: 10 MIN; TOTAL: 30 MIN

MAKES 1⅓ CUPS ● ●

This sweet-tart condiment is a great complement to meat loaf and sausages as well as simply cooked duck and pork.

- 1 cup pitted prunes
- 1 cup water
- ¼ cup unsulfured molasses
- ¼ cup sherry vinegar
- 2 tablespoons sugar
- 1 star anise pod

Salt and freshly ground black pepper

1. In a medium saucepan, bring all of the ingredients to a boil. Simmer over moderate heat until the pitted prunes are very soft, about 20 minutes. Discard the star anise pod.

2. Puree the ketchup in a food processor. Transfer the prune ketchup to a bowl and season it with salt and pepper. —*G.A.*

MAKE AHEAD The prune ketchup can be refrigerated for up to 1 week.

Beef Chili with Beans

ACTIVE: 30 MIN; TOTAL: 2 HR 30 MIN

8 SERVINGS

"Chili means Halloween to me," chef Grant Achatz of Alinea in Chicago says. When he was growing up, his mother always served it to him and his cousins before they went trick-or-treating as a way to counteract the sugar buzz to come. This smoky, spicy version is a slightly modified version of his mother's chili, made with ancho, pasilla and chipotle powders, plus a homemade blend of seasonings and fresh herbs.

- 3 tablespoons vegetable oil
- 3 pounds ground beef chuck
- 2 large onions, finely chopped
- 1 green bell pepper, finely chopped
- 5 garlic cloves, finely chopped
- 3 tablespoons pure ancho chile powder
- 3 tablespoons pure pasilla chile powder
- 3 tablespoons ground cumin
- 2 tablespoons ground coriander
- 1 tablespoon sugar
- 2 teaspoons chopped thyme
- 2 teaspoons chopped oregano
- 1 teaspoon freshly ground black pepper
- 1 teaspoon cayenne pepper
- 3 cups low-sodium beef broth

One 15-ounce can pinto beans

One 14-ounce can diced tomatoes with their juices

- 5 chipotle chiles in adobo sauce, seeded and finely chopped
- 1 cup tomato sauce
- ¼ cup tomato paste
- 1 tablespoon cider vinegar

Juice of 1 lime

Salt

1. In a large, heavy pot or a medium enameled cast-iron casserole, heat the vegetable oil. Add half of the ground beef chuck and cook it over high heat, breaking the ground meat up with a wooden spoon, until it is browned, about 5 minutes; transfer it to a large bowl with a slotted spoon. Brown the remaining beef. Return the first batch of beef to the casserole. Add the onions and green bell pepper and cook over moderate heat, stirring occasionally, until the onions are translucent, about 8 minutes.

2. Add the garlic, ancho chile powder, pasilla chile powder, cumin, coriander, sugar, thyme, oregano, black pepper and cayenne and cook the chili for 10 minutes, stirring occasionally.

3. Stir in the beef broth, pinto beans, tomatoes with their juices, chipotles in adobo sauce, tomato sauce, tomato paste and the cider vinegar. Simmer the beef chili on low heat for 1½ hours, stirring occasionally. Add the lime juice to the chili, season it with salt and serve right away. —*Grant Achatz*

WINE Intense, fruity Zinfandel.

BEEF CHILI WITH BEANS

beef & lamb

Indian-Style Grilled Short Ribs

TOTAL: 30 MIN PLUS 3 DAYS MARINATING

4 SERVINGS

These succulent, crusty ribs are marinated in an Indian-inspired combination of garlic, ginger, tomato and coriander.

- 6 garlic cloves, coarsely chopped
- 2 tablespoons minced fresh ginger
- ¼ cup dry red wine
- 3 tablespoons red wine vinegar
- 3 tablespoons pure maple syrup
- 3 tablespoons vegetable oil
- 3 tablespoons tomato paste
- 1 tablespoon rosemary leaves
- 1 tablespoon kosher salt
- 2 teaspoons thyme
- 1½ teaspoons freshly ground pepper
- 1 teaspoon ground coriander
- ½ teaspoon ground allspice
- ½ teaspoon sweet paprika
- ¼ teaspoon ground ginger
- ¼ teaspoon ground cloves
- ¼ teaspoon cayenne pepper
- 8 beef short ribs on the bone (1 pound each), fat trimmed

Celery Root and Apple Slaw (p. 262), for serving

1. In a blender, puree the garlic, ginger and wine. Scrape into a bowl and stir in all of the remaining ingredients except for the ribs. Pour into 2 resealable plastic bags. Add the ribs, tightly seal and refrigerate for 3 days.

2. Light a grill. Remove the ribs from the marinade, scraping off any excess. Grill over moderately high heat until lightly charred and medium rare, 5 minutes per side. Serve with Celery Root and Apple Slaw on the side. —*Floyd Cardoz*

WINE Fruity, luscious Shiraz.

Lamb Chops with Vinaigrette

TOTAL: 25 MIN

4 SERVINGS ●

"Everything in this recipe is Greek but you just might not realize it," says Michael Psilakis, chef and owner of Onera and Dona in Manhattan. The lamb, almonds, lemon and onion show up on tables all over Greece, and the bulgur is ubiquitous on the Greek island of Crete.

- ½ cup plus 3 tablespoons extra-virgin olive oil
- 1 small onion, halved and thinly sliced
- 1 cup medium-grind cracked bulgur wheat
- 1½ cups chicken stock or broth
- ¼ cup fresh lemon juice
- 1½ teaspoons Dijon mustard
- 1½ teaspoons dried Greek oregano
- 2 teaspoons roasted garlic paste from a tube (see Note)

Kosher salt and freshly ground pepper

- ½ cup slivered almonds
- 8 lamb loin chops (about 1¾ pounds)
- 4 ounces prewashed baby arugula (5 cups)

1. In a saucepan, heat 1 tablespoon of the olive oil. Add the onion and cook over moderate heat until translucent. Add the bulgur and stir to coat. Add the stock; bring to a boil. Reduce the heat, cover and simmer over low heat until the stock is absorbed and the bulgur is tender, 10 minutes.

2. In a blender, combine the lemon juice with the mustard, oregano and garlic paste and puree until smooth. With the machine on, slowly pour in ½ cup of the olive oil. Season with salt and pepper.

3. In a very large skillet, toast the almonds over moderate heat, stirring, until golden, about 3 minutes. Transfer to a plate.

4. In the same skillet, heat the remaining 2 tablespoons of oil until shimmering. Season the lamb chops generously with salt and pepper, add to the skillet and cook over moderately high heat, turning once, for 6 minutes total for medium rare.

5. Stir ⅓ cup of the dressing into the bulgur. Add the almonds and season with salt and pepper. In another bowl, toss the arugula with 3 tablespoons of the vinaigrette. Spoon the bulgur onto plates and top with the chops. Mound the arugula alongside and serve, passing the remaining vinaigrette at the table. —*Michael Psilakis*

NOTE Look for roasted garlic paste at specialty food markets.

WINE Cherry-inflected, earthy Sangiovese.

tools
fire starters

1. BARREL CHIPS
Made from pieces of the barrels used to age bourbon. **Details $7 for 2 lbs; northwoodssmokeofmn.com.**

2. BINCHOTAN CHARCOAL
A centuries-old low-smoke charcoal used in Japan for robata grilling and to grill seafood and vegetables. **Details $13 for 500 gm of briquettes at Korin; 800-626-2172.**

3. BAMBOO CHARCOAL
A clean-burning, virtually smokeless charcoal great for grilling meat, poultry, fish and vegetables. **Details $5 for 100 gm of briquettes at Korin; 800-626-2172.**

4. GROOVED CHARCOAL
Kingsford's Sure Fire Grooves provide air channels for fast heating and even burning. **Details $3 for 4½ lbs; kingsford.com.**

Lamb Cutlets with Romesco

TOTAL: 40 MIN

4 SERVINGS ● ●

1½ pounds boneless lamb leg steaks, cut ½ inch thick and lightly pounded

Salt and freshly ground pepper

½ cup all-purpose flour

2 large eggs, beaten

1½ cups *panko* (Japanese bread crumbs)

1 medium tomato, seeded and chopped

1 roasted red pepper from a jar

1 garlic clove

¼ cup salted roasted almonds

2 tablespoons red wine vinegar

Pinch of sugar

¼ cup extra-virgin olive oil, plus more for frying

2 ounces fresh goat cheese, crumbled (¼ cup)

2 tablespoons snipped chives

2 tablespoons coarsely chopped flat-leaf parsley

1. Season the lamb with salt and pepper. Put the flour, eggs and *panko* in 3 shallow bowls; season each with salt and pepper. Dredge the lamb in the flour, then dip in the eggs and coat with *panko.* Transfer the lamb to a plate.

2. In a blender, combine the tomato, roasted pepper, garlic, almonds, vinegar and sugar and process until smooth. With the machine on, add the ¼ cup of olive oil in a thin stream and blend until creamy. Season the sauce with salt and pepper.

3. In a large skillet, heat ¼ inch of olive oil until shimmering. Add the breaded cutlets and cook over moderately high heat, turning once, until golden and crisp, 7 minutes. Drain on paper towels; transfer to plates. Spoon some of the *romesco* sauce over the lamb and garnish with the goat cheese, chives and parsley. Serve the remaining sauce on the side. —*Jose Garces*

WINE Juicy, spicy Grenache.

Minty Lamb and Sausage Orzo with Grilled Artichokes

TOTAL: 30 MIN

4 SERVINGS ● ●

½ pound ground lamb

½ pound sweet Italian sausage, casings removed

¼ cup plus 2 tablespoons Mint Pesto (recipe follows)

2 tablespoons extra-virgin olive oil, plus more for brushing

1 cup marinated artichoke hearts, drained (6 ounces)

Salt

1 cup orzo

1 large ripe tomato, diced

¼ pound feta cheese, crumbled

Freshly ground pepper

1. Light a grill. Bring a medium saucepan of water to a boil. In a medium bowl, mix the lamb and sausage with 3 tablespoons of the pesto. Form the mixture into eight 3-inch patties and brush with olive oil. Thread the artichoke hearts onto skewers. Grill over high heat until the meat is cooked through and the artichokes are lightly charred, about 8 minutes.

2. Salt the boiling water. Add the orzo and cook until al dente; drain. Transfer to a bowl. Add the tomato, feta and remaining pesto. Remove the artichokes from the skewers and add to the orzo. Crumble the patties into the orzo and add 2 tablespoons of olive oil. Season with salt and pepper, toss well and serve.—*Grace Parisi*

WINE Fresh, fruity rosé.

MINT PESTO

TOTAL: 10 MIN

MAKES ½ CUP ● ●

¾ cup packed mint leaves

¼ cup flat-leaf parsley leaves

2 scallions, thickly sliced

2 medium garlic cloves

½ teaspoon finely grated lemon zest

2 tablespoons extra-virgin olive oil

Salt

In a food processor, pulse the mint, parsley, scallions, garlic and lemon zest until chopped. With the machine on, add the olive oil in a thin stream; process until smooth. Season with salt.—*G.P.*

Braised Lamb with Peppers and Oregano

ACTIVE: 45 MIN; TOTAL: 3 HR

6 SERVINGS ●

¼ cup extra-virgin olive oil

3 pounds boneless lamb shoulder, cut into 3-inch chunks

Salt and freshly ground pepper

½ cup water

4 Italian frying peppers, chopped

3 large tomatoes, coarsely chopped

2 large onions, coarsely chopped

2 tablespoons minced oregano

1. Preheat the oven to 300°. If you have an unglazed clay pot like a Römertopf, soak it in warm water for 30 minutes. Pat the clay pot dry.

2. Meanwhile, heat the olive oil in a large skillet. Season the lamb with salt and pepper. Add half of the lamb to the skillet and cook over high heat until browned, about 10 minutes. Transfer the lamb to the clay pot or a medium enameled cast-iron casserole. Repeat with the remaining lamb.

3. Pour off the fat in the skillet. Add the water and bring to a boil, scraping up any browned bits stuck to the bottom. Pour the liquid into the clay pot and add the peppers, tomatoes, onions and oregano. Cover and bake for 2 hours and 15 minutes, or until the lamb is very tender.

4. Pour the stew into a large strainer set over a large saucepan. Skim the fat from the juices and boil until reduced to ¾ cup, 10 minutes. Return the lamb and vegetables to the sauce; cook just until warmed through. —*Foteini Sioni*

MAKE AHEAD The braised lamb can be refrigerated for up to 4 days.

WINE Firm, complex Cabernet Sauvignon.

beef & lamb

Marinated Lamb Kebabs with Sumac-Onion Salad

ACTIVE: 25 MIN; TOTAL: 4 HR 25 MIN
4 SERVINGS ●

- 2 tablespoons extra-virgin olive oil
- 1 tablespoon tomato paste
- 1 tablespoon Aleppo pepper (see Note)
- 1 garlic clove, minced
- 1½ teaspoons Turkish Baharat (recipe follows)
- 1½ pounds boneless well-trimmed lamb, preferably from the loin, cut into 1-inch cubes

Kosher salt
- 2 medium white onions, halved lengthwise, thinly sliced crosswise
- ¼ cup chopped flat-leaf parsley
- 1 teaspoon ground sumac (see Note)

Warm pita bread, for serving

1. In a large bowl, combine the olive oil with the tomato paste, Aleppo pepper, garlic and Turkish Baharat. Add the lamb and stir to coat evenly. Cover and refrigerate for at least 4 hours or overnight. Bring to room temperature before grilling.

2. Light a grill. Thread the lamb cubes onto 4 long skewers and season with salt. Grill the lamb kebabs, turning, over moderately high heat for about 5 minutes for medium meat.

3. Meanwhile, in a medium bowl, thoroughly toss the sliced onions with 1 tablespoon of salt. Let stand until the onions are slightly soft, about 5 minutes. Rinse the onions and drain well. In a serving bowl, toss the onion slices with the chopped parsley and ground sumac. Serve the lamb kebabs with the onion salad and warm pita bread. —*Burhan Cagda*

NOTE Aleppo pepper and sumac are available at spice shops and online from kalustyans.com.

WINE Cherry-inflected, earthy Sangiovese.

TURKISH BAHARAT

TOTAL: 5 MIN
MAKES 3 TABLESPOONS ● ●

- 1 tablespoon dried oregano
- 1 tablespoon pickling spice
- 1 teaspoon freshly ground pepper
- ½ teaspoon cinnamon
- ½ teaspoon ground cumin
- ½ teaspoon dried mint
- ¼ teaspoon freshly grated nutmeg

In a small bowl, combine all of the herbs and spices.

Grilled Spiced Lamb Chops with Vegetable Ragout

ACTIVE: 45 MIN; TOTAL: 1 HR
4 SERVINGS

- 1 teaspoon fennel seeds
- 1 teaspoon coriander seeds
- ½ teaspoon cumin seeds
- 2 teaspoons minced rosemary
- 8 lamb rib chops (2 pounds), bones frenched (have your butcher do this)

Salt
- 1 pint cherry tomatoes
- ¼ cup plus 2 tablespoons extra-virgin olive oil
- 2 garlic cloves, thinly sliced
- 2 bay leaves
- 3 thyme sprigs
- 2 tablespoons balsamic vinegar
- 1 small shallot, thinly sliced
- 1½ cups shelled fresh peas (1½ pounds in the pod)
- 1 cup shelled fava beans (1 pound in the pod)
- 6 ounces chanterelles, trimmed, caps quartered if large
- 3 tablespoons unsalted butter
- ½ cup red pearl onions, peeled and halved lengthwise
- 2 cups chicken stock
- 1 tablespoon chopped mint
- 1½ teaspoons chopped tarragon
- 1½ teaspoons chopped marjoram

Freshly ground pepper

1. Preheat the oven to 300°. Grind the fennel, coriander and cumin seeds to a powder in a spice grinder. Transfer to a small bowl and stir in the rosemary. Season the lamb chops with salt and coat with the ground spice mixture; refrigerate the lamb chops for 1 hour.

2. In a shallow glass or ceramic baking dish, toss the tomatoes, ¼ cup of oil, garlic, bay leaves, thyme sprigs, vinegar and shallot. Add a pinch of salt. Bake for 30 minutes, until the tomatoes are soft.

3. Bring a medium saucepan of salted water to a boil. Add the peas and cook until just tender, 3 minutes. Transfer to a medium bowl. Add the favas to the pan and cook until bright green, 1 minute. Drain and squeeze each lightly to pop the bean from its skin. Add to the peas.

4. In a large skillet, heat the remaining olive oil until shimmering. Add the chanterelles, season with salt and cook over moderately high heat until softened, 3 minutes. Reduce the heat to moderate and cook, stirring occasionally, until the chanterelles are tender and browned, 5 minutes. Add 1 tablespoon of butter and the pearl onions, cut side down, and cook over moderate heat until golden on the bottom, 3 minutes. Add the stock and simmer over moderate heat until the onions are tender, 3 minutes. Stir the peas and fava beans into the chanterelles and onions.

5. Light a grill. Discard the bay leaves and thyme sprigs. Add the tomato mixture to the vegetables; simmer for 3 minutes. Remove from the heat and stir in the mint, tarragon and marjoram. Add the remaining 2 tablespoons of butter, 1 tablespoon at a time, stirring until the butter is melted. Season the ragout with salt and pepper.

6. Grill the lamb chops over high heat until nicely charred on the outside and medium rare within, 3 minutes per side. Spoon the ragout into 4 shallow bowls, top with the chops and serve at once. —*Jason Wilson*

WINE Earthy, medium-bodied Tempranillo.

GRILLED SPICED LAMB CHOPS
WITH VEGETABLE RAGOUT

LUSCIOUS TANDOORI LAMB CHOPS

LAMB STEW WITH ROOT VEGETABLES

Luscious Tandoori Lamb Chops

ACTIVE: 30 MIN; TOTAL: 1 HR 10 MIN PLUS OVERNIGHT MARINATING

4 SERVINGS

- 8 lamb rib chops (2½ pounds)
- ¾ cup Greek yogurt
- ¼ cup heavy cream
- 3 tablespoons fresh lemon juice

One 3-inch piece of fresh ginger, peeled and minced

- 4 large garlic cloves, minced
- 1 tablespoon malt vinegar
- 1 tablespoon garam masala
- 1 tablespoon ground cumin
- 1 tablespoon paprika
- ½ teaspoon cayenne pepper
- ¼ teaspoon ground mace (optional)
- ¼ teaspoon freshly grated nutmeg

Kosher salt

- 2 tablespoons vegetable oil
- 3 tablespoons unsalted butter, melted

1. Using a paring knife, cut a few ¼-inch-deep slashes into each lamb chop. In a large bowl, whisk the yogurt with the heavy cream, lemon juice, minced ginger and garlic, the malt vinegar, garam masala, cumin, paprika, cayenne, mace, nutmeg and 1 teaspoon of kosher salt. Transfer the lamb chops to the marinade and turn to coat them, then cover and refrigerate overnight.

2. Add the vegetable oil to the marinade and toss with the lamb chops. Remove the lamb chops from the marinade, scrape off excess and let them stand at room temperature for 30 minutes.

3. Light a grill. Season the lamb chops with salt. Grill over moderately high heat for 8 minutes, turning once, until well browned. Brush both sides with the melted butter and grill for another 2 minutes per side for medium rare. *—Suvir Saran*

WINE Fruity, luscious Shiraz.

Lamb Stew with Root Vegetables

ACTIVE: 1 HR; TOTAL: 3 HR

8 SERVINGS ●

- ½ cup all-purpose flour

Salt and freshly ground pepper

- 4 pounds boneless lamb shoulder or top round, cut into 2-inch cubes
- ½ cup olive oil
- 2 cups dry red wine
- 2 tablespoons sherry vinegar
- 4 cups chicken stock
- 2 tablespoons chopped tarragon
- 1 pound baby carrots, peeled
- 1 pound baby parsnips, peeled
- 1 pound small fingerling potatoes
- ½ pound baby turnips, halved
- 8 baby fennel bulbs, trimmed, fronds reserved and chopped
- 1 large shallot, minced
- 2 tablespoons minced flat-leaf parsley

1. Preheat the oven to 350°. Put the flour in a large bowl; season generously with salt and pepper. Add the lamb cubes in 4 batches, tossing to coat thoroughly.

2. In a large enameled cast-iron casserole, heat 2 tablespoons of the oil until shimmering. Add one-fourth of the lamb and cook over moderately high heat until browned, 6 minutes; transfer to a plate. Brown the remaining floured lamb in 3 batches, adding 2 tablespoons of oil to the pot per batch. Reduce the heat if the casserole bottom darkens too much.

3. Return the lamb to the casserole. Add the wine and vinegar; bring to a boil. Add the stock and tarragon and return to a boil. Season with salt and pepper. Cover and braise the stew in the oven for about 1 hour, or until the meat is nearly tender.

4. Add the carrots, parsnips, potatoes, turnips, fennel and shallot to the lamb stew. Season with salt and pepper and bring to a boil, stirring to distribute the vegetables. Cover the casserole, return it to the oven and cook until the meat and vegetables are tender, about 1 hour longer. Season with salt and pepper. Stir in the parsley and fennel fronds and serve the stew in deep bowls. —*Jim Clendenen*
WINE Ripe, juicy Pinot Noir.

Lamb Chops with Fennel Relish
TOTAL: 30 MIN
2 SERVINGS ●

- 3 tablespoons extra-virgin olive oil
- **Four 1-inch-thick lamb loin chops (about 6 ounces each)**
- **Salt and freshly ground black pepper**
- 1 small fennel bulb, cored and diced
- 1 garlic clove, very finely chopped
- 1 shallot, minced
- 2 anchovy fillets, rinsed and very finely chopped
- 2 tablespoons minced parsley
- 1 tablespoon chopped kalamata olives
- 1 tablespoon drained small capers
- ¼ teaspoon crushed red pepper
- 1 teaspoon sherry vinegar

1. In a medium skillet, heat 1 tablespoon of oil until shimmering. Season the chops with salt and pepper, add to the skillet and cook over moderately high heat, turning once, until browned, 7 minutes. Transfer to a plate and keep warm.

2. In another medium skillet, heat the remaining oil. Add the fennel, garlic and shallot and season with salt and pepper. Cook over high heat, stirring occasionally, until crisp-tender, 4 minutes. Off the heat, add the anchovies, parsley, olives, capers, crushed pepper and vinegar and mound on plates. Top with the lamb chops, drizzle with any juices; serve.—*Stuart Brioza*
WINE Intense, spicy Syrah.

Garlic-Rubbed Leg of Lamb with Leeks
ACTIVE: 1 HR; TOTAL: 4 HR
8 TO 10 SERVINGS

- 1 head of garlic, cloves separated but not peeled
- 3 tablespoons extra-virgin olive oil, plus more for drizzling
- 2 tablespoons kosher salt
- 2 tablespoons cracked black pepper
- 1 tablespoon chopped oregano
- 1 tablespoon chopped thyme
- 12 leeks, white part only, split
- 1 cup dry red wine
- **One 7-pound semi-boneless leg of lamb (aitchbone removed)**

1. Preheat the oven to 400°. In a small baking dish, toss the garlic with 1 tablespoon of oil. Cover with foil and bake for 1 hour, until golden. Let cool slightly, then squeeze the garlic cloves out of the skins. Transfer to a mini processor. Add the salt, pepper, oregano, thyme and remaining oil and process to a paste.

2. Arrange the leeks in a large roasting pan, cut sides up. Drizzle with oil and the wine. Rub 1 tablespoon of the paste on the underside of the lamb and lay on the leeks. Spread the remaining paste on the lamb and roast for 30 minutes. Lower the oven to 350° and roast for 1 hour and 10 minutes, until an instant-read thermometer inserted into the thickest part registers 130° to 135° for medium rare. Transfer to a carving board; let rest for 20 minutes.

3. Turn the leeks. Roast for 5 minutes, until the liquid in the pan is nearly evaporated. Carve the lamb, transfer to a platter and serve with the leeks. —*Tim Love*
WINE Rich, ripe Cabernet Sauvignon.

Five-Spice Lamb with Spinach
TOTAL: 30 MIN
4 SERVINGS ●

- 1 tablespoon ground cumin
- 1 tablespoon ground coriander
- 1 tablespoon sweet paprika
- 1 tablespoon freshly ground black pepper
- 1 teaspoon cayenne pepper
- **Eight 8-ounce lamb loin chops**
- **Salt**
- ¼ cup extra-virgin olive oil, plus more for drizzling
- 5 tablespoons unsalted butter
- 3 medium shallots, thinly sliced
- 1 pound cleaned bagged spinach, tough ends discarded

1. In a bowl, mix the spices. Season the lamb with salt; drizzle with olive oil. Coat both sides of the chops with the spices.

2. In a very large skillet, heat the ¼ cup of olive oil until shimmering. Add the chops and cook over moderate heat until browned and medium rare, 7 minutes per side.

3. Meanwhile, in a large, deep skillet, melt the butter. Add the shallots and cook over moderate heat until softened and golden. Add handfuls of the spinach to the skillet and cook over moderate heat, stirring and adding more spinach after each batch wilts. Season with salt, mound on plates and serve with the lamb. —*Ryan Poli*
WINE Round, deep-flavored Syrah.

beef & lamb

Lamb Chops with Pomegranate-Pistachio Couscous

TOTAL: 6 HR 40 MIN

4 SERVINGS ●

- 1 cup cilantro leaves
- 2 garlic cloves
- 1 tablespoon ground cumin
- ¼ teaspoon cayenne pepper
- ¼ cup fresh lemon juice
- 1 teaspoon finely grated lemon zest
- 2 tablespoons plus 1 teaspoon extra-virgin olive oil

Salt and freshly ground pepper

Four 7-ounce lamb loin chops, 1¼ inches thick, trimmed of excess fat

- 1½ cups water
- ¼ teaspoon cinnamon
- 1 cup couscous
- 2 tablespoons chopped mint
- 2 tablespoons chopped unsalted pistachios
- ¼ cup pomegranate seeds
- ¼ cup plus 2 tablespoons pomegranate juice

1. Preheat the oven to 375°. In a blender or food processor, combine the cilantro, garlic, cumin, cayenne and lemon juice with ½ teaspoon of the lemon zest and 1 tablespoon of the olive oil. Season with salt and pepper and process to a paste. Spread all but 1 tablespoon of the seasoning paste over the lamb chops and let stand for 10 minutes.

2. Meanwhile, in a small saucepan, bring the water to a boil. Add the cinnamon, 1 tablespoon of the olive oil and ½ teaspoon of salt. Stir in the couscous, cover and remove from the heat; let stand until all the water has been absorbed, about 10 minutes. Transfer the couscous to a large bowl and fluff with a fork. Stir in the mint, pistachios, half of the pomegranate seeds and the remaining ½ teaspoon of lemon zest. Cover and keep warm.

3. Heat the remaining 1 teaspoon of olive oil in a medium ovenproof skillet. Scrape off the seasoning paste on the chops. Add the chops to the pan and cook over moderate heat, turning once, until browned, about 5 minutes. Transfer the skillet to the oven and roast for 6 minutes for medium-rare meat. Transfer the lamb to a plate and pour off the fat in the skillet.

4. Set the skillet over moderate heat and add the pomegranate juice and the reserved 1 tablespoon of the seasoning paste. Cook, scraping up any bits stuck to the pan. Simmer over moderate heat until reduced to ¼ cup, about 2 minutes.

5. Mound the couscous on plates and top with the chops. Spoon the sauce on the meat, sprinkle with the remaining pomegranate seeds and serve right away.
—*Annie Wayte*

WINE Juicy, spicy Grenache.

health
superfruits

Like grapes, **pomegranates** (a key ingredient in the recipe above) contain polyphenols, which are potent antioxidants that protect against heart disease. **To remove the red seeds** (known as arils) cut off the blossom end and then score the rind four to six times. Submerge in a large bowl of water and break it into segments. Still working underwater, loosen the arils. The rind and membranes will float to the surface while the arils will drop to the bottom.

Braised Lamb with Pickled Onions

ACTIVE: 1 HR 30 MIN; TOTAL: 4 HR 30 MIN

10 SERVINGS

One 5-pound boneless lamb shoulder, tied

- 3 bell peppers—1 red, 1 yellow and 1 green, cut into ½-inch dice
- 2 large white onions, 1 diced and 1 thinly sliced lengthwise

One 14½-ounce can diced tomatoes

Kosher salt and freshly ground pepper

- 4 whole cloves
- 2 teaspoons coriander seeds

Two 3-inch cinnamon sticks

- ½ cup distilled white vinegar
- 1 teaspoon sugar
- 1 pound masa harina (4 cups)
- ¾ cup pure olive oil
- ½ cup cilantro leaves

1. Preheat the oven to 325°. Put the lamb in a deep roasting pan with 4 cups of water, the peppers, diced onion and tomatoes with their juices. Season the lamb with salt and pepper. Tie the cloves, coriander and 1 cinnamon stick in cheesecloth and add to the roasting pan. Cover tightly with foil. Braise for 2½ to 3 hours, until an instant-read thermometer inserted in the thickest part registers 180°. Discard the spice bundle.

2. In a bowl, mix the sliced onion, vinegar, sugar, 2 tablespoons of salt and remaining cinnamon stick; let stand at room temperature for at least 2 and up to 4 hours.

3. Transfer the meat to a cutting board; let cool slightly. Transfer the vegetables to a bowl; reserve. Strain the liquid into a heatproof measuring cup, skim off the fat and transfer to a large, deep skillet. Simmer over moderate heat until reduced to 1½ cups, 20 minutes. Return the vegetables to the sauce. When the lamb is cool enough to handle, remove the strings and shred, discarding any excess fat. Add to the sauce; season with salt and pepper.

4. In a bowl, mix the masa harina with 2½ cups of water; stir until a stiff dough forms. If it's very dry and crumbly, add a few tablespoons of water. Add the oil. Knead until smooth and divide into 20 pieces. Roll into 20 balls; keep covered with a lightly moistened towel. Flatten, a few at a time, into 3-inch tortillas, a scant ⅓ inch thick. Heat a cast-iron griddle or skillet

until hot. Add the tortillas in batches and cook over moderately high heat, turning once, until lightly browned and slightly crisp. Serve the lamb over the warm tortillas, garnished with the pickled onions and cilantro leaves. —*Mateo Granados*
WINE Round, deep-flavored Syrah.

Braised Lamb Shanks with Roasted Broccoli and Squash
ACTIVE: 1 HR 20 MIN; TOTAL: 4 HR
6 SERVINGS

- ¼ cup plus 3 tablespoons extra-virgin olive oil
- 6 medium lamb shanks (about 6 pounds)
- Salt and freshly ground pepper
- 2 cups dry white wine
- 4 cups chicken stock or broth
- 2 medium onions, coarsely chopped
- 1 celery rib, coarsely chopped
- 1 large carrot, thinly sliced
- 4 thyme sprigs
- 2 bay leaves
- 2 garlic cloves, thinly sliced
- 1 small onion, finely chopped
- 1 teaspoon yellow mustard seeds
- ½ teaspoon cumin seeds
- 4 large canned Italian plum tomatoes, drained and chopped
- 3 pounds small delicata squash— scrubbed, halved, seeded and cut crosswise 1 inch thick
- One 2-pound head of broccoli, cut into 1½-inch florets
- One 15-ounce can chickpeas, rinsed and drained
- 1½ cups couscous
- 2 tablespoons unsalted butter
- Spicy Cilantro Pesto (recipe follows)

1. Preheat the oven to 325°. In a large skillet, heat 1 tablespoon of oil. Season the lamb with salt and pepper. Add 3 shanks to the pan; cook over moderately high heat until browned all over, 10 minutes. Transfer to a large roasting pan and repeat with oil and remaining shanks. Pour off the oil.

2. Add the wine. Boil for 1 minute, scraping up any browned bits; pour into the pan with the lamb. Add the stock, coarsely chopped onions, celery, carrot, thyme and bay leaves. Bring to a boil over high heat. Cover with foil and braise in the oven for 2½ hours, turning once, until very tender. Remove the foil. Cool slightly.

3. Meanwhile, in a medium skillet, heat 2 tablespoons of oil. Add the garlic, finely chopped onion, yellow mustard and cumin seeds; cook over moderate heat until the onion is golden, 7 minutes. Add the tomatoes and cook until reduced to ⅔ cup, 4 minutes. Season with salt and pepper.

4. Increase the oven temperature to 400°. On each of 2 large rimmed baking sheets, toss the squash with 1 tablespoon of oil. Season with salt and pepper. Arrange in an even layer. Roast the squash for 45 minutes, until tender. On another large rimmed baking sheet, toss the broccoli and remaining oil; season with salt and pepper. Roast for 25 minutes, until lightly browned and tender.

5. Transfer the shanks to a work surface; cover to keep warm. Strain the liquid into a saucepan; skim off the fat. Add the chickpeas, *sofrito* and shanks, cover and simmer over low heat for 5 minutes. Season with salt. Stir in the squash and broccoli.

6. Cook the couscous according to package instructions, then toss with the butter and season with salt. Keep covered.

7. Set the shanks in shallow bowls and spoon the couscous alongside. Ladle the vegetables on top; pass the Spicy Cilantro Pesto at the table. —*Troy MacLarty*
WINE Rich, ripe Cabernet Sauvignon.

SPICY CILANTRO PESTO
TOTAL: 15 MIN
MAKES ⅔ CUP ● ● ●

- 1 cup cilantro leaves and small sprigs
- ½ cup flat-leaf parsley leaves and small sprigs
- 1 garlic clove, chopped
- One 1-inch piece of fresh ginger, peeled and finely chopped
- ½ large jalapeño, seeded and chopped
- ½ cup vegetable oil
- Salt

In a blender, mince the cilantro, parsley, garlic, ginger and jalapeño. With the machine on, gradually add the oil in a steady stream and puree. Scrape the pesto into a bowl and season with salt. —*T.M.*

Syrah-Braised Lamb Shoulder
ACTIVE: 30 MIN; TOTAL: 4 HR
6 SERVINGS ● ●

- 2 tablespoons ground cumin
- 3 tablespoons extra-virgin olive oil
- Salt and freshly ground pepper
- One 5-pound boneless lamb shoulder roast, tied
- 1 bottle Syrah
- 4 cups chicken stock or broth
- 12 thyme sprigs, tied with string
- Herbed Potato Soufflé (p. 266)

1. Preheat the oven to 350°. In a bowl, mix the cumin, 2 tablespoons of the oil and a big pinch each of salt and pepper. Rub the mixture all over the lamb.

2. Heat the remaining 1 tablespoon of oil in a large, heavy casserole or Dutch oven. Add the lamb and brown it well over moderately high heat, 15 minutes. Transfer to a large plate. Wipe out the casserole.

3. Return the lamb to the casserole. Add the wine, stock and thyme sprigs; bring to a boil. Cover with a tight-fitting lid. Transfer to the oven and braise for 2½ to 3 hours, turning occasionally, until tender.

4. Transfer the lamb roast to a large platter and cover with foil. Discard the thyme sprigs. Boil the braising liquid until reduced to 1½ cups, about 40 minutes.

5. Remove the strings from the roast. Slice the lamb, transfer to plates or a platter and spoon the sauce on top. Serve with the Herbed Potato Soufflé. —*Mike Davis*
WINE Round, deep-flavored Syrah.

beef & lamb

Paprika-Roasted Leg of Lamb

ACTIVE: 15 MIN; TOTAL: 1 HR 15 MIN
12 SERVINGS

- 3 tablespoons sweet paprika
- 1 tablespoon pure chile powder, such as ancho or pasilla
- 1½ teaspoons ground cardamom
- One 6½-pound boneless leg of lamb, butterflied
- 2 tablespoons extra-virgin olive oil
- Salt
- 6 whole garlic cloves
- 4 rosemary sprigs
- 2 thyme sprigs
- 1 lemon, sliced ¼ inch thick

1. Preheat the oven to 500°. In a bowl, mix the paprika, chile powder and cardamom. Rub the lamb with olive oil; season with salt. Sprinkle the spices over the lamb.

2. Lay the lamb, fat side down, on a large rimmed baking sheet. Scatter the garlic, rosemary, thyme and lemon around the lamb and roast on the top rack of the oven for 25 minutes, or until nicely browned. Turn the lamb fat side up and roast for 25 minutes longer, or until an instant-read thermometer inserted in the thickest part registers 130° for medium rare. Transfer the lamb to a carving board; let rest for 10 minutes. Slice the lamb ¼ inch thick and serve right away. —*Marcus Samuelsson*
SERVE WITH Spicy Quince Sambal (recipe follows).
WINE Intense, spicy Syrah.

SPICY QUINCE SAMBAL

ACTIVE: 20 MIN; TOTAL: 30 MIN
MAKES 1½ CUPS ● ● ●

- 2 tablespoons vegetable oil
- 4 garlic cloves, minced
- 3 red Thai chiles, minced
- One 2-inch piece of ginger, peeled and minced
- 1 small red onion, finely chopped
- 2 tablespoons salted roasted peanuts, coarsely chopped
- 2 small quinces—peeled, halved, cored and cut into ¼-inch dice
- 2 tablespoons fresh lime juice
- 1 tablespoon sugar
- 1 teaspoon salt
- 1 tablespoon coarsely chopped mint
- 1 tablespoon coarsely chopped cilantro

In a large skillet, heat the oil. Cook the garlic, chiles, ginger and onion over moderate heat until softened, 4 minutes. Add the peanuts and cook until sizzling, about 3 minutes. Add the quinces, lime juice, sugar and salt. Cover and simmer, stirring a few times, until the quinces are barely tender, 3 minutes. Let cool slightly. Stir in the mint and cilantro; serve. —*M.S.*

Ground Lamb and Shallot Kebabs with Pomegranate Molasses

ACTIVE: 25 MIN; TOTAL: 1 HR
4 SERVINGS

- 2 tablespoons crème fraîche
- 1 garlic clove, minced
- 1¼ teaspoons salt
- ½ teaspoon freshly ground pepper
- 1 pound ground lamb
- 12 large shallots—peeled, halved lengthwise and root ends trimmed but kept intact
- 2 tablespoons extra-virgin olive oil
- ⅓ cup water
- 1½ teaspoons pomegranate molasses
- 1 teaspoon fresh lemon juice
- 2 tablespoons chopped scallions
- 1 tablespoon chopped parsley
- Warm pita bread, for serving

1. Light a grill. In a medium bowl, gently knead the crème fraîche, garlic, salt and pepper into the lamb. Using moistened hands, roll into 16 balls. On each of 8 short metal skewers (10 inches or less), alternate 3 shallot halves with 2 lamb balls. Brush with oil. Grill over moderately high heat, turning once, until browned on the outside (but not cooked through), 3 minutes.

2. Transfer the kebabs to a very large (12 to 14 inches), deep skillet. Add the water, 1 teaspoon of the pomegranate molasses and the lemon juice; bring to a boil. Cover and simmer gently over low heat until the shallots are very tender and the meatballs cooked through, 30 minutes.

3. Uncover and increase the heat to high. Add the remaining ½ teaspoon of pomegranate molasses and cook, basting occasionally, until the meatballs and shallots are glazed, about 5 minutes.

4. Transfer the kebabs to a platter and drizzle with any remaining sauce. Garnish with the scallions and parsley and serve with warm pita bread. —*Paula Wolfert*
WINE Juicy, fresh Dolcetto.

Olive-Crusted Lamb with Adzuki Bean Stew

ACTIVE: 1 HR; TOTAL: 1 HR 15 MIN PLUS OVERNIGHT SOAKING
4 SERVINGS ●

- ¼ cup black olives (see Note), pitted and quartered
- ½ teaspoon light brown sugar
- 1 pound boneless lamb loin, trimmed, or 1 pound boneless leg of lamb, trimmed
- Salt and freshly ground pepper
- 1 lemon
- 2 teaspoons honey
- 3 tablespoons extra-virgin olive oil
- 1 medium onion, finely chopped
- 1 fennel bulb, cored and minced
- 2 cups chicken stock or broth
- 1 cup water
- 1 bay leaf
- 1 teaspoon ketchup
- 1 cup dried adzuki beans, soaked in water overnight and drained
- 1 tablespoon Worcestershire sauce
- 2 small zucchini (¼ pound each), cut into thin rounds
- 1 teaspoon chopped thyme
- Fleur de sel, for garnish

1. Preheat the oven to 450°. Spread the olives on a microwave-safe plate and microwave at 50 percent power for 30 minutes, until dry. Cool, then grind in a mini food processor to a coarse powder. Stir the brown sugar into the olive powder. Season the lamb with salt and pepper and rub all over with the olive powder.

2. Bring a small saucepan of water to a boil. Using a vegetable peeler, remove the zest from the lemon, leaving behind the bitter white pith. Slice into thin julienne strips. Add to the pan. Simmer over moderate heat until softened, 10 minutes. Drain and mix with the honey.

3. In a medium saucepan, heat 1 tablespoon of oil. Add the onion and fennel. Cook over moderate heat until softened, 8 minutes. Add the stock, water, bay leaf and ketchup and bring to a boil Add the beans and simmer over low heat, stirring occasionally, until tender, 1 hour. Transfer the beans to a bowl. Boil the liquid until reduced to ½ cup, 8 minutes. Return the beans to the pan. Stir in the Worcestershire sauce, lemon zest and honey; season with salt and pepper. Discard the bay leaf.

4. In an ovenproof skillet, heat 1 tablespoon of oil until shimmering . Add the lamb. Cook over moderately high heat until browned on the bottom, 2 minutes. Turn and cook for 1 minute. Transfer to the oven and roast until medium rare, 8 minutes for the loin and 12 for the leg. Transfer to a carving board. Let rest for 5 minutes.

5. Wipe out the skillet; add the remaining oil and zucchini. Cook over moderately high heat, stirring, until crisp-tender, 3 minutes. Season with salt and pepper.

6. Spoon the beans onto plates. Top with the zucchini and sprinkle with the thyme and fleur de sel. Carve the lamb and serve alongside.—*Cyril Renaud*

NOTE Dry, smooth Moroccan olives (available at Sahadi's; 718-624-4550) are ideal for making the olive powder.

WINE Intense, spicy Syrah.

GROUND LAMB AND SHALLOT KEBABS

OLIVE-CRUSTED LAMB WITH ADZUKI BEAN STEW

beef & lamb

Roasted Leg of Goat Stuffed with Swiss Chard and Lime Pickle

ACTIVE: 20 MIN; TOTAL: 2 HR

8 SERVINGS ●

- 1½ pounds Swiss chard, stems and inner ribs discarded
- ½ cup lime pickle (see Note)
- One 6-pound leg of goat, boned and butterflied
- Salt and freshly ground pepper
- ¼ cup extra-virgin olive oil
- 1¼ pounds cherry tomatoes (4 cups)
- 2 tablespoons shredded basil leaves

1. Preheat the oven to 400°. Fill a large, deep skillet with 1 inch of salted water and bring to a boil. Add the chard and cook until just wilted. Drain and rinse under cold water; squeeze dry and coarsely chop.

2. In a mini food processor, coarsely puree the lime pickle. Set the meat on a work surface, boned side up, and season with salt and pepper. Spread the pickle over the meat and then the chard. Roll into a roast; tie it at 1-inch intervals using kitchen string. Season with salt and pepper.

3. In a heavy roasting pan, heat 2 tablespoons of the olive oil. Add the roast and cook over moderately high heat until browned all over, 10 minutes. Transfer to the oven and roast for 1 hour and 10 minutes, or until an instant-read thermometer inserted into the thickest part of the meat registers 130°. Let rest for 15 minutes.

4. In a large, flameproof baking dish, heat the remaining oil. Add the tomatoes; cook over moderate heat until the skins begin to blister, 2 to 3 minutes. Season with salt and pepper. Transfer to the oven and roast for 5 minutes, until softened. Sprinkle with the basil. Snip the strings from the goat and slice. Pour the juices into a heatproof cup; spoon off the fat. Serve with the tomatoes. Pass the jus. —*David Myers*

NOTE Look for lime pickle, a tangy Indian condiment, at Indian markets or online at indiaplaza.com.

WINE Intense, fruity Zinfandel.

Braised Rabbit with Mustard and Summer Savory

ACTIVE: 50 MIN; TOTAL: 2 HR

6 SERVINGS ●

- Two 4-pound rabbits (see Note)
- Salt and freshly ground pepper
- 6 summer savory sprigs
- 4 thyme sprigs
- 6 tablespoons Dijon mustard
- 3 tablespoons unsalted butter
- 3 tablespoons extra-virgin olive oil
- 12 whole garlic cloves
- 3 large shallots, minced
- 1 medium onion, chopped
- 1 cup dry white wine
- 2 large tomatoes—peeled, seeded and chopped
- 1 quart chicken stock
- 1 cup heavy cream

1. Cut each rabbit into 6 pieces: 2 hind legs, 2 front legs, neck and loin with flaps attached. Season the rabbit with salt and pepper. Press 2 savory and 2 thyme sprigs on the underside of each loin and fold the flaps over the herbs; secure the flaps with toothpicks. Spread the mustard all over the rabbit pieces.

2. In a very large enameled cast-iron casserole, melt 2 tablespoons of the butter in 2 tablespoons of the olive oil. Add 4 rabbit pieces and cook over moderately high heat until they are browned on the bottom, about 2 minutes. Turn and cook the rabbit over moderate heat until browned, about 3 minutes. Transfer the rabbit pieces to a large bowl. Repeat in 2 batches with the remaining rabbit, adding the remaining 1 tablespoon each of butter and olive oil for the last batch.

3. Add the garlic, shallots and onion to the casserole and cook over moderately low heat, stirring occasionally, until the onion is softened, about 8 minutes. Add half of the wine and boil over moderately high heat, scraping up any bits stuck to the bottom, until reduced by half, 4 minutes. Repeat with the remaining wine. Add the

tomatoes, stock and the remaining savory. Nestle the rabbit pieces in the casserole and bring to a simmer. Cover the casserole and cook the rabbit over low heat, turning the pieces a few times, until the pieces are tender, about 1 hour.

4. Transfer the rabbit pieces to a bowl. Boil the cooking liquid over high heat until it is reduced to 5 cups, about 15 minutes. Discard the savory. Add the cream and boil until thickened, about 5 minutes; season with salt and pepper. Return the rabbit to the casserole and simmer until it is heated through. Serve. —*Christophe Emé*

NOTE Rabbits are available at farmers' markets or dartagnan.com.

WINE Full-bodied, minerally Riesling.

Lamb Salad with Arugula and Raspberry Vinaigrette

TOTAL: 30 MIN

4 SERVINGS ●

- 1 cup pecan halves (4 ounces)
- 1 tablespoon Dijon mustard
- 1 tablespoon raspberry vinegar
- 1 tablespoon raspberry preserves
- 3 tablespoons extra-virgin olive oil
- 1 teaspoon chopped basil
- 1 teaspoon finely chopped thyme
- Salt and freshly ground pepper
- One 5-ounce bag baby arugula
- 1 cup crumbled fresh goat cheese (4 ounces)
- 1 pound leftover roasted lamb (see p. 145), cut into bite-size pieces

1. Preheat the oven to 350°. Toast the pecans in a pie plate in the oven for 7 minutes, or until they are golden. Let the pecans cool.

2. In a large bowl, whisk the mustard with the vinegar and preserves. Whisk in the oil until the dressing is emulsified. Whisk in the basil and thyme; season with salt and pepper. Add the arugula, goat cheese, pecans and lamb to the bowl and toss. Serve. —*Tim Love*

WINE Juicy, fresh Dolcetto.

LAMB SALAD WITH ARUGULA
AND RASPBERRY VINAIGRETTE

CHINESE-STYLE RIBS WITH
GUAVA BARBECUE SAUCE (P. 156)

pork & veal

"There comes a time when every griller wants to cook 'low and slow' in the style of a Southern or Texas pit master."

–Steven Raichlen, barbecue expert

LEMONGRASS-BARBECUED PORK WITH RICE-VERMICELLI SALAD　　**STUFFED PORK TENDERLOINS WITH BACON AND APPLE-RIESLING S**

Lemongrass-Barbecued Pork with Rice-Vermicelli Salad

ACTIVE: 1 HR; TOTAL: 3 HR INCLUDING MARINATING

6 SERVINGS ●

BARBECUED PORK

- 4 large garlic cloves, thickly sliced
- 3 large stalks of fresh lemongrass, tender inner white bulbs only, sliced crosswise
- 2 large shallots, thickly sliced
- 1½ tablespoons sugar
- 3 tablespoons Asian fish sauce
- 3 tablespoons fresh lime juice
- 3 tablespoons vegetable oil
- 2 tablespoons soy sauce
- 1½ pounds boneless pork loin, sliced ¼ inch thick

RICE-VERMICELLI SALAD

- ½ pound rice vermicelli
- 4 medium garlic cloves, quartered

- 3 Thai chiles or 1 large jalapeño, thickly sliced
- 3 tablespoons sugar
- ¼ cup Asian fish sauce
- ½ cup finely chopped cilantro
- ½ cup finely chopped mint
- ¼ cup fresh lime juice
- ⅓ cup water
- 2 large cucumbers—peeled, halved lengthwise, seeded and thinly sliced crosswise

Carrot and Daikon Pickles (recipe follows), for serving

1. PREPARE THE BARBECUED PORK: In a food processor, finely chop the garlic, lemongrass and shallots. Add the sugar, fish sauce, lime juice, oil and soy sauce; process to a paste. In a glass dish, coat the pork slices with the marinade. Cover and refrigerate for at least 1 hour.

2. MAKE THE RICE-VERMICELLI SALAD: In a bowl, cover the rice vermicelli with

cold water and soak until pliable, 20 minutes. In a mortar, using a pestle, pound the garlic cloves to a paste with the chiles and sugar. Stir in the fish sauce, cilantro, mint, lime juice and water.

3. Bring a saucepan of water to a boil over high heat. Drain the noodles; add to the boiling water. Cook, stirring, until barely tender, about 1 minute; drain. Rinse in cold water; drain thoroughly. Transfer to a large bowl, add the dressing and toss well. Scatter the cucumbers over the salad.

4. Light a grill. Lift the pork slices from the marinade, leaving on some of the flavorings. Grill over a hot fire until nicely charred, 2 minutes per side. Transfer to plates and serve with the rice-vermicelli salad. Pass the Carrot and Daikon Pickles at the table. —*Marcia Kiesel*

MAKE AHEAD The marinated pork and the dressing can be refrigerated overnight.

WINE Tart, citrusy Riesling.

CARROT AND DAIKON PICKLES
ACTIVE: 15 MIN; TOTAL: 2 HR 15 MIN
6 SERVINGS ● ●

- ¾ cup white vinegar
- 2 tablespoons sugar
- 2 teaspoons kosher salt
- 3 large carrots, peeled and sliced crosswise ⅛ inch thick
- 1 pound daikon, peeled and cut into 1½-inch-long matchsticks

In a medium bowl, combine the vinegar, sugar and kosher salt; stir to dissolve the sugar and salt. Add the carrots and daikon. Cover the vegetables with a small plate and top with a heavy can to keep them submerged in the pickling liquid. Let stand at room temperature for 2 hours. —*M.K.*

Stuffed Pork Tenderloins with Bacon and Apple-Riesling Sauce
ACTIVE: 1 HR; TOTAL: 1 HR 20 MIN
4 SERVINGS ●
PORK

- 1 tablespoon extra-virgin olive oil
- ¼ cup minced onion
- ¼ pound pork breakfast sausage, casings removed
- 1 Granny Smith apple—peeled, cored and cut into ⅓-inch dice
- 1 garlic clove, minced
- ½ teaspoon chopped thyme
- ½ teaspoon chopped sage
- ½ cup finely chopped collard greens (2 large leaves, stemmed)
- 4 ounces fresh goat cheese, at room temperature

Kosher salt and freshly ground pepper
Two 1-pound pork tenderloins
- 6 slices of bacon

SAUCE
- 1 tablespoon extra-virgin olive oil
- 1 garlic clove, minced
- 1 Granny Smith apple—peeled, cored and cut into ⅓-inch dice
- ¾ cup apple cider
- ½ cup dry Riesling wine
- ¼ cup chicken stock or broth
- ½ teaspoon chopped sage
- ½ teaspoon chopped thyme

Kosher salt and freshly ground pepper

1. MAKE THE PORK: In a skillet, heat the oil until shimmering. Add the onion. Cook over moderate heat until translucent, 3 minutes. Add the sausage and cook, breaking it up, until cooked through, 3 minutes. Add the apple, garlic, thyme and sage. Cook until the apple begins to soften, 2 minutes. Stir in the greens. Cook until wilted, 2 minutes. Transfer to a bowl. Let cool to room temperature. Mix in the cheese; season with salt and pepper.

2. Light a grill. Using a long, thin knife and beginning at a thick end, cut a 1-inch-wide pocket through the center of each tenderloin, using the handle of a wooden spoon to widen it if necessary. Fill the pocket with stuffing, poking it in with the wooden spoon. Season the tenderloins with salt and pepper and wrap the bacon securely around them; try to cover any exposed stuffing with the bacon. Grill over moderately high heat, turning 4 times, until they are browned on every side, 25 minutes, or the internal temperature reaches 140°. Transfer to a cutting board, cover tightly with foil and let rest for 10 to 15 minutes.

3. MAKE THE SAUCE: In a saucepan, heat the oil. Add the garlic and cook over moderate heat until fragrant, 1 minute. Add the apple, cider, wine, stock, sage and thyme and simmer until the apple softens, 7 minutes. Transfer to a blender and puree until smooth. Strain back into the pan and boil until it coats the back of a spoon, 5 minutes. Season with salt and pepper.

4. Slice the pork tenderloins crosswise about 1 inch thick and arrange on plates. Spoon the sauce around the meat and serve.—*Debra Whiting*

MAKE AHEAD The wrapped, stuffed pork and finished sauce can be refrigerated separately overnight. Bring the tenderloins to room temperature before grilling.

WINE Vivid, lightly sweet Riesling.

Asian Ribs with Five-Spice Rub and Hoisin Glaze
TOTAL: 40 MIN
4 SERVINGS ●

- 4 pounds pork spareribs
- ⅓ cup Asian Five-Spice Rub (recipe follows)
- ½ cup hoisin sauce
- 2 tablespoons ketchup

Vegetable oil, for brushing

1. Using a sharp knife, make ¼-inch-deep slashes in the rib meat between the bones, without cutting through. Spread all but 1 tablespoon of the spice rub over the ribs and into the slashes and let stand for 5 minutes.

2. Meanwhile, in a small saucepan, combine the hoisin sauce, ketchup and the remaining 1 tablespoon of spice rub and bring to a boil. Cook for 1 minute, then transfer to a bowl.

3. Light a grill. Lightly brush the ribs with oil and grill them over a moderately high fire, turning frequently, until they are sizzling and cooked through, about 25 minutes. Brush the ribs with half of the hoisin glaze and grill for 2 minutes longer. Transfer them to a cutting board and cut in between the bones. Serve the ribs with the remaining hoisin glaze on the side. —*Grace Parisi*

WINE Fruity, luscious Shiraz.

ASIAN FIVE-SPICE RUB
TOTAL: 5 MIN
MAKES ABOUT ⅓ CUP ● ●

- 3 tablespoons Chinese five-spice powder
- 1 tablespoon light brown sugar
- 1 tablespoon kosher salt
- 1 teaspoon cayenne pepper
- ½ teaspoon garlic powder

In a small bowl, combine all of the ingredients, pressing out any lumps in the brown sugar. —*G.P.*

OTHER USES Try the rub on rib eye steaks, beef ribs, pork or chicken thighs.

● FAST   ● HEALTHY   ● MAKE AHEAD   ● STAFF FAVORITE

pork & veal

Crispy Deep-Fried Ribs

ACTIVE: 45 MIN; TOTAL: 3 HR

6 SERVINGS ●

One reason these ribs are so impossibly good is that they're braised for hours and then deep-fried so they're supercrisp. The sauce—which includes ketchup and plenty of garlic—was originally concocted for chicken wings.

- 14 large garlic cloves, 8 peeled and smashed, 6 minced
- ½ cup sliced fresh ginger plus ¼ cup minced (6 ounces total)
- 6 scallions, thinly sliced, white and green parts separated
- 4 star anise pods
- 3 cups soy sauce
- 2 quarts water
- 2 cups ginger ale
- ½ cup dry white wine
- Strips of zest and juice from 1 navel orange
- 1 cup granulated sugar
- ½ cup cilantro stems plus ¼ cup coarsely chopped cilantro
- 3 racks of baby back ribs (5½ pounds)

- ¼ cup vegetable oil, plus more for frying
- 2 cups lightly packed brown sugar
- 1 cup ketchup
- 1 teaspoon crushed red pepper
- ½ cup all-purpose flour
- ½ cup cornstarch

1. Preheat the oven to 400°. In a large roasting pan, combine the smashed garlic with the sliced ginger, the scallion whites, star anise, 1½ cups of the soy sauce, the water, ginger ale, white wine, orange zest and juice, granulated sugar and cilantro stems. Set the roasting pan over 2 burners and bring the braising liquid to a boil over moderately high heat.

2. Add the baby back ribs to the roasting pan, cover tightly with foil and bake the ribs for about 2 hours, or until they are very tender. Let cool to room temperature, then spread the ribs out in a single layer on a baking sheet and refrigerate until they are chilled and firm, about 30 minutes. Discard the braising liquid.

3. Meanwhile, in a large saucepan, heat the ¼ cup of vegetable oil. Add the minced garlic with the minced ginger and the scal-

lion greens and cook the aromatics over moderately high heat, stirring, until they are fragrant, about 1 minute. Add the remaining 1½ cups of soy sauce along with the brown sugar, ketchup and crushed red pepper and bring the rib sauce to a boil. Cook the rib sauce over moderately high heat for 3 minutes, stirring occasionally. Remove the sauce from the heat and add the chopped cilantro. Transfer the rib sauce to a large bowl.

4. In a large sturdy pot, heat 1½ inches of vegetable oil to 375°. In a large bowl, whisk the flour with the cornstarch. Cut the racks into individual ribs. Toss the ribs in the flour mixture and shake off the excess flour. Working in batches, fry the ribs until the coating is lightly golden and crisp, about 2 minutes. Transfer the deep-fried ribs to paper towels to drain briefly, then add them to the sauce in the bowl and toss to coat. Pile the deep-fried ribs on a serving platter and serve them hot. —*Ola Fendert*

MAKE AHEAD The recipe can be prepared through Step 3; refrigerate the ribs and sauce separately for up to 2 days.

WINE Intense, fruity Zinfandel.

Chinese-Style Ribs with Guava Barbecue Sauce

ACTIVE: 45 MIN; TOTAL: 2 HR

4 SERVINGS ●

- 2 tablespoons sugar
- 1 tablespoon kosher salt
- 1 tablespoon dry mustard
- 1 teaspoon Chinese five-spice powder
- ½ teaspoon freshly ground pepper
- ½ teaspoon ground cinnamon
- ¼ teaspoon ground cloves
- 5 pounds baby back ribs
- ½ cup medium-dry sherry
- Guava Barbecue Sauce (recipe follows), for glazing and serving

1. Light a grill. When the coals are covered with a light gray ash, push them to opposite sides of the grill and set a disposable drip pan in the center. If using a gas grill, turn off the center burners.

2. In a bowl, combine the sugar, salt, dry mustard, Chinese five-spice powder, pepper, cinnamon and cloves. Sprinkle the mixture over the ribs. Pour the sherry into a spray bottle.

3. Place the ribs on the hot grate above the drip pan and away from the coals, bony side down. Cover and grill for 30 minutes. Spray the ribs with sherry. Cover and grill for another 30 minutes. Shift the ribs around (but keep them bony side down) and spray once more with sherry. Cover and grill for about 30 minutes longer, until the meat is tender. Replenish the coals as necessary throughout grilling.

4. Take the ribs off the grill and spread the coals out evenly. Brush the Guava Barbecue Sauce on both sides of the ribs and grill directly over the fire for about 1 minute per side, until glazed and bubbling. Transfer the ribs to a platter and let rest for 5 minutes. Cut down between the bones and arrange the ribs on a platter. Pass the remaining sauce at the table.
—*Steven Raichlen*

WINE Intense, fruity Zinfandel.

GUAVA BARBECUE SAUCE
ACTIVE: 10 MIN; TOTAL: 25 MIN
MAKES ABOUT 1¼ CUPS ● ●

- 8 ounces canned guava paste (see Note), cut into ½-inch pieces (1 cup)
- ⅓ cup cider vinegar
- ¼ cup dark rum
- 3 tablespoons tomato paste
- 3 tablespoons fresh lime juice
- 1 tablespoon soy sauce
- 1 tablespoon Worcestershire sauce
- 2 teaspoons minced fresh ginger
- 1 scallion, white part only, minced
- 1 garlic clove, minced
- ¼ cup water
- Salt and freshly ground pepper

In a small saucepan, combine the guava paste with the vinegar, rum, tomato paste, lime juice, soy sauce, Worcestershire sauce, ginger, scallion, garlic and water and bring to a boil. Simmer over low heat, stirring occasionally, until reduced to 1¼ cups, about 15 minutes. Season the sauce with salt and pepper. —*S.R.*

NOTE Guava paste is usually sold in flat metal cans. It is available at many supermarkets as well as at Latin markets.

MAKE AHEAD The barbecue sauce can be refrigerated for up to 5 days.

Roasted Pork with Sticky Mango Glaze
ACTIVE: 20 MIN; TOTAL: 1 HR 45 MIN
12 SERVINGS ●

Mangoes, ubiquitous in the Caribbean, flavor this sticky, slightly spicy glaze for roasted pork. Sweet-and-sour tamarind paste adds tartness to the glaze.

- ½ large mango, peeled and cut into ½-inch chunks (1 cup)
- 2 tablespoons sugar
- 1½ teaspoons tamarind paste (see Note)
- 1 teaspoon Worcestershire sauce
- ½ teaspoon soy sauce
- ¼ teaspoon crushed red pepper
- ½ teaspoon vegetable oil
- 1 garlic clove, minced
- Salt and freshly ground pepper
- 1 tablespoon extra-virgin olive oil
- One 4-pound pork loin roast, tied
- ½ cup dry white wine
- ¾ cup chicken stock or low-sodium broth

1. Preheat the oven to 300°. In a blender, combine the mango chunks with the sugar, tamarind paste, Worcestershire sauce, soy sauce and crushed red pepper and puree them until smooth.

2. In a small saucepan, heat the vegetable oil until shimmering. Add the minced garlic and cook over moderate heat until fragrant, about 1 minute. Add the mango puree, season with salt and pepper and bring the glaze to a simmer. Cook the glaze over low heat until it is slightly thickened, about 5 minutes.

3. In a large ovenproof skillet, heat the olive oil until shimmering. Season the pork roast with salt and pepper. Add the roast to the skillet and cook over high heat, turning occasionally with tongs, until browned all over, about 7 minutes.

4. Transfer the skillet to the oven and roast the pork for about 45 minutes, until an instant-read thermometer inserted in the thickest part registers 130°. Brush the mango glaze all over the roast, turning to coat it evenly. Continue to roast the pork until an instant-read thermometer inserted in the center registers 135°, about 5 minutes longer.

5. Light the broiler. Brush some of the mango glaze and pan drippings over the pork; broil 8 inches from the heat for about 5 minutes, or until the mango glaze is slightly sticky and golden. Transfer the roast to a cutting board and let rest for 15 minutes.

6. Meanwhile, pour off the fat from the skillet and set the skillet over moderately high heat. Add the white wine and cook, scraping up any browned bits from the bottom of the skillet. Transfer the jus to a small saucepan and simmer the jus until it is reduced by half, about 5 minutes. Add the chicken stock and simmer until slightly reduced, about 3 minutes longer. Season the jus with salt and pepper.

7. Discard the strings from the roast and slice ⅓ inch thick. Serve with the jus.
—*Carolina Buia and Isabel González*

NOTE Tamarind paste is available at Latin, Asian and Indian markets and specialty food shops.

WINE Bright, tart Barbera.

BRAISED PORK SHANKS

Braised Pork Shanks

ACTIVE: 1 HR; TOTAL: 3 HR 30 MIN

6 SERVINGS ●

Pork shanks, which come from the front leg of the pig, can be chewy when cooked incorrectly. When prepared properly, however, they become succulent and flavorful. The best way to cook them is a long, slow braise, as in the recipe here. Don't let the liquid boil, or it will toughen the meat.

- ½ cup all-purpose flour
- 2 tablespoons chile powder

Kosher salt and freshly ground pepper

Six 1½-pound pork shanks

- ¼ cup extra-virgin olive oil
- 1 medium onion, chopped
- 2 medium carrots, chopped
- 2 medium celery ribs, chopped
- 6 garlic cloves, minced
- 1 cup dry white wine
- 6 cups chicken stock or broth
- 3 rosemary sprigs
- 2 bay leaves
- 2 thyme sprigs

1. In a large, sturdy resealable plastic bag, combine the flour and chile powder with 1 tablespoon each of salt and pepper. Add the pork shanks, one at a time, and shake to coat thoroughly.

2. In a large skillet, heat 2 tablespoons of the olive oil until shimmering. Add 3 of the pork shanks and cook over moderately high heat until browned all over, about 10 minutes. Transfer the browned shanks to a deep, heavy casserole. Wipe out the skillet and brown the remaining shanks in the remaining olive oil; lower the heat if necessary. Add the shanks to the casserole.

3. Add the onion, carrots, celery and garlic to the skillet. Cook over moderate heat until softened, about 5 minutes. Add the wine and bring to a boil. Simmer until slightly reduced, about 2 minutes. Pour the wine and vegetables over the pork. Add the stock, rosemary, bay leaves and thyme, season with salt and pepper and bring to a boil. Tuck the shanks into the liquid so they're mostly submerged. Cover and cook over moderately low heat for 2½ hours, or until very tender. Turn the pork shanks every 30 minutes to keep them submerged. Transfer the braised shanks to a large, deep platter, cover and keep warm.

4. Strain the liquid, pressing hard on the solids; discard the solids. Return the liquid to the casserole and boil until reduced to 4 cups, about 20 minutes. Spoon off the fat, pour the pork gravy over the braised shanks and serve. —*Tim Love*

MAKE AHEAD The recipe can be refrigerated for up to 2 days.

WINE Firm, complex Cabernet Sauvignon.

Sautéed Pork Cutlets with Prosciutto, Sage and Lemon

TOTAL: 30 MIN

6 SERVINGS ●

Two 1-pound pork tenderloins, each cut on the bias into 6 slices

Freshly ground pepper

- 12 sage leaves
- 12 thin slices of prosciutto (6 ounces)
- ¼ cup extra-virgin olive oil
- 3½ tablespoons unsalted butter
- ½ cup chicken stock or broth
- 3 tablespoons fresh lemon juice

1. Lay the pork slices on a work surface and pound to ¼-inch thickness. Season with pepper. Set a sage leaf in the center of each cutlet. Top each cutlet with a slice of prosciutto; thread 2 toothpicks through each one to secure the prosciutto.

2. In a very large skillet, heat 2 tablespoons of the olive oil until shimmering. Add 1 tablespoon of the butter. Arrange 6 of the cutlets in the skillet, prosciutto side down, and cook over moderately high heat until the prosciutto is crisp, about 1 minute. Turn the cutlets and cook until they are barely pink in the center, about 3 minutes. Transfer the cutlets to a warm platter. Wipe out the skillet and repeat with 1 tablespoon of butter and the remaining 2 tablespoons of olive oil and 6 cutlets.

3. Wipe out the skillet. Add the stock, lemon juice and any accumulated juices. Boil over high heat until reduced to ½ cup, about 2 minutes. Off the heat, swirl in the remaining butter. Pour the sauce over the pork and serve. —*Morgan Brownlow*

WINE Full-bodied, minerally Riesling.

Curried Pork and Squash

TOTAL: 25 MIN

2 SERVINGS ●

One 12-ounce pork tenderloin, cut into 6 medallions and flattened slightly

- 1 teaspoon Madras curry powder

Salt and freshly ground pepper

- 2 tablespoons extra-virgin olive oil
- 2 tablespoons unsalted butter
- ½ cup butternut squash, cut into ⅓-inch dice
- 1 small red onion, thinly sliced lengthwise
- 2 large shiitake mushrooms, stemmed, caps thickly sliced
- 1 tablespoon balsamic vinegar
- 1 teaspoon thyme leaves

1. Heat a large, heavy skillet until hot to the touch. Season the pork medallions with the curry powder, salt and pepper. Add the olive oil to the skillet, then add the pork medallions and cook over moderately high heat until lightly browned on one side, about 2 minutes. Turn the medallions and add the butter. Move the pork to one side of the skillet and add the squash. Cook, stirring the squash occasionally, until crisp-tender, 2 minutes. Transfer the pork medallions to a plate and keep warm.

2. Add the onion and shiitakes to the squash, season with salt and pepper and cook, stirring until all of the vegetables are tender, about 3 minutes. Add the balsamic vinegar, thyme and any accumulated pork juices to the squash. Spoon the vegetables onto plates, arrange the pork medallions around them and serve. —*Stuart Brioza*

WINE Intense, fruity Zinfandel.

pork & veal

Pork and Leeks in Avgolemono Sauce

ACTIVE: 30 MIN; TOTAL: 1 HR 40 MIN

6 SERVINGS ●●

- 2½ pounds boneless pork shoulder, cut into 1½-inch pieces
- 2 cups beef broth
- 2 cups water
- 2 celery ribs, cut into 1-inch pieces
- 1 large carrot, cut into 1-inch pieces
- 1 tablespoon extra-virgin olive oil
- 4 large leeks, white and tender green parts only, sliced crosswise ¾ inch thick
- 3 large egg yolks
- 1 large egg
- ¼ cup fresh lemon juice
- 2 tablespoons cold water
- 1½ tablespoons all-purpose flour
- 2 tablespoons chopped dill

1. In a large enameled cast-iron casserole, bring the pork, beef broth, water, celery, carrot and olive oil to a simmer. Cook over moderately low heat, skimming occasionally, until the meat is tender, 1 hour.
2. Using a slotted spoon, transfer the meat and vegetables to a bowl. Add the leeks and bring to a boil, then simmer over moderately low heat, stirring occasionally, until softened, 20 minutes. Ladle 2 cups of the broth into a glass measuring cup.
3. In a medium bowl, whisk the yolks with the whole egg, then whisk in the lemon juice. In a small bowl, whisk the cold water with the flour, then whisk into the eggs. Gradually add the reserved broth to the egg mixture, whisking constantly. Add to the casserole and simmer over moderate heat, stirring, until the sauce thickens, 2 to 3 minutes. Return the meat and vegetables to the casserole and reheat. Stir in the dill. Serve. —*Evangelos Gerovassiliou*

SERVE WITH Noodles, crusty bread, rice or orzo.

MAKE AHEAD The stew can be refrigerated for up to 2 days.

WINE Fresh, lively Soave.

Pork Roast with Sausage, Fruit and Nut Stuffing

ACTIVE: 45 MIN; TOTAL: 3 HR 30 MIN

12 SERVINGS

Pork and fruit is a classic pairing around the world, but this dish gets a particularly Spanish flavor from the combination of dried fruit and *butifarra* (a Catalan cured pork sausage) in the stuffing. The stuffing cooks inside the roast, which gives it a deep, marvelously porky flavor.

- ¼ cup pine nuts
- ¼ cup walnut halves
- 1 cup brandy
- 12 dried apricots
- 12 pitted prunes
- 1 teaspoon finely grated clementine zest
- 1 pound *butifarra* or sweet Italian sausage, meat removed from the casings
- ¼ cup extra-virgin olive oil
- 4 garlic cloves, minced
- Salt and freshly ground pepper
- Two 6-rib pork loin roasts (8½ pounds total)
- 1½ teaspoons minced thyme
- 1½ teaspoons minced rosemary
- 3 tablespoons all-purpose flour
- 2 cups chicken stock or low-sodium broth

1. Preheat the oven to 350°. Spread the pine nuts and walnuts in a pie plate and bake them for about 3 minutes, or until they are lightly toasted. Coarsely chop the walnuts.
2. In a small saucepan, bring the brandy to a simmer. Add the dried apricots, cover and simmer for 2 minutes. Add the pitted prunes and the clementine zest. Remove the saucepan from the heat and let the fruit stand in the brandy for 20 minutes. With a slotted spoon, transfer the fruit to a work surface. Simmer the brandy over moderately high heat until it is reduced to ¼ cup, about 7 minutes. Cut the apricots and prunes into quarters.
3. In a medium nonstick skillet, cook the sausage over moderate heat, breaking it up with a spoon, until almost no pink remains, about 5 minutes. Transfer the sausage to a food processor and process until finely ground. Transfer to a large bowl.
4. Heat 2 tablespoons of the olive oil in the skillet. Add the garlic and cook over moderate heat until fragrant, about 3 minutes. Add to the sausage in the bowl, along with the nuts, apricots, prunes and the reduced brandy and season with salt and pepper.
5. Carve a 3½-inch pocket along the length of each roast, sliding the knife between the bones and the meat. Fill the pockets with the stuffing. Put the roasts on a large rimmed baking sheet, rib bones up. Rub the roasts with the remaining 2 tablespoons of olive oil. Sprinkle the roasts with the thyme and rosemary and season with salt and pepper.
6. Roast the meat for about 1 hour and 45 minutes, rotating the baking sheet halfway through, until an instant-read thermometer inserted in the thickest part registers 140°. Transfer the roasts to a carving board and let rest in a warm spot for 15 to 20 minutes.
7. Tilt the baking sheet and pour off most of the fat. Put the baking sheet over moderate heat. Sprinkle the flour over the sheet and stir in ½ cup of the chicken stock, scraping up the browned bits. Transfer to a medium saucepan and whisk in the remaining 1½ cups of stock. Simmer over low heat, whisking often, until the gravy is thickened and no floury taste remains, about 5 minutes. Pour into a gravy boat.
8. Using a carving knife, carve the roasts into chops. Transfer the chops to plates and pass the gravy at the table.
—*José Andrés*

MAKE AHEAD The stuffed roasts can be refrigerated overnight. Bring to room temperature before roasting.

WINE Complex, elegant Pinot Noir.

PORK ROAST WITH SAUSAGE,
FRUIT AND NUT STUFFING

BRAISED PORK WITH PEARL ONIONS AND GRAPES

Braised Pork with Pearl Onions and Grapes

ACTIVE: 45 MIN; TOTAL: 1 HR 30 MIN

4 SERVINGS ●

One 2-pound boneless rib-end
    pork loin roast
Salt and freshly ground pepper
5 tablespoons unsalted butter,
    2 tablespoons softened
½ cup dry white wine
2 cups low-sodium chicken broth
2 garlic cloves, thinly sliced
1 bay leaf
1 thyme sprig plus 1 teaspoon
    chopped thyme
½ small yellow onion, coarsely
    chopped
¾ pound pearl onions
2 tablespoons all-purpose flour
½ pound red and green grapes

1. Season the pork with salt and pepper. In a small enameled cast-iron casserole, melt 2 tablespoons of butter. Add the pork and brown well over moderately high heat, about 10 minutes; transfer to a plate. Pour off the fat. Add the wine and boil over high heat, scraping up the browned bits, until reduced by half, 3 minutes. Add the broth and bring to a boil. Add the garlic, bay leaf, thyme sprig, onion and the pork. Cover and simmer over very low heat, turning once, until an instant-read thermometer inserted in the center registers 160°, about 1 hour.

2. Meanwhile, in a medium saucepan of water, boil the pearl onions until almost tender, 5 minutes; drain and peel. In a bowl, blend the 2 tablespoons of softened butter with the flour to form a paste.

3. Transfer the pork to a plate. Strain the cooking liquid and return to the casserole; boil until reduced to 2 cups, 4 minutes. Whisk ½ cup of the cooking liquid into the flour paste until smooth, then whisk the mixture into the cooking liquid. Simmer over moderately high heat, whisking, until thickened. Simmer over low heat, stirring, until no floury taste remains, 5 minutes. Stir in the chopped thyme and season with salt and pepper. Return the pork and its juices to the casserole and add the onions. Cover and bring just to a simmer, turning the pork a few times in the sauce to heat it up.

4. In a skillet, melt the remaining butter. Add the grapes and cook over moderately high heat, shaking the skillet, until they start to burst. Thickly slice the pork and transfer to plates. Spoon the sauce, pearl onions and grapes on top; serve. —*Marcia Kiesel*

WINE Fruity, low-oak Chardonnay.

Spicy Ginger Pork in Lettuce Leaves

ACTIVE: 20 MIN; TOTAL: 30 MIN

6 FIRST-COURSE SERVINGS ● ● ●

¾ pound ground pork
1 red bell pepper, finely diced
1 garlic clove, minced
1 tablespoon minced peeled ginger
1 tablespoon Thai sweet chile sauce
1 tablespoon Asian fish sauce
1 teaspoon Asian sesame oil
1 tablespoon plus 1 teaspoon
    grapeseed oil
One 8-ounce can whole water
    chestnuts, drained and diced
2 scallions, thinly sliced
2 tablespoons oyster sauce
2 tablespoons chopped cilantro
24 Boston lettuce leaves

1. In a bowl, mix the pork, bell pepper, garlic, ginger, chile sauce, fish sauce, sesame oil and 1 tablespoon of grapeseed oil.

2. In a large skillet or wok, heat the remaining 1 teaspoon of grapeseed oil until shimmering. Add the pork; stir-fry over high heat, breaking it up, until cooked through and starting to brown, 8 minutes. Stir in the water chestnuts, scallions, oyster sauce and cilantro. Remove from the heat.

3. Spoon the pork into bowls. Stack the lettuce leaves on plates. To eat, spoon the pork onto the lettuce leaves, roll up and eat. —*Annabel Langbein*

WINE Full-bodied, rich Pinot Gris.

Grilled Pork Tenderloin Salad

TOTAL: 30 MIN

4 TO 6 SERVINGS ● ●

⅓ cup red wine vinegar
1 garlic clove
1 small shallot, chopped
1 teaspoon Dijon mustard
1 large basil leaf
½ teaspoon dried Greek oregano
½ cup extra-virgin olive oil
Kosher salt and freshly ground pepper
Two ¾-pound pork tenderloins
2 medium tomatoes, quartered
1 small onion, sliced crosswise
    ⅓ inch thick
1 pound medium asparagus
5 ounces prewashed mesclun
    greens (6 cups)
3 ounces thinly sliced prosciutto,
    cut into strips

1. In a blender, combine the vinegar with the garlic, shallot, mustard, basil, and oregano and puree. With the machine on, pour in ¼ cup plus 2 tablespoons of the oil; season with salt and pepper.

2. Light a grill or preheat a grill pan. Season the pork with salt and pepper. Grill the pork over moderately high heat, turning once, until browned and cooked through, about 10 minutes. Transfer to a cutting board and let rest for 5 minutes.

3. In a medium bowl, toss the tomatoes, onion and asparagus with the remaining olive oil; season with salt and pepper. Grill the vegetables over moderately high heat until lightly browned, about 2 minutes for the tomatoes and 4 minutes for the onions and asparagus. Transfer to a plate.

4. In a large bowl, toss the mesclun with the prosciutto, grilled onion and half of the vinaigrette. Mound the salad onto plates. Thinly slice the pork and arrange it on the plates, along with grilled tomatoes and asparagus. Drizzle the pork and vegetables with the remaining vinaigrette and serve. —*Michael Psilakis*

WINE Peppery, refreshing Grüner Veltliner.

pork & veal

Pork and Purple Taro Stew

ACTIVE: 25 MIN; TOTAL: 50 MIN

6 SERVINGS ●

If you can't find purple taro root, a vividly colored variety of this starchy, slightly sweet root vegetable, substitute ordinary taro root or purple or yellow potatoes.

- ¼ cup vegetable oil
- 1½ pounds trimmed pork shoulder, cut into ½-inch dice
- Salt and freshly ground pepper
- 2 large shallots, thinly sliced
- 2 large garlic cloves, very finely chopped
- 2 tablespoons soy sauce
- 4 cups water
- 1 pound taro root, preferably purple, or 1 pound purple or yellow potatoes, peeled and sliced ¼ inch thick
- ¾ cup diagonally sliced garlic chives or onion chives

1. In a large saucepan, heat 3 tablespoons of the oil. Add half of the pork at a time, season with salt and pepper and cook over high heat, stirring once, until lightly browned, about 4 minutes. With a slotted spoon, transfer the pork to a bowl.
2. Add the remaining 1 tablespoon of oil to the saucepan. Add the shallots and garlic and cook over low heat, stirring occasionally, until softened, about 5 minutes. Add the soy sauce, increase the heat to high and cook for 2 minutes. Add the water and bring to a boil. Add the sliced taro and the browned pork and its juices.
3. Simmer the stew over moderately low heat, stirring occasionally, until the pork and taro are tender, 15 minutes. Season with salt and pepper and stir in the garlic chives. Let the stew stand for 5 minutes before serving. —*Marcia Kiesel*

SERVE WITH Steamed rice.

MAKE AHEAD The pork stew can be made 1 day ahead and refrigerated. Gently rewarm the stew and stir in the chives.

WINE Intense, spicy Syrah.

Choucroute Garnie

ACTIVE: 30 MIN; TOTAL: 2 HR 40 MIN PLUS OVERNIGHT CURING

10 SERVINGS ●

Families in Alsace generally eat choucroute garnie during the winter because it's such a hearty dish. Here, F&W contributing editor Jacques Pépin adapted the recipe to make it quicker and easier—calling for store-bought sauerkraut instead of the homemade kind, for instance. Serve it with two or three types of mustard, such as a hot Dijon, a grainy Pommery and a tarragon-flavored mustard.

- ⅓ cup kosher salt, plus more for seasoning
- 2 tablespoons light brown sugar
- 3 pounds pork back ribs or baby back ribs, cut into 3 sections
- 6 pounds sauerkraut (in plastic bags), drained
- ¼ cup duck or goose fat or peanut oil
- 1 large onion, coarsely chopped
- 4 large garlic cloves, coarsely chopped
- 20 juniper berries
- 3 large bay leaves
- ½ teaspoon caraway seeds
- 1 teaspoon freshly ground pepper
- 3 cups chicken stock
- 1½ cups Riesling or Pinot Gris
- 2 pounds Polish kielbasa, skinned and cut into 2-inch pieces
- 10 skinless hot dogs
- One 2-pound piece of boneless boiled ham (3 to 4 inches wide), sliced ¼ inch thick
- 2 pounds medium potatoes (about 10), peeled
- Assorted mustards, for serving

1. In a large, sturdy, resealable plastic bag, combine the ⅓ cup of kosher salt with the sugar. Add the pork ribs; shake well to thoroughly coat the ribs with the seasonings. Seal the bag and refrigerate the ribs overnight or for up to 24 hours.

2. The next day, preheat the oven to 300°. Rinse the sauerkraut in cold water; squeeze dry. Melt the duck fat in a large roasting pan set over 2 burners on high heat. Add the onion and garlic. Cook over moderately low heat, stirring, until softened, 7 minutes. Stir in the sauerkraut, juniper berries, bay leaves, caraway, pepper, stock and wine and bring to a rolling boil over high heat.
3. Meanwhile, rinse the pork ribs under cold water and pat dry. Nestle the pork ribs in the sauerkraut and bring back to a boil over moderately high heat. Cover tightly with foil and bake for 1½ hours.
4. Remove the ribs from the sauerkraut. Cut between the ribs; return to the sauerkraut and nestle in the kielbasa, hot dogs and ham. Cover and bake until hot, 5 minutes. Discard the bay leaves.
5. Meanwhile, in a large saucepan, cover the potatoes with cold water, add salt and bring to a boil over high heat; cook the potatoes until tender when pierced. Drain the potatoes and cover to keep warm.
6. To serve, mound the sauerkraut in the center of very hot dinner plates and partially tuck in the ribs and kielbasa. Arrange the hot dogs and ham around the sauerkraut. Alternatively, pile the sauerkraut on a large heated platter and garnish with the meats. Serve with the boiled potatoes and assorted mustards. —*Jacques Pépin*

MAKE AHEAD The choucroute can be prepared through Step 3 and refrigerated for 3 days. Reheat before proceeding.

WINE Full-bodied, minerally Riesling.

Lemon-and-Pickled-Pepper-Glazed Ham

ACTIVE: 30 MIN; TOTAL: 3 HR

10 SERVINGS

Any pickled pepper will work in this recipe but F&W's Grace Parisi loves hot Peppadews for their fruity flavor and sweet-and-sour brine. Since the heat level of pickled peppers can vary, you should add them gradually while making the glaze.

One 7½ pound bone-in smoked ham
1 lemon, thinly sliced
1 large white onion, thinly sliced
3 cups chicken stock or broth
¾ cup lemon-lime marmalade
  (17 ounces; see Note) or lemon,
  orange or grapefruit marmalade
¼ cup seeded, coarsely chopped
  pickled peppers, such as hot
  Peppadew, Italian cherry peppers
  or jalapeños
¼ cup grainy mustard
3 tablespoons fresh lemon juice
2 tablespoons bourbon
2 tablespoons cornstarch dissolved
  in 3 tablespoons water

1. Preheat the oven to 375°. Using a sharp knife, remove the rind from the ham, leaving a ¼-inch layer of fat all around it. Deeply score the fat in a crosshatch pattern at ½-inch intervals. Transfer to a large roasting pan. Scatter around the lemon and onion and add the stock.

2. In a food processor, process the marmalade, pickled peppers, mustard, lemon juice and bourbon to a coarse puree. Brush the top of the ham with 2 tablespoons of the glaze. Cover with foil and bake for 1 hour. Remove the foil. Brush the ham with a scant ½ cup of glaze and bake for 1 hour. Brush with another scant ½ cup of glaze and bake until the ham is browned and an instant-read thermometer inserted in the thickest part registers 155°, 30 minutes.

3. Transfer the ham to a cutting board. Strain the juices into a large glass measuring cup and skim the fat; boil in a saucepan until reduced to 2½ cups, 5 minutes. Whisk the cornstarch slurry and add to the juices with the remaining ½ cup of glaze. Simmer over moderately high heat, stirring, until thickened, 3 minutes. Slice the ham and serve with the sauce. —*Grace Parisi*

NOTE Lemon-lime marmalade (we like Thursday Cottage brand) is available at supermarkets and specialty shops.

WINE Dry, fruity sparkling wine.

CHOUCROUTE GARNIE

LEMON-AND-PICKLED-PEPPER-GLAZED HAM

pork & veal

Grilled Pork Chops with Orange Barbecue Sauce

ACTIVE: 25 MIN; TOTAL: 1 HR 25 MIN
PLUS 4 HR MARINATING
8 SERVINGS

Chef and restaurateur Mario Batali brushes citrusy-spicy barbecue sauce on pork chops after they're almost cooked through so that the sauce doesn't burn on the grill. He prefers flavoring the sauce with blood orange juice, which is less acidic than classic orange juice, but both are good.

- 1 quart plus ¼ cup fresh orange juice, preferably blood orange juice

tools

grill

WEBER RANCH KETTLE
Most people own one grill. Steven Raichlen, the author of *The Barbecue Bible* and host of PBS's *Barbecue University with Steven Raichlen,* has 60. The Weber kettle grill above is one of his favorites. It's a kettle grill on steroids, an enormous charcoal grill that measures three feet across and can even be used to smoke a whole hog. (Raichlen's recipe for Patio Pig Pickin' is on p. 167.) **Details** $1,199; weber.com.

- 2 tablespoons light brown sugar
- 2 tablespoons extra-virgin olive oil
- 2 teaspoons ancho chile powder, or other pure chile powder
- 1 teaspoon ground cumin
- 8 bone-in pork chops, about 1 inch thick (10 to 12 ounces each)
- 1 cup ketchup
- 6 garlic cloves, thinly sliced
- 4 jalapeños, thinly sliced crosswise
- ¼ cup red wine vinegar
- 1 tablespoon fennel seeds
Salt
- 1 orange, preferably a blood orange, sliced crosswise (8 slices)

1. In each of 2 large resealable plastic bags, combine 2 tablespoons of the orange juice, 1 tablespoon of brown sugar, 1 tablespoon of olive oil, 1 teaspoon of ancho chile powder and ½ teaspoon of cumin. Seal the bags and shake to mix the marinade. Add 4 pork chops to each bag, seal and shake again to coat the chops with the sauce. Refrigerate for at least 4 hours.

2. Light a grill. In a large saucepan, combine the remaining 1 quart of orange juice with the ketchup, garlic cloves, jalapeños, red wine vinegar and fennel seeds and bring to a boil, stirring once or twice. Simmer the barbecue sauce over moderate heat, stirring occasionally, until reduced to 2 cups, about 30 minutes. Season the barbecue sauce with salt.

3. Season the pork chops with salt and grill over a medium-hot fire until nicely charred and just pink in the center, about 12 minutes per side. Brush a thick layer of barbecue sauce on each chop, cover the grill and cook until the pork is nicely glazed, about 3 minutes. Top each chop with an orange slice and serve. —*Mario Batali*
MAKE AHEAD The pork chops can be marinated overnight. The barbecue sauce can be refrigerated for up to 2 days.
WINE Deep, velvety Merlot.

Cider-Braised Ham with Apple-Onion Compote

ACTIVE: 30 MIN; TOTAL: 4 HR
10 TO 12 SERVINGS

- ¼ cup pure maple syrup
- ¼ cup Dijon mustard
- 2 tablespoons dark brown sugar
One 10-pound bone-in smoked ham from the shank end
- 3 Granny Smith apples—peeled cored and thinly sliced
- 1 large onion, thinly sliced
- 1 cup apple cider
- 1 cup chicken stock or low-sodium broth

1. Preheat the oven to 375°. In a small bowl, combine the maple syrup, mustard and brown sugar. Using a sharp knife, remove the rind from the ham, leaving a layer of fat at least ¼ inch thick all over. Score the fat in a crosshatch pattern at ½-inch intervals. Set the ham in a large roasting pan. Brush the ham with two tablespoons of the maple mustard glaze, and scatter the apple and onion slices around it. Add the cider and chicken broth to the pan. Cover the ham with foil and braise in the oven for 2 hours. Uncover the ham, and brush it with all but 2 tablespoons of the maple-mustard glaze. Bake uncovered about 1½ hours longer, until the ham is deeply browned and an instant-read thermometer inserted in the thickest part of the ham registers 155°.

2. Transfer the ham to a cutting board and let rest 20 minutes. Strain the gravy into a large glass measuring cup, gently shaking the strainer to extract as much liquid as possible. Reserve the apple-onion compote left in the strainer. Spoon off as much fat from the gravy as possible. In a saucepan, boil the gravy until reduced to 1½ cups, 15 minutes. Whisk in the remaining 2 tablespoons of glaze. Slice the ham, and serve with the apple-onion compote and the gravy. —*Grace Parisi*
WINE Vivid, lightly sweet Riesling.

Patio Pig Pickin'

ACTIVE: 3 HR 15 MIN; TOTAL: 8 HR

15 TO 18 SERVINGS

Instead of a whole hog, barbecue expert Steven Raichlen's recipe calls for slow smoking a whole fresh ham North Carolina style. Raichlen, the award-winning author of 27 cookbooks, uses a large kettle grill like the one shown at the far left when he makes this version of pulled pork because of its sheer size and high-domed lid. Serve the pulled pork on a bun with the peppery vinegar sauce and mustard slaw that follow.

Coarse salt

- 2 tablespoons sweet paprika
- 1 tablespoon brown sugar
- 1 tablespoon garlic powder

Freshly ground black pepper

One 15- to 16-pound fresh ham

- 6 cups hickory wood chips or chunks, soaked for 1 hour in water, then drained

Vinegar Sauce (recipe follows)

15 to 18 hamburger buns or kaiser rolls

- 1 stick unsalted butter, melted

Mustard Slaw (recipe follows)

1. Light a grill. When the coals are covered with a light gray ash, push them to opposite sides of the grill and set a disposable drip pan in the center. If using a gas grill, turn off the center burners.

2. In a small bowl, mix 3 tablespoons of the coarse salt with the sweet paprika, brown sugar, garlic powder and 1 tablespoon of freshly ground black pepper. Sprinkle the seasoning mixture all over the fresh ham, concentrating on the exposed part of the meat.

3. When the fire is medium low (275° to 300°), toss 1½ cups of the hickory wood chips on the coals. (If using a gas grill, toss the chips into a smoker box.) Set the fresh ham, skin side up, in the center of the hot grate above the drip pan and away from the coals. Cover the grill and cook the ham until it is darkly browned on the outside, cooked through and very tender inside, about 7 to 8 hours. You'll need to replenish the coals every 1 to 2 hours, the wood chips every hour for the first 4 hours. To test for doneness, use an instant-read meat thermometer: The internal temperature of the ham should be about 190°. (Yes, this is very well done—that's how you get meat tender enough to pull.) If the ham starts to brown too much, cover it loosely with aluminum foil for the last 2 hours or so, but remember that those browned bits are good, too.

4. Transfer the cooked ham to a cutting board. Cover the ham loosely with aluminum foil and let it rest for 20 minutes. Pull any crisp skin off the ham and, if you're so inclined, finely chop the skin with a cleaver. (Southern pit masters call the crispy bits "brownies" and mix a little in with their pulled pork.)

5. Wearing heatproof food gloves, pull the meat off the bones in large pieces; discard any bones or lumps of fat. Using your fingers or 2 forks, pull each piece of pork into thin shreds, or finely chop the pork with a cleaver. Transfer the pulled pork to a large heatproof pan and stir in about 2½ cups of the Vinegar Sauce, enough to keep the meat moist; add more as it is needed. Season the pulled pork with salt and pepper. If you are not quite ready to serve the pork, cover the pan with aluminum foil and place it on a warm (not hot) grill or in an oven set on low.

6. Lightly brush the cut sides of the hamburger buns with the melted butter. Lightly toast the buns on the warm grill. Just before serving, mound the pulled pork on the toasted hamburger buns, top the sandwiches with the Mustard Slaw and serve the sandwiches with the remaining Vinegar Sauce on the side.
—*Steven Raichlen*

WINE Fresh, fruity rosé.

VINEGAR SAUCE

TOTAL: 5 MIN

MAKES ABOUT 6 CUPS ● ●

This super sour sauce is designed to be a counterpoint to the richness and fattiness of the pulled pork.

- 4 cups distilled white vinegar
- 1⅓ cups water
- ⅔ cup ketchup
- ½ cup firmly packed brown sugar
- ¼ cup salt
- 2 tablespoons crushed red pepper
- 1 tablespoon freshly ground pepper

Combine all of the ingredients in a medium glass or ceramic bowl and whisk until the sugar and salt are thoroughly dissolved. If it's necessary, season the vinegar sauce with additional salt and pepper to taste; the sauce should be piquant and flavorful. —*S.R.*

MUSTARD SLAW

TOTAL: 20 MIN

15 TO 18 SERVINGS ● ● ●

- ⅓ cup Dijon mustard
- ⅓ cup sugar
- ⅓ cup distilled white vinegar
- ⅓ cup vegetable oil

2 to 3 tablespoons hot sauce

- 1 teaspoon celery seeds

Salt and freshly ground pepper

- 1 large head green cabbage, cored and finely chopped (about 10 cups)
- 4 carrots, finely grated

In a very large bowl, whisk the Dijon mustard with the sugar. Gradually whisk in the distilled white vinegar, the vegetable oil, hot sauce and celery seeds. Season the dressing with salt and pepper; the dressing should be highly seasoned. Add the cabbage and the carrots to the dressing in the bowl and toss the slaw thoroughly. Serve the slaw. —*S.R.*

PORK CHOP WITH STICKY RICE AND THAI GREEN-CHILE SAUCE

MIXED GRILL WITH CHIMICHURRI SAUCES AND ROASTED PEPPE

Pork Chops with Sticky Rice and Thai Green-Chile Sauce

**ACTIVE: 40 MIN; TOTAL: 3 HR 15 MIN
PLUS OVERNIGHT MARINATING**

4 SERVINGS ●

Here, in a play on Vietnamese pork chops, the meat is marinated in a mix of hoisin, orange juice and chiles, then served with sticky rice and a side of sweet, crunchy watermelon.

- ¼ cup plus 3 tablespoons Asian fish sauce
- ¼ cup hoisin sauce
- ¼ cup fresh orange juice
- ¼ cup coarsely chopped fresh ginger
- 2 tablespoons honey
- 1 tablespoon Chinese black bean sauce
- ½ teaspoon Asian sesame oil
- Eight ½-inch-thick, bone-in pork loin chops (about 5 ounces each)
- 2 garlic cloves, thinly sliced
- 10 Thai bird chiles or 2 serrano chiles, stemmed and thinly sliced
- 3 tablespoons sugar
- ¼ cup fresh lime juice
- 2 tablespoons water
- 2 tablespoons chopped cilantro, plus leaves for garnish
- 2 cups white sticky rice, soaked overnight (see Note)

Chilled watermelon slices, for serving

1. In a medium bowl, whisk ¼ cup of the fish sauce with the hoisin, orange juice, ginger, honey, black bean sauce and sesame oil; transfer to a shallow baking dish. Add the chops and turn to coat, then refrigerate for at least 3 hours or overnight.

2. Meanwhile, in a mortar, pound the garlic, chiles and 1 tablespoon of the sugar to a coarse paste; gradually add the remaining 2 tablespoons of sugar until pasty.

Add the lime juice, the remaining 3 tablespoons of fish sauce and the water. Stir in the chopped cilantro.

3. Line a bamboo steamer basket with moistened cheesecloth. Drain the soaked rice and spread it in the steamer in an even layer. Set the basket over a pot of boiling water, cover and steam the rice until tender but chewy, about 30 minutes. Cover, remove from the heat and keep warm.

4. Light a grill. Remove the pork from the marinade and grill over high heat, turning once, until lightly charred, about 6 minutes. Serve with the sticky rice, chile sauce, watermelon and cilantro. *—Pino Maffeo*

NOTE Sticky rice is often sold as sweet rice or Thai sticky rice.

MAKE AHEAD The marinating pork chops and Thai green-chile sauce can be refrigerated overnight.

WINE Vivid, lightly sweet Riesling.

Mixed Grill with Chimichurri Sauces and Roasted Peppers

TOTAL: 1 HR 30 MIN PLUS 2 HR FOR ACCOMPANIMENTS

6 SERVINGS ●

In Argentina, a mixed grill is called a *parrillada* (*parilla* is "grill" in Spanish) and is often served in a rustic style, with whole pieces of meat like chicken hearts and sausage brought to the table. For a more elegant presentation of the dish, Michelle Bernstein, chef of Michy's in Miami, grills the meat on skewers. She also serves chicken livers instead of chicken hearts and presents the mixed grill with a trio of different chimichurri sauces.

- 1 **pound fresh chorizo sausage, cut into 8 pieces**
- 1 **pound boneless chicken breasts with skin, cut into 8 pieces**
- 8 **large chicken livers, trimmed**
- 1 **pound skirt steak, cut into 8 pieces**

Extra-virgin olive oil, for drizzling

Salt and freshly ground pepper

Traditional Chimichurri, Sweet Paprika Chimichurri, Spicy Chimichurri (recipes follow), for serving

Roasted Bell Peppers (p. 254), for serving

1. Light a grill. Place the chorizo, chicken, chicken livers and skirt steak in 4 separate dishes and drizzle with oil; season the chicken and steak with salt and pepper. Grill the chorizo and chicken pieces over high heat until lightly charred and cooked through, about 3 minutes per side. Transfer to plates. Grill the chicken livers and skirt steak until lightly charred outside and rare within, for about 2 minutes per side.

2. Thread an assortment of the meats onto 6 long metal skewers and grill them just until they are heated through. Serve the mixed grill with the chimichurri sauces and the roasted bell peppers.
—*Michelle Bernstein*

WINE Rustic, peppery Malbec.

TRADITIONAL CHIMICHURRI

TOTAL: 10 MIN

MAKES ABOUT ¾ CUP ● ● ●

Michelle Bernstein, who was born and raised in Miami by an Argentinean mother and Minnesotan father, says that her mother taught her how to make this recipe when she was five years old. Chimichurri is an essential part of Argentinean cuisine; a bowl of chimichurri can be found on every dinner table. This chimichurri is typically served with steak, but it also tastes great on grilled fish and chicken.

- ¼ **cup coarsely chopped flat-leaf parsley**
- 3 **tablespoons red wine vinegar**
- 4 **large garlic cloves, very finely chopped (2½ tablespoons)**
- 2 **tablespoons oregano leaves**
- 2 **teaspoons crushed red pepper**

Kosher salt and freshly ground black pepper

- ½ **cup extra-virgin olive oil**

In a food processor, combine the chopped flat-leaf parsley with the red wine vinegar, very finely chopped garlic, oregano leaves and the crushed red pepper. Process the chimichurri sauce until it is smooth. Season the sauce with salt and pepper. Transfer the sauce to a small bowl and pour the olive oil over the mixture. Let the chimichurri sauce stand for at least 20 minutes before serving. —*M.B.*

MAKE AHEAD The chimichurri can be refrigerated overnight. Let the chimichurri sauce return to room temperature before serving.

SWEET PAPRIKA CHIMICHURRI

TOTAL: 10 MIN

MAKES ABOUT ¾ CUP ● ●

This recipe is traditionally made with *ají molido,* a sweet pepper powder similar to paprika, but slightly smokier.

- ½ **cup extra-virgin olive oil**
- ¼ **cup sweet paprika**
- 4 **garlic cloves, very finely chopped**

Juice of 1 lemon

- 1 **tablespoon water**

Salt and freshly ground black pepper

In a food processor, combine the olive oil, with the sweet paprika, very finely chopped garlic, the lemon juice and water and process until the chimichurri sauce is smooth. Season the sauce with salt and pepper. —*M.B.*

MAKE AHEAD The chimichurri can be refrigerated overnight. Let the chimichurri sauce return to room temperature before serving.

SPICY CHIMICHURRI

TOTAL: 10 MIN

MAKES ABOUT ½ CUP ● ●

Michelle Bernstein created this chimichurri for her Mexican husband, who loves jalapeños. Because the sauce is pureed, it is far from authentic. As she says, "This is not a chimichurri I would serve to my mother," who is Argentinean.

- ¾ **cup finely chopped cilantro**
- ¼ **cup extra-virgin olive oil**
- 1 **garlic clove, very finely chopped**
- 2 **tablespoons fresh lime juice**
- 1 **jalapeño, with seeds, chopped**

Salt and freshly ground black pepper

In a blender, pulse the chopped cilantro with the olive oil, very finely chopped garlic, lime juice and chopped jalapeño until the sauce is smooth. Season the chimichurri with salt and pepper.
—*M.B.*

MAKE AHEAD The spicy chimichurri sauce can be refrigerated for up to 4 hours. Let the sauce return to room temperature before serving.

pork & veal

Pork Meat Loaf with Chickpeas

ACTIVE: 30 MIN; TOTAL: 1 HR 15 MIN

8 SERVINGS ● ●

Four 1-inch slices of Italian bread,
crusts removed, bread soaked in
1 cup of milk and squeezed dry

- 4 ounces sliced bacon
- 4 ounces sliced prosciutto
- 1 medium onion, thinly sliced
- 2 garlic cloves, very finely chopped
- 4 oil-packed sun-dried tomatoes
- 1 roasted red pepper from a jar
- 2 large eggs
- 2 tablespoons chopped parsley
- 1 teaspoon chopped thyme
- 1 teaspoon crushed red pepper
- ½ teaspoon dried oregano

Kosher salt and freshly ground pepper

2½ pounds lean ground pork

Extra-virgin olive oil

- 1 cup tomato puree
- 1 cup chicken stock or broth
- ½ cup prepared plain hummus

1. Preheat the oven to 350°. In a food processor, pulse the bread, bacon and prosciutto. Add the onion, garlic, tomatoes, roasted pepper and eggs; process to a paste. Pulse in the parsley, thyme, crushed pepper, oregano and 1 teaspoon each of salt and pepper. Transfer to a bowl and knead in the pork. Preheat the broiler.

2. Pat the pork into two 8-inch loaves. In a large nonstick roasting pan, heat 1 tablespoon of oil. Transfer the loaves to the pan. Cook over moderate heat until the bottoms are browned, 6 minutes. Brush the tops with oil and broil until slightly browned, 8 minutes. Lower the oven to 350°.

3. In a cup, mix the tomato puree, stock and hummus; pour into the roasting pan and cook for 30 minutes, until an instant-read thermometer inserted into the center of a loaf registers 180°. Light the broiler.

4. Spoon some of the sauce over the loaves and broil for 5 minutes, until browned. Serve with the gravy. —*Andrew Carmellini*

WINE Fruity, light-bodied Beaujolais.

Feijoada

ACTIVE: 25 MIN; TOTAL: 2 HR 30 MIN

8 TO 10 SERVINGS ●

- 2 tablespoons vegetable oil
- 3 garlic cloves, thinly sliced
- 1 large onion, finely chopped
- 1½ pounds dried black beans,
  soaked overnight and drained
- 3½ quarts water
- 1 pound fresh spicy sausage,
  such as linguiça
- ¾ pound dried beef (*carne seca*)
  or corned beef, in one piece
- 1½ pounds smoked pork chops
- ¾ pound lean slab bacon
- ¾ pound chorizo, in one piece
- 1 dried red chile

Salt

Toasted Manioc Flour (recipe follows)

1. Heat the oil in a large, heavy casserole. Add the garlic and onion and cook over moderately low heat, stirring occasionally, until softened, 7 minutes. Stir in the beans. Add the water. Bring to a boil over moderately high heat. Reduce the heat to low and simmer for 1 hour, stirring occasionally. Add all of the meats and the chile and cook until the beans are tender, 1 hour.

2. Remove the meats from the casserole and thickly slice; discard any bones. Pick out and discard the chile. Season the beans with salt, ladle into shallow bowls and serve with the sliced meats. Pass the Toasted Manioc Flour at the table for sprinkling over the feijoada. —*Eric Ripert*

SERVE WITH Sautéed collard greens.

WINE Rustic, peppery Malbec.

TOASTED MANIOC FLOUR

TOTAL: 20 MIN

MAKES ABOUT 2 CUPS ●

- 3 tablespoons unsalted butter
- 1 small onion, very thinly sliced
- 1 large egg, beaten
- 1½ cups manioc flour (see Note)
- 2 tablespoons minced parsley

Salt

Melt the butter in a large skillet. Add the onion. Cook over low heat until softened, 7 minutes. Stir in the egg and cook, stirring, until dry and crumbly, 30 seconds. Add the flour and cook over moderate heat, stirring occasionally, until lightly toasted, 8 minutes. Stir in the parsley and season with salt. Serve with the feijoada. —*E.R.*

NOTE Manioc flour, or cassava flour, is available at Latin markets.

Marinated Pork Chops with Herb Salsa

ACTIVE: 30 MIN; TOTAL: 1 HR 30 MIN

6 SERVINGS ●

- ¼ cup plus 2 tablespoons
  extra-virgin olive oil
- 3 tablespoons fresh lemon juice
- 1 tablespoon chopped rosemary
- 3 garlic cloves, minced

Freshly ground pepper

Six 5-ounce boneless pork rib chops

- 1 tablespoon drained capers
- 1 tablespoon Dijon mustard
- 1 tablespoon white wine vinegar
- 1 cup flat-leaf parsley leaves
- ½ cup basil leaves
- ½ cup mint leaves

Salt

1. In a large bowl, whisk ¼ cup of the olive oil with the lemon juice, rosemary and two-thirds of the garlic; season with pepper. Add the pork chops and turn to coat. Let stand at room temperature for 1 hour.

2. In a food processor, pulse the remaining garlic with the capers, mustard and vinegar just to combine. Add the parsley, basil and mint and pulse to chop. Add the remaining 2 tablespoons of olive oil and pulse just to combine. Transfer the salsa to a bowl; season with salt and pepper. Light a grill.

3. Remove the pork from the marinade; season with salt. Grill over high heat, turning once, until just cooked, 8 to 9 minutes. Let rest for 5 minutes. Serve with the salsa. —*Hugo Matheson and Kimbal Musk*

WINE Fresh, fruity rosé.

MARINATED PORK CHOPS
WITH HERB SALSA

BOUDIN BLANC WITH LEEKS
AND MUSTARD SAUCE

Boudin Blanc with Leeks and Mustard Sauce

ACTIVE: 30 MIN; TOTAL: 1 HR

4 SERVINGS

This recipe is based on the classic French veal and pork sausage boudin blanc, often served with a black truffle–flecked cream sauce. F&W's Marcia Kiesel replaces the pungent truffles with smooth Dijon and grainy mustards.

- 3 **cups chicken stock or low-sodium broth**
- 2 **large leeks, white and tender green parts only, halved lengthwise**
- **Salt and freshly ground pepper**
- 2 **pounds white potatoes, peeled and cut into 2-inch chunks**
- 1 **tablespoon unsalted butter, at room temperature**
- 1 **cup milk, warmed**
- 1 **tablespoon vegetable oil**
- 8 **white veal and pork sausages such as boudin blanc or bockwurst, halved lengthwise**
- 1 **cup heavy cream**
- 2 **teaspoons grainy mustard**
- 1 **teaspoon Dijon mustard**
- 1 **tablespoon chopped parsley**

1. In a large skillet, bring the stock to a boil. Add the leeks and a pinch each of salt and pepper. Cover partially and simmer over low heat, carefully turning the leeks once, until tender, about 10 minutes. Using a slotted spoon, transfer to a plate. Pour the stock into a large glass measuring cup.

2. In a large saucepan, cover the potatoes with water. Add a large pinch of salt and bring to a boil over moderately high heat until tender, about 12 minutes. Pour off the water. Set the saucepan over the hot burner and shake the potatoes for 1 minute to dry them out. Pass the potatoes through a ricer into a medium saucepan. Gently stir in the butter, then stir in the milk. Season the potatoes with salt and pepper and cover.

3. In the large skillet, heat the oil until shimmering. Add the sausages and cook over high heat until lightly browned, about 1 minute per side. Pour in the reserved leek cooking broth, cover and simmer over moderately low heat for 5 minutes. Transfer the sausages to a warmed platter and cover with foil.

4. Boil the broth in the skillet over high heat until reduced to 2 cups, about 3 minutes. Add the cream and boil until reduced by one-third, about 10 minutes. Stir in both mustards and season with salt and pepper. Add the leeks to the sauce and simmer over low heat until heated through.

5. Rewarm the potatoes, still covered, over moderately high heat, stirring once. Spoon the potatoes onto plates and set the sausages and leeks next to them. Spoon the mustard sauce over the leeks and potatoes, sprinkle with the parsley and serve. —*Marcia Kiesel*

WINE Ripe, luxurious Chardonnay.

Veal Scallopine with Paprika Sauce and Grapefruit-Watercress Salad

TOTAL: 45 MIN

4 SERVINGS ●

- 2 **pink grapefruit**
- 1 **cup dry white wine**
- 2 **large shallots, thinly sliced**
- 1 **bay leaf**
- 1½ **cups chicken stock or low-sodium broth**
- ½ **cup heavy cream**
- 1½ **teaspoons hot paprika**
- 2 **tablespoons unsalted butter**
- **Salt and freshly ground pepper**
- 2 **large eggs**
- 2 **tablespoons water**
- **All-purpose flour, for dredging**
- 2 **cups *panko* (Japanese bread crumbs)**
- **Four 5- to 6-ounce slices of veal scallopine, pounded about ⅛ inch thick**
- **Vegetable oil, for frying**
- 3 **cups cleaned watercress**
- 4 **sage leaves, minced**
- 1 **tablespoon chopped capers**
- 2 **teaspoons extra-virgin olive oil**

1. Using a sharp knife, peel the grapefruit, removing all of the bitter white pith. Working over a strainer set over a medium bowl, cut in between the grapefruit membranes to release the sections into the strainer. Squeeze 1 tablespoon of grapefruit juice from the membranes and reserve.

2. In a medium saucepan, combine the wine, shallots and bay leaf and boil over high heat until almost all of the liquid has evaporated, about 6 minutes. Add the chicken stock; boil until reduced to ½ cup, about 5 minutes.

3. Add the cream and paprika to the saucepan and bring to a boil. Reduce the heat to moderately low and simmer until thickened slightly. Discard the bay leaf. Remove the sauce from the heat and swirl in the butter. Season the sauce with salt and pepper and keep warm.

4. In a shallow bowl, beat the eggs with the water. Put the flour and *panko* in two other shallow bowls. Season the veal with salt and pepper. Dredge the veal in the flour and shake off the excess, then dip the veal in the egg mixture and coat with *panko*.

5. In a very large skillet, heat ¼ inch of vegetable oil until shimmering. Add the veal and cook over moderately high heat, turning once, until golden brown and crisp, about 6 minutes; reduce the heat to moderate halfway through cooking. Drain the veal on paper towels.

6. Meanwhile, in a medium bowl, toss the grapefruit and the 1 tablespoon of reserved juice with the watercress, sage and capers. Drizzle on the olive oil, season with salt and pepper and toss well.

7. Transfer the veal to plates. Top with the salad and spoon the sauce on the side. —*Dennis Leary*

WINE Minerally, complex Sauvignon Blanc.

---

pork & veal

Pork with Gingersnap Sauce

TOTAL: 35 MIN

4 SERVINGS ● ●

This sauerbraten-like dish uses ginger-snaps two ways: as a sweet crust for pork medallions and as a flavoring for the rich, appley sauce.

- ¼ cup finely ground gingersnaps, plus 3 tablespoons coarsely crushed gingersnaps, for garnish
- 2 tablespoons all-purpose flour

Two 12-ounce pork tenderloins

Salt and freshly ground pepper

- 2 tablespoons unsalted butter
- 1 tablespoon extra-virgin olive oil
- 1 medium shallot, minced
- ¼ cup Calvados or other apple brandy
- 1 cup low-sodium chicken broth
- ½ cup apple cider
- 1 tablespoon cider vinegar
- 2 tablespoons chopped chives

1. On a sheet of wax paper, mix 2 table-spoons of the ground gingersnaps with the flour. Slice the pork crosswise about 2 inches thick. Gently pound each piece to a 1-inch thickness. Season with salt and pepper and dredge in the flour mixture.

taste test
gingersnaps

Beth's Triple Gingersnaps are all-natural and loaded with ginger, perfect for the pork recipe above. **Details** $4.69 for 7 oz; dereuze.com.

2. In a large skillet, melt 1 tablespoon of butter in the oil. Add the pork all at once and cook over moderately high heat, turning once, until browned and nearly cooked through, 6 minutes. Transfer to a plate.

3. Add the shallot to the skillet; cook over moderate heat until softened, 1 minute. Add the Calvados and cook, stirring, until reduced by half, 1 to 2 minutes. Add the broth and cider. Simmer until reduced to 1 cup, scraping up any browned bits, 5 minutes. Add the vinegar, remaining ground gingersnaps and 1 tablespoon of butter and cook, stirring, until thickened, 1 minute. Return the pork to the skillet. Cook for 1 minute. Transfer to plates and spoon on the sauce. Garnish with chives and crushed gingersnaps. —*Grace Parisi*

WINE Fruity, light-bodied Beaujolais.

Spicy Stewed Sausages with Three Peppers

ACTIVE: 20 MIN; TOTAL: 35 MIN

8 SERVINGS ●

"This is my take on the Little Italy classic," says Mario Batali, TV chef, restaurateur and cookbook author (most recently of *Mario Tailgates Nascar Style*). He was speaking of the sausage and peppers that are a mainstay of the iconic Manhattan neighborhood and its annual street festival. Stewing the bell peppers in red wine gives them richness; so does a generous garnish of grated pecorino. The stewed sausages and peppers are delicious tossed with pasta.

- 2 pounds sweet Italian sausage, pricked all over with a fork
- 3 tablespoons extra-virgin olive oil, plus more for brushing
- 2 red bell peppers, cut into 1-inch dice
- 2 green bell peppers, cut into 1-inch dice
- 2 yellow bell peppers, cut into 1-inch dice
- 1 medium red onion, thinly sliced

- 1 small fennel bulb—trimmed, cored and thinly sliced
- 4 serrano chiles, seeded and thinly sliced crosswise
- 1 habanero chile, seeded and thinly sliced

Salt

- 1 cup dry red wine
- 1 cup freshly grated pecorino cheese (3 ounces)

Crusty bread, for serving

1. Light a grill. Brush the Italian sausages lightly with olive oil and grill them over a medium-hot fire, turning, until they are nicely charred and just cooked through, about 16 minutes total.

2. Meanwhile, set a large cast-iron skillet on the grill and add the 3 tablespoons of olive oil. Add the red, green and yellow bell peppers, the sliced onion, sliced fennel and the sliced serrano and habanero chiles and cook, stirring occasionally, until the vegetables are softened, about 15 minutes. Season with salt. Add the reserved sausages and the red wine to the skillet and simmer until the wine has reduced by half, about 4 minutes. Remove the skillet from the grill and sprinkle half of the pecorino cheese over the sausages and peppers. Serve the stew with crusty bread, passing the remaining pecorino at the table. —*Mario Batali*

WINE Juicy, fresh Dolcetto.

Baked Rice and Beans with White Veal Sausage

ACTIVE: 1 HR; TOTAL: 2 HR PLUS OVERNIGHT SOAKING

8 SERVINGS ●

This satisfying dish fuses the classic Latin combination of rice and beans with the sausages and bread-crumb topping of cassoulet, the much-loved French casserole.

- ¾ cup dried white navy beans , soaked overnight and drained
- 1 carrot
- 1 celery rib

1 small onion, peeled, plus
1 medium onion, finely chopped

1 pound slab bacon

4 whole cloves

5 thyme sprigs

1 teaspoon whole black
peppercorns

8 cups water

1¼ pounds white veal sausages,
such as bockwurst

7 tablespoons unsalted butter,
4 tablespoons melted

2 large garlic cloves, minced

2 bay leaves

7 ounces carnaroli or arborio rice
(1 cup)

1 cup heavy cream

Salt and freshly ground white pepper

1½ cups *panko* (Japanese bread
crumbs)

1. In a large enameled cast-iron casserole, combine the navy beans with the carrot, celery rib, whole onion and bacon. Wrap the cloves, thyme sprigs and black peppercorns in a large square of cheesecloth, tie with kitchen string and add to the casserole along with the water. Bring to a boil, then cover partially and simmer over moderate heat until the beans are tender, about 1 hour. Add the veal sausages during the last 10 minutes of cooking.

2. Drain the beans in a colander set over a bowl; reserve 3 cups of the cooking liquid. Discard the carrot, celery, onion and the cheesecloth bundle. Transfer the bacon to a cutting board and cut into ½-inch pieces. Slice the sausages diagonally ¾ inch thick. Add the bacon and sausages to the beans.

3. Preheat the oven to 400°. Wipe out the casserole and melt 3 tablespoons of the butter in it. Add the chopped onion, the garlic and bay leaves, cover and cook over moderate heat, stirring occasionally, until the onion is softened but not browned, about 6 minutes. Add the rice and stir to coat with the butter. Add the reserved 3 cups of cooking liquid and bring to a boil. Cover and cook over moderately low heat until the rice is just tender, about 15 minutes; the rice should be a little soupy. Stir in the heavy cream and the beans and season with salt and white pepper. Discard the bay leaves.

4. Butter a shallow 3-quart baking dish. Spoon the rice and beans into the dish and smooth the top. In a small bowl, toss the *panko* with the 4 tablespoons of melted butter so the crumbs are evenly moistened. Sprinkle the *panko* over the rice and beans. Bake the rice and beans about 15 minutes, or until heated through.

5. Preheat the broiler. Broil the rice and beans for about 2 minutes, shifting the baking dish once or twice, until the crumbs are evenly golden and crisp. Serve right away. —*Grace Parisi*

MAKE AHEAD The casserole can be baked a day ahead and refrigerated overnight. Rewarm before serving.

WINE Creamy, supple Pinot Blanc.

Blanquette de Veau

ACTIVE: 40 MIN; TOTAL: 2 HR 20 MIN

4 SERVINGS ●●

Chef Daniel Boulud, with five cookbooks and five restaurants to his name, now has yet another cookbook, *Braise.* This recipe shows his mastery of the technique.

2 pounds trimmed, boneless veal
shoulder, cut into 2-inch chunks

1½ quarts low-sodium vegetable
broth

3 parsley stems plus 2 tablespoons
chopped flat-leaf parsley

2 thyme sprigs

1 bay leaf

½ teaspoon black peppercorns

½ teaspoon coriander seeds

1 small white onion stuck with
6 cloves

1 leek, white part only, halved and
cut into 1-inch pieces

1 large carrot, cut into 1-inch pieces

1 medium celery rib, cut into
1-inch pieces

1 cup heavy cream

1 tablespoon unsalted butter,
softened

1 tablespoon all-purpose flour

1 tablespoon fresh lemon juice

Pinch of cayenne pepper

Salt and freshly ground pepper

2 tablespoons minced chives

1. In a medium enameled cast-iron casserole, cover the veal shoulder with the vegetable broth and bring to a simmer over moderately high heat. Tie the parsley stems, thyme sprigs, bay leaf, peppercorns and coriander seeds in a piece of cheesecloth and add the bundle to the casserole along with the onion. Simmer over low heat for 1 hour, skimming occasionally. Add the leek, carrot and celery and simmer until the veal is tender, 45 minutes longer. Drain the meat and vegetables, reserving the broth. Discard the herb and spice bundle and onion. Cover the meat and vegetables to keep them from drying out.

2. Return the broth to the casserole; you should have about 4 cups. Boil the broth over high heat until it is reduced by half, about 8 minutes. Add the heavy cream to the broth and simmer over moderately low heat until the sauce is reduced by a third, about 6 minutes.

3. In a small bowl, blend the butter and flour to form a paste. Whisk ½ cup of the hot liquid into the paste until it is smooth, then whisk into the remaining liquid in the casserole. Simmer the sauce over moderate heat, whisking often, until it is thickened and no floury taste remains, about 5 minutes. Return the veal and vegetables along with the lemon juice and cayenne to the sauce and simmer over low heat until the meat is hot. Season the blanquette de veau with salt and pepper. Stir in the chopped parsley and chives and serve at once. —*Daniel Boulud.*

WINE Light, crisp white Burgundy.

GRILLED SWORDFISH STEAKS WITH
BASIL-CAPER BUTTER (P. 202)

fish

"If you've got good spinach, a nice piece of fish and lemon, that's all it takes. If you taste two or three flavors in clean form, that makes for happy cooking."

—**Hugo Matheson,** chef and co-owner, The Kitchen, Boulder, Colorado

SPICY BUTTER-STEAMED BASS

HALIBUT WITH MIXED BEANS AND LEMON-BUTTER SAUCE

Spicy Butter-Steamed Bass

TOTAL: 30 MIN

4 SERVINGS ●

Topping fillets with butter before steaming them creates an instant sauce as the butter melts into the fragrant fish. F&W's Grace Parisi uses cultured butter (traditionally made with fermented cream), available in most supermarkets.

Four 7-ounce sea bass or red snapper fillets with skin

One 1½-inch piece of fresh ginger, peeled and cut into very thin matchsticks

1 serrano chile, thinly sliced

1 small garlic clove, minced

Finely grated zest and juice of 1 lime

Salt and freshly ground pepper

4 tablespoons unsalted butter, cut into small pieces

Chopped cilantro leaves and sliced scallion, for garnish

1. With a knife, make 4 shallow slashes in the skin of each fish fillet and place them in a large glass or ceramic pie plate, skin side up. In a small bowl, combine the ginger with the sliced serrano chile, minced garlic and lime zest and sprinkle the mixture over the fish. Season with salt and pepper and dot with the butter. Drizzle the lime juice on top.

2. Make a steamer by arranging 3 small balls of aluminum foil in a large, deep skillet. Add 1 inch of water to the skillet and bring to a boil. Set the pie plate on the foil balls, cover the skillet with a tight-fitting lid or aluminum foil and steam the fish for 5 minutes, or until it can be flaked with a fork. Using a spatula, transfer the fish fillets to shallow bowls and spoon the buttery broth on top. Garnish with the cilantro and scallion and serve. Serve right away.
—*Grace Parisi*

WINE Vivid, lightly sweet Riesling.

Halibut with Mixed Beans and Lemon-Butter Sauce

TOTAL: 1 HR

8 SERVINGS

2 pounds fresh cranberry beans, shelled (2 cups)

4 garlic cloves—2 whole, 2 minced

3 thyme sprigs, plus 1 teaspoon chopped thyme

2 pounds fresh fava beans, shelled (2 cups)

½ pound haricots verts

½ pound sugar snap peas

1 cup thawed frozen baby peas

1 stick plus 6 tablespoons unsalted butter, 12 tablespoons cubed and chilled

2 shallots, minced

1 cup dry white wine

1 cup chicken stock

3 tablespoons fresh lemon juice

Salt and freshly ground pepper

2 tablespoons canola oil

Eight 1-inch-thick skinless halibut
  fillets (6 to 7 ounces each)

Micro-greens, for garnish (optional)

1. Bring 2 medium saucepans of water to a boil and prepare a large bowl of ice water. Add the cranberry beans, whole garlic cloves and thyme sprigs to one saucepan and simmer over moderate heat until the beans are tender, about 30 minutes. Drain the beans and discard the garlic and thyme. Wipe out the saucepan and return the beans to it.

2. Meanwhile, preheat the oven to 425°. Add the fava beans to the second saucepan of boiling water and cook for 5 minutes. Using a slotted spoon, transfer the favas to the ice water to cool.

3. Add the haricots verts to the boiling water and cook until crisp-tender, about 4 minutes. Using a slotted spoon, transfer the haricots verts to the ice water to cool. Add the sugar snaps to the boiling water and cook for 2 minutes. Drain and add them to the ice water. Drain all the beans and peas and pat dry; pop the favas out of their outer skins. Add the beans, sugar snaps and baby peas to the cranberry beans.

4. Wipe out the medium saucepan and melt the 2 tablespoons of butter. Add the shallots and minced garlic and cook over moderate heat, stirring occasionally, until softened. Add the wine and cook until nearly evaporated, about 10 minutes. Add the stock and cook until reduced to ¼ cup, about 6 minutes. Reduce the heat to moderately low and whisk in the butter cubes, a few at a time, until a creamy sauce forms. Add 1 tablespoon of the lemon juice and season lightly with salt and pepper. Pour all but ¼ cup of the butter sauce over the vegetables; keep warm.

5. Heat the oil in a very large ovenproof skillet. Pat the halibut fillets dry and season with salt and pepper. Add them to the skillet and cook over high heat until lightly browned, about 3 minutes. Transfer the

skillet to the oven and cook until the fillets are almost opaque throughout, about 5 minutes; carefully turn them. Add the remaining butter sauce to the skillet with the remaining 2 tablespoons of lemon juice and the chopped thyme. Cook over moderate heat just until the sauce is bubbling and the fish is just cooked through. Transfer the fillets to plates and spoon the lemon-butter sauce on top. Garnish with micro-greens and serve with the beans.
—Colin Devlin

MAKE AHEAD The recipe can be prepared through Step 3 one day ahead. Refrigerate the vegetables; let return to room temperature before proceeding.

WINE Light, crisp white Burgundy.

Seared Hamachi with Carrot Salad and Yuzu Dressing

TOTAL: 45 MIN

6 SERVINGS ● ● ●

Hamachi, a young fish of the jack family found in Pacific waters, can be difficult to find on the East Coast, but is well worth seeking out. Raw, the fish has a lovely, firm texture; seared, it becomes buttery and practically melts in your mouth. Mahimahi is a fine substitute.

⅛ teaspoon ground cardamom
⅛ teaspoon ground coriander
⅛ teaspoon ground star anise
⅛ teaspoon ground allspice
Pinch of cayenne pepper
Freshly ground black pepper
1 pound carrots, peeled and cut into batons
1 teaspoon very finely grated orange zest, plus ¼ cup plus 2 tablespoons fresh orange juice
½ teaspoon very finely grated yuzu or lemon zest, plus 2 tablespoons fresh yuzu juice or fresh lemon juice
1 tablespoon pickled ginger, minced, plus 2 tablespoons pickled ginger juice from the jar

3 tablespoons vegetable oil
Kosher salt
1 small shallot, minced
1 tablespoon snipped chives
1 tablespoon finely shredded mint leaves
Six 6-ounce *hamachi* or mahimahi fillets
Lemon wedges, for serving

1. In a small skillet, combine the ground cardamom, coriander, star anise, allspice, cayenne and ⅛ teaspoon of freshly ground black pepper and cook over moderate heat until fragrant, about 10 seconds. Transfer to a plate and let cool completely.

2. Fill a medium bowl with cold water and ice cubes. In a medium saucepan of boiling salted water, blanch the carrots just until crisp-tender, 1 to 2 minutes. Drain and immediately plunge them into the ice water bath to cool. Drain thoroughly and pat dry with paper towels.

3. Transfer ⅓ cup of the carrots to a blender. Add the toasted spices, orange zest and juice, yuzu zest and juice, the 2 tablespoons of pickled ginger juice and 1 tablespoon of the vegetable oil. Puree the carrot dressing until smooth. Season with kosher salt.

4. In a bowl, toss ⅓ cup of the carrot dressing with the minced pickled ginger, shallot, chives, shredded mint leaves and the remaining carrots.

5. In a large nonstick skillet, heat the remaining 2 tablespoons of oil until shimmering. Season the fillets with salt and pepper and add to the pan. Cook over moderately high heat, turning once until just cooked through, about 6 minutes. Spoon the carrot salad in the centers of 6 plates and set a fillet on top of each. Drizzle the remaining dressing over the fish and serve with lemon wedges.
—Douglas Keane

MAKE AHEAD The dressing and carrots can be refrigerated separately overnight.

WINE Full-bodied, rich Pinot Gris.

fish

Pan-Fried River Trout with Corn Cakes and Red-Pepper Coulis

ACTIVE: 1 HR 20 MIN

4 SERVINGS

- 8 trout fillets (see Note)
- 2 cups milk
- 20 saltine crackers, broken
- 1½ cups all-purpose flour
- ¼ cup vegetable oil
- Salt and freshly ground pepper
- 3 tablespoons unsalted butter
- Grilled Corn Cakes and Roasted Red-Pepper Coulis (recipes follow)

1. In a large, shallow dish, cover the trout fillets with the milk and refrigerate for at least 10 minutes or up to 30 minutes.

2. In a food processor, pulse the crackers to fine crumbs. Transfer the crumbs to a large plate and mix with the flour.

3. Heat a very large skillet. Add the oil. Remove the trout from the milk and season with salt and pepper. Dredge in the cracker-crumb mixture and add to the skillet, skin side down. Add the butter and tilt the skillet to melt and distribute it evenly. Cook the trout over moderately high heat until browned and crisp, 3 minutes per side.

4. Arrange the warm Grilled Corn Cakes on plates and set the trout fillets on top. Garnish with the Roasted Red-Pepper Coulis and serve. —*Rollie Wesen*

NOTE For boned whole trout, simply follow the method for fillets and increase the cooking time by 1 to 2 minutes per side.

WINE Fruity, low-oak Chardonnay.

GRILLED CORN CAKES

ACTIVE: 40 MIN; TOTAL: 55 MIN

MAKES ABOUT 12 CORN CAKES ● ●

- 4 large ears of corn
- 1 cup all-purpose flour
- 1 teaspoon salt
- ½ teaspoon baking powder
- ½ teaspoon Old Bay seasoning
- Cayenne pepper
- 1 large egg, beaten
- ½ cup buttermilk
- ½ cup whole milk
- Vegetable oil
- 1½ tablespoons unsalted butter

1. Light a grill. Shuck the corn, leaving on the last thin layer of green husk. Grill over a hot fire, turning the ears frequently, until charred all over, about 10 minutes. Transfer them to a large bowl. Cover with plastic wrap and let steam for about 20 minutes. Then cut the kernels off the cobs; you should have about 2 cups.

2. Preheat the oven to 350°. In a large bowl, whisk together the flour, salt, baking powder, Old Bay and a pinch of cayenne. In a small bowl, beat the egg with the buttermilk and whole milk and pour the mixture over the flour. Add the corn kernels. Using a rubber spatula, stir lightly just until blended.

3. Lightly oil a large cast-iron skillet and set it over moderately high heat. When the skillet is hot, add four ¼-cup-size dollops of batter, spacing them evenly. Add ½ tablespoon of butter and tilt the skillet to let it run under the cakes. Cook the corn cakes until browned on the bottom, about 3 minutes. Turn and cook until lightly browned on the second side, about 1 minute longer. Transfer them to a rimmed baking sheet; repeat with the remaining batter and butter. Reheat the corn cakes in the oven for about 3 minutes and serve hot. —*R.W.*

MAKE AHEAD The corn can be grilled up to 2 days ahead and refrigerated. The corn cakes can be made early in the day and reheated before serving.

ROASTED RED-PEPPER COULIS

ACTIVE: 20 MIN; TOTAL: 45 MIN

MAKES ABOUT 2 CUPS ● ● ●

- 3 large red bell peppers
- 3 tablespoons extra-virgin olive oil
- 1 medium shallot, thinly sliced
- 1 tablespoon sherry vinegar or red wine vinegar
- Salt and freshly ground white pepper

1. Roast the red peppers directly over a gas flame or under the broiler, turning occasionally, until the peppers are blackened all over. Transfer them to a bowl and let cool completely. Peel the peppers and discard the skins, seeds and cores, then coarsely chop them.

2. In a food processor, combine the peppers with the olive oil, shallot and vinegar and puree until very smooth. Season the coulis with salt and white pepper. —*R.W.*

MAKE AHEAD The red-pepper coulis can be refrigerated overnight. Bring to room temperature before serving.

Pan-Seared Halibut with Tomato Vinaigrette

TOTAL: 25 MIN

4 SERVINGS ● ●

Chicago chef Shawn McClain serves this halibut at the Green Zebra, with labor-intensive lobster dumplings and tomato water. To make the tomato water, he blends sea salt with heirloom tomatoes, then strains the mixture through cheesecloth. Here, F&W's test kitchen streamlines his recipe to make it fast and light. We omit the lobster dumplings and substitute a fresh and chunky tomato vinaigrette for the tomato water.

- 1½ pounds heirloom tomatoes, coarsely chopped and juices reserved
- 2 tablespoons very finely chopped shallots
- 1 garlic clove, minced
- 1 tablespoon white balsamic vinegar
- 1 tablespoon snipped chives
- 1 tablespoon chopped flat-leaf parsley
- 3 tablespoons extra-virgin olive oil
- 1 teaspoon ground fennel seeds
- Salt and freshly ground pepper
- Four 6-ounce skinless halibut fillets
- 1 tablespoon unsalted butter

PAN-SEARED HALIBUT WITH TOMATO VINAIGRETTE

GUINNESS-GLAZED HALIBUT

1. In a medium bowl, combine the heirloom tomatoes and their juices with the minced shallots and garlic, the white balsamic vinegar, chives, parsley, 2 tablespoons of the olive oil and ¼ teaspoon of the ground fennel. Season the tomato vinaigrette with salt and pepper.

2. In a small bowl, mix the remaining ¾ teaspoon of ground fennel with ½ teaspoon each of salt and pepper. Sprinkle all over the fillets. In a medium nonstick skillet, heat the remaining 1 tablespoon of olive oil until shimmering. Add the fillets and cook over moderately high heat until browned on the bottom, about 5 minutes. Turn them and add the butter to the skillet. Spoon the butter over the fillets as they cook, about 2 minutes longer. Transfer the fillets to plates, spoon the tomato vinaigrette on top and serve right away.
—*Shawn McClain*

WINE Fresh, fruity rosé.

Guinness-Glazed Halibut

ACTIVE: 20 MIN; TOTAL: 50 MIN PLUS OVERNIGHT MARINATING

4 SERVINGS ●

Two 12-ounce bottles of Guinness
    stout
⅓ cup honey
1 tablespoon fresh lemon juice
½ teaspoon hot sauce
Salt
Four 6-ounce skinless halibut
    fillets
4 large carrots, cut into
    2-by-½-inch sticks
Extra-virgin olive oil, for brushing
Freshly ground pepper

1. In a skillet, boil the stout with the honey. Simmer over moderate heat for 25 minutes, skimming a few times, until reduced to ½ cup. Pour into a heatproof bowl and stir in the lemon juice, hot sauce and ½ teaspoon of salt; cool to room temperature.

2. In a shallow dish, pour half of the glaze over the fillets and turn to coat thoroughly. Cover the dish and refrigerate overnight, turning the fillets a few times. Reserve the remaining glaze.

3. Preheat the broiler. Bring a saucepan of water to a boil. Add the carrots and boil until just tender, 4 minutes; drain. Pour the reserved glaze into the pan and boil over high heat until thickened and reduced to ⅓ cup, about 2 minutes. Add the carrots and simmer until glazed, about 1 minute.

4. Remove the fillets from the marinade and arrange on a rimmed baking sheet. Brush with olive oil and season with pepper. Broil 4 inches from the heat until richly browned and just cooked through, 4 minutes. Transfer to plates and serve with the carrots. —*Melissa Clark*

MAKE AHEAD The stout glaze can be refrigerated for up to 3 days.

WINE Full-bodied, rich Pinot Gris.

fish

Halibut with Soy-Ginger Dressing

ACTIVE: 15 MIN; TOTAL: 50 MIN

6 SERVINGS ● ●

For this recipe, select dense, thick fillets of the freshest fish so they stay moist throughout cooking.

- 1 tablespoon sesame seeds
- ¼ cup plus 2 tablespoons soy sauce
- 3 tablespoons unseasoned rice vinegar
- 2 tablespoons mirin
- 2 tablespoons grapeseed oil
- 2 teaspoons Asian sesame oil
- 2 scallions, thinly sliced on the diagonal
- ¼ cup finely julienned peeled fresh ginger (1 ounce)

Six 6-ounce halibut fillets, skinned

Freshly ground pepper

Steamed short-grain rice and steamed spinach or pea shoots, for serving

1. In a small skillet, toast the sesame seeds over moderate heat, stirring a few times, until golden, 3 to 4 minutes. In a small bowl, mix the soy sauce with the rice vinegar, mirin, grapeseed and sesame oils, scallions and ginger. In a large, shallow dish, brush the halibut fillets with half of the soy-ginger dressing. Cover and refrigerate for 30 minutes.

2. Preheat the oven to 450°. Transfer the fillets to a large, rimmed baking sheet and season with pepper. Bake in the upper third of the oven for 10 to 12 minutes, or until glazed and just cooked through.

3. Spoon the rice into shallow bowls. Set the halibut fillets on top and spoon the spinach alongside. Pour the remaining dressing over the fish, sprinkle with the toasted sesame seeds and serve.
—*Annabel Langbein*

MAKE AHEAD The dressing can be refrigerated overnight. The halibut can marinate for up to 3 hours.

WINE Lively, tart Sauvignon Blanc.

Grilled Striped Bass with Plums and Potato-Mushroom Papillotes

ACTIVE: 30 MIN; TOTAL: 45 MIN

4 SERVINGS ● ●

- 1 pound fingerling potatoes, scrubbed
- ½ pound hen-of-the-woods or oyster mushrooms, thickly sliced lengthwise
- 1 tablespoon plus 1 teaspoon tamari
- 1 tablespoon plus 1 teaspoon balsamic vinegar
- 3 tablespoons extra-virgin olive oil

Salt and freshly ground pepper

Four 6-ounce striped bass fillets, skinned

- 2 teaspoons chopped rosemary
- 4 round purple plums, halved and pitted

Watercress sprigs, for garnish

1. Light a grill. Preheat the oven to 500°. In a medium saucepan of boiling salted water, cook the potatoes until tender, about 10 minutes. Drain and let cool. Then peel and halve them lengthwise.

2. Tear off four 20-by-14-inch sheets of parchment or foil. Spread equal amounts of potatoes and mushrooms on half of each sheet. In a small bowl, mix the tamari with the vinegar and 1 tablespoon of olive oil. Drizzle over the potatoes and mushrooms and season with salt and pepper. Fold the sheets over the vegetables and crimp to seal if using parchment; if using foil, fold in the edges to seal the packages. Transfer to 2 baking sheets and bake for about 15 minutes, or until sizzling.

3. Drizzle the bass fillets with 1½ tablespoons of the olive oil, sprinkle with the chopped rosemary and season with salt and pepper. Drizzle the purple plums with the remaining ½ tablespoon of olive oil. Grill the bass fillets over high heat until nicely charred and just cooked through, 3 to 4 minutes per side. Grill the plums, cut side down, until lightly charred, about 2 minutes per side.

4. Transfer the fish and plums to plates. Open a papillote on each plate and pour out the potatoes, mushrooms and any juices, watching out for the hot steam. Serve with watercress. —*Cyril Renaud*

MAKE AHEAD The cooked, peeled potatoes can be refrigerated overnight. Bring to room temperature before using.

WINE Lush, fragrant Viognier.

Grilled Sea Bass with Parsley-Anchovy Sauce

TOTAL: 45 MIN

6 SERVINGS ● ●

- 9 oil-packed anchovy fillets, drained
- 3 garlic cloves
- 1 large serrano chile, seeded
- ¼ cup fresh lemon juice, plus lemon wedges for serving
- 1½ cups flat-leaf parsley leaves
- 6 tablespoons extra-virgin olive oil, plus more for brushing

Salt and freshly ground pepper

Three 2-pound sea bass, pan-dressed

- 18 small thyme sprigs

1. In a food processor, combine the anchovies, garlic, serrano and lemon juice and process until finely chopped. Add the parsley and pulse until finely chopped. Add the 6 tablespoons of olive oil, season with salt and pepper and pulse just to combine. Transfer to a bowl.

2. Light a grill. Make 3 slashes in both sides of each fish at 2-inch intervals; slice to the bone. Tuck a thyme sprig into each slash. Season with salt and pepper; brush with oil. Brush the grate with oil and grill the fish over high heat, turning once, until it flakes easily, 15 minutes. Alternatively, preheat the broiler and position a rack 10 inches from the heat. Place the fish on a sturdy baking sheet, brush generously with oil and broil, turning once, 20 minutes.

3. Transfer the fish to a large platter and serve with the sauce and lemon wedges.
—*Hugo Matheson and Kimbal Musk*

WINE Light, crisp white Burgundy.

Crispy Sea Bass with Noodles
TOTAL: 35 MIN
4 SERVINGS ● ● ●

½ pound soba noodles
2 tablespoons sesame seeds
¼ cup chicken stock or broth
2 tablespoons soy sauce
1 teaspoon sugar
1 teaspoon Asian sesame oil
3 tablespoons vegetable oil
½ pound young bok choy, sliced
    ½ inch thick on the diagonal
1 tablespoon minced fresh ginger
1 large garlic clove, minced
3 scallions, white and light green
    parts only, thinly sliced
Four 6-ounce sea bass fillets with skin
Salt
¼ cup rice flour

1. Bring a saucepan of salted water to a boil. Add the soba and cook until al dente, 3 minutes; drain. Rinse under cold water and drain, shaking off any excess water.
2. In a skillet, toast the sesame seeds over moderate heat, stirring, until they begin to pop, 2 minutes. Transfer to a plate.
3. In a bowl, combine the stock, soy sauce, sugar and sesame oil. In a large skillet, heat 1 tablespoon of the vegetable oil. Add the bok choy, ginger, garlic and scallions and stir-fry over high heat until the bok choy is crisp-tender, 5 minutes. Add the noodles and cook, tossing, for 2 minutes. Add the soy mixture and bring to a boil, tossing. Remove from the heat and keep warm.
4. In a large nonstick skillet, heat the remaining 2 tablespoons of vegetable oil. Season the fish with salt and dust with the rice flour. Add to the skillet, skin side down, and cook over high heat until crisp, 4 minutes. Turn the fish and cook until just opaque throughout, 2 minutes.
5. Transfer the soba and bok choy to shallow bowls and top with the fish, skin side up. Sprinkle with the toasted sesame seeds and serve. —*Shawn McClain*
WINE Lively, tart Sauvignon Blanc.

Sautéed Bass with Lemongrass
ACTIVE: 1 HR; TOTAL: 1 HR 30 MIN
4 SERVINGS

"When you travel a lot," says French super-chef Joël Robuchon, "you pick up ideas all over the place." Thai ingredients were the inspiration for this beguiling dish topped with frizzled leeks.

1 medium tomato, quartered
    and seeded
2 teaspoons extra-virgin olive oil
1 small garlic clove, finely chopped
1 thyme sprig
Salt and freshly ground pepper
¾ cup vegetable oil, plus more
    for frying
10 lemongrass stalks, bottom
    two-thirds of tender inner bulbs
    only, thinly sliced
3 tablespoons unsalted butter
1 small shallot, sliced
One 3-inch-long strip lemon zest
¼ cup dry white wine
1 cup heavy cream
4 scallions, white and pale green
    parts only
1 medium leek, white part only,
    cut into fine julienne
Four 6-ounce skinless sea bass fillets
2 teaspoons fresh lemon juice

1. Preheat the oven to 300°. In a small baking dish, drizzle the tomato quarters with the olive oil and scatter the garlic on top. Add the thyme sprig and season with salt and pepper. Toss well and arrange the tomatoes skin side up. Bake for about 1 hour, or until very soft. Peel the tomato quarters. Leave them in the dish and discard the thyme sprig. Leave the oven on.
2. Meanwhile, in a small saucepan, combine the ¾ cup of vegetable oil with a little more than half of the sliced lemongrass and bring to a boil. Simmer over low heat for 10 minutes. Remove from the heat and let steep for 30 minutes. Strain.
3. In a medium saucepan, melt 2 tablespoons of the butter. Add the shallot and cook over moderate heat until softened, about 3 minutes. Add the remaining lemongrass and the lemon zest and cook over low heat for 10 minutes, stirring occasionally. Add the wine and simmer until reduced by half, about 3 minutes. Add the cream and simmer over low heat until reduced to ½ cup, about 15 minutes. Strain the sauce into a small saucepan.
4. In a medium saucepan of boiling water, cook the scallions for 1 minute. Using tongs, transfer them to a plate. Cut the scallions into 2-inch lengths. Add the leek julienne to the water and blanch for 1 minute. Drain and pat dry with paper towels.
5. In a medium skillet, heat ¼ inch of vegetable oil until shimmering. Add the leeks and fry over moderate heat until crisp but not browned, about 3 minutes. Using a slotted spoon, transfer the leeks to paper towels and drain. Season with salt.
6. Put the scallions in the dish with the tomato and warm in the oven. Meanwhile, in a large skillet, warm ¼ cup of the lemongrass oil until shimmering. Season the bass fillets with salt and pepper, add them to the skillet and cook over moderately high heat until lightly browned and just opaque, about 3 minutes per side. Transfer the fillets to plates and arrange the tomato and scallions on top.
7. Bring the sauce to a boil. Remove from the heat and stir in the lemon juice, then whisk in the remaining 1 tablespoon of butter until smooth; season with salt. If desired, froth the sauce using an immersion blender. Spoon the sauce around the fish and drizzle some of the lemongrass oil around the plate. Top with the fried leeks. Serve right away.
—*Joël Robuchon*
NOTE The remaining lemongrass oil can be refrigerated for up to one week. It can be used to sauté seafood, chicken or pork. Or it can be used to make a vinaigrette or as a garnish for finished dishes.
WINE Minerally, complex Sauvignon Blanc.

SNAPPER AND SPICED CRAB WITH LIME-CORIANDER BROTH

Snapper and Spiced Crab with Lime-Coriander Broth

TOTAL: 1 HR

6 SERVINGS ●

Pan-fried correctly, this snapper develops a crispy skin. Start with a very hot, well-oiled pan, says chef Douglas Keane of Cyrus in Healdsburg, California. To prevent the skin from sticking, gently shake the pan so the fish glides on the oil "like a car glides on water when it hydroplanes."

LIME-CORIANDER BROTH

- 1 tablespoon unsalted butter
- 1 onion, thinly sliced
- 1 small celery rib, thinly sliced
- 2 garlic cloves, smashed
- One 1-inch piece fresh ginger, smashed
- 1 teaspoon coriander seeds
- ½ teaspoon crushed red pepper
- 6 cardamom pods, crushed
- ½ star anise pod
- ¼ teaspoon black peppercorns
- 10 cilantro sprigs
- 2 basil sprigs
- 2 kaffir lime leaves (see Note)
- ½ cup dry white wine
- ¼ cup Asian fish sauce
- ¼ cup fresh lime juice
- 2 cups water
- Kosher salt

SNAPPER AND SPICED CRAB

- 1½ teaspoons cumin seeds
- 1 teaspoon cardamom seeds (from 12 pods)
- ¼ teaspoon coriander seeds
- ¼ teaspoon fennel seeds
- 1 star anise pod, broken
- 5 tablespoons vegetable oil
- 1 small red onion, finely chopped
- ½ pound lump crabmeat, picked over
- 2 tablespoons chopped cilantro
- 1½ tablespoons fresh lemon juice
- 1½ tablespoons fresh lime juice
- Salt and freshly ground pepper
- Six 5-ounce red snapper fillets

1. MAKE THE LIME-CORIANDER BROTH: Melt the butter in a large saucepan. Add the onion, celery, garlic and ginger and cook over moderate heat until softened, about 5 minutes. Add the coriander seeds, crushed red pepper, cardamom, star anise, peppercorns, cilantro and basil sprigs and lime leaves and cook for 1 minute. Add the wine and cook over moderate heat until reduced by half, 5 minutes. Add the fish sauce, lime juice and water and bring to a boil. Simmer over moderately low heat for 15 minutes. Strain into a small saucepan, season with salt; keep warm.

2. PREPARE THE SNAPPER AND SPICED CRAB: In a small skillet, combine the cumin, cardamom, coriander, fennel and star anise. Toast over moderately high heat until fragrant, about 1 minute. Let cool. Grind to a fine powder in a spice grinder.

3. In a skillet, heat 2 tablespoons of the oil. Add the chopped red onion and cook over moderate heat, stirring occasionally, until the onion is softened and just beginning to brown, about 5 minutes. Add the ground spices and cook over low heat for 1 minute. Fold in the crab, cilantro and lemon and lime juices; remove from the heat. Season with salt and pepper.

4. In each of the 2 large nonstick skillets, heat 1½ tablespoons of the remaining oil until shimmering. Season the snapper with salt and pepper; add to the skillets, skin side down. Cook over high heat, gently shaking the skillets, until the skin is golden brown and crisp, about 5 minutes. Turn the fillets and cook for 2 minutes.

5. Mound the spiced crab mixture in warmed shallow bowls and top with the snapper fillets, skin side up. Spoon the broth all around and serve right away.
—Douglas Keane

NOTE You can substitute two 1-inch strips of lime zest for the kaffir lime leaves.

MAKE AHEAD The broth can be refrigerated overnight and reheated gently.

WINE Lively, tart Sauvignon Blanc.

Poached Red Snapper with Papaya and Mango Sauce Vierge

TOTAL: 25 MIN

4 SERVINGS ● ●

Chef Eric Ripert of New York City's Le Bernardin often vists the remote Brazilian beach town of Trancoso to relax and to find new inspiration for his seafood repertoire. "Brazilians eat rich and heavy," he said. "I wanted something light and healthy." His idea was to poach a local fish and top it with a tropical version of his *sauce vierge,* replacing the pickles, capers and tomatoes with papaya, mango and ginger.

- ½ cup diced papaya
- ½ cup diced mango
- 2 tablespoons diced red onion
- 1 tablespoon plus 1 teaspoon coarsely chopped tarragon
- 1 tablespoon very finely chopped shallot
- 2 teaspoons very finely chopped fresh ginger
- 1 small garlic clove, very finely chopped
- Four 7- to 8-ounce skinless red snapper fillets
- Sea salt
- Cayenne pepper
- ¼ cup extra-virgin olive oil
- 2 tablespoons fresh lime juice
- Freshly ground black pepper

1. In a medium bowl, mix the papaya with the mango, red onion, tarragon, shallot, ginger and garlic.

2. Fill a large, high-sided skillet with ½ inch of water and bring to a simmer. Season both sides of the fillets with salt and cayenne pepper. Add them to the skillet, cover and simmer gently until just cooked through, about 7 minutes. Transfer the fillets to plates with a slotted spatula.

3. Add the olive oil and lime juice to the papaya-mango mixture and season with salt and black pepper. Spoon the sauce over the snapper and serve.—Eric Ripert

WINE Complex, aromatic Chenin Blanc.

fish

Pan-Fried Snapper with Buttery Parsnip Puree

ACTIVE: 40 MIN; TOTAL: 1 HR 45 MIN

8 SERVINGS

Avant-garde artists Mary Ellen Carroll and Donna Wingate prepared this dish at a dinner party to inaugurate Boston's new Institute of Contemporary Art on the museum's construction site. Carroll's friend Michael Isabell, who filmed the event, used to be a fishmonger; for this dish, he suggested using a seasonal fish caught off Cape Cod that day. Any meaty flaky white fish like snapper, sea bass or cod would work.

- **2 pounds parsnips, peeled and cut into 1-inch lengths**

THE FRUIT COMPANY
Orchard Fresh Gifts Since 1942

ingredient
citrus fruits

Kosher salt
- **6 tablespoons unsalted butter, at room temperature**
- **1 cup all-purpose flour**

Eight 6-ounce flaky white fish fillets with skin, such as red snapper, sea bass or cod

Freshly ground pepper

Balsamic-Glazed Red Onions (recipe follows), for serving

1. In a very large saucepan, cover the parsnips with cold water; add a large pinch of salt and bring to a boil. Simmer over moderate heat until very tender, 25 minutes. Drain well, reserving ½ cup of cooking liquid.

2. In a food processor, pulse the parsnips until coarsely chopped. Add the reserved cooking liquid and 2 tablespoons of the butter and season with salt; process until smooth. Return the parsnip puree to the saucepan and keep warm.

3. Put the flour in a shallow bowl. Season the fish with salt and pepper, then dredge in the flour; tap to remove any excess flour. Melt 2 tablespoons of butter in each of 2 large nonstick skillets. Add 4 fillets to each skillet, skin side down. Cook over moderately high heat, turning once, until golden brown and cooked through, 8 minutes.

4. Spoon the parsnip puree onto 8 warmed plates. Top with the fish, skin side up, and garnish with Balsamic-Glazed Red Onions. Serve right away.

—Mary Ellen Carroll and Donna Wingate

MAKE AHEAD The parsnip puree can be refrigerated overnight. Reheat gently

WINE Fruity, low-oak Chardonnay.

BALSAMIC-GLAZED RED ONIONS

ACTIVE: 15 MIN; TOTAL: 1 HR

8 SERVINGS ● ●

You'll know the onions are done when they are very tender and their juices are syrupy. Don't overcook them or the sweetness will be cloying. Leftovers can be slathered on slices of buttered baguette.

- **2 tablespoons unsalted butter**
- **2 tablespoons extra-virgin olive oil**
- **2 large red onions, halved and thinly sliced**
- **1 cup water**
- **½ cup balsamic vinegar**
- **3 tablespoons sugar**
- **1 rosemary sprig**

Kosher salt

In a medium saucepan, melt the butter in the olive oil. Add the onions and cook over moderate heat until softened, 7 minutes. Add the water, balsamic vinegar, sugar and rosemary and season with salt. Cover partially and simmer the onions over low heat until they are tender, 30 minutes. Uncover them and simmer until the juices are syrupy, 15 minutes longer. Discard the rosemary and serve warm.

—M.E.C. and D.W.

MAKE AHEAD The onions can be refrigerated overnight. Reheat gently.

Red Snapper with Citrus and Fennel Salad

TOTAL: 40 MIN

4 SERVINGS ● ●

- **4 small radishes, thinly sliced**
- **½ small fennel bulb—halved, cored and shaved paper-thin**
- **½ small red or yellow bell pepper, finely diced**
- **1 jalapeño, seeded and thinly sliced**
- **¼ cup coarsely chopped cilantro**
- **1 tablespoon snipped chives**
- **1 tablespoon finely shredded mint leaves**
- **1 grapefruit**
- **1 navel orange**
- **2 tablespoons extra-virgin olive oil, plus more for brushing**
- **1 tablespoon fresh lemon juice**

Salt and freshly ground pepper

Four 6-ounce skinless red snapper fillets

RED SNAPPER WITH CITRUS AND FENNEL SALAD

PAN-FRIED FLOUNDER WITH POBLANO-CORN RELISH

1. Preheat the broiler. In a large bowl, toss the sliced radishes, shaved fennel, diced bell pepper, jalapeño slices, chopped cilantro, snipped chives and shredded mint. Using a sharp knife, peel the grapefruit and the navel orange, removing all of the bitter white pith. Working over the bowl, cut between the membranes and release the sections into the bowl. To release the juice in the membranes, squeeze them over the bowl. Add the 2 tablespoons of olive oil and the lemon juice, and season the citrus and fennel salad with salt and pepper.

2. Set the fillets on a well-oiled, sturdy baking sheet and brush with olive oil; season with salt and pepper. Broil 6 inches from the heat for 4 minutes, on one side only, just until white throughout. Using a spatula, transfer the fillets to plates. Top with the salad and serve. —*Daniel Boulud*

WINE Vivid, lightly sweet Riesling.

Pan-Fried Flounder with Poblano-Corn Relish

TOTAL: 35 MIN

4 SERVINGS ● ● ●

- 1 large poblano chile pepper, cut into thin strips
- ¼ cup plus 1 teaspoon extra-virgin olive oil
- 1 small onion, thinly sliced
- 1 ear of corn, kernels cut off
- 1 garlic clove, minced
- ½ large Hass avocado, diced
- Juice of ½ lemon
- ¼ cup chopped cilantro
- **Salt and freshly ground black pepper**
- **Four 6-ounce flounder fillets**
- **All-purpose flour, for dredging**
- **Lemon wedges, for serving**

1. In a large nonstick skillet, spread the poblano strips in an even layer and cook over high heat, without stirring, until they are lightly charred, 3 minutes. Add 1 teaspoon of the olive oil and the onion to the skillet and cook over moderate heat until the onion is lightly browned, 3 minutes. Add the corn and garlic and cook, stirring, until heated through, about 2 minutes. Transfer the relish to a bowl and let cool to room temperature. Gently fold in the avocado, lemon juice and cilantro and season with salt and pepper.

2. Season the fillets with salt and pepper. Dredge them in the flour, shaking off the excess. In each of 2 large, nonstick skillets, heat 2 tablespoons of the olive oil until shimmering. Cook 2 fillets in each skillet over moderately high heat until golden brown on the bottom, about 3 minutes. Turn and cook just until the fillets are white throughout, about 1 minute longer. Transfer the fillets to plates and top with the poblano relish. —*Brian Talley*

WINE Fruity, low-oak Chardonnay.

fish

Cornmeal-Crusted Flounder

TOTAL: 30 MIN
4 SERVINGS ●

- 1 teaspoon extra-virgin olive oil
- 6 ounces thinly sliced pancetta, cut into ½-inch squares
- 1¼ pounds medium asparagus
- Salt and freshly ground pepper
- 1 cup buttermilk
- 2 large eggs
- 2 cups yellow cornmeal
- ¼ cup plus 2 tablespoons vegetable oil
- Four 6- to 8-ounce flounder fillets

1. Preheat the oven to 425°. Spread the olive oil on a large rimmed baking sheet and heat in the oven for 1 minute. Scatter the pancetta on the sheet and bake for 5 minutes, or until sizzling. Add the asparagus and roll in the fat until coated. Season with salt and pepper. Bake for 15 minutes, or until lightly browned and just tender.

2. In a shallow bowl, beat the buttermilk with the eggs. In another shallow bowl, mix the yellow cornmeal with 2 teaspoons of salt and ½ teaspoon of pepper.

3. In a large skillet, heat the vegetable oil until shimmering. Dip each flounder fillet in the buttermilk mixture, let the excess drip off, then carefully coat in the cornmeal. Fry over moderate heat until golden brown and crisp, about 4 minutes per side. Transfer to paper towels to drain, then transfer to plates. Serve with the asparagus and pancetta. —*Amy Tornquist*
WINE Peppery, refreshing Grüner Veltliner.

Tea-Steamed Cod Baked in Paper

ACTIVE: 30 MIN; TOTAL: 1 HR
8 SERVINGS ●

- 1 teaspoon Chinese citrus tea
- ⅔ cup boiling water
- Eight 6-ounce skinless cod fillets
- 32 very small sage leaves
- ¼ cup *furikake* (Japanese seaweed and sesame seasoning; see Note)
- Salt and freshly ground pepper

1. Preheat the oven to 350°. In a cup, cover the tea with the boiling water and let steep for 5 minutes. Strain the tea and let cool to room temperature.

2. Cut out eight 14-inch squares of brown parchment paper. Lay a square on a work surface and set a cod fillet in the center. Make 4 deep, evenly spaced slashes in the cod and place a sage leaf and ¼ teaspoon of the *furikake* in each. Pour 1 tablespoon of tea over the cod and season it with salt and pepper. Gather the paper up and around the fish and twist, then tie the top with kitchen string. Set the packet on a large rimmed baking sheet. Repeat with the remaining fish, sage leaves, *furikake,* tea and seasonings.

3. Bake the packets in the center of the oven for about 30 minutes, until simmering gently. Transfer them to plates and serve, letting guests untie and carefully open them at the table. —*Han Feng*
NOTE *Furikake,* the Japanese seaweed and sesame seasoning for rice, is available at Asian markets and specialty food shops.
WINE Light, fresh Pinot Grigio.

Chorizo-Crusted Cod

TOTAL: 30 MIN
4 SERVINGS ● ●

- 1½ ounces Spanish chorizo, peeled and thinly sliced
- ½ cup coarse dry bread crumbs
- Salt and freshly ground pepper
- Extra-virgin olive oil
- Four 6-ounce skinless cod or halibut fillets, about 1½ inches thick

1. Preheat the oven to 400°. In a mini food processor, finely chop the chorizo. Add the bread crumbs and pulse until combined. Season with salt and pepper and transfer the crumbs to a plate. Lightly oil a medium glass or ceramic baking dish. Dip one side of each fillet into the crumbs, pressing to help them adhere; arrange the in the baking dish, crumb side up. Pack the remaining chorizo crumbs on top.

2. Roast the fillets for 12 minutes, or until they are white throughout and flake with a fork. Preheat the broiler and broil them 6 inches from the heat for 20 to 30 seconds, or until the chorizo crust is crisp and lightly browned. Serve. —*Peter Ireland*
WINE Fruity, light-bodied Beaujolais.

Cod with Cockles and White Wine

TOTAL: 30 MIN
4 SERVINGS ● ● ●

- Four 6-ounce skinless cod or hake fillets (1¼ inch thick)
- Salt and freshly ground pepper
- 2 tablespoons all-purpose flour
- 2 tablespoons extra-virgin olive oil
- 2 garlic cloves, minced
- 1 pound cockles, scrubbed
- ½ cup dry white wine
- ½ cup bottled clam broth
- 2 tablespoons unsalted butter
- 2 tablespoons chopped parsley
- Pinch of smoked sweet paprika (optional)

1. Preheat the oven to 375°. Season the fish with salt and pepper and dust lightly with the flour.

2. In a medium ovenproof skillet, heat 1 tablespoon of olive oil until shimmering. Add the cod and cook over high heat until golden on the bottom, about 4 minutes; turn the cod. Transfer to the oven and roast for about 10 minutes, or until the flesh flakes with a fork. Transfer to bowls.

3. In another large skillet, heat the remaining olive oil until shimmering. Add the garlic and cockles. Cook over high heat for 1 minute. Add the wine and cook, stirring, for 1 minute. Add the broth and cook, stirring, until the cockles open and the liquid is reduced to ¼ cup, about 7 minutes. Tilt the skillet so the liquid pools to one side. Add the butter and swirl until melted. Toss the cockles in the sauce; add the parsley. Spoon the cockles over the fish, sprinkle with paprika and serve. —*Jose Garces*
WINE Zesty, fresh Albariño.

fish

Prosecco-Battered Cod with Mint Aioli

ACTIVE: 30 MIN; TOTAL: 1 HR 30 MIN

6 SERVINGS ●

The cod here has an amazingly light and crunchy crust. One secret to the perfect coating: lightening the batter with a sparkling wine like Prosecco.

Six 6-ounce skinless cod fillets
Salt
2 garlic cloves, very finely chopped
1 cup mint leaves
¾ cup mayonnaise
Freshly ground pepper
Vegetable oil, for frying
1½ cups all-purpose flour, plus more for dredging
2 cups Prosecco or other sparkling wine
Lemon wedges, for serving

1. Lightly season the cod fillets with salt. Cover the fish fillets and refrigerate them for 1 hour.
2. Meanwhile, in a food processor, combine the chopped garlic and the mint leaves and process until finely chopped. Add the mayonnaise to the food processor and pulse to blend. Scrape the mint aioli into a bowl and season with salt and pepper.
3. In a large saucepan, heat 2 inches of vegetable oil to 325°. Set a wire rack over a baking sheet. In a large bowl, whisk the 1½ cups of flour with the Prosecco. Spread a handful of flour in a shallow bowl. Dredge each cod fillet in the flour, then dip the fillets in the batter to coat; let any excess batter drip back into the bowl. Working in 2 batches, carefully add the cod fillets to the hot oil and fry, turning once, until they are browned and crisp, about 3 minutes. With a slotted spoon, transfer the fish fillets to the rack to drain for 1 minute. Serve the fried cod fillets immediately with the mint aioli and lemon wedges.
—*Tommy Habetz*

WINE Dry, fruity sparkling wine.

Seared Tuna with Kimchi and Scallion Pancakes

TOTAL: 1 HR PLUS 2 WEEKS FOR THE KIMCHI

4 SERVINGS ●

The simple grilled tuna and crispy-chewy scallion pancakes are terrific, but what makes the dish so sensational is the homemade kimchi, a version of the traditional Korean pickled-vegetable condiment. Sweetened with honey and orange juice, it is both utterly original and completely delicious.

¼ cup canola oil, plus more for brushing
1 small shallot, minced
2 tablespoons minced fresh ginger
2 tablespoons soy sauce
2 tablespoons rice vinegar
1 teaspoon Chinese chile garlic sauce
1 pound center-cut tuna steak (1½ inches thick)
Salt and freshly ground pepper
2 cups baby arugula
1 cup Kimchi (recipe follows)
Scallion Pancakes (recipe follows)

1. In a small skillet, heat the ¼ cup of canola oil until shimmering. Add the shallot and ginger and cook over moderately low heat for 3 minutes, stirring, until softened. Remove from the heat. Add the soy sauce, vinegar and chile sauce; let cool.
2. Light a grill. Brush the tuna with oil and season with salt and pepper. Grill over high heat, turning, until browned on all sides and still rare in the center, about 8 minutes. Transfer the tuna to a work surface and cut into ⅓-inch slices.
3. Drizzle some of the shallot-ginger dressing onto 4 plates and arrange the tuna slices on top. Mound the arugula next to the tuna and drizzle lightly with some of the shallot-ginger dressing. Serve with the Kimchi and Scallion Pancakes.
—*Christopher Lee*

WINE Complex, aromatic Chenin Blanc.

KIMCHI

ACTIVE: 30 MIN; TOTAL: 2 WEEKS

MAKES 2 CUPS ● ●

3 cups coarsely shredded napa cabbage (8 ounces)
1 medium carrot, julienned
½ medium red bell pepper, peeled and julienned
½ medium yellow bell pepper, peeled and julienned
One 3-inch piece of daikon, peeled and julienned
1 scallion, thinly sliced
2 tablespoons soy sauce
1 tablespoon honey
2 tablespoons julienned ginger
2 garlic cloves, thinly sliced
1 tablespoon Asian fish sauce
2 teaspoons Chinese chile sauce
2 tablespoons fresh lime juice
2 tablespoons fresh lemon juice
2 tablespoons fresh orange juice
2 teaspoons sweet paprika

1. In a large pan of boiling salted water, cook the napa cabbage for 1 minute; drain and rinse under cold water. Squeeze the cabbage to get rid of excess water and pat it dry. In a bowl, toss the cabbage with the carrot, peppers, daikon and scallion.
2. In a medium saucepan, combine the soy sauce with the honey, ginger and garlic and 1 cup of water and bring to a boil. Remove the brine from the heat and add the fish sauce, chile sauce and the lime, lemon and orange juices with the paprika. Pour the brine over the vegetables and toss well. Let cool. Transfer to a tall, airtight jar, cover the kimchi and refrigerate it for 2 weeks. —*C.L.*

SCALLION PANCAKES

TOTAL: 30 MIN

MAKES TWO 10-INCH PANCAKES ● ●

1 cup all-purpose flour
3 tablespoons rice flour
½ teaspoon onion powder

SEARED TUNA WITH KIMCHI AND SCALLION PANCAKES

FRESH TUNA SALAD WITH AVOCADO

Pinch of cayenne pepper

Salt and freshly ground pepper

1⅓ cups seltzer

4 scallions, green parts only, thinly sliced

½ cup canola oil

1. In a medium bowl, whisk both flours with the onion powder, cayenne and a generous pinch of salt and pepper. Whisk in the seltzer and scallions. The batter should be the consistency of pancake batter.

2. Heat ¼ cup of the canola oil in each of two 10-inch skillets until shimmering. Divide the batter between the pans, gently shaking them and swirling to coat the bottom. Cook over high heat until the pancakes are nearly set and golden on the bottom, about 3 minutes. Flip and cook until golden and crisp, about 3 minutes. Drain the pancakes on paper towels and sprinkle with salt. Cut each pancake into quarters and serve. —*C.L.*

Fresh Tuna Salad with Avocado

TOTAL: 30 MIN

4 SERVINGS ● ● ●

½ cup extra-virgin olive oil

1 tablespoon fennel seeds

1 tablespoon black peppercorns

One ¾-pound tuna steak, 1 inch thick

Salt

½ cup plus 2 tablespoons mayonnaise

2 anchovy fillets, minced

2 tablespoons capers, drained and chopped

1 garlic clove, minced

2 tablespoons fresh lemon juice

2 celery ribs, sliced crosswise ¼ inch thick

1 small red onion, finely diced

⅓ cup pitted oil-cured black olives, chopped

4 Hass avocados, halved and pitted

Pea shoots or alfalfa sprouts (optional)

1. In a saucepan, combine the olive oil, fennel seeds and peppercorns; bring to a simmer over moderately low heat. Season the tuna with salt and add. Simmer over low heat, turning once, until barely pink in the center, 15 minutes. Transfer to a plate; scrape off the fennel and peppercorns. Strain and reserve the oil.

2. In a bowl, mix the mayonnaise, anchovies, capers, garlic and 1 tablespoon of lemon juice. Stir in the celery, onion and olives. With a fork, break the tuna into 1-inch pieces and fold in; season with salt.

3. Set 2 avocado halves on each of 4 plates. Drizzle them with some of the spice-infused olive oil and the remaining 1 tablespoon of fresh lemon juice. Spoon about ½ cup of the tuna salad into the center of each avocado half. Top the tuna salad with the pea shoots or alfalfa sprouts. Serve right away. —*Nan McEvoy*

WINE Fresh, lively Soave.

fish

Smoky Tuna and Bacon Burgers with Lemongrass Aioli

TOTAL: 30 MIN

4 SERVINGS ● ●

- 1 pound tuna steak, well chilled
- 1 strip of bacon, minced
- ¼ cup plus 1 tablespoon Lemongrass Wet Rub (recipe follows)

Salt and freshly ground pepper

Vegetable oil, for brushing

- ¼ cup mayonnaise
- 4 brioche rolls or hamburger buns

Sliced red onion, for serving

tools

japanese knives

Kershaw Shun A "D-shaped" handle provides an excellent grip; metrokitchen.com.

Misono The sharp, elegant superthin blades are great for slicing and fine dicing; korin.com.

MAC The company's "Chef" series is more affordable than many Japanese knives; korin.com.

Masamoto It's known for its good balance and weight; korin.com.

1. Light a grill. On a work surface, using a sharp knife, cut the tuna into thin strips. Stack the strips and cut into cubes. Add the bacon and chop until the tuna is fine and the bacon is evenly mixed in. Transfer to a bowl. Stir in ¼ cup of the Lemongrass Wet Rub and season lightly with salt and pepper. Using slightly moistened hands, form the tuna mixture into four 4-inch patties. Brush the patties with oil and season with salt and pepper. Grill over moderately high heat, turning once, until browned on the outside, about 6 minutes.

2. Mix the mayonnaise with the remaining 1 tablespoon of the Lemongrass Wet Rub and season the aioli with salt and pepper. Set the tuna burgers on the rolls and serve with the aioli and onion slices. —*Grace Parisi*

WINE Minerally, complex Sauvignon Blanc.

LEMONGRASS WET RUB

TOTAL: 10 MIN

MAKES A SCANT ½ CUP ● ●

- 2 stalks of fresh lemongrass, the bottom 5 inches of the inner bulb only, thinly sliced
- ¼ cup chopped fresh ginger
- 1 garlic clove
- 1 medium jalapeño, halved
- 2 tablespoons vegetable oil
- 2 tablespoons cilantro leaves

Salt

In a processor, mince the lemongrass, ginger, garlic and jalapeño. Add the oil and process to a coarse paste. Add the cilantro and process until fairly smooth. Season generously with salt. —*G.P.*

OTHER USES Try the lemongrass rub on other lean fish, or blend it with a little more vegetable oil and use as the base for chicken or vegetable stir-fries. Rub it onto chicken, seafood, pork and beef, or stir into ground pork or turkey for meatballs, meat loaf or burgers.

MAKE AHEAD The rub can be refrigerated for up to 3 days.

Grilled Tuna with Fried Manchego

TOTAL: 30 MIN

4 SERVINGS ●

- 1 large tomato, finely diced
- 1 tablespoon white wine vinegar
- 1 tablespoon minced shallot
- 1 teaspoon chopped thyme
- 1 teaspoon honey
- 1 garlic clove, minced
- ¼ teaspoon crushed red pepper

Extra-virgin olive oil

Salt

- 1 pound center-cut tuna steak (about 1½ inches thick)

Freshly ground pepper

- ¼ cup all-purpose flour
- 1 large egg, beaten
- ½ cup fine dry bread crumbs
- ½ pound Manchego cheese, sliced ¼ inch thick and cut into triangles
- 1 large heart of romaine—large leaves coarsely chopped, small leaves left whole

1. In a large bowl, mix the tomato, vinegar, shallot, thyme, honey, garlic, crushed red pepper and ¼ cup of olive oil until emulsified. Season generously with salt.

2. Heat a grill pan and brush with olive oil. Brush the tuna with olive oil; season with salt and pepper. Grill over moderately high heat, turning, until seared on the outside but still rare on the inside, 13 minutes. Let the tuna rest for 5 minutes and slice.

3. Heat ¼ inch of olive oil in a large skillet until shimmering. Put the flour, egg and crumbs in 3 shallow bowls. Dip the cheese triangles in the flour, then the egg and finally the crumbs, pressing to help them adhere. Add the cheese to the hot oil and fry over moderately high heat, turning once, until golden and crisp, 2 to 3 minutes. Drain on a rack. Sprinkle lightly with salt.

4. Add the romaine to the bowl. Toss well and mound on large plates. Arrange the tuna on the plates and stack the fried cheese alongside. Serve. —*Jose Garces*

WINE Fresh, fruity rosé.

Tuna and Potato Salad

TOTAL: 40 MIN

4 SERVINGS ●

- 2 Yukon Gold potatoes, peeled and cut into ½-inch pieces
- 1 medium carrot, peeled and cut into ¼-inch pieces
- ½ cup frozen baby peas
- ¼ cup plus 2 tablespoons mayonnaise
- 2 tablespoons crème fraîche
- 1 tablespoon Dijon mustard
- 2 tablespoons fresh lemon juice

Salt and freshly ground black pepper
- ¼ cup coarsely chopped flat-leaf parsley
- 2 tablespoons snipped chives

One 6-ounce can or jar solid white tuna in olive oil, preferably Spanish or Italian, drained and flaked
- 2 tablespoons extra-virgin olive oil
- 4 ounces baby arugula (4 cups)

1. Put the potatoes and carrot in a steamer basket set over a pot of simmering water and steam until just tender, about 9 minutes. Sprinkle the frozen baby peas on top of the steamed vegetables and steam just until the peas are heated through, about 1 minute longer. Transfer the vegetables to a plate and refrigerate until they are cooled slightly, about 10 minutes.

2. Meanwhile, in a medium bowl, whisk the mayonnaise with the crème fraîche, mustard and 1 tablespoon of the lemon juice; season the dressing with salt and pepper. Fold in the chopped parsley, chives, flaked tuna and cooled vegetables.

3. In a medium bowl, whisk the olive oil with the remaining 1 tablespoon of lemon juice and season with salt and pepper. Add the baby arugula and toss. Mound the greens on plates, top with the tuna and potato salad and serve right away.
—*Jose Garces*

WINE Zesty, fresh Albariño.

Stuffed Whole Wild Salmon

ACTIVE: 25 MIN; TOTAL: 1 HR 25 MIN

12 SERVINGS ●

- 6 garlic cloves, thinly sliced
- 2 serrano chiles, thinly sliced crosswise
- 1 medium red onion, thinly sliced
- 1 whole orange, thinly sliced
- 1 whole lemon, thinly sliced
- ½ small fennel bulb, cored and very thinly sliced
- 2 tablespoons pure ancho chile powder

Extra-virgin olive oil
One 8- to 9-pound whole wild salmon, scaled and cleaned
Salt and freshly ground pepper

1. Preheat the oven to 425°. In a large bowl, toss the garlic, chiles, onion, orange, lemon, fennel, 1 tablespoon of the chile powder and 3 tablespoons of olive oil. Lay the salmon diagonally on a very large rimmed baking sheet. Season the cavity with salt and pepper; stuff with the aromatics and tie with kitchen string at 3-inch intervals. Rub all over with olive oil, season with salt and pepper and sprinkle with the remaining chile powder. Wrap the head and tail with foil if they touch the oven's sides.

2. Roast the salmon on the bottom rack of the oven for about 1 hour, until just cooked through and an instant-read thermometer inserted into the thickest part registers 135° to 140°; remove from the oven. Preheat the broiler. Set the rack 6 inches from the heat. Broil the salmon for about 3 minutes, until richly browned.

3. With 2 forks, carefully lift off the skin from the top of the salmon and reserve. Lift the flesh from the top and transfer to a platter. Lift the skeletal bone and discard. Carefully pour the pan juices into a bowl. Cut the second side of the salmon into sections and transfer to the platter. Discard the aromatics. Serve with the juices, crispy skin and olive oil. —*Tim Love*

WINE Ripe, luxurious Chardonnay.

Potato-Crusted Salmon with Herb Salad

TOTAL: 30 MIN

4 SERVINGS ● ●

Pre-shredded potatoes, sold in plastic bags in the supermarket frozen-food department, usually end up as hash browns. This recipe suggests an entirely new use for them: seared onto fat fillets of salmon to form a fantastic crisp crust.

- 4 cups frozen shredded potatoes (hash browns), thawed and squeezed dry
- 2 tablespoons snipped chives
- 2 tablespoons all-purpose flour

Salt and freshly ground pepper
Four 8-ounce skinless salmon fillets
- 1 cup vegetable oil
- 1½ teaspoons fresh lemon juice
- 1 teaspoon Dijon mustard
- 1½ tablespoons extra-virgin olive oil
- 4 ounces herb salad mix (6 cups)

1. In a medium bowl, toss the shredded potatoes with the chives and flour and season with salt and pepper. Lay the salmon fillets on a work surface and season with salt and pepper. Evenly pat a quarter of the shredded potatoes onto the top of each fillet.

2. In a large nonstick skillet, heat the oil until shimmering. Carefully add the salmon fillets to the oil, potato side down, and cook over moderately high heat, undisturbed, until browned, about 8 minutes. Carefully turn the salmon and cook for 1 minute longer. Using a slotted spatula, transfer the potato-crusted salmon to 4 plates. Blot off any excess oil.

3. In a medium bowl, whisk the lemon juice with the mustard and olive oil to make a dressing. Season the dressing with salt and pepper. Add to the herb salad mix and toss to coat. Put salad on the plates of salmon and serve right away.
—*Grace Parisi*

WINE Creamy, supple Pinot Blanc.

fish

Gingery Panko-Crusted Salmon with Asian Vegetables

ACTIVE: 45 MIN; TOTAL: 1 HR

4 SERVINGS

Chef Daniel Martinez uses Japanese bread crumbs, called *panko,* for almost everything he breads at Portland's Thirst wine bar. "I love its crispy texture and lightness," he says. Here, he creates a gingery *panko* crust for luscious salmon served with a side of Asian-scented eggplant.

- 3 tablespoons unsalted butter
- 1 small shallot, very finely chopped
- 1 garlic clove, very finely chopped
- 1 tablespoon plus 2 teaspoons minced fresh ginger (from a 1½-inch piece)
- ½ cup *panko*
- Kosher salt and freshly ground black pepper
- 5 tablespoons extra-virgin olive oil
- 1 medium eggplant (1¼ pounds), cut into ½-inch dice
- 2 tablespoons freshly squeezed lime juice
- 1 tablespoon Dijon mustard
- Four 6-ounce salmon fillets with skin
- ¾ pound shiitake mushrooms, stems discarded, caps thinly sliced
- 1 scallion, thinly sliced
- 2 tablespoons unseasoned rice vinegar
- 1 tablespoon chopped basil
- 2 teaspoons chopped mint
- ¼ cup tamari (see Note) or low-sodium soy sauce
- 1 tablespoon honey

1. Preheat the oven to 400°. In a medium skillet, melt the butter. Add the chopped shallot, chopped garlic and 1 tablespoon of the minced ginger and cook over moderate heat until the shallot is translucent, about 4 minutes. Add the *panko* and stir to coat evenly with the butter. Cook, stirring frequently, until the *panko* is lightly toasted, about 3 minutes. Season the topping lightly with salt and black pepper.

2. In a large skillet, heat 3 tablespoons of the olive oil until shimmering. Add the diced eggplant and cook over moderately high heat until lightly browned, about 5 minutes. Reduce the heat to moderate, cover and cook until the eggplant is softened, about 5 minutes longer. Transfer the eggplant to a small bowl.

3. In a shallow bowl, whisk the lime juice with the mustard. Add the salmon fillets and turn to coat. Set the salmon fillets on a parchment paper–lined baking sheet and season them with salt and pepper. Pack the *panko* mixture on top of the salmon fillets and roast for 12 minutes, or until they are just cooked through.

4. Meanwhile, heat the remaining 2 tablespoons of olive oil in the skillet. Add the thinly sliced shiitake caps and cook over moderately high heat, stirring occasionally, until the mushrooms are tender, about 3 minutes. Reduce the heat to moderate. Add the sliced scallion and the remaining 2 teaspoons of minced ginger and cook for 1 minute. Return the softened eggplant to the skillet and season the vegetables with salt and pepper. Add the rice vinegar and cook until reduced by half, about 1 minute. Remove from the heat and stir in the chopped basil and mint.

5. In a small saucepan, simmer the tamari over moderate heat until reduced by half, about 2 minutes. Stir in the honey. Mound the vegetables in the center of each plate. Top with the salmon fillets, drizzle with the tamari sauce and serve.
—*Daniel Martinez*

NOTE Tamari, a soy sauce made without wheat, has a fuller-bodied flavor than regular soy sauce and complements fish well; low-sodium soy sauce is a fine substitute.

WINE Full-bodied, rich Pinot Gris.

Chive Salmon with Remoulade

TOTAL: 30 MIN

4 SERVINGS ● ●

A classic French remoulade is usually prepared with homemade mayonnaise. The recipe here calls for the store-bought kind, combining it with capers, Granny Smith apples and celery.

- ½ cup mayonnaise
- 1 tablespoon fresh lemon juice
- 1 tablespoon Dijon mustard
- ½ tablespoon chopped drained capers
- ½ cup plus 1 tablespoon minced chives
- 2 Granny Smith apples, peeled and cut into matchsticks
- 2 celery ribs, sliced diagonally ¼ inch thick
- Salt and freshly ground pepper
- 2 tablespoons extra-virgin olive oil
- Four 6-ounce skinless salmon fillets
- 8 medium radishes, thinly sliced crosswise

1. In a medium bowl, mix the mayonnaise, lemon juice, mustard, capers and 1 tablespoon of the chives. Stir in the apples and celery and season the remoulade with salt and pepper.

2. In a small bowl, stir 1 tablespoon of the olive oil into the remaining ½ cup of chives. Season the salmon fillets with salt and pepper. Press the chive paste onto one side of each salmon fillet.

3. In a large nonstick skillet, heat the remaining 1 tablespoon of olive oil. Add the salmon fillets, chive side down, and cook them over moderately high heat until they are lightly browned, about 3 minutes. Turn the fillets over and cook for 3 minutes longer. Transfer the salmon fillets to serving plates. Spoon the remoulade alongside the salmon, scatter the radishes on top of the fillets and serve right away.
—*Amy Tornquist*

WINE Fruity, low-oak Chardonnay.

Olive Oil–Poached Salmon with Fresh Horseradish

TOTAL: 1 HR

4 SERVINGS ●

- ½ pound fresh horseradish, peeled and finely grated on a Microplane
- 2¼ cups boiling water
- 2 medium leeks, white parts only, julienned
- 1 medium carrot, julienned
- 1 medium fennel bulb—halved, cored and julienned
- 1½ cups plus 2 tablespoons extra-virgin olive oil
- 2 tablespoons Dijon mustard

Salt and freshly ground pepper

Four 6-ounce skinless salmon fillets

Fleur de sel or sea salt, for sprinkling

1. Set a medium strainer lined with a coffee filter over a small saucepan. Put the grated horseradish in the filter and gradually pour the boiling water over it.

2. In a large saucepan of boiling water, blanch the leeks, carrot and fennel for 1 minute. Drain in a colander and transfer the vegetables to a bowl.

3. In a large skillet, heat the 2 tablespoons of olive oil. Add the leeks, carrot and fennel and cook over moderate heat, tossing, until hot. Stir in the mustard and season with salt and pepper. Remove from the heat.

4. In a saucepan, bring the remaining 1½ cups of olive oil to a simmer over moderate heat. Season the salmon fillets with salt and pepper and add to the oil. Gently simmer them over low heat for 4 minutes. Turn and simmer until they are just cooked, about 3 minutes longer.

5. Meanwhile, gently reheat the horseradish broth and season with salt. Rewarm the vegetables. Pour the broth into 4 shallow bowls. Spoon the vegetables into the bowls and top with the fillets. Sprinkle with fleur de sel and pepper and serve.

—*Gabriel Kreuther*

WINE Full-bodied, minerally Riesling.

CHIVE SALMON WITH REMOULADE

OLIVE OIL–POACHED SALMON WITH FRESH HORSERADISH

fish

Tasmanian-Pepper Poached Salmon

ACTIVE: 15 MIN; TOTAL: 45 MIN

4 SERVINGS ●

Tasmanian pepper berries are dark purple, with a lovely sweetness and a pungent kick. They can be found at Le Sanctuaire (310-581-8999). For a spicier dish, use a sprinkle of ground pepper berries, but be warned—they tend to turn food purple.

- 1 **lemon**
- 1 **cup extra-virgin olive oil**
- 1 **tablespoon whole Tasmanian pepper berries or ¼ cup pink peppercorns**

Four 6-ounce salmon fillets, skinned

Salt and freshly ground pepper

Ground Tasmanian pepper berries (optional)

- 2 **tablespoons fresh orange juice**
- 2 **tablespoons cold unsalted butter**

1. Finely grate ½ teaspoon of lemon zest and wrap in plastic. Using a vegetable peeler, remove the remaining zest in wide strips and cut into thin julienne. Squeeze and reserve 1 tablespoon of lemon juice.

2. In a medium skillet, mix the olive oil with the pepper berries and lemon julienne and bring to a boil. Simmer over low heat for 20 minutes. Strain through a fine sieve set over a bowl, pressing on the solids; return the infused oil to the skillet and bring to a simmer. Add the salmon, season with salt and pepper and simmer over moderately low heat until cooked, 5 minutes. Carefully turn the fish; cook until opaque throughout, 5 minutes. Transfer the fish to warmed plates.

3. Ladle out all but ¼ cup of the olive oil and set the skillet over moderately high heat. Add the lemon juice and orange juice and boil for 1 minute. Remove the skillet from the heat. Add the grated lemon zest and gradually whisk in the butter. Season the sauce with salt, pour it over the salmon fillets and serve. —*Jing Tio*

WINE Full-bodied, rich Pinot Gris.

Cedar-Planked Salmon with Grainy Mustard Glaze

ACTIVE: 20 MIN; TOTAL: 1 HR

8 SERVINGS ●

Eight 7-inch square cedar planks

- ½ **cup whole-grain mustard**
- 1 **tablespoon dry mustard**
- ¼ **cup mayonnaise**
- 1 **tablespoon soy sauce**
- 2 **teaspoons honey**
- ½ **teaspoon finely grated lemon zest**

Salt and freshly ground pepper

Eight 7-ounce salmon fillets, skinned

1. Light a grill. Soak the planks in water for 30 minutes. When the coals are covered with a light gray ash, push them to opposite sides of the grill and set a disposable drip pan in the center. In a bowl, mix the mustards, mayonnaise, soy sauce, honey and zest; season with salt and pepper. Season the fish with salt and pepper.

2. Drain the planks and pat dry. Set the salmon, skinned side down, on the planks. Spread the glaze over the top and sides. Arrange the planks on the grate above the drip pan and away from the coals. Cover and cook the salmon for 15 minutes, until browned and just cooked through; transfer to plates. —*Steven Raichlen*

WINE Ripe, luxurious Chardonnay.

Salmon with Roasted Shiitakes and Mushroom Sauce

ACTIVE: 35 MIN; TOTAL: 1 HR

4 SERVINGS ●

- 3 **tablespoons olive oil**
- 1 **pound small shiitakes, stems reserved for Mushroom Syrup**
- 16 **medium garlic cloves**
- 1 **jalapeño, sliced 1 inch thick**

Salt

- 2 **tablespoons grapeseed oil**

Four 6-ounce salmon fillets with skin

Freshly ground white pepper

- ¼ **cup Mushroom Syrup (recipe follows)**

Lemon wedges, for serving

1. Preheat the oven to 450°. Heat a 12-inch cast-iron skillet until very hot. Add the olive oil, shiitake caps, garlic and jalapeño slices and stir well. Season with salt. Transfer the skillet to the oven and roast the shiitake caps, stirring a few times, for about 20 minutes, or until richly browned and crisp.

2. In a large, nonstick skillet, heat the grapeseed oil. Season the salmon fillets with salt and white pepper and add them to the skillet, skin side down. Cook the salmon over high heat for 5 minutes, then reduce the heat to moderate and cook until the skin is browned and very crisp, about 12 minutes longer. Turn and cook for 2 minutes on the other side, until barely cooked through.

3. Transfer the salmon fillets to plates, skin side up. Gently lift the skin off and lean it against the fillet. Spoon the roasted shiitake caps on the salmon. Drizzle the plates with Mushroom Syrup and serve with lemon wedges.

—*Jean-Georges Vongerichten*

MAKE AHEAD The Mushroom Syrup can be refrigerated overnight. Melt it in a microwave oven before serving.

WINE Ripe, juicy Pinot Noir.

MUSHROOM SYRUP

ACTIVE: 10 MIN; TOTAL: 35 MIN

MAKES ABOUT ½ CUP ● ●

- 4 **tablespoons grapeseed oil**
- 14 **ounces shiitake stems (from 2 pounds shiitakes), chopped**
- 3 **cups water**
- 3 **cups low-sodium chicken broth**

In a skillet, heat the oil until shimmering. Add the shiitake stems and cook over moderate heat, stirring a few times, until deeply browned, 5 minutes. Add the water and broth and bring to a boil over high heat. Boil until reduced to 1 cup, 12 minutes. Strain the broth and return to the saucepan. Boil over high heat until reduced to ¼ cup, 7 minutes. —*J.G.V.*

SALMON WITH ROASTED SHIITAKES

SALMON WITH MUSHROOM SAUCE

Salmon with Mushroom Sauce

TOTAL: 30 MIN

4 SERVINGS ●

Briefly soaking the salmon in fresh orange juice before broiling creates a deeply cara-melized glaze that is so delicious you will never want to cook salmon any other way.

Four 6-ounce skinless center-cut
    salmon fillets
¼ cup fresh orange juice
Salt
  4 tablespoons plus 2 teaspoons
    unsalted butter
  1 garlic clove, minced
  1 pound sliced cremini mushrooms
Freshly ground pepper
  8 medium scallions or ramps,
    cut into 2-inch lengths
  ½ cup dry white wine
  ½ cup vegetable stock, fish stock
    or low-sodium broth
  ¼ cup heavy cream

1. Preheat the broiler. Lay the fish in a bak-ing dish and pour the orange juice over it. Season with salt; let stand 5 minutes. Turn and let stand for 5 minutes more.

2. In a large skillet, melt 4 tablespoons of the butter. Add the garlic and cook over moderately high heat until fragrant. Add the mushrooms; season with salt and pep-per. Cover and cook over moderately high heat, until the mushrooms have released their liquid, 5 minutes. Stir in the scallions and cook uncovered over high heat, stirring occasionally, until browned, 5 minutes. Add the wine; boil for 1 minute. Add the stock and cream and simmer for 3 minutes. Season with salt and pepper.

3. While the sauce simmers, transfer the fillets to a rimmed baking sheet, skinned side down. Top each with ½ teaspoon of the remaining butter. Broil 5 inches from the heat for 5 minutes, without turning, until browned and just cooked. Spoon the sauce on plates, set the fish on top and serve. —*Ian Garrone and Allen Kuehn*

WINE Complex, elegant Pinot Noir.

Grilled Salmon with Sweet Onions and Red Bell Peppers

ACTIVE: 55 MIN; TOTAL: 2 HR

4 SERVINGS ●

Red bell peppers are fabulous when grilled alongside sweet onion halves and salmon fillets marinated in a blend of soy sauce, brown sugar and olive oil.

  ¼ cup soy sauce
  ¼ cup light brown sugar
  2 tablespoons extra-virgin olive oil,
    plus more for drizzling
Four 6-ounce salmon fillets with skin
  2 small sweet onions, halved
    crosswise but not peeled
  2 red bell peppers—stemmed,
    cored and quartered lengthwise
  1 teaspoon balsamic vinegar
Salt and freshly ground pepper
  1 teaspoon chopped thyme
  1 tablespoon chopped marjoram

1. In a large, shallow dish, combine the soy sauce and brown sugar with the 2 table-spoons of oil; add the salmon and coat well. Cover and refrigerate for 1 hour.

2. Light a grill. Drizzle the cut sides of the onions with oil and grill over moderately high heat, cut side down, until nicely charred and starting to soften, about 15 minutes. Turn them and cook until tender, about 15 minutes longer.

3. Push the onions to the side of the grill. Oil the peppers and grill them, skin side down, away from the hottest part of the grill until lightly charred, about 5 minutes. Turn and grill for 5 minutes. Push them over to the onions. Remove the salmon from the marinade and grill, skin side down, for 8 minutes. Turn and grill until just cooked through, 4 minutes longer.

4. Drizzle the onions with oil and the bal-samic vinegar. Season with salt and pepper and sprinkle with the thyme. Transfer the salmon, peppers and onions to plates, sprinkle with the marjoram and serve. —*Brian Talley*

WINE Ripe, juicy Pinot Noir.

Poached Salmon with Caper-Butter Sauce

ACTIVE: 20 MIN; TOTAL: 40 MIN

4 SERVINGS ●

"You'd think salmon is so rich you wouldn't want a butter sauce with it," says F&W's Marcia Kiesel. "But beurre blanc is com-plex. It tastes shallot-y and wine-y. It really complements the flavor of the fish."

  2 tablespoons extra-virgin olive oil
  2 medium shallots, finely minced
  1¼ cups dry white wine
  1 stick cold unsalted butter, cut
    into tablespoons
  1 tablespoon capers, drained and
    rinsed
Salt and freshly ground pepper
  2 cups water
Four 6- to 7-ounce skinless salmon
    fillets
  2 cups shredded romaine lettuce

1. In a skillet, heat the olive oil. Add the shallots. Cook over low heat until softened, 4 minutes. Add ¾ cup of wine and boil over high heat until reduced to 2 tablespoons, 7 minutes. Reduce the heat to moderate. Remove the skillet and whisk in the butter, 1 tablespoon at a time, occasionally mov-ing the skillet back to the burner to keep the sauce very warm. Stir in the capers; season with salt and pepper.

2. In a large skillet, combine the water with the remaining ½ cup of wine and bring to a boil. Season the salmon with salt and pepper and add to the skillet. Simmer very gently over low heat, turning once, until just cooked through, 4 minutes per side.

3. When the salmon is almost done, gently reheat the sauce over moderate heat, whisking constantly just until hot; do not let it boil. Spread the shredded lettuce on plates. Using a slotted spatula, remove the salmon fillets from the skillet and quickly pat them dry with a paper towel, then set them on the lettuce. Pour the sauce over the salmon and serve. —*Marcia Kiesel*

WINE Rich, complex white Burgundy.

---

fish

Grilled Wild Salmon Skewers with Orange Tomato Jam

ACTIVE: 40 MIN; TOTAL: 2 HR 30 MIN

12 SERVINGS ● ●

- 4 medium orange tomatoes (about 1¾ pounds)—peeled, seeded and coarsely chopped
- ¼ cup cider vinegar
- 3 tablespoons honey
- 1 tablespoon minced fresh ginger
- ½ teaspoon ground cumin

Pinch of cayenne pepper

- 3 tablespoons extra-virgin olive oil
- 4 garlic cloves, minced
- 1 tablespoon chopped basil

Kosher salt and freshly ground pepper

equipment
hibachi grill

The rugged, compact, hibachi-style **Lodge Logic Sportman's Grill** is large enough to cook yakitoris, satays, small cuts of meat and kebabs for a crowd yet small enough to fit on a table. (We like it for grilling the wild salmon skewers in the recipe above.) It's made of preseasoned heavy cast iron and features a fire door for stoking charcoal without removing the grate. It is easy to carry to a patio, balcony, campsite or tailgate party. **Details** $115; lodgemfg.com.

- 3¼ pounds skinless wild salmon fillet, cut crosswise into twenty-four ½-inch-thick slices

1. In a saucepan, bring the tomatoes, vinegar, honey, minced ginger, cumin, cayenne, 1 tablespoon of the olive oil and half the garlic to a boil. Simmer over moderate heat, stirring occasionally, until thick, 45 minutes. Transfer to a bowl and refrigerate until cool, 1 hour. Stir the basil into the jam and season with salt and pepper.

2. Meanwhile, in a shallow bowl, combine the remaining 2 tablespoons of olive oil with the remaining garlic and season with salt and pepper. Add the salmon, toss well to coat and refrigerate for 1 hour.

3. Light a grill. Thread the salmon slices onto twenty-four 8-inch bamboo skewers. Grill the salmon over moderate heat, turning once, until cooked through, 4 to 5 minutes. Serve the salmon skewers with the tomato jam. —*Joe Vitale*

MAKE AHEAD The tomato jam can be refrigerated for up to 3 days.

WINE Fresh, fruity rosé.

Grilled Salmon with Teriyaki Shiitake

TOTAL: 30 MIN

4 SERVINGS ● ●

Sake combined with soy sauce, sesame oil and brown sugar make an Asian-accented glaze for shiitakes. Using the meaty-tasting mushrooms as a topping for salmon creates a dish loaded with heart-protective omega-3 fatty acids as well as B vitamins and protein.

- ¼ cup plus 1 tablespoon sake
- 2½ tablespoons soy sauce
- 2½ teaspoons light brown sugar
- 2 teaspoons Asian sesame oil
- 1 tablespoon canola oil
- ¾ pound shiitake mushrooms, stemmed and caps thickly sliced

Four 6-ounce skinless salmon fillets

- 1 tablespoon snipped chives

---

1. Preheat the broiler. In a small bowl, whisk the sake with the soy sauce, brown sugar and sesame oil. In a large nonstick, ovenproof skillet, heat 2 teaspoons of the canola oil. Add the shiitakes and cook over high heat, stirring occasionally, until lightly browned in spots and tender, about 8 minutes. Add all but 1 tablespoon of the sake mixture and cook, stirring, until the skillet is dry and the mushrooms are glazed, about 2 minutes. Transfer to a plate.

2. Wipe out the skillet and heat the remaining 1 teaspoon of canola oil. Add the salmon fillets and cook over high heat, turning once, until lightly browned, about 4 minutes. Spoon off any fat in the skillet. Remove the skillet from the heat, add the reserved 1 tablespoon of the sake mixture and turn the fillets to coat.

3. Broil the fillets until the tops are golden, lightly glazed and just cooked through, 1½ to 2 minutes. Transfer to plates and top with the mushrooms. Sprinkle with the snipped chives and serve.
—*Dr. Andrew Weil*

WINE Complex, elegant Pinot Noir.

Sautéed Spanish Mackerel with Black-Eyed Pea Salad

ACTIVE: 20 MIN; TOTAL: 1 HR 15 MIN

4 SERVINGS ●

Le Bernardin chef Eric Ripert's vivid black-eyed pea salad was inspired by *acarajé*, a traditional Brazilian dish made by pounding raw peas into a paste and mixing them with dried shrimp. Ripert uses whole peas and tosses them with a lime vinaigrette and chopped dried shrimp.

- ½ pound dried black-eyed peas, rinsed (1⅓ cups)
- ⅓ cup dried shrimp (see Note)
- ½ cup extra-virgin olive oil
- ¼ cup fresh lime juice
- ¼ cup chopped cilantro
- 2 scallions, white and light green parts only, thinly sliced
- 1 medium shallot, minced

fish

1 medium tomato—halved crosswise, seeded and cut into ¼-inch dice

1 small garlic clove, minced

1 jalapeño, seeded and minced

Salt and freshly ground pepper

2 tablespoons vegetable oil

Four 6-ounce skinless Spanish mackerel fillets

1. In a medium saucepan, cover the black-eyed peas with 2 inches of water and bring to a boil. Simmer over low heat, stirring occasionally, until the peas are tender, about 45 minutes. Drain the peas.

2. Meanwhile, in a small bowl, cover the dried shrimp with hot water and let stand until softened, about 30 minutes. Drain and coarsely chop.

3. In a large bowl, combine the olive oil, lime juice, cilantro, scallions, shallot, tomato, garlic and jalapeño. Fold in the peas and dried shrimp; season with salt and pepper. Let the black-eyed pea salad stand at room temperature for about 15 minutes, stirring once or twice.

4. In each of two large nonstick skillets, heat 1 tablespoon of the vegetable oil until shimmering. Season the mackerel fillets with salt and pepper. Add them to the skillets and cook over high heat until lightly browned, about 3 minutes. Turn them and cook until they are just opaque throughout, about 2 minutes longer.

5. Using a slotted spoon, scoop the black-eyed pea salad onto 4 plates and set the sautéed mackerel fillets on top. Drizzle any dressing remaining from the salad around the plates and serve. —*Eric Ripert*

NOTE Dried shrimp are available at Asian markets in a variety of sizes and forms. Choose headless shrimp that are still slightly pliable; they shouldn't crumble when they are pressed.

MAKE AHEAD The salad can be made early in the day; cover and refrigerate. Serve lightly chilled or at room temperature.

WINE Lively, tart Sauvignon Blanc.

Fried Spanish Mackerel with Cilantro Sauce

ACTIVE: 30 MIN; TOTAL: 45 MIN

6 SERVINGS ●

F&W's Marcia Kiesel recently set out to find the best home cooks in the Vietnamese seaside town of Nha Trang. One cook prepared crisp little fish fried in freshly rendered pork fat. Kiesel substitutes fish fillets here; to make this dish as the Vietnamese do, fry whole smelts or *rougets*.

5 garlic cloves, thickly sliced

3 Thai chiles or 1 large jalapeño, thickly sliced

3 medium shallots, 1 thickly sliced, 2 thinly sliced

3 tablespoons sugar

3 packed cups cilantro leaves and small sprigs

3 tablespoons Asian fish sauce

3 tablespoons fresh lime juice

¼ cup plus 2 tablespoons water

4 ounces fresh pork fat, cut into small dice, or ½ cup rendered lard

Six 6-ounce Spanish mackerel fillets with skin

Salt and freshly ground black pepper

1. In a large mortar, pound the garlic to a paste with the chiles, thickly sliced shallot and sugar. Add the cilantro and pound to a paste. Stir in the fish sauce, lime juice and water.

2. In a skillet, cook the pork fat over moderately low heat until ½ cup of fat is rendered, 20 minutes. Discard any solid fat. Season the fish with salt and pepper. Heat the fat until shimmering; add the fish, skin side down, and cook over moderately high heat until browned and crisp, 4 minutes. Reduce the heat to moderate, turn the fish and cook for 2 minutes. Transfer to plates. Add the remaining shallots to the pan and fry, stirring, until browned and crisp. Scatter over the fish. Spoon some sauce alongside and pass the rest. —*Marcia Kiesel*

WINE Vivid, lightly sweet Riesling.

Indian Swordfish Packets

TOTAL: 30 MIN

4 SERVINGS ● ●

Cooking in foil is a great way to keep food moist and minimize cleanup. Here, swordfish packets with cauliflower, scallions, raisins and an Indian spice mix make a wonderfully tangy, sweet and spicy dish.

1 tablespoon finely grated fresh ginger

2 garlic cloves, minced

1 teaspoon garam masala

½ teaspoon ground cumin

¼ teaspoon turmeric

⅛ teaspoon cayenne pepper

½ teaspoon finely grated lime zest

3 tablespoons fresh lime juice

Salt and freshly ground pepper

Four 6-ounce skinless swordfish steaks

½ small head cauliflower (1 pound), cut into 1-inch florets

2 scallions, green parts only, cut into 1-inch lengths

⅓ cup golden raisins

2 tablespoons extra-virgin olive oil

1. Preheat the oven to 500°. In a saucepan, bring 1 inch of water to a boil. In a bowl, mix the ginger, garlic, garam masala, cumin, turmeric, cayenne, lime zest and juice; season with salt and pepper. Spread the spice paste all over the swordfish.

2. Put the cauliflower in a steamer basket, add to the saucepan and steam until crisp-tender, about 3 minutes. Spread the cauliflower on a plate.

3. Lay four 14-inch-long sheets of foil on a large work surface. Spoon one-fourth of the cauliflower in the center of each. Top with the scallion greens, raisins and fish. Drizzle each steak with ½ tablespoon of oil; season with salt and pepper. Fold up the foil to form packets. Transfer to a sturdy baking sheet. Bake for 15 minutes, until the fish is cooked through. Carefully transfer to plates and serve. —*Annie Wayte*

SERVE WITH Steamed rice.

WINE Fresh, fruity rosé.

fish

Grilled Swordfish Steaks with Basil-Caper Butter

ACTIVE: 30 MIN; TOTAL: 45 MIN

4 SERVINGS ●

When grilling over wood—the connoisseur's choice—the idea is to keep the focus on the flavor of the wood smoke. A simple dish like these swordfish steaks, marinated in olive oil and lemon juice and topped with basil-caper butter, is a great choice.

- 6 tablespoons unsalted butter, softened
- 2 tablespoons chopped basil
- 2 teaspoons drained capers, chopped
- 1 tablespoon plus 1 teaspoon fresh lemon juice

Salt and freshly ground pepper

- 1 tablespoon extra-virgin olive oil

Four 8-ounce swordfish steaks, cut 1 inch thick

Arugula and Endive Salad with Pine Nuts and Parmesan, for serving (p. 39)

1. Light a grill. In a small bowl, blend the softened butter with the chopped basil, the capers and 1 teaspoon of the lemon juice. Season the basil-caper butter with salt and pepper, and refrigerate while you prepare the swordfish.

2. In a large, shallow dish, mix the olive oil with the remaining 1 tablespoon of lemon juice. Season the swordfish steaks with salt and pepper and turn them in the olive oil mixture. Refrigerate them for 15 minutes to marinate.

3. Grill the swordfish steaks over a hot fire until they are nicely charred on the outside and just cooked within, about 4 minutes per side. Transfer them to plates, top each with a dollop of the basil-caper butter and serve right away with the Arugula and Endive Salad with Pine Nuts and Parmesan. —*Steven Raichlen*

MAKE AHEAD The basil-caper butter can be refrigerated for up to 2 days.

WINE Zippy, fresh Pinot Bianco.

Red Fish Curry

ACTIVE: 40 MIN; TOTAL: 1 HR

6 SERVINGS ●

- ½ cup vegetable oil
- ½ cup fresh curry leaves (see Note)
- 15 garlic cloves, smashed
- 4 medium shallots, thinly sliced

One 2-inch piece of ginger, peeled and julienned (¼ cup)

- 4 long hot green chiles, seeded and thinly sliced crosswise
- 1 tablespoon ground coriander
- ½ teaspoon turmeric
- ¼ teaspoon cayenne
- 2 tablespoons tamarind puree (see Note)
- 1 cup tomato puree or one 14-ounce can of whole tomatoes with juice, pureed in a food processor

Six 6-ounce skinless tilapia fillets

Salt and freshly ground black pepper

Cilantro leaves, for garnish

1. In a very large, deep skillet, heat the oil. Add the curry leaves and cook over low heat until fragrant, about 2 minutes. Add the garlic and cook until softened, about 3 minutes. Add the shallots, ginger and chiles and cook for 5 minutes. Add the coriander, turmeric and cayenne and cook, stirring, until fragrant, about 2 minutes. Add the tamarind and tomato purees and simmer over low heat until thickened, about 10 minutes.

2. Season the tilapia fillets with salt and black pepper and nestle them in the sauce. Cover and simmer over moderately low heat, turning once, until the fish is just cooked through, about 4 minutes per side. Transfer the fish to plates and spoon the sauce on top. Garnish with the cilantro and serve. —*Aniamma Philip*

SERVE WITH White rice and lime wedges.

NOTE Fresh curry leaves and tamarind puree are available at specialty Indian markets and by mail order from Kalustyan's (800-352-3451) or kalustyans.com.

WINE Rich Alsace Gewürztraminer.

Grouper with Jicama and Black Bean Sauce

TOTAL: 30 MIN

4 SERVINGS ● ●

When legendary chef Jacques Pépin needs a break, he escapes to the bustling beach town of Playa del Carmen, Mexico, where he watches the waves, drinks chilled rosé and transforms the best local ingredients into simple recipes that showcase his elegant French technique. This dish was inspired by the delicious local grouper Pépin picks up at the beach when the fishermen return with their catch. Here, the skinned fillets are steamed over a bed of simmering local vegetables, including a dice of juicy jicama, which Pépin usually adds raw to salads for a cool crunch.

SAUCE

- 1 cup cooked dried or canned black beans with some of their liquid
- 2 tablespoons cilantro leaves
- 1½ tablespoons extra-virgin olive oil
- 2 teaspoons fresh lime juice

Salt and freshly ground pepper

FISH

- 1 tablespoon extra-virgin olive oil
- ¼ cup dry white wine
- 2 scallions, thinly sliced crosswise
- 1½ cups diced peeled jicama (½-inch dice)
- 1 medium tomato, cut into 1-inch dice
- ½ poblano chile, seeded and cut into ½-inch dice

Salt and freshly ground pepper

Four 6-ounce skinless grouper, striped bass or red snapper fillets

- ¼ cup cilantro leaves, for garnish

1. MAKE THE SAUCE: In a food processor, combine the black beans, cilantro, olive oil and lime juice and process until pureed. Scrape the puree into a small saucepan and bring to a simmer. Season with salt and pepper and remove from the heat.

GROUPER WITH JICAMA AND BLACK BEAN SAUCE

CRISPY MONKFISH WITH CAPERS

2. PREPARE THE FISH: In a skillet, combine the olive oil, wine, scallions, jicama, tomato and poblano; season with salt and pepper. Boil for 1 minute. Season the grouper with salt and pepper and arrange in the skillet, skinned side down. Cover and simmer over moderate heat until just cooked, 5 to 6 minutes.

3. Reheat the sauce. Transfer the fish to a platter. Strain the cooking liquid into the sauce, reserving the vegetables. Spoon the sauce onto plates and top with the fish and reserved vegetables. Garnish with the cilantro and serve. —*Jacques Pépin*
WINE Minerally, complex Sauvignon Blanc.

Crispy Monkfish with Capers
TOTAL: 40 MIN
4 SERVINGS ●
This riff on Wiener schnitzel, a breaded and fried veal cutlet, is lightened by substituting thinly sliced monkfish for the veal.

1¼ **pounds monkfish fillet**
¼ **cup all-purpose flour**
3 **large eggs, 2 beaten with 2 tablespoons of water, 1 hard cooked and finely chopped**
1 **cup *panko* (Japanese bread crumbs)**
Salt and freshly ground black pepper
4 **tablespoons unsalted butter**
¼ **cup vegetable oil**
1 **tablespoon finely chopped flat-leaf parsley**
1 **tablespoon capers, drained**
1 **teaspoon finely grated lemon zest**
Steamed asparagus and lemon wedges, for serving

1. Using a sharp knife, cut the monkfish fillet on the diagonal into ½-inch-thick slices. Put the flour, beaten eggs and *panko* into 3 shallow bowls. Season the monkfish slices with salt and pepper and dust each on one side only with flour, tapping off the excess. Dip the floured side in the egg and then in the *panko,* pressing so that the bread crumbs adhere.

2. In a large skillet, melt 2 tablespoons of the butter in 2 tablespoons of the oil. Add half of the monkfish slices, breaded side down, and cook over high heat until golden, about 3 minutes. Carefully turn the fillets and cook just until white throughout, 2 to 3 minutes longer. Transfer the finished fillets to plates, breaded side up. Repeat with the remaining butter, oil and fillets.

3. Sprinkle the crispy monkfish with the chopped parsley, capers, grated lemon zest and chopped hard-cooked egg. Serve the garnished monkfish at once with steamed asparagus and lemon wedges.
—*Daniel Boulud*
WINE Dry, light Champagne.

fish

Sardinian-Style Paella

ACTIVE: 20 MIN; TOTAL: 1 HR

12 SERVINGS ●

Fregola, the pearl-size Sardinian pasta that is quite similar to couscous, is used in place of rice in this paella-style dish; it soaks up a lot of the cooking liquid from the seafood, tomato and chorizo stew and still stays nicely chewy. For such an impressive main course, this Paella can be prepared surprisingly quickly.

Large pinch of saffron threads
6½ cups warm water
3 tablespoons extra-virgin olive oil
1 medium onion, finely chopped
3 large garlic cloves, thinly sliced
1 pound *fregola* (2¼ cups)
½ pound chorizo, thinly sliced
1 cup canned diced tomatoes, drained
1 cup dry white wine
Salt and freshly ground black pepper
2 pounds large shrimp, shelled and deveined
2 pounds red snapper, cod or monkfish, cut into 2-inch pieces
1 pound mussels, scrubbed and debearded
1 pound cockles, scrubbed
2 tablespoons chopped flat-leaf parsley

1. In a small bowl, crumble the saffron threads into ½ cup of the warm water and let stand for 10 minutes.

2. Meanwhile, heat the olive oil in a very large, deep sauté pan. Add the finely chopped onion and the sliced garlic and cook over high heat, stirring, until the onion and garlic are lightly browned, about 2 minutes. Add the *fregola* and the sliced chorizo to the pan and cook, stirring, until the chorizo releases some of its fat and starts to brown, about 2 minutes. Add the diced tomatoes, dry white wine, the saffron and its soaking liquid and the remaining 6 cups of warm water to the sauté pan and bring to a boil. Stir in 1½ teaspoons of salt and ½ teaspoon of pepper, cover the sauté pan and cook over low heat until the *fregola* becomes very chewy and soupy, about 10 minutes.

3. Season the large shrimp and the red snapper pieces with salt and pepper and add them to the sauté pan along with the mussels and cockles, nestling the fish pieces and the shellfish into the *fregola.* Bring the paella to a boil. Cover the sauté pan and cook over low heat until the *fregola* is al dente, the fish is just cooked through and the mussels and cockles have opened, about 12 minutes longer.

4. Remove the sauté pan from the heat and let the paella stand for 5 minutes; the *fregola* will absorb a bit more of the liquid, but the dish should still be a bit brothy. Discard any mussels and cockles whose shells haven't opened. Sprinkle the *fregola* with the chopped flat-leaf parsley and serve the paella right away.
—*Maria Helm Sinskey*
WINE Fresh, fruity rosé.

Bouillabaisse

ACTIVE: 1 HR 30 MIN; TOTAL: 2 HR

4 SERVINGS ●

When Cathal Armstrong, one of F&W's Best New Chefs 2006, was growing up in Ireland, his father (a travel agent and avid cook) made all kinds of Spanish and French dishes, including a great bouillabaisse. Now Armstrong serves his own phenomenal bouillabaisse, packed with shrimp, mussels, clams and monkfish, at Restaurant Eve, in Old Town Alexandria, Virginia. One of the first customers to taste the dish was his mother, who was visiting from Ireland. She loved it, Armstrong reports, adding wryly. " Why wouldn't she? She's my mother."

BROTH
⅓ cup extra-virgin olive oil
8 shallots, coarsely chopped
2 leeks, white and tender green parts, coarsely chopped
1 medium fennel bulb, cored and coarsely chopped
1 head of garlic, cloves peeled and coarsely chopped
1 teaspoon tightly packed saffron
3 large tomatoes, coarsely chopped
2 tablespoons tomato paste
2 pounds nonoily white fish bones and heads
3 quarts of water
4 thyme sprigs
4 parsley sprigs
2 bay leaves
Salt
Freshly ground black pepper
ROUILLE
1 baking potato (8 ounces), peeled and cut into 1-inch dice
2 large egg yolks
2 large garlic cloves, chopped
½ roasted red pepper
1 tablespoon plus 1 teaspoon *harissa*
¾ cup extra-virgin olive oil
Salt
SOUP
¼ cup extra-virgin olive oil
2 garlic cloves, minced
1 leek, white and tender green parts, finely diced
½ medium fennel bulb, cored and cut into ½-inch dice
1 baking potato, peeled and cut into ½-inch dice
1 large tomato—peeled, seeded and cut into ½-inch dice
12 littleneck clams, scrubbed and rinsed
16 mussels, debearded
8 large shrimp (½ pound), shelled and deveined

SARDINIAN-STYLE PAELLA

BOUILLABAISSE

1½ pounds snapper or monkfish fillets, cut into 2-inch chunks

1 tablespoon fresh lemon juice

3 tablespoons chopped basil

8 thin slices of baguette, brushed with olive oil and toasted

Lemon wedges, for serving

1. MAKE THE BROTH: In a large pot, heat the olive oil. Add the chopped shallots, leeks, fennel and garlic and cook over moderate heat until the vegetables are softened, about 8 minutes. Add the saffron to the pot and cook, stirring, for 1 minute. Add the chopped tomatoes and the tomato paste to the broth and cook over moderately high heat, stirring, for 2 minutes. Add the fish bones and heads, the 3 quarts of water, the thyme sprigs, parsley sprigs and bay leaves and bring to a boil. Simmer the broth over moderately low heat for 45 minutes.

2. Strain the broth and discard the solids. Return the broth to the pot and boil over high heat until it is reduced to 6 cups, about 20 minutes. Season the broth with salt and pepper.

3. MAKE THE ROUILLE: In a small saucepan of boiling salted water, cook the diced baking potato until it is tender, about 7 minutes. Drain the potato well and transfer to a food processor. With the machine running, add the egg yolks, chopped garlic, roasted red pepper and the *harissa* and process to a puree. Add the olive oil and process very briefly until it is just incorporated. Scrape the rouille into a bowl and season with salt. Cover and refrigerate the rouille.

4. MAKE THE SOUP: In a large pot, heat the olive oil. Add the minced garlic, diced leek and fennel and cook over moderately low heat, stirring occasionally, until the vegetables are tender, about 8 minutes.

Add the diced potato and cook until just tender, about 5 minutes. Add the tomato and cook, stirring, for 3 minutes. Stir in the broth and bring to a boil. Add the clams and cook over moderate heat until they start to open. Add the mussels, the large shrimp and the snapper and simmer the paella until the seafood is just cooked, about 4 minutes. Discard any clams or mussels whose shells don't open. Stir the lemon juice and basil into the paella; season with salt and pepper.

5. To serve, spread the baguette toasts with some of the rouille. Spoon the bouillabaisse into 4 large, shallow bowls and serve with the toasts and lemon wedges on the side. Pass the remaining rouille at the table. —*Cathal Armstrong*

MAKE AHEAD The broth can be refrigerated overnight. The rouille can be refrigerated for up to 4 hours.

WINE Fresh, fruity rosé.

●FAST   ●HEALTHY   ●MAKE AHEAD   ●STAFF FAVORITE

LIGURIAN SEAFOOD STEW

Ligurian Seafood Stew

TOTAL: 45 MIN

6 SERVINGS ● ●

At A Voce, chef Andrew Carmellini's Manhattan restaurant, this recipe includes blanched peas, snap peas and fingerling potatoes in a mussel broth along with sea bass, clams, an herb pesto and little seafood meatballs of shrimp, chorizo and scallops. Here, the F&W test kitchen narrows the ingredient list to the basics and uses bottled clam juice flavored with spicy chorizo as a stand-in for mussel broth.

- ¼ cup plus 2 tablespoons extra-virgin olive oil
- 2 shallots, thinly sliced
- 2 garlic cloves, thinly sliced
- 2 tablespoons finely diced chorizo

Pinch of crushed red pepper
- 1 cup dry white wine
- 2 cups bottled clam broth
- ½ cup water
- 1 cup basil leaves
- 1 tablespoon pine nuts
- 1 tablespoon freshly grated Parmesan cheese

Salt
- 2 dozen littleneck clams
- 1 pound shelled and deveined large shrimp
- 1 pound sea bass fillets, cut into 2-inch pieces
- ½ cup frozen baby peas

Crusty bread, for serving

1. In a medium soup pot, heat 2 tablespoons of the olive oil. Add the shallots, garlic, chorizo and crushed red pepper and cook over high heat until the shallots are softened, about 5 minutes. Add the wine and cook until reduced by half, about 8 minutes. Add the clam broth and water and bring to a boil.

2. Meanwhile, in a food processor, pulse the basil, pine nuts, Parmesan and the remaining ¼ cup of oil. Season with salt.

3. Add the clams to the soup pot and cook over high heat, stirring occasionally, until they open, about 8 minutes; transfer the clams to a bowl as they open. Discard any that do not open. Add the shrimp and fish to the broth, season with salt and cook until the fish is opaque and firm, about 5 minutes. Return the clams to the pot, add the peas and cook until warmed through. Ladle the stew into deep bowls, drizzle with the pesto and serve with crusty bread. —*Andrew Carmellini*

WINE Fresh, minerally Vermentino.

Grilled Sardines with Eggplant Puree and Tarragon Dressing

TOTAL: 1 HR 15 MIN

4 SERVINGS ●

The local sardines now sold throughout California are so rich and lush-tasting that they can stand up to the smoky, charred flavors of grilling. Chef David LeFevre of Los Angeles's Water Grill adds even more character to these incredible little fish by serving them with a puckery tarragon, caper and pine nut relish. A fishmonger can bone and butterfly the sardines, making them especially easy to cook and eat.

- 1 medium eggplant, halved lengthwise
- ¼ cup plus 2 tablespoons extra-virgin olive oil, plus more for grilling
- 2 tablespoons white wine vinegar
- 2 tablespoons water
- ¼ cup plus 2 tablespoons chopped tarragon
- 1 small shallot, finely chopped
- 3 garlic cloves, very finely chopped
- ½ cup chicken stock or low-sodium broth

Salt and freshly ground black pepper
- 3 tablespoons pine nuts
- 1 teaspoon finely grated lemon zest
- 1 tablespoon finely chopped roasted red pepper
- 2 teaspoons capers, drained and chopped
- 2 tablespoons fresh lemon juice
- 12 fresh sardines, boned, heads and tails intact

1. Preheat the oven to 375°. Brush the cut sides of the eggplant halves with 2 tablespoons of olive oil and place, cut side down, on a rimmed baking sheet. Bake the eggplants for about 45 minutes, or until they are very soft. Let cool, then carefully scoop out and coarsely chop the flesh. Transfer to a medium bowl.

2. In a small saucepan, combine the white wine vinegar with the 2 tablespoons of water, 2 tablespoons of the chopped tarragon, half of the chopped shallot and two-thirds of the chopped garlic and bring to a boil. Simmer over low heat until the liquid is nearly evaporated, about 5 minutes. Transfer the liquid to a blender. Add the chicken stock and one-fourth of the eggplant and puree until smooth. Stir into the remaining eggplant and season with salt and pepper.

3. In a small skillet, toast the pine nuts over moderately high heat, shaking the pan occasionally, until golden, about 3 minutes; transfer to a plate. In the same skillet, heat the remaining ¼ cup of olive oil. Add the remaining shallot and garlic and cook over low heat until softened, about 2 minutes. Transfer the shallot and garlic to a bowl and let cool. Whisk in the lemon zest, roasted red pepper, capers and lemon juice and season with salt and pepper. Stir in the remaining ¼ cup of tarragon and the pine nuts.

4. Preheat a grill. Brush the sardines with olive oil and season both sides of the fish generously with salt and pepper. Grill the sardines over high heat, turning them once, until they are lightly charred, 2 to 3 minutes. Spoon the eggplant puree onto plates and top with the sardines. Spoon the tarragon dressing on top of the sardines and serve. —*David LeFevre*

WINE Fresh, minerally Vermentino.

fish

Vinegar-Poached Sturgeon with Thyme-Butter Sauce

ACTIVE: 35 MIN; TOTAL: 2 HR

4 SERVINGS ●

- 4 medium zucchini (1½ pounds), sliced crosswise ½ inch thick
- Salt
- 2 tablespoons unsalted butter, softened
- 1 teaspoon chopped thyme
- Freshly ground pepper
- 3 tablespoons extra-virgin olive oil
- Four 6-ounce skinless farmed sturgeon or wild Pacific halibut fillets
- 3 tablespoons homemade red wine vinegar or good-quality store-bought red wine vinegar (see Note)
- ¾ cup water
- Bouquet garni made with 2 parsley sprigs, 1 bay leaf and the leafy top of 1 celery rib, tied with kitchen string
- 1 medium shallot, thinly sliced
- 3 tablespoons capers, drained and rinsed

1. Preheat the oven to 375°. On a large rimmed baking sheet, sprinkle the zucchini slices with salt. Arrange them in an even layer and let stand for 1 hour. In a small bowl, blend the butter with the thyme and season with salt and pepper.

2. Rinse the zucchini and pat dry; wipe the baking sheet. Return the zucchini to the sheet and toss with 2 tablespoons of olive oil. Spread the slices in an even layer and bake until golden brown on the bottom, 30 minutes. Transfer to a platter.

3. Sprinkle the fish with 1 tablespoon of vinegar; refrigerate for 10 minutes. In a large, heavy skillet, boil the remaining 2 tablespoons of vinegar with the water, bouquet garni and shallot. Season the poaching liquid lightly with salt and pepper and add the fillets. Cover tightly and simmer over low heat, turning once, until barely cooked through, about 8 minutes. Transfer to a large plate. Strain the liquid into a bowl.

4. Wipe out the skillet and set it over high heat. Add the remaining olive oil and heat until shimmering. Add the fillets, boned side down, and cook until golden brown on the bottom, about 2 minutes. Turn and cook for 1 minute longer. Set the fillets on the zucchini and cover with foil to keep warm.

5. Add the strained poaching liquid to the skillet and boil over high heat until reduced to ⅓ cup, about 5 minutes. Stir in the capers and remove from the heat. Swirl in the thyme butter and season the sauce with salt and pepper. Transfer the fillets and zucchini to plates, spoon the sauce on top and serve. —Paula Wolfert

NOTE if you are planning to make your own red wine vinegar, see Box, p. 48.

WINE Lush, fragrant Viognier.

White Anchovy and Crisp Pita Bread Salad

TOTAL: 25 MIN

4 SERVINGS ●

- Two 6-inch pita breads, split into 4 rounds
- 4 tablespoons unsalted butter, softened
- 1 medium shallot, thinly sliced and separated into rings
- 1½ tablespoons white balsamic vinegar or balsamic vinegar
- 1 tablespoon extra-virgin olive oil
- ¾ cup sour cream
- 1 garlic clove, minced
- Salt and freshly ground white pepper
- 2 large Belgian endives, cored and sliced crosswise ½ inch thick
- 12 marinated white anchovies, cut into 1-inch pieces

1. Preheat the oven to 350°. Arrange the pitas on a baking sheet, rough sides up, and spread each round with 1 tablespoon of butter. Bake for about 8 minutes, until crisp. Let cool and break into large pieces.

2. Meanwhile, in a small bowl, steep the shallot in the vinegar for 5 minutes. Stir in the olive oil, then add the sour cream and garlic and season with salt and pepper.

3. In a large bowl, toss the endive with the anchovies and toasted pita. Add the sour cream dressing and toss well. Spoon onto 4 plates and serve. —Marcia Kiesel

WINE Dry, earthy sparkling wine.

equipment

crocks

If you are planning to make homemade red wine vinegar, as used in the recipe above (see Box, p. 48 for method), here are some crocks Paula Wolfert likes:

Emile Henry's 4.2-quart crock doubles as an ice tea server and features a boxwood spigot. Details $100; cooking.com.

Clay Coyote Pottery one-gallon crocks are individually hand thrown and feature wooden spigots. Details $65; claycoyote.com.

Fish Tacos with Crispy Pickled Jalapeños

TOTAL: 40 MIN

4 SERVINGS ● ● ●

- 8 corn tortillas
- 1 cup plus 1 tablespoon vegetable oil

One 4-ounce can green chiles, drained and rinsed

- 1 tablespoon sliced green olives
- 1 garlic clove, peeled and smashed
- ⅓ cup cilantro leaves, plus more for garnish
- 1 scallion, white and green parts, cut into 1-inch lengths
- 1 tablespoon fresh lime juice

Salt and freshly ground pepper

- 8 ounces prepackaged shredded coleslaw mix (4 cups)
- 1¼ pounds sea bass fillets with skin, cut into 1-inch-wide strips
- ½ cup cornstarch
- ½ cup drained pickled sliced jalapeños

1. Preheat the oven to 200°. Lightly brush the tortillas with 1 tablespoon of the oil. Stack, wrap in foil and bake them until warmed through.

2. Meanwhile, in a mini food processor, combine the green chiles with the sliced olives, smashed garlic, cilantro, scallion and 1 teaspoon of the lime juice and process until a coarse puree forms. Transfer the green salsa to a small bowl and season with salt and pepper.

3. In a medium bowl, combine the shredded coleslaw mix with the remaining 2 teaspoons of lime juice and season with salt and pepper. Toss well.

4. In a large nonstick skillet, heat the remaining 1 cup of oil until shimmering. Place the fillets in a large resealable, sturdy plastic bag. Add the cornstarch and a pinch of salt. Seal the bag and shake to coat. Remove the fillets, tapping off the excess cornstarch, and add to the hot oil. Fry over moderately high heat, turning occasion-

ally, until golden, crisp and cooked through, about 5 minutes. Drain on paper towels and sprinkle lightly with salt.

5. Add the jalapeños to the cornstarch in the bag; shake to coat. Remove the jalapeños and tap off excess cornstarch. Add to the hot oil and fry over moderately high heat until crisp, 2 to 3 minutes. Using a slotted spoon, transfer to paper towels to drain. Sprinkle with salt and pepper.

6. Place the fried fish and warm tortillas on a serving platter and serve with the crispy jalapeños, coleslaw, green salsa and cilantro leaves. —*Grace Parisi*

WINE Vivid, lightly sweet Riesling.

Spicy Fish Cakes with Nuoc Cham Sauce and Fried Garlic Chips

ACTIVE: 1 HR; TOTAL: 1 HR 15 MIN

MAKES 18 FISH CAKES ●

F&W's Marcia Kiesel based this recipe on one prepared by chef David Thai, a Vietnam war refugee who grew up in France. Today he cooks Vietnamese dishes with classic French technique at Ana Mandara, a seaside resort in Nha Trang, Vietnam, that Kiesel visited.

Vegetable oil

- 4 large eggs, lightly beaten
- 2½ tablespoons Thai red curry paste
- 2 tablespoons sugar
- 1½ tablespoons Asian fish sauce
- 1 large shallot, thinly sliced
- 7 large garlic cloves, 1 minced, 6 thinly sliced
- 2 pounds skinless halibut or cod fillets, finely chopped by hand (about 3 cups)
- 1¼ cups fine dry bread crumbs
- ½ teaspoon freshly ground white pepper
- 1 large head of green leaf lettuce, separated into leaves
- 1 large cucumber, peeled and thinly sliced
- 1 bunch of mint, separated into small sprigs and large leaves

- 1 bunch of basil, separated into small sprigs and large leaves
- 1 bunch of cilantro, separated into small sprigs and large leaves
- 1 cup mung bean sprouts

Nuoc Cham Sauce (p. 29)

1. In a food processor, combine 2½ tablespoons of vegetable oil with the eggs, red curry paste, sugar, fish sauce, shallot, the minced garlic clove and ½ cup of the chopped fish and process until a fairly smooth paste forms.

2. Put the remaining fish in a large bowl. Add the fish paste, ¼ cup of the bread crumbs and the white pepper and stir to combine thoroughly. Cover the mixture and refrigerate until chilled, at least 1 hour or overnight.

3. In a saucepan, heat ¼ inch of vegetable oil until shimmering. Add the sliced garlic and cook over moderately low heat until golden brown and crisp, about 3 minutes. With a slotted spoon, transfer to a plate.

4. Add enough oil to the saucepan to reach 2 inches up the side. Heat the oil to 300°. Meanwhile, spread the remaining 1 cup of bread crumbs in a shallow bowl. Gently form the fish mixture into 18 oval cakes. Dredge the cakes in the bread crumbs until lightly coated.

5. Fry 4 fish cakes at a time, turning them a few times, until browned and crisp, about 3 minutes. Adjust the heat to keep the oil at 300°. Drain the fish cakes on a wire rack set over a large baking sheet. Transfer them to a platter and sprinkle the fried garlic chips on top.

6. Arrange the lettuce, cucumber and herbs on a platter. Put the bean sprouts and Nuoc Cham Sauce in separate bowls. Place a fish cake in a lettuce leaf, add cucumber slices, herb sprigs and bean sprouts and roll up to make a package. Dip in the sauce and eat. —*Marcia Kiesel*

MAKE AHEAD The fish cake mixture can be refrigerated overnight.

WINE Lush, fragrant Viognier.

SPICY SHRIMP AND CELLOPHANE-
NOODLE SALAD (P. 220)

shellfish

"Shrimp toast doesn't exist in China.
You don't find spaghetti and meatballs in Italy either."

—**Jean-Georges Vongerichten,** chef and restaurateur

CREOLE GRILLED SHRIMP ROLLS

SMOKY CITRUS SHRIMP WITH PARSLEY

Creole Grilled Shrimp Rolls

TOTAL: 30 MIN

4 SERVINGS ● ●

- 1 pound shelled and deveined jumbo shrimp, butterflied
- ¼ cup plus 1 tablespoon Creole Spice Paste (recipe follows)
- 2 tablespoons vegetable oil
- ¼ cup mayonnaise
- 1 celery rib, finely chopped
- 1 tablespoon finely chopped celery leaves
- 2 sour gherkins, finely chopped (2 tablespoons)
- 4 hot dog buns

1. Light a grill. In a medium bowl, toss the shrimp with ¼ cup of the spice paste and the oil and let stand at room temperature for 10 minutes.

2. Meanwhile, in a small bowl, mix the mayonnaise with the chopped celery, celery leaves, gherkins and the remaining 1 tablespoon of spice paste; refrigerate.

3. Grill the shrimp over high heat until pink and charred in spots, about 2 minutes. Transfer to a plate and freeze just until cooled, 5 minutes. Chop the shrimp and stir it into the mayonnaise. Mound the shrimp salad in the buns and serve.
—*Grace Parisi*

WINE Creamy, supple Pinot Blanc.

CREOLE SPICE PASTE

TOTAL: 15 MIN

MAKES 1 CUP ● ●

F&W's Grace Parisi has tried this aromatic spice paste on lots of foods, but her favorite way to use it is on butterflied jumbo shrimp.

- 2 garlic cloves
- ½ small onion, coarsely chopped
- 1 jalapeño, halved lengthwise and seeded
- 1 tablespoon flat-leaf parsley leaves
- 1 teaspoon thyme leaves
- ½ medium green bell pepper, coarsely chopped
- 1½ teaspoons kosher salt
- ½ teaspoon cayenne pepper
- ½ teaspoon freshly ground black pepper
- 2 tablespoons vegetable oil

In a food processor, puree the garlic with the onion, jalapeño, parsley and thyme. Add the green bell peppers, salt, cayenne and black pepper and pulse until finely chopped. Transfer the spice paste to a bowl and stir in the oil. —*G.P.*

OTHER USES Mix the spice paste into mayonnaise to use in chicken or tuna salad. You can also rub it on steak, chicken and pork.

MAKE AHEAD The Creole spice paste can be refrigerated for up to 3 days.

Smoky Citrus Shrimp with Parsley

TOTAL: 40 MIN

4 SERVINGS ● ●

Grub co-author Bryant Terry eats these tangy, garlicky shrimp piled high on crispy toasts, but sometimes he sandwiches them inside a quesadilla oozing with shredded Jack cheese. He recommends buying wild-caught or sustainably raised shrimp from the United States or Canada, where environmental standards are stricter than in places like Latin America and Southeast Asia. For more information on sustainable sources of shrimp, look at the Monterey Bay Aquarium's Seafood Watch (seafoodwatch.org).

- 2 pounds large shrimp, shelled and deveined
- ¾ teaspoon chipotle powder

Kosher salt

- 2 tablespoons extra-virgin olive oil
- 6 garlic cloves, very finely chopped
- ½ cup fresh orange juice
- 2 tablespoons fresh lemon juice
- 2 tablespoons fresh lime juice
- ½ cup flat-leaf parsley leaves, minced

Lightly toasted baguette slices

1. In a bowl, toss the shrimp with the chipotle powder and 1 teaspoon of salt. In a large skillet, heat the olive oil. Add the shrimp and cook over high heat, stirring frequently, until they begin to turn pink but are still raw in the center, 2 minutes. Using a slotted spoon, transfer them to a plate.

2. Reduce the heat to moderately high. Add the garlic to the skillet and cook until lightly golden, 1 minute. Add the orange, lemon and lime juices and boil until slightly thickened, scraping up any brown bits from the bottom of the skillet, 2 minutes.

3. Return the shrimp to the pan and toss to coat. Cook until white throughout, 1 minute. Stir in the parsley and season with salt. Transfer to bowls and serve with baguette toasts. *—Bryant Terry*

WINE Minerally, complex Sauvignon Blanc.

Grilled Citrus Shrimp with Vegetable Slaw

TOTAL: 40 MIN

6 SERVINGS ● ●

- ½ cup plus 1 tablespoon fresh lime juice
- ½ cup fresh orange juice
- ½ cup pineapple juice
- 2 tablespoons sugar
- 2 star anise pods, broken
- 1 rosemary sprig
- 1 cinnamon stick, broken
- 1 pound large shrimp, shelled and deveined
- 2 tablespoons extra-virgin olive oil, plus more for brushing
- 2 tablespoons coarsely chopped cilantro
- 1 large carrot, julienned
- 1 small yellow squash, julienned
- 1 small red onion, thinly sliced

Salt and freshly ground black pepper

- ½ teaspoon crushed red pepper

1. Light a grill or preheat the broiler. In a shallow dish, combine ½ cup of the lime juice with the orange juice, pineapple juice, sugar, star anise, rosemary and cinnamon stick. Add the shrimp, toss to coat and refrigerate for 10 minutes.

2. Meanwhile, in a medium bowl, combine the 2 tablespoons of olive oil with the cilantro and the remaining 1 tablespoon of lime juice. Add the carrot, squash and onion and season with salt and black pepper.

3. Remove the shrimp from the marinade. Transfer the marinade to a small saucepan, add the crushed red pepper and boil over high heat until reduced to ⅓ cup, about 8 minutes. Strain the sauce into a bowl.

4. Brush the shrimp with olive oil and season with salt and pepper. Grill over a hot fire or broil until nicely charred and just cooked through, 1 minute per side. Add to the sauce and toss. Arrange the shrimp on plates. Top with a little citrus sauce. Spoon the slaw alongside and serve. *—E. Michael Reidt*

WINE Vivid, lightly sweet Riesling.

Moo Shu Shrimp

TOTAL: 40 MIN

4 SERVINGS ●

- 12 small flour tortillas
- 6 tablespoons vegetable oil
- 1 pound shelled and deveined medium shrimp
- 3 large eggs, beaten

Salt and freshly ground pepper

- 2 tablespoons minced fresh ginger
- 1 large garlic clove, minced
- 3 ounces sliced mixed wild mushrooms (1 packed cup)
- 8 ounces shredded coleslaw mix (3 cups)
- 3 scallions, halved lengthwise and cut into 1-inch lengths
- 1 tablespoon hoisin sauce, plus more for serving

Cilantro leaves, for serving

1. Preheat the oven to 200°. Stack the tortillas and wrap in foil. Heat in the oven until warmed through.

2. Heat a large wok or skillet until very hot to the touch. Add 1 tablespoon of the oil and heat until smoking. Add the shrimp and stir-fry over high heat until lightly browned and cooked through, 2 minutes. Scrape the shrimp onto a large platter. Add 2 tablespoons of the oil to the wok. Stir the eggs, season them with salt and pepper and add to the wok. Cook, stirring, until large soft curds form, 2 minutes. Scrape the eggs onto the platter.

3. Add 2 tablespoons of oil to the wok. Add the ginger, garlic and mushrooms and stir-fry over high heat for 4 minutes, until lightly browned. Add the remaining 1 tablespoon of oil. Add the coleslaw mix and scallions, season with salt and pepper and stir-fry until the cabbage is wilted but still crunchy, about 4 minutes. Return the shrimp and eggs to the wok, add 1 tablespoon of hoisin and stir-fry until combined. Transfer to a bowl. Serve with the tortillas, cilantro and hoisin sauce. *—Grace Parisi*

WINE Vivid, lightly sweet Riesling.

---

shellfish

Shrimp Salad with Croutons

TOTAL: 30 MIN

4 SERVINGS ● ●

- 3 tablespoons red wine vinegar
- 2 teaspoons honey
- 1 teaspoon Dijon mustard
- ¼ cup plus 1 tablespoon extra-virgin olive oil, plus more for brushing
- 1 cup coarsely chopped, drained jarred roasted red peppers, 1 tablespoon of oil from the jar reserved
- Salt and freshly ground pepper
- Four 1-inch-thick slices of ciabatta bread
- 2 garlic cloves, minced
- 1 pound shelled and deveined medium shrimp
- 1 medium Vidalia or other sweet onion, thinly sliced
- ¼ cup minced chives

1. Light a grill. In a small bowl, combine the red wine vinegar with the honey, Dijon mustard, ¼ cup of the olive oil and the reserved 1 tablespoon of red pepper oil. Season the vinaigrette with salt and pepper and set aside.

tools

double-prong skewers

These **Bamboo Skewers** prevent kebabs from spinning or slipping. **Details** From $8 for 16; bestofbarbecue.com.

2. Brush the ciabatta slices on both sides with olive oil and grill the bread over high heat until the slices are slightly charred, about 1 minute per side. Let the toasted bread cool slightly, then cut it into 1-inch cubes.

3. In a large skillet, heat the remaining 1 tablespoon of olive oil. Add the minced garlic and the shrimp, season with salt and pepper and cook over moderate heat until the shrimp are pink and curled, about 1 minute per side. Scrape the cooked shrimp and garlic into a medium bowl and let cool slightly.

4. Add the roasted red peppers, onion, chives and croutons to the bowl with the shrimp. Pour the vinaigrette over the shrimp salad and toss well to coat. Transfer the shrimp salad to plates and serve.
—*Amy Tornquist*

WINE Full-bodied, rich Pinot Gris.

Vietnamese-Style Jumbo Shrimp on Sugarcane

ACTIVE: 40 MIN; TOTAL: 1 HR 10 MIN
PLUS 2 HR MARINATING

4 SERVINGS ● ●

- 4 garlic cloves, coarsely chopped
- 3 tablespoons sugar
- 2 large shallots, coarsely chopped
- ¼ cup Asian fish sauce
- 3 tablespoons fresh lime juice
- 1 teaspoon freshly ground pepper
- 3 stalks of fresh lemongrass, tender inner white bulbs only, thinly sliced crosswise
- ¼ cup vegetable oil, plus more for brushing
- 24 jumbo shrimp, shelled and deveined
- 12 sugarcane swizzle sticks (see Note)
- 3 tablespoons chopped peanuts
- 3 tablespoons coarsely chopped cilantro
- Vietnamese Dipping Sauce (recipe follows), for serving

1. In a food processor, combine the garlic, sugar, shallots, fish sauce, lime juice and pepper. Add the lemongrass and the ¼ cup of vegetable oil; process to a puree. Arrange the shrimp in a large, shallow glass dish in a single layer and pour the marinade on top; turn the shrimp to coat thoroughly. Cover and refrigerate for 2 hours.

2. Light a grill. Cut each sugarcane stick in half on a sharp diagonal so each piece has a sharp point. Scrape off most of the marinade. Working with the shrimp's natural curl, use a small, sharp knife to make 2 slits—one near the tail end and one near the head. Thread a sugarcane stick through the slits; the shrimp should lie flat. Repeat with the remaining shrimp.

3. Grill the shrimp over a hot fire, brushing them once or twice with oil, until lightly charred and just cooked through, about 3 minutes per side. Transfer the shrimp to a platter and sprinkle the peanuts and cilantro on top. Serve the shrimp with the Vietnamese Dipping Sauce.
—*Steven Raichlen*

NOTE Sugarcane swizzle sticks are available in the fruit department of many large supermarkets. Alternatively, look for canned sugarcane in syrup at Asian markets; you'll have to drain the sugarcane and cut it into sticks lengthwise with a sharp knife.

MAKE AHEAD The lemongrass marinade can be refrigerated overnight.

WINE Rich Alsace Gewürztraminer.

VIETNAMESE DIPPING SAUCE

TOTAL: 10 MIN

MAKES ABOUT 1 CUP ● ●

- One 2-inch piece of carrot
- 2 garlic cloves, minced
- 2 tablespoons sugar
- ½ cup warm water
- ¼ cup Asian fish sauce
- ¼ cup fresh lime juice
- 2 tablespoons white vinegar
- 1 red Thai chile, thinly sliced

VIETNAMESE-STYLE JUMBO SHRIMP ON SUGARCANE

CRISPY SHRIMP IN KATAIFI CRUST

1. Slice the carrot lengthwise with a sturdy vegetable peeler. Stack the slices and cut lengthwise into very fine julienne strips.
2. In a small bowl, mash the garlic with the sugar. Add the water, Asian fish sauce, lime juice, vinegar, Thai chile and carrots and stir well. —S.R.

Crispy Shrimp in Kataifi Crust
TOTAL: 40 MIN
4 FIRST-COURSE SERVINGS ● ●
Superchef Joël Robuchon was inspired to create this dish when he tasted a dish of Vietnamese shrimp rolled in soft vermicelli. "But I'm more into Mediterranean flavors at the moment," he says. He also wanted a crispy crust, so instead of vermicelli he uses *kataifi*, a Middle Eastern pastry that resembles shredded phyllo.

- ¾ **cup fresh orange juice**
- ½ **teaspoon jasmine tea**
- 4 **rosemary leaves**
- ½ **teaspoon cornstarch mixed with 1 teaspoon cold water**
- ¼ **teaspoon balsamic vinegar**
- **Salt**
- ¼ **pound *kataifi* dough (see Note), snipped into 4-inch lengths**
- ⅓ **cup basil leaves, finely shredded**
- ⅓ **cup chives, cut in 1-inch lengths**
- 1 **large egg**
- 1 **tablespoon water**
- **All-purpose flour, for dredging**
- 16 **large shrimp, shelled (but with tail shells left on) and deveined**
- **Freshly ground pepper**
- **Vegetable oil, for frying**

1. In a saucepan, combine the orange juice, tea and rosemary. Simmer over moderate heat until reduced to ¼ cup, 5 minutes. Strain and return to the pan. Bring to a simmer and whisk in the cornstarch mixture; cook until thickened, 30 seconds. Stir in the vinegar and season with salt.
2. In a large, shallow dish, separate the *kataifi* dough into individual threads using your fingers. Add the basil and chives and toss to distribute throughout the pastry.
3. In a shallow bowl, beat the egg with the water. Spread the flour in another shallow bowl. Season the shrimp with salt and pepper. Holding the shrimp by the tail, dredge them in the flour and shake off the excess, then dip them in the beaten egg and roll in the *kataifi*; press to help it adhere.
4. Set a rack over a baking sheet. In a large, deep skillet, heat ½ inch of oil to 350°. Fry 4 or 5 shrimp at a time until the *kataifi* is golden brown and crisp, about 1 minute per side. Drain the shrimp on the rack. Season with salt. Serve with the orange-rosemary sauce. —*Joël Robuchon*
NOTE *Kataifi* dough is available at Middle Eastern shops or Kalustyan's (800-352-3451; kalustyans.com).
WINE Light, crisp white Burgundy.

shellfish

Shrimp-Stuffed Triple-Baked Potatoes

ACTIVE: 30 MIN; TOTAL: 1 HR 15 MIN

4 SERVINGS

- 6 medium white potatoes (about 5 ounces each), scrubbed
- 1 cup crème fraîche
- 2 garlic cloves, minced
- Salt and freshly ground white pepper
- 3½ tablespoons unsalted butter, softened
- ⅔ cup heavy cream, warmed
- 12 medium shrimp—shelled, deveined and halved lengthwise

1. Preheat the oven to 400°. Prick the potatoes a few times with a fork and bake on a rack in the oven for about 40 minutes, or until tender.

2. Meanwhile, in a small bowl, blend the crème fraîche with the garlic; season with salt and white pepper and let stand for at least 15 minutes.

3. Increase the oven temperature to 450°. When the roasted potatoes are cool enough to handle, cut them in half lengthwise and scoop the flesh into a medium bowl, leaving a thin wall around the skins. Reserve 8 of the potato skin halves; set aside the rest for another use or discard. Mash the flesh well with a potato masher, then gently mash in 2½ tablespoons of the butter and the warm cream and season with salt and white pepper.

4. Rub the remaining 1 tablespoon of butter all over the outsides of the 8 reserved potato skins and season with salt and pepper. Arrange the potato skins, cut side up, on a baking sheet. Bake in the upper third of the oven for about 3 minutes, or until the skins are lightly crisp. Spoon the filling into the potato skins and continue baking for about 10 minutes, or until heated through and glazed on top.

5. In a medium saucepan, heat the crème fraîche. Add the shrimp and cook over moderate heat, stirring occasionally, until pink and starting to curl, about 3 minutes.

Using a slotted spoon, transfer the shrimp to a plate. Increase the heat to moderately high and simmer the crème fraîche until slightly reduced, about 2 minutes. Return the shrimp to the sauce.

6. Set 2 baked potato halves on each plate. Spoon the shrimp and crème fraîche sauce over the stuffed potatoes and serve immediately. —*Marcia Kiesel*

WINE Ripe, luxurious Chardonnay.

Shrimp and Papaya Salad

TOTAL: 30 MIN

4 SERVINGS ● ●

- 1 pound shelled and deveined large shrimp
- 2 tablespoons extra-virgin olive oil
- 1½ tablespoons fresh lime juice
- ½ teaspoon finely grated lime zest
- 1 small hot chile, such as Thai or serrano, very finely chopped
- Salt
- 1 small ripe papaya (1½ pounds)— peeled, seeded and cut into ¾-inch chunks
- ½ small red onion, thinly sliced into rings
- 1 celery rib, thinly sliced diagonally
- 1 bunch watercress (6 ounces), thick stems discarded
- ½ cup cilantro leaves
- ¼ cup salted cashews, coarsely chopped

1. Fill a large bowl with ice water. In a large saucepan of salted boiling water, cook the shrimp until pink and curled, about 2 minutes. Drain and plunge the shrimp into the ice water to cool. Drain and pat them dry.

2. In a large bowl, whisk the olive oil with the lime juice, lime zest and chile and season with salt. Add the papaya, onion, celery, watercress, cilantro and shrimp and toss gently. Scatter the cashews on top and serve. —*Annie Wayte*

WINE Tart, citrusy Riesling.

Peel-and-Eat Shrimp with Barbecue Spices

TOTAL: 25 MIN

6 SERVINGS ● ● ●

During a visit to Savannah, New York City chef Bobby Flay (Mesa Grill, Bolo, Bar Americain) ate as much shrimp and barbecue as humanly possible, then came back and created a recipe that cleverly combines them both. He loves to rub large peel-and-eat shrimp with a barbecue-inspired blend of paprika, chile powder, sugar and cumin before sautéing them.

- 1½ tablespoons sweet pimentón de la Vera (Spanish smoked paprika)
- 1 tablespoon ancho chile powder
- 1 tablespoon light brown sugar
- 1 teaspoon ground cumin
- 1 teaspoon kosher salt
- ½ teaspoon freshly ground black pepper
- 8 garlic cloves, coarsely chopped
- 2 pounds large shrimp, deveined but not shelled
- ½ cup vegetable oil
- 2 tablespoons unsalted butter
- 4 scallions, thinly sliced

1. In a large bowl, mix the smoked paprika with the ancho chile powder, light brown sugar, cumin, salt, pepper and chopped garlic. Add the shrimp to the bowl and toss to coat the shrimp with the spices.

2. Heat ¼ cup of the vegetable oil in 2 large skillets until shimmering. Add half of the shrimp to each of the skillets and cook over moderately high heat, stirring occasionally, until the shrimp are curled and white throughout, about 4 minutes. Add half of the butter and half of the scallions to each skillet and swirl them in. Transfer the shrimp to a platter and serve right away. —*Bobby Flay*

NOTE If you don't want to fuss with shells, you can use shelled shrimp. Cut the cumin in half and cook over moderate heat.

WINE Vivid, lightly sweet Riesling.

PEEL-AND-EAT SHRIMP
WITH BARBECUE SPICES

shellfish

Spicy Shrimp and Cellophane-Noodle Salad

ACTIVE: 30 MIN; TOTAL: 60 MIN
6 FIRST-COURSE SERVINGS ● ●

- 3 tablespoons fresh lime juice
- 2 tablespoons Asian fish sauce
- 1 tablespoon sugar
- 1 tablespoon grapeseed oil
- 1 red Thai chile, sliced paper-thin
- 1 kaffir lime leaf, minced, or
- ½ teaspoon grated lime zest
- 1 teaspoon oyster sauce
- 1¼ pounds large shrimp, shelled, or small squid bodies, halved lengthwise

Two 2-ounce packages dried cellophane noodles

Boiling water

Salt and freshly ground pepper
- 2 scallions, thinly sliced
- 1½ cups mint leaves
- ¾ cup cilantro leaves
- ¾ cup basil leaves
- ½ cup chopped salted roasted peanuts

Lime wedges, for serving

1. In a bowl, mix the lime juice, fish sauce, sugar, oil, chile, lime leaf and oyster sauce. In another bowl, toss the shrimp with half of the dressing. Refrigerate, covered, for 30 minutes. In a large heatproof bowl, cover the cellophane noodles with warm water. Let stand until pliable, 5 minutes.

2. Light a grill. Drain the noodles. Using scissors, cut them into 2-inch lengths and return to the bowl. Cover the noodles with the boiling water and let stand until they are softened, about 1 minute. Drain well.

3. Season the shrimp with salt and pepper and grill over high heat until just tender, 1 minute per side. In a bowl, toss them with the noodles, scallions, mint, cilantro, basil and the remaining dressing. Mound the salad on plates or a platter. Sprinkle with the peanuts and serve with lime wedges. —*Annabel Langbein*
WINE Tart, citrusy Riesling.

Grilled Oysters with Spicy Tarragon Butter

TOTAL: 40 MIN
6 SERVINGS ●

- 2 sticks unsalted butter, softened
- 3 tablespoons chopped tarragon
- 2 tablespoons hot sauce
- ½ teaspoon kosher salt
- ¼ teaspoon freshly ground pepper
- 3 dozen medium to large oysters, such as Gulf Coast or bluepoint

1. Light a grill. In a food processor, pulse the butter, tarragon, hot sauce, salt and pepper until blended. Transfer to a sheet of plastic wrap and roll into a 2-inch-thick log. Refrigerate until slightly firm, 15 minutes. Slice the butter into 36 pats.

2. Place the oysters on the hot grill, flat-side up. Cover the grill and cook until the oysters open, 5 minutes. Using tongs, transfer the oysters to a platter, trying to keep the liquor inside. Quickly remove the top shells and loosen the oysters from the bottom shells. Top each oyster with a pat of tarragon butter and return them to the grill. Cover the grill and cook until the butter is mostly melted and the oysters are hot, 1 minute. Serve. —*Bobby Flay*
WINE Fresh, minerally Vermentino.

Shrimp with Fresh Citrus Sauce

TOTAL: 30 MIN
6 SERVINGS ● ●

- 1 tablespoon fresh lemon juice
- ½ teaspoon *harissa* or hot sauce
- 3 tablespoons extra-virgin olive oil
- 1 large fennel bulb—halved, cored and shaved paper-thin
- 4 celery ribs, very thinly sliced
- 2 navel oranges, peeled and thinly sliced crosswise

Salt and freshly ground pepper
- 1½ pounds shelled and deveined large shrimp
- ½ cup fresh grapefruit juice
- 2 tablespoons unsalted butter
- 1 tablespoon snipped chives

1. In a medium bowl, whisk the lemon juice and *harissa* with 2 tablespoons of the olive oil. Add the fennel, celery and orange slices, season with salt and pepper and toss. Transfer the salad to plates.

2. In a large skillet, heat the remaining 1 tablespoon of olive oil until smoking. Season the shrimp with salt and pepper and add to the skillet. Cook, stirring once, until just pink and curled, about 2 minutes. Transfer the shrimp to a plate.

3. Add the grapefruit juice to the large skillet and cook until reduced by half. Swirl the butter into the reduced grapefruit juice, then add the chives and the cooked shrimp; simmer for 2 minutes, stirring. Top the fennel and celery salad with the shrimp and its sauce and serve. —*Andrew Carmellini*
WINE Lively, tart Sauvignon Blanc.

Tunisian Prawns with Kerkennaise Sauce

ACTIVE: 25 MIN; TOTAL: 1 HR 15 MIN
4 SERVINGS

The Kerkennah Islands off the coast of Tunisia are known for their date palms, olive trees and caper bushes. The Kerkennaise capers are very similar to the famous plump capers of Pantelleria, the Sicilian island just 30 miles away.

- 1¼ pounds tomatoes, halved crosswise
- ½ cup chopped scallions (4 large)
- 1 serrano chile, minced
- ¾ teaspoon ground coriander
- ¼ teaspoon ground caraway seeds
- ¼ cup chopped flat-leaf parsley

Pinch of sugar
- 1 tablespoon white wine vinegar
- 1 small garlic clove, minced

Salt
- ¼ cup plus 2 tablespoons extra-virgin olive oil
- 1¾ pounds jumbo shrimp, shelled and deveined

Freshly ground pepper
- 2 teaspoons drained capers

TUNISIAN PRAWNS WITH KERKENNAISE SAUCE

MANILA CLAMS WITH HOT SOPPRESSATA AND SWEET VERMOUTH

1. Grate the cut sides of the tomatoes against the large holes of a box grater set in a shallow bowl. Discard the tomato skins. Add the scallions, chile, coriander, caraway, parsley, sugar and vinegar to the grated tomatoes. Using the flat side of a chef's knife, mash the garlic to a paste with ¼ teaspoon of salt. Stir the garlic paste and 3 tablespoons of the olive oil into the sauce and season it with salt. Let the Kerkennaise sauce stand at room temperature for 1 hour.

2. Light a grill. In a medium bowl, toss the shrimp with the remaining 3 tablespoons of olive oil. Season the shrimp with salt and pepper and grill over a moderately hot fire until just cooked through, about 8 minutes. Transfer the shrimp to plates and sprinkle with the capers. Serve the shrimp at once with the Kerkennaise sauce.

—*Abderrazak Haouari*

WINE Fresh, fruity rosé.

Manila Clams with Hot Soppressata and Sweet Vermouth

TOTAL: 30 MIN

6 SERVINGS ● ●

This dish combines hot soppressata with Manila clams, a very common West Coast shellfish; cooks on the East Coast can use either littleneck clams or cockles.

- ¼ cup extra-virgin olive oil
- 4 garlic cloves, thinly sliced
- 3 ounces thinly sliced hot soppressata, cut into ¼-inch strips
- ½ medium sweet onion, very thinly sliced
- ½ teaspoon crushed red pepper
- ⅓ cup dry white wine
- ⅓ cup sweet vermouth
- 5 pounds Manila or littleneck clams or cockles, scrubbed and rinsed
- 2 tablespoons minced parsley
- 2 tablespoons fresh lemon juice

1. In a large, deep skillet, heat the olive oil until it is shimmering. Add the garlic, soppressata, the onion slices and the crushed red pepper and cook over moderate heat until the onion is softened, about 5 minutes. Add the white wine and sweet vermouth to the skillet and bring to a boil over high heat. Add the clams, cover the skillet and cook, shaking the skillet a few times, until all of the clam shells have opened, about 5 minutes. Discard any clams whose shells do not open.

2. Using a slotted spoon or a Chinese wire skimmer, transfer the cooked clams to shallow soup bowls. Add the chopped flat-leaf parsley and the lemon juice to the broth in the skillet and then bring it to a simmer. Ladle the hot clam broth over the clams in the bowl and serve at once.

—*Tommy Habetz*

SERVE WITH Grilled bread.

WINE Fresh, minerally Vermentino.

● FAST ● HEALTHY ● MAKE AHEAD ● STAFF FAVORITE

STEAMED COCKLES IN
SCALLION BROTH

Steamed Cockles in Scallion Broth

TOTAL: 35 MIN

4 SERVINGS ● ●

For a more substantial meal, toss in pasta and chopped tomatoes.

- 1 tablespoon extra-virgin olive oil
- 1 large shallot, minced
- 6 medium scallions, green parts only, thinly sliced crosswise
- ½ jalapeño, seeded and minced
- ½ cup dry white wine

Freshly cracked black pepper

- 2½ pounds cockles, scrubbed and rinsed
- 4 slices toasted baguette
- 2 tablespoons chopped parsley

1. In a large pot, heat the oil. Add the shallot and cook over moderately high heat until golden brown, about 5 minutes. Add the scallions, jalapeño and wine; bring to a boil. Sprinkle with cracked pepper and add the cockles. Cover and cook over high heat, shaking the saucepan a few times, until all the cockles have opened, about 4 minutes; discard the ones that don't.

2. Place a slice of toast in each bowl. Sprinkle the parsley into the cockles and transfer to the bowls. Pour the broth over the cockles and serve. —*Susan Spungen*

WINE Zesty, fresh Vinho Verde.

Pan-Fried Oysters with Creamy Radish and Cucumber Salad

TOTAL: 45 MIN

8 SERVINGS ● ●

Chef Paul Kahan (an F&W Best New Chef 1999) loves the intense flavor of oysters, and, like most chefs, he adores anything fried. Here he serves crunchy oysters with a creamy raita-like cucumber mixture.

- ¼ cup mayonnaise
- ¼ cup plain Greek yogurt
- 2 tablespoons buttermilk
- 1½ tablespoons lemon juice
- 1 garlic clove, mashed
- ½ teaspoon yellow mustard seeds, coarsely cracked
- ½ teaspoon black peppercorns, coarsely cracked
- ¼ teaspoon dill seeds, coarsely cracked
- 2 tablespoons grapeseed oil
- 1 small red onion, thinly sliced
- 1 small bunch radishes, cut into ¼-inch wedges
- 1 seedless cucumber—peeled, halved, seeded and thinly sliced

Salt

- 1 cup all-purpose flour
- 2 large eggs
- 2½ cups *panko* (Japanese bread crumbs)

Freshly ground black pepper

- 2 dozen oysters, shucked
- 1½ cups canola oil
- 1 small bunch watercress, thick stems discarded

1. In a medium bowl, combine the mayonnaise with the yogurt, buttermilk and lemon juice. Whisk in the mashed garlic, mustard seeds, peppercorns and dill seeds until combined. Whisk in the grapeseed oil. Add the sliced red onion, radish wedges and cucumber slices and season well with salt. Cover the salad and refrigerate.

2. Put the flour, eggs and *panko* in 3 shallow bowls and season each with salt and black pepper. Lightly beat the eggs. Pat the oysters dry with paper towels. Lightly dredge in the flour, then dip in the eggs and then in the *panko,* pressing lightly to help the crumbs adhere. Transfer to a baking sheet lined with wax paper.

3. In a large skillet, heat the canola oil until shimmering. Working in batches, fry the oysters over high heat, turning once, until the coating is crisp and golden, 2 to 3 minutes. Transfer to paper towels to drain. Season the oysters with salt.

4. Arrange the fried oysters on a platter and spoon the creamy radish and cucumber salad on the side. Garnish with the watercress and serve. —*Paul Kahan*

WINE Dry, light Champagne.

Viognier-Steamed Clams with Bacon and Parsnips

TOTAL: 45 MIN

6 SERVINGS ●

- 1 pound small parsnips, peeled
- ¼ cup extra-virgin olive oil, plus more for brushing

Salt and freshly ground pepper

- 6 ounces thickly sliced bacon, cut crosswise into ½-inch strips
- 1½ cups Viognier
- 2 tablespoons unsalted butter
- 1 shallot, minced
- 4 dozen littleneck clams, scrubbed and rinsed
- 1 cup heavy cream
- 2 tablespoons snipped chives

Oyster crackers, for garnish

1. Preheat the oven to 350°. On a baking sheet, brush the parsnips with olive oil. Season the parsnips with salt and pepper and roast, turning once or twice, until tender, 40 minutes. Let cool slightly; quarter lengthwise and slice ¼ inch thick.

2. In a large, deep skillet, cook the bacon over moderately high heat until browned and crisp, 6 minutes. Drain on paper towels; wipe out the skillet. In the skillet, bring the wine, butter and shallot to a boil. Add the clams, cover and cook over high heat until open, 6 to 8 minutes. Transfer to a large bowl. Discard any that don't open.

3. Pour the broth into a glass measuring cup. Rinse out the skillet. Slowly pour the broth into the skillet, stopping before you reach the grit. Add the cream and boil until reduced by half, 8 minutes. If the sauce separates, transfer to a blender and puree until smooth, then return to the skillet.

4. Add the parsnips, bacon, chives and the clams in their shells to the skillet. Season generously with pepper, cover and bring to a boil. Spoon into bowls, sprinkle with crackers and serve. —*Dean Maupin*

SERVE WITH White Cheddar and Scallion Muffins (p. 304).

WINE Lush, fragrant Viognier.

shellfish

Seared Scallops and Corn Cakes with Bacon Vinaigrette

TOTAL: 1 HR

4 SERVINGS

- ¼ pound thickly sliced bacon
- 7 tablespoons extra-virgin olive oil
- 1 small shallot, very finely chopped
- 2 tablespoons sherry vinegar
- ¼ cup chicken stock
- 1 tablespoon Dijon mustard
- 1 tablespoon whole-grain mustard
- Salt and freshly ground black pepper
- ¾ cup all-purpose flour
- ¾ teaspoon baking powder
- Pinch of cayenne pepper
- ¾ cup milk
- 2 large eggs, separated
- 1 tablespoon unsalted butter, melted, plus 1 teaspoon unsalted butter
- ¾ cup fresh corn kernels
- 12 jumbo sea scallops (about 1½ pounds)
- 1 head of frisée, leaves torn

technique

prepping soft-shells

Purchasing Buy live crabs if possible and choose ones with soft, moist shells.

Cleaning Turn the crab upside down; with scissors, cut off the "face." Remove the brain sac from behind the eyes. Lift up the "apron" from the abdomen of the crab and cut it off where it joins the body. Turn the crab right side up and lift each flap where the shell comes to a point; scrape off the spongy gills.

1. In a medium skillet, cook the bacon over moderate heat, stirring occasionally, until browned and crisp, about 5 minutes. Transfer to a bowl and pour off all but 2 tablespoons of the fat. Add 2 tablespoons of the olive oil and the shallot to the skillet and cook over moderate heat, stirring, until the shallot is softened. Add the vinegar and stock and simmer for 2 minutes. Remove from the heat and whisk in the mustards. Season with salt and pepper.

2. In a bowl, whisk the flour, baking powder, ½ teaspoon of salt and the cayenne. In another bowl, whisk the milk, egg yolks and melted butter. Stir in the dry ingredients and the corn. In a small bowl, beat the egg whites until firm peaks form, fold them into the corn batter.

3. Preheat the oven to 200°. In a large skillets, heat 2 tablespoons of the olive oil. Add several 2-tablespoon-size dollops of batter to the skillet, forming 3-inch cakes. Cook over moderate heat until the edges are deeply browned and the tops are bubbling, about 2 minutes. Turn the cakes and cook until lightly browned on the bottom, about 2 minutes longer. Drain the corn cakes on paper towels and repeat with the remaining batter, adding up to 2 more tablespoons of oil to the skillet. Transfer the corn cakes to a wire rack set over a baking sheet and keep warm in the oven.

4. In a large skillet, heat the remaining tablespoon of olive oil with the remaining teaspoon of butter. Season the scallops with salt and pepper and add them to the skillet. Cook over high heat, undisturbed, until browned on the bottom, 2 to 3 minutes. Turn the scallops and cook until golden, about 3 minutes longer.

5. Stir the bacon into the vinaigrette. In a bowl, toss the frisée with 2 tablespoons of the dressing and mound on plates. Arrange the scallops and corn cakes on the plates, drizzle with the rest of the dressing and serve. —*Stewart Woodman*
WINE Dry, rich Champagne.

Grilled Soft-Shell Crabs with Lemon Mayonnaise and Apple-Fennel Salad

TOTAL: 1 HR

8 SERVINGS

Chef Mario Batali cooks soft-shell crabs on the grill to give them a smoky flavor and an appealingly chewy texture. This salad is his Italian riff on coleslaw, made with very thinly sliced apples and fennel.

- ¼ cup plus 2 tablespoons apple cider vinegar
- ¼ cup extra-virgin olive oil, plus more for brushing
- 2 tablespoons pink peppercorns, coarsely chopped
- 1 teaspoon celery seeds
- 4 Granny Smith apples—peeled, cored and very thinly sliced, preferably on a mandoline
- 2 fennel bulbs—trimmed, cored and very thinly sliced, preferably on a mandoline
- Salt and freshly ground black pepper
- 1½ cups mayonnaise
- 3 tablespoons fresh lemon juice
- Finely grated zest of 1 lemon
- 16 soft-shell crabs, cleaned

1. Light a grill. In a bowl, stir the cider vinegar, ¼ cup of olive oil, 1 tablespoon of peppercorns and celery seeds. Add the apples and fennel and toss; season with salt and pepper. Refrigerate until chilled.

2. In a bowl, blend the mayonnaise, lemon juice and zest and the remaining 1 tablespoon of pink peppercorns; season with salt and pepper. Refrigerate until chilled.

3. Season the crabs with salt and pepper and brush with olive oil. Grill over a hot fire, top shell down, until lightly charred and crisp, 5 minutes. Turn and grill until just cooked through, 1 minute longer. Spoon the salad onto plates and top each with 2 grilled crabs. Serve the lemon mayonnaise on the side. —*Mario Batali*
WINE Zippy, fresh Pinot Bianco.

Soft-Shell Crabs with Lemon Aioli and Sweet Onion

TOTAL: 40 MIN PLUS 1 HR MARINATING

8 SERVINGS

"Soft-shell crabs were one of the first things I tasted as a young cook that completely flipped me out," says Paul Kahan, chef at Blackbird and Avec in Chicago. "I couldn't get enough of them."

- 3 tablespoons red wine vinegar
- 1 small shallot, minced
- 1¼ cups extra-virgin olive oil
- 1 small Vidalia or other sweet onion, cut into thin rings

Salt and freshly ground pepper

- ½ cup mayonnaise
- ½ teaspoon finely grated lemon zest
- 1½ tablespoons fresh lemon juice
- 1½ cups rice flour (see Note)
- 8 soft-shell crabs, cleaned

1. In a large bowl, whisk the vinegar with the shallot and ½ cup of the olive oil. Add the onion rings, season with salt and pepper and refrigerate for 1 hour.

2. Meanwhile, in a small bowl, whisk the mayonnaise with the lemon zest and juice. Gradually whisk in ¼ cup of the olive oil and season with salt and pepper. Refrigerate the aioli until chilled.

3. In a large skillet, heat the remaining ½ cup of olive oil until shimmering. Spread the rice flour in a shallow bowl. Lightly dust the soft-shell crabs with rice flour and fry over high heat, turning once, until browned and crisp, 6 to 7 minutes. Drain the fried crabs on paper towels and season with salt and pepper.

4. Using a slotted spoon, transfer the marinated onion rings to a serving platter. Top with the fried soft-shell crabs and serve with the lemon aioli. —*Paul Kahan*

NOTE Rice flour is available at most supermarkets and at specialty and health food stores.

MAKE AHEAD The lemon aioli can be refrigerated overnight.

WINE Complex, aromatic Chenin Blanc.

Crab Salad with Ginger and Dried Orange Peel

TOTAL: 15 MIN

4 SERVINGS ● ●

Jing Tio, owner of Le Sanctuaire cookware and design shop in Los Angeles, dries his own orange peel in a high-tech L'Equip machine, then grinds it to create a citrus powder with a beautifully smooth flavor—delicious with his simple crab and scallion salad. If you don't want to buy a dehydrator, simply purchase granulated orange peel at a specialty food shop.

- 3 tablespoons vegetable oil
- 3 large scallion whites, thinly sliced, plus 1 scallion green, thinly sliced
- 1 tablespoon minced fresh ginger
- 2 tablespoons sake
- 1 tablespoon rice vinegar
- 1 teaspoon soy sauce
- 1 teaspoon sugar
- 1 pound crabmeat, preferably Dungeness, Maine claw or lump, picked over

Salt and freshly ground pepper

- ½ teaspoon granulated dried orange peel

In a large skillet, heat the vegetable oil. Add the white scallion slices and the minced ginger to the skillet and cook them over moderate heat until the scallion slices start to brown, about 3 minutes. Add the sake, rice vinegar, soy sauce and sugar to the scallions and cook over moderate heat, stirring to dissolve the sugar, about 1 minute. Add the crabmeat and green scallion slices and toss lightly to coat them with the dressing. Season the crabmeat and scallions with salt and pepper. Transfer the crab salad to a platter and sprinkle it with the granulated dried orange peel. Serve the crab salad at room temperature or lightly chilled.
—*Jing Tio*

WINE Spicy American Gewürztraminer.

Pride of Baltimore Crab Cakes

ACTIVE: 20 MIN; TOTAL: 45 MIN

6 SERVINGS ● ●

- 1 cup mayonnaise
- ¼ cup extra-virgin olive oil
- ¼ cup plus 2 tablespoons grapeseed oil
- 1½ tablespoons fresh lemon juice

Cayenne pepper

- 1 garlic clove, peeled and chopped

Fine sea salt

- 1 pound jumbo lump crabmeat, picked over
- 1 cup finely crushed saltine crackers (3½ ounces)
- 1 large egg, lightly beaten
- 1 tablespoon Dijon mustard
- 1 tablespoon Worcestershire sauce
- ½ teaspoon Tabasco sauce

1. In a medium bowl, whisk the mayonnaise. Gradually whisk in the olive oil and ¼ cup of the grapeseed oil. Add the lemon juice and season with cayenne. Transfer ½ cup of the mayonnaise to a small bowl and reserve. Using the flat side of a chef's knife, mash the garlic to a paste with a generous pinch of salt. Whisk the garlic paste into the bowl of mayonnaise, then transfer the aioli to a serving bowl.

2. In a large bowl, gently mix the crabmeat with the crumbs, egg, mustard, Worcestershire sauce, Tabasco and the reserved ½ cup of mayonnaise. Shape the mixture into six 1-inch-thick crab cakes and transfer to a wax paper–lined plate. Refrigerate until firm, at least 20 minutes.

3. Preheat the oven to 400°. Heat the remaining 2 tablespoons of grapeseed oil in a large cast-iron skillet. Add the crab cakes and cook over moderate heat until golden on the bottom, about 4 minutes. Carefully turn the crab cakes, then transfer them to the oven and bake until golden and cooked through, about 10 minutes. Transfer the crab cakes to plates and serve with the garlic aioli. —*David Lentz*

WINE Zesty, fresh Albariño.

shellfish

Scallops with Brussels Sprouts

TOTAL: 25 MIN
2 SERVINGS ●

- ¼ cup crème fraîche
- ¼ teaspoon finely grated lemon zest
- 1 teaspoon fresh lemon juice
- 1 tablespoon snipped chives
- 3 tablespoons extra-virgin olive oil
- Salt and freshly ground pepper
- 6 jumbo scallops (about ¾ pound)
- 6 thin slices pancetta (about 2 ounces)
- ½ pound brussels sprouts, thinly sliced
- 1 shallot, thinly sliced
- 1 tablespoon unsalted butter
- 1 garlic clove, minced

1. In a small bowl, whisk the crème fraîche with the finely grated lemon zest and the fresh lemon juice, the snipped chives and 1 tablespoon of the olive oil. Season the lemon-chive crème fraîche to taste with salt and pepper.

2. In a medium skillet, heat the remaining 2 tablespoons of olive oil until shimmering. Generously season the scallops with salt and pepper and add them to the skillet. Cook the scallops over moderately high heat, turning once, until they are golden and just cooked through, about 5 minutes. Transfer the scallops to a plate; tent with aluminum foil to keep warm.

3. Meanwhile, in another medium skillet, cook the pancetta over moderately high heat, turning once, until browned and crisp, about 4 minutes. Add the brussels sprouts and shallot and cook, stirring, until the brussels sprouts are softened but still bright green, about 2 minutes. Off the heat, stir in the butter and garlic and season with salt and pepper; transfer to 2 plates and top with the scallops. Serve with the lemon-chive crème fraîche.
—*Stuart Brioza*

WINE Peppery, refreshing Grüner Veltliner.

Grilled Squid Salad with Celery Leaf Pesto

TOTAL: 45 MIN
6 SERVINGS ● ●

- 2 tablespoons pine nuts
- 1½ cups flat-leaf parsley leaves
- 3 celery ribs, thinly sliced, plus ½ cup celery leaves
- 2 garlic cloves
- 6 tablespoons extra-virgin olive oil, plus more for grilling
- 3 tablespoons Parmesan cheese
- Salt and freshly ground pepper
- One 15-ounce can imported butter beans, drained and rinsed
- ½ cup pickled sweet peppers or cherry peppers, thinly sliced
- ½ small red onion, finely chopped
- 1½ pounds small squid, cleaned
- ½ cup torn basil leaves

1. Light a grill. In a small skillet, toast the pine nuts over high heat until lightly browned. Transfer to a plate to cool.

2. In a food processor, combine ½ cup of the parsley with the celery leaves, garlic and pine nuts and process until minced. Add the 6 tablespoons of olive oil and the Parmesan and process until smooth. Season the pesto with salt and pepper and transfer to a large bowl.

3. Bring a medium saucepan of salted water to a boil. Add the celery and blanch for 30 seconds; drain. Rinse under cold water and pat dry. Add the celery, butter beans, pickled peppers, onion and the remaining 1 cup of parsley to the pesto.

4. In a medium bowl, toss the squid with a little olive oil and season with salt and pepper. Grill the squid over high heat for 5 minutes, or it is until charred in spots. Cut the squid bodies into rings; leave the tentacles whole. Add the squid to the salad and toss. Season with salt and pepper, garnish with the basil and serve.
—*Melissa Kelly*

WINE Light, fresh Pinot Grigio.

Crab Salad with Caesar Vinaigrette

TOTAL: 30 MIN
4 SERVINGS ● ●

Chef Shawn McClain uses a mortar and pestle to combine the ingredients for this piquant anchovy-and-Parmesan dressing, but a blender does the job more easily. McClain loves tossing roasted peppers with the crunchy greens, crab and anchovy.

- 8 white anchovies (see Note)
- 1 garlic clove
- 2 tablespoons red wine vinegar
- 1 teaspoon Dijon mustard
- 1 teaspoon Worcestershire sauce
- ¼ cup extra-virgin olive oil
- Salt and freshly ground pepper
- ¼ cup freshly grated Parmigiano-Reggiano cheese
- 1 pound jumbo lump crabmeat, picked over for cartilage
- 1 tablespoon snipped chives
- 1½ teaspoons chopped tarragon
- ¼ cup finely diced roasted red pepper
- ½ pound baby romaine lettuce leaves

1. In a blender or mini processor, combine 4 of the white anchovies with the garlic clove, red wine vinegar, Dijon mustard and Worcestershire sauce and puree until the dressing is smooth. With the machine on, add the olive oil and blend until incorporated. Season the vinaigrette with salt and pepper; add the grated Parmiggiano-Reggiano and blend briefly.

2. In a large bowl, gently toss the crabmeat, snipped chives, tarragon and roasted red pepper with the vinaigrette. Add the baby romaine and toss. Transfer the salad to plates, top with the remaining 4 white anchovies and serve. —*Shawn McClain*

NOTE Marinated white anchovies are available at Italian food markets, specialty food stores as well as in the deli case at some supermarkets.

WINE Fruity, low-oak Chardonnay.

CRAB SALAD WITH CAESAR VINAIGRETTE

SCALLOPS WITH SUMMER SQUASH

Scallops with Summer Squash

TOTAL: 30 MIN

4 SERVINGS ● ●

At his restaurants in Chicago, chef Shawn McClain prepares a rich herb dressing for tender scallops by blanching parsley, tarragon and chervil, then blending them with an egg yolk and olive oil. To make this recipe the easy way, omit the egg and make a very fresh herb sauce with olive oil and unblanched parsley, tarragon and chives (simpler to find than chervil).

1 **cup flat-leaf parsley leaves**
¼ **cup snipped chives**
2 **tablespoons tarragon leaves**
½ **cup plus 2 tablespoons extra-virgin olive oil**
Salt and freshly ground pepper
1½ **pounds mixed small yellow squash and zucchini, halved lengthwise and cut into 1-inch pieces**
1 **teaspoon finely chopped thyme**
2 **slices of prosciutto (1 ounce), cut into thin ribbons**
12 **jumbo scallops (about 1¼ pounds)**
½ **cup loosely packed Parmesan cheese shavings (½ ounce)**

1. In a blender or a mini processor, chop the flat-leaf parsley leaves, snipped chives and tarragon leaves to a coarse paste. With the machine on, pour in ½ cup of the olive oil and blend until the sauce is fairly smooth. Season the herb sauce with salt and pepper.

2. In a large skillet, heat 1 tablespoon of the olive oil until it is shimmering. Add the yellow squash and zucchini pieces and cook over high heat, stirring occasionally, until the summer squash is crisp-tender, about 5 minutes. Stir in the chopped thyme and 2 tablespoons of the herb sauce; season the summer squash with salt and pepper. Add the prosciutto to the skillet and keep warm.

3. In a medium skillet, heat the remaining tablespoon of oil until it is shimmering. Season the scallops with salt and pepper and add them to the skillet. Cook the scallops over high heat, turning them once, until they are golden brown and just barely opaque throughout, about 5 minutes. Add 1 tablespoon of the herb sauce to the scallops and stir to coat.

4. Spoon the summer squash onto 4 warmed plates and top with the sautéed scallops. Drizzle the scallops and squash with the remaining herb sauce, then garnish with the Parmesan cheese shavings and serve right away.
—*Shawn McClain*

WINE Fruity, low-oak Chardonnay.

BAY SCALLOP PAN ROAST

Bay Scallop Pan Roast

TOTAL: 25 MIN

4 SERVINGS ● ●

F&W's Marcia Kiesel vastly prefers sweet and fresh bay scallops to the semi-cooked calico scallops generally sold in supermarkets.

- 3 tablespoons unsalted butter
- ½ cup fresh bread crumbs, preferably from brioche

Salt and freshly ground pepper

- 1 tablespoon vegetable oil
- 1½ pounds bay scallops
- 4 large white mushrooms, thinly sliced
- 1 large shallot, thinly sliced
- 1 tablespoon fresh lemon juice
- ¼ cup water
- 1 tablespoon chopped parsley

1. In a large skillet, melt 1 tablespoon of the butter. Add the bread crumbs, season lightly with salt and pepper and cook over moderate heat, stirring, until the crumbs are golden brown and crisp, about 3 minutes. Scrape the crumbs onto a plate.

2. Wipe out the skillet. Add the oil and heat until it is shimmering. Add 1 tablespoon of the butter and let melt. Add the scallops, season with salt and pepper and brown over high heat, about 2 minutes total. Transfer to a large, shallow dish.

3. Melt the remaining 1 tablespoon of butter in the skillet. Add the mushrooms, season with salt and pepper and cook over moderate heat until their liquid is almost evaporated, about 4 minutes. Add the shallot and cook, stirring, until softened, about 3 minutes. Add the lemon juice and cook for 30 seconds. Add the water and simmer for 1 minute.

4. Return the scallops and any accumulated juices to the skillet and season with salt and pepper. Remove from the heat and stir in the parsley. Spoon the scallops and mushrooms onto plates, sprinkle with the crumbs and serve. —*Marcia Kiesel*

WINE Light, crisp white Burgundy.

Thai Red Curry Mussels with Fried Potatoes

TOTAL: 1 HR 15 MIN

6 SERVINGS

Chef Douglas Keane of Cyrus in Healdsburg, California, prepared this dish for his wife, Lael Newman, on one of their first dates; today, she asks him to make it whenever they can find beautiful fresh mussels at the fish market. For Keane, the fragrant combination of coconut milk and red curry is comforting and restorative—an equivalent to chicken noodle soup.

- ¼ cup plus 2 tablespoons vegetable oil
- 2 medium shallots, very finely chopped
- 1 celery rib, finely chopped
- 1 carrot, finely chopped
- 1½ teaspoons minced fresh ginger
- 3 garlic cloves, smashed
- 2½ teaspoons Thai red curry paste
- ½ cup coarsely chopped cilantro
- ½ cup coarsely chopped basil, plus several whole basil leaves, for garnish
- ¼ cup coarsely chopped mint
- 2¼ cups dry white wine
- 2 cups water

One 13-ounce can unsweetened coconut milk

- 1½ teaspoons light brown sugar
- 2 kaffir lime leaves (see Note)
- ¼ cup fresh lime juice
- 3 tablespoons Asian fish sauce
- 1 pound fingerling potatoes or small red potatoes
- 1 tablespoon unsalted butter

Salt and freshly ground black pepper

- 8 scallions, thinly sliced
- 3 pounds mussels, scrubbed

1. In a medium saucepan, heat 2 tablespoons of the vegetable oil. Add the chopped shallots, celery, carrot, minced ginger and smashed garlic and cook over moderate heat until the vegetables are softened, about 5 minutes. Add the Thai red curry paste and cook, stirring, for 2 minutes. Add the chopped cilantro, basil and mint and cook for 2 minutes. Stir in 2 cups of the dry white wine and boil until reduced by three-fourths, about 12 minutes. Add the water and boil until it is reduced by half, about 10 minutes. Add the coconut milk, brown sugar and kaffir lime leaves and boil for 5 minutes. Remove the sauce from the heat and stir in the lime juice and Asian fish sauce. Strain the curry sauce into a bowl.

2. Meanwhile, in a medium saucepan of boiling water, cook the fingerling potatoes until they are just tender, about 10 minutes. Drain and let cool slightly. Peel the potatoes and cut them in half lengthwise.

3. Heat 2 tablespoons of the vegetable oil in a large nonstick skillet. Add the potato halves, cut side down, and cook over high heat until they are golden brown on the bottom, about 5 minutes. Add the butter, season with salt and black pepper and cook, stirring occasionally, until the potatoes are golden all over, about 4 minutes longer. Using a slotted spoon, transfer the potatoes to a plate, top with the whole basil leaves and keep warm.

4. In a large, deep skillet, heat the remaining 2 tablespoons of vegetable oil until shimmering. Add the sliced scallions and cook over high heat for 1 minute. Add the remaining ¼ cup of wine and bring it to a boil. Add the curry sauce and bring it to a boil. Add the mussels and cook them over high heat, stirring occasionally, until they open, 4 to 5 minutes. Discard any mussels that don't open. Spoon the mussels and the curry sauce into deep bowls and serve immediately with the crisp potatoes.

—*Douglas Keane*

NOTE You can substitute two 1-inch strips of lime zest for the kaffir lime leaves.

MAKE AHEAD The curry sauce can be refrigerated overnight.

WINE Spicy American Gewürztraminer.

shellfish

Pickled Vegetable–Seafood Salad

TOTAL: 50 MIN
6 FIRST-COURSE SERVINGS ● ●

- 4 large celery ribs, cut into 3-by-½-inch sticks
- 2 large carrots, cut into thin julienne (on a mandoline)
- 2 teaspoons kosher salt
- 1 tablespoon plus 2 teaspoons sugar
- 1 tablespoon plus 1 teaspoon distilled white vinegar
- 2 large cucumbers—peeled, halved lengthwise, seeded and cut into 3-by-½-inch sticks
- ½ pound medium shrimp—shelled, deveined and halved lengthwise
- ½ pound small, cleaned squid, bodies sliced into ¼-inch rings, tentacles left whole
- 2 large garlic cloves, thickly sliced
- 2 red Thai chiles or 1 medium jalapeño chile pepper, thickly sliced
- ¼ cup Asian fish sauce
- 2 tablespoons fresh lime juice
- 2 tablespoons water
- ½ cup salted roasted peanuts, chopped

ingredient
cardamom

In an F&W survey, chefs singled out **cardamom** as the most underused spice. Although it's commonly found in Indian recipes such as the Shrimp Masala at right, TV chef Ming Tsai values its versatility: "It's a great spice that can be sweet or savory."

1. In a bowl, toss the celery and carrots with 1 teaspoon each of the salt and sugar. Add the vinegar and gently squeeze the vegetables with your hands to work in the seasonings. Let stand in the vinegar and sugar for 5 minutes. In another bowl, toss the cucumbers with the remaining salt. Using your fingers, work the salt into the cucumbers. Let stand for 5 minutes.
2. Rinse the pickled celery, carrots and cucumbers under cold water and squeeze dry; transfer to a large bowl.
3. In a medium saucepan of boiling salted water, cook the shrimp just until pink and curled, 1 minute. With a slotted spoon, transfer the shrimp to the bowl with the vegetables. Add the squid to the water and cook until opaque, 1 minute; transfer the squid to the large bowl.
4. In a mortar, pound the garlic, chiles and the remaining sugar to a paste. Stir in the fish sauce, lime juice and water. Add the dressing to the large bowl and toss the salad well. Sprinkle the peanuts over the salad and serve. —*Marcia Kiesel*
WINE Zesty, fresh Vinho Verde.

Shrimp Masala

TOTAL: 40 MIN
4 TO 6 SERVINGS ● ●

Make the masala paste in large quantities; it's great as a dry rub or in a marinade for fish and chicken.

MASALA PASTE

- 1½ teaspoons coriander seeds
- Seeds from 1 cardamom pod
- ⅛ teaspoon anise seeds
- 1 whole clove
- ½ teaspoon crushed red pepper
- One ½-inch piece of cinnamon stick, broken
- ¼ teaspoon black peppercorns
- 1 tablespoon vegetable oil
- 1 tablespoon cider vinegar
- 2 teaspoons finely grated fresh ginger
- 1 garlic clove, very finely chopped

- ½ teaspoon turmeric
- Salt

SHRIMP

- 3 tablespoons vegetable oil
- 10 fresh curry leaves
- 2 garlic cloves, minced
- 1 large onion, thinly sliced
- One ½-inch piece of ginger, peeled and sliced paper-thin
- ½ cup canned whole tomatoes with juice, chopped
- 1 pound large shrimp, shelled and deveined
- Salt
- Pineapple Pachadi (recipe follows)

1. MAKE THE MASALA PASTE: In a spice grinder, combine the coriander, cardamom and anise seeds, clove, crushed pepper, cinnamon and peppercorns and grind to a fine powder. Transfer to a small bowl and stir in the oil, vinegar, ginger, garlic and turmeric. Season the paste with salt.
2. MAKE THE SHRIMP: In a large skillet, heat the oil until shimmering. Add the curry leaves and cook over moderately high heat until they sizzle, 10 seconds. Add the garlic, onion and ginger. Cook over moderate heat, stirring occasionally, until softened and starting to brown, 10 minutes. Add the masala paste and cook, stirring, until fragrant, 5 minutes. Add the tomatoes and their juice. Cook, scraping up any browned bits from the bottom of the skillet.
3. Add the shrimp to the skillet in an even layer and season with salt. Simmer, turning once, until just cooked through, about 3 minutes; serve with Pineapple Pachadi. —*Aniamma Philip*
SERVE WITH Steamed white rice.
MAKE AHEAD The masala paste can be made 1 day in advance and stored in an airtight container at room temperature or it can be kept in the refrigerator for up to a week. The recipe can be made through Step 2 up to 4 hours ahead. Reheat before adding the shrimp.
WINE Fruity, soft Chenin Blanc.

PINEAPPLE PACHADI

ACTIVE: 15 MIN; TOTAL: 30 MIN
6 TO 8 SERVINGS ●

- 2 tablespoons vegetable oil
- 12 fresh curry leaves
- ½ teaspoon black mustard seeds
- ½ teaspoon crushed red pepper
- 6 medium shallots, minced
- 2 long hot green chiles, seeded and minced
- 1 cup finely chopped fresh pineapple
- ½ cup water
- ½ cup finely shredded unsweetened coconut
- 1½ cups plain whole milk yogurt
- Salt

1. Heat the oil in a small saucepan. Add 6 curry leaves, the mustard seeds and red pepper and cook over high heat until the curry leaves sizzle and the mustard seeds pop, 30 seconds; remove from the heat.
2. In a medium skillet, simmer the shallots, chiles, pineapple, water and remaining curry leaves over moderately low heat until most of the water has evaporated, 10 minutes. Add the coconut and yogurt and cook, stirring, until heated through but not boiling, about 3 minutes. Remove the pan from the heat, stir in the fried curry leaf mixture and season the pineapple *pachadi* with salt. Let the *pachadi* cool to room temperature and serve. —*A.P.*

Bahian Seafood Stew with Coconut and Tomato

TOTAL: 45 MIN
4 SERVINGS ● ●

- 2 tablespoons canola oil
- 2 shallots, minced (½ cup)
- 2 medium garlic cloves, minced
- 1 small onion, cut into ½-inch dice
- 1 red bell pepper, cut into ½-inch dice
- 1 tablespoon minced fresh ginger
- 1 stalk of lemongrass, tough outer leaves discarded and stalk smashed
- 3 tomatoes—halved, seeded and cut in ¼-inch dice
- Salt and freshly ground pepper
- 1½ pounds large shrimp, shelled and deveined
- 1 cup unsweetened coconut milk
- 12 cilantro leaves, plus 1 tablespoon chopped cilantro
- ½ pound skinless grouper fillet, cut into 1-inch pieces
- 2 tablespoons fresh lime juice

Heat the oil in a medium enameled cast-iron casserole; cook the shallots, garlic, onion, bell pepper, ginger and lemongrass over moderate heat until softened, 7 minutes. Add the tomatoes, season with salt and pepper and cook for 3 minutes. Season the shrimp with salt and pepper and add to the stew with the coconut milk and cilantro leaves. Cover and cook for 2 minutes. Season the grouper with salt and pepper; add to the stew, cover and cook for 3 minutes. Discard the lemongrass. Add the lime juice and season the stew with salt and pepper. Garnish with the chopped cilantro; serve. —*Eric Ripert*

SERVE WITH Steamed white rice and thin lime wedges.

WINE Spicy American Gewürztraminer.

Lobster with Udon Noodles, Bok Choy and Citrus

TOTAL: 40 MIN
4 SERVINGS ●

- Two 1¼-pound live lobsters
- 2 heads of baby bok choy
- ¼ pound dried Japanese udon noodles
- ¼ cup plus 3 tablespoons vegetable oil
- 2 small shallots, thinly sliced
- Salt
- 1 orange or grapefruit
- 1 medium onion, thinly sliced
- ½ pound oyster mushrooms, large caps quartered
- 1 tablespoon light brown sugar
- ½ cup vegetable stock or broth
- 2 tablespoons sake
- Freshly ground pepper
- 2 tablespoons unsalted butter

1. Bring a large pot of water to a rolling boil over high heat. Add the lobsters headfirst and cook for 5 minutes. Using tongs, transfer to a rimmed baking sheet. Return the water to a boil. Add the bok choy and cook for 30 seconds. Transfer to a work surface and quarter each head lengthwise.
2. Add the udon to the boiling water and cook, stirring often, until al dente, about 6 minutes; drain. Return to the pot and cover with cold water. Drain and rinse the udon 2 more times, then drain thoroughly, lifting the noodles a few times to help dry.
3. In a small skillet, heat ¼ cup of the oil. Add the shallots and cook over moderate heat, stirring a few times, until browned and crisp, 3 minutes. Transfer to paper towels to drain, then salt lightly.
4. Crack the lobster claws and remove the meat in one piece. Twist off the lobster tails. Using kitchen shears, slit one side of each tail shell; remove the meat in one piece. Cut the tail meat in half lengthwise and discard the intestinal veins.
5. Using a sharp knife, peel the orange, taking care to remove all of the bitter white pith. Cut in between the membranes to release the sections.
6. In a large skillet, heat the remaining oil. Add the onion and mushrooms. Cook over high heat for 5 minutes, stirring occasionally. Add the sugar, bok choy, stock and sake and bring to a simmer. Add the udon, season with salt and pepper and stir well.
7. In a skillet, melt the butter. Add the lobster. Cook over moderately low heat, turning, until warmed through, 2 minutes. Crush the fried shallots over the lobster and stir to coat. Season with salt and pepper. Transfer the noodles and vegetables to a serving bowl, top with the lobster and oranges and serve. —*Ludovic Lefebvre*
WINE Rich, complex white Burgundy.

shellfish

Lobster Paella on the Grill

ACTIVE: 1 HR; TOTAL: 1 HR 20 MIN
8 SERVINGS

This impressive paella cooks on the grill in one big pan. You'll need a large pile of coals that will stay hot for an hour or so.

- 6 cups chicken stock or broth
- ¼ cup extra-virgin olive oil
- 8 skinless, boneless chicken thighs, trimmed of excess fat (about 2 pounds)

Salt and freshly ground black pepper

- 3 chorizo sausages, cut into 1-inch chunks (about ½ pound)
- 2 medium onions, coarsely chopped
- 3 bell peppers—preferably 1 red, 1 yellow and 1 orange, cut lengthwise into 1-inch strips
- 6 garlic cloves, thinly sliced
- 3 cups medium-grain Spanish rice, such as Valencia, or arborio rice (18 ounces)
- ½ teaspoon saffron threads

Two 1¼-pound lobsters—tails split lengthwise, claws and knuckles cracked and heads discarded (see Note)

- 2 pounds large shrimp, shelled and deveined
- 1 pound littleneck clams, scrubbed
- 1 pound mussels, scrubbed and debearded

Lemon wedges, for serving

1. Light a grill. In a medium saucepan, cover the chicken stock and bring to a simmer on the grill. Set aside, covered.

2. Set a paella pan or a very large skillet over the hot fire and add the olive oil. Add the chicken thighs and season with salt and pepper. Add the chorizo and cook until the chicken and sausage are lightly browned on both sides, about 6 minutes; transfer to a plate. Add the onions, peppers and garlic to the pan and cook, stirring occasionally, until all the vegetables are softened, about 6 minutes.

3. Add the rice to the pan and cook, stirring, until golden, about 3 minutes. Stir in the stock, crumble in the saffron and add a large pinch of salt. Add the chicken thighs and chorizo. Cover the grill and cook until the stock has reduced to 2 cups, about 12 minutes. Nestle the lobster pieces in the rice, cover the grill and cook for 3 minutes. Arrange the shrimp, clams and mussels in the rice, cover the grill and simmer until the chicken, shrimp and lobster are cooked through and the clams and mussels are open, about 10 minutes. Discard any shellfish that don't open. Spoon the paella into shallow bowls and serve piping hot with lemon wedges. —*Mario Batali*

NOTE You can ask your fishmonger to cut up the lobster for you.

WINE Fruity, luscious Shiraz.

Lobster Fideos

ACTIVE: 1 HR 15 MIN; TOTAL: 1 HR 45 MIN
12 FIRST-COURSE SERVINGS ● ●

Rossejat de fideos, a traditional seafood dish of Spain's Catalonia region, resembles paella, but instead of rice it calls for *fideos,* fine vermicelli-like pasta.

Six 1¼-pound live lobsters

- ¾ cup plus 1 tablespoon extra-virgin olive oil
- 6 garlic cloves, coarsely chopped
- 2 large carrots, coarsely chopped
- 2 large sweet onions, chopped

One 35-ounce can peeled whole tomatoes, drained and chopped

- 1½ tablespoons sweet pimentón de la Vera (smoked Spanish paprika)
- ½ cup brandy
- 3 quarts water
- 2 tablespoons unsalted butter, melted

Salt and freshly ground pepper

- 1½ pounds *fideos* or angel-hair pasta, broken into 3-inch lengths

1. In a large, heavy pot of boiling water, cook the lobsters for 5 minutes; the water need not return to a boil. Transfer to 2 large rimmed baking sheets. Drain the pot. When the lobsters are cool, twist off the tails and claws. Break the bodies and legs into 3-inch pieces. With scissors, cut down the center of the tails; remove the meat in one piece. Discard the intestinal veins. Crack the claws; remove the meat in one piece. Cover the meat and refrigerate.

2. Heat 6 tablespoons of olive oil in the pot. Add the body pieces and legs and cook over high heat, stirring often, until beginning to brown, 7 minutes. Add the garlic, carrots and onions and cook over high heat, stirring occasionally, until softened, 8 minutes. Add the tomatoes and cook until any liquid has evaporated, 5 minutes. Add the pimentón and cook, stirring, until fragrant, 3 minutes. Add the brandy and cook until almost evaporated, 3 minutes. Add the water and bring to a boil. Simmer over moderate heat for 30 minutes, skimming. Strain into a large saucepan, bring to a simmer, cover and keep hot.

3. Preheat the oven to 400°. Wash out the large pot and return to the stove. Slice the tails crosswise ½ inch thick; transfer to a large rimmed baking sheet, fanning slightly. Put the claws on the sheet. In a small bowl, combine the melted butter with 1 tablespoon of the oil. Brush the tails and claws with the mixture; season with salt and pepper. Cover with foil and bake for 12 minutes, until just heated through.

4. In the large pot, heat the remaining olive oil until shimmering. Add the *fideos* and cook over moderately high heat, stirring constantly, until browned, 5 minutes. Stir in half of the stock, cover and cook for 3 minutes. Add half of the remaining stock, cover and cook until almost absorbed, 3 minutes. Add the remaining stock and cook, stirring, until the *fideos* are al dente, about 2 minutes. Season with salt and pepper.

5. Spoon the *fideos* into shallow bowls and top with lobster. —*José Andrés*

WINE Rich, complex white Burgundy.

LOBSTER FIDEOS

LOBSTER PAPPARDELLE WITH CHIVE BUTTER

Lobster Pappardelle with Chive Butter

ACTIVE: 50 MIN; TOTAL: 1 HR 15 MIN

4 SERVINGS ●

Two 1½-pound live lobsters, preferably female

2 tablespoons vegetable oil

2 medium shallots, thinly sliced

2 thyme sprigs

1 medium tomato, coarsely chopped

½ cup dry white wine

½ cup heavy cream

¾ pound dried pappardelle

5 tablespoons cold unsalted butter, cut into tablespoons

Salt and freshly ground black pepper

¼ cup snipped chives

1. Boil a large pot of water. Add the lobsters, headfirst, and cook for 5 minutes; the water may not come back to a boil. They will be almost cooked through. Using tongs, transfer to a large rimmed baking sheet. Reserve 3 cups of cooking liquid.

2. Crack the claws and knuckles; remove the meat. With scissors, cut along the inside of the tails; remove the meat. Discard the dark veins. Refrigerate the meat in a bowl. Remove the dark green eggs from the bodies and tails; reserve. Using poultry shears, cut the shells into 2-inch pieces.

3. In a large saucepan, heat the oil. Add the shells and cook over high heat, stirring, until sizzling and starting to brown, 5 minutes. Add the shallots and thyme. Cook over moderately high heat until softened, 4 minutes. Add the tomato and cook until the juices evaporate. Add the wine and boil until reduced by half, 4 minutes. Add the reserved liquid; bring to a boil. Reduce over moderately low heat to 3 cups, 20 minutes. Strain in a fine sieve; return to the pan.

4. Simmer the broth over moderately high heat. Put the reserved eggs in a small sieve that fits in the pan of lobster broth and simmer until they turn bright red, 1 minute. Remove the sieve from the broth and press the eggs through the mesh into a bowl.

5. Return the broth to a boil, add the cream and boil over high heat until reduced to 1 cup, 7 minutes. Reduce the heat to low. Slice the lobster tails ⅓ inch thick.

6. In a large pot of boiling salted water, cook the noodles, stirring, until al dente. Drain and return to the pot. Add 1 tablespoon of the butter, toss well and cover.

7. Add the lobster and eggs; bring to a simmer. Season with salt and pepper. Remove from the heat and whisk in the remaining butter, 1 tablespoon at a time, occasionally moving back to the burner to keep very warm. Stir in the chives. Pour the sauce over the pappardelle and toss. Serve in shallow bowls. —*Marcia Kiesel*

WINE Ripe, luxurious Chardonnay.

SUGAR SNAPS AND SNOW PEAS WITH
GRATED FRESH HORSERADISH (P. 246)

vegetables

"My mother served Birds Eye frozen squash with nothing added to it. When I was a kid I'd go behind her back and throw cinnamon in it, just to jazz it up."

–**Barbara Lynch,** chef and restaurateur, Boston

GRILLED BROCCOLI WITH ANCHOVY DRESSING

GREEN BEAN—CHILE STIR-FRY

Grilled Broccoli with Anchovy Dressing

TOTAL: 30 MIN

6 SERVINGS ● ● ●

- 3 pounds broccoli, ends trimmed
- ½ cup plus 2 tablespoons extra-virgin olive oil

Salt and freshly ground pepper

- 12 oil-packed anchovy fillets, drained
- ⅓ cup fresh lemon juice
- 1 teaspoon finely chopped rosemary

1. Light a grill. Bring a medium pot of water fitted with a steamer insert to a boil. Cut the heads of broccoli lengthwise into quarters, leaving the florets attached to the long stem. Peel the stems. Steam the broccoli until bright green, about 5 minutes. Transfer the broccoli to a large bowl and toss with 2 tablespoons of the olive oil. Season with salt and pepper.

2. In a blender or a mini processor, mix the anchovies, lemon juice and rosemary and puree until smooth. With the blender on, slowly pour in the remaining ½ cup of olive oil. Season with salt and pepper.

3. Grill the broccoli over high heat, turning, until lightly charred all over, 5 minutes. Transfer to a platter and drizzle with some of the dressing. Serve with the remaining dressing. —*Hugo Matheson and Kimbal Musk*

Green Bean—Chile Stir-Fry

TOTAL: 20 MIN

4 SERVINGS ● ● ●

According to chef Sai Viswanath of De-Wolf Tavern in Bristol, Rhode Island, this classic southern Indian dish—spicy with chile peppers and aromatic with ginger and mustard seeds—is too good to change: "I've eaten it forever and the flavor memory is so persistent, I just can't change it."

- 2 pounds green or yellow wax beans
- ¼ cup vegetable oil
- ½ teaspoon black mustard seeds
- 1 jalapeño, seeded and minced
- ½ teaspoon minced fresh ginger
- 10 curry leaves or ¼ cup chopped cilantro

Salt

1. In a saucepan of boiling salted water, cook the beans until crisp-tender, 2 minutes. Drain, let cool and pat dry.

2. In a large skillet, heat 2 tablespoons of the oil until shimmering. Add half of the mustard seeds and when they pop, add half each of the jalapeño, ginger and curry leaves; cook over high heat until fragrant, 30 seconds. Add half of the beans and toss until hot, 30 seconds. Season with salt. Transfer to a platter. Repeat with the remaining oil, mustard seeds, jalapeño, ginger, curry leaves and beans. Serve hot or at room temperature. —*Sai Viswanath*

Roasted Broccoli with Fondue

TOTAL: 30 MIN

2 LARGE SERVINGS ●

Roasting broccoli brings out its sweetness in a way that steaming or boiling does not. Here the broccoli is served with a generous portion of crunchy croutons and a creamy Fontina cheese fondue for dipping.

One 1½-pound head of broccoli, cut into long spears

Two 1½-inch-thick slices of peasant bread, crust removed, bread cut into 1½-inch cubes

¼ cup plus 2 tablespoons extra-virgin olive oil

1 large garlic clove, minced

Salt and freshly ground pepper

¼ cup plus 2 tablespoons heavy cream

1 large egg yolk

2 ounces Fontina cheese, shredded

1 tablespoon very finely chopped fresh marjoram

½ tablespoon balsamic vinegar

1. Preheat the oven to 450°. Heat a large rimmed baking sheet in the oven until it is very hot to the touch. In a large bowl, toss the broccoli spears with the bread cubes, olive oil and garlic and season generously with salt and pepper. Spread the broccoli and bread cubes on the hot baking sheet and roast for about 15 minutes, turning once, until the broccoli is tender and browned in spots and the bread cubes are crisp and golden.

2. Meanwhile, in a small saucepan, heat the cream until boiling. In a small bowl, whisk the egg yolk. Gradually whisk in the hot cream. Return the mixture to the saucepan and cook over low heat, whisking constantly, until it is slightly thickened, about 2 minutes. Off the heat, add the Fontina and stir until melted. Pour the fondue into a bowl. Transfer the broccoli and bread to plates and sprinkle with the marjoram and balsamic vinegar. Serve with the fondue. —*Stuart Brioza*

Swiss Chard with Smoked Bacon and Jalapeño Vinegar

ACTIVE: 25 MIN; TOTAL: 40 MIN PLUS 2 HR PICKLING

6 SERVINGS ●

Stewed greens, often slow cooked with bits of smoky bacon, are ubiquitous in the South. Here, mild Swiss chard gets an irresistibly spicy flavor from a side of vinegared jalapeños.

1 cup white wine vinegar

3 large jalapeños, coarsely chopped

Kosher salt

½ pound thickly sliced bacon, cut crosswise into ⅓-inch strips

3 shallots, thinly sliced

1 cup chicken stock or low-sodium broth

2 pounds Swiss chard, stems removed and chopped, leaves coarsely chopped separately

Freshly ground pepper

1. In a small saucepan, bring the white wine vinegar to a boil. Remove from the heat. Add the chopped jalapeños and ½ teaspoon of salt and let the jalapeños stand for 2 hours. Strain, reserving the jalapeños and vinegar separately.

2. In a large enameled cast-iron casserole or Dutch oven, cook the bacon over moderate heat until browned and crisp, about 6 minutes. Using a slotted spoon, transfer the bacon to a plate.

3. Add the shallots to the casserole and cook over moderate heat until softened, about 3 minutes. Add ½ cup of the stock and bring to a boil. Add the chard stems, cover and cook until softened, about 4 minutes. Add the chard leaves and the remaining ½ cup of stock and season with salt and pepper. Cover and cook, stirring occasionally, until the leaves are tender, about 5 minutes. Stir in the crispy bacon and 2 tablespoons of the jalapeño vinegar and transfer to a bowl. Serve the pickled jalapeños and the remaining jalapeño vinegar on the side. —*Bobby Flay*

Gingery Creamed Kale and Cabbage

ACTIVE: 30 MIN; TOTAL: 1 HR

12 SERVINGS ●

Chef Marcus Samuelsson, author of *The Soul of a New Cuisine* and *Aquavit*, stirs ginger and turmeric into this African-inspired vegetable side dish to give it a kick, then adds cream and buttermilk to smooth and soften the spicy flavors. This easy recipe can be made ahead of time and would be great with any kind of feast.

Salt

3 pounds kale, tough stems discarded

¼ cup plus 2 tablespoons vegetable oil

1 large white onion, coarsely chopped

1 pound green cabbage, coarsely shredded

1½ tablespoons finely grated fresh ginger

½ teaspoon turmeric

2 cups heavy cream

1 cup buttermilk

1. Bring a large pot of water to a boil and salt the water. Add the kale and cook until tender, about 6 minutes. Drain and let cool, then coarsely chop.

2. In a large pot, heat the oil. Add the onion. Cook over moderate heat until softened, 7 minutes. Add the cabbage, ginger and turmeric and season with salt. Cook over moderate heat, stirring occasionally, until the cabbage is wilted, 5 minutes. Add the cream, cover and simmer over moderately low heat, stirring occasionally, until the cream has thickened, 8 minutes. Stir in the kale, season with salt and cook for 3 minutes, stirring a few times. Remove from the heat; stir in the buttermilk. Bring to a simmer. Serve. —*Marcus Samuelsson*

MAKE AHEAD The kale can be refrigerated overnight. Reheat it gently and stir in the buttermilk shortly before serving.

● FAST   ● HEALTHY   ● MAKE AHEAD   ● STAFF FAVORITE

vegetables

Tarragon-Roasted Zucchini with Goat Cheese and Black Olives

ACTIVE: 30 MIN; TOTAL: 1 HR 10 MIN

10 SERVINGS ● ●

You can substitute any variety of summer squash, such as pattypan and crookneck, for the zucchini.

- 3 **pounds medium zucchini, cut into 1-inch pieces**
- ½ **cup tarragon leaves**
- 2 **large garlic cloves, coarsely chopped**
- 1 **teaspoon sugar**
- ½ **cup plus 2 tablespoons extra-virgin olive oil**

Salt and freshly ground pepper

- 1 **medium white onion, sliced ½ inch thick crosswise and separated into rings**

One 5½-ounce log fresh goat cheese, crumbled (1 cup)

- ¾ **cup pitted kalamata olives, coarsely chopped**

1. Preheat the oven to 425°. Place a large roasting pan in the oven and heat until very hot. In a large bowl, toss the zucchini with the tarragon, garlic, sugar and ¼ cup plus 2 tablespoons of the olive oil; season the zucchini with salt and pepper.

2. Pour the remaining ¼ cup of olive oil into the roasting pan, add the onion rings and roast them for 5 minutes, until they are softened. Add the zucchini mixture to the roasting pan in an even layer and roast, stirring occasionally, for about 15 minutes, until the zucchini is tender and lightly browned in spots. Let the zucchini cool for 20 minutes.

3. Add half each of the fresh goat cheese and the kalamata olives to the zucchini and toss gently. Transfer the roasted zucchini to a platter, garnish with the remaining fresh goat cheese and kalamata olives and serve at once. —*Mateo Granados*

MAKE AHEAD The recipe can be prepared up to 2 hours ahead and served at room temperature.

Creamy Swiss Chard with Crisp Bread Crumbs

ACTIVE: 1 HR 10 MIN;
TOTAL: 2 HR 10 MIN

12 SERVINGS ●

Cookbook author Maria Helm Sinskey claims that a rich gratin topped with cheesy bread crumbs is the only way her children, Ella, 8, and Lexi, 6, will eat Swiss chard. "I've learned that a little cream and cheese gets my kids to finish their vegetables," she says.

BÉCHAMEL SAUCE

- 3 **tablespoons unsalted butter**
- ½ **cup all-purpose flour**
- 1 **quart whole milk**
- 1 **cup heavy cream**
- 1 **small onion, quartered**
- 2 **bay leaves**
- ½ **pound Italian Fontina cheese, shredded (2 cups)**

Salt and freshly ground pepper

FILLING AND TOPPING

- 7 **tablespoons unsalted butter, 4 tablespoons melted**
- 1 **tablespoon extra-virgin olive oil**
- 4 **large garlic cloves, thinly sliced**
- 3 **pounds Swiss chard, tough stems discarded and leaves cut into bite-size pieces**

Salt and freshly ground pepper

- 2 **cups fresh bread crumbs**
- ¼ **cup freshly grated Parmesan cheese**

1. MAKE THE BÉCHAMEL SAUCE: In a large saucepan, melt the butter. Stir in the flour over moderate heat. Gradually whisk in the milk until smooth, then whisk in the cream and bring to a boil over moderately high heat, whisking constantly. Add the onion and bay leaves. Simmer over low heat, whisking often, until thickened and no floury taste remains, 15 minutes. Discard the onion and bay leaves and add the Fontina; season with salt and pepper.

2. MAKE THE FILLING AND TOPPING: Preheat the oven to 375°. Butter a 15-by-

10-inch baking dish. In a large, deep skillet, melt the 3 tablespoons of butter in the oil. Add the garlic; cook over moderately high heat until fragrant, 1 minute. Add the chard. Cook over high heat, stirring, until the leaves are wilted and any liquid has evaporated, 10 minutes. Season with salt and pepper. Transfer to a colander to drain thoroughly, pressing down on the chard. Spread the chard in the prepared baking dish in an even layer; pour on the sauce.

3. In a medium bowl, mix the bread crumbs with the 4 tablespoons of melted butter. Stir in the Parmesan. Spread the bread crumbs evenly over the gratin and bake for about 45 minutes, or until golden brown and bubbling. Let rest for about 10 minutes before serving. —*Maria Helm Sinskey*

MAKE AHEAD The recipe can be prepared through Step 2 and refrigerated overnight. Bring to room temperature before spreading the bread crumbs over the gratin.

Tangy Swiss Chard with Slivered Carrots

TOTAL: 20 MIN

8 SERVINGS ● ●

A healthy dose of rice wine vinegar adds a great tangy edge to these quick-sautéed vegetables.

- ¼ **cup extra-virgin olive oil**
- 2 **large carrots (¾ pound), halved lengthwise and thinly sliced on the diagonal**
- 4 **pounds Swiss chard, stems chopped, leaves cut into 1-inch strips**
- 2 **tablespoons rice wine vinegar**

Kosher salt and freshly ground pepper

Heat the oil in a very large skillet. Add the carrots. Cook over moderately high heat until crisp-tender, 3 minutes. Add the chard stems and cook for 1 minute, then stir in the chard leaves and toss until wilted, about 3 minutes. Stir in the vinegar, season with salt and pepper and serve.

—*Mary Ellen Carroll and Donna Wingate*

Indian-Spiced String Beans

TOTAL: 30 MIN

4 SERVINGS ● ●

- ¼ cup vegetable oil
- 1 onion, halved and thinly sliced
- 2 long hot green chiles, split
- 12 fresh curry leaves
- ¾ teaspoon freshly ground black pepper
- ⅛ teaspoon turmeric
- 1 pound green beans, cut into 2-inch lengths

Kosher salt

In a large, deep skillet, heat the oil. Add the onion and chiles. Cook over moderately high heat, stirring, for 2 minutes. Stir in the curry leaves, pepper and turmeric. Reduce the heat to moderate. Add the green beans and cook, stirring occasionally, until the onion is translucent, about 4 minutes. Cover and cook, stirring occasionally, until the beans are tender, 6 minutes longer. Season with salt and serve. —*Aniamma Philip*

Turmeric-Ginger Cauliflower

ACTIVE: 15 MIN; TOTAL: 45 MIN

4 SERVINGS ● ● ●

- 2 tablespoons vegetable oil
- 1 medium tomato, seeded and finely chopped
- 1 tablespoon black mustard seeds
- ½ jalapeño, seeded and minced
- 1 teaspoon minced peeled fresh ginger
- ½ teaspoon turmeric
- 1 head cauliflower (2¼ pounds), cut into 1-inch florets

Salt

Preheat the oven to 425°. In a small bowl, combine the oil, tomato, mustard seeds, jalapeno, ginger and turmeric. On a large rimmed baking sheet, toss the cauliflower florets with the flavored oil. Season with salt and spread in an even layer. Roast for about 25 minutes, or until lightly browned and barely tender. Serve hot or at room temperature. —*Sai Viswanath*

INDIAN-SPICED STRING BEANS

TURMERIC-GINGER CAULIFLOWER

vegetables

Spicy Braised Escarole

TOTAL: 35 MIN

6 SERVINGS ● ● ○

- 3 tablespoons extra-virgin olive oil
- ¼ pound thickly sliced soppressata, cut into ¼-inch dice
- 2 garlic cloves, minced
- ½ teaspoon crushed red pepper
- 4 heads of escarole (2½ pounds), dark outer leaves removed, inner leaves coarsely chopped

One 14-ounce can diced tomatoes

- 1 tablespoon minced oregano

Salt and freshly ground pepper

- ¼ cup panko (Japanese bread crumbs)
- 2 tablespoons freshly grated Parmesan cheese

1. In a large soup pot, heat 2 tablespoons of the oil. Add the soppressata, garlic and crushed pepper and cook over high heat, stirring, until the garlic is golden, 2 minutes. Add the escarole in batches and cook. Add the tomatoes and oregano, season with salt and pepper and bring to a boil. Cook over low heat until the escarole is tender, about 15 minutes; transfer to a bowl.

2. In a small skillet, heat the remaining 1 tablespoon of olive oil. Add the panko and cook over moderate heat, stirring, until golden, 1 minute. Off the heat, stir in the Parmesan. Sprinkle the escarole with the crumbs and serve right away.
—*Andrew Carmellini*

Cabbage Gratin with Potatoes

TOTAL: 30 MIN

4 SERVINGS ●

- 2 pounds red potatoes, cut into 1-inch cubes
- 2 tablespoons plus 1 teaspoon extra-virgin olive oil

Salt and freshly ground pepper

- ½ pound lean slab bacon, sliced ¼ inch thick, cut into 1-inch pieces
- 1 pound green cabbage, cored and thinly sliced (8 cups)
- 2 garlic cloves, minced
- ½ cup heavy cream

One 7½-ounce package of farmer cheese

1. Preheat the oven to 425°. Spread the potatoes on 2 large rimmed baking sheets. Pour 1 tablespoon of olive oil over each pan and toss to coat the potatoes; season with salt and pepper. Roast the potatoes for about 25 minutes, until browned on the bottom and tender. Remove the potatoes from the oven. Preheat the broiler.

2. Meanwhile, in a large, deep ovenproof skillet, heat the remaining 1 teaspoon of olive oil. Add the bacon and cook over moderate heat until lightly browned, about 4 minutes. Add the cabbage, cover and cook, stirring a few times, until tender, about 12 minutes. Stir in the garlic and cook until fragrant, about 2 minutes. Stir in the roasted potatoes, season with salt and pepper and add the cream. Simmer for 1 minute. Dollop the farmer cheese all over the top and broil for 1 minute, or until the cheese is browned. Serve right away.
—*Amy Tornquist*

Crispy Swiss Chard Cakes with Mascarpone-Creamed Spinach

TOTAL: 1 HR 30 MIN

6 FIRST-COURSE SERVINGS

This recipe is based on a Japanese pressed spinach dish called *gomae* that is usually served cold. The trick to making perfect Swiss chard cakes is to press them long and hard enough to squeeze out any excess moisture. That keeps the bread-crumb crust crunchy and concentrates the chard flavor.

- 3 tablespoons unsalted butter
- 2 shallots, minced
- 1 garlic clove, minced
- 5 pounds Swiss chard (about 3 bunches), thick stems discarded

Salt and freshly ground pepper

- ½ cup all-purpose flour
- ½ cup cornstarch
- 1½ cups panko or coarse dry bread crumbs

Dijon mustard, for brushing

- 1 pound baby spinach
- ¼ cup mascarpone cheese
- ½ cup pure olive oil

1. In a large pot, melt 2 tablespoons of the butter. Add half of the minced shallots and the garlic and cook over moderate heat until softened. Add the Swiss chard and cook, tossing, until wilted. Transfer the chard to a colander and let cool. Press out as much liquid as possible and coarsely chop. Season with salt and pepper and press the chard into 6 patties; don't worry if they don't hold together.

2. In a small bowl, whisk the flour with the cornstarch and 1 teaspoon of salt. Sprinkle the mixture onto a work surface and set the chard cakes on top. Turn the cakes, pressing and squeezing them into compact patties and working in a little of the flour mixture as you go.

3. Spread the panko on a plate. Brush the tops of the cakes with mustard and invert them one at a time into the panko. Brush the bottoms with mustard and sprinkle panko on top; press to adhere. Transfer the cakes to a wax paper–lined plate and refrigerate until firm, about 20 minutes.

4. In a large skillet, melt the remaining 1 tablespoon of butter. Add the remaining minced shallot and cook over moderate heat until softened. Add the spinach and cook, tossing, until wilted, about 5 minutes. Transfer the spinach to a colander and press out as much liquid as possible. Return the spinach to the skillet. Stir in the mascarpone and season with salt and pepper. Keep warm.

5. Heat the olive oil in a large nonstick skillet. Add the chard cakes and fry over moderately high heat, turning once, until golden and crisp, about 6 minutes. Spoon the spinach onto plates and top with the chard cakes. Serve right away.
—*Douglas Keane*

CRISPY SWISS CHARD CAKES WITH
MASCARPONE-CREAMED SPINACH

vegetables

Roasted Beets with Horseradish Cream

ACTIVE: 15 MIN; TOTAL: 2 HR
8 SERVINGS ● ●

- 3 pounds medium beets, scrubbed
- Extra-virgin olive oil
- ¾ cup sour cream
- ¼ cup drained prepared horseradish
- 1 tablespoon fresh lemon juice
- Salt and freshly ground pepper
- 2 tablespoons chopped flat-leaf parsley

1. Preheat the oven to 400°. Set the beets in a medium roasting pan. Drizzle with olive oil. Cover with foil. Bake for 1 hour and 30 minutes, until tender. Let cool slightly.

2. In a small bowl, whisk the sour cream, horseradish and lemon juice. Season with salt and pepper.

3. Peel the beets and cut into wedges. Transfer to a bowl, drizzle with half of the horseradish cream and sprinkle with the parsley. Serve the remaining horseradish cream on the side. —*Vitaly Paley*

MAKE AHEAD The beet wedges and horseradish cream can be refrigerated separately overnight. Bring to room temperature before serving.

health
mushrooms

Mushrooms haven't been lauded for their healthy benefits. That should change: A three-ounce **portobello** cap provides more than 400 mg of potassium, about as much as a small banana. One serving of **cremini** mushrooms delivers 32 percent of the daily recommended intake of immunity-boosting selenium. **Shiitake, oyster** and **maitake,** the best sources of the disease-fighting antioxidant ergothioneine, contain 40 times more of it than wheat germ does.

Creamy Mustard Greens with Fried Shallots

ACTIVE: 1 HR; TOTAL: 1 HR 30 MIN
8 SERVINGS

- 2 tablespoons extra-virgin olive oil
- 1 medium onion, finely chopped
- ½ teaspoon crushed red pepper
- 6 pounds mustard greens, tough stems discarded and leaves torn
- 1 cup chicken stock
- ⅓ cup all-purpose flour
- ¼ teaspoon cayenne pepper
- Kosher salt and freshly ground black pepper
- 10 medium shallots, thinly sliced
- Vegetable oil, for frying
- 1¼ cups heavy cream
- 1 garlic clove, smashed

1. Heat the oil in a pot. Add the onion and the crushed red pepper and cook over moderate heat, stirring, until the onion is translucent, 5 minutes. Add the greens in batches, stirring each to wilt before adding more. Add the stock and bring to a simmer. Cover and cook over moderately low heat until the greens are tender, 15 minutes. Drain the greens and return them to the pot.

2. In a bowl, mix the flour with the cayenne and a generous pinch each of salt and pepper. Add the shallots and toss to coat with the flour mixture; transfer to a strainer and shake to remove the excess flour.

3. In a deep skillet, heat ½ inch of vegetable oil. Fry the shallots in batches over moderate heat until crisp, 2 minutes. Using a slotted spoon, transfer to paper towels to drain.

4. In a saucepan, simmer the cream and garlic over low heat until reduced to 1 cup, 10 minutes. Strain the cream over the greens and simmer over moderate heat until very thick, 5 minutes; season with salt and pepper. Stir in half the fried shallots and transfer to a serving dish. Sprinkle the remaining shallots on top and serve. —*Melissa Rubel*

MAKE AHEAD The stewed greens can be refrigerated overnight. The fried shallots can stand at room temperature for 4 hours.

Leeks Two Ways with Wild Mushrooms

ACTIVE: 40 MIN; TOTAL: 1 HR
12 SERVINGS ●

The leek, like its relatives onion and garlic, is generally used to flavor other foods. Washington DC chef José Andrés feels this is a mistake. "Listen to me: Leek is a vegetable," he says emphatically. "It can be the center of a dish." Here, he pairs it with black trumpet mushrooms for a sensational tapa.

- ¼ ounce dried black trumpet mushrooms
- ½ cup hot water
- 12 medium leeks, halved crosswise where they start to become green, green tops thoroughly cleaned
- 1½ tablespoons unsalted butter
- Salt
- 2 thyme sprigs
- ¼ cup plus 1 tablespoon extra-virgin olive oil
- 1 tablespoon white wine vinegar
- Freshly ground black pepper
- 1 tablespoon small mint leaves

1. Put the black trumpet mushrooms in a bowl and cover them with the hot water. Let the mushrooms stand until softened, about 10 minutes. Lift the mushrooms out of the water and rinse. Cut any large mushrooms in half lengthwise.

2. Cut the white part of each leek crosswise into ⅓-inch-thick slices, keeping the rings intact. Thinly slice enough leek greens to make ½ cup; reserve the rest of the leek greens for another use.

3. In a small saucepan of simmering water, cook the leek greens for 1 minute; drain well. In a small skillet, melt ½ tablespoon of the butter. Add the greens and cook over moderate heat for 1 minute, stirring. Transfer the greens to a blender. Add 2 tablespoons of water and blend the greens until smooth; season the puree with salt.

4. In a large, deep skillet, bring 6 cups of water to a boil with the thyme sprigs and remaining 1 tablespoon of butter. Season with salt, cover and cook for 2 minutes. Uncover and add the sliced leeks. Simmer over moderately low heat until tender, about 12 minutes. Line a large baking sheet with paper towels. With a slotted spoon, transfer the leeks to the paper towels to drain; pat dry.

5. In a small bowl, mix ¼ cup of the olive oil with the vinegar and season with salt and pepper. In a small skillet, heat the remaining 1 tablespoon of olive oil. Add the mushrooms, season with salt and pepper and toss over moderately high heat until warmed through, about 1 minute.

6. Dollop the pureed leek greens onto a serving platter. Arrange the sliced leeks on the platter and spoon the vinaigrette on top. Scatter the mushrooms and mint over the leeks and serve.
—*José Andrés*

MAKE AHEAD The recipe can be prepared one day ahead through Step 3. Refrigerate the mushrooms, pureed leek greens and poached sliced leeks separately. Bring to room temperature before proceeding.

Leeks Vinaigrette with Fried Eggs and Smoked Prosciutto
TOTAL: 45 MIN
8 SERVINGS ● ●

- 8 medium leeks (4 pounds), white and tender green parts only, halved lengthwise
- 3 tablespoons Champagne vinegar
- 1 small shallot, minced
- 1 teaspoon whole-grain mustard
- ½ teaspoon finely chopped tarragon
- ½ cup plus 2 tablespoons extra-virgin olive oil
- Kosher salt and freshly ground pepper
- 8 slices of *speck* (½ pound) (see Note)
- 1 tablespoon unsalted butter
- 8 large eggs
- 2 tablespoons minced chives

1. Prepare a large bowl of ice water. In a large pot of boiling salted water, cook the leeks, covered, until tender, 5 minutes. Transfer the leeks to the ice water to cool. Drain well, then transfer the leeks to paper towels to dry, cut side down.

2. In a small bowl, whisk the vinegar with the shallot, mustard and tarragon. Slowly whisk in ¼ cup plus 2 tablespoons of the olive oil. Season with salt and pepper.

3. In a large skillet, heat the remaining olive oil. Working in batches, fry the *speck* over moderately high heat, turning once, until crisp around the edges, about 3 minutes. Drain on paper towels.

4. Add the butter to the skillet. Reduce the heat to moderate. Crack 2 eggs into the skillet and fry, basting the eggs with fat, until the whites are set and the yolks are still slightly runny, 3 minutes. Transfer to a plate. Repeat with the remaining eggs. Season the eggs with salt and pepper.

5. In a large bowl, coat the leeks with the vinaigrette, keeping them intact. Arrange on a platter or on individual plates and top with the *speck* and fried eggs. Drizzle any remaining vinaigrette on top, sprinkle with the chives and serve. —*Paul Kahan*

NOTE *Speck*, a type of smoked prosciutto, is available at specialty food stores. If you can't find it, use regular prosciutto.

Poblano-and-Cheddar-Stuffed Portobello Mushrooms
ACTIVE: 40 MIN; TOTAL: 1 HR
2 MAIN-COURSE SERVINGS ● ●

- 2 poblano chiles
- 4 jumbo portobello mushrooms (about 6 ounces each), stemmed
- 3 tablespoons plus 1 teaspoon extra-virgin olive oil
- Salt and freshly ground black pepper
- ⅓ cup finely chopped onion
- 1 cup baby spinach
- ½ cup cooked rice
- ¼ cup shredded sharp cheddar cheese
- 2 tablespoons chopped cilantro

1. Light a grill or preheat the broiler. Roast the poblanos over the grill or under the broiler, turning, until blackened, 3 to 4 minutes. Transfer to a bowl, cover with plastic and let cool. Peel, core and seed the poblanos, then finely chop them.

2. Brush the mushrooms with 3 tablespoons of oil; season with salt and pepper. Grill or broil over high heat, turning, until softened, 10 to 12 minutes. Transfer to a plate, stem side down; drain and cool.

3. In a medium skillet, heat the remaining oil. Add the onion and cook over moderate heat until softened, 6 minutes. Add the baby spinach and cook until wilted, about 1 minute. Transfer the spinach to a sieve and press out the liquid. In a bowl, mix the spinach with the rice, cheese, cilantro and poblanos. Season with salt and pepper.

4. Preheat the oven to 325°. Season the mushroom caps with salt and pepper. Spoon the rice mixture into the mushrooms, mounding it slightly. Transfer to a baking dish and bake for about 20 minutes, or until the cheese is melted and the top is lightly browned. Serve warm or at room temperature. —*Grace Parisi*

vegetables

Roasted Eggplant and Tomatoes with Anchovy Crumbs

ACTIVE: 30 MIN; TOTAL: 1 HR 30 MIN

6 SERVINGS ● ● ●

Cookbook author Annabel Langbein visited Trapani, on the western coast of Sicily, when she was researching her 2001 cookbook *Savour Italy*. That's where she discovered the wonderful cooking at the *agriturismo* (farmhouse hotel) Duca Di Castelmonte. Sicilian cooks use a lot of crisp bread crumbs in their dishes, as a crunchy accent, inspiring Langbein to top slices of soft, baked eggplant and tomato with toasted crumbs mixed with anchovies, capers and lemon zest.

Two 1-pound long, slender eggplants, sliced lengthwise ¾ inch thick

Salt

¼ cup extra-virgin olive oil, plus more for brushing

4 cups crustless country bread in 1-inch pieces (4 ounces)

4 anchovy fillets, chopped

2 tablespoons chopped parsley

1 tablespoon chopped capers

1 garlic clove, minced

Finely grated zest of ½ lemon

4 ounces crumbled feta cheese (about 1 cup)

4 large tomatoes (about 2 pounds), thinly sliced

Freshly ground black pepper

1. Preheat the oven to 450°. Sprinkle the eggplant slices with salt and let stand until beads of water appear on the surface, about 15 minutes. Pat the eggplant slices dry; transfer them to a lightly oiled, large rimmed baking sheet. Brush the eggplant slices with oil and bake in the upper third of the oven for about 20 minutes, or until golden brown and tender. Using a spatula, loosen the eggplant slices from the sheet. Reduce the oven temperature to 400°.

2. Meanwhile, in a food processor, combine the bread with the anchovies, parsley, capers, garlic, lemon zest and ½ teaspoon of salt. Add the ¼ cup of olive oil and process until coarse crumbs form.

3. Sprinkle the feta on the eggplant and top with the sliced tomatoes. Season with salt and pepper. Scatter the crumbs over the tomatoes and bake in the upper third of the oven for 50 minutes, or until browned and crisp on top. Let cool for 5 to 10 minutes, then serve. —*Annabel Langbein*

Shredded Parmesan Brussels Sprouts

ACTIVE: 20 MIN; TOTAL: 50 MIN

8 SERVINGS ● ●

Why are these ridiculously easy brussels sprouts so good? First they're coarsely shredded, which gives them an appealing texture. Then the sprouts are roasted in a hot oven until they're lightly charred, which enhances their nutty sweetness. They're finished with a sprinkling of Parmesan cheese, which melts into the leaves.

3 pounds brussels sprouts, trimmed

½ cup extra-virgin olive oil

Kosher salt and freshly ground black pepper

½ cup freshly grated Parmesan cheese

Preheat the oven to 425°. In a food processor fitted with a slicing blade, coarsely shred the brussels sprouts. On 2 large rimmed baking sheets, toss the brussels sprouts with the olive oil, season with salt and pepper and spread in an even layer. Roast in the oven for 30 minutes, until the brussels sprouts are tender and browned in spots; rotate the pans and stir the brussels sprouts halfway through roasting. Sprinkle with the Parmesan cheese, toss and bake for 1 more minute, or until the cheese is melted. Transfer the brussels sprouts to a bowl and serve right away. —*Melissa Rubel*

MAKE AHEAD The brussels sprouts can be baked up to 2 hours ahead; rewarm them before serving.

Beet-and-Goat-Cheese "Ravioli"

ACTIVE: 30 MIN; TOTAL: 1 HR 30 MIN

8 SERVINGS ●

When fashion designer Han Feng develops a menu for a dinner party, she focuses on balancing the colors as well as the flavors and textures. For her gorgeous riff on the classic combination of beets and goat cheese, she tucks the creamy cheese between magenta-hued disks of cooked beet and then adds a light soy-sauce dressing.

8 medium beets (2 pounds)

4½ ounces fresh goat cheese (¾ cup), softened

1 tablespoon minced chives, plus 3 tablespoons chives cut in 1-inch lengths

Salt and freshly ground black pepper

2 tablespoons turbinado sugar

2 tablespoons unseasoned rice vinegar

2 tablespoons light soy sauce

Extra-virgin olive oil, for drizzling

1. In a large saucepan, cover the beets with water and bring to a boil. Simmer the beets over moderate heat until tender, about 1 hour. Drain the beets and let cool. Peel the beets and slice them crosswise ¼ inch thick; you'll need 64 slices.

2. In a small bowl, blend the goat cheese with the minced chives and season with salt and pepper. Arrange 32 beet rounds on a work surface. Dollop a teaspoon of the goat cheese filling in the center of each round and top with the remaining 32 rounds; press lightly. Transfer the beet ravioli to plates or a platter.

3. In a small bowl, combine the sugar, vinegar and soy sauce and stir to dissolve the sugar. Spoon the dressing over the ravioli and drizzle with olive oil. Garnish with the chives and serve.—*Han Feng*

MAKE AHEAD The cooked beets and the seasoned goat cheese can be refrigerated separately overnight.

BEET-AND-GOAT-CHEESE "RAVIOLI"

vegetables

Spring Pea Falafel with Marinated Radishes and Minted Yogurt

TOTAL: 45 MIN PLUS 4 HR MARINATING

4 SERVINGS ● ● ●

MARINATED RADISHES

- 1 tablespoon vegetable oil
- 1 large shallot, thinly sliced
- 2 thyme sprigs
- 2 tablespoons honey
- ¼ cup Champagne vinegar
- 1 bunch red radishes, thinly sliced

FALAFEL

- ½ cup dried green split peas
- 1½ cups frozen peas, thawed
- ½ cup chopped onion
- 1 tablespoon all-purpose flour
- 2 tablespoons chopped parsley
- 2 garlic cloves, chopped
- 1 teaspoon ground coriander
- 1 teaspoon ground cumin
- ½ teaspoon baking powder
- ¼ teaspoon cayenne pepper
- 1 tablespoon fresh lemon juice
- Salt
- 3 tablespoons extra-virgin olive oil

MINTED YOGURT

- ½ cup plain low-fat Greek yogurt
- 1 tablespoon chopped mint

superfast
side dish

BROCCOLI RABE WITH ALMONDS AND ORANGE VINAIGRETTE

Steam chopped broccoli rabe in a little white wine until tender and the wine has almost evaporated. Add extra-virgin olive oil and stir until the broccoli rabe is coated. Top with chopped marcona almonds, orange sections and a simple dressing made with fresh orange juice, finely grated orange zest, olive oil, Dijon mustard and a pinch of grated nutmeg.
—*Edward Lee*

- 1 teaspoon sumac (optional), see Note
- Salt and freshly ground pepper

FOR SERVING

- 1 tablespoon sesame seeds
- ½ small red onion, thinly sliced
- 1 cup pea shoots or watercress
- 2 tablespoons fresh lemon juice

1. MARINATE THE RADISHES: In a small saucepan, heat the oil. Add the shallot and thyme and cook over moderately low heat until the shallot is softened, 4 minutes. Add the honey and vinegar and simmer for 2 minutes. Let cool. Put the radishes in a shallow dish and pour the marinade over them. Cover and refrigerate for at least 4 hours or overnight.

2. MAKE THE FALAFEL: Working in 2 batches, grind the split peas to a powder in a spice grinder. In a food processor, pulse the thawed peas a few times. Add the ground split peas, onion, flour, parsley, garlic, coriander, cumin, baking powder, cayenne, lemon juice and 1 teaspoon of salt and process until thoroughly combined. Form the mixture into 12 falafel patties using a scant ¼ cup per patty. Refrigerate the falafel until firm.

3. MAKE THE MINTED YOGURT: In a bowl, combine the yogurt, mint and sumac and season with salt and pepper.

4. Preheat the oven to 400°. In a large nonstick skillet, heat the olive oil. Add the falafel patties in two batches to the skillet and cook over moderately high heat until browned, crisp and heated through, about 3 minutes per side. Transfer the falafel to a cookie sheet. Rewarm all of the patties in the oven, about 4 minutes.

5. Drain the radishes; discard the thyme sprigs. Spoon the minted yogurt onto plates and top with the radishes and falafel. Scatter the sesame seeds, red onion and pea shoots all around, drizzle with the lemon juice and serve. —*Nicki Reiss*

NOTE Sumac is a Middle Eastern spice that's used to add a tangy flavor.

Haricots Verts and Chestnuts with Date Vinaigrette

TOTAL: 40 MIN

10 SERVINGS ● ● ● ●

- 2 cups vacuum-packed peeled chestnuts (10 ounces)
- 2 pounds haricots verts
- 2 small shallots, chopped
- ¼ cup cider vinegar
- ½ cup grapeseed oil
- ¼ cup chopped pitted dates
- 1 teaspoon fresh thyme leaves
- Freshly ground pepper
- Salt

1. Preheat the oven to 350°. Spread the chestnuts on a baking sheet and bake until slightly dry, about 5 minutes. Let cool, then thinly slice and transfer to a large bowl.

2. Bring a large saucepan of salted water to a boil. Add the haricots verts and cook until crisp-tender, about 5 minutes. Drain them in a colander and cool under running water. Pat thoroughly dry. Add the haricots verts to the chestnuts.

3. In a blender, combine the shallots, cider vinegar and grapeseed oil and pulse until smooth. Add the dates, thyme and ¼ teaspoon of pepper and pulse until the dates are finely chopped but not pureed. Add the vinaigrette to the haricots verts, season with salt and toss. Serve at room temperature or chilled. —*Barbara Lynch*

MAKE AHEAD The cooked haricots verts and dressing can be refrigerated separately overnight.

Sugar Snaps and Snow Peas with Grated Fresh Horseradish

TOTAL: 30 MIN

4 SERVINGS ● ●

Be sure to grate the horseradish at the very last minute since it loses potency quickly as it sits.

- ¼ pound snow peas
- 1 cup chicken stock
- ½ pound sugar snap peas, trimmed
- 2 tablespoons soy sauce

2 tablespoons unsalted butter, cut into cubes

1 tablespoon water

Freshly ground pepper

6 medium radishes, such as watermelon radishes, thinly sliced

1½ tablespoons coarsely grated fresh horseradish

Sea salt, for sprinkling

1. Bring a medium saucepan of salted water to a boil. Add the snow peas and cook until bright green and crisp-tender, about 1 minute. Drain and rinse under cold water. Pat dry and cut into 1-inch pieces.
2. In a large skillet, boil the stock over moderately high heat until reduced to ¼ cup, 5 minutes. Add the sugar snaps and cook until bright green, 2 minutes. Add the snow peas, soy sauce, butter and water and cook over moderate heat, stirring, until the vegetables are glazed, 2 minutes. Season with pepper. Off the heat, add the radishes. Transfer the vegetables to bowls along with any liquid in the skillet. Sprinkle with the horseradish and sea salt and serve right away. —David Chang

Bok Choy with Black Bean Sauce
TOTAL: 30 MIN
4 SERVINGS ● ●

1 tablespoon vegetable oil

1 garlic clove, minced

1 tablespoon very finely chopped fresh ginger

2 scallions, thinly sliced

2 tablespoons black bean sauce

1 tablespoon dry sherry

½ cup chicken broth

¼ teaspoon Asian chile paste

1¼ pounds baby bok choy, quartered lengthwise

1 bunch watercress (6 ounces), thick stems discarded

1 teaspoon cornstarch mixed with 1 tablespoon water

Steamed rice, for serving

1. In a large skillet, heat the vegetable oil until shimmering. Add the minced garlic, ginger and scallions and cook over moderate heat until softened, about 2 minutes. Add the black bean sauce, sherry, chicken broth and chile paste, bring to a boil and simmer the sauce for 1 minute.
2. Meanwhile, place the bok choy in a steamer and steam until crisp-tender, about 3 minutes. Add the watercress to the steamer and cook just until it wilts, about 1 minute longer.
3. Add the bok choy and watercress to the skillet with the sauce. Stir the cornstarch mixture; add it to the skillet and stir-fry over high heat until the sauce is thickened, about 1 minute. Transfer the vegetables to a bowl and serve with rice.
—Shawn McClain

Spinach-Feta Pie
ACTIVE: 30 MIN; TOTAL: 1 HR 20 MIN
8 SERVINGS ●

2½ pounds fresh spinach, stems trimmed

8 large eggs, beaten

6 ounces feta cheese, crumbled (1¼ cups)

¼ cup plus 2 tablespoons freshly grated Pecorino Romano cheese

¼ cup plus 2 tablespoons freshly grated Parmesan cheese

Freshly ground pepper

2 tablespoons extra-virgin olive oil

1. Preheat the oven to 375°. Fill a large pot halfway with water and bring to a boil. Add the spinach by the handful and cook until wilted, 1 minute. Drain and let cool slightly, then squeeze out as much liquid as possible. Coarsely chop the spinach.
2. In a large bowl, whisk the eggs with the feta, ¼ cup each of the pecorino and Parmesan and a generous pinch of pepper. Stir in the spinach. Pour the mixture into a shallow, buttered 2-quart baking dish and sprinkle the remaining 2 tablespoons each of pecorino and Parmesan on top.

Drizzle the oil over the pie and bake for about 40 minutes, or until golden and sizzling. Let cool for 10 minutes then serve. —Dave Alhadeff

MAKE AHEAD The baked pie can be refrigerated overnight; reheat before serving.

Spinach and Scallion Dutch Baby
ACTIVE: 20 MIN; TOTAL: 45 MIN
8 SERVINGS ● ● ●

This addictive pancake is a savory riff on the traditional Dutch baby, the sweet eggy pastry invariably dusted with confectioners' sugar. Pouring the batter into a hot skillet creates a crisp crust.

1 pound baby spinach

4 large eggs

1 cup milk

1 cup all-purpose flour

Kosher salt and freshly ground pepper

Pinch of freshly grated nutmeg

4 tablespoons unsalted butter

4 large scallions, thickly sliced

2 tablespoons freshly grated Parmesan cheese

1. Remove the top rack in the oven and preheat to 450°. In a large pot of boiling salted water, cook the spinach until wilted, about 1 minute. Drain and let cool. Squeeze the spinach dry and coarsely chop it.
2. In a blender, mix the eggs, milk, flour, the 1½ teaspoons of salt, ⅛ teaspoon of pepper and nutmeg until smooth.
3. In a 12-inch cast-iron skillet, melt the butter. Add the scallions and cook over moderate heat until tender, 3 minutes. Add the spinach and cook until heated through, about 1 minute; season with salt and pepper. Increase the heat to high and cook for 1 minute without stirring. Pour in the batter, sprinkle with the Parmesan and transfer the skillet to the oven. Bake for 25 minutes or until golden. Cut into wedges and serve hot or warm. —Melissa Rubel

MAKE AHEAD The Dutch baby can be baked up to 4 hours ahead; reheat in the skillet in a 425° oven for 5 minutes.

vegetables

Red Spinach with Homemade Curry Oil

ACTIVE: 25 MIN; TOTAL: 2 DAYS

4 TO 6 SERVINGS ●

Last year, Tom Chino of the legendary Chino Farms in Rancho Sante Fe, California, became one of the first growers in America to plant Bordeaux red spinach, named for its striking red stems and leaf veins. Here, the tender spinach is sautéed with a fragrant homemade curry oil; any leftover oil is wonderful with salads and other cooked vegetables.

- 2 **tablespoons cumin seeds**
- 2 **tablespoons coriander seeds**
- 1 **tablespoon brown mustard seeds**
- 1 **tablespoon fennel seeds**
- 1 **tablespoon cardamom pods**
- 1 **tablespoon pink peppercorns**
- 1 **teaspoon white peppercorns**
- 1 **tablespoon fenugreek seeds**
- 2 **tablespoons paprika**
- 1 **teaspoon cayenne pepper**
- 3 **garlic cloves, coarsely chopped**
- 2 **shallots, coarsely chopped**
- 1½ **cups extra-virgin olive oil**
- 2 **pounds red spinach or baby green spinach, washed but not dried**

Salt

1. In a large skillet, combine the cumin, coriander, mustard and fennel seeds with the cardamom and pink and white peppercorns and toast over moderate heat, shaking the pan, until fragrant, about 2 minutes. Transfer to a spice grinder and let cool. Add the fenugreek, paprika and cayenne and finely grind the spices.

2. In a food processor, combine the ground spices with the garlic and shallots and process until fine. With the machine on, add the olive oil and process until a thin paste forms. Return the mixture to the skillet and warm over low heat, about 10 minutes. Transfer the curry oil to a large jar and refrigerate for 2 days.

3. Line a sieve with a double layer of cheesecloth and set it over a bowl. Add the curry oil and strain, pressing on the solids to extract as much oil as possible. You should have about ⅔ cup. Discard the spices.

4. Fill a soup pot with ½ inch of water and bring to a boil. Add the spinach and cook, tossing, until wilted, about 2 minutes for red spinach and about 5 minutes for green. Drain the spinach and press it dry, then coarsely chop. Wipe the pot dry.

5. Add ¼ cup of the strained curry oil to the pot and heat until shimmering. Add the spinach, season with salt and cook over moderately high heat, tossing, just until heated through, about 5 minutes. Transfer the spinach to a bowl and serve.
—*David Myers*

MAKE AHEAD The strained curry oil can be refrigerated for up to 1 month.

Garlicky Eggplant Puree with Crumbled Feta

ACTIVE: 15 MIN; TOTAL: 1 HR 45 MIN

6 SERVINGS ● ●

A topping of finely chopped garlic mixed with parsley and crumbled feta cheese turns this silken eggplant puree into an exquisite salad.

Two 1-pound eggplants
- 3 **tablespoons chopped flat-leaf parsley**
- 2 **large garlic cloves, minced**

Salt and freshly ground pepper
- 4 **ounces feta, crumbled (1 cup)**
- 3 **tablespoons extra-virgin olive oil**

1. Preheat the oven to 425°. On a baking sheet, roast the eggplants, turning once, until they are very soft and blackened, about 1 hour. Let cool slightly.

2. Slash the eggplants lengthwise. Using a spoon, scoop the pulp into a strainer. Let drain for 10 minutes, shaking the strainer occasionally.

3. On a work surface, finely chop the parsley with the garlic. Transfer the eggplant pulp to a food processor and pulse until chopped. Add three-fourths of the parsley mixture, and season with salt and pepper and pulse just until blended. Transfer the eggplant to a bowl; stir in three-quarters of the feta. Sprinkle with the remaining parsley mixture and feta, drizzle with olive oil and serve. —*Dionisis Papanikolauo*

SERVE WITH Toasted pita or crusty bread.

Mashed Winter Squash with Indian Spices

ACTIVE 40 MIN; TOTAL: 1 HR 20 MIN

8 SERVINGS ● ●

Fragrant Indian spices—coriander, turmeric and black mustard seeds—are a wonderful accent for creamy mashed butternut squash. The squash can be roughly smashed until chunky, or thoroughly mashed until smooth.

- 8 **pounds butternut or buttercup squash, halved lengthwise and seeded**
- ⅓ **cup plus 1 tablespoon vegetable oil, plus more for drizzling**

Salt and freshly ground pepper
- 2 **tablespoons black mustard seeds**
- 2 **garlic cloves, very finely chopped**
- 1 **medium onion, finely chopped**
- 1 **teaspoon ground coriander**
- 1 **teaspoon turmeric**
- ¼ **teaspoon crushed red pepper**
- ¼ **cup water**

1. Preheat the oven to 400°. On 2 large rimmed baking sheets, drizzle the cut sides of the squash with oil and season with salt and pepper. Turn the squash cut sides down and roast for about 45 minutes, or until tender.

2. Meanwhile, in a large pot, heat 1 tablespoon of the oil. Add the mustard seeds and cook over moderately high heat, shaking the pot, until they pop, about 1 minute. Transfer the seeds to a small bowl. Add the remaining ⅓ cup of oil to the pot. Add the garlic and onion and cook over

MASHED WINTER SQUASH WITH INDIAN SPICES

TOASTED CORN BREAD HASH WITH BRUSSELS SPROUTS

moderate heat, stirring occasionally, until softened, about 7 minutes. Add the coriander, turmeric and crushed red pepper and cook, stirring, until fragrant, about 1 minute. Remove from the heat.

3. Using a large spoon, scrape the squash flesh from the skins into the pot. Add the water and cook over moderately high heat, stirring and lightly mashing the squash, until blended and heated through. Season the squash with salt and pepper. Transfer to a bowl, top with the toasted mustard seeds and serve.—*Marcia Kiesel*

Toasted Corn Bread Hash with Brussels Sprouts
ACTIVE: 25 MIN; TOTAL: 50 MIN
4 SERVINGS
In this Indian-inspired dish, lightly browned cubes of sweet corn bread are tossed with cabbagelike brussels sprouts, mustard oil and crushed red pepper.

1¼ cups all-purpose flour
¾ cup cornmeal
1 tablespoon baking powder
Salt
2 large eggs
1 cup milk
6 tablespoons unsalted butter, melted
2 tablespoons honey
1 pound brussels sprouts
2 tablespoons mustard oil or vegetable oil
Pinch of crushed red pepper
Freshly ground black pepper

1. Preheat the oven to 400°. Butter and flour a 9-inch square baking pan. In a large bowl, whisk the flour with the cornmeal, baking powder and ½ teaspoon of salt. In a medium bowl, whisk the eggs to mix, then whisk in the milk, butter and honey. Using a rubber spatula, lightly stir the wet ingredients into the dry; stir until just blended. Scrape the batter into the prepared pan and bake for about 25 minutes, or until the corn bread springs back when lightly pressed. Transfer the corn bread to a rack to cool. Cut half of the corn bread into ¾-inch cubes. Wrap the remaining corn bread and reserve for another use.

2. In a medium saucepan of boiling salted water, cook the brussels sprouts until crisp-tender, about 3 minutes. Drain and slice lengthwise ⅓ inch thick.

3. In a large nonstick skillet, heat 1 tablespoon of oil until shimmering. Add the corn bread, sprinkle with the crushed pepper and cook over high heat until browned all over, 30 seconds per side. Transfer to a platter. Add the remaining 1 tablespoon of oil and the brussels sprouts and cook over moderately high heat, stirring, until hot, 1 minute. Season with salt and black pepper. Gently stir in the corn bread. Transfer to the platter and serve. —*Sai Viswanath*

● FAST ● HEALTHY ● MAKE AHEAD ● STAFF FAVORITE

249

vegetables

Shredded Brussels Sprouts with Truffle Oil

ACTIVE: 20 MIN; TOTAL: 40 MIN

8 SERVINGS ● ● ●

1½ sticks unsalted butter
2½ pounds brussels sprouts, shredded
Kosher salt and freshly ground pepper
1 tablespoon fresh lemon juice
1 tablespoon white truffle oil

In a very large skillet, melt the butter. Add the brussels sprouts, season them with salt and pepper and cook over moderate heat until they are very tender, about 20 minutes. Remove the brussels sprouts from the heat. Stir in the lemon juice and truffle oil. Transfer to a bowl and serve immediately. —*Octavio Becerra*

Asparagus with Sesame Dressing

TOTAL: 20 MIN

4 SERVINGS ● ● ● ●

The sweet and tangy sesame dressing here is also great served as a dip for crudités, as a spread for a roast beef sandwich or as a flavoring for fish, chicken or shrimp.

Kosher salt
Juice of 1 lemon
¼ cup sesame seeds
1½ pounds asparagus, cut into 3-inch lengths
2 small carrots, quartered lengthwise and cut into 3-inch lengths
¼ cup plus 1 tablespoon mayonnaise
2 teaspoons rice vinegar
1 teaspoon soy sauce
1 teaspoon sugar
Pinch of cayenne pepper

1. Bring a large saucepan of water to a boil. Add a large pinch of salt and the lemon juice to the saucepan of water. In a medium skillet, toast the sesame seeds over moderate heat, shaking the pan a few times, until the seeds are golden brown, about 4 minutes. Spread the sesame seeds on a plate and let them cool completely.

2. Add the asparagus and carrots to the boiling water and cook for 2 minutes. Drain the vegetables and spread out on a baking sheet to cool.

3. In a mini food processor, pulse the sesame seeds until coarsely ground. Add the mayonnaise, rice vinegar, soy sauce, sugar and cayenne and process to blend. Season the dressing with salt.

4. Transfer the asparagus and carrots to a platter. Drizzle the dressing on top or mix with the vegetables and serve.
—*Kozo Iwata*

Collard Cobbler with Cornmeal Biscuits

ACTIVE: 1 HR; TOTAL: 2 HR

8 TO 10 SERVINGS ● ●

Cornmeal biscuits make a delicious crust for these smoky, spicy collard greens.

BISCUITS
1 cup all-purpose flour
½ cup coarse yellow cornmeal
2½ teaspoons baking powder
1 teaspoon sugar
½ teaspoon salt
5 tablespoons cold unsalted butter, cut into small pieces
¾ cup half-and-half

COLLARDS
½ pound slab bacon, cut into 1-by-½-inch sticks
1 large sweet onion, thinly sliced
3 garlic cloves, minced
4 ounces spicy andouille sausage, halved lengthwise and sliced ¼ inch thick
4 cups Turkey Stock (p. 109) or low sodium chicken broth
4 pounds collard greens—thick stems and inner ribs removed, leaves cut into 1-inch ribbons
1 cup plus 2 tablespoons half-and-half
2 tablespoons cornstarch dissolved in ¼ cup water
Salt and freshly ground pepper

1. MAKE THE BISCUITS: In a food processor, pulse the flour with the cornmeal, baking powder, sugar and salt. Add the butter and pulse until the pieces are the size of small peas. Add the half-and-half and pulse just until the dough comes together. Transfer the biscuit dough to a lightly floured work surface and knead it 2 or 3 times. Flatten the dough slightly and roll it out to a 10-inch square. Cut the dough into 2-inch squares and refrigerate the squares on a baking sheet.

2. MAKE THE COLLARDS: In a large pot, cook the bacon over moderate heat until it is golden and the bacon fat is rendered, about 8 minutes. Using a slotted spoon, transfer the bacon to a plate. Discard all but 1 tablespoon of fat from the pot. Add the onion and garlic to the pot and cook over moderate heat, stirring, until the onion is softened, about 6 minutes. Add the bacon, andouille and 3 cups of the Turkey Stock and bring to a boil over high heat. Add the collard greens in 3 batches, stirring so each batch wilts before adding more of the collards. Cover the pot and simmer the collard greens over low heat until they are very tender, about 30 minutes.

3. Preheat the oven to 375°. Add 1 cup of the half-and-half and the remaining 1 cup of Turkey Stock to the collard greens and bring to a boil. Stir the cornstarch slurry and add it to the pot. Cook the collards, stirring, until the sauce is thickened, 2 to 3 minutes. Season the collard greens with salt and pepper.

4. Transfer the collard greens to a large ceramic or glass baking dish. Top the greens with the biscuit squares, overlapping them slightly, and brush the tops of the biscuit squares with the remaining 2 tablespoons of half-and-half. Season the biscuits well with pepper and bake the cobbler for 50 minutes, or until the greens are bubbling and the biscuits are golden. Let the cobbler rest for 20 minutes before serving. —*Grace Parisi*

Broccoli Rabe with Lemon Butter

ACTIVE: 45 MIN; TOTAL: 1 HR

8 SERVINGS

In this recipe, tangy *ricotta salata* cheese, a rich and tart lemon butter and toasted pine nuts embellish broccoli rabe.

- **6 pounds broccoli rabe, thick stems discarded**
- **1 stick plus 1 tablespoon unsalted butter, softened**
- **Finely grated zest of 2 lemons**
- **Salt and freshly ground pepper**
- **3 tablespoons extra-virgin olive oil**
- **½ cup pine nuts**
- **5 garlic cloves, finely chopped**
- **1½ tablespoons fresh lemon juice**
- **¾ cup *ricotta salata,* crumbled**

1. In a large pot of boiling salted water, cook half of the broccoli rabe until tender, about 3 minutes. Using a slotted spoon, transfer the broccoli rabe to a colander to drain. Repeat with the remaining greens. Squeeze the excess water from the broccoli rabe and coarsely chop.

2. In a bowl, blend the butter with the lemon zest; season with salt and pepper.

3. In the large pot, heat 1½ tablespoons of the olive oil. Add the pine nuts and cook over moderate heat until golden, about 4 minutes. Using a slotted spoon, transfer the pine nuts to a plate. Heat the remaining 1½ tablespoons of olive oil in the pot. Add the garlic and cook over moderate heat until sizzling, about 3 minutes. Add the chopped broccoli rabe and toss well. Add the lemon butter and lemon juice and stir well. Season with salt and pepper and transfer to a serving bowl. Top with the pine nuts and *ricotta salata* and serve.

—*Marcia Kiesel*

MAKE AHEAD The recipe can be prepared up to 1 day ahead through Step 2; cover and refrigerate the butter and the broccoli rabe separately.

ASPARAGUS WITH SESAME DRESSING

COLLARD COBBLER AND BROCCOLI RABE WITH LEMON BUTTER

STUFFED YELLOW PEPPERS WITH SPICY
SWISS CHARD AND SCALLION PILAF

Stuffed Yellow Peppers with Spicy Swiss Chard and Scallion Pilaf

ACTIVE: 35 MIN; TOTAL: 1 HR 45 MIN

4 SERVINGS ●

- 1½ cups short-grain (sushi) rice, rinsed and drained
- 3 cups water
- ¾ pound Swiss chard, ribs removed and reserved for another use
- ¼ cup extra-virgin olive oil
- 6 medium scallions, thinly sliced
- 1 garlic clove, minced
- ¾ teaspoon turmeric
- ¾ teaspoon ground cumin
- ¾ teaspoon ground ginger
- ¼ teaspoon cinnamon
- ¼ teaspoon cayenne pepper
- 1 medium tomato, diced
- 2 tablespoons currants
- 1 tablespoon fresh lemon juice
- Salt and freshly ground pepper
- 4 yellow bell peppers (½ pound each)
- 1 cup vegetable broth or water

1. Preheat the oven to 400°. In a medium saucepan, cover the rice with the water and bring to a boil. Cover the saucepan and cook the rice over low heat until the water is absorbed, about 15 minutes. Remove from the heat and let the rice stand for 5 minutes. Fluff the rice.

2. Meanwhile, in a large skillet, bring ½ inch of water to a boil. Add the Swiss chard and cook over high heat until tender, about 2 minutes. Drain the chard and let cool, then squeeze dry and coarsely chop.

3. In the skillet, heat the olive oil. Add the scallions and garlic and cook over moderate heat until softened, about 4 minutes. Add the turmeric, cumin, ginger, cinnamon and cayenne and cook, stirring, for 2 minutes. Add the tomato and cook, stirring, until the liquid evaporates, about 2 minutes. Add the currants and chopped Swiss chard, cover and cook for 2 minutes. Add the lemon juice and rice. Season with salt and pepper and stir well.

4. Cut the tops off the peppers and reserve. Scoop out the seeds and ribs. Spoon the filling into the peppers and replace the tops. Pour the broth into a shallow baking dish that will hold the peppers snugly. Stand the stuffed peppers in the broth. Cover tightly with foil and bake for 1 hour and 10 minutes, or until the peppers are tender. Serve the peppers warm or at room temperature. —*Celia Brooks Brown*

Roasted Squash with Maple Syrup and Sage Cream

ACTIVE: 1 HR; TOTAL: 2 HR 10 MIN

10 SERVINGS ●

- 1 buttercup or kabocha squash (about 2 pounds)—peeled, seeded and cut into 1-inch wedges
- 1 butternut squash (about 2 pounds), peeled and cut into 1-inch cubes
- ¼ cup extra-virgin olive oil
- ¼ cup light brown sugar
- Salt and freshly ground pepper
- 1 acorn squash (about 1½ pounds)—halved, seeded and cut into 1-inch wedges (with skin)
- 1 delicata squash (about 1 pound), cut into 1-inch rings (with skin)
- 2 tablespoons pure maple syrup
- 1 cup heavy cream
- 20 sage leaves, coarsely chopped
- 2 tablespoons unsalted butter
- Baby watercress and shaved pecorino cheese, for garnish

1. Preheat the oven to 350°. In a large bowl, toss the buttercup and butternut squash with 2 tablespoons of the olive oil and 2 tablespoons of the brown sugar. Season with salt and pepper. Spread the squash on a large rimmed nonstick baking sheet. Add the acorn and delicata squash to the bowl. Toss with the remaining 2 tablespoons each of olive oil and brown sugar and season with salt and pepper. Spread on another large rimmed baking sheet and roast for 1 hour, turning once after 30 minutes, until tender and lightly caramelized in spots. Arrange the squash on a large platter and drizzle with the maple syrup.

2. In a small saucepan, bring the cream to a simmer with the sage and cook over moderate heat for 5 minutes. Remove from the heat and let stand for 5 minutes, then add the butter and season lightly with salt and pepper. Strain the cream into a heat-proof cup. Drizzle it over the roasted squash, garnish with the watercress and pecorino and serve. —*Barbara Lynch*

MAKE AHEAD The roasted squash and sage cream can be refrigerated separately overnight. Reheat in a 350° oven, loosely covered with foil.

New Delhi–Style Stir-Fried Mixed Summer Squash

TOTAL: 20 MIN

6 SERVINGS ● ● ● ●

- ⅓ cup canola oil
- 1 tablespoon black mustard seeds
- 3 whole dried red chiles
- ¼ cup unsweetened shredded coconut
- 1 small jalapeño, finely chopped
- 1 teaspoon cumin seeds
- 12 fresh or frozen curry leaves
- ¼ teaspoon ground turmeric
- 2½ pounds mixed small zucchini and yellow squash, halved lengthwise and cut into ⅓-inch half-moons
- Salt

In a large skillet, heat the oil until shimmering. Add the mustard seeds. Cook over moderately high heat until they begin to pop, 1 minute. Add the dried chiles, coconut, jalapeño, cumin seeds, curry leaves and turmeric. Cook over low heat, stirring, until the coconut begins to brown, 2 minutes. Increase the heat to moderately high, add the zucchini and squash and cook, stirring and tossing, until tender, 7 to 8 minutes. Season with salt and cook for 1 minute. Transfer the vegetables to a large bowl and serve. —*Suvir Saran*

vegetables

Roasted Bell Peppers

ACTIVE: 25 MIN; TOTAL: 1 HR 25 MIN

6 SERVINGS ● ●

- 4 red bell peppers, stemmed and cored but left whole
- 4 yellow bell peppers, stemmed and cored but left whole

Extra-virgin olive oil, for brushing

Salt and freshly ground pepper

1. Preheat the oven to 350°. On a large rimmed baking sheet, rub all the peppers generously with olive oil. Bake for 1 hour, or until the skins are blistered and peppers soft.
2. When the peppers are cool enough to handle, peel and cut them into ½-inch-thick strips. Season them with salt and pepper.
—*Michelle Bernstein*

tools
$10 gadgets

Peelers A wide, sturdy handle and a flexible blade make plastic peelers the most useful small kitchen tool.

Citrus Reamers Some chefs prefer easy-to-grip-and-maneuver handheld reamers over tabletop juicers.

Egg Toppers This stainless steel tool removes the tops of soft-boiled eggs for an elegant presentation.

Paring Knives "These refute the idea that the bigger the knife, the better," says chef Laurent Manrique of Aqua in San Francisco.

MAKE AHEAD The roasted peppers can be refrigerated overnight. Bring to room temperature before serving.

Grilled Corn with Queso Fresco and Lime-Tarragon Butter

ACTIVE: 30 MIN; TOTAL: 1 HR 30 MIN

6 SERVINGS

This recipe is based on a street food staple in Oaxaca, Mexico. The corn is typically smothered in mayonnaise, dipped in cheese and then covered with a spicy chile powder. Here, melted butter is added for an American accent. Use a powdered-sugar shaker to apply an even coating of the chile powder.

- 6 ears of corn, unhusked
- 1 stick unsalted butter, softened
- 2 tablespoons fresh lime juice
- 1 tablespoon finely chopped tarragon

Salt and freshly ground black pepper

- 2 tablespoons chile powder
- ¼ teaspoon cinnamon
- ¼ pound *queso fresco* or mild feta, finely crumbled

1. Soak the corn in a large bowl of water for 1 hour.
2. Light a grill. On a large plate, blend the butter with the lime juice and tarragon and season with salt and pepper. Spread the butter in a ⅓-inch layer in the center of the plate. In a small bowl, mix the chile powder and cinnamon. Grill the corn over moderately high heat, turning often, until evenly charred all over, 25 minutes.
3. Carefully peel back the corn husks but leave them attached to the cobs. Discard the corn silk and use the husks as a handle. Roll the corn in the softened butter, top with a thick layer of crumbled cheese and sprinkle with the chile powder mixture. Serve right away.
—*Michelle Bernstein*

MAKE AHEAD The lime-tarragon butter can be refrigerated overnight. Bring to room temperature before using.

Grilled Corn with Chipotle Butter

TOTAL: 20 MIN

8 SERVINGS ● ●

The contrast of sweet corn and spicy chipotles reminds TV chef Mario Batali of the unbeatable combination of tortilla chips and salsa. This dish is incredibly simple to make, especially because the rich, spicy butter can be prepared ahead of time.

- 1½ sticks unsalted butter, softened
- 2 canned chipotle chiles—stemmed, seeded and minced, plus 1 tablespoon adobo sauce from the can
- 1 large garlic clove, minced

Salt and freshly ground black pepper

- 8 ears of corn, shucked

1. Light a grill. In a medium bowl, blend the butter with the chipotle, adobo sauce and garlic and season with salt and pepper. Let stand at room temperature.
2. Grill the corn over a medium-hot fire, turning often, until nicely browned, about 12 minutes. Serve the corn hot off the grill with the chipotle butter. —*Mario Batali*

MAKE AHEAD The chipotle butter can be refrigerated overnight. Let return to room temperature before serving.

Creamed Edamame and Pearl Onions

TOTAL: 45 MIN

8 SERVINGS ●

This clever riff on the classic creamed peas and pearl onions combines onions with edamame (soy beans) and a topping of *panko* (Japanese bread crumbs). To make the crumb topping extra crispy, the dish is quickly toasted under the broiler before serving.

- 1 pound frozen shelled edamame
- 10 ounces white pearl onions
- 1½ tablespoons unsalted butter, 1 tablespoon melted

Pinch of sugar

- ¾ cup heavy cream

1 teaspoon finely chopped
thyme

½ cup Turkey Stock (p. 109)
or chicken stock

Salt and freshly ground black
pepper

1¼ teaspoons cornstarch dissolved
in 1 tablespoon of water

½ cup *panko* (Japanese bread
crumbs)

1. Bring a medium saucepan of water to a boil and fill a bowl with ice water. Add the edamame to the boiling water and cook until tender, about 5 minutes. Using a slotted spoon, transfer the edamame to a plate and pat dry.

2. Cook the pearl onions in the saucepan of boiling water for 3 minutes. Drain the onions and transfer them to the bowl of ice water to cool completely. Using a paring knife, trim off the root ends, peel the onions and pat dry.

3. Melt the ½ tablespoon of butter in a medium deep skillet. Add the peeled onions and the sugar and cook over moderately low heat, stirring, until they are lightly browned, about 15 minutes. Add the heavy cream and thyme to the skillet and simmer until the cream is slightly reduced, about 5 minutes. Add the edamame and Turkey Stock and bring to a boil. Season the cream sauce with salt and pepper. Stir the cornstarch slurry, then add it to the cream sauce and cook, stirring, until thickened, about 2 minutes.

4. Preheat the broiler and place a rack 6 to 8 inches from the heat. Pour the edamame mixture into a 2-quart shallow baking dish. In a small bowl, mix the 1 tablespoon of melted butter with the *panko*. Sprinkle the bread crumbs over the edamame and broil for about 3 minutes, or until golden and bubbling. Serve the edamame and pearl onion hot. —*Grace Parisi*

MAKE AHEAD The recipe can be prepared through Step 3 and refrigerated for up to 2 days. Rewarm before proceeding.

Yuca with Tangy Bell Pepper Sauce
ACTIVE: 20 MIN; TOTAL: 50 MIN
12 SERVINGS ●

In Cuba, yuca, a starchy tuber, is often boiled and topped with a garlic *mojo,* a citrus-based marinade. But a red pepper sauce is also tasty and vibrant. Frozen yuca is available at Latin food stores.

5 pounds frozen yuca in large
pieces

1 large bay leaf

2 tablespoons salt, plus more
for seasoning

1 cup extra-virgin olive oil

1 slice white country bread,
roughly torn

3 red bell peppers, cut into
2-inch pieces

3 garlic cloves

2 tablespoons oregano leaves

1 tablespoon sherry vinegar

¼ teaspoon sugar

Freshly ground pepper

1. Put the yuca and bay leaf in a large pot and cover with water. Add the 2 tablespoons of salt and bring to a boil. Cover partially and cook over moderately low heat until just tender, 35 to 40 minutes.

2. Meanwhile, in a small skillet, heat 1 tablespoon of the olive oil until shimmering. Add the bread and cook over moderate heat until golden, about 5 minutes.

3. Transfer the bread to a blender. Add the bell peppers, garlic, oregano, sherry vinegar and sugar and pulse until finely chopped. With the machine on, pour in the remaining olive oil and blend until smooth. Season the pepper sauce with salt and pepper and transfer to a bowl.

4. Drain the yuca well and transfer to a large platter. Drizzle with some of the pepper sauce and serve the remaining pepper sauce on the side.
—*Carolina Buia*

MAKE AHEAD The pepper sauce can be refrigerated overnight. Bring to room temperature before serving.

Mixed Vegetable Thoren
TOTAL: 30 MIN
6 SERVINGS ●

This *thoren* is a dry, sauceless curry from Kerala, India. *Thorens* are usually prepared with just one vegetable and made sweet and fragrant with green chiles, fresh coconut, turmeric, mustard seeds and curry leaves. Here, three vegetables—green beans, carrots and shredded cabbage—are combined to create a dish that can be the centerpiece of a vegetarian meal.

2 tablespoons vegetable oil

2 teaspoons black mustard
seeds

8 fresh curry leaves

½ teaspoon crushed red pepper

6 cups finely chopped green
cabbage (1½ pounds)

3 large carrots, finely chopped

½ pound green beans, thinly sliced
on the bias

1 large onion, finely chopped

1¾ cups shredded unsweetened
coconut

2 long hot green chiles, thinly sliced
crosswise on the bias

½ teaspoon turmeric

Salt

Heat the vegetable oil in a large, deep skillet. Add the black mustard seeds to the skillet and cook over high heat until the seeds pop, about 1 minute. Add the fresh curry leaves and crushed red pepper and cook until the curry leaves sizzle, about 30 seconds. Add the chopped cabbage and carrots with the sliced beans, chopped onion, shredded coconut and sliced green chiles and turmeric and cook over moderately high heat, stirring, until the vegetables start to soften, about 3 minutes. Continue cooking over moderate heat, stirring occasionally, until the vegetables are crisp-tender, about 5 minutes longer. Season with salt to taste and serve the mixed vegetable *thoren* immediately.
—*Aniamma Philip*

vegetables

Confit of Piquillo Peppers

ACTIVE: 20 MIN; TOTAL: 1 HR 50 MIN

12 SERVINGS ● ● ●

Confiting (the process of cooking meat very slowly in its own fat) is a technique that both preserves food and makes it ultratender. Here, in a riff on the traditional preparation, piquillo peppers are cooked in olive oil. The key here is cooking the peppers slowly and patiently over low heat, being very careful not to scald the oil.

40 ounces jarred piquillo peppers, drained

Salt

4 garlic cloves, minced

¾ cup Spanish extra-virgin olive oil

1. Preheat the oven to 300°. Put one-fourth of the drained peppers in a food processor and puree. Season with salt.
2. In a large, shallow baking dish, arrange half of the remaining whole peppers in a single layer. Season with salt and scatter the garlic on the peppers. Top with half of the pepper puree and the remaining whole peppers. Season with salt. Spread the remaining pepper puree in an even layer and season again with salt. Pour the olive oil over the peppers and cover with aluminum foil. Bake for 1½ hours. Let stand, covered, until warm. —*José Andrés*

SERVE WITH Toasted bread.

MAKE AHEAD The pepper confit can be refrigerated overnight. Reheat to serve.

Grilled Vegetable Salad with Croutons, Haloumi and Anchovy Sauce

TOTAL: 15 MIN

6 SERVINGS ● ●

½ pound shiitake mushrooms, stemmed

¾ pound small eggplant, sliced lengthwise ½ inch thick

¾ pound zucchini, sliced lengthwise ½ inch thick

Four 1-inch-thick slices of peasant bread

½ pound haloumi cheese or *queso blanco*, sliced ⅓ inch thick

Olive oil, for brushing

½ cup Provençal Anchovy Sauce (recipe follows)

Salt and freshly ground pepper

1. Light a grill. Brush the shiitakes, eggplant, zucchini, bread and cheese with olive oil. Grill the shiitakes, eggplant and zucchini over a moderately high fire, turning occasionally, until tender and charred in spots, 8 to 10 minutes; transfer to a platter. Grill the bread until toasted, 3 to 4 minutes; transfer to the platter. Grill the cheese, turning once or twice, until softened and charred in spots, 2 minutes.
2. Cut the vegetables and cheese into 1-inch pieces and transfer to a bowl. Add the anchovy sauce and toss. Cut the bread into 1-inch pieces, add to the bowl and toss. Season the salad lightly with salt and pepper and serve. —*Grace Parisi*

PROVENÇAL ANCHOVY SAUCE

TOTAL: 10 MIN

MAKES ABOUT ½ CUP ● ●

6 oil-packed anchovies, rinsed

2 garlic cloves

¼ teaspoon chopped rosemary

½ teaspoon finely grated lemon zest

½ teaspoon crushed red pepper

2 tablespoons fresh lemon juice

6 tablespoons extra-virgin olive oil

1 tablespoon finely chopped flat-leaf parsley

In a blender or food processor, pulse the anchovies with the garlic, rosemary, lemon zest and crushed red pepper until the garlic is finely chopped. Add the lemon juice and olive oil and puree until smooth. Add the parsley and pulse just to incorporate. —*G.P.*

OTHER USES Mix the anchovy sauce into potato or grain salads, or brush on vegetables, bread, chicken, steaks, lamb and pork while grilling. You can also serve it as a side dish with grilled fish.

Pearl Onions au Gratin

TOTAL: 1 HR 30 MIN

10 SERVINGS ●

Inspired by the pickled pearl onions that she ate as a child, chef Barbara Lynch prepares this rich onion dish with cream, garlic, shallots and bacon and tops it with a crispy *panko* crust.

2½ pounds red or white pearl onions

4 thick strips of bacon, finely diced

2 tablespoons unsalted butter

2 shallots, finely chopped

2 garlic cloves, minced

1½ cups heavy cream

Salt and freshly ground pepper

¾ cup *panko* (Japanese bread crumbs) or coarse, dry bread crumbs

2 tablespoons chopped parsley

1. Preheat the oven to 350°. Bring a pot of water to a boil. Add the onions and cook for 5 minutes. Drain; rinse under cold water. Trim off the root ends, then pinch the onions to remove the skins.
2. In a medium, deep skillet, cook the bacon over moderately high heat until the fat is rendered, 3 to 4 minutes. Pour the bacon fat into a heatproof cup and reserve 1½ teaspoons. Drain the bacon on paper towels.
3. Add the butter to the skillet along with the shallots and garlic. Cook over moderate heat, stirring, until softened, 3 minutes. Add the cream and simmer until reduced by half, 10 minutes; season with salt and pepper. Transfer to a large, shallow baking dish and cover with the cream.
4. In a small bowl, toss the *panko* with the bacon, parsley and the 1½ teaspoons of reserved bacon fat. Season lightly with salt and pepper. Spread the *panko* mixture over the onions and bake until the crumbs are toasted and the onions are bubbling, about 30 minutes. —*Barbara Lynch*

MAKE AHEAD The onions can be prepared through Step 3 and refrigerated overnight. Return to room temperature before adding the *panko* mixture and baking.

PEARL ONIONS AU GRATIN

SUPERCRISPY ONION RINGS

NAPA CABBAGE SALAD

Supercrispy Onion Rings

TOTAL: 30 MIN

8 SERVINGS ● ●

- 2 quarts vegetable oil, for frying
- 3 cups cake flour
- 1 cup cornstarch
- 2 teaspoons baking soda
- 2 teaspoons kosher salt, plus more for sprinkling

2½ to 3 cups chilled club soda

- 2 large Spanish onions, cut into ½-inch slices and separated into rings

In a very large pot or deep fryer, heat the oil to 365°. In a bowl, whisk the flour with the cornstarch, baking soda and 2 teaspoons of salt. Add 2½ cups of the club soda and whisk until smooth; the batter should be thick but pourable. If necessary, add the remaining ½ cup of club soda, a few tablespoons at a time. Working with 6 to 8 onion rings at a time, dip them in the batter until completely coated; as you pull the rings from the batter, scrape off some of the excess against the side of the bowl. Carefully add the onions to the hot oil and fry until golden and crisp, 2 minutes. Drain the onion rings on paper towels, sprinkle with salt and serve immediately or keep warm in an oven on low heat while you coat and fry the rest. —*Colin Devlin*

Napa Cabbage Salad

TOTAL: 15 MIN

4 SERVINGS ● ●

- ½ cup slivered almonds
- 3 tablespoons vegetable oil
- 2 tablespoons rice vinegar
- 1 tablespoon soy sauce
- ½ teaspoon sugar
- 1 pound napa cabbage, chopped
- 2 scallions, thinly sliced
- ¼ cup chopped cilantro

Freshly ground black pepper

1. Preheat the oven to 350°. In a pie plate, toast the almonds in the oven for 5 minutes. Let the almonds cool.

2. In a serving bowl, combine the oil, vinegar, soy sauce and sugar. Add the napa cabbage, scallions and cilantro and toss the salad. Add the toasted almonds and season the salad with pepper. Toss the salad again and serve immediately. —*Sarah Matthews*

Eight-Treasure Stir-Fry

TOTAL: 30 MIN

8 SERVINGS (AS PART OF A MULTICOURSE MEAL) ● ●

In China, *ba* (eight) is a lucky number because it sounds like the word *fa,* which means "to become wealthy." For this eight-ingredient dish, three types of mushrooms are stir-fried with scallions, green chile, bean sprouts, tofu and apple and then seasoned with softened tea leaves.

½ cup plus 1 tablespoon boiling water

1 teaspoon loose tea, preferably Longjing

¼ ounce dried wood ear mushrooms (⅓ cup)

3 tablespoons vegetable oil

8 shiitake mushrooms, stems discarded, caps thinly sliced

1 long, thin green chile, split lengthwise, seeded and thinly sliced crosswise

Salt and freshly ground pepper

4 scallions, thinly sliced crosswise

1 small Granny Smith apple— peeled, cored and sliced ⅛ inch thick

One 14-ounce can whole straw mushrooms, drained and rinsed

8 ounces firm tofu, sliced ⅓ inch thick and cut into 1-inch strips

3 ounces mung bean sprouts (1 cup)

1. In a cup, pour the 1 tablespoon of boiling water over the tea; let steep for 5 minutes. Strain the tea, reserving the leaves.

2. In a small, heatproof bowl, soak the wood ear mushrooms in the remaining ½ cup of boiling water until they are softened, about 5 minutes. Drain the wood ears well. Cut off any hard bits; slice the wood ears into thin strips.

3. Set a wok or large skillet over high heat for 3 minutes. Add the oil and when it begins to smoke, add the shiitake mushrooms and chile and season with salt and pepper. Stir-fry until the chile is browned, about 2 minutes. Add the scallions and apple and stir-fry until the apple is almost tender, about 2 minutes. Add the wood ears and straw mushrooms and stir-fry until sizzling, about 2 minutes. Add the tofu and the tea leaves and stir gently until sizzling, about 2 minutes longer. Season with salt and pepper and remove from the heat. Fold in the bean sprouts. Mound the vegetables on small plates and serve. —Han Feng

Fresh Cranberry Bean and Tomato Stew

ACTIVE: 20 MIN; TOTAL: 1 HR 20 MIN

4 SERVINGS ● ●

Real Food author Nina Planck was raised on a farm in Virginia in the 1970s, where her family grew vegetables, including heirloom tomatoes. At their farm stand, the Plancks sold unsightly tomato "seconds" in gallon baskets, at dirt-cheap prices, for use in sauces, juices, salsas and soups. To this day, Planck prepares this stew with tomato seconds and just-picked cranberry beans, topping servings with a big dollop of cold, tangy sour cream.

3 pounds very ripe tomatoes, coarsely chopped

3 tablespoons extra-virgin olive oil

1 onion, cut into ½-inch dice

1 large poblano chile, seeded and cut into ½-inch dice

3 large garlic cloves, minced

1½ pounds fresh cranberry beans, shelled (1 pound)

Kosher salt and freshly ground pepper

¼ cup chopped cilantro

Sour cream, for serving

1. In a food processor, puree the tomatoes until the sauce is smooth. In a large soup pot, heat the olive oil. Add the diced onion and poblano chile and the minced garlic and cook the vegetables over moderate heat until beginning to soften, about 3 minutes. Add the tomato puree and the cranberry beans to the soup pot, then cover the pot and simmer until the cranberry beans are tender, about 1 hour.

2. Season the cranberry bean and tomato stew with salt and pepper. Ladle the stew into bowls, sprinkle with the cilantro and serve immediately with sour cream on the side. —Nina Planck

MAKE AHEAD The cranberry bean and tomato stew can be refrigerated overnight. Reheat gently before serving.

Slow-Roasted Balsamic Turnips

ACTIVE: 40 MIN; TOTAL: 2 HR 15 MIN

12 SERVINGS ●

Balsamic vinegar mixed with butter and caramel makes an inspired glaze for these roasted turnips.

4 tablespoons unsalted butter

3 pounds medium turnips, peeled and cut lengthwise into 6 wedges each

Salt and freshly ground black pepper

¼ cup plus 2 tablespoons sugar

¼ cup balsamic vinegar

2 cups chicken stock

4 thyme sprigs

1. Preheat the oven to 400°. Melt 2 tablespoons of the butter in each of 2 large skillets. Add half of the turnip wedges, flat side down, to each of the skillets and season the turnips with salt and pepper. Cook the turnips over moderately high heat, turning once, until they are browned, about 3 minutes per side. Transfer the turnips to a large bowl.

2. Scrape the butter from one skillet into the other skillet. Evenly sprinkle the sugar over the butter. Cook the butter and sugar over moderate heat until a rich brown caramel forms, about 6 minutes. Slowly add the balsamic vinegar to the skillet, taking care that it doesn't bubble over, and stir to dissolve the sugar. Boil the caramel mixture over high heat for 2 minutes. Stir in the chicken stock and bring to a boil.

3. Arrange the turnips in concentric circles in a large oval baking dish. Pour the caramel over the turnips, top with the thyme sprigs and bake for 15 minutes. Baste the turnips. Reduce the oven temperature to 350° and bake for 50 minutes. Baste the turnips again and increase the oven temperature to 400°. Continue baking for 30 minutes longer, or until the turnips are very tender and the caramel mixture has reduced to a glaze. Discard the thyme sprigs and serve. —Maria Helm Sinskey

vegetables

Shaved Sunchoke Salad with Parmesan and Arugula

TOTAL: 30 MIN

6 SERVINGS ● ●

Sunchokes (also known as Jerusalem artichokes) are knobby tubers that resemble fresh ginger. They have a potato-like texture and a sweet, slightly nutty taste.

- 1 **pound sunchokes (Jerusalem artichokes)**
- 6 **tablespoons extra-virgin olive oil**
- 2 **tablespoons fresh lemon juice**
- 1 **tablespoon white wine vinegar**
- 1 **tablespoon minced shallot**
- 2 **tablespoons finely chopped flat-leaf parsley**
- 1 **bunch arugula, thick stems discarded**
- ¾ **cup Parmesan shavings (2 ounces)**

Salt and freshly ground black pepper

1. Bring a medium saucepan of salted water to a boil. Add the sunchokes and simmer for 2 minutes. Drain the sunchokes and rinse them under cold water.

2. Using a mandoline or a sharp knife, very thinly slice the sunchokes. Transfer the sunchoke slices to a large bowl and add the olive oil, lemon juice, white wine vinegar, shallot and parsley and toss to coat the sunchokes with the dressing. Add the arugula and half of the Parmesan shavings to the large bowl and season the salad with salt and pepper. Toss the salad and transfer it to a platter. Scatter the remaining Parmesan shavings on top of the salad and serve it immediately.
—*Brian Bistrong*

Fried Sweet Plantains

TOTAL: 35 MIN

12 SERVINGS ● ●

Plantains are abundant all over the Caribbean. One popular way to eat them is to pan-fry the sweet banana-like slices until they're warm and tender.

- 1 **cup vegetable oil**
- 6 **very ripe plantains (about ¾ pound each), peeled and cut on the diagonal into ½-inch slices**

Salt (optional)

In 2 very large nonstick skillets, heat the oil until shimmering. Working in batches, fry the plantains in a single layer over moderate heat, turning occasionally, until deep golden and tender, 7 to 8 minutes per batch. Drain the plantains on a paper towel–lined rack and, if desired, sprinkle lightly with salt. Serve warm.
—*Carolina Buia*

MAKE AHEAD The plantains can be fried early in the day and kept at room temperature. Reheat in a warm oven and sprinkle with salt before serving.

Mashed Plantains with Rum

ACTIVE: 10 MIN; TOTAL: 25 MIN

6 SERVINGS ● ● ●

The classic Cuban version of West African *fufu* (mashed plantains) mixes in bits of crispy pork.

- 4 **very ripe plantains (almost fully black), peeled and cut into 1-inch pieces**
- 4 **tablespoons unsalted butter**
- ¼ **cup packed light brown sugar**
- 1 **teaspoon pure vanilla extract**
- ¼ **teaspoon ground cinnamon**
- 1 **tablespoon dark rum**
- 2 **teaspoons fresh lime juice**

Kosher salt and freshly ground pepper

In a medium saucepan, combine the plantains, butter, brown sugar, vanilla and cinnamon. Add enough water to just cover the plantains and bring to a simmer over moderate heat. Cook until the plantains are very tender, 15 minutes. Using a slotted spoon, transfer the plantains to a medium bowl. Add the rum and lime juice and coarsely mash the plantains. Season with salt and pepper and serve.
—*Michelle Bernstein*

Crispy Okra Salad

TOTAL: 50 MIN

4 SERVINGS ●

The usual Indian way of preparing okra is to cut it into rounds. But when chef Suvir Saran was 7 years old, he insisted that the family cook slice the okra into wispy, long strips. The supercrunchy result was a hit and the story became a family legend.

- 1¼ **teaspoons garam masala**
- ¼ **teaspoon *amchoor* powder (optional), see Note**

Vegetable oil, for frying

- 1 **pound young okra, halved lengthwise and cut into long, thin strips**

Kosher salt

- ½ **small red onion, very thinly sliced (¾ cup)**
- 1 **medium tomato—cored, seeded and sliced into thin strips**
- ¼ **cup coarsely chopped cilantro**
- 2 **tablespoons fresh lemon juice**

1. In a small bowl, combine the garam masala with the *amchoor* powder and set aside.

2. In a large, deep skillet, add 1 inch of vegetable oil and heat to 350°. Working in batches, fry the okra strips, stirring a few times, until they are golden and crisp, about 4 minutes per batch. Using a slotted spoon, transfer the fried okra to a large paper towel–lined plate to drain. Sprinkle with some of the reserved spice mixture and season with salt.

3. In a large bowl, gently toss the fried okra with the red onion slices, tomato strips, the chopped cilantro and the lemon juice. Season the salad with more of the spice mixture and salt and serve immediately.
—*Suvir Saran*

NOTE *Amchoor* powder, which is made from dried green mangoes, adds a fruity, tangy note to this dish. It's available at Indian markets and from Kalustyan's (800-352-3451 or kalustyans.com).

CRISPY OKRA SALAD

vegetables

Mango-Cucumber Relish

ACTIVE: 20 MIN; TOTAL: 50 MIN

MAKES 5 CUPS ● ●

- ¼ cup fresh lime juice
- 1 tablespoon apple cider vinegar
- ½ teaspoon sugar
- Salt
- 2 large, ripe mangoes (about 1 pound each), peeled and cut into ½-inch dice
- 1 large seedless cucumber—peeled, seeded and cut into ¼-inch dice
- 1 large jalapeño, seeded and minced
- 1 tablespoon finely chopped basil

In a bowl, mix the lime juice with the vinegar, sugar and a generous pinch of salt. Add the mangoes, cucumber, jalapeño and basil and toss well. Cover and refrigerate until chilled, about 30 minutes.
—Carolina Buia and Isabel González

MAKE AHEAD The relish can be refrigerated overnight. Add the chopped basil just before serving.

Caramelized Endives with Apples

ACTIVE: 20 MIN; TOTAL: 40 MIN

4 SERVINGS ● ●

- 1 Granny Smith apple—peeled, halved, cored and sliced ¹⁄₁₆ inch thick on a mandoline
- 4 Belgian endives, halved lengthwise
- 1 tablespoon unsalted butter
- 1 tablespoon vegetable oil
- Salt and freshly ground pepper
- ½ cup water

Carefully tuck 6 apple slices between the leaves in each endive half. In a large skillet, melt the butter in the oil over high heat. Add the endives, cut sides down, and cook over moderate heat until nicely browned, about 6 minutes. Carefully turn the endives. Season with salt and pepper and add the water to the skillet. Cover and simmer over low heat until the endives are tender, 12 to 15 minutes. Uncover and cook until the liquid has evaporated. Serve hot.
—Jean-Georges Vongerichten

Celery Root and Apple Slaw

TOTAL: 25 MIN

4 SERVINGS ● ● ●

- 2 tablespoons coarsely chopped cilantro
- 2 tablespoons snipped chives
- 2 tablespoons extra-virgin olive oil
- 1 tablespoon fresh lime juice
- ½ teaspoon garam masala
- 2 Granny Smith apples— peeled, cored and julienned (2 cups)
- 1¼ pounds celery root, peeled and julienned (2 cups)
- 4 ounces daikon radish, peeled and julienned (1 cup)
- Salt and freshly ground black pepper

In a large bowl, combine the cilantro, chives, olive oil, lime juice and garam masala. Add the apples, celery root and daikon, season with salt and pepper and toss well. Serve the slaw lightly chilled or at room temperature. —Floyd Cardoz

MAKE AHEAD The slaw can be refrigerated for up to 4 hours.

Bread and Butter Pickles

ACTIVE: 20 MIN; TOTAL: 1 HR 20 MIN

MAKES ABOUT 6 CUPS ● ● ●

Homemade condiments are key to truly superlative burgers. These puckery bread and butter pickles also make a great hot dog topping.

- 2 cups light brown sugar
- 2 cups cider vinegar
- ¼ cup kosher salt
- 1 tablespoon mustard seeds
- ½ teaspoon turmeric
- 10 whole cloves
- 10 allspice berries
- 1¾ pounds Kirby cucumbers, sliced crosswise ¼ inch thick (about 6 cups)
- 2 medium yellow onions, thinly sliced

In a large saucepan, combine the brown sugar, vinegar, salt, mustard seeds, turmeric, cloves and allspice and bring to a boil, stirring to dissolve the sugar and salt. Add the cucumbers and onions and simmer over moderate heat, stirring a few times, until the cucumbers darken, about 5 minutes. Remove from the heat. Let cool, then refrigerate until chilled, about 1 hour.
—Sue Moore

Tomato-Cucumber Chutney

ACTIVE: 20 MIN; TOTAL: 45 MIN

MAKES 3 CUPS ● ● ●

- 2 tablespoons vegetable oil
- 4 garlic cloves, minced
- 2 red Thai chiles, minced
- 1 medium red onion, finely chopped
- 6 medium tomatoes, cut into ½-inch dice
- 1 tablespoon curry powder
- 2 tablespoons honey
- 1 English cucumber, halved lengthwise, seeded and finely diced
- Salt and freshly ground pepper
- 2 tablespoons coarsely chopped basil
- 2 teaspoons sesame seeds

In a large skillet, heat the vegetable oil. Add the minced garlic, red Thai chiles and onion and cook, stirring occasionally, over moderate heat until the onion is softened, about 5 minutes. Add the chopped tomatoes and the curry powder and simmer until the tomato liquid starts to thicken, about 10 minutes. Add the honey and simmer for 5 minutes. Add the cucumber and simmer until crisp-tender, about 3 minutes. Remove the skillet from the heat and season the chutney with salt and pepper. Let cool slightly. Stir in the basil, sprinkle with the sesame seeds and serve. —Marcus Samuelsson

MAKE AHEAD The chutney can be refrigerated overnight.

Roasted Fall-Vegetable Hash

TOTAL: 40 MIN

4 SERVINGS ● ●

- ½ pound brussels sprouts, quartered
- ½ pound butternut squash, peeled and cut into ½-inch dice
- 3 tablespoons extra-virgin olive oil

Salt and freshly ground black pepper

- ¼ pound thickly sliced bacon, cut into ¼-inch dice
- ½ pound sweet onions, such as Vidalia or Texas sweets, finely chopped
- 1 small Granny Smith apple—peeled, cored and cut into ¼-inch dice
- 10 sage leaves, thinly sliced crosswise
- 1 cup apple cider

1. Preheat the oven to 400°. On a large rimmed baking sheet, toss the brussels sprouts and squash with 2 tablespoons of the olive oil and season with salt and pepper. Roast the vegetables for about 20 minutes, or until they are tender.

2. In a large, deep skillet, heat the remaining 1 tablespoon of olive oil. Add the diced bacon and cook over moderate heat until it is crisp, about 5 minutes. Add the onions and cook, stirring occasionally, until they are browned, about 10 minutes. Stir in the diced apple and cook until it starts to soften, about 2 minutes. Gently stir in the roasted brussels sprouts and squash and the sage leaves, then pour the apple cider into the skillet. Simmer the vegetables over moderately high heat until the cider has almost evaporated, about 10 minutes. Season the vegetable hash with salt and pepper. Transfer the vegetable hash to a bowl and serve immediately. —Kenny Callaghan

MAKE AHEAD The vegetable hash can be refrigerated overnight.

Anu's Avial

TOTAL: 45 MIN

4 TO 6 SERVINGS ●

Avial is a traditional Indian stew made with ordinary vegetables like cucumbers, carrots, potatoes and string beans. What makes the combination exotic is the pungent mixture of fresh coconut, green chiles, garlic and cumin that's folded in at the end, cooled by a bit of creamy whole milk yogurt.

- 1 medium cucumber—peeled, seeded and cut into 3-by-⅓-inch sticks
- 1 baking potato (½ pound), peeled and cut into 1-by-¼-inch matchsticks
- 1 medium carrot, cut into 1-by-¼-inch matchsticks
- 3 ounces green beans, cut into 1-inch lengths
- 1 medium tomato, chopped
- 5 long hot green chiles—3 halved lengthwise and seeded, 2 halved lengthwise, seeded and thinly sliced crosswise
- 5 tablespoons vegetable oil
- 1 cup water
- 1 teaspoon turmeric
- 1½ cups (5¼ ounces) shredded unsweetened coconut
- 3 medium shallots, thinly sliced
- 1 garlic clove, thinly sliced
- ½ teaspoon cumin seeds
- 12 fresh curry leaves
- 1 underripe banana, cut into 1-by-¼-inch sticks
- 1 cup plain whole milk yogurt

Salt

1. In a large saucepan, combine the cucumber, potato, carrot, green beans, tomato, the halved chiles and 2 tablespoons of the vegetable oil. Add the water and turmeric and bring the vegetables to a simmer over high heat. Reduce the heat to moderate, cover and cook, stirring occasionally, until the vegetables are tender, about 10 minutes.

2. In a food processor, combine the sliced chiles with the coconut, shallots, garlic and cumin seeds and process to a paste. Stir the paste into the vegetables and simmer for 4 minutes.

3. In a small skillet, heat the remaining oil until shimmering. Add the curry leaves and fry over high heat until sizzling, 10 seconds. Add the oil and fried curry leaves to the stew, along with the banana and simmer for 1 minute. Stir in the yogurt. Season with salt and serve. — Aniamma Philip

SERVE WITH Steamed white rice.

Curried Parsnips and Carrots

ACTIVE: 30 MIN; TOTAL: 1 HR 15 MIN

12 SERVINGS ●

- 3 pounds slender carrots, halved lengthwise and cut into 2-inch pieces
- 2 pounds slender parsnips, halved lengthwise and cut into 2-inch pieces
- ½ cup extra-virgin olive oil

Salt and freshly ground pepper

- ½ cup pine nuts
- 3 tablespoons Banyuls vinegar or red wine vinegar
- 2 teaspoons Madras curry powder
- ¼ cup dried currants
- 2 tablespoons chopped parsley

1. Preheat the oven to 375°. In a large roasting pan, toss the carrots and parsnips with ¼ cup of the oil and season with salt and pepper. Roast for 45 minutes, stirring a few times, until tender and lightly caramelized in spots. Remove from the oven. Spread the pine nuts in a pie plate and toast for 5 minutes, or until golden.

2. In a bowl, whisk the vinegar and curry powder; whisk in the remaining ¼ cup of oil. Add the roasted vegetables, pine nuts, currants and parsley; season with salt and pepper and toss well. Serve warm. —Maria Helm Sinskey

GRITS WITH WILD MUSHROOMS
AND SHERRY BROTH (P. 274)

potatoes, grains & beans

"You know, you're walking through the woods and you smell something, and all of a sudden, you're five years old? That's what this rice dish is like for me."

–**Jacques Pépin,** cooking teacher extraordinaire

CRANBERRY-GLAZED SWEET POTATOES

HERBED POTATO SOUFFLÉ

Cranberry-Glazed Sweet Potatoes

ACTIVE: 35 MIN; TOTAL: 2 HR

8 SERVINGS ● ● ○

This ingenious dish uses the liquid from simmered cranberries as a tart glaze for sweet potatoes while the cooked berries make an attractive garnish. Because the potatoes are spread out in a single layer, the dish resembles an apple tart.

- 4 **pounds slender sweet potatoes, peeled and sliced crosswise ¼ inch thick**
- 1 **cup water**
- 4 **tablespoons unsalted butter, melted**
- 2 **tablespoons bourbon**

Salt and freshly ground black pepper

- ¾ **cup cranberries**
- ⅓ **cup light brown sugar**
- ⅛ **teaspoon cayenne pepper**
- ⅛ **teaspoon cinnamon**

1. Preheat the oven to 350°. Butter a large oval, shallow baking dish. Arrange the sweet potato slices in concentric circles in the baking dish, overlapping the potato slices slightly. Pour ½ cup of the water over the sweet potatoes in the dish. Cover the sweet potatoes with aluminum foil and bake them for about 40 minutes, or until they are just tender. Increase the oven temperature to 425°.

2. In a small bowl, mix the melted butter with the bourbon. Spoon the bourbon mixture over the sweet potatoes. Season the potatoes with salt and black pepper and bake in the upper third of the oven for about 25 minutes, basting halfway through cooking, until the bourbon mixture is almost completely absorbed.

3. Meanwhile, in a saucepan, combine the cranberries, the remaining ½ cup of water and the brown sugar and boil over moderately high heat until the cranberries start to burst, about 10 minutes. Drain the cranberries, reserving the liquid separately.

4. Stir the cayenne and cinnamon into the cranberry liquid and spoon it over the sweet potatoes. Bake in the upper third of the oven, basting well after 5 minutes, for 20 minutes longer, until the potatoes are nicely glazed and most of the liquid has been absorbed. During the last 5 minutes of baking, scatter the cranberries on top. Serve hot or warm. —*Marcia Kiesel*

MAKE AHEAD The potatoes can be baked 8 hours ahead; rewarm before serving.

Herbed Potato Soufflé

ACTIVE: 20 MIN; TOTAL: 1 HR 30 MIN

6 SERVINGS

"Most people are afraid of soufflés because they think they're so delicate," says Mike Davis, chef and owner of 26brix in Walla Walla, Washington. Starchy potatoes prevent this soufflé from falling.

2 tablespoons unsalted butter,
plus more for brushing
1½ pounds baking potatoes,
peeled and quartered
¾ cup half-and-half
½ pound Cantal cheese or
Gruyère cheese, shredded
(2 cups)
1 teaspoon finely chopped oregano
1 teaspoon finely chopped
thyme
1 tablespoon finely chopped
flat-leaf parsley
Salt and freshly ground black
pepper
5 large eggs, separated
2 large egg whites
Pinch of cream of tartar

1. Preheat the oven to 375°. Butter and flour a 2-quart soufflé dish. In a medium saucepan, cover the baking potatoes with cold water and bring to a boil. Simmer until tender, about 20 minutes.

2. Drain the potatoes and return them to the saucepan. Shake the pan over high heat to dry out the potatoes, about 1 minute. Add the 2 tablespoons of butter and mash the potatoes. Stir in the half-and-half and let the potatoes cool slightly. Stir in the shredded Cantal cheese and the oregano, thyme and parsley and season the mashed potatoes with salt and black pepper. Stir in the 5 egg yolks. Transfer the potato mixture to a large bowl.

3. In another large bowl, using an electric mixer, beat the 7 egg whites until they are foamy. Add the cream of tartar and beat until the egg whites form stiff peaks. Stir one-third of the beaten whites into the potato mixture. Using a rubber spatula, fold in the remaining whites until no streaks of white remain. Scrape the soufflé mixture into the prepared soufflé dish and bake in the bottom third of the oven for about 45 minutes, or until the soufflé is puffed and richly browned. Serve the potato soufflé immediately. —*Mike Davis*

Crunchy Potato Wedges with Romesco Sauce
ACTIVE: 45 MIN; TOTAL: 1 HR 30 MIN
8 SERVINGS ● ● ●

Boiling potatoes briefly before roasting them, a restaurant technique, creates an outrageously crunchy crust.

2 ancho chiles
2 cups boiling water
4 pounds medium Yukon Gold
potatoes, scrubbed
Salt
¾ cup extra-virgin olive oil
Freshly ground pepper
½ cup salted, roasted almonds,
coarsely chopped
2 tablespoons fresh bread crumbs
¾ cup drained piquillo peppers
from a 7.6-ounce jar
3 garlic cloves, chopped
1 medium tomato, seeded and
chopped
2 tablespoons chopped flat-leaf
parsley
1 tablespoon sherry vinegar
1 cup pitted green olives such as
Sicilian or Greek, chopped

1. Preheat the oven to 425°. Put the anchos in a heatproof bowl and cover with the boiling water. Set a small plate on top to keep the anchos submerged and let soak until softened, about 20 minutes. Discard the soaking liquid, stems and seeds and chop the anchos.

2. Meanwhile, in a large heavy pot, cover the potatoes with water and bring to a boil. Add a large pinch of salt and cook over moderately high heat until just tender when pierced with a knife, about 25 minutes. Drain and let cool slightly, then peel the potatoes and cut into wedges. Transfer the potatoes to 2 large rimmed baking sheets. Drizzle with ¼ cup plus 2 tablespoons of the olive oil, turn to coat and season with salt and pepper.

3. Roast the potatoes on the upper and lower racks of the oven for 40 minutes, switching the pans once, until the potatoes are browned and crisp.

4. Meanwhile, in a large skillet, heat the remaining ¼ cup plus 2 tablespoons of olive oil. Add the chopped almonds and cook over moderate heat, shaking the skillet a few times, until lightly browned, about 4 minutes. Add the bread crumbs and cook until lightly toasted, about 1 minute. Let cool slightly, then transfer to a food processor. Add the anchos, piquillos, garlic, tomato, parsley and vinegar and process to a coarse paste; season with salt and pepper. Spoon the *romesco* sauce over the potatoes, sprinkle the olives on top and serve. —*Vitaly Paley*

Sweet Potato Soufflé
ACTIVE: 25 MIN; TOTAL: 2 HR 50 MIN
12 SERVINGS

3 pounds large sweet potatoes
6 tablespoons unsalted butter,
softened
½ cup heavy cream
½ cup shredded Gruyère cheese
2 tablespoons light brown sugar
1 teaspoon chopped thyme
Salt and freshly ground pepper
3 large eggs

1. Preheat the oven to 350°. Bake the sweet potatoes for 1½ hours, or until tender. Raise the oven temperature to 425°.

2. Peel the sweet potatoes as soon as they are cool enough to handle; transfer to a bowl. Using a handheld electric mixer, beat the sweet potatoes with the butter until smooth. Beat in the cream, Gruyère, brown sugar and thyme; season with salt and pepper. Beat in the eggs one at a time, beating well after each addition.

3. Transfer the sweet potato puree to a buttered 11-by-8-inch baking dish; bake for 15 minutes. Reduce the oven to 400°. Bake for 30 minutes, or until the sweet potatoes are lightly puffed and browned. Let the soufflé rest for 10 minutes before serving. —*Maria Helm Sinskey*

potatoes, grains & beans

Sweet Potato Fries

ACTIVE: 20 MIN; TOTAL: 2 HR 20 MIN

4 SERVINGS

> 4 medium sweet potatoes (about 2 pounds), peeled and cut into ½-inch-thick batons
>
> Vegetable oil, for frying
>
> 1 teaspoon *furikake* (see Note)
>
> Kosher salt

1. In a large bowl, cover the sweet potato batons with cold water and let them stand for 2 hours.

2. Fill a large pot with 4 inches of oil; heat to 300°. Drain the potatoes; pat thoroughly dry with paper towels. Working in batches, fry the potatoes until softened but not browned, 4 minutes. Transfer to a paper towel–lined platter to drain and cool.

3. Heat the vegetable oil to 350°. Fry the sweet potatoes again until golden, about 4 minutes. Transfer to a paper towel–lined platter to drain. Sprinkle with *furikake* and salt and serve. —*Terry Crandall*

NOTE *Furikake* is a Japanese seasoning of dried chiles, nori and sesame that's available at Asian markets. You can substitute chile powder.

chef idea

side dish

SPANISH FINGERLING POTATOES

Boil fingerling potatoes, then cut them in half and sauté them in olive oil until golden. Sauté diced onion until caramelized. Add diced tomatoes and simmer until their liquid has evaporated. Add red wine vinegar, mayonnaise, chopped oregano, cayenne, ground cumin and salt. Toss the sautéed potatoes with the tomato mixture and Spanish smoked paprika and serve garnished with sliced scallions.
—*Andy Nusser*

Sausage-Stuffed Potato Galette

ACTIVE: 30 MIN; TOTAL: 1 HR 45 MIN

8 SERVINGS

Any sage-spiked pork sausage can be used as the filling for this luscious potato cake (if the sausages come in casings, remove the meat and discard them). Don't be alarmed that the sausage isn't browned before it's layered with the potato—as the galette bakes, the sausage cooks through.

> 3 pounds large Yukon Gold potatoes
>
> Salt and freshly ground pepper
>
> 3 tablespoons extra-virgin olive oil
>
> 1 fennel bulb—halved, cored and thinly sliced lengthwise
>
> 1 small onion, sliced
>
> 1 pound pork breakfast sausage

1. In a large saucepan, cover the potatoes with water and bring to a boil. Simmer until partially cooked, 8 to 10 minutes. Transfer to a plate and let cool. Peel the potatoes and coarsely shred them on a box grater. Spread the shredded potatoes on a baking sheet; season very lightly with salt and pepper.

2. In a 12-inch nonstick ovenproof skillet, heat 1 tablespoon of the oil. Add the fennel and onion, cover and cook over moderate heat until softened, 5 minutes. Uncover and cook, stirring occasionally, until lightly browned, 5 minutes longer. Let cool slightly, then transfer to a food processor. Add the sausage and pulse to combine.

3. Preheat the oven to 375°. Wipe out the skillet and coat with 1 tablespoon of the olive oil. Press half of the shredded potatoes in the bottom of the skillet and partially up the side. Spread the sausage mixture over the potatoes, leaving a 1-inch border all around. Press the remaining potatoes on top in an even layer, sealing the edges. Cook over moderately high heat until the bottom is golden, 15 minutes.

4. Carefully slide the potato galette onto a large plate and cover with the skillet. Invert the galette into the skillet. Drizzle the remaining 1 tablespoon of oil around the edge of the galette and cook over moderately high heat for 5 minutes. Transfer the skillet to the oven and bake for 45 minutes, until the bottom is well browned and the sausage cooked through. Slide the galette onto a cutting board, cut into wedges and serve. —*Grace Parisi*

Grilled Potato and Onion Salad with Blue Cheese and Bacon

TOTAL: 30 MIN

12 SERVINGS ● ◐

> 1 pound sliced meaty bacon
>
> 3 red onions, sliced ½ inch thick
>
> ¼ cup extra-virgin olive oil
>
> Kosher salt and freshly ground pepper
>
> 3½ pounds small new potatoes (about 1½ inches in diameter), scrubbed
>
> ½ cup mayonnaise
>
> ½ pound blue cheese, such as Gorgonzola, Roquefort or Maytag Blue, crumbled

1. Preheat the oven to 400°. Spread the bacon in a single layer on a baking sheet. Bake until brown and crisp, 15 minutes. Transfer to paper towel–lined plates to drain. Crumble into ½-inch pieces.

2. Light a grill. In a large bowl, toss the onions with 1 tablespoon of the olive oil. Season with salt and pepper. Grill over moderately high heat, turning once, until lightly charred and tender, about 5 minutes. Cut the onions into ½-inch pieces.

3. In a large pot of salted cold water, bring the potatoes to a boil. Simmer until they are beginning to get tender, about 5 minutes. Drain the potatoes and cut them in half. In a large bowl, toss the potatoes with the remaining 3 tablespoons of olive oil and season with salt and pepper. Grill the potatoes over moderately high heat, turning once, until they are tender and browned, about 5 minutes.

4. In a large bowl, mix the mayonnaise with the blue cheese. Add the bacon, onions and potatoes and toss to coat. Transfer to a clean bowl and serve. —*Jeri Ryan*

Mashed Fingerling Potatoes with Cucumber Vinaigrette

TOTAL: 30 MIN

6 SERVINGS ● ● ●

- 2 pounds large fingerling potatoes, peeled
- 1 Kirby cucumber—peeled, halved and seeded
- ¼ cup cider vinegar
- ¼ cup extra-virgin olive oil
- 2 shallots, thinly sliced
- 1 tablespoon sugar

Salt and freshly ground pepper

- 2 tablespoons snipped chives
- 2 tablespoons chopped celery leaves

1. In a large saucepan of boiling salted water, cook the potatoes until tender, about 15 minutes. Drain; transfer the potatoes to a bowl and coarsely mash.

2. Meanwhile, in a blender, puree the cucumber and vinegar until smooth. Strain the cucumber vinegar into a bowl, pressing on the solids; discard the solids.

3. In a skillet, heat the olive oil until shimmering. Add the shallots and cook over moderately low heat until softened, about 4 minutes. Add the cucumber vinegar and sugar, season with salt and pepper and bring to a simmer. Pour the vinaigrette over the potatoes. Add the chives and celery leaves, season with salt and pepper and stir gently to combine. Serve warm or at room temperature. —*Brian Bistrong*

MAKE AHEAD The potato salad can be refrigerated overnight.

Skirlie Potato Cakes

ACTIVE: 45 MIN; TOTAL: 2 HR

4 SERVINGS

Skirlie is a classic Scottish dish, a kind of poor man's haggis made with sheep innards—but don't worry, these cakes substitute potatoes. Typically served as a meal in itself, they're even better as a side dish because they soak up other flavors so beautifully.

- 1½ pounds baking potatoes, scrubbed

Salt

- ¼ cup plus 2 tablespoons vegetable oil, plus more for oiling
- 2 tablespoons unsalted butter
- 1 large shallot, minced
- 1 garlic clove, minced
- 2 ounces lean smoked bacon, cut into ¼-inch dice (⅓ cup)
- 3 tablespoons old-fashioned rolled oats
- 2 tablespoons chopped parsley
- 1 teaspoon chopped thyme

Freshly ground pepper

- ½ cup all-purpose flour, for dredging

1. Put the potatoes in a medium saucepan, cover with water and bring to a boil. Add a large pinch of salt and boil over moderately high heat until tender, 35 minutes. Oil an 8-inch square glass baking dish.

2. In a medium skillet, melt the butter. Add the shallot and garlic. Cook over moderate heat until softened, 3 minutes. Add the bacon and cook until most of the fat has been rendered, 3 minutes. Add the oats and cook, stirring, until lightly golden, 2 minutes. Remove from the heat and stir in the parsley and thyme.

3. Drain and peel the potatoes. Halve each potato crosswise. Working over a bowl, pass the hot potatoes through a ricer. Alternatively, mash them by hand until smooth. Stir in the oat mixture; season with salt and pepper. Spread the potatoes in the prepared baking dish. Cover with plastic wrap and refrigerate until firm, at least 1 hour.

4. Bring the potatoes to room temperature. Cut the mixture into 4 squares, then cut each square in half again. Carefully lift the cakes out of the dish with an offset metal spatula. In a large nonstick skillet, heat ¼ cup of the oil until shimmering. Spread the flour in a shallow bowl; season with ½ teaspoon of salt. Carefully dredge the potato cakes in the flour; shake off any excess. Add the cakes to the skillet. Cook over moderately high heat until browned, 2 minutes. Turn the cakes and add the remaining 2 tablespoons of oil to the skillet. Cook until richly browned and heated through, 2 minutes. Transfer the cakes to a platter. Serve hot. —*Nick Nairn*

Lemony Salt–Roasted Fingerling Potatoes

ACTIVE: 15 MIN; TOTAL: 45 MIN

8 SERVINGS ● ●

This lemon-scented herb salt makes a great seasoning for everything from roasted white fish to grilled chicken and pork to steamed vegetables—and of course, any kind of potato. Grinding the sage, rosemary and thyme into the salt, rather than just stirring it in, helps intensify and meld the flavors.

- 2 large sage leaves, chopped
- 1 teaspoon chopped rosemary
- 1 teaspoon thyme leaves
- 1 teaspoon finely grated lemon zest
- 1 tablespoon kosher salt
- 4 pounds fingerling potatoes, halved lengthwise
- 2 tablespoons extra-virgin olive oil
- 2 tablespoons unsalted butter, melted

Freshly ground pepper

1. Preheat the oven to 425°. In a mini food processor, pulse the sage, rosemary and thyme until finely chopped. Add the lemon zest and pulse to blend. Add the salt and pulse until finely ground. Transfer the herb salt to a small bowl.

2. In a large bowl, toss the potatoes with the oil and butter and season with pepper. Spread in a single layer on 2 large rimmed baking sheets and roast for 25 minutes. Season the potatoes generously with the herb salt, toss well and continue baking for 5 minutes, or until the potatoes are tender and golden. Transfer to a bowl and serve hot or warm. —*Melissa Rubel*

potatoes, grains & beans

Yukon Golds with Shallot Butter

ACTIVE: 10 MIN; TOTAL: 20 MIN

6 SERVINGS ● ●

2¼ pounds small Yukon Gold potatoes, scrubbed but not peeled

1 teaspoon yellow mustard seeds

4 tablespoons unsalted butter, softened

1 tablespoon minced parsley

1 medium shallot, minced

2 teaspoons fresh lemon juice

Salt and freshly ground pepper

1. In a saucepan, boil the potatoes in water to cover until tender, about 15 minutes.

2. Meanwhile, in a small skillet, toast the mustard seeds over moderate heat until they pop, about 3 minutes. In a small bowl, mix the butter with the parsley, shallot, lemon juice and mustard seeds. Season generously with salt and pepper.

3. Drain and halve the potatoes lengthwise. In a large dish, toss the potatoes with the shallot butter and serve. —Andy Ayers

Celery Root and Potato Puree

ACTIVE: 20 MIN; TOTAL: 50 MIN

4 SERVINGS ●

1 large celery root (1½ pounds), peeled and cut into ½-inch dice

1 medium baking potato (½ pound), peeled and cut into ½-inch dice

1 garlic clove

1 cup heavy cream

1 cup whole milk

Salt and freshly ground pepper

1. In a medium saucepan, combine the celery root, potato, garlic, cream and milk and bring to a boil. Reduce the heat to moderately low and simmer until tender, about 40 minutes; drain in a colander set over a bowl and reserve the cooking liquid.

2. Working in batches, puree the celery root and potato in a blender, adding as much of the reserved cooking liquid as necessary to form a soft puree. Transfer the puree to the saucepan, season with salt and pepper and reheat before serving. —Andy Arndt

Mashed Potatoes with Manchego and Olive Oil

ACTIVE: 35 MIN; TOTAL: 1 HR 10 MIN

12 SERVINGS ●

2 heads of garlic, top third of each cut off

¼ cup Spanish extra-virgin olive oil, plus more for drizzling

6 pounds baking potatoes, peeled and cut into 2-inch chunks

Water

Salt

3 cups heavy cream, heated

½ pound young Manchego cheese, cut into ¼-inch dice

1. Preheat the oven to 350°. Stand the garlic heads on a large sheet of heavy-duty foil. Drizzle with olive oil and wrap in the foil. Bake for about 1 hour, until the garlic is very soft. Squeeze the soft cloves from the papery skins into a small bowl and mash with a fork.

2. Put the potatoes in a large pot, cover with water and bring to a boil. Salt the water and boil over moderately high heat until tender, about 20 minutes. Drain and return the potatoes to the pot. Shake the pot over moderately high heat for about 1 minute to dry the potatoes.

3. Mash the potatoes with a potato masher, then mash in half of the hot cream. Add the remaining cream and mash again. Stir in the Manchego to melt. Slowly stir in the mashed garlic and 3 tablespoons of the oil. Season with salt. Transfer to a warmed serving bowl. Drizzle with the remaining oil and serve. —José Andrés

Roasted Sweet Potato and Okra Salad

ACTIVE: 45 MIN; TOTAL: 1 HR 20 MIN

12 SERVINGS ● ● ●

1 pound red potatoes, scrubbed but not peeled and cut into 1-inch cubes

¾ cup plus 1 tablespoon extra-virgin olive oil

Salt and freshly ground pepper

3 pounds orange sweet potatoes, peeled and cut into 1-inch cubes

1 tablespoon mustard seeds

5 ounces spinach, large stems discarded, leaves rinsed (8 cups packed)

1 pound small okra, thawed if frozen

¼ cup plus 1 tablespoon red wine vinegar

3 tablespoons drained and chopped capers

1. Preheat the oven to 350°. On a rimmed baking sheet, toss the red potatoes with 1 tablespoon of the olive oil and spread them in an even layer. Season with salt and pepper. Bake the potatoes in the middle of the oven for about 30 minutes, or until they're lightly browned and just tender. Let cool.

2. On each of 2 large rimmed baking sheets, toss half of the sweet potatoes with 2 tablespoons of the olive oil. Spread the sweet potatoes in an even layer and season with salt and pepper. Bake the sweet potatoes on the upper and lower racks of the oven for about 20 minutes, or until lightly browned and just tender; switch the sheets halfway through for even cooking. Let the sweet potatoes cool.

3. In a large skillet, toast the mustard seeds over moderately high heat until they start popping, about 3 minutes. Transfer the seeds to a small bowl. Add the rinsed spinach leaves—they will still be wet—to the skillet and cook over moderately high heat, tossing with tongs, until completely wilted. Transfer the spinach to a colander to cool. Lightly squeeze the spinach dry and then coarsely chop.

4. Wipe out the skillet. Add 2 tablespoons of olive oil and heat until shimmering. Add the okra, season with salt and pepper and cook over moderate heat, turning a few times, until the okra is lightly browned, about 5 minutes.

ROASTED SWEET POTATO AND OKRA SALAD

FARRO AND GREEN BEAN SALAD

5. In a very large bowl, mix the vinegar, capers and remaining ¼ cup plus 2 tablespoons of olive oil; season with salt and pepper. Add the red potatoes, sweet potatoes, mustard seeds, spinach and okra and toss well to coat. Transfer the salad to a platter and serve. —*Marcus Samuelsson*

Farro and Green Bean Salad

TOTAL: 45 MIN

6 SERVINGS ● ●

- 1   cup farro
- Water
- Salt
- 6   ounces thin green beans
- 1   cup pure olive oil, for frying
- 4   large shallots—3 thinly sliced, 1 minced
- 1   cup all-purpose flour
- 3   cremini mushrooms, thinly sliced
- 2   tablespoons sherry vinegar
- 1   tablespoon balsamic vinegar
- 1   garlic clove, minced
- 1   teaspoon thyme leaves
- ¼   cup plus 2 tablespoons extra-virgin olive oil
- 3   tablespoons salted toasted hazelnuts, coarsely chopped
- Freshly ground pepper

1. In a medium saucepan, cover the farro with 2 cups of water and bring to a boil. Cover the pan, remove from the heat and let the farro stand for 15 minutes. Drain the farro and return it to the saucepan. Add 2 more cups of water and a pinch of salt and bring to a boil. Cook the farro over high heat until it is al dente, 10 minutes longer; drain well.

2. Meanwhile, in a saucepan of boiling salted water, cook the thin green beans until they are crisp-tender, about 5 minutes; drain. Rinse the green beans under cold water and pat them dry.

3. Heat the pure olive oil in a medium saucepan. In a bowl, toss the sliced shallots with the flour, separating them into rings. Transfer to a strainer and tap off the excess flour. Add the shallots to the hot oil and fry over high heat, stirring, until golden, 5 minutes. Using a slotted spoon, transfer the shallots to paper towels to drain thoroughly; season lightly with salt.

4. Pour off all but 1 tablespoon of the oil from the saucepan. Add the mushrooms and cook over high heat, stirring, until browned. Transfer to a plate.

5. In a medium bowl, whisk the vinegars with the minced shallot, garlic and thyme. Whisk in the extra-virgin olive oil. Add the farro, green beans, hazelnuts and three-fourths of the fried shallots and gently toss. Season with salt and pepper and transfer to a platter or shallow bowl. Garnish with the remaining fried shallots and serve. —*Melissa Kelly*

potatoes, grains & beans

Warm Farro and Mushroom Salad with Sherry Vinaigrette

ACTIVE: 35 MIN; TOTAL: 1 HR 15 MIN

8 SERVINGS ●

Farro, an ancient grain from the wheat family, holds it shape nicely, making it an ideal make-ahead dish.

- ¾ cup walnuts
- 1½ pounds shiitake mushrooms, stems discarded, caps quartered
- ¾ cup plus 2 tablespoons extra-virgin olive oil
- Kosher salt and freshly ground pepper
- 1 shallot, finely chopped
- ⅓ cup sherry vinegar
- 1 teaspoon chopped thyme
- 6 cups chicken stock
- ½ ounce dried porcini mushrooms
- 1 medium onion, coarsely chopped
- 1 garlic clove, minced
- 2 cups farro
- 1 bay leaf
- ⅓ cup chopped flat-leaf parsley

1. Preheat the oven to 350°. In a pie plate, toast the walnuts for 10 minutes, or until well browned. Let cool, then coarsely chop.

2. Increase the oven temperature to 425°. In a bowl, toss the shiitakes with ¼ cup of the oil and season with salt and pepper. Spread the shiitakes on the baking sheet and roast for about 25 minutes, or until tender and browned around the edges.

3. In a small bowl, cover the shallot with the sherry vinegar and let stand for 10 minutes. Add the thyme and whisk in ½ cup of the oil. Season with salt and pepper.

4. Heat 1 cup of the chicken stock in a microwave oven. Add the porcini and let stand for 10 minutes. Remove the porcini and coarsely chop; pour the soaking liquid into a bowl, stopping before you reach the grit.

5. In a saucepan, heat the remaining oil. Add the onion and garlic and cook over moderate heat until translucent, 6 minutes. Add the farro, porcini and their soaking liquid, the remaining stock and the bay leaf. Bring to a simmer, then cover and cook over moderately low heat until the farro is tender, about 20 minutes. Drain well; discard the bay leaf.

6. Return the farro to the pan and toss with the walnuts, shiitakes, vinaigrette and parsley and season with salt and pepper. Transfer to a bowl and serve warm or at room temperature. —*Melissa Rubel*

Warm Winter Farro Salad

TOTAL: 30 MIN

4 SERVINGS ● ●

As with pasta, the trick to cooking farro is to use lots of liquid with a pinch of salt.

- ¼ cup extra-virgin olive oil
- 1 each small onion, small carrot and celery rib, diced
- 1 small rosemary sprig
- ⅔ cup farro
- 2 cups chicken stock or low-sodium broth
- 2 cups water
- Salt
- 1 pound broccoli rabe, thick stems trimmed
- 1 tablespoon unsalted butter
- 4 scallions, thinly sliced
- 1 shallot, minced
- Freshly ground pepper
- 1½ teaspoons sherry vinegar
- ¼ cup red grapes, halved
- 1 tablespoon chopped pecans

1. In a large saucepan, heat 2 tablespoons of the oil. Add the onion, carrot, celery and rosemary; cook over high heat, stirring, until just softened. Add the farro and cook, stirring for 1 minute. Add the stock, water and a pinch of salt; bring to a boil. Cook over moderately high heat, stirring occasionally, until the farro is tender, 15 minutes; drain, reserving ¼ cup of the cooking liquid. Discard the rosemary sprig.

2. Meanwhile, pour 1 inch of water into a large skillet and bring to a boil. Add the broccoli rabe and cook over high heat until just wilted. Drain the broccoli rabe well, then coarsely chop. In the skillet, melt the butter in the remaining oil. Add the scallions, shallot and broccoli rabe. Season with salt and pepper; cook over moderately high heat until tender, 2 to 3 minutes. Add the farro and its reserved liquid; cook, stirring until heated through. Stir in the vinegar, grapes and pecans. Season with salt and pepper, transfer to a bowl and serve. —*Gabriel Frasca*

Herbed Brown Rice Salad with Corn, Fava Beans and Peas

TOTAL: 1 HR

8 SERVINGS ● ●

French chef Cyril Renaud of New York City's Fleur de Sel had brown rice for the first time when his Irish-American wife, Brigette, introduced him to it. Now he loves this heart-healthy, nutty-flavored grain, especially because its chewy texture holds up well in salads, like this slightly spicy one full of vegetables and herbs.

- 3 tablespoons extra-virgin olive oil
- 1 large onion, chopped
- 2 cups short-grain brown rice
- 2 cups rice milk
- 2 cups water
- 2 cups corn kernels (from 4 ears)
- 1 cup shelled fresh peas (from 1 pound in the pod)
- 1 cup shelled fava beans (from 1 pound in the pod)
- 3 tablespoons fresh orange juice
- 2 tablespoons white wine vinegar
- 1 tablespoon Tabasco
- ¼ cup chopped basil
- 1 tablespoon coarsely chopped tarragon
- Salt
- 8 medium scallions, white and light green parts only, thinly sliced crosswise
- 1 bunch small radishes (4 ounces), thinly sliced crosswise
- 1 bunch arugula (6 ounces)

ERBED BROWN RICE SALAD WITH CORN, FAVA BEANS AND PEAS

BULGUR WITH TANGY ARTICHOKES

1. In a medium saucepan, heat 1 tablespoon of the olive oil. Add the onion and cook over moderately low heat until softened, about 7 minutes. Stir in the rice, then add the rice milk and water and bring to a boil. Cover and cook over low heat until the liquid has been absorbed and the rice is tender, about 35 minutes. Transfer the rice to a large bowl and let cool to room temperature, stirring a few times.

2. Meanwhile, in a medium saucepan of boiling salted water, cook the corn until just tender, about 3 minutes. Using a slotted spoon, transfer the corn to a shallow bowl. Repeat with the peas, then the fava beans, cooking them for about 2 minutes. Peel the fava beans.

3. In a small bowl, combine the orange juice with the vinegar, Tabasco and the remaining olive oil. Add the basil and tarragon and season with salt. Fold the corn, peas, favas, scallions and radishes into the cooled rice. Add the dressing to the rice and toss to coat. Season with salt. Spread the arugula on a platter, spoon the rice salad on top and serve.
—*Cyril Renaud*

MAKE AHEAD The recipe can be prepared through Step 2 and refrigerated for up to 1 day. Bring the rice and vegetables to room temperature before proceeding.

Bulgur with Tangy Artichokes
TOTAL: 30 MIN
4 SERVINGS ● ● ●

2½ cups vegetable stock, preferably homemade or low-sodium broth

9 ounces medium bulgur (1½ cups)

1 bunch medium asparagus, stalks peeled

2 tablespoons fresh lemon juice

¼ cup extra-virgin olive oil

4 ounces marinated artichoke hearts, drained and quartered (1 cup)

¼ cup chopped flat-leaf parsley

½ teaspoon finely grated lemon zest

Salt and freshly ground pepper

2 ounces marcona almonds (½ cup), coarsely chopped

1. In a saucepan, bring the stock to a boil. Add the bulgur and bring to a boil. Cover and remove from the heat. Let stand until the liquid is completely absorbed, 10 minutes. Fluff with a fork.

2. Meanwhile, steam the asparagus until crisp-tender, about 5 minutes. Pat dry and cut the asparagus into ½-inch pieces.

3. In a medium bowl, whisk the lemon juice and oil. Add the bulgur, asparagus, artichokes, parsley and lemon zest; season with salt and pepper. Add two-thirds of the almonds and toss. Sprinkle the remaining nuts on top and serve. —*Shawn McClain*

potatoes, grains & beans

Bean Salad with Basil Vinaigrette

TOTAL: 25 MIN

8 SERVINGS ● ●

- 1 pound green beans or Romano beans, trimmed
- 1 pound yellow wax beans, trimmed
- ¼ cup plus 2 tablespoons extra-virgin olive oil
- ¼ cup balsamic vinegar
- 3 tablespoons shredded basil leaves
- 1 garlic clove, thinly sliced
- ½ teaspoon crushed red pepper

Two 15-ounce cans cannellini beans, drained

Salt and freshly ground black pepper

1. Bring a large pot of salted water to a boil. Add the green beans and yellow wax beans and cook until just tender, about 4 minutes. Drain, pat dry and let cool. Cut the beans into 2-inch lengths.

2. In a large bowl, mix the olive oil, balsamic vinegar, basil, garlic and crushed pepper. Fold in the cannellini beans and green and yellow beans. Season with salt and pepper, toss well. Serve. —*Mario Batali*

MAKE AHEAD The cooked green and yellow beans can be refrigerated overnight.

ingredient

grits

A type of corn porridge, grits consist of coarsely ground corn, traditionally produced by a stone mill. After grinding, the corn is passed through a screen; the finer part becomes cornmeal and the coarser becomes grits. In an F&W survey, chef Edward Lee of 610 Magnolia in Louisville, Kentucky, singled out grits as his pantry must-have. "Everyone should have a good bag of grits, preferably from Anson Mills." **Details** $4.95 for 12 oz; ansonmills.com.

Corn and Goat Cheese Grits

TOTAL: 1 HR

6 SERVINGS

This hearty yet elegant recipe for grits has been "citified" by the addition of lots of chopped garlic and fresh goat cheese. The end result is a tangy, creamy, corn-flecked side dish.

- 4 cups water
- ½ cup whole milk
- 2 tablespoons unsalted butter

Kosher salt

- 1 cup stone-ground cornmeal
- 2 tablespoons extra-virgin olive oil
- 1 large Spanish onion, coarsely chopped (1½ cups)
- 3 garlic cloves, coarsely chopped
- 1½ cups fresh corn kernels (3 ears) or one 10-ounce package frozen corn kernels

Freshly ground pepper

- 4 ounces fresh goat cheese

1. In a medium saucepan, combine the water with the milk, butter and 1 teaspoon of salt and bring to a boil. Slowly whisk the cornmeal into the boiling liquid. Cook the grits over moderate heat, stirring them frequently with a wooden spoon, until they are thickened and the grains are tender, about 40 minutes.

2. Meanwhile, in a medium skillet, heat the olive oil. Add the chopped onion and cook over moderate heat until the onion is softened, about 5 minutes. Add the garlic and the fresh corn kernels and cook, stirring occasionally, until the garlic is softened, about 5 minutes. Season the corn mixture with salt and pepper. Transfer the corn mixture to a food processor or blender and puree until the mixture is just smooth.

3. Stir the pureed corn and the goat cheese into the grits and season them with salt and pepper. Cook the grits just until heated through. Transfer the grits to a bowl and serve right away. —*Bobby Flay*

Grits with Wild Mushrooms and Sherry Broth

ACTIVE: 1 HR; TOTAL: 1 HR 30 MIN

6 SERVINGS

- 2 cups milk
- 1 cup stone-ground grits (see Note)

Salt

- 1 ounce dried porcini mushrooms (1 cup)
- 3 cups boiling water
- ¼ cup plus 1 tablespoon extra-virgin olive oil
- 1 small carrot, thinly sliced crosswise
- 1 small onion, thinly sliced crosswise
- 1 medium celery rib, thinly sliced crosswise
- 3 medium garlic cloves, lightly smashed
- 4 ounces large white or cremini mushrooms, thickly sliced
- ¼ teaspoon fennel seeds
- ¼ teaspoon black peppercorns
- 2 bay leaves
- 2 parsley sprigs
- 1 tarragon sprig
- 5 thyme sprigs
- 1 cup dry white wine
- 1 cup dry sherry
- 1 stick unsalted butter

Freshly ground pepper

- 1¼ pounds fresh porcini, chanterelles or stemmed shiitake mushrooms, thickly sliced
- ½ cup freshly grated Parmesan cheese
- ⅓ cup snipped chives

1. Preheat the oven to 300°. In a large ovenproof saucepan, bring the milk and 2 cups of water to a boil. Whisk in the grits and 1 teaspoon of salt and bring back to a boil, whisking constantly. Cover the grits with a tight-fitting lid and bake for 1 hour, or until the liquid is nearly absorbed and the grits are just tender; stir at least once with a wooden spoon while baking.

2. Meanwhile, in a heatproof bowl, combine the dried porcini with the 3 cups of boiling water and let soak until the porcini are softened, about 15 minutes. Drain the porcini and reserve 2 cups of the soaking liquid. Finely chop the porcini.

3. In a large saucepan, heat 3 tablespoons of the olive oil. Add the carrot, onion, celery and garlic and cook over moderate heat until the vegetables are softened, about 8 minutes. Add the white mushrooms and the chopped porcini mushrooms and cook until the mushrooms begin to brown, about 8 minutes. Add the fennel seeds, peppercorns, bay leaves, parsley, tarragon and 2 of the thyme sprigs. Stir in the wine and sherry and cook over moderate heat until reduced to ½ cup, about 10 minutes. Add the reserved 2 cups of porcini soaking liquid and boil until reduced to ¾ cup, about 15 minutes.

4. Strain the sherry broth into a small saucepan, pressing hard on the solids with a ladle or wooden spoon. Whisk in 3 tablespoons of the butter. Season the sherry broth with salt and pepper.

5. In a large, deep skillet, heat the remaining olive oil. Add the fresh porcini mushrooms and the remaining thyme sprigs; cook over moderately high heat until the mushrooms are golden brown, 10 minutes. Season with salt and pepper.

6. Return the grits to low heat and vigorously whisk in the remaining 5 tablespoons of butter and the Parmesan cheese. Stir in the chives, then season the grits with salt and pepper. Spoon the grits into warmed shallow bowls. Top the grits with the sautéed porcini and spoon the sherry broth all around. —*Douglas Keane*

NOTE Keane prefers stone-ground grits from Anson Mills (ansonmills.com) because of their intense corn flavor.

MAKE AHEAD The sautéed porcini and sherry broth can be refrigerated separately overnight. Gently reheat the porcini and the sherry broth separately.

Herbed Polenta and Parmesan Gratin

ACTIVE: 35 MIN; TOTAL: 4 HR

12 SERVINGS ● ○

These indulgent polenta squares, made with plenty of Parmesan, are just as good when made ahead and reheated.

- 1 **quart milk**
- 1 **quart water**
- 1 **stick unsalted butter**
- 1 **tablespoon plus 2 teaspoons kosher salt**
- 1 **tablespoon chopped rosemary**
- 12 **ounces polenta, not instant (2 cups)**
- 2 **large eggs**
- 1½ **cups freshly grated Parmesan cheese**
- 1½ **cups heavy cream**

1. Lightly oil a 15-by-12-inch rimmed baking sheet. In a saucepan, bring the milk, water and butter to a boil. Add the kosher salt and rosemary. Gradually whisk in the polenta until smooth. Bring to a simmer, whisking, until thickened. Cook over low heat for 15 minutes, stirring with a wooden spoon. Remove from the heat; cool for 10 minutes, stirring occasionally.

2. Whisk the eggs, one at a time, into the polenta, then whisk in 1 cup of cheese. Spread on the prepared baking sheet in an even layer. Let cool to room temperature. Cover with plastic and refrigerate until firm, at least 2 hours or overnight.

3. Preheat the oven to 400°. Lightly butter a 15-by-10-inch baking dish. Cut the polenta into 2-inch squares. Arrange the squares in the prepared dish in a single layer, overlapping them slightly. Pour the cream over the polenta and sprinkle the remaining Parmesan on top. Bake for 40 minutes, or until puffed and golden brown. Let stand for 10 to 15 minutes before serving. —*Maria Helm Sinskey*

MAKE AHEAD The recipe can be prepared through Step 2 and refrigerated for up to 2 days.

Fragrant Bean, Chickpea and Lentil Stew

ACTIVE: 25 MIN TOTAL: 2 HRS 30 MIN PLUS OVERNIGHT SOAKING

4 SERVINGS

- 1 **stick unsalted butter**
- 1 **medium onion, finely chopped**
- 1 **garlic clove, minced**
- 1 **teaspoon minced, peeled fresh ginger**
- ¼ **cup tomato paste**
- 2 **tablespoons plus 1½ teaspoons garam masala**
- 4 **cups water**
- ⅓ **cup dried French green lentils, rinsed and soaked overnight**
- ⅓ **cup dried black beans, rinsed and soaked overnight**
- ⅓ **cup dried chickpeas, rinsed and soaked overnight**
- ⅓ **cup dried red or pink beans, rinsed and soaked overnight**
- 1 **tablespoon fresh lemon juice**

Salt

1. In a large saucepan, melt 2 tablespoons of the butter. Add the chopped onion and cook over moderately low heat until softened, about 7 minutes. Add the garlic and ginger and cook over moderate heat until fragrant, about 1 minute. Add the tomato paste and the garam masala and cook, stirring, until glossy, about 3 minutes. Gradually stir in the water until the mixture is smooth.

2. Drain the soaked lentils, black beans, chickpeas and red beans. Add the lentils and beans to the saucepan and bring to a boil. Add the remaining 6 tablespoons of butter to the pan and simmer over low heat, stirring occasionally, until the beans are tender and the cooking liquid is thick, about 2½ hours. Stir in the lemon juice, season the stew with salt and serve. —*Sai Viswanath*

NOTE The stew can be refrigerated for up to 2 days. Reheat gently.

THAI SUMMER BEAN STEW
WITH CHICKEN

Thai Summer Bean Stew with Chicken

TOTAL: 1 HR

4 SERVINGS ● ● ●

    1 pound chicken cutlets,
       about ¼ inch thick
Salt and freshly ground pepper
    2 tablespoons canola oil
    1 tablespoon fresh lime juice, plus
       lime wedges for serving
    1 pound fresh fava beans, shelled
    1 cup light coconut milk
    2 teaspoons Thai green curry paste
    1 cup low-sodium chicken broth
    2 tablespoons Asian fish sauce
    1 tablespoon sugar
   10 basil leaves, plus more for garnish
   ¼ cup cilantro leaves, plus more
       for garnish
    1 small onion, thinly sliced
    1 pound mixed green beans and
       yellow wax beans, cut into
       1½-inch lengths
    2 ears of corn, shucked and
       cut crosswise into
       ½-inch thick rounds
Steamed jasmine rice, for serving

1. Light a grill. Season the chicken with salt and pepper and rub with 1 tablespoon of the oil and the lime juice. Grill over high heat until browned and cooked through, about 2½ minutes per side. Transfer the chicken to a carving board.

2. In a medium saucepan of boiling water, cook the fava beans just until bright green, about 2 minutes; drain and rinse under cold water. Working over a bowl, pop the beans out of their skins with your fingers.

3. In the same saucepan, whisk half of the coconut milk with the green curry paste. Whisk in the remaining coconut milk, ½ cup of the chicken broth, the fish sauce and the sugar and bring to a boil. Simmer over low heat for 5 minutes. Transfer the sauce to a blender. Add the 10 basil leaves and the ¼ cup of cilantro and puree.

4. In a large skillet, heat the remaining tablespoon of oil. Add the onion and cook over moderately high heat until lightly browned. Add the green beans, wax beans and corn and cook over high heat for 2 minutes, tossing frequently. Add the remaining ½ cup of broth. Cover the skillet and simmer the beans until tender, 3 minutes. Stir in the sauce and fava beans and simmer until just heated through. Season the stew with salt and pepper.

5. Slice the chicken crosswise into ½-inch strips. Ladle the stew into shallow bowls. Top with the chicken and garnish with basil and cilantro. Serve with lime wedges and jasmine rice.—*Susan Spungen*

Dirty Hoppin' John

ACTIVE: 20 MIN; TOTAL: 40 MIN

6 SERVINGS ● ●

Hoppin' John, a black-eyed pea dish said to have been invented by slaves, appears on holiday tables throughout the South. In this version, another Southern staple is included—dirty rice (white rice with chicken livers).

    3 tablespoons extra-virgin olive oil
    1 pound chicken livers, trimmed
Kosher salt and freshly ground pepper
    1 large red onion, finely chopped
    1 red bell pepper, finely chopped
    2 garlic cloves, minced
  1½ cups long-grain white rice
One 15-ounce can black-eyed peas,
       drained and rinsed, or
       one 10-ounce box frozen
       black-eyed peas, thawed
  2¾ cups chicken stock or broth
    4 thyme sprigs
    2 tablespoons chopped parsley
Hot sauce, for serving

1. In a saucepan, heat the olive oil. Add the chicken livers, season with salt and pepper; and sauté over high heat, turning once, until nearly cooked through, about 4 minutes. Using a slotted spoon, transfer the chicken livers to a plate and let cool. Chop the livers into ½-inch pieces.

2. Add the onion and bell pepper to the saucepan and cook over high heat, stirring until softened, about 5 minutes. Add the garlic and cook for 1 minute. Add the rice and stir for 1 minute, until coated. Add the peas, stock, thyme and 1½ teaspoons of salt and bring to a boil. Cover and cook over low heat until the rice is tender and the stock is absorbed, about 18 minutes.

3. Discard the thyme sprigs. Fluff the rice with a fork. Stir in the chicken livers and parsley, cover and let stand for 5 minutes. Transfer the rice to a bowl, fluff with a fork and serve right away with hot sauce. —*Bobby Flay*

Jasmine Rice with Spring Garlic

ACTIVE: 15 MIN; TOTAL: 30 MIN

10 SERVINGS ● ●

Spring garlic is young garlic that hasn't yet formed a large bulb; it has a long green stem that resembles a scallion. Here, it is used to add a delicate garlic-onion flavor to fragrant toasted jasmine rice.

    3 tablespoons extra-virgin olive oil
   10 ounces jasmine rice (1½ cups),
       rinsed
  1¼ cups thinly sliced spring garlic
       or 1 medium white onion,
       finely chopped, plus 6 garlic
       cloves, thinly sliced
    3 cups chicken stock or broth
    1 tablespoon kosher salt

1. Preheat the oven to 375°. In a medium cast-iron casserole, heat the olive oil until shimmering. Add the rice and spring garlic and cook over moderately high heat, stirring constantly, until the rice is lightly browned, about 5 minutes. Add the stock and salt and bring to a boil over high heat. Boil uncovered for 5 minutes, until the liquid is nearly absorbed.

2. Cover the rice and bake for 10 minutes, until tender but firm and the liquid is completely absorbed. Let stand, covered, for 5 minutes. Fluff the rice with a fork, transfer to a bowl. Serve. —*Mateo Granados*

potatoes, grains & beans

Crispy Grits with Sweet-and-Sour Beets and Mushrooms

ACTIVE: 1 HR; TOTAL: 3 HR

8 SERVINGS

- 3 large golden or red beets (1¼ pounds)
- 1½ cups extra-virgin olive oil, plus more for rubbing
- 1½ cups stone-ground white grits (see Note)
- 3 cups milk
- 3 cups water
- Salt
- 6½ tablespoons unsalted butter
- 1 large egg yolk
- Freshly ground pepper
- ½ pound mixed wild mushrooms, such as chanterelles and oysters, trimmed and thickly sliced
- 1 thyme sprig
- 2 tablespoons dry white wine
- 3 large shallots, thinly sliced
- ¼ cup white wine vinegar
- 1 tablespoon sugar
- ¼ cup snipped chives
- 1 cup rice flour
- 1 cup baby greens, for garnish

1. Preheat the oven to 350°. Line a 9-inch square baking dish with plastic wrap. Rub the beets lightly with olive oil and wrap individually in foil. Bake the beets for about 1 hour, or until tender when pierced with a fork. Let cool slightly.

2. In a medium enameled cast-iron casserole or Dutch oven, whisk the grits, milk, water and 1 teaspoon of salt. Bring to a boil over moderate heat, whisking constantly. Cover the grits. Bake in the oven for about 50 minutes, stirring 3 or 4 times. The grits are done when they're tender and the liquid has been absorbed.

3. Whisk 6 tablespoons of the butter and the egg yolk into the grits. Season with pepper. Spoon the grits into the prepared baking dish and press a sheet of plastic wrap directly onto the surface. Refrigerate them until firm, about 1 hour.

4. Peel the roasted beets and cut them into 1-inch pieces. Transfer the beet pieces to a large bowl.

5. In a medium skillet, heat 1 tablespoon of the olive oil until shimmering. Add the mushrooms and thyme sprig and season with salt and pepper. Cook over moderately high heat, stirring occasionally, until the liquid has evaporated and the mushrooms are lightly browned, about 8 minutes. Add the wine and the remaining ½ tablespoon of butter and cook, stirring, until evaporated, about 1 minute. Add the mushrooms to the beets. Discard the thyme sprig.

6. Wipe out the skillet. Add 2 tablespoons of the olive oil and heat until shimmering. Add the shallots and cook over moderate heat, stirring, until they are softened. Add the vinegar, sugar and a pinch of salt and cook until the liquid is slightly reduced, about 3 minutes. Stir in ¼ cup of the olive oil and add the dressing to the beets and mushrooms. Stir in the chives and season with salt and pepper.

7. Spread the rice flour on a plate. Turn the grits out onto a work surface; discard the plastic. Cut the grits in half, then cut each half into eight narrow 4½-inch-long rectangles. Dust the grits with rice flour. Divide the remaining 1 cup plus 1 tablespoon of olive oil between 2 large nonstick skillets and heat until shimmering. Add the grit cakes and fry over moderately high heat until golden and crisp all over, about 8 minutes total. Drain on paper towels and season lightly with salt. Transfer the cakes to a platter and top with the sweet-and-sour beets and mushrooms. Garnish with the baby greens and serve. —*Paul Kahan*

NOTE Kahan favors the white grits made by Byrd Mill in Ashland, Virginia. They're available at byrdmill.com.

MAKE AHEAD The recipe can be prepared through Step 4 and refrigerated for up to 2 days. Return the vegetables to room temperature before serving.

Polenta Gratin with Spinach and Wild Mushrooms

ACTIVE: 30 MIN; TOTAL: 1 HR 15 MIN

8 SERVINGS ●

Commercial wild mushroom mixes (usually a combination of shiitake, cremini and oyster mushrooms) are a godsend: Some invisible helper has already cleaned, stemmed and sliced the mushrooms for you. In this recipe, they are mixed with spinach and cream, then baked in a gratin under smooth rounds of precooked polenta until bubbling hot.

- 2 tablespoons extra-virgin olive oil
- 12 ounces sliced mixed wild mushrooms (5 cups)
- 1 large shallot, minced
- 8 ounces prewashed baby spinach (8 lightly packed cups)
- ½ teaspoon thyme
- Pinch of freshly grated nutmeg
- Salt and freshly ground pepper
- 1 tablespoon unsalted butter
- 1 tablespoon all-purpose flour
- ¾ cup chicken stock or low-sodium broth
- ½ cup cream
- One 18-ounce log of prepared polenta, cut into ¼-inch slices
- 3 ounces Gruyère cheese, shredded (1 cup)

1. Preheat the oven to 350°. In a large nonstick skillet, heat the olive oil. Add the mushrooms and cook over high heat, stirring occasionally, until lightly browned, about 6 minutes. Add the shallot and cook over moderately low heat for 3 minutes. Add the spinach, thyme and nutmeg and cook over high heat until the spinach has wilted, about 2 minutes. Season with salt and pepper. Spread the spinach evenly in a 2-quart baking dish.

2. In a small saucepan, melt the butter. Whisk in the flour over moderately high heat. Add the stock and cream and whisk until thickened, 5 minutes. Season lightly with salt and pepper; pour over the spin-

POLENTA GRATIN WITH SPINACH AND WILD MUSHROOMS

BUTTERNUT SQUASH RISOTTO WITH CRISPY PANCETTA

ach. Arrange the polenta on top of the spinach in overlapping concentric circles, pressing to submerge the polenta slightly. Sprinkle the Gruyère on the polenta, cover with foil and bake for 40 minutes.

3. Preheat the broiler. Uncover the polenta and broil 6 inches from the heat for 2 minutes, or until golden. Let stand for 10 minutes before serving. —*Grace Parisi*

MAKE AHEAD The unbaked gratin can be refrigerated overnight.

Butternut Squash Risotto with Crispy Pancetta

TOTAL: 45 MIN

8 SERVINGS

¼ pound thinly sliced pancetta, cut into ¼-inch strips

3 tablespoons extra-virgin olive oil

One 1½-pound butternut squash— peeled, halved, seeded and cut into 1½-by-¼-inch sticks

8 sage leaves

Kosher salt and freshly ground pepper

5½ cups chicken stock or low-sodium broth

4 tablespoons unsalted butter

1 medium onion, finely diced

19 ounces arborio rice (2½ cups)

1 cup dry white wine

½ cup freshly grated Parmesan cheese, plus more for serving

1. In a large skillet, cook the pancetta over moderate heat until crisp, about 4 minutes. Using a slotted spoon, transfer the pancetta to a medium bowl. Add 1 tablespoon of the olive oil to the fat in the skillet. Add the squash and cook over moderately high heat, stirring occasionally, until tender, about 8 minutes. Add the sage, season with salt and pepper and cook until aromatic, about 1 minute longer. Transfer the squash to the bowl with the pancetta.

2. In a medium saucepan, bring the stock to a simmer over moderately high heat. Reduce the heat to low and keep warm.

3. In a large saucepan, melt 3 tablespoons of the butter in the remaining 2 tablespoons of oil. Add the onion and cook over moderate heat, stirring occasionally, until softened. Add the rice and cook, stirring, for 2 minutes. Add the wine and cook, stirring constantly, until absorbed. Add ½ cup of the hot stock and cook, stirring, until absorbed. Continue adding the stock, about ½ cup at a time, and stirring constantly until it is nearly absorbed before adding more. The risotto is done when the rice is just tender and the liquid is creamy, about 20 minutes.

4. Stir the remaining 1 tablespoon of butter and the ½ cup of Parmesan into the risotto. Gently fold in the squash and pancetta. Spoon the risotto into warmed bowls, sprinkle with Parmesan and serve. —*Mary Ellen Carroll and Donna Wingate*

●FAST ●HEALTHY ●MAKE AHEAD ●STAFF FAVORITE

potatoes, grains & beans

Fregola and Blood Orange Salad with Arugula

ACTIVE: 25 MIN; TOTAL: 35 MIN

6 SERVINGS ● ●

Sardinian *fregola*, a cross between pasta and couscous, is made from a dough of coarsely ground semolina and water that is dried, toasted and grated into tiny pearls. Here, it's tossed with tender, juicy citrus sections for a hearty grain salad.

- 12 ounces *fregola* (2 cups)
- 2 thyme sprigs
- 1 bay leaf
- 1 small celery rib with leaves
- 1 large shallot, minced
- ¼ cup sherry vinegar
- 1 tablespoon fresh lemon juice
- 2 teaspoons minced preserved lemon peel (optional)
- 1 teaspoon Dijon mustard
- 1 teaspoon honey
- ½ cup extra-virgin olive oil
- Salt
- 4 blood oranges
- 6 ounces arugula (12 cups)
- Aged pecorino cheese shavings, for garnish

ingredients
new grains

Kalustyans house brand barley couscous is nuttier and has a grainier texture than classic couscous made from semolina. **Details** $2.99 for 1 lb at kalustyans.com.

Bangali brown Kalijira rice from Lotus Foods is distinguished by its surprisingly delicate texture and taste. This tiny aromatic brown rice grown in Bangladesh cooks in only 25 minutes, producing firm yet tender grains. **Details** $3.99 for 15 oz; lotusfoods.com.

1. In a large saucepan of boiling, salted water, cook the *fregola*, thyme, bay leaf and celery until al dente, about 12 minutes. Drain the *fregola* and spread on a large rimmed baking sheet to cool. Discard the thyme, bay leaf and celery.

2. In a small bowl, soak the shallot in the vinegar and lemon juice for 10 minutes. Stir in the preserved lemon peel, Dijon mustard and honey. Whisk in the olive oil and season the salad dressing with salt.

3. Using a sharp knife, peel the blood oranges, removing all of the bitter white pith. Working over a bowl, cut in between the membranes to release the sections.

4. In a bowl, toss the oranges with 2 tablespoons of dressing. In a large bowl, fold ½ cup of dressing into the *fregola*, then spoon into the center of a platter. Put the arugula in the bowl; toss with the remaining dressing. Arrange the arugula and oranges around the *fregola*, garnish with the cheese. Serve. —*Naomi Hebberoy*

Wild Rice Stuffing with Chestnuts and Sausage

ACTIVE: 1 HR; TOTAL: 2 HR 40 MIN

12 SERVINGS ●

- Water
- 1½ cups wild rice
- 4 tablespoons unsalted butter
- 3 onions, 1 finely chopped, 2 thinly sliced
- 2 garlic cloves, minced
- 1 celery rib, finely chopped
- 2 cups jasmine rice
- Kosher salt
- 1 pound pork breakfast sausage, casings removed
- ⅓ cup snipped chives
- 1 teaspoon chopped sage
- 1 teaspoon chopped thyme
- 8 ounces vacuum-packed chestnuts, coarsely chopped
- Freshly ground black pepper
- 3 cups Turkey Stock (p. 109) or low-sodium chicken broth
- 2 tablespoons cornstarch mixed with 2 tablespoons water

1. Preheat the oven to 350°. Butter a shallow 13-by-9-inch baking dish. Bring a large saucepan of water to a boil. Add the wild rice to the saucepan, cover partially and simmer over moderately low heat until tender, 45 minutes. Drain the rice well.

2. Meanwhile, melt 2 tablespoons of the butter in a medium saucepan. Add the chopped onion, garlic and celery and cook over moderately high heat, stirring occasionally, until the vegetables are softened, about 6 minutes. Add the jasmine rice to the saucepan and cook for 2 minutes, stirring. Add 2½ cups of water and 1 teaspoon of salt and bring to a boil. Cover and simmer over low heat until the water is absorbed and the rice is tender, about 18 minutes. Fluff the jasmine rice with a fork and transfer it to a large bowl.

3. In a medium skillet, melt the remaining tablespoons of butter. Add the sliced onions and cook over moderate heat, stirring occasionally, until softened and golden, about 15 minutes; add a few tablespoons of water if the onions dry out. Add the onions to the jasmine rice.

4. Add the sausage to the skillet. Cook over moderately high heat, breaking it up, until browned and cooked through, about 8 minutes. Stir in the chives, sage and thyme and scrape the mixture into the bowl. Add the chestnuts and drained wild rice, season with salt and pepper and stir gently.

5. Add the Turkey Stock to the skillet and scrape up any browned bits stuck to the bottom of the pan. Boil until the stock is reduced to 1½ cups, about 10 minutes. Stir the cornstarch slurry, then add it to the reduced stock and cook, stirring, until thickened, 2 to 3 minutes. Stir the stock into the stuffing and spread in the prepared baking dish. Cover the stuffing with aluminum foil and bake until sizzling, about 30 minutes. Serve hot. —*Grace Parisi*

Gnocchi with Wild Mushrooms

TOTAL: 30 MIN

6 SERVINGS ●

This simplified version of a restaurant recipe uses store-bought gnocchi and chicken stock instead of homemade. The topping is Parmesan cheese and truffle oil.

- 2 tablespoons extra-virgin olive oil
- 2 tablespoons unsalted butter
- 2 pounds mixed wild mushrooms, stemmed if necessary and thickly sliced (10 cups)
- 2 shallots, minced
- ¼ cup dry vermouth
- ¾ cup chicken stock or broth
- ½ cup heavy cream
- 1 teaspoon chopped thyme

Salt and freshly ground pepper
- 2 pounds fresh or frozen prepared gnocchi
- 6 tablespoons freshly grated Parmesan cheese
- 1 teaspoon white truffle oil (optional)

1. Preheat the broiler. In a large ovenproof skillet, heat the olive oil with the butter. Add the mushrooms and shallots and cook over high heat, stirring occasionally, until the mushrooms are browned, about 12 minutes. Add the vermouth and cook until it has evaporated. Add the chicken stock, cream and thyme, season with salt and pepper and bring to a boil.

2. Meanwhile, in a large pot of boiling salted water, cook the gnocchi until they float to the surface, about 3 minutes. Drain the gnocchi well. Add the gnocchi to the mushrooms and simmer, stirring, for 1 minute. Stir in ¼ cup of the Parmesan and sprinkle the remaining Parmesan on top.

3. Broil the gnocchi 6 inches from the heat for 2 to 3 minutes, until they are golden and bubbling. Drizzle the gnocchi and mushrooms with truffle oil and serve. —*Andrew Carmellini*

Greek-Style Vegetable Risotto

TOTAL: 30 MIN

4 TO 6 SERVINGS ● ●

- 6 cups vegetable stock or low-sodium broth
- ¼ cup extra-virgin olive oil
- 1 small onion, finely chopped
- 1 pound arborio rice (2 cups)
- 1 large zucchini (10 ounces), cut into ½-inch dice
- 4 scallions, thinly sliced crosswise
- ½ cup frozen peas, thawed

One ½-pound bunch of arugula, large stems discarded, leaves coarsely chopped

Kosher salt and freshly ground black pepper

Freshly grated Parmesan cheese, for serving

1. In a medium saucepan, bring 5 cups of the vegetable stock to a simmer. In another medium saucepan, heat 2 tablespoons of the olive oil. Add the onion to the oil and cook over moderate heat, stirring occasionally, until translucent, about 3 minutes. Add the rice and cook, stirring, for 1 minute. Add 1 cup of the hot stock and cook, stirring, until the stock is absorbed. Continue adding the hot stock, 1 cup at a time and stirring occasionally until completely absorbed before adding more. Continue cooking until the rice is al dente and the liquid is thickened, 20 minutes total.

2. Meanwhile, in a large skillet, heat the remaining olive oil. Add the zucchini and scallions and cook over moderately high heat until just tender, about 2 minutes. Add the peas and arugula and cook until the arugula is wilted, about 1 minute. Add the remaining 1 cup of vegetable stock, season with salt and pepper and bring to a simmer. Remove from the heat.

3. Stir the vegetables and their liquid into the risotto and cook until creamy, 1 minute. Season the risotto with salt and pepper. Spoon the risotto into bowls and serve with Parmesan cheese. —*Michael Psilakis*

White Beans with Escarole

ACTIVE: 35 MIN; TOTAL: 50 MIN

12 SERVINGS ● ●

This white bean salad, which could be made with any leftover cooked beans, features toasted croutons and a dressing flavored with lemon juice and shallot.

- 1 tablespoon minced shallot
- 2 teaspoons finely grated lemon zest
- ¼ cup fresh lemon juice

Pinch of sugar

Salt and freshly ground pepper
- ½ cup extra-virgin olive oil

Two 15-ounce cans cannellini beans, drained and rinsed
- 1 tablespoon chopped parsley
- ½ pound pancetta, sliced ¼ inch thick and cut into ½-inch pieces

Two 1-inch-thick slices of peasant bread, torn into ½-inch pieces (2 cups), toasted

Two 1-pound heads of escarole, tough dark leaves discarded, inner leaves torn into bite-size pieces

1. In a small bowl, combine the minced shallot with the lemon zest, lemon juice and sugar. Season the salad dressing with salt and pepper and let sit for 10 minutes. Whisk in 6 tablespoons of the olive oil. Transfer ¼ cup of the dressing to a large bowl, add the beans and parsley and let stand for 30 minutes.

2. In a skillet, cook the pancetta over moderate heat, stirring, until crisp, about 7 minutes. Using a slotted spoon, transfer the pancetta to a plate. Heat the remaining 2 tablespoons of oil in the skillet, then stir in the toasted bread and toss to coat.

3. Add the bread to the beans along with the escarole and the remaining dressing. Season with salt and pepper and toss. Serve right away. —*Maria Helm Sinskey*

MAKE AHEAD The salad can be prepared through Step 2 up to 4 hours ahead.

GOLDEN BASMATI RICE WITH APRICOTS (LEFT)
AND BARLEY AND ROASTED SQUASH PILAF

Golden Basmati Rice with Apricots

ACTIVE: 30 MIN; TOTAL: 1 HR 30 MIN

8 SERVINGS

- ¼ teaspoon saffron threads
- ¼ cup warm water
- 7 tablespoons unsalted butter
- 1 medium onion, finely chopped
- 2 garlic cloves, minced
- ¼ teaspoon cinnamon
- 2½ cups basmati rice
- 4 cups chicken stock
- 2 teaspoons salt
- 2 scallions, thinly sliced
- ⅔ cup salted roasted almonds, coarsely chopped
- 6 dried apricots, cut into ½-inch pieces
- 1 large Granny Smith apple, cored and cut into 1-inch pieces

Freshly ground pepper

1. Preheat the oven to 375°. In a small bowl, crumble the saffron over the warm water and let stand for 5 minutes. In a large skillet, melt 4 tablespoons of butter. Add the onion and garlic and cook over moderate heat until softened, about 7 minutes. Stir in the cinnamon. Add the rice and stir to coat. Add the stock, saffron, soaking liquid and salt and bring to a boil. Transfer to a 13-by-9-inch glass baking dish. Cover with foil and bake for 45 minutes, or until the stock is absorbed and the rice tender.

2. In a large skillet, melt the remaining butter. Cook the scallions over moderately high heat for 30 seconds. Add the almonds and apricots and cook until the apricots start to brown, 2 minutes. Add the apple and cook, stirring, just until warmed, 1 minute; stir into the rice, season with pepper and serve. —*Marcia Kiesel*

Barley and Roasted Squash Pilaf

ACTIVE: 45 MIN; TOTAL: 2 HR

8 TO 10 SERVINGS ●

- 4 cups peeled, diced (1-inch) butternut squash (1⅓ pounds)
- 17 small peeled shallots, 1 minced
- 12 small sage leaves
- 2 tablespoons extra-virgin olive oil

Salt and freshly ground pepper

- 3 tablespoons unsalted butter
- 14 ounces pearl barley (2 cups)
- 8 cups Turkey Stock (p. 109) or chicken stock
- 1½ cups vacuum-packed whole, roasted peeled chestnuts (about 9 ounces), coarsely chopped
- 2 tablespoons chopped parsley

1. Preheat the oven to 375°. On a large rimmed baking sheet, toss the diced squash with the whole shallots, sage and 1 tablespoon of the oil and season well with salt and pepper. Roast for 40 minutes, turning once, until the squash and shallots are softened and browned in spots. Crumble the sage. Leave the oven on.

2. In a large enameled cast-iron casserole, melt 1 tablespoon of butter in the remaining oil. Cook the barley over moderate heat, stirring, until golden, 7 minutes. Add the minced shallot and cook until softened. Add the stock and bring to a boil. Season with salt and pepper. Cover and bake for 35 minutes, until the barley is al dente.

3. Stir the chestnuts into the barley and simmer over moderate heat until the liquid is thickened and nearly absorbed, 5 minutes. Stir in the remaining butter, squash, shallots, sage and parsley. Season with salt and pepper. Serve. —*Grace Parisi*

Buckwheat Salad with Mushrooms and Parsley Oil

ACTIVE: 35 MIN; TOTAL: 50 MIN

4 SERVINGS ●

- 2 cups lightly packed parsley leaves (8 ounces), 1 cup chopped parsley
- ⅓ cup plus 2 tablespoons extra-virgin olive oil

Salt

- 1½ cups buckwheat groats (kasha)
- ½ pound each shiitake and oyster mushrooms, stemmed, large caps quartered

Freshly ground black pepper

- 2 tablespoons balsamic vinegar
- 2 tablespoons fresh lemon juice, plus lemon wedges, for serving
- 1 garlic clove, minced
- 1 tablespoon dark soy sauce
- 2 large scallions, thinly sliced
- 1 medium fennel bulb, diced

1. Bring a saucepan of water to a boil. Prepare a bowl of ice water. Blanch the 1 cup of parsley leaves in the boiling water for 20 seconds. With a slotted spoon, transfer the parsley to the ice water. Drain the parsley, squeeze out the excess water and pat thoroughly dry. In a blender, puree the blanched parsley with ⅓ cup of the olive oil. Transfer to a bowl and season with salt.

2. Bring a medium saucepan of water to a boil. In a large skillet, toast the groats over moderately high heat, shaking the pan often, until lightly browned, 3 minutes. Let cool slightly, then transfer to the boiling water. Simmer over low heat, stirring often, until just tender but still holding its shape, 5 minutes. Drain the groats, spread out on a large rimmed baking sheet and let cool to room temperature.

3. Heat the remaining 2 tablespoons of olive oil in the large skillet. Add the mushrooms and season generously with salt and pepper. Cover and cook over moderate heat, stirring occasionally, until the mushrooms have released their liquid, about 5 minutes. Uncover and cook, stirring occasionally, until the mushrooms are golden brown, about 5 minutes longer.

4. In a small bowl, mix all but 1 tablespoon of the parsley oil with the balsamic vinegar, lemon juice, garlic and soy sauce.

5. In a large bowl, toss the buckwheat groats, sliced scallions, diced fennel and the 1 cup of chopped parsley with the dressing; season with salt and pepper and transfer to a platter. Top the salad with the sautéed mushrooms and drizzle with the remaining 1 tablespoon of parsley oil. Serve with the lemon wedges. —*Melissa Clark*

ROASTED RED PEPPER SANDWICHES (P. 294)

breads, pizzas & sandwiches

"Our agenda is understanding everyone's role in the final product—the farmer, miller, server, pizzamaker. We don't slide pizza under your door in a white box."

—**Chris Bianco,** chef and owner, Pizzeria Bianco, Phoenix, Arizona

ONION-MUSTARD MONKEY BREAD AND MAPLE-THYME BISCUITS

SHRIMP AND CHORIZO FLATBREADS

Onion-Mustard Monkey Bread

ACTIVE: 30 MIN; TOTAL: 3 HR 30 MIN

10 TO 12 SERVINGS ●

These buttery, onion-flecked, pull-apart rolls are an irresistible cross between classic Parker House rolls and bialys.

- 1 **stick unsalted butter, plus more for coating**
- 1½ **cups milk**
- 2 **tablespoons sugar**
- 1 **envelope dry active yeast**
- 4 **cups all-purpose flour, plus more for dusting**

Salt

- 1 **medium onion, finely chopped**
- 3 **tablespoons whole-grain mustard**
- 2 **tablespoons snipped chives**
- 1 **teaspoon chopped thyme**

1. In a medium saucepan, melt 3 tablespoons of the butter. Add the milk and sugar and heat just until warm. Transfer the mixture to a large bowl, stir in the yeast and let stand until foamy, about 5 minutes. Stir in the flour and 1½ teaspoons of salt until a sticky dough forms. Turn the dough out onto a lightly floured work surface and knead until smooth, about 5 minutes. Oil the bowl and return the dough to it. Cover the bowl with plastic wrap and let stand in a draft-free spot until doubled in bulk, about 1 hour.

2. Butter a 10-inch tube or Bundt pan. Punch down the dough and divide it into 4 pieces. Roll each piece into a 12-inch-long log and cut each log into 12 equal pieces. Roll each piece into a ball.

3. Heat 1 tablespoon of the butter in a medium skillet. Add the onion and cook over moderate heat until softened, about 6 minutes. Stir in the whole-grain mustard, snipped chives and chopped thyme. Add the remaining 4 tablespoons of butter; stir until melted. Season the onion mixture lightly with salt and transfer to the large

bowl to cool slightly. Add half of the dough balls to the bowl and turn to coat with the onion mixture. Arrange the dough balls in the bottom of the prepared pan. Repeat with the remaining dough balls. Cover the monkey bread loosely with plastic wrap and let stand until it has risen to the top of the pan, about 1 hour.

4. Preheat the oven to 425°. Bake the bread in the lower third of the oven for 25 minutes, or until the top is golden. Cover the pan loosely with foil, reduce the oven temperature to 375° and bake for 30 minutes longer, or until risen. Let the bread cool in the pan for 15 minutes. Set an inverted plate on top and turn the bread out onto it. Set another plate on top and invert the bread so it's right side up. Break into rolls or cut into slices. —*Grace Parisi*

MAKE AHEAD The monkey bread can be prepared through Step 3 and refrigerated overnight.

Shrimp and Chorizo Flatbreads

TOTAL: 30 MIN

4 SERVINGS ● ●

One 14-ounce can diced tomatoes,
    drained, ¼ cup of juices reserved
2 tablespoons extra-virgin olive oil
1 tablespoon honey
1 tablespoon white wine vinegar
1 teaspoon chopped thyme
1 small shallot, minced
1 garlic clove, minced
2 tablespoons coarsely chopped
    flat-leaf parsley
Pinch of crushed red pepper
Salt and freshly ground pepper
½ cup prepared hummus
4 pocketless pita breads
½ cup thinly sliced chorizo
    (2 ounces)
½ pound shelletrd and deveined raw
    medium shrimp, halved
    lengthwise
¼ pound Manchego cheese,
    shredded (1 cup)

1. Preheat the oven to 500° and position a rack in the center. In a bowl, mix the tomatoes and their juices with the olive oil, honey, vinegar, thyme, shallot, garlic, parsley and crushed pepper; season the tomato dressing with salt and pepper.

2. Spread the hummus on the pitas and top with the chorizo, shrimp and cheese. Bake directly on the oven rack for about 4 minutes, or until the shrimp are cooked and the cheese is melted. Transfer the flatbreads to a work surface. Using a slotted spoon, top with the dressing. Quarter the flatbreads and serve. —*Jose Garces*

Buttery Maple-Thyme Biscuits

ACTIVE: 20 MIN; TOTAL: 1 HR 10 MIN

MAKES 8 BISCUITS

2 thyme sprigs plus 1 teaspoon
    coarsely chopped thyme
¼ cup pure maple syrup
2¼ cups all-purpose flour, plus
    more for dusting
1 tablespoon baking powder
½ teaspoon table salt
1½ sticks cold unsalted butter,
    cut into ½-inch pieces
¾ cup plus 1 tablespoon milk
Coarse sea salt

1. In a small saucepan, cover the thyme sprigs with the maple syrup and simmer over moderate heat for 1 minute; set the maple syrup aside to cool. When it is cool, discard the thyme sprigs.

2. In a large bowl, whisk the flour with the baking powder, table salt and the 1 teaspoon of chopped thyme. Cut the chilled butter into the flour until the pieces are pea size. Make a well in the center of the flour mixture and pour in the milk. Stir with a fork until the dough is evenly moistened. Turn the dough out onto a lightly floured work surface and gather into a ball.

3. Roll out the biscuit dough until ¾ inch thick. Using a floured 2¾-inch round cookie cutter, stamp out the biscuits as close together as possible. Gather the scraps, press them together and stamp out more biscuits. Transfer the biscuits to a parchment paper–lined baking sheet and refrigerate for 30 minutes.

4. Preheat the oven to 400°. Using a pastry brush, brush the biscuits with the glaze and then sprinkle with sea salt. Bake in the upper third of the oven for 20 minutes, or until they are golden. Serve the biscuits while still warm. —*Melissa Rubel*

Grilled Camp Bread

ACTIVE: 30 MIN; TOTAL: 3 HR 30 MIN

MAKES 4 LARGE FLATBREADS

1 envelope instant dry yeast
1⅔ cups warm water
Pinch of sugar
5 cups all-purpose flour
1 tablespoon kosher salt
1 tablespoon coarsely ground
    black pepper
¼ cup extra-virgin olive oil, plus
    more for brushing

1. In the bowl of a standing electric mixer fitted with a dough hook, combine the yeast, warm water and sugar and let stand until foamy, 5 minutes. Add the flour, salt, pepper and the ¼ cup of olive oil and mix at medium-low speed until a soft, supple dough forms, 5 minutes. Form the dough into a ball and cut into fourths. Lightly oil each piece and wrap individually in plastic. Refrigerate for at least 3 hours.

2. Light a grill. On a lightly oiled work surface, unwrap one piece of dough and press and stretch into a 12-by-8-inch rectangle. Transfer to an oiled baking sheet. Repeat with the remaining dough. Brush the dough on both sides with oil. Grill the bread over moderate heat (working in batches, if necessary), turning occasionally, until puffed and lightly charred in spots, 4 minutes total. Serve right away. —*Tim Love*

Herbed Garlic Bread

TOTAL: 20 MIN

6 SERVINGS ●

1 stick unsalted butter
6 large garlic cloves, thickly
    sliced (¼ cup)
4 thyme sprigs
1 rosemary sprig
Coarse sea salt
1 large baguette, halved and then
    split lengthwise
Pimentón de la Vera (smoked Spanish
    paprika) (optional)

1. Preheat the broiler. Melt the butter in a skillet. Add the garlic, thyme and rosemary and cook over moderately low heat, stirring occasionally, until the garlic is softened and golden, 12 minutes. Discard the herb sprigs. Using a slotted spoon, transfer the garlic and any loose herbs to a bowl and mash to a paste; season with salt.

2. Spread the bread with the garlic paste; brush with the butter left in the skillet. Sprinkle lightly with salt and paprika. Broil 8 inches from the heat for 1 minute, or until sizzling and browned. —*Grace Parisi*

breads, pizzas & sandwiches

Fontina, Prosciutto and Caramelized Onion Flatbreads

ACTIVE: 45 MIN; TOTAL: 1 HR 40 MIN

4 SERVINGS

DOUGH

- 1 envelope active dry yeast
- 1 cup warm water

Pinch of sugar

- 1 teaspoon extra-virgin olive oil, plus more for coating
- 1 teaspoon chopped thyme
- 1 teaspoon salt

About 2⅓ cups all-purpose flour

TOPPINGS

- 3 tablespoons extra-virgin olive oil
- 2 pounds white onions, thinly sliced and separated into rings

Salt and freshly ground pepper

- ¾ pound Italian Fontina cheese, sliced
- 8 thin slices of prosciutto
- 2 tablespoons grapeseed oil
- 1 tablespoon white truffle oil
- 2 tablespoons sherry vinegar
- 1 tart-sweet apple, such as Fuji— peeled, cored and cut into matchsticks
- 4 ounces arugula (6 cups)

ingredient
truffle salt

Most coveted new ingredient: truffle salt from **FungusAmongUs**. It's far more fragrant than truffle oil and is great on pizzas. **Details** $17 for 3.5 oz; fungusamongus.com.

---

1. In a bowl, mix the yeast, water and sugar. Let stand until foamy, 5 minutes. Add the olive oil, thyme and salt. Add 2 cups of the flour and stir until a very soft, wet dough forms. Turn the dough out onto a lightly floured work surface and knead, working in about ⅓ cup more flour, until soft and silky. Shape into a ball and place in a large, oiled bowl. Cover and let rise at room temperature until doubled in bulk, 1 hour.

2. Preheat the oven to 450°. Oil 2 large baking sheets. Heat the olive oil in a large, deep skillet. Add the onions and stir to coat. Cover and cook over moderate heat, stirring occasionally, until the onions are softened, 5 minutes. Raise the heat to high and cook uncovered, until the onions are golden brown, 8 minutes. If the onions dry out, add a few tablespoons of water to the skillet. Season with salt and pepper, transfer to a plate and let cool slightly.

3. Punch down the dough and turn out onto a lightly floured work surface. Divide into 8 equal pieces. Roll each piece out to a 9-by-3-inch rectangle and arrange on the prepared baking sheets. Top with the Fontina, onions and prosciutto. Bake until golden and crisp, 25 minutes.

4. In a large bowl, whisk the grapeseed oil with the truffle oil and vinegar and season with salt and pepper. Add the apple and arugula and toss. Top the hot flatbreads with the arugula salad and serve.
—*Betty Fraser and Cliff Crooks*

Pizza Bianca with Truffle Oil

TOTAL: 45 MIN

4 SERVINGS ●

Ricotta and creamy Taleggio cheeses top these wonderful white pizzas. In a final touch of decadence, the pies are drizzled with a little truffle oil right before serving.

- 1 tablespoon unsalted butter
- 1 medium onion, halved lengthwise and thinly sliced
- 1 tablespoon water
- 1 teaspoon white wine vinegar

Salt and freshly ground white pepper

- 1½ cups ricotta, preferably fresh
- 2 tablespoons extra-virgin olive oil, plus more for brushing
- 2 teaspoons fresh lemon juice
- 2 heads frisée, inner white leaves only (3 cups)
- 1½ pounds frozen pizza dough, thawed and shaped into 2 balls
- ½ pound Taleggio cheese, rind removed, cheese cut into 1-inch pieces
- 2 tablespoons pine nuts

White truffle oil, for drizzling

1. Preheat the oven to 500°. Set a pizza stone in the bottom of the oven and heat for at least 30 minutes.

2. Meanwhile, in a medium saucepan, melt the butter. Add the onion, cover and cook over moderately low heat, stirring occasionally, until softened but not browned, about 10 minutes. Add the water when the pan gets dry. Add the vinegar, transfer the onion to a bowl and season with salt and pepper. In a medium bowl, season the ricotta with salt and pepper.

3. In another medium bowl, whisk the 2 tablespoons of olive oil with the lemon juice. Add the frisée and season with salt and pepper.

4. On a lightly floured work surface, roll or stretch one ball of dough into a 14-inch round. Transfer the dough to a lightly floured pizza peel or inverted baking sheet and brush the edge with olive oil. Spread half of the ricotta on the dough, leaving a 1-inch border. Top with half each of the onion, Taleggio and pine nuts. Slide the pizza onto the preheated stone and bake for 5 to 6 minutes, until golden and bubbling. Drizzle lightly with truffle oil, cut into wedges and serve at once with half of the frisée salad on the side. Repeat with the remaining ingredients to make the second pizza and serve hot, with the rest of the frisée salad. —*Grace Parisi*

Grilled Margherita and Olive-Fontina Pizzas

ACTIVE: 45 MIN; TOTAL: 1 HR 45 MIN
PLUS OVERNIGHT RESTING
MAKES FOUR 10-INCH PIZZAS (8 SERVINGS)

DOUGH

- 2 tablespoons honey
- 3 cups warm water
- 2 packages dry active yeast
- 7 cups all-purpose flour, plus more for dusting
- ¼ cup extra-virgin olive oil, plus more for rubbing
- 3 tablespoons kosher salt

OLIVE-FONTINA TOPPING

- ½ cup pine nuts
- ½ pound Italian Fontina cheese, coarsely shredded (2 cups)
- ½ cup pitted black Moroccan olives, chopped

MARGHERITA TOPPING

- 2 cups tomato sauce
- ½ pound mozzarella, coarsely shredded (2 cups)
- ½ cup torn basil leaves

Maldon salt, for sprinkling (see Note)

1. MAKE THE DOUGH: In a very large bowl, stir the honey into the water until dissolved. Sprinkle the yeast over the water and let stand until foamy, about 8 minutes. Stir in the flour, the ¼ cup of olive oil and the salt until blended. Turn the dough out onto a lightly floured surface and knead until smooth. Place the dough in an oiled bowl, cover with plastic wrap and let stand in a warm place until doubled in volume, about 1 hour.

2. On the floured work surface, punch down the dough and cut into 4 pieces. Roll each piece into a ball and place on an oiled baking sheet. Rub the dough balls with oil, cover with plastic and refrigerate overnight.

3. Light a grill. When the coals are hot, push two-thirds to one side for a hot fire; spread the remaining coals on the other side for a medium-hot fire.

4. PREPARE THE OLIVE-FONTINA PIZZAS: In a small cast-iron skillet, toast the pine nuts over the medium-hot fire, shaking the pan, until the nuts are golden and fragrant, about 1 minute. Arrange all the topping ingredients near the grill.

5. On a lightly oiled work surface or sheet pan, press 1 dough ball into a thin, roughly shaped, 10-inch round. Repeat with the remaining balls. Carefully set 1 round over the hot fire and grill until firm on the bottom and easy to lift, 1 minute. Using tongs, move the crust to the medium-hot fire and continue grilling until the bottom is deeply browned and blistered, 2 minutes. Carefully flip the crust and return to the hot fire until cooked through, 1 minute.

6. Slide the crust back to the medium-hot fire and top with 1 cup of the Fontina and ¼ cup each of the olives and pine nuts. Cover the grill and cook until the cheese is melted, about 2 minutes. Transfer to a cutting board; cut into pieces and serve. Grill another round, and top it with the remaining Fontina, olives and pine nuts.

7. PREPARE THE MARGHERITA PIZZAS: Grill another round on both sides. Slide the pizza to a medium-hot fire; spread it with 1 cup of the tomato sauce and top with 1 cup of the cheese. Cover the grill and cook until the cheese melts, 2 minutes. Transfer to a cutting board and scatter half of the basil on top. Sprinkle the pizza with Maldon salt, cut into pieces and serve. Repeat with the remaining ingredients.
—*Mario Batali*

NOTE English Maldon salt—which has a mild flavor—is available at specialty food stores.

Spicy Snapper Sandwiches

TOTAL: 30 MIN
4 SERVINGS ●●

- 1 teaspoon finely grated lime zest
- 2 tablespoons fresh lime juice
- 2 garlic cloves, minced
- 1 Thai or serrano chile, minced
- 1 tablespoon extra-virgin olive oil

Four 6-ounce red snapper fillets

Salt and freshly ground pepper

- ¼ cup mayonnaise
- ½ tablespoon capers, chopped
- 4 rolls or buns, split
- 4 Bibb or romaine lettuce leaves
- 4 thin slices red onion

1. Preheat the oven to 400°. In a bowl, mix half of the lime zest and half of the lime juice with half of the garlic and half of the chile. Stir in the olive oil. Make 3 shallow 2-inch slashes in the skin of each fish fillet. Spread the garlic-chile paste over the fish. Transfer to a baking dish, skin side up, and season with salt and pepper. Bake for 8 minutes, or until the fish flakes easily.

2. Meanwhile, in another small bowl, combine the mayonnaise, capers and remaining lime zest, lime juice, garlic and chile. Season the sauce with salt and pepper.

3. Toast the rolls. Spread the sauce on the rolls and top with the fish, lettuce and onion. Close the sandwiches and serve.
—*Annie Wayte*

Mortadella Sandwiches with Grapes, Mushrooms and Tapenade

TOTAL: 25 MIN
MAKES 2 SANDWICHES ●

- 2 ounces trumpet royal or oyster mushrooms
- 1 tablespoon extra-virgin olive oil

Salt and freshly ground pepper

- 3 tablespoons mayonnaise
- 3 tablespoons jarred tapenade
- 4 slices toasted sourdough bread
- ½ cup sliced red grapes
- 6 ounces sliced mortadella
- 1 teaspoon chopped parsley

In a medium skillet, sauté the mushrooms in the olive oil until tender; season with salt and pepper. Mix the mayonnaise with the tapenade and spread on the toast. Top half of the slices with the mushrooms, grapes, mortadella and parsley. Close the sandwiches, halve and serve. —*Harold Dieterle*

breads, pizzas & sandwiches

Open-Faced Reuben Sandwiches

TOTAL: 40 MIN

4 SERVINGS ●

½ small head of green cabbage, cored and finely shredded (3 cups)

1½ tablespoons kosher salt

2 tablespoons sugar

2 tablespoons cider vinegar

¼ small red bell pepper, thinly sliced

¼ yellow bell pepper, thinly sliced

½ small red onion, thinly sliced

2 scallions, thinly sliced

2 teaspoons poppy seeds

1½ tablespoons Dijon mustard

Freshly ground pepper

2 tablespoons extra-virgin olive oil

Four ½-inch-thick slices of pastrami (about 1¼ pounds)

4 slices rye bread

¼ pound sliced Swiss cheese

1. In a large bowl, toss the cabbage, salt and sugar. Using your hands, crush and squeeze the cabbage to release the liquid. Let stand for 10 minutes, crushing and squeezing until very soupy; transfer to a colander. Rinse briefly with cold water and squeeze out as much liquid as possible; you should have about 1 cup of cabbage. Transfer to a medium bowl and add the vinegar, bell peppers, onion, scallions, poppy seeds and ½ tablespoon of the mustard. Season the slaw with pepper.

2. Preheat a broiler. In a small bowl, combine the remaining 1 tablespoon of mustard with 1 tablespoon of the olive oil. Brush the pastrami slices with the mustard oil and the bread with the remaining 1 tablespoon of olive oil. Transfer the bread to a baking sheet and toast under the broiler, turning, until golden, 3 minutes. Top the toasted bread with the cheese and the pastrami. Broil just until the cheese is melted and the pastrami is warmed through, 2 minutes. Transfer the open-face sandwiches to plates, garnish with the cabbage slaw and serve. —*David Burke*

Crispy Fried Chicken Sandwiches

TOTAL: 30 MIN

4 SERVINGS ●

Executive chef John Hennigan of LuLu Petite in San Francisco substitutes a creamy artichoke tapenade here for the mayonnaise usually used in fried chicken sandwiches.

½ cup all-purpose flour

1 large egg

2 tablespoons water

1 cup *panko* (Japanese bread crumbs) or coarse dry bread crumbs

Four 4-ounce chicken cutlets, pounded ¼ inch thick

Salt and freshly ground pepper

Vegetable oil

4 teaspoons honey, warmed in the microwave, for drizzling

Eight ⅓-inch-thick slices ciabatta or other chewy country bread, lightly toasted

½ cup jarred artichoke tapenade, preferably with truffles

4 crisp romaine lettuce leaves

2 plum tomatoes, thinly sliced

1. Spread the flour in a shallow bowl. In another shallow bowl, beat the egg with the water. Put the *panko* in a third shallow bowl. Season the chicken cutlets with salt and pepper, then dredge them in the flour, shaking off any excess. Dip the cutlets in the egg, letting any excess drip off, and then coat with the *panko*.

2. In a very large skillet, heat ¼ inch of oil until shimmering. Add the cutlets and fry over high heat until golden brown and cooked through, about 2½ minutes per side. Drain the cutlets on paper towels.

3. Lightly drizzle the honey on 4 of the toast slices. Spread 2 tablespoons of the tapenade on each of the remaining 4 slices. Set a lettuce leaf on the tapenade and top with the cutlets and tomatoes. Close the sandwiches, cut in half and serve. —*John Hennigan*

Grilled Salmon Sandwiches

TOTAL: 30 MIN

4 SERVINGS ●

One of the great things about roasting a whole salmon is that there are usually leftovers. Any extra salmon can be used in this exquisite riff on the BLT, which layers the fish with bacon and watercress. The sandwich would be equally good made with another kind of roasted fish, such as bluefish or cod.

8 slices of ciabatta or peasant bread

3 tablespoons extra-virgin olive oil

12 slices of bacon (about ¾ pound)

½ cup mayonnaise

1¼ pounds leftover roasted salmon or other leftover roasted fish (approximately 3 cups)

1 tablespoon fresh lemon juice

Salt and freshly ground pepper

1 bunch of watercress (6 ounces), thick stems discarded

1. Light a grill. Brush the slices of ciabatta bread on both sides with 2 tablespoons of the olive oil and grill the bread over high heat until it is toasted on both sides, about 2 minutes.

2. Meanwhile, in a large skillet, cook the bacon slices over moderately high heat until crisp, about 6 minutes. Drain the bacon on paper towels.

3. Spread the mayonnaise on the slices of toasted bread. Divide the salmon between 4 of the toasted slices and top the fish with the crispy bacon. In a medium bowl, combine the lemon juice with the remaining 1 tablespoon of olive oil. Season the dressing with salt and pepper. Add the watercress to the dressing in the bowl and toss to coat the greens. Mound the dressed watercress on top of the bacon. Close the grilled salmon sandwiches, cut them in half and serve immediately. —*Tim Love*

GRILLED SALMON SANDWICHES

PULLED-CHICKEN SANDWICH

MEAT LOAF CLUB SANDWICH

Pulled-Chicken Sandwiches

TOTAL: 30 MIN

4 SERVINGS ● ●

- 2 cups cider vinegar
- 1½ cups water
- 1 cup dry white wine
- ⅓ cup vegetable oil
- 3 tablespoons Worcestershire sauce
- 2 tablespoons dry mustard
- 1 tablespoon sweet paprika
- 2 teaspoons kosher salt
- 1 teaspoon freshly ground black pepper
- ½ teaspoon cayenne pepper

One 3½-pound rotisserie chicken

- 4 hamburger buns, split
- 1 cup prepared coleslaw

1. In a medium saucepan, combine the vinegar with the water, wine, oil, Worcestershire sauce, mustard, paprika, salt, black pepper and cayenne and boil over high heat until reduced to 1¼ cups, about 15 minutes. Remove the warm vinegar sauce from the heat.

2. Meanwhile, remove all of the meat from the chicken and shred it. Discard the skin. Add the chicken to the warm vinegar sauce and heat through, stirring gently. Pile the pulled chicken on the buns and drizzle with extra vinegar sauce. Top with the coleslaw, close the sandwiches and serve right away.
—*Amy Tornquist*

Meat Loaf Club Sandwiches

TOTAL: 30 MIN

4 SERVINGS ● ●

- 10 slices of bacon, 2 slices coarsely chopped
- 2 garlic cloves
- 3 tablespoons dry bread crumbs
- 3 tablespoons freshly grated Parmesan cheese
- 3 tablespoons milk
- 1 large egg
- ½ teaspoon chopped thyme
- ¼ teaspoon finely chopped rosemary

½ teaspoon hot sauce

Kosher salt and freshly ground pepper

¾ pound lean ground sirloin

12 slices white or sourdough bread

2 tablespoons extra-virgin olive oil

¼ cup mayonnaise

1 chipotle chile in adobo sauce, stemmed and chopped

2 beefsteak tomatoes, thinly sliced

4 Bibb or romaine lettuce leaves

Cornichons and mustard, for serving

1. Preheat the oven to 375°. Line a baking sheet with a wire rack. In a food processor, pulse the chopped bacon with the garlic cloves until minced. Add the bread crumbs, Parmesan, milk, egg, thyme, rosemary and hot sauce, season generously with salt and pepper and process to a paste. Transfer the paste to a medium bowl and knead in the ground sirloin.

2. Preheat a griddle or grill pan. Spread the meat mixture evenly on 4 slices of the white bread. Top with another 4 slices of bread and brush both sides of the sandwiches with olive oil. Brush the remaining 4 slices of white bread lightly with olive oil and set aside. Place the sandwiches on the griddle and top with a heavy skillet. Cook over moderate heat, turning the sandwiches once, until they are golden, about 6 minutes total. Transfer the sandwiches to the rack and bake until the meat is cooked through, about 8 minutes.

3. Meanwhile, in a medium skillet, cook the remaining 8 slices of bacon until crisp, about 6 minutes. Drain on paper towels. Toast the remaining 4 slices of white bread on the griddle until golden, about 2 minutes per side.

4. In a small bowl, blend the mayonnaise with the chopped chipotle chile. Spread the mayonnaise on the meat loaf sandwiches and top with the bacon, tomatoes, lettuce and toasted bread. Cut each meat loaf sandwich in half. Secure each half with a toothpick and serve with cornichons and mustard. —David Burke

Beef Tenderloin Sandwiches with Shiitake Sauce

ACTIVE: 1 HR; TOTAL: 1 HR 30 MIN

6 SERVINGS

1 stick unsalted butter, cut into tablespoons

6 garlic cloves, minced

4 scallions, minced

1½ pounds shiitake mushrooms, stemmed, caps thinly sliced

1½ teaspoons chile powder

1½ teaspoons dried thyme

Coarsely ground pepper

2 cups beef stock or broth

2 cups dry red wine

1 tablespoon soy sauce

1 teaspoon cornstarch dissolved in 1 tablespoon cold water

Salt

2 baguettes

2 pounds filet mignon, sliced ½ inch thick

Extra-virgin olive oil, for brushing

1. In a large, deep skillet, melt 4 tablespoons of butter. Add one-third of the garlic and all of the scallions and cook over moderately high heat for 1 minute. Add the shiitakes and cook until slightly softened, about 2 minutes. Add the chile powder, thyme and 1 teaspoon of pepper and cook over moderate heat, stirring occasionally, until the shiitakes begin to brown, 5 minutes. Add the stock, wine and soy sauce; bring to a boil. Simmer gently until reduced to 1 cup, 40 minutes. Stir the cornstarch slurry and whisk into the liquid. Cook, stirring, until slightly thickened, 2 minutes. Season with salt; keep warm.

2. Preheat the broiler. Cut the baguettes into thirds and split lengthwise, taking care not to cut all the way through. In a saucepan, melt the remaining butter and add the remaining garlic. Cook over low heat until fragrant. Brush the bread with the butter, sprinkle lightly with salt and broil for 1 minute, cut side up, until golden.

3. Preheat a grill pan. Brush the steak with oil; season with salt and pepper. Grill the meat in batches over high heat, turning once, until charred and medium rare, about 5 minutes. Dip the meat in the mushroom sauce and arrange on the baguettes. Spoon the mushroom sauce on top, close the sandwiches and serve —Andy Ayers

Philly Cheesesteak Panini

TOTAL: 20 MIN

6 SERVINGS ●

This is an ingenious way to transform packaged garlic bread: Scrape out the garlic butter, spread it all over the crust, then stuff the bread with beef and cheese and grill it: The result is a crisp panini.

¼ cup drained pickled peppers, such as peperoncini, stemmed and chopped

One 6½-ounce jar marinated artichokes, drained and chopped

3 tablespoons sliced green olives

2 tablespoons chopped dill pickles

2 loaves frozen garlic bread (each about 12 inches long), thawed

1 pound sliced lean, rare roast beef

7 ounces sliced provolone cheese

1. Preheat a panini press or cast-iron griddle. In a bowl, mix the peppers, artichokes, olives and pickles. Open the garlic bread and scrape off most of the spread; transfer the spread to a small plate.

2. Spread the pickle mixture on the bread bottoms. Top with the roast beef and provolone and close the sandwiches. Spread the reserved spread on the outside of the loaves. Grill in a panini press until the cheese is melted and the bread is browned and crisp, 5 minutes. Alternatively, set the loaves on a griddle and top with a heavy skillet. Cook over moderate heat until browned on the bottom, 5 minutes. Turn, cover with the skillet and cook until the cheese is melted, 3 minutes. Cut each loaf into thirds and serve. —Grace Parisi

breads, pizzas & sandwiches

Cajun-Spiced, Open-Faced Red Pepper Frittata Sandwiches

ACTIVE: 30 MIN; TOTAL: 45 MIN

4 SERVINGS ● ●

- 2 tablespoons extra-virgin olive oil, plus more for brushing
- 1 medium onion, finely diced
- ½ teaspoon crushed red pepper
- ¼ teaspoon garlic powder
- ¼ teaspoon sweet paprika
- ⅛ teaspoon chile powder
- Salt
- 1 red bell pepper, cut into ¼-inch dice
- 1 teaspoon chopped thyme, plus 1 teaspoon thyme leaves for garnish
- ½ teaspoon coarsely chopped oregano leaves
- ½ teaspoon finely grated lemon zest
- 6 large eggs
- ½ cup whole milk
- 2½ ounces aged Asiago cheese, coarsely shredded (¾ cup)
- Freshly ground black pepper
- 1 whole wheat baguette, ends trimmed, loaf halved lengthwise and crosswise

1. In a 10-inch, ovenproof nonstick skillet, heat 1 tablespoon of the olive oil. Add the diced onion, crushed red pepper, garlic powder, paprika, chile powder and a large pinch of salt to the skillet and cook over low heat, stirring a few times, until the onion is browned, about 10 minutes. Add the remaining 1 tablespoon of olive oil to the skillet along with the diced red bell pepper and cook until the pepper is softened, about 5 minutes. Remove the skillet from the heat and stir the chopped thyme, oregano and lemon zest into the onion and pepper mixture.

2. Preheat the broiler. In a medium bowl, whisk the eggs well. Whisk in the whole milk and ¼ teaspoon of salt. Return the skillet to moderately low heat and stir in the Asiago cheese. Pour in the beaten eggs and stir lightly to mix the vegetables and eggs. Season with black pepper, cover and cook until the eggs pull away from the side of the skillet, about 8 minutes.

3. Meanwhile, brush the cut sides of the baguette with olive oil and arrange on a cookie sheet, cut sides up. Broil the bread 6 inches from the heat for about 3 minutes, or until toasted.

4. Uncover the frittata and place under the broiler until just set and lightly browned, about 2 minutes.

5. Carefully slide the frittata onto a work surface and using a sharp knife, cut it into 4 pieces, each about same size as the bread slices. Set the warm frittata pieces on the baguette toasts, sprinkle with the thyme leaves and serve immediately.
—*Bryant Terry*

Roasted Red Pepper Sandwiches with Tapenade and Basil

TOTAL: 45 MIN PLUS OVERNIGHT MARINATING

12 SERVINGS ● ● ●

For a more substantial sandwich, add tuna or chicken.

- 5 large red bell peppers
- 2 garlic cloves, minced
- 2 teaspoons chopped thyme
- 2 teaspoons chopped rosemary
- 1 can anchovy fillets (3 ounces), drained and minced
- Salt and freshly ground pepper
- Two 24-inch baguettes, halved lengthwise
- ⅓ cup black olive tapenade from a jar
- 20 basil leaves

1. Roast the red bell peppers over a gas flame until they are charred all over. Transfer the roasted bell peppers to a bowl and let cool. Discard the skin and seeds and quarter the peppers. In a bowl, toss the peppers with the garlic, thyme, rosemary and about one-fourth of the anchovies and season with salt and pepper. Refrigerate the roasted red peppers overnight.

2. Light a grill. Toast the baguettes over a hot fire, cut sides down. Spread the bottom halves of the baguettes with the black olive tapenade. Top with the marinated peppers and their juices, and then basil leaves and the remaining anchovies. Close the sandwiches and cut them into 12 pieces. Wrap in napkins and serve immediately.
—*Christophe Emé*

Steak-and-Egg-Salad Sandwiches

TOTAL: 40 MIN

4 SERVINGS ●

For this sandwich, soft pita bread is stuffed with deviled egg salad and thin slices of grilled beef.

- 4 large eggs
- ¼ cup mayonnaise
- ½ teaspoon paprika
- ½ teaspoon dry mustard
- 2 tablespoons snipped chives
- Dash of Worcestershire sauce
- Dash of hot sauce
- 1 celery rib, diced
- Salt and freshly ground pepper
- Two 1-pound strip steaks, cut 1 inch thick
- 4 large pocketless pita breads
- 2 tablespoons extra-virgin olive oil, plus more for brushing
- 1 tablespoon fresh lemon juice
- 1 bunch watercress

1. Put the eggs in a medium saucepan filled with cold water and bring to a rapid boil. Cover and let stand off the heat for 10 minutes. Drain and fill the pan with cold water, shaking the eggs against the side of the pan to crack them. Peel the eggs and coarsely chop them. In a medium bowl, combine the mayonnaise, paprika, dry mustard, chives, Worcestershire and hot sauce. Add the chopped eggs and celery and season with salt and pepper. Refrigerate the egg salad.

STEAK-AND-EGG-SALAD SANDWICHES

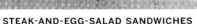

PULLED PORK AND GOAT CHEESE QUESADILLAS

2. Meanwhile, light a grill. Brush the strip steaks and the pita breads with olive oil. Grill the pita breads for 30 seconds per side, until they are just heated through and lightly toasted. Immediately wrap the pita breads in aluminum foil to keep them soft. Season the steaks with salt and pepper and grill them over moderately high heat for about 10 minutes, turning once, for medium-rare meat. Transfer the grilled steaks to a cutting board and let them rest for 10 minutes. Thinly slice the steaks across the grain.

3. In a medium bowl, whisk the lemon juice with the 2 tablespoons of olive oil. Add the watercress to the bowl, season with salt and pepper and toss to coat. Spread the egg salad over the pitas. Arrange the sliced steak on one half of each pita bread and top with the watercress. Fold the pita breads to close and serve the sandwiches right away. —*David Burke*

Pulled Pork and Goat Cheese Quesadillas

TOTAL: 30 MIN

4 SERVINGS ●

- 2 tablespoons vegetable oil, plus more for brushing
- 1 small green bell pepper, cut into strips
- 1 small red bell pepper, cut into strips
- 1 large jalapeño, thinly sliced
- 1 small onion, finely chopped
- 3 garlic cloves, minced
- 2 Braised Pork Shanks (p. 159), meat pulled from the bones and thinly sliced
- ½ cup pork gravy (from Braised Pork Shanks, p. 159)

Eight 8-inch flour tortillas

One 5-ounce log of fresh goat cheese, softened

1. In a large, deep skillet, heat the 2 tablespoons of oil. Add the green and red bell peppers and cook them over moderately high heat, stirring, until the peppers are softened, about 10 minutes. Add the jalapeño, onion and garlic, cover and cook over moderate heat, stirring occasionally, until softened, about 5 minutes. Add the meat from the Braised Pork Shanks and the gravy and cook for 3 minutes longer.

2. Arrange the tortillas on a work surface and spread a thin layer of goat cheese over each one. Spoon the pork and bell pepper mixture over the goat cheese and fold the tortillas in half. Brush the tortillas with oil.

3. Heat 2 large skillets and preheat the oven to 300°. Working in batches, cook the tortillas over moderate heat, turning once, until crisp, about 7 minutes. Transfer the quesadillas to a baking sheet and keep warm in the oven. Cut the quesadillas in half and serve right away. —*Tim Love*

● FAST ● HEALTHY ● MAKE AHEAD ● STAFF FAVORITE

breads, pizzas & sandwiches

Greek Salad with Bulgur in Pita Pockets

ACTIVE: 45 MIN; TOTAL: 1 HR
MAKES 12 MINI PITA
SANDWICHES ●

- ¾ cup water
- ½ cup bulgur wheat
- Salt
- 3 tablespoons extra-virgin olive oil
- 3 tablespoons fresh lemon juice
- ¼ cup chopped cilantro
- ¼ cup pitted kalamata olives, chopped
- 2 tablespoons chopped mint, plus 2 mint sprigs (optional)
- ½ teaspoon sweet paprika
- ½ teaspoon ground cumin
- Freshly ground pepper
- 1 cup plain low-fat Greek yogurt
- ½ small European cucumber— peeled, halved, seeded and thinly sliced
- ½ small red onion, thinly sliced
- 1 small garlic clove, minced
- 24 Isis Candy or other cherry tomatoes, halved
- 12 mini pitas, top third cut off
- 4 ounces mixed baby greens

chef idea

bread salad

For this autumn bread salad, combine toasted Italian bread cubes (about 1 inch), sautéed diced bacon, chopped red onion, shredded raw green cabbage, thinly sliced Fuyu persimmons and apples, baby spinach, pomegranate seeds and currants. Mix balsamic vinegar, apple cider vinegar, extra virgin olive oil, Dijon mustard and a little heavy cream and season with salt, pepper and allspice. Drizzle the dressing; toss well. —*Kathleen Weber and Kay Baumhefner*

1. In a small saucepan, boil the water. Add the bulgur and ½ teaspoon of salt; return to a boil. Cover, remove from the heat and let stand until the water is absorbed, about 25 minutes. Drain the bulgur in a fine sieve, pressing to remove any excess liquid and spread the bulgur on a plate to cool.
2. In a bowl, whisk 2 tablespoons of olive oil with 2 tablespoons of lemon juice. Stir in the cilantro, olives, chopped mint, paprika and cumin. Add the bulgur and toss well. Season with salt and pepper.
3. In a bowl, mix the yogurt, cucumber, onion, garlic and remaining lemon juice. Season with salt and pepper. In a medium bowl, toss the tomatoes with the remaining olive oil; season with salt and pepper.
4. Spoon the bulgur salad into the pitas then tuck in the baby greens and tomatoes. Top with the yogurt, garnish with the mint sprigs and serve. —*Joe Vitale*

German Soft Pretzel Sticks

ACTIVE: 30 MIN; TOTAL: 2 HR 10 MIN
MAKES 2 DOZEN PRETZEL STICKS

- ½ cup light brown sugar
- 2 envelopes active dry yeast
- ¼ cup vegetable oil
- About 5¾ cups all-purpose flour, plus more for kneading
- Butter for greasing
- ¾ cup baking soda
- 1 large egg beaten with 1 tablespoon of water
- Flaky salt, such as Maldon
- Yellow mustard, for serving

1. In a bowl, stir the brown sugar into 2 cups of warm water until dissolved. Sprinkle the yeast over the water and let stand until foamy, about 5 minutes. Stir in the vegetable oil and 3 cups of the flour. Knead in the remaining 2¾ cups of flour; the dough will be slightly sticky.
2. Transfer the dough to a floured work surface and knead until silky, about 3 minutes; if the dough is very sticky, knead in up to ¼ cup more flour. Transfer the dough

to a large, oiled bowl, cover with plastic wrap and let stand at room temperature until doubled in bulk, about 45 minutes.
3. Preheat the oven to 450°. Line 3 large cookie sheets with parchment paper and butter the paper. Punch down the dough and turn it out onto a floured work surface. Knead the dough lightly, flatten it out and cut it into 24 pieces. Roll each piece into a 9-inch stick about ½ inch thick. Transfer the sticks to the prepared cookie sheets, leaving at least 2 inches between them. Let stand uncovered until puffed, about 25 minutes.
4. In a large, deep skillet, stir the baking soda into 2 quarts of water and bring to a simmer over high heat. Reduce the heat to moderate. Using 2 slotted spoons, carefully dip 6 of the pretzels at a time in the simmering water for 30 seconds, turning once; add about 1 cup of hot water before dipping the second batch of pretzels. Transfer the pretzels to paper towels to drain, then return them to the paper-lined cookie sheets, spacing them evenly.
5. Brush the pretzels with the egg wash and sprinkle with salt. Bake the pretzels until they are richly browned, about 10 minutes. Serve the pretzels warm or at room temperature. —*Grant Achatz*

Wild Mushroom Whole Wheat Stuffing with Tarragon

ACTIVE: 1 HR; TOTAL: 1 HR 45 MIN
MAKES 16 CUPS ●
This recipe can be used to stuff a 17-pound turkey or baked on its own.

- 1½ loaves whole wheat bread (3 pounds), cut into 1-inch cubes
- 1½ sticks unsalted butter
- 4 ounces thickly cut bacon or *speck*, cut into ¼-inch dice
- 6 celery ribs, cut into ¼-inch dice (2 cups)
- 1 large white onion, cut into ¼-inch dice
- 6 garlic cloves, minced

2 pounds mixed wild mushrooms, such as chanterelle, oyster and hen-of-the-woods, thickly sliced

¼ cup chopped flat-leaf parsley

¼ cup finely chopped tarragon

¼ cup snipped chives

4 cups Turkey Stock (p. 309) or low-sodium chicken broth

Salt and freshly ground pepper

1. Preheat the oven to 350°. Spread the bread on 2 large rimmed baking sheets and bake for 15 minutes, until slightly firm and golden. Transfer to a large bowl.

2. Meanwhile, in a deep skillet, melt 2 tablespoons of the butter. Add the bacon and cook over moderately high heat until browned, about 6 minutes. Drain well. Add the celery, onion and garlic to the pan and cook over moderate heat, stirring, until softened, about 10 minutes. Add the mixture and the bacon to the large bowl.

3. Melt 4 tablespoons of the butter in the skillet. Add the mushrooms and cook over high heat, stirring occasionally, until golden, about 10 minutes. Add the remaining 6 tablespoons of butter and melt, then scrape the mushrooms into the bowl. Stir in the herbs and Turkey Stock, season with salt and pepper and mix well. Let the stuffing cool to room temperature.

4. Stuff the turkey. Spread the remaining stuffing in a large baking dish. Alternatively, spread all of the stuffing in 2 baking dishes. Cover the dishes with foil and bake the stuffing for about 30 minutes, or until heated through. Remove the foil and bake the stuffing until the top is crusty and golden, about 15 minutes longer.
—*Barbara Lynch*

Pumpernickel, Rye and Red Cabbage Stuffing
ACTIVE: 45 MIN; TOTAL: 2 HR 45 MIN
12 SERVINGS ●

¾ pound loaf rye bread with caraway seeds, cut into ¾-inch dice (8 cups)

¾ pound loaf pumpernickel bread, cut into ¾-inch dice (8 cups)

1 pound smoky kielbasa, quartered lengthwise and sliced ½ inch thick

4 tablespoons unsalted butter, melted

1 medium onion, halved and thinly sliced

2 garlic cloves, minced

1 pound red cabbage, finely shredded (6 cups)

1 large Granny Smith apple— peeled, cored and thinly sliced

2 tablespoons red wine vinegar

2 teaspoons chopped thyme

4 cups Turkey Stock (p. 109) or low-sodium chicken broth

Kosher salt and freshly ground pepper

2 large eggs, beaten

1. Preheat the oven to 350°. Butter a shallow 13-by-9-inch baking dish. Spread the rye bread and the pumpernickel bread on 2 large baking sheets and bake until slightly dry, about 20 minutes.

2. Meanwhile, in a large, deep skillet, cook the kielbasa over moderately high heat, stirring occasionally, until browned, about 5 minutes. Transfer to a large bowl. Add 2 tablespoons of the melted butter to the skillet along with the onion and garlic and cook over moderate heat for 4 minutes. Add the red cabbage, apple, vinegar and thyme and cook, stirring occasionally, until the cabbage is wilted, about 6 minutes.

3. Add the cabbage mixture to the kielbasa. Stir in the toasted bread and stock. Season with salt and pepper, then stir in the eggs. Spread the stuffing in the prepared baking dish and brush with the remaining melted butter.

4. Cover the stuffing with aluminum foil and bake until set, about 45 minutes. Uncover the baking dish and bake the stuffing until the top is crisp, about 40 minutes longer. Let the stuffing rest for 15 minutes before serving. —*Grace Parisi*

Cranberry-Pecan Bread Pudding with Bacon
ACTIVE: 40 MIN; TOTAL: 2 HR 30 MIN
12 SERVINGS ●

Two 1-pound loaves of cranberry-pecan bread, bottom crusts removed, the rest of the loaf cut into 1-inch cubes (12 cups)

1 pound thickly sliced bacon, cut into ½-inch pieces

1 large onion, finely chopped

1 celery rib, finely chopped

2 garlic cloves, minced

1 tablespoon chopped sage

2 teaspoons chopped thyme

4 cups Turkey Stock (p. 109) or low-sodium chicken broth

Kosher salt and freshly ground pepper

2 large eggs, beaten

2 tablespoons unsalted butter, melted

1. Preheat the oven to 350°. Butter a shallow 13-by-9-inch baking dish. Spread the bread on a large baking sheet and bake until golden and crisp, 25 minutes.

2. Meanwhile, in a large, deep skillet, cook the bacon over moderately high heat, stirring occasionally until browned, 7 minutes. Transfer the bacon to a plate and pour off all but ¼ cup of the fat. Add the onion, celery and garlic and cook over moderately high heat, stirring occasionally, until softened, 6 minutes. Add the sage and thyme. Scrape the onion mixture into a large bowl and stir in the toasted bread cubes, bacon and Turkey Stock. Season with salt and pepper, then add the beaten eggs and stir well. Let the mixture stand, stirring occasionally, until most of the liquid has been absorbed, 15 minutes. Spread the mixture in the prepared baking dish and brush the top with the melted butter.

3. Cover with foil and bake for 45 minutes, until just set. Remove the foil and bake until golden, 40 minutes longer. Let the bread pudding rest for 15 minutes before serving. —*Grace Parisi*

GLAZED SWEET ROLLS (P. 308)

breakfast & brunch

"One of my fondest memories is waking up at 4:30, going to the restaurant, filling up the griddle with bacon and breathing in that intoxicating, smoky smell."

—**Grant Achatz,** chef and co-owner, Alinea Restaurant, Chicago

POACHED EGGS WITH PARMESAN AND SMOKED SALMON TOASTS

SOUFFLÉED STRAWBERRY-JAM OMELET

Poached Eggs with Parmesan and Smoked Salmon Toasts

TOTAL: 30 MIN

4 SERVINGS ● ●

Dipping a crisp toast finger in a soft egg yolk is one of life's great pleasures. "When I was a kid, I loved it," says F&W contributing editor Jean-Georges Vongerichten. Evidently, he's still fond of it. He makes an adult version that's elegant enough to serve as a first course at a dinner party: He wraps smoked salmon around half of the toasts and sprinkles the rest with grated Parmesan, which bakes into a salty crust.

Four ½-inch-thick slices of sourdough bread, each slice cut into four 4-by-½-inch rectangles

Extra-virgin olive oil, for brushing

¼ cup freshly grated Parmesan

2 ounces thinly sliced smoked salmon, cut into 8 long strips

4 large eggs

1. Preheat the oven to 425°. Fill a medium skillet with water and bring to a boil. Put the bread on a baking sheet and brush it all over with olive oil. Bake for about 8 minutes, or until the bread is crisp. Reserve 8 of the toasts. Push the remaining 8 toasts close together on the baking sheet and sprinkle the Parmesan on top in a thick layer. Bake the toasts for about 2 minutes, or until the cheese is melted. Wrap the smoked salmon around the remaining 8 toasts.

2. Reduce the heat under the skillet to moderately low so the water simmers. One at a time, break the eggs into a small bowl and slide them into the simmering water. Cook until the whites are just firm and the yolks are still runny, about 3 minutes. Using a slotted spoon, transfer the eggs to paper towels and gently blot dry. Put each egg in a small, warmed bowl. Serve immediately with the Parmesan and smoked salmon toasts.
—*Jean-Georges Vongerichten*

Souffléed Strawberry-Jam Omelets

ACTIVE: 15 MIN; TOTAL: 25 MIN

4 SERVINGS ● ● ●

⅓ cup superfine sugar, plus more for dusting

4 large egg whites

3 large egg yolks

¼ cup strawberry jam

Confectioners' sugar, for dusting

1. Preheat the oven to 425°. Position a rack in the upper third of the oven. Generously butter a large rimmed baking sheet and dust it generously with superfine sugar. In a large mixing bowl, using a handheld electric mixer, beat the egg whites until soft peaks form. Beat the superfine sugar into the whites, 1 tablespoon at a time, beating well after each addition, until the whites form firm, glossy peaks. In a small bowl, whisk the egg yolks until pale yellow. Gently fold the yolks into the beaten whites.

2. With a spatula, form half of the egg mixture into four 5-by-3-inch ovals on the prepared baking sheet. With the back of a spoon, make a 2-inch-long indent in the center of each oval; fill with 1 tablespoon of the jam. Cover with the remaining egg.

3. Bake the soufflés for about 10 minutes, until puffed, golden brown and still slightly jiggly in the center. With a metal spatula, gently lift the omelets off the baking sheet and transfer to plates. Dust with confectioners' sugar and serve. —*Marcia Kiesel*

Eggs Cocotte with Mushrooms and Parsley Puree
ACTIVE: 1 HR; TOTAL: 1 HR 15 MIN
4 FIRST-COURSE SERVINGS

At The Mansion in Las Vegas, chef Joël Robuchon cooks these eggs in martini glasses in a professional steam oven; the F&W test kitchen got great results by steaming the eggs in ramekins (*en cocotte*) in a water bath. Either way, the runny eggs are delicious with the creamy mushrooms and super-silky parsley puree.

- **6** ounces flat-leaf parsley, leaves only
- **½** pound white mushrooms, coarsely chopped
- **1** tablespoon vegetable oil
- Salt and freshly ground pepper
- **2** tablespoons water
- **½** cup heavy cream
- **2** tablespoons unsalted butter
- **1** small shallot, thinly sliced
- **¼** pound small chanterelles or other wild mushrooms, sliced ¼ inch thick
- **4** large eggs

1. In a saucepan of boiling water, blanch the parsley until tender but still bright green, about 3 minutes. Drain well. Transfer to a food processor and puree; scrape into a bowl and clean the processor.

2. Add the white mushrooms to the processor and pulse to mince. In a large nonstick skillet, heat the oil. Add the minced mushrooms, season with salt and pepper and cook over high heat until the liquid has evaporated, about 5 minutes. Add the water and stir to scrape up any browned bits. Add the cream, cover and simmer over low heat for 10 minutes. Strain through a fine strainer into a small saucepan, pressing on the solids. Simmer over moderately high heat until reduced to ⅓ cup, about 2 minutes. Season with salt.

3. In a large skillet, melt the butter. Add the shallot and cook over moderately high heat until softened, 2 minutes. Add the chanterelles, season with salt and pepper and cook over moderate heat, stirring occasionally, until browned, 10 minutes.

4. Set a round rack in a large, wide pot. Add enough water to reach just under the rack without touching it. Cover the pot and bring the water to a boil. Butter four 1¼-cup heatproof porcelain bowls, about 4½ inches wide at the top tapering down to 2 inches wide at the bottom. Alternatively, use ramekins. Spoon the parsley puree into the bowls. Crack 1 egg into each of the porcelain bowls; season with salt and pepper. Cover each bowl with plastic wrap. Carefully set on the rack in the pot, cover and steam over low heat until the whites are firm and the yolks are runny, about 12 minutes. Discard the plastic wrap.

5. Reheat the mushroom cream and chanterelles. Spoon the cream over the eggs, top with the chanterelles and serve. —*Joël Robuchon*

Polenta Gratins with Poached Eggs and Sheep's-Milk Cheese
TOTAL: 1 HR
6 SERVINGS

It's hard to go wrong with a recipe that features soft-poached eggs, warm polenta and gooey, salty cheese. Make sure to check the expiration date on the polenta or stone-ground cornmeal; fresh polenta has a distinctive, sweet corn aroma that transforms this dish.

- **4** cups water
- Salt
- **1** cup artisanal polenta or stone-ground cornmeal
- **1** tablespoon unsalted butter
- **1** tablespoon extra-virgin olive oil
- **3** tablespoons freshly grated Parmesan cheese
- Freshly ground pepper
- **1** tablespoon distilled white vinegar
- **6** large eggs
- **3** ounces young sheep's-milk cheese, such as Cacio di Roma or Manchego, shredded (1 cup)

1. In a medium saucepan, bring the water to a simmer with a pinch of salt. Slowly whisk in the polenta until smooth. Cook over low heat, whisking often, until the polenta is tender and very thick, about 40 minutes. Stir the butter, olive oil and Parmesan cheese into the polenta and season with salt and pepper. Cover the polenta and keep warm.

2. In a very large skillet, bring 3 quarts of water to a boil. Reduce the heat enough to maintain the water at a steady simmer and add the vinegar. Break the eggs into ramekins and, one by one, add them to the simmering water. Poach the eggs until the whites are firm but the yolks are still runny, about 3 minutes.

3. Preheat the broiler. Whisk the polenta over moderately high heat for 2 minutes to break up any lumps that may have formed and to heat it through. Spoon the polenta into 6 individual gratin dishes and set the dishes on a sturdy baking sheet. Using a slotted spoon, transfer one of the poached eggs onto the top of each serving of polenta, patting the bottom of the spoon with paper towels to dry the eggs before transferring them. Sprinkle the shredded cheese over the eggs and broil for 30 seconds, or until the cheese is bubbling. Season with freshly ground pepper and serve. —*Morgan Brownlow*

breakfast & brunch

Asparagus with Soft-Cooked Eggs and Brown-Butter Hollandaise

ACTIVE: 40 MIN; TOTAL: 1 HR

4 SERVINGS

F&W contributing editor Jacques Pépin loves eggs in any form, but this recipe is one of his absolute favorites, with its nutty hollandaise sauce, runny eggs and crisp, buttery crumbs.

- 1 cup crustless 1-inch bread cubes, cut from thickly sliced, firm-textured country bread
- 1 tablespoon extra-virgin olive oil

Salt

- 16 fat asparagus, tough ends snapped off, stalks peeled
- 4 large eggs
- 1 stick unsalted butter, cut into tablespoons
- 2 large egg yolks
- 1½ tablespoons hot water
- 2 teaspoons fresh lemon juice

Freshly ground pepper

Cayenne pepper

1. Preheat the oven to 400°. In a pie plate, toss the bread cubes with the olive oil and season with salt. Bake for 8 minutes, or until golden brown. Let cool completely. Transfer the bread to a sturdy plastic bag and crush with a rolling pin until coarse crumbs form. Reduce the oven to 350°.

2. Bring a large, deep skillet of salted water to a boil. Add the asparagus and boil until just tender, 5 minutes. Drain the asparagus and transfer to a large gratin dish.

3. Bring a medium saucepan of water to a boil. Add the eggs and boil over moderate heat for 5 minutes. Pour off the water and gently shake the pan to crack the egg shells. Fill the pan with ice water and let the eggs cool for 5 minutes; drain. Carefully shell the eggs and transfer to a plate.

4. In a small saucepan, cook the butter over moderate heat until it smells like roasted hazelnuts and the milk solids are lightly browned, about 7 minutes. Remove from the heat and let the butter cool slightly.

5. Bring a medium saucepan of water to a simmer over moderate heat. In a blender, combine the egg yolks and hot water; blend for 2 seconds. With the blender on medium, gradually add the hot butter, a few drops at a time at first and then in a thin stream, until fully incorporated. Add any browned bits from the bottom of the pan and the lemon juice. Season the sauce with salt, pepper and a pinch of cayenne.

6. Reheat the asparagus in the oven. One by one, carefully lower the peeled whole eggs into the hot water in the medium saucepan and warm just until heated through, about 1 minute.

7. Meanwhile, arrange 4 of the asparagus spears on each of 4 plates. Pat the eggs dry and set one on top of each plate of asparagus. Spoon the hollandaise over the eggs and asparagus, sprinkle with the crushed croutons and serve right away. —*Jacques Pépin*

MAKE AHEAD The recipe can be prepared through Step 2 up to 1 day ahead. Store the bread crumbs in an airtight container. Cover the cooked asparagus with plastic wrap and refrigerate overnight.

Ham-and-Cheese Turnovers

ACTIVE: 15 MIN; TOTAL: 45 MIN

4 SERVINGS ●

Customers line up at the Frog Hollow Farm shop in San Francisco's Ferry Building Marketplace for both amazing fruit pastries and delicious yet simple savory turnovers like the ham-and-cheese ones here. The turnovers freeze well, so make extra batches and store them for whenever a craving hits; they're best eaten straight out of the oven.

- ½ pound frozen all-butter puff pastry, thawed
- 4 thin slices of smoked ham, such as Black Forest (4 ounces)
- 3 ounces Gruyère cheese, shredded (1 cup)
- 1 large egg, lightly beaten

1. Preheat the oven to 400°. Line a rimmed baking sheet with parchment paper. On a lightly floured work surface, gently roll out the puff pastry to a roughly 13-inch square ¹⁄₁₆ inch thick. Cut out four 6-inch squares and transfer to the prepared baking sheet. Refrigerate the pastry for 5 minutes.

2. Meanwhile, lay the ham slices on a work surface. Spoon ¼ cup of the shredded Gruyère on one side of each slice of ham, then fold the other side of the ham over the cheese to form a neat package.

3. Lightly brush the edges of the pastry squares with water. Set the ham-and-cheese packages on the squares and fold the pastry corner to corner to form triangles. Press the edges of the turnovers together and crimp decoratively with a fork. Brush the turnovers with the beaten egg and bake them for about 30 minutes, or until golden brown and puffed. Let cool slightly and serve. —*Rebecca Courchesne*

SERVE WITH Whole-grain mustard.

Spicy Honey-Glazed Bacon

ACTIVE: 5 MIN; TOTAL: 25 MIN

6 SERVINGS ●

- 1 pound thick-cut bacon
- 2 tablespoons honey
- ¼ teaspoon ground coriander
- ⅛ teaspoon cayenne pepper
- 1 tablespoon sesame seeds

Preheat the oven to 375°. Line 2 rimmed baking sheets with parchment paper. Arrange the bacon on the paper in a single layer. In a small skillet, combine the honey, coriander and cayenne and cook over high heat until melted, about 1 minute. Brush the honey on one side of the bacon and bake for 10 minutes. Sprinkle with the sesame seeds and bake for 5 to 10 minutes longer, depending on the thickness and fattiness of the bacon, until sizzling and browned. Transfer the bacon to paper towels, glazed side up, to drain and cool slightly. Serve right away. —*Grace Parisi*

SPICY HONEY-GLAZED BACON

breakfast & brunch

White Cheddar and Scallion Muffins

ACTIVE: 15 MIN; TOTAL: 40 MIN

MAKES 2 DOZEN MINI MUFFINS ● ●

- 1½ cups all-purpose flour
- 1½ teaspoons baking powder
- 1¼ teaspoons salt
- ¼ teaspoon cayenne pepper
- 4 tablespoons cold unsalted butter, cut into small cubes
- ¼ cup minced scallion greens
- 3 ounces extra-sharp, white cheddar cheese, shredded (1 cup)
- ½ cup plus 2 tablespoons cold milk

1. Preheat the oven to 375°. Lightly coat two 12-cup mini-muffin tins with vegetable oil spray. In a bowl, mix the flour, baking powder, salt and cayenne. Using 2 knives or a pastry blender, work in the butter until the mixture resembles coarse meal with some small pieces of butter visible. Add the scallions, cheese and milk; stir with a wooden spoon just until the dough comes together.

2. Scoop the dough into the tins. Bake for about 25 minutes, until lightly browned on top. Transfer the tins to a wire rack to cool slightly. Serve warm. —*Dean Maupin*

taste test
butter

F&W editors tasted over 20 supermarket butters (both salted and unsalted ones and even a goat's-milk variety) and picked **Organic Valley's Cultured Unsalted Sweet Cream Butter** as having the freshest butter flavor.

Fresh Corn Soufflé with Bacon and Comté

ACTIVE: 35 MIN; TOTAL: 1 HR 15 MIN

4 SERVINGS

F&W's Marcia Kiesel likes to feature corn in main courses because "it's so substantial." She uses it here as a base for a decadent cheese soufflé with smoky bacon.

- Unsalted butter
- Freshly grated Parmesan cheese, for coating
- Salt
- 4 ears of corn, shucked
- ¼ pound thickly sliced bacon, cut crosswise into ⅓-inch strips
- 1 cup milk
- Freshly ground pepper
- 3 large egg yolks
- 6 ounces shredded Comté cheese (2 cups)
- ½ teaspoon chopped thyme
- 6 large egg whites

1. Preheat the oven to 350°. Generously butter a 1½-quart soufflé dish and coat it with Parmesan, tapping out the excess. Bring a large saucepan of water to a boil. Add salt and the corn and boil over high heat just until tender, about 5 minutes.

2. Meanwhile, in a small skillet, cook the bacon over high heat for 1 minute, then reduce the heat to moderate and cook until browned, about 5 minutes longer.

3. Using tongs, transfer the corn to a plate. Drain off the water and return the saucepan to the stove. Cut the corn kernels from the cobs; you should have 2½ cups. Put 2 cups of the kernels in the saucepan and add the milk. Simmer over moderate heat until the milk has reduced by one-third, about 5 minutes. Transfer the corn and milk to a blender and puree until very smooth. Scrape the puree into a large bowl and stir in the bacon and the remaining ½ cup of corn kernels. Season lightly with salt and pepper and stir in the egg yolks, Comté and thyme. Cover with plastic wrap and let cool to room temperature.

4. In a large stainless steel bowl, using an electric mixer, beat the egg whites with a pinch of salt at high speed until they hold firm peaks. Stir one-third of the egg whites into the corn base to lighten it, then gently fold the remaining egg whites into the mixture until just blended. Scrape the mixture into the prepared soufflé dish and bake for 45 minutes, or until nicely browned on top and slightly jiggly in the center. Serve the soufflé right away. —*Marcia Kiesel*

Golden Corn Cakes

TOTAL: 30 MIN

4 SERVINGS ●

- 1½ cups fresh corn kernels (from about 3 ears)
- ½ cup milk
- ¼ cup heavy cream
- 2 large eggs
- 2 large egg yolks
- 1¼ cups all-purpose flour
- ½ teaspoon baking powder
- 1 teaspoon salt
- 2 tablespoons unsalted butter
- 2 tablespoons extra-virgin olive oil

1. Preheat the oven to 325°. In a blender, combine 1 cup of the corn kernels with the milk and puree until smooth. Add the heavy cream, eggs and egg yolks and blend. Transfer the corn mixture to a bowl and whisk in the flour, baking powder, salt and the remaining ½ cup of corn kernels.

2. In a large nonstick skillet, melt 1 tablespoon of the butter in 1 tablespoon of the olive oil. Spoon rounded 2-tablespoon-size dollops of batter into the hot skillet and cook over moderately high heat, turning once, until the corn cakes are golden, about 5 minutes. Transfer the corn cakes to a rack set over a baking sheet and keep warm in the oven. Repeat with the remaining corn cake batter, using the remaining 1 tablespoon each of butter and olive oil; adjust the heat under the skillet if necessary. Serve the corn cakes hot.
—*Jean-Georges Vongerichten*

Corn Cakes and Spiced Cranberries

TOTAL: 30 MIN

6 SERVINGS ● ●

- 4 tablespoons unsalted butter, plus more for coating
- 1⅓ cups sugar, plus more for coating
- ¾ cup milk
- ⅓ cup stone-ground yellow cornmeal
- 2 large eggs, separated
- 1 small star anise pod
- ½ teaspoon black peppercorns
- 1 cinnamon stick
- 2 cups dry red wine
- 2 cups fresh or frozen cranberries

1. Preheat the oven to 350°. Butter and sugar six ¾-cup ramekins. In a small saucepan, bring the milk and butter to a boil. Off the heat, whisk in the cornmeal until smooth. Cover and let sit until the liquid is completely absorbed.

2. Meanwhile, in a bowl, beat the egg whites until firm peaks form. In another bowl, whisk the egg yolks with ⅓ cup of the sugar. Add the cornmeal and whisk until smooth. Fold in the whites completely. Spoon the batter into the ramekins. Run your thumb around the edge of each ramekin so the cakes rise straight. Bake the cakes for 22 minutes, or until golden, risen and firm to the touch. Let cool slightly.

3. Meanwhile, tie the star anise, peppercorns and cinnamon stick in a small cheesecloth bundle. In a small saucepan, combine the wine, the remaining 1 cup of sugar and the spice bundle and bring to a boil, stirring to dissolve the sugar. Add the cranberries and cook over moderate heat until they start to pop, about 5 minutes. Using a slotted spoon, transfer the cranberries to a bowl. Discard the spice bundle and boil the liquid over moderate heat until thick and syrupy, about 15 minutes. Return the cranberries to the syrup. Run a knife around the sides of the cakes and unmold. Serve the corn cakes with the spiced cranberries. —*Peter Ireland*

Crumbly Date-Nut Corn Bread

ACTIVE: 20 MIN; TOTAL: 45 MIN

MAKES ONE 10-INCH CORN BREAD ● ●

The key to this corn bread is coarse stone-ground cornmeal. The cornmeal from War Eagle Mill in Arkansas is especially good; the yellow kind makes the prettiest bread (wareaglemill.com).

- ½ teaspoon cumin seeds
- ¾ cup pecan halves
- 1 tablespoon vegetable oil
- 1¾ cups coarse yellow cornmeal, preferably stone-ground
- ¾ cup all-purpose flour
- 2½ teaspoons baking powder
- 1 teaspoon salt
- ½ teaspoon baking soda
- 6 Medjool dates, pitted and cut into ½-inch pieces
- 2 large eggs, lightly beaten
- 1 cup milk
- 3 tablespoons honey
- 6 tablespoons unsalted butter, melted

1. Preheat the oven to 400°. In a 10-inch cast-iron skillet, toast the cumin seeds over moderate heat until fragrant, about 1 minute. Let cool, then transfer to a mortar and grind to a powder. Spread the pecans in a pie plate and toast in the oven for 5 minutes, or until lightly browned. Let cool, then coarsely chop them.

2. Add the oil to the skillet and heat in the oven. In a large bowl, whisk the cornmeal with the flour, baking powder, salt and baking soda. Stir in the dates, pecans and cumin. In a medium bowl, mix the eggs, milk, honey and butter, then gently stir into the cornmeal just until blended.

3. Tilt the hot skillet to coat it with oil. Pour the batter into the skillet and bake for 20 minutes, or until golden brown and the top springs back when lightly pressed. Transfer the corn bread to a wire rack to cool, then cut into wedges. Serve the bread warm or at room temperature. —*Marcia Kiesel*

Light and Crispy Popovers

ACTIVE: 10 MIN; TOTAL: 35 MIN

MAKES 6 POPOVERS ●

If you don't own a 6-cup popover pan, you can substitute a 12-cup nonstick muffin pan. Use only 10 of the cups, adding ½ teaspoon of oil to the bottom of each before pouring in the batter. Both the baking temperature and cooking time will remain the same.

- 3 tablespoons vegetable oil, such as canola or corn oil
- 2 large eggs, at room temperature
- 1 cup whole milk

Pinch of salt

- 1 cup all-purpose flour

Softened butter and jam or preserves, for serving

1. Preheat the oven to 425°. Pour 1 teaspoon of the vegetable oil into each cup of a 6-cup popover pan. Set the popover pan in the fully preheated oven.

2. In a blender, combine the eggs with the whole milk and blend at medium speed until well mixed. Add the pinch of salt and the remaining 1 tablespoon of vegetable oil and blend at medium speed just until combined. Add the flour and blend at medium speed until the batter is completely smooth.

3. Pour the batter into the hot popover-pan, filling each cup about halfway up the side. Bake the popovers in the center of the oven for about 15 minutes, or until they are nicely risen. Reduce the oven temperature to 350° and bake for 10 minutes longer, or until the popovers are golden brown and nicely puffed. Transfer the popovers to a cloth napkin–lined basket and serve right away with butter and jam or preserves. —*Amy Hase*

MAKE AHEAD The popover batter can be prepared earlier in the day and refrigerated. Let the batter stand at room temperature for 30 minutes, then stir it well before filling the popover pan.

● FAST ● HEALTHY ● MAKE AHEAD ● STAFF FAVORITE

breakfast & brunch

Date Quick Bread with Pecan Streusel

ACTIVE: 25 MIN; TOTAL: 1 HR 30 MIN

MAKES 3 MINI LOAVES

STREUSEL TOPPING

Vegetable oil spray

½ cup pecan halves

½ cup all-purpose flour

1½ tablespoons light brown sugar

1 tablespoon granulated sugar

½ teaspoon baking powder

Pinch of salt

3 tablespoons unsalted butter, melted

BREAD

¾ cup whole milk

¾ cup finely chopped pitted dates

2 cups all-purpose flour

2¼ teaspoons baking powder

½ teaspoon salt

1 cup sugar

2 large eggs

½ cup canola oil

1 teaspoon pure vanilla extract

GLAZE

½ cup confectioners' sugar

2 tablespoons unsalted butter, softened

1 tablespoon milk

½ teaspoon pure vanilla extract

1. Preheat the oven to 375°. Lightly coat three 6-by-3-inch mini loaf pans with vegetable oil spray.

2. MAKE THE STREUSEL TOPPING: Toast the nuts on a baking sheet until fragrant and lightly browned, 8 minutes. Cool, then break into large pieces. In a bowl, mix the flour, sugars, baking powder and salt. Stir in the melted butter. Add the nuts and squeeze the streusel into large clumps.

3. MAKE THE BREAD: In a saucepan, simmer the milk and the dates; set aside. In a bowl, whisk the flour, baking powder and salt. In another bowl, using a electric mixer, beat the sugar, eggs and oil until blended. Beat in the milk, dates and vanilla until combined. Add the dry ingredients and beat at low speed just until smooth. Spread in the pans and sprinkle with the streusel. Bake for 45 minutes, or until golden and a toothpick inserted in the center comes out with a few moist crumbs. Cool for 20 minutes, then turn out on a rack.

4. MAKE THE GLAZE: Stir the sugar, butter, milk and vanilla until smooth. Drizzle over the warm loaves and cool. —*Grace Parisi*

ingredient

3 great honeys

APIPHARM
Wildflower Honey An intensely floral, smooth, golden honey (photo at right) from Macedonia in northern Greece. **Details** $8 for 8.8 oz; demeterspantry.com.

MOON SHINE TRADING COMPANY
Yellow Star Thistle Honey A spicy, light-amber honey made from bright California wildflowers. **Details** $10 for 16 oz; moonshinetrading.com.

BLUE HILLS HONEY
Meadow Honey An explosively sweet honey cultivated in Tasmania's Tarkine wilderness. **Details** $15 for 500 g; tassienaturals.com.

Crispy Mushroom Strudels

ACTIVE: 40 MIN; TOTAL: 1 HR

6 FIRST-COURSE SERVINGS ●

1 stick unsalted butter plus 4 tablespoons melted butter

3 medium shallots, minced

1 pound shiitakes, stems discarded and caps sliced ¼ inch thick

1 pound white mushrooms, sliced ¼ inch thick

Salt and freshly ground pepper

½ cup dry sherry

1 tablespoon sherry vinegar

9 sheets phyllo dough

Sour cream, for serving

1. Preheat the oven to 375°. In a very large skillet, melt the stick of butter. Add the shallots and cook over moderate heat until softened, 4 minutes. Add the mushrooms, season with salt and pepper and cook over moderately high heat, stirring occasionally, until lightly browned and the liquid has evaporated, 8 minutes. Add the sherry and vinegar and cook for 1 minute. Season with salt and pepper. Transfer the mushrooms to a food processor and process until finely chopped but still a bit chunky.

2. Lay 1 sheet of phyllo on a work surface and brush with melted butter; top and repeat with 2 more phyllo sheets; keep the rest covered with plastic. Cut the layered phyllo in half to form two 8½-by-12-inch rectangles. Spoon ½ cup of the mushrooms at the bottom of each half, leaving a 1-inch border. Roll the phyllo over the mushrooms; fold in the sides and continue to roll up like a cigar. Brush each strudel with melted butter and transfer to a large baking sheet. Repeat with the remaining phyllo, mushrooms and butter.

3. Bake the strudels for 15 minutes, or until nicely browned and crisp. Let rest for 3 minutes. With a serrated knife, cut the strudels on the bias into 2-inch lengths. Transfer the strudels to a platter, cut side up, and top with small dollops of sour cream. Serve hot. —*Tommy Habetz*

RASPBERRY SCONES

CINNAMON-BANANA BREAD

Raspberry Scones

ACTIVE: 20 MIN; TOTAL: 40 MIN

MAKES 1 DOZEN SCONES ● ● ●

- 2 cups spelt flour
- 1 tablespoon baking powder
- ½ teaspoon salt
- ⅓ cup canola oil
- ⅓ cup agave nectar
- 1 tablespoon pure vanilla extract
- ⅓ cup hot water
- 1 cup fresh raspberries

1. Preheat the oven to 375°. Line a baking sheet with parchment paper. In a bowl, whisk the spelt with the baking powder and salt. Stir in the oil, agave nectar and vanilla. Stir in the hot water, then the raspberries.
2. Scoop 12 mounds of batter ⅓ cup each onto the prepared baking sheet and lightly brush the tops with oil. Bake the scones for 20 minutes, or until golden. Let the baking sheet cool completely on top of a rack. —*Erin McKenna*

Cinnamon-Banana Bread

ACTIVE: 20 MIN; TOTAL: 1 HR 15 MIN

8 SERVINGS ● ●

This healthy recipe from vegan baker Erin McKenna of BabyCakes NYC is full of potassium-packed bananas. Instead of processed sugar, it calls for agave nectar, a natural sweetener; a little canola oil replaces the usual butter. The bread is an improvement on the one McKenna often made with her mother when she was growing up:"I thought it was so healthy, because of the bananas. I didn't factor in all the sugar and butter."

- ¼ cup canola oil, plus more for coating
- 1 cup Bob's Red Mill gluten-free, all-purpose baking flour
- 1 teaspoon baking soda
- 1 teaspoon baking powder
- 1 teaspoon cinnamon
- ½ teaspoon xanthan gum
- ¼ teaspoon salt
- 3 overripe bananas, mashed
- ⅓ cup agave nectar
- ⅓ cup unsweetened soy milk
- 2 teaspoons pure vanilla extract

1. Preheat the oven to 350°. Lightly oil an 8½-by-4½-inch loaf pan. Line the bottom and sides of the loaf pan with parchment paper and set aside.
2. In a medium bowl, whisk the baking flour with the baking soda, baking powder, cinnamon, xanthan gum and salt. In another bowl, whisk the bananas with the oil, agave nectar, soy milk and vanilla. Add the banana mixture to the dry ingredients and whisk until smooth. Pour the batter into the prepared loaf pan and bake for 45 minutes, or until a toothpick inserted in the center comes out clean. Let the banana bread cool on a rack for 20 minutes before turning it out. Let cool completely before slicing. —*Erin McKenna*

breakfast & brunch

Glazed Sweet Rolls

ACTIVE: 30 MIN; TOTAL: 2 HR 10 MIN

MAKES 32 ROLLS ●

2 sticks unsalted butter, softened, plus more for coating

2 cups milk

1 tablespoon instant dry yeast

6¼ cups all-purpose flour, plus more for dusting

1¾ cups sugar

1 teaspoon salt

1 tablespoon cinnamon

¼ cup water

1. In a small saucepan, melt 1 stick of the butter in 1 cup of the milk over moderate heat. Remove from the heat and add the remaining 1 cup of milk. Pour this mixture into the bowl of a standing electric mixer fitted with a paddle. Add the yeast and beat until dissolved. Add the flour, ¾ cup of the sugar and the salt and beat at medium speed until a dough forms.

2. Transfer the dough to a lightly floured surface and knead until smooth, about 1 minute. Lightly oil a large bowl, add the dough and turn to coat. Cover the dough with plastic wrap and let stand in a warm place until it has almost doubled in bulk, about 40 minutes.

3. Line the bottoms of two 10-inch round cake pans with parchment paper and lightly butter the paper. Divide the dough into 4 equal pieces. Roll 1 piece into a 12-by-6-inch rectangle about ⅓ inch thick, with a long edge facing you. In a small bowl, combine ½ cup of the sugar with the cinnamon. Spread 2 tablespoons of the butter on the dough and sprinkle with 2 tablespoons of the cinnamon sugar, leaving a 1-inch border at one long edge. Roll up the dough jelly roll style and pinch to seal. Repeat with the remaining dough and cinnamon sugar.

4. Cut each roll into 8 slices; arrange the slices in the pans, cut side up and about ½ inch apart. Cover the pans with a damp towel and set in a warm place until slightly risen, 30 minutes.

5. Preheat the oven to 375°. Bake the rolls for 30 minutes, or until golden. In a saucepan, stir the water and remaining sugar; simmer over moderately high heat until dissolved, 2 minutes. Remove the rolls from the oven. Generously brush the tops with hot syrup. Cool in the pans for 15 minutes and serve warm. —*Annabel Langbein*

Summer Fruit Pudding

TOTAL: 30 MIN PLUS OVERNIGHT CHILLING

10 SERVINGS ● ●

1 loaf challah (1¼ pounds), sliced, crusts trimmed

1 pound strawberries, quartered

3½ pints raspberries

3½ pints blackberries

½ cup sugar

½ teaspoon finely grated lemon zest

1. Line a 2½-quart soufflé dish with plastic wrap, leaving at least 6 inches of overhang all around. Line the bottom with several slices of challah, overlapping slightly. Line the side with challah, overlapping slightly. Reserve a few slices for the top.

2. In a saucepan, simmer the berries, sugar and lemon zest over low heat just until the sugar is dissolved and the berries release some of their juices, about 5 minutes.

3. Spoon the berries and their juices into the challah-lined dish, mounding them slightly above the top. Top with the remaining challah and press down until flush with the rim. Fold the plastic wrap over the pudding. Top with a small plate and weigh down with a heavy can. Refrigerate overnight.

4. Remove the plate and peel back the plastic wrap. Invert a plate over the pudding; flip both the plate and the soufflé dish, then lift off the dish. Discard the plastic. Cut the pudding into wedges and serve.
—*Hugo Matheson and Kimbal Musk*

SERVE WITH Lightly whipped cream or vanilla ice cream.

MAKE AHEAD The recipe can be prepared through Step 3 and refrigerated for 2 days.

Pear Bruschetta with Hazelnut Cream

ACTIVE: 25 MIN; TOTAL: 55 MIN

4 SERVINGS ●

Chef Jean-Georges Vongerichten has been making rustic fruit bruschetta (essentially a fruit tart with a bread crust) in the pizza oven at New York's Mercer Kitchen for years. This pear bruschetta, with its hazelnut frangipane flavored with amaretto, is a comforting late-winter incarnation.

Four ⅓-inch-thick slices of sourdough bread, 5 by 3 inches (6 ounces)

3 ounces roasted, skinned and salted hazelnuts (¾ cup), chopped

½ cup confectioners' sugar, plus more for dusting

4 tablespoons unsalted butter, softened

2 teaspoons amaretto liqueur

½ teaspoon pure vanilla extract

1 large egg, chilled

2 large ripe Bartlett pears

1 tablespoon fresh lemon juice

1. Preheat the oven to 350°. Put the bread slices on a large rimmed baking sheet and lightly toast for about 7 minutes.

2. In a food processor, finely grind ½ cup of the hazelnuts. Transfer to a bowl. Add the confectioners' sugar and butter and beat at medium-high speed until light and fluffy, about 3 minutes. Add the amaretto and vanilla and beat for 1 minute. Add the egg and beat until incorporated. Spread the hazelnut cream on the toasts.

3. Peel, halve and core the pears. Slice each pear half lengthwise ¼ inch thick; spread the halves into fans. Brush with the lemon juice. Using a spatula, transfer the pear fans to the toasts. Dust the pears with confectioners' sugar. Bake for about 30 minutes, or until the hazelnut cream is set and nicely browned. Dust the toasts with confectioners' sugar, scatter the remaining ¼ cup of chopped hazelnuts over the top and serve right away.
—*Jean-Georges Vongerichten*

PEAR BRUSCHETTA WITH
HAZELNUT CREAM

MARA DES BOIS STRAWBERRY
NAPOLEONS (P. 330)

pies & fruit desserts

"Pie is a symbol of community, and giving the first slice is like giving the best."

–Mary Ellen Diaz, founder of First Slice (soup kitchen), Chicago

CAMPARI MERINGUES WITH BAKED PEACHES AND RASPBERRY SAUCE

LEMON VERBENA TART WITH CAPE GOOSEBERRY COMPOTE

Campari Meringues with Baked Peaches and Raspberry Sauce

ACTIVE: 30 MIN; TOTAL: 3 HR 15 MIN

4 SERVINGS

Baking peaches brings out their sweetness and makes them meltingly soft. But if you can find ripe and drippy summer peaches, don't bake them. Simply blanch them in boiling water for about 10 seconds to loosen the skins, then peel and slice.

- 4 firm, ripe freestone peaches (6 ounces each)
- 2 large egg whites
- 1 tablespoon Campari
- ⅓ cup granulated sugar
- ½ cup plus 1 tablespoon confectioners' sugar
- 1½ tablespoons turbinado or dark brown sugar
- 1 tablespoon water
- 6 ounces fresh raspberries
- 1 cup heavy cream

1. Preheat the oven to 300°. Arrange the peaches in a deep baking dish without touching; cover tightly with foil and bake for about 1 hour, until tender. Let cool. Carefully peel the peaches, then halve and pit. Cut into ½-inch wedges and return to the baking dish with any juices. Refrigerate for at least 2 hours or overnight.

2. Lower the oven to 225°. Line a baking sheet with parchment. In a bowl, using an electric mixer, beat the whites and Campari until soft peaks form. Beat in the granulated sugar, 1 tablespoon at a time, until stiff and glossy. Sift the ½ cup of confectioners' sugar on top and quickly beat in.

3. Spoon the meringue onto the baking sheet in 4 mounds. Using the back of a spoon, make a well in the center of each to create bowls. Bake in the center of the oven for 1 hour; turn the oven off and let cool in the oven for 1½ hours. The centers of the meringues will be slightly soft.

4. In a microwave-safe bowl, heat the turbinado sugar and the water at high power for 1 minute; stir until dissolved. Transfer to a blender, add the berries and puree. Strain through a sieve to remove the seeds. Refrigerate until chilled. In a bowl, beat the cream and remaining confectioners' sugar at medium-high speed until just firm. Fill the meringues with the cream. Top with the peaches. Drizzle with the sauce and serve.—*Will Goldfarb*

Lemon Verbena Tart with Cape Gooseberry Compote

ACTIVE: 1 HR; TOTAL: 1 HR 40 MIN

PLUS 3 HR CHILLING

MAKES ONE 10½-INCH TART ●

PASTRY

- 2 cups cake flour, sifted
- ½ teaspoon cinnamon
- 1 cup toasted, skinned hazelnuts, finely ground

2 sticks unsalted butter, softened

¾ cup sugar

1 large egg

½ teaspoon pure vanilla extract

Finely grated zest of ½ lemon

Finely grated zest of ½ orange

LEMON CURD FILLING

4 extra-large egg yolks

3 extra-large eggs

1 cup plus 1 tablespoon sugar

1 cup fresh lemon juice

½ cup dried lemon verbena leaves or 6 fresh lemon verbena leaves

1 stick plus 2 tablespoons cold unsalted butter, cut into tablespoons

Salt

COMPOTE AND GARNISH

1½ cups water

1 cup sugar

⅔ cup fresh orange juice

¼ cup Cointreau or Grand Marnier

½ vanilla bean, seeds scraped

3 pints cape gooseberries

¼ teaspoon freshly ground pepper

Lightly sweetened whipped cream and fresh lemon verbena, for serving

1. MAKE THE PASTRY: In a bowl, stir the flour, cinnamon and hazelnuts. In another bowl, using an electric mixer, beat the butter and sugar at high speed until light and fluffy, 2 minutes. Beat in the egg, then the vanilla extract and zests. Beat in the dry ingredients in 3 batches until almost incorporated. Stir until thoroughly combined. Divide in half, pat into 2 disks and wrap in plastic. Refrigerate one disk for 1 hour, until firm. Freeze the other for another use.

2. Preheat the oven to 325°. Roll the pastry between 2 sheets of heavy-duty plastic to a 12-inch round. Chill until firm. Unwrap and press into the bottom and up the side of a 10½-inch fluted tart pan with a removable bottom. Refrigerate for 15 minutes, or until firm. Line the pastry with foil and fill with pie weights or dried beans. Bake for 45 minutes, or until browned on

the edges. Remove the foil and weights and bake for 25 minutes, or until crisp on the bottom. Transfer to a rack to cool.

3. MAKE THE LEMON CURD FILLING: In a large, heavy saucepan, whisk the egg yolks and whole eggs with the sugar, lemon juice and lemon verbena leaves. Cook over moderate heat, whisking constantly, until hot and thickened, about 5 minutes. Remove from the heat and whisk in the butter, 1 tablespoon at a time, until blended. Add a pinch of salt. Strain the curd through a sieve set over a bowl. Pour the curd into the tart shell and smooth the surface. Refrigerate until firm, about 2 hours.

4. MAKE THE COMPOTE: In a saucepan, whisk together the water, sugar, orange juice, Cointreau and vanilla seeds; bring to a boil. Add the gooseberries and simmer over moderately high heat, stirring gently, until soft, about 5 minutes. Stir in the pepper and let cool to room temperature.

5. Cut the tart into wedges. Garnish with the compote. Serve with whipped cream and lemon verbena. —*Mary Dumont*

Double-Chocolate Peanut Butter Pie

ACTIVE: 45 MIN; TOTAL: 4 HR INCLUDING CHILLING

MAKES ONE 9-INCH PIE ●

This incredibly chocolaty and creamy quick-bake pie is a grown-up version of a Reese's Peanut Butter Cup.

CHOCOLATE CRUST

4 ounces semisweet chocolate, chopped (½ cup)

½ stick unsalted butter, cut into tablespoons

8 ounces chocolate wafer cookies (from a 9-ounce package), finely ground (2 cups)

PEANUT BUTTER FILLING

8 ounces cream cheese, softened (1 cup)

1 cup chunky peanut butter

½ cup sugar

2 teaspoons pure vanilla extract

1 cup well-chilled heavy cream

¾ cup salted roasted peanuts, chopped

Kosher salt

TOPPING

4 ounces semisweet chocolate, chopped (½ cup)

½ cup heavy cream

1. MAKE THE CHOCOLATE CRUST: Preheat the oven to 375°. In a glass bowl, microwave the chocolate and butter at high power in 20-second intervals until melted. Stir well, then stir in the cookie crumbs and press over the bottom of a 9-inch springform pan and 1½ inches up the side. Bake for 10 minutes, or until set; the crust will firm up as it cools.

2. MAKE THE PEANUT BUTTER FILLING: In a large bowl, using a handheld electric mixer, beat the cream cheese, peanut butter, sugar and vanilla until blended. In another large bowl, using the same beaters, whip the chilled cream until firm. Fold one-third of the cream into the peanut butter mixture to loosen it, then fold in the remaining cream and ½ cup of the peanuts. Spoon the filling into the crust; smooth the surface. Sprinkle lightly with salt and refrigerate until set, 3 hours.

3. MAKE THE TOPPING: In a medium glass bowl, microwave the chocolate and cream at high power in 20-second intervals until the chocolate is melted and the cream is hot. Stir until blended; cool to barely warm, stirring occasionally.

4. Spread the topping on the filling and refrigerate until firm, 15 minutes. Sprinkle the remaining peanuts around the edge of the pie. Carefully run a thin knife around the crust to loosen it, then remove the springform ring. Using a sharp knife, cut into wedges. Run the knife under hot water and dry between each cut. —*Vitaly Paley*

MAKE AHEAD The pie can be covered and refrigerated overnight. Garnish before serving. Serve chilled or slightly cool.

pies & fruit desserts

Flaky Pear Pie

ACTIVE: 40 MIN; TOTAL: 2 HR 30 MIN
PLUS 3 HR COOLING
MAKES ONE 10-INCH PIE ●
CRUST
 2 cups all-purpose flour
 1 teaspoon salt
 ⅔ cup cold vegetable shortening,
   cut into tablespoons
 ½ cup ice water
FILLING
 ½ cup sugar
 ¼ cup all-purpose flour
 ¼ teaspoon cinnamon
 ⅛ teaspoon ground cloves
 8 firm Bartlett or Anjou pears—
   peeled, cored and sliced
   ½ inch thick
 1 tablespoon unsalted butter,
   cut into small bits
MILK GLAZE
 1 tablespoon milk
 1 tablespoon sugar
 1 tablespoon unsalted butter,
   melted

1. MAKE THE CRUST: In a large bowl, mix the flour and salt. Cut in the shortening until the mixture resembles coarse meal. Sprinkle on the ice water and mix lightly with a fork. Gently knead the dough until it just comes together; cut in half and flatten each piece into a disk. Wrap in plastic and refrigerate until firm, about 30 minutes.

2. MAKE THE FILLING: Preheat the oven to 350°. In a large bowl, stir together the sugar, flour, cinnamon and cloves. Add the pears and toss to coat.

3. On a lightly floured work surface, roll out 1 disk of dough to an 11½-inch round. Fit into a 10-inch aluminum pie pan without stretching. Roll out the second disk to an 11-inch round. Transfer the pear filling to the pan and arrange the slices so there are no gaps. Dot the pears with the butter. Cover the pie with the top crust and press all around the edge to seal. Trim any overhang and crimp the edge decoratively.

4. MAKE THE MILK GLAZE: In a bowl, mix the milk, sugar and butter and brush this glaze over the pie. With a knife, make 5 evenly spaced slits in the top crust.

5. Bake the pie for 1 hour and 50 minutes, or until the crust is golden and the filling begins to bubble through the vents. Let the pie cool on a rack, 3 hours. Serve warm or at room temperature. —Grant Achatz

Georgia Peach Pie

ACTIVE: 45 MIN; TOTAL: 2 HR 30 MIN
PLUS COOLING
MAKES ONE 9-INCH PIE ● ●
CRUST
 2⅔ cups all-purpose flour
 2 teaspoons sugar
 ¾ teaspoon salt
 1 stick cold unsalted butter, cut into
   ½-inch pieces
 ½ cup plus 1 tablespoon cold solid
   vegetable shortening
 ½ cup ice water
FILLING
 8 large, ripe but firm peaches
   (3½ pounds)
 ¾ cup sugar
 1½ tablespoons fresh lemon juice
 5 tablespoons all-purpose flour
 1½ tablespoons unsalted butter,
   thinly sliced
Egg wash made with 1 large egg yolk
   mixed with 2 tablespoons water
Bourbon Whipped Cream (recipe
   follows), for serving

1. MAKE THE CRUST: In a food processor, pulse the flour, sugar and salt until combined. Add the butter and shortening and pulse until the mixture resembles coarse meal. Transfer to a large bowl and sprinkle the ice water on top. Stir with a fork until a crumbly dough forms. Turn the dough out onto a work surface and knead 2 or 3 times, just until the dough comes together. Cut the dough in half and form into 2 disks; wrap the dough in plastic and refrigerate until firm, at least 30 minutes or overnight.

2. On a lightly floured surface, roll out each disk of dough to a 12-inch round. Ease one into a 9-inch glass pie plate. Transfer the other to a baking sheet and refrigerate.

3. MAKE THE FILLING: Preheat the oven to 400°. Bring a pan of water to a boil and fill a bowl with ice water. With a knife, mark a shallow X in the bottom of each peach. Blanch the peaches in the boiling water for 1 minute. Using a slotted spoon, transfer to the ice water to cool. Drain and peel the peaches and cut into ¾-inch wedges. Transfer the peaches to a bowl. Add the sugar, lemon juice and flour, toss well and let stand for 5 minutes.

4. Pour the peaches and their juices into the chilled pie shell and scatter the butter on top. Brush the edge of the pie crust with the egg wash and lay the second round of dough on top. Press the edges of the pie crust together to seal and trim the overhang to ½ inch. Fold the edge of the pie dough under and crimp decoratively. Brush the remaining egg wash on top and cut a few slits for venting steam.

5. Transfer the peach pie to the oven. Place a baking sheet in the bottom of the oven to catch any drips. Bake the pie for 30 minutes. Reduce the oven temperature to 375°, cover the edge of the pie with foil and bake for about 40 minutes longer, until the filling is bubbling and the crust is deeply golden on the top and bottom. Transfer the pie to a rack to cool completely. Serve with the Bourbon Whipped Cream. —Angie Mosier

BOURBON WHIPPED CREAM
TOTAL: 5 MIN
MAKES 2 CUPS ●
 1 cup heavy cream, chilled
 1 tablespoon bourbon
 ½ teaspoon sugar
 ¼ teaspoon pure vanilla extract
Using an electric mixer, beat the ingredients together in a bowl until the heavy cream is softly whipped. —A.M.

GEORGIA PEACH PIE

pies & fruit desserts

Chilled Grapefruit-Caramel Meringue Pie

ACTIVE: 1 HR; TOTAL: 3 HR PLUS 5 HR FREEZING

12 SERVINGS ●

- 1 cup fresh pink grapefruit juice
- Coarsely shredded zest of 3 pink grapefruit (½ cup)
- 1 dozen large eggs, 6 eggs lightly beaten, 6 eggs separated
- ¾ cup plus 1⅓ cups sugar
- 2 sticks unsalted butter, softened, plus 4 tablespoons melted
- 9 whole graham crackers
- ½ pound cream cheese, softened
- Caramel Sauce (recipe follows)
- ¾ cup heavy cream

1. Fill a medium saucepan with 2 inches of water and simmer over moderate heat. In a medium heatproof bowl, whisk the grapefruit juice and zest, the 6 whole eggs, 6 egg yolks and ¾ cup of sugar. Set the bowl over the pan and cook, stirring, until a thick curd forms, about 15 minutes; don't worry if it looks slightly curdled. Strain through a fine sieve set over a bowl; press on the solids, then discard them. Whisk in the softened butter until blended. Place a sheet of plastic directly on the curd and refrigerate until set, about 3 hours.

2. In a food processor, crush the graham crackers; pour in the melted butter and pulse just to combine. Pat the crumbs over the bottom of a 9-inch springform pan. Refrigerate the crust for 30 minutes.

3. In a medium bowl, using an electric mixer, beat the cream cheese until fluffy. Beat in ¾ cup of the Caramel Sauce. In another medium bowl, beat the heavy cream until soft peaks form. Fold the heavy cream into the caramel cream cheese.

4. Spoon the grapefruit curd into the springform and tap gently to form an even layer. Spoon the caramel cream on top in a smooth layer. Drizzle the remaining ¾ cup of caramel all over the caramel cream and freeze until slightly set, 1 hour.

5. Fill a medium saucepan with 2 inches of water and simmer. In the bowl of a standing mixer, mix the 6 whites and the remaining sugar. Set over the simmering water; whisk over low heat until the sugar dissolves and the whites are hot to the touch. Transfer to the mixer fitted with a whisk and beat at medium-high speed until stiff and glossy, 8 minutes. Spread the meringue over the caramel. Swirl in decorative peaks. Freeze the pie until firm, at least 4 hours.

6. Preheat the broiler and position a rack 8 inches from the heat. Broil the meringue until it begins to brown, 2 minutes, shifting the pan for even browning. Alternatively, brown with a propane torch. Carefully remove the ring. Chill on a platter in the refrigerator for 30 minutes before serving.—*Deborah Snyder*

CARAMEL SAUCE

TOTAL: 15 MIN

MAKES 1½ CUPS ●

- 1½ cups sugar
- 2 tablespoons water
- ¾ cup heavy cream

In a saucepan, mix the sugar and water. Using a wet pastry brush, wash down the side of the pan to remove any sugar crystals. Cook on high heat until an amber caramel forms, 8 minutes. Remove from the heat, stir in the cream and then return and cook for 1 minute, stirring until smooth. Transfer to a bowl and cool. —*D.S.*

Blueberry-Raspberry Tart

ACTIVE: 30 MIN; TOTAL: 2 HR

12 SERVINGS ●

PASTRY

- 2½ cups all-purpose flour, plus more for dusting
- ¼ cup sugar
- ½ teaspoon kosher salt
- 1½ sticks cold unsalted butter, cut into ½-inch pieces
- 3 tablespoons sour cream
- ⅓ cup ice water

FILLING

- 4 cups raspberries
- 3 cups blueberries
- ½ cup plus 2 tablespoons sugar
- 3 tablespoons plus 1 teaspoon cornstarch
- 2 tablespoons fresh lemon juice
- 1 tablespoon milk
- Confectioners' sugar, for dusting

1. MAKE THE PASTRY: In a food processor, pulse the 2½ cups of flour with the sugar and salt. Add the butter and sour cream and pulse until the mixture resembles small peas. Sprinkle on the ice water and pulse until the pastry just comes together. Transfer to a sheet of plastic wrap and pat into a disk. Wrap and refrigerate for at least 30 minutes or overnight.

2. MAKE THE FILLING: Preheat the oven to 400°. In a bowl, gently toss the berries with the sugar, cornstarch and lemon juice until well combined.

3. Line a rimmed baking sheet with parchment. On a lightly floured work surface, roll out the pastry to a 15-inch round, about ⅛ inch thick. Transfer to the baking sheet. Spread the filling on the pastry, leaving a 1½-inch border. Fold the border up and over the berries, pinching together any cracks. Brush the border with milk and bake the tart for 45 to 50 minutes, or until the pastry is golden and the fruit is bubbling. Let cool on the sheet for 20 minutes, then dust with confectioners' sugar; carefully remove from the sheet. Transfer to a plate, cut into wedges and serve. —*Jeri Ryan*

VARIATION To make 12 individual tarts, increase the pastry recipe by half. Divide into 12 equal portions and pat into disks. Refrigerate for at least 30 minutes or overnight. Roll out into 7-inch rounds ⅛ inch thick. Spread ½ cup of the berry filling on each round, leaving a 1-inch border. Proceed with the rest of Step 3.

MAKE AHEAD The tart can be baked up to 6 hours ahead and kept at room temperature until serving.

Old-Fashioned Strawberry-Rhubarb Crisp

ACTIVE: 30 MIN; TOTAL: 2 HR

6 SERVINGS ● ●

FILLING

- 2 pounds rhubarb stalks, sliced ½ inch thick
- 1¼ cups sugar
- 1 pound strawberries, hulled and quartered
- 3 tablespoons cornstarch
- 2 teaspoons fresh lemon juice
- 1 teaspoon pure vanilla extract

TOPPING

- 1 stick unsalted butter, softened
- 1½ cups light brown sugar
- 1½ cups all-purpose flour
- 1¼ cups quick-cooking rolled oats
- 3 tablespoons canola oil
- 1½ teaspoons cinnamon
- ¾ teaspoon salt

1. MAKE THE FILLING: Preheat the oven to 375°. In a bowl, toss the rhubarb with ¾ cup of the sugar. Let stand for 15 minutes, stirring occasionally. In another bowl, toss the berries with the remaining ½ cup sugar and let stand for 10 minutes, stirring occasionally. Using a slotted spoon, transfer the rhubarb to the berries; discard any rhubarb juice. Add the cornstarch, lemon juice and vanilla; stir well. Transfer to a 13-by-9-inch glass baking dish.

2. MAKE THE TOPPING: Combine the ingredients in a medium bowl. Using your fingers, mix until large crumbs form.

3. Sprinkle the topping evenly over the filling and bake for 30 minutes. Reduce the oven temperature to 325° and continue baking for about 30 minutes longer, until the filling is bubbling and the topping nicely browned. Let rest for 10 to 20 minutes before serving. —*Rollie Wesen*

SERVE WITH Vanilla ice cream.

MAKE AHEAD The topping can be refrigerated overnight; bring it to room temperature before using.

Maple Custards with Sugared Pecans

ACTIVE: 30 MIN; TOTAL: 1 HR 30 MIN PLUS 6 HR CHILLING

12 SERVINGS ● ●

- 3¼ cups pure maple syrup
- 16 large egg yolks
- 4 large whole eggs
- 4 tablespoons unsalted butter
- 2 cups pecan halves (½ pound)
- ¼ cup sugar
- Salt
- Boiling water
- Whipped cream, for serving

1. Preheat the oven to 325°. Spoon 1 teaspoon of maple syrup into each of twelve ½-cup ramekins, swirling to coat the bottoms. Arrange the ramekins in a large roasting pan.

2. In a bowl, whisk the yolks and whole eggs until blended. Whisk in the remaining maple syrup. Pour into the ramekins. Carefully pour enough hot water into the roasting pan to reach halfway up the sides of the ramekins. Cover the pan with foil and bake the custards for 55 minutes, or until just set.

3. Using tongs, immediately remove the ramekins from the hot water and let cool to room temperature. Refrigerate the custards for at least 6 hours or overnight.

4. Meanwhile, in a large skillet, melt the butter. Add the pecans and stir to coat. Cook over moderate heat until lightly browned, about 5 minutes. Put the sugar in a bowl. With a slotted spoon, transfer the pecans to the bowl with the sugar and toss to coat. Transfer the pecans to a baking sheet, shaking off any excess sugar. Sprinkle the nuts lightly with salt. Set aside to cool.

5. Carefully run a thin knife around each custard. Dip each ramekin in a bowl of boiling water, then quickly invert the custard onto a plate. Spoon whipped cream over the custards, garnish with the sugared pecans and serve. —*José Andrés*

MAKE AHEAD The custards can be refrigerated for 2 days. The sugared pecans can be stored overnight in an airtight container.

Sweet and Tart Lime Bars

ACTIVE: 30 MIN; TOTAL: 2 HR PLUS 6 HR CHILLING

MAKES 16 BARS ●

PASTRY

- 2 tablespoons salted roasted almonds with skin
- ¼ cup confectioners' sugar
- 1 stick unsalted butter, softened
- 1 large egg
- ½ teaspoon pure vanilla extract
- 1 cup all-purpose flour

LIME CURD

- 2 large eggs
- ¼ cup plus 2 tablespoons sugar
- ⅓ cup fresh lime juice
- ½ teaspoon finely grated lime zest
- 9 tablespoons cold unsalted butter, cut into ½-inch pieces

1. MAKE THE PASTRY: In a food processor, pulse the almonds and sugar until finely ground. Add the butter and pulse until smooth. Pulse in the egg and vanilla then the flour until smooth. Press evenly into an 11-by-8-inch glass baking dish, pressing 1 inch up the side. Trim the edge to ¾ inch; chill until firm, at least 1 hour.

2. Preheat the oven to 350°. Prick the pastry with a fork and bake for 25 minutes, or until golden. Let cool completely.

3. MAKE THE LIME CURD: In a heatproof bowl set over a pan of simmering water, cook the eggs, sugar, lime juice and zest, whisking, until an instant-read thermometer registers 180°, about 7 minutes. Set the bowl in an ice water bath; stir until the temperature drops to 130°, about 3 minutes. Whisk in the butter. Cool at room temperature for 1 hour.

4. Pour the lime curd over the pastry and refrigerate until firm, at least 6 hours or overnight. Cut into bars and serve. —*Ludovic Augendre*

pies & fruit desserts

Apple Pies with Orange Muscat Cream Sauce

ACTIVE: 40 MIN; TOTAL: 3 HR

8 SERVINGS ●

APPLE PIES

- ½ cup golden raisins
- 2 tablespoons Orange Muscat wine
- 3 cups all-purpose flour
- ½ cup sugar plus 1 teaspoon
- ¾ teaspoon salt
- ½ cup cold solid vegetable shortening, cut into 4 pieces
- 1 stick cold unsalted butter, cut into ½-inch pieces
- ½ cup plus 1 tablespoon ice water
- 4 medium Granny Smith apples

ORANGE MUSCAT CREAM SAUCE

- 1½ cups apple juice
- 1 cup Orange Muscat wine
- ½ teaspoon cinnamon
- ¼ teaspoon freshly grated nutmeg
- 1 teaspoon finely grated tangerine zest
- 6 tablespoons unsalted butter
- 1 cup heavy cream

1. MAKE THE APPLE PIES: In a small saucepan, simmer the golden raisins in the Orange Muscat over low heat, covered, for 2 minutes; set aside.

2. In a food processor, pulse the all-purpose flour with the teaspoon of sugar and salt several times. Add the shortening and pulse 5 or 6 times, until it is the size of peas; add the butter and pulse 5 or 6 times, until it is the size of peas. Pour the ice water on top and pulse 5 or 6 times, just until the pastry is moistened.

3. Transfer the pastry to a lightly floured work surface and knead several times. Divide the pastry in half and pat it into two 6-inch disks; wrap in plastic and refrigerate until firm, at least 30 minutes.

4. Preheat the oven to 375°. Peel, halve and core the apples; slice them ¼ inch thick, keeping the halves together.

5. On a lightly floured surface, roll out 1 disk of pastry to a 12-inch square, and cut it in quarters. Sprinkle ⅛ of the raisins and ½ tablespoon of the sugar in the center of each pastry square; set a sliced apple half over the raisins, fan slightly and sprinkle each one with ½ tablespoon of the sugar. Fold the pastry up around the apple halves and crimp decoratively. Set the pies on a rimmed baking sheet. Repeat with the remaining ingredients to make 4 more pies. Spoon any remaining Muscat from the raisins over the apples. Bake the pies for 1 hour and 20 minutes, or until the pastry is golden brown and the apples are lightly caramelized.

6. MEANWHILE, MAKE THE ORANGE MUSCAT CREAM SAUCE: Combine all of the ingredients in a medium saucepan and simmer until the sauce is reduced to 1½ cups, about 50 minutes.

7. Serve the pies warm or at room temperature with the Muscat cream sauce.

—Jim Clendenen

Granny Smith Apple and Brown Butter Custard Tart

ACTIVE: 1 HR; TOTAL: 3 HR

8 TO 10 SERVINGS ● ○

Pastry chef Kate Neumann of Chicago's MK The Restaurant often showcases rich, nutty, fragrant browned butter in her desserts. Here, she adds it to a sweet custard loaded with caramelized apples and baked in a buttery tart shell.

TART SHELL

- Vegetable oil spray
- 1⅓ cups all-purpose flour
- ½ cup sugar
- ½ teaspoon baking powder
- ¼ teaspoon salt
- 1 stick unsalted butter, softened
- 1 large egg yolk mixed with 1 tablespoon water

FILLING

- 10 tablespoons unsalted butter
- 1 cup sugar
- 5 large Granny Smith apples (6 to 8 ounces each)—peeled, cored and cut into 6 wedges each
- Salt and freshly ground pepper
- 2 large eggs
- ¼ cup all-purpose flour

1. MAKE THE TART SHELL: Preheat the oven to 350°. Spray an 11-inch fluted tart pan with a removable bottom with vegetable oil spray. In a food processor, pulse the flour with the sugar, baking powder and salt. Add the butter and egg yolk mixture and process just until the pastry comes together. Turn the pastry out onto a work surface and knead 2 or 3 times. Press the pastry evenly into the tart pan and refrigerate until chilled, at least 30 minutes.

2. Line the tart shell with parchment paper and fill loosely with pie weights. Bake for about 35 minutes, until the edge is set. Remove the parchment and pie weights and bake for about 20 minutes longer, until the tart shell is lightly browned all over.

3. MEANWHILE, MAKE THE FILLING: In a very large skillet, melt 2 tablespoons of the butter. Add ½ cup of the sugar; cook over high heat until just brown. Add the apples, season lightly with salt and pepper and cook over moderate heat, turning once, until lightly caramelized, 12 minutes.

4. In a small saucepan, cook the remaining stick of butter over moderate heat until the milk solids brown and the butter is fragrant, about 7 minutes. In a medium bowl, using an electric mixer, beat the eggs with the remaining ½ cup of sugar until thick and fluffy, about 3 minutes. Beat in the flour and ¼ teaspoon of salt, then beat in the browned butter, scraping the milk solids into the custard mixture.

5. Pour the custard into the shell and arrange the apples in a single layer of slightly overlapping circles. Bake the tart in the lower third of the oven for 45 to 50 minutes, until the custard is puffed and richly browned. Transfer to a rack and cool before serving.

—Kate Neumann

pies & fruit desserts

Maple Pecan Tart

ACTIVE: 30 MIN; TOTAL: 2 HR 40 MIN
PLUS COOLING
MAKES ONE 11½-INCH TART ●

PASTRY
- 2 cups all-purpose flour
- ¼ teaspoon salt
- 1 stick plus 3 tablespoons cold unsalted butter, cut into ½-inch pieces
- ¼ cup ice water
- 1 large egg white, beaten

FILLING
- 5 large eggs
- ¼ cup sugar
- 1 cup pure maple syrup
- 1 tablespoon pure vanilla extract
- ¼ cup all-purpose flour
- 1 teaspoon salt
- 4 tablespoons unsalted butter, melted
- 2 cups pecan halves (½ pound)

1. MAKE THE PASTRY: In a food processor, pulse the flour and salt. Add the butter and pulse just until pea-size clumps form. Drizzle in the ice water and pulse until the pastry is evenly moistened. Turn out onto a work surface and pat into a disk. Wrap the pastry in plastic and refrigerate until firm, at least 30 minutes.

2. Preheat the oven to 375°. On a lightly floured surface, roll out the pastry to a scant ¼ inch thick. Fit the pastry into an 11½-inch tart pan with a removable bottom and trim the overhang. Using the pastry scraps, patch any cracks in the shell. Refrigerate for 30 minutes.

3. Using a fork, prick the bottom of the tart shell several times. Line the shell with parchment and fill with pie weights or dried beans. Bake in the lower third of the oven for 30 minutes, until set. Carefully remove the parchment and weights and bake the shell for about 22 minutes, until golden and firm. Lightly brush the hot pastry with the egg white until thoroughly coated, being careful to fill any holes or cracks.

4. MAKE THE FILLING: In a large bowl, using an electric mixer, beat the eggs and sugar at medium speed until light and frothy, 2 minutes. Beat in the maple syrup and vanilla. Add the flour and salt; beat for 1 minute. Beat in the butter.

5. Reduce the oven temperature to 325°. Set the tart pan on the oven rack and carefully pour the filling into the shell. Sprinkle evenly with the pecans. Bake for 28 minutes, until the filling is just set in the center. Transfer to a rack; cool completely.

6. Remove the pan's ring. Slide the tart onto a plate and serve. —Marc Aumont

SERVE WITH Vanilla ice cream.

MAKE AHEAD The tart can be made 1 day ahead and kept at room temperature.

Poached Plum Tart

ACTIVE: 1 HR 10 MIN; TOTAL: 2 HR
15 MIN PLUS 4 HR CHILLING
8 SERVINGS ●

PASTRY
- 1¼ cups all-purpose flour
- ¼ teaspoon salt
- 1 stick cold unsalted butter, cut into small pieces
- 3 tablespoons ice water

PASTRY CREAM
- 1 teaspoon powdered gelatin
- 2 teaspoons water
- 2 cups plus 2 teaspoons whole milk
- 6 large egg yolks
- ½ cup sugar
- ½ cup plus 2 tablespoons all-purpose flour
- 1 tablespoon pure vanilla extract

Pinch of salt

PLUMS
- 2 cups fruity red wine, such as Beaujolais
- ½ cup sugar
- 6 whole cloves
- 6 black peppercorns

One 3-inch cinnamon stick, broken
- ½ vanilla bean, split lengthwise, seeds scraped

- 6 medium purple or greengage plums (2¼ pounds), pitted and cut into eighths

1. MAKE THE PASTRY: In a food processor, pulse the flour and salt. Add the butter and pulse just until pea size. Sprinkle on the ice water and pulse until the pastry comes together. Turn out onto a work surface and flatten into a disk. Wrap in plastic and refrigerate until firm, at least 1 hour.

2. Preheat the oven to 350°. Turn the pastry out onto a floured work surface and roll out to a 12-inch round. Transfer to an 11-inch tart pan with a removable bottom; gently press the pastry up the side of the pan and trim any overhang. Refrigerate until firm, about 20 minutes.

3. Line the pastry with foil and fill with pie weights or dried beans. Bake for about 40 minutes, until dry and lightly golden. Remove the foil and pie weights and bake for about 15 minutes longer, until the shell is golden brown. Transfer to a rack to cool.

4. MAKE THE PASTRY CREAM: In a small saucepan, sprinkle the gelatin in an even layer on the water. Let stand until softened, 5 minutes. In a medium saucepan, warm the milk. In a medium bowl, whisk the yolks with the sugar until thick and pale. Whisk in the flour, then gradually whisk in the hot milk until smooth. Stir in the vanilla and salt. Scrape into the medium saucepan and cook over moderate heat, whisking constantly, until bubbling, 4 minutes. Reduce the heat to low and cook, whisking, until no floury taste remains, 5 minutes longer. Remove from the heat.

5. Warm the gelatin over low heat, swirling the pan until melted, 3 minutes; stir into the pastry cream. Scrape the cream into a bowl and cover directly with plastic. Let cool to room temperature. Refrigerate until chilled and firm, 4 hours or overnight.

6. POACH THE PLUMS: In a skillet, boil the wine, sugar, cloves, peppercorns, cinnamon and vanilla bean and seeds, whisking to dissolve the sugar. Add the plums and

POACHED PLUM TART

CARAMELIZED BANANA TART

simmer over moderate heat, stirring until tender, about 10 minutes. Using a slotted spoon, transfer the plums to a plate; let cool to room temperature. Boil the liquid until it has reduced to ⅓ cup, about 6 minutes. Strain the syrup into a bowl and pat the plums dry.

7. Spread the pastry cream in the shell. Arrange the plums in concentric circles over the cream. Brush some of the syrup over the plums. (If the syrup is too thick, reheat it gently.) Refrigerate the tart 1 hour, or until just set. Cut into wedges; serve the syrup on the side.—*Nina Planck*

Caramelized Banana Tart

ACTIVE: 25 MIN; TOTAL: 1 HR 40 MIN

6 SERVINGS ● ●

14 ounces all-butter puff pastry, thawed in the refrigerator

1 large egg yolk mixed with 1½ tablespoons water

5 small just-ripe bananas, halved lengthwise

1½ tablespoons fresh lemon juice

½ cup sugar

6 tablespoons unsalted butter

½ vanilla bean, split, seeds scraped

2 tablespoons water

Sweetened whipped cream or vanilla ice cream, for serving

1. Preheat the oven to 375°. Line a baking sheet with parchment. On a lightly floured surface, roll out the pastry to a rough 15-by-10-inch rectangle, then trim to a neat 14-by-9-inch rectangle. Using a ruler, cut a ¾-inch-wide strip of dough from each side to make 2 long and 2 short strips. Transfer the dough to the baking sheet; brush with the egg wash. Set the strips on each side to form a border, pressing firmly to help the dough adhere. Brush the strips with the egg wash. Freeze the tart shell until chilled, about 10 minutes.

2. Prick the bottom of the tart shell all over with a fork. Bake the shell in the lower third of the oven for 40 minutes, or until puffed and golden. Press down on the center of the shell lightly. Increase the oven temperature to 425°.

3. Rub the bananas all over with the lemon juice. In a skillet, cook the sugar over moderate heat, stirring, until melted. Cook the syrup without stirring until a medium-amber caramel forms, 5 minutes. Remove from the heat; whisk in the butter, vanilla seeds and water. Add the bananas and gently turn to coat with caramel. Arrange the bananas in the tart shell, cut side up, leaving most of the caramel in the skillet. Drizzle ¼ cup of the caramel over the bananas. Bake the tart for about 20 minutes, until the bananas are slightly tender. Cool slightly. Serve with whipped cream, passing the remaining caramel. —*Zoe Behrens*

pies & fruit desserts

Bananas in Coffee Bean Syrup

ACTIVE: 15 MIN; TOTAL: 2 HR 45 MIN

6 SERVINGS ● ●

On a recent trip to Vietnam, F&W test kitchen supervisor Marcia Kiesel topped her yogurt every morning at breakfast with these bananas steeped in warm, bittersweet coffee. Make sure the bananas you choose are ripe but still firm so they don't get mushy.

- 2 cups water
- ½ cup whole espresso coffee beans
- ½ cup sugar
- Two 3-inch strips of lemon zest
- One 3-inch cinnamon stick, broken into pieces
- 8 firm, medium bananas
- 1 tablespoon fresh lemon juice
- Plain whole milk yogurt, for serving

1. In a medium saucepan, combine the water with the whole espresso coffee beans and bring to a boil. Simmer the coffee beans over low heat for 20 minutes. Add the sugar, strips of lemon zest and pieces of cinnamon stick and simmer the mixture over moderate heat for about 5 minutes, or until it is syrupy.

2. Meanwhile, peel the bananas and slice them ½ inch thick on the diagonal. In a large, shallow dish, toss the sliced bananas with the lemon juice to prevent them from turning dark.

3. Pour the coffee bean syrup over the sliced bananas and let them stand until they have cooled to room temperature, then refrigerate the bananas and syrup until they are thoroughly chilled, about 2 hours. Spoon the bananas and coffee bean syrup over the yogurt and serve right away.
—*Marcia Kiesel*

MAKE AHEAD The coffee bean syrup can be prepared up to 1 day ahead; let the syrup cool, then refrigerate it overnight. Gently reheat the syrup before pouring it over the sliced bananas.

Sweet Potato Tart with Red Wine Caramel

ACTIVE: 45 MIN; TOTAL: 2 HR 30 MIN

MAKES ONE 10-INCH TART ●

TART SHELL

- ¼ cup finely chopped blanched almonds
- ¼ cup plus 2 tablespoons sugar
- 1 stick unsalted butter, softened
- 1 large egg
- 1½ cups all-purpose flour
- ¼ teaspoon baking powder

FILLING

- Two 1-pound sweet potatoes
- 2 large eggs, beaten
- ½ cup granulated sugar
- ½ cup light brown sugar
- ½ teaspoon salt
- ½ teaspoon cinnamon
- ½ teaspoon ground ginger
- 1 vanilla bean, split and seeds scraped
- ¾ cup heavy cream
- ¾ cup milk
- Red Wine Caramel (recipe follows) and lightly sweetened whipped cream, for serving

1. MAKE THE TART SHELL: Preheat the oven to 350°. In a food processor, combine the almonds and sugar and process until finely ground. Add the butter and egg and process until creamy, scraping down the side of the bowl. Add the flour and baking powder and process just until a dough forms, scraping down the side of the bowl. Using your fingers, press the dough evenly into a 10-inch fluted tart pan with a removable bottom. Refrigerate for 15 minutes.

2. Line the tart shell with aluminum foil and fill with pie weights or dried beans. Bake the tart shell for about 25 minutes, or until it is just set. Carefully remove the aluminum foil and pie weights and bake the tart shell for 15 to 20 minutes longer, until the shell is crisp and lightly browned all over. Let cool slightly.

3. MEANWHILE, MAKE THE FILLING: Poke the sweet potatoes all over with a fork and roast them in the oven alongside the tart shell for about 1 hour, or until they are soft. Let the potatoes cool. Turn the oven temperature down to 325°.

4. Peel and puree the sweet potatoes; you should have about 1½ cups (reserve any leftovers for another use). In a medium bowl, whisk the eggs with the granulated sugar and light brown sugar, salt, cinnamon, ginger and vanilla seeds until smooth. Add the 1½ cups of sweet potato puree along with the heavy cream and milk and whisk until blended.

5. Pour the filling into the tart shell and bake for 20 minutes. Using strips of foil or a 10-inch pie crust ring, cover the rim of the shell to prevent overbrowning. Bake the tart for 40 minutes longer, or until the filling is set. Transfer to a rack and let cool completely. Slice into wedges, top with the Red Wine Caramel and whipped cream, and serve.—*Michael Laiskonis*

MAKE AHEAD The tart dough can be patted into a disk, wrapped in plastic and refrigerated for up to 1 week. The finished tart can be refrigerated for up to 2 days.

RED WINE CARAMEL

TOTAL: 15 MIN

MAKES ABOUT ¾ CUP ●

- ¾ cup sugar
- 2 tablespoons water
- ¾ cup red wine

In a medium saucepan, bring the sugar and water to a boil over moderately high heat, washing down the side of the saucepan with a moistened pastry brush. Cook the syrup without stirring until a pale-amber caramel forms, about 6 minutes. Remove the caramel from the heat and carefully add the red wine. Cook, stirring to dissolve the hardened caramel, until slightly reduced, about 3 minutes. Transfer the red wine caramel to a pitcher and serve warm. —*M.L.*

SWEET POTATO TART WITH
RED WINE CARAMEL

BLUEBERRY COBBLER WITH
HONEY BISCUITS

Blueberry Cobbler with Honey Biscuits

ACTIVE: 25 MIN; TOTAL: 1 HR 30 MIN

8 SERVINGS ●

- 1 cup all-purpose flour
- ⅔ cup finely ground cornmeal
- 5 tablespoons granulated sugar
- 1½ teaspoons baking powder
- Scant ½ teaspoon cinnamon
- ½ teaspoon kosher salt
- 6 tablespoons unsalted butter, cut into small pieces and chilled
- ⅔ cup plus 1 tablespoon heavy cream
- 6 cups blueberries (2 pounds)
- 2 tablespoons honey
- 3 tablespoons fresh orange juice
- ½ teaspoon finely grated lemon zest
- 1 tablespoon potato starch or cornstarch
- 1 tablespoon turbinado sugar
- Vanilla ice cream, for serving

1. Preheat the oven to 350°. In a food processor, pulse the flour, cornmeal, 3 tablespoons of the granulated sugar, the baking powder, cinnamon and salt to combine. Add the butter and pulse until the mixture resembles coarse meal. Add the ⅔ cup of heavy cream and pulse just until a smooth dough forms. On a lightly floured surface, pat the dough into a ball. Flatten slightly, then roll out ½ inch thick. Using a floured 1½-inch round biscuit cutter, stamp out 32 rounds; reroll the scraps if necessary.

2. In a medium bowl, toss the berries with the honey, orange juice, lemon zest, potato starch and the remaining 2 tablespoons of granulated sugar. Pour the berries into a 2-quart baking dish. Arrange the biscuit rounds over the fruit in rows so they touch but do not overlap. Brush the rounds with the remaining 1 tablespoon of cream and sprinkle with the turbinado sugar. Bake for about 50 minutes, or until the fruit juices are bubbling and thickened and the biscuits are golden brown. Let cool slightly, then serve with ice cream. —*Colin Devlin*

Oaty Mixed Berry Crumble

ACTIVE: 20 MIN; TOTAL: 1 HR 10 MIN

4 TO 6 SERVINGS ● ●

Scottish cooking school owner and celebrity chef Nick Nairn likes to use finely cut oats in this topping, but you can also grind rolled oats in a food processor to achieve the same texture.

TOPPING

- ¾ cup all-purpose flour
- ¾ cup old-fashioned rolled oats
- 1¼ cups plain granola
- ½ cup sugar
- 1½ sticks chilled unsalted butter, cut into cubes

FILLING

- ¾ cup sugar
- Finely grated zest of 1 lemon
- ½ teaspoon cinnamon
- ¼ teaspoon ground allspice
- ¼ teaspoon freshly grated nutmeg
- 1 pound blackberries
- ¾ pound blueberries
- ¾ pound raspberries
- 2 tablespoons unsalted butter, cut into small pieces
- Devonshire cream, vanilla ice cream or lightly whipped cream, for serving

1. MAKE THE TOPPING: Preheat the oven to 400°. In a food processor, pulse the flour, oats, granola and sugar until coarsely ground. Add the butter and pulse until the mixture resembles fine meal.

2. MAKE THE FILLING: In a large bowl, toss the sugar with the lemon zest, cinnamon, allspice and nutmeg. Add the berries and toss well. Carefully spread the berries in a 13-by-9-inch glass or ceramic baking dish and dot with the butter. Spoon the topping over the berries and bake for 40 to 45 minutes, until the fruit is bubbling and the topping is browned. Let the crumble cool slightly and serve warm with the Devonshire Cream. —*Nick Nairn*

MAKE AHEAD The mixed berry crumble can be made up to 4 hours ahead. Reheat it gently before serving.

Quick Apple Crumble with Lebneh

TOTAL: 20 MIN

4 SERVINGS ● ●

The blend of flavors and textures in this quick dessert—nutty, sweet, tart, crunchy and smooth—makes this simple dessert irresistible. *Lebneh*, a thick Middle Eastern–style yogurt, stays creamy underneath the warm apples topped with a quick granola crumble. If you can't find *lebneh*, substitute Greek-style yogurt.

- 6 tablespoons unsalted butter
- 2 large Granny Smith apples— peeled, halved, cored and thinly sliced (see Note)
- ¼ cup plus 2 tablespoons light brown sugar
- ½ teaspoon ground cinnamon
- Pinch of freshly grated nutmeg
- 1 tablespoon fresh lemon juice
- ¼ cup water
- 16 ounces *lebneh* (2 cups)
- 1 cup granola

1. Heat the butter in a large skillet. Add the Granny Smith apple slices and cook them over high heat, stirring occasionally, until they are just tender and lightly browned, 5 to 6 minutes. Add the brown sugar, cinnamon, nutmeg and lemon juice to the apples and cook, stirring and shaking the skillet, until the sugar is melted and the apples are lightly caramelized, about 5 minutes longer. Add the water and stir gently until a sauce forms.

2. Spoon the *lebneh* into bowls and spoon the caramelized apples and sauce on top. Sprinkle the apple crumbles with the granola and serve right away.
—*Grace Parisi*

NOTE Wedges of firm, ripe peaches, nectarines and plums would be delicious in place of the apples.

MAKE AHEAD The recipe can be prepared through Step 1 up to 6 hours ahead. Rewarm the caramelized apples before assembling the crumble.

Cast-Iron Skillet Apple Crisp

ACTIVE: 30 MIN; TOTAL: 1 HR 25 MIN
8 SERVINGS

This rustic apple dessert—a mixture of sweet and tart apples and buttery bread crumbs—slow cooks on the grill over indirect heat, which is created by piling all the hot coals on one side, away from the food, to make a kind of outdoor oven.

- 2 cups fine fresh bread crumbs
- ½ cup light brown sugar
- 1 stick unsalted butter, melted
- 3 medium McIntosh apples—peeled, cored and sliced ¾ inch thick
- 3 medium Granny Smith apples—peeled, cored and sliced ¾ inch thick
- 3 tablespoons fresh lemon juice

Finely grated zest of 1 lemon
- 1 cup dark brown sugar
- ¾ teaspoon cinnamon
- ¼ teaspoon freshly grated nutmeg

Pinch of ground cloves
- 1½ cups plain yogurt, preferably goat's milk
- 1 cup confectioners' sugar

1. Light a grill. When the coals are hot, push them to one side of the grill. Put the bread crumbs in a large cast-iron skillet. Set the skillet on the grill opposite the coals; cover and cook, stirring occasionally, until the bread crumbs are nicely toasted, about 5 minutes. Transfer the bread crumbs to a large bowl and stir in the light brown sugar and half of the melted butter.

2. In a large bowl, toss the apple slices with the lemon juice and zest. Add the dark brown sugar, cinnamon, nutmeg and cloves and toss well.

3. Set the skillet back on the grill opposite the coals and scatter half of the bread crumb mixture over the bottom. Spread the apple slices in the skillet in an even layer. Top the apples with the remaining bread crumbs and drizzle with the remaining melted butter. Cover the grill and cook until the apples are tender and bubbling and the crisp is nicely browned, about 45 minutes. Remove the skillet from the grill and let the apple crisp rest for at least 10 minutes before serving.

4. Meanwhile, in a medium bowl, mix the yogurt with the confectioners' sugar. Serve the apple crisp, warm or at room temperature, with the sweetened yogurt.
—*Mario Batali*

MAKE AHEAD The recipe can be prepared through Step 2 up to one day ahead. Refrigerate the apple mixture; let the crumb mixture stand at room temperature.

Cherry-Mascarpone Tart

ACTIVE: 1 HR; TOTAL: 4 HR
8 SERVINGS ●

CRUST
- 6 tablespoons unsalted butter, softened
- ¼ cup sugar
- 2 large egg yolks
- 1 teaspoon pure vanilla extract
- ⅔ cup all-purpose flour
- ½ cup yellow cornmeal
- ½ teaspoon salt

Vegetable oil spray

FILLING
- 2 tablespoons unsalted butter, softened
- ¼ cup sugar
- 1¼ cups mascarpone cheese
- 1 large egg
- 1 teaspoon pure vanilla extract

Finely grated zest of 1 lemon
- 2 tablespoons heavy cream

CHERRIES
- ½ cup sugar
- ½ cup Black Muscat wine

Juice of 1 lemon
- 1 pound cherries—stemmed, pitted and halved

1. MAKE THE CRUST: Preheat the oven to 350°. In a bowl, using an electric mixer, beat the butter and sugar at medium speed until fluffy, 2 minutes. Beat in the egg yolks and vanilla. Beat in the flour, cornmeal and salt until a dough forms. Gather the dough into a ball and transfer to a large nonstick baking sheet. Cover with plastic and roll out to a 9-inch square, a scant ¼ inch thick. Bake for 10 minutes, or until the edges are lightly browned. Immediately transfer to a food processor; pulse until fine. Lower the oven temperature to 300°.

2. Line a 13¾-by-4-inch, straight-sided rectangular tart pan with a removable bottom with foil. Spray the foil with vegetable spray. Press a ½-inch layer of the crumbs evenly over the bottom and up the side of the pan. Refrigerate until firm, 20 minutes.

3. MEANWHILE, MAKE THE FILLING: In a medium bowl, using an electric mixer, beat the butter with the sugar at medium speed until fluffy, about 2 minutes. Add half of the mascarpone cheese and beat at low speed until combined. Add the remaining mascarpone cheese, the egg, vanilla, lemon zest and cream and beat just until smooth, about 1 minute. Pour the filling into the crust and smooth the surface.

4. Set the tart pan on a sturdy baking sheet. Position racks in the bottom and center of the oven. On the bottom rack, place a roasting pan filled with 1 inch of water. Place the tart on the center rack and bake for 35 to 40 minutes, until the filling is puffed and set. Let cool to room temperature, then refrigerate until chilled, at least 2 hours. Lift the tart from the pan and remove the foil. Transfer to a platter.

5. PREPARE THE CHERRIES: In a saucepan, bring the sugar, Muscat and lemon juice to a boil. Reduce the heat to moderate and simmer until syrupy, 10 minutes. Let cool slightly, then transfer to a bowl and add the cherries. Let stand for 10 minutes. Using a slotted spoon, transfer the cherries to the tart and serve. —*Spencer Budros*

pies & fruit desserts

Roasted Pear Sundaes with Balsamic-Caramel Sauce

TOTAL: 45 MIN

4 SERVINGS ● ●

High-quality balsamic vinegar is dense and complex, so a little goes a long way in this sweet-tangy caramel sauce, which is also great drizzled over fresh fruit.

- 1 cup sugar
- 3 tablespoons water
- ½ cup heavy cream
- 2 tablespoons aged balsamic vinegar
- 2 large firm but ripe Bartlett pears, cored and cut into ¾-inch pieces
- 2 tablespoons unsalted butter, melted

Pinch of kosher salt
- ¼ cup hazelnuts
- 1 pint vanilla ice cream

1. Preheat the oven to 425°. In a medium saucepan, combine the sugar with the water. Boil the syrup over moderately high heat, without stirring, washing down any crystals that form on the side of the pan, until a deep amber caramel forms, 6 to 8 minutes. Remove the syrup from the heat and stir in the cream; the hot sauce will bubble up. Pour the caramel sauce into a heatproof cup and let cool slightly. Stir in the balsamic vinegar; keep warm.

2. Heat a rimmed baking sheet in the oven. In a bowl, toss the pears with the melted butter and salt. Spread the pears on the baking sheet; roast, stirring once, until golden around the edges and tender, 15 minutes; transfer to a plate to cool.

3. Reduce the oven temperature to 350°. Spread the hazelnuts in a pie plate and toast for 7 minutes; transfer to a cutting board and coarsely chop.

4. Spoon the pears into bowls and top with vanilla ice cream. Pour the balsamic-caramel sauce on top, sprinkle with the hazelnuts and serve right away.
—*Melissa Rubel*

Blackberry Corn Cakes with Peach-Maple Ice Cream

ACTIVE: 1 HR 15 MIN; TOTAL: 3 HR

MAKES 24 TO 30 CORN CAKES

Corn cakes, often referred to as hoe cakes or johnnycakes, are basically cornmeal pancakes; they can be savory or sweet. This version is topped with big scoops of homemade Peach-Maple Ice Cream.

- 1 cup all-purpose flour
- ⅔ cup stone-ground yellow cornmeal
- 1½ teaspoons baking powder
- 3 tablespoons granulated sugar
- ½ teaspoon salt
- 2 ears of corn, kernels removed, cobs reserved
- 1½ cups milk
- 2 large eggs, separated
- 5 tablespoons unsalted butter, melted, plus more for the griddle
- 1 pint blackberries, halved lengthwise

Confectioners' sugar, for dusting
Peach-Maple Ice Cream
(recipe follows)

1. Preheat the oven to 200°. In a large bowl, whisk the flour, cornmeal, baking powder, granulated sugar and salt. Working over a blender, use a table knife to scrape the milky liquid from the corn cobs. Add half of the corn kernels, the milk and the egg yolks to the blender and puree until smooth. Whisk the corn puree into the dry ingredients. Fold in the melted butter and the remaining corn kernels.

2. Using an electric mixer, beat the egg whites until stiff peaks form. Fold the beaten whites into the batter, then carefully fold in the blackberries.

3. Heat a large griddle. Brush the griddle lightly with butter. For each corn cake, pour a scant ¼ cup of batter onto the griddle and cook the cake over moderate heat until small bubbles appear on the surface, about 3 minutes. Flip the corn cakes and cook until golden, about 2 minutes longer. Transfer the corn cakes to a baking sheet and keep them warm in the oven while you prepare the rest.

4. Stack 4 or 5 warm corn cakes on each plate and dust with confectioners' sugar. Top each stack with a scoop of Peach-Maple Ice Cream and serve right away.
—*Bobby Flay*

ingredient
balsamic vinegar

LA VECCHIA DISPENSA
Italian Balsamic Sampler A set aged for 8, 10, 20 and 40 years—great for comparison tastings. **Details** $25; zingermans.com.

MALETTI
12-Year Balsamic Vinegar A rich condiment made from the wine and must of Lambrusco and Trebbiano grapes. **Details** $65 for 100 ml; ritrovo.com.

TONDO
12-Year Balsamic Vinegar An inky, complex vinegar perfect for drizzling over a variety of cheese and fruit. **Details** $72 for 100 ml; 888-225-3679.

ROASTED PEAR SUNDAE WITH BALSAMIC-CARAMEL SAUCE

BLACKBERRY CORN CAKES WITH PEACH-MAPLE ICE CREAM

PEACH-MAPLE ICE CREAM

ACTIVE: 40 MIN; TOTAL: 2 HR 30 MIN

MAKES 1 QUART ●

- ¾ pound ripe peaches
- 1 tablespoon fresh lemon juice
- 1 cup heavy cream
- ½ cup milk
- ½ vanilla bean, split, seeds scraped
- 2 large egg yolks
- ¼ cup plus 2 tablespoons sugar

Pinch of salt

- ¼ cup pure maple syrup
- 1 tablespoon bourbon, or more to taste

1. Bring a small pot of water to a boil over high heat and fill a medium bowl with ice water to loosen the skin of the peaches for peeling. Cut a shallow X in the bottom of each peach, then carefully drop the peaches into the boiling water. After 30 seconds, remove the peaches with a slotted spoon and transfer to the ice water to cool. Peel the peaches and cut them into ½-inch wedges; reserve the peach skins and pits and set aside. Transfer the peach wedges to a bowl and toss with the lemon juice. Cover the peach wedges and refrigerate them while you make the rest of the ice cream recipe.

2. In a medium saucepan, combine the heavy cream and milk. Add the vanilla bean and scraped seeds and the peach skins and pits and bring to a simmer. Cover the saucepan and remove from the heat. Let the mixture steep for 20 minutes. Strain the infused cream into a bowl.

3. In a medium bowl, whisk the egg yolks with the sugar and salt. Whisk in half of the infused cream, then transfer the mixture back to the saucepan, along with the remaining infused cream. Cook the custard over moderate heat, stirring constantly with a wooden spoon, until it is slightly thickened and an instant-read thermometer inserted in the custard registers 165°, about 5 minutes. Immediately strain the custard into a clean bowl and stir in the maple syrup and bourbon. Refrigerate the custard until it is chilled, about 30 minutes.

4. In a blender, puree the peach wedges with 1 cup of the custard until smooth. Transfer the pureed peaches and the remaining custard to an ice cream maker and freeze according to the manufacturer's instructions. Transfer the frozen peach-maple ice cream to a plastic container. Press a sheet of plastic wrap directly onto the surface of the ice cream, cover and freeze until firm, about 1 hour. —B.F.

MAKE AHEAD The peach-maple ice cream can be prepared several days ahead and kept in the freezer.

● FAST   ● HEALTHY   ● MAKE AHEAD   ● STAFF FAVORITE

329

pies & fruit desserts

Warm Peach Shortcake with Brandy Whipped Cream

ACTIVE: 40 MIN; TOTAL: 1 HR 15 MIN
8 SERVINGS

SHORTCAKE

Vegetable spray

½ cup plus 1 tablespoon sugar

¼ teaspoon ground cinnamon

2 cups all-purpose flour

2 teaspoons baking powder

½ teaspoon freshly grated nutmeg

½ teaspoon salt

¼ teaspoon baking soda

1 stick cold unsalted butter, cut into ½-inch pieces, plus 1 tablespoon unsalted butter, melted

¾ cup buttermilk

2 large eggs, beaten

FILLING

3 tablespoons brandy

¼ cup golden raisins

3 tablespoons unsalted butter

4 firm, ripe peaches—halved, pitted and sliced ½ inch thick

½ cup packed light brown sugar

¼ teaspoon ground cinnamon

1 cup heavy cream

pairing

dessert and demi-sec

Sweet sparkling wine is one of the wine world's great secrets. Labeled sec or demi-sec, these are dosed with just enough sugar to make them ideal partners to desserts—like the strawberry napoleons at right.

Schramsberg 2002 Crémant Demi-Sec Delicately sweet.

Mumm Cuvée M Lush and fruity, moderately sweet.

Korbel Sec Apricot-inflected.

1. MAKE THE SHORTCAKE: Preheat the oven to 375°. Spray a 9-inch round cake pan with vegetable spray. In a small bowl, combine 1 tablespoon of the sugar with the cinnamon.

2. In a large bowl, whisk the flour with the remaining ½ cup of sugar, the baking powder, nutmeg, salt and baking soda. Using a pastry blender or 2 knives, cut the cold butter into the flour mixture until the pieces are the size of small peas. Make a well in the center of the flour and butter mixture and add the buttermilk and the beaten eggs. Stir with a fork, until a dough forms. Scrape the dough into the prepared cake pan and bake for 35 minutes, until the top is golden. Brush the top of the hot shortcake with the remaining 1 tablespoon of melted butter and sprinkle all over with the cinnamon sugar. Transfer the short-cake to a rack to cool for 10 minutes.

3. MEANWHILE, MAKE THE FILLING: In a small bowl, pour the brandy over the raisins and let stand for 20 minutes, to soften the raisins. In a large skillet, melt the butter. Add the peaches, cover and cook over moderately low heat until just softened, about 6 minutes. Reserve 1 tablespoon of brandy. Add the remaining brandy with the raisins, brown sugar and cinnamon to the skillet. Cook the peaches over moderate heat, stirring often, until glazed and crisp-tender, about 8 minutes.

4. In a medium bowl, whip the heavy cream with the reserved 1 tablespoon of brandy until soft peaks form. Remove the shortcake from the pan and transfer to a plate. Using a serrated knife, slice the cake in half horizontally; slide the top half of the cake onto a plate. Spoon the peaches and sauce over what is now the bottom of the shortcake. Top with the other half. Cut the cake into wedges and serve with a dollop of brandy whipped cream.
—*Constance Snow*

MAKE AHEAD The shortcake can be baked up to 1 day ahead.

Mara des Bois Strawberry Napoleons

ACTIVE: 45 MIN; TOTAL: 2 HR PLUS 4 TO 6 HR CHILLING
4 SERVINGS ●

Mara des Bois are small, wildly aromatic strawberries. Pastry sous-chef Michael Brock of Los Angeles's Boule layers them in a stellar napoleon with crisp puff pastry and pillowy lemon verbena cream.

½ pound cold all-butter puff pastry

⅔ cup whole milk

¼ cup sugar

¼ cup loosely packed fresh or dried whole lemon verbena leaves (see Note)

½ vanilla bean, split, seeds scraped

2 large egg yolks

1½ teaspoons cornstarch

2 teaspoons all-purpose flour

½ teaspoon unflavored gelatin

1 tablespoon water

½ cup heavy cream

1 tablespoon seedless raspberry jam, melted

2 tablespoons melted and strained apricot jam

1½ cups whole Mara des Bois or thinly sliced strawberries

1. Preheat the oven to 375°. Line a large baking sheet with parchment. On a lightly floured work surface, roll out the puff pastry to a 12-by-6-inch rectangle. Trim into 4 neat rectangles, 6-by-3 inches each. Cut each rectangle into 3 equal pieces and transfer to the prepared baking sheet. Chill for 10 minutes. Poke each piece 3 times with a fork. Cover the pastry with parchment paper and top with another baking sheet to prevent the pastry from puffing. Bake for about 35 minutes, until the pastry is deep golden and crisp. Remove the top baking sheet and parchment and let the pastry pieces cool completely.

2. Meanwhile, in a medium saucepan, bring the milk and sugar to a simmer. Add the lemon verbena and the vanilla bean and seeds. Remove from the heat, cover and let stand for 15 minutes. Strain the milk into a heatproof measuring cup.

3. In a medium bowl, whisk the egg yolks with the cornstarch and flour. Gradually whisk in the hot milk. Pour the mixture into the saucepan and cook over moderate heat, whisking constantly, until the pastry cream is very thick, about 4 minutes. Transfer the pastry cream to a bowl.

4. In a small glass bowl, sprinkle the gelatin over the water and let stand until softened. Microwave the gelatin for 5 seconds, or until melted; whisk into the pastry cream. Press a sheet of plastic directly onto the pastry cream and refrigerate for about 1 hour, or until thoroughly chilled.

5. In a medium bowl, using an electric mixer, beat the heavy cream until stiff. Beat half of the whipped cream into the pastry cream. Fold in the remaining whipped cream with a rubber spatula. Refrigerate the pastry cream until chilled.

6. Arrange the puff pastry pieces on a work surface. Brush 4 of the pieces with the raspberry jam and the remaining 8 pieces with the apricot jam. Spoon a scant ¼ cup of the pastry cream onto the 4 raspberry-topped pieces and 4 of the apricot-topped pieces. Arrange the strawberries over the cream filling; reserve 4 of the whole or sliced strawberries for garnish. Dollop any remaining cream over the strawberries. Stack the raspberry layers on top of the cream-filled apricot layers, pressing lightly. Top the stacks with the remaining apricot-topped layers. Refrigerate the napoleons until chilled, 4 to 6 hours. Garnish the napoleons with the reserved strawberries and serve. —*Michael Brock*

NOTE Fresh lemon verbena is available at farmers' markets and at specialty food stores. Dried, whole lemon verbena leaves can be found wherever fine teas are sold.

MAKE AHEAD The puff pastry can be stored in an airtight container for 2 days and the pastry cream refrigerated for 2 days.

Strawberry-and-Cream Fraisier
ACTIVE: 1 HR; TOTAL: 2 HR 45 MIN
12 SERVINGS ●

When the first berries of the season appear, French *pâtissiers* start making *fraisiers*, light, sugar syrup–moistened cakes filled with sliced strawberries and pastry cream then covered with a thin sheet of almond paste. In this version, the cake is layered with fresh fruit, vanilla cream and almond paste in a glass bowl, like a trifle.

PASTRY CREAM
- 2 cups milk
- 1 vanilla bean, split and scraped
- ⅛ teaspoon kosher salt
- 6 large egg yolks
- ½ cup sugar
- ¼ cup all-purpose flour
- 2 tablespoons unsalted butter, cut into pieces

CAKE
- 4 large eggs, separated
- ¾ cup plus 3 tablespoons sugar
- 1 teaspoon pure vanilla extract
- ¾ cup all-purpose flour
- ¼ teaspoon kosher salt
- 4 tablespoons unsalted butter, melted
- 3 tablespoons water
- 1 tablespoon kirsch
- ¾ pound strawberries, thinly sliced

Confectioners' sugar, for dusting
- 4 ounces almond paste (½ cup)

1. MAKE THE PASTRY CREAM: In a medium saucepan, bring the milk, vanilla bean, vanilla seeds and salt just to a boil. Remove the pan from the heat.

2. In a bowl, whisk the yolks and sugar until pale; whisk in the flour. Whisk 1 cup of the hot milk into the egg mixture. Pour the mixture into the hot milk and whisk over low heat until the pastry cream is thickened, 3 minutes. Whisk in the butter. Strain the pastry cream into a large bowl. Press a piece of plastic directly on the surface; refrigerate until chilled, 2 hours.

3. MAKE THE CAKE: Preheat the oven to 350°. Butter and flour a 9-inch round cake pan. In a bowl, using a handheld electric mixer, beat the egg whites at medium-high speed until they hold firm peaks. Add 6 tablespoons of the sugar and continue beating until stiff and glossy, 1 minute.

4. In another medium bowl, beat the egg yolks with another 6 tablespoons of sugar, the vanilla extract and the salt at medium-high speed until thick and light in color, about 1 minute. Fold half of the whites into the yolk mixture, then fold in half of the flour. Repeat with the remaining whites and flour. Fold in the butter.

5. Scrape the batter into the prepared cake pan and bake for about 20 minutes, or until the cake is golden and pulls away from the edge of the pan. Set the pan on a rack and let cool for 10 minutes. Invert the cake onto a rack and let cool completely.

6. In a saucepan, mix 3 tablespoons of the sugar with the water; cook over moderate heat, stirring, until dissolved. Remove from the heat and add the kirsch.

7. Using a serrated knife, slice the cake in half horizontally. Transfer the cake bottom to a round 9-inch straight-sided glass bowl and brush with half of the syrup. Arrange a row of strawberry slices around the dish, then top the cake with the remaining sliced strawberries in an even layer. Spread all but 1 tablespoon of the pastry cream over the strawberries. Brush the cut side of the top with the remaining syrup and set, cut side down, on the pastry cream.

8. Lightly dust a work surface with confectioners' sugar and roll out the almond paste to a 9-inch round ¹⁄₁₆ inch thick. Spread the remaining 1 tablespoon of pastry cream on the top of the *fraisier* and cover with the round of almond paste. —*Christophe Emé*

MAKE AHEAD The recipe can be made through Step 6 up to 1 day ahead. Wrap the cake tightly in plastic and refrigerate the pastry cream and kirsch syrup.

pies & fruit desserts

Blancmange with Nectarines

ACTIVE: 30 MIN; TOTAL: 40 MIN PLUS 4 HR CHILLING

6 TO 8 SERVINGS ●

BLANCMANGE

- 2 cups whole blanched almonds
- 2 cups half-and-half
- ¼ cup sugar
- 4 drops pure almond extract
- 1 tablespoon plus 1 teaspoon unflavored gelatin
- ⅓ cup water
- 1 cup heavy cream

NECTARINES

- 3 large white nectarines
- 1 cup Sauternes or other dessert wine
- ½ cup water
- ½ cup sugar

1. MAKE THE BLANCMANGE: Preheat the oven to 350°. Lightly oil six 4-ounce ramekins. On a rimmed baking sheet, toast the almonds until they are golden, about 7 minutes. Let cool, then coarsely chop.

2. In a small saucepan, warm the half-and-half over low heat. Stir in the sugar until it is dissolved. Pour into a blender, add the almonds and blend until very thick and smooth. Strain the mixture through a fine strainer set over a medium bowl, pressing hard on the solids with a rubber spatula. You should have about 1½ cups liquid. Stir in the almond extract.

3. In a small saucepan, sprinkle the gelatin over the water and let stand until softened, about 5 minutes. Set the saucepan over low heat and when the water is warm, remove from the heat and swirl the pan to dissolve the gelatin. Scrape the gelatin into the almond milk. Set the stainless steel bowl over an ice water bath and stir the mixture often until it begins to thicken, about 10 minutes. In a large stainless steel bowl, beat the heavy cream until softly whipped. Fold it into the almond mixture and spoon it into the prepared ramekins. Cover and refrigerate until the blancmanges are set, at least 4 hours or overnight.

4. PREPARE THE NECTARINES: Set an ice water bath next to the stove. Using a paring knife, make an X on the bottom of each nectarine. Bring a medium saucepan of water to a boil and add the nectarines. After 10 seconds, transfer them to the ice water until they are cool enough to handle. Rub off the skins, then pit and quarter the nectarines. Wipe out the saucepan.

5. In the saucepan, combine the Sauternes, water and sugar and bring to a boil to dissolve the sugar. Add the nectarines and simmer over low heat, stirring occasionally, until tender, 3 to 8 minutes, depending on the ripeness of the fruit. Remove from the heat and let cool to room temperature.

6. Run a small knife around the edge of each ramekin, and loosen the blancmanges by dipping the bottoms of the ramekins into a bowl of hot water. Unmold onto plates. Spoon the nectarines and syrup around each blancmange; serve.—*Dennis Leary*

MAKE AHEAD The blancmanges can be refrigerated in their ramekins for up to 2 days. The poached nectarines can be refrigerated overnight. Serve lightly chilled or at room temperature.

equipment
coffee grinder

Instead of blades, the **KitchenAid Pro Line** burr grinder uses discs and works as well as models twice the price. **Details** $210; kitchenaid.com.

Graham Cracker Ice Cream Sundaes with Raspberries

ACTIVE: 25 MIN; TOTAL: 55 MIN

8 SERVINGS

Tara Lane, the pastry chef at Blackbird in Chicago, created this ridiculously simple ode to the classic campfire dessert s'mores. "I love hidden flavors," she says, which is why she folds nutty graham cracker crumbs into vanilla ice cream and adds a splash of balsamic vinegar to the luscious brown butter sauce. Instead of serving a dessert wine with this sundae, try a lightly sweet, fruity Lindemans Framboise raspberry lambic ale from Belgium. It will echo the ripe berries served with the ice cream.

- 2 pints vanilla ice cream, softened slightly
- 1½ cups graham cracker crumbs (7 ounces)
- 1 stick unsalted butter
- 2½ tablespoons balsamic vinegar
- 2 pints raspberries

1. In a standing mixer or working in batches in a food processor, blend the softened ice cream with the graham cracker crumbs. Transfer the ice cream to a plastic container, press plastic wrap directly onto the surface of the ice cream, cover and freeze until it is firm, at least 30 minutes.

2. In a small saucepan, cook the butter over moderate heat, stirring it occasionally, until it becomes golden brown and fragrant, about 5 minutes. Transfer the browned butter to a heatproof bowl and stir in the balsamic vinegar.

3. Spoon the raspberries into dessert bowls and drizzle with the warm brown-butter balsamic sauce. Scoop the graham cracker ice cream over the raspberries and serve the dessert right away.
—*Tara Lane*

MAKE AHEAD The graham cracker ice cream can be prepared up to 2 days ahead and kept in the freezer.

Swirled Summer Berry Soufflés

ACTIVE: 20 MIN; TOTAL: 30 MIN

6 SERVINGS ● ● ●

- 2 cups raspberries
- 1 cup blackberries
- ½ cup granulated sugar
- ¼ cup water
- 1 teaspoon pure vanilla extract
- 1 teaspoon fresh lemon juice
- 1 tablespoon cornstarch mixed with 1 tablespoon water
- 3 large egg whites
- ½ cup superfine sugar
- ¼ cup chopped unsalted pistachios

1. Preheat the oven to 400°. In a medium saucepan, combine the raspberries and blackberries with the granulated sugar, water, vanilla and lemon juice. Bring to a simmer over moderate heat, stirring often. Stir in the cornstarch mixture and cook, stirring, until thickened, about 1 minute.

2. In a large bowl, beat the egg whites until they hold very soft peaks. Gradually beat in the superfine sugar, 2 tablespoons at a time, and continue beating until glossy peaks form, about 3 minutes longer. Swirl in ¾ cup of the berry mixture gently, leaving streaks in the beaten whites.

3. Spoon the remaining berry mixture into six ½-cup ramekins. Top with the soufflé mixture, mounding it slightly. Sprinkle with the pistachios. Bake the soufflés for 6 minutes, or until they are golden on top. Serve at once. —Annabel Langbein

Blackberry Mousse and Honey-Tuile Napoleons

ACTIVE: 1 HR; TOTAL: 2 HR

4 SERVINGS

This easy but impressive dessert is from pastry chef Sue McCown of Coco La Ti Da in Seattle, who came up with this recipe as part of an F&W challenge to create a late-summer dessert using only seasonal fruit and pantry staples. Be sure to layer the tuiles with the mousse just before serving or they can become soggy.

TUILES

- 2 tablespoons unsalted butter, at room temperature
- 2 tablespoons honey
- ¼ cup confectioners' sugar, plus more for dusting
- ¼ cup plus 2 tablespoons all-purpose flour
- 1 large egg white, lightly beaten

MOUSSE

- 1 teaspoon unflavored gelatin
- 3 tablespoons cold water
- 1 cup blackberries
- ¼ cup sugar
- 1 large egg white
- ¾ cup heavy cream

SYRUP

- ¾ cup water
- ⅓ cup sugar
- 2 tablespoons fresh or dried lemon verbena leaves
- Finely grated zest of 1 lemon
- 1 cup blackberries, plus more for garnish

1. MAKE THE TUILES: Preheat the oven to 325°. Line 3 baking sheets with parchment paper. In a medium bowl, using an electric mixer, cream the butter and honey. Beat in the ¼ cup of confectioners' sugar and the flour, then add the egg white and beat until smooth. Spoon 5 well-rounded teaspoons of batter onto each of the prepared baking sheets, about 4 inches apart. Using an offset spatula, spread the batter evenly into 3- to 3½-inch rounds. Bake the tuiles for about 12 minutes, or until lightly browned, shifting the baking sheets from top to bottom and front to back for even baking. Transfer the tuiles to a wire rack and let cool until crisp. Repeat with the remaining batter to make 5 more tuiles.

2. MAKE THE MOUSSE: In a small bowl, sprinkle the gelatin over 1 tablespoon of the water and let stand until softened, about 5 minutes. In a blender, puree the blackberries with the remaining 2 tablespoons of water. Strain the puree into a

small saucepan; there should be about ¾ cup. Add the sugar and bring to a boil. Simmer the berry mixture over moderate heat, stirring occasionally, until slightly reduced, about 5 minutes. Stir in the softened gelatin until dissolved. Set aside to cool.

3. In a medium bowl, using an electric mixer, beat the white until firm peaks form. Using a rubber spatula, fold the cooled blackberry puree into the white until no streaks remain. In another bowl, beat the cream until softly whipped. Fold the cream into the berry mixture and refrigerate the mousse until chilled, about 1 hour.

4. MAKE THE SYRUP: In a saucepan, combine the water and sugar and bring to a boil. Remove from the heat. Add the lemon verbena and lemon zest and let the syrup stand for 30 minutes. Strain the syrup into a cup. Wipe out the saucepan and return the syrup to it. Add the blackberries and bring to a boil over high heat. Reduce the heat to low and cook the syrup over moderate heat, crushing the blackberries against the side of the pan, until the liquid is slightly reduced and the berries have broken down, about 15 minutes. Strain the syrup into a heatproof cup without pressing on the berries in the strainer. Refrigerate the blackberry syrup until chilled.

5. ASSEMBLE THE DESSERT: Place 8 tuiles on a work surface. Scoop a slightly rounded ¼-cup mound of mousse onto each tuile. Stack one mousse-topped tuile on another to make 4 stacks. Top each stack with a plain tuile and press lightly to flatten each stack slightly (in case of breakage, use the extra tuiles). Dust the tops of the napoleons with confectioners' sugar. Using a metal spatula, carefully transfer each napoleon to a plate. Garnish with blackberries, drizzle with the syrup and serve right away.—Sue McCown

MAKE AHEAD The recipe can be prepared through Step 4 up to 2 days ahead. Store the tuiles in an airtight container. Refrigerate the mousse and the syrup.

pies & fruit desserts

Frozen Raspberry and Chocolate-Chip Semifreddo Parfaits

TOTAL: 30 MIN PLUS 8 HR FREEZING

16 SERVINGS ●

2½ cups chilled heavy cream
3 large eggs
2 large egg yolks
1 cup sugar
¼ cup plus 1 tablespoon fresh lemon juice
1 tablespoon pure vanilla extract
½ teaspoon salt
4 pints fresh raspberries
9 ounces mini chocolate chips or chopped bittersweet chocolate

1. Line two 9-by-4-inch loaf pans with plastic wrap, leaving a 4-inch overhang all around. In a bowl, using an electric mixer, whip the heavy cream until firm, then chill.

2. In a stainless bowl set over a pan of simmering water, whisk the eggs, yolks and ¾ cup of the sugar until the mixture reaches 155° on an instant-read thermometer. Remove the bowl from the heat. Using an electric mixer, beat the eggs at medium speed until fluffy and pale, about 5 minutes. Beat in 1 tablespoon of the lemon juice, the vanilla and the salt. Add 2 pints of the raspberries and, at low speed, mix briefly, just until the raspberries are slightly broken up. Fold in the chocolate chips and the whipped cream. Spoon the parfait into the loaf pans. Tap the pans lightly on a surface and cover the parfaits with the overhanging plastic wrap. Freeze until firm, at least 8 hours.

3. Meanwhile, in a medium bowl, toss the remaining 2 pints of raspberries with the remaining ¼ cup each of sugar and lemon juice. Refrigerate for up to 8 hours.

4. Unwrap the parfaits and invert them onto platters. Peel off the plastic. Using a hot knife, slice the parfaits and serve with the raspberry compote. —*Pichet Ong*

MAKE AHEAD The wrapped parfaits can be frozen in the loaf pans for 1 week.

Passion Fruit and Coconut Cream Parfaits

ACTIVE: 45 MIN; TOTAL: 3 HR

6 SERVINGS ●

PASSION FRUIT CURD

8 large egg yolks
3 large eggs
⅓ cup sugar
¾ cup plus 2 tablespoons passion fruit puree (7 ounces) (see Note)
6 tablespoons unsalted butter

COCONUT CREAM

2½ cups unsweetened coconut milk
⅔ cup sugar
3 tablespoons unsalted butter
½ vanilla bean, split, seeds scraped
2½ tablespoons cornstarch
2 tablespoons water

POACHED PINEAPPLE

1½ cups sugar
2 cups water
10 thin lemon slices, seeded
½ vanilla bean, split, seeds scraped
One 3-pound pineapple—peeled, cored and cut into ½-inch cubes (4 cups)

CASHEW PRALINE

½ cup granulated sugar
1 tablespoon light corn syrup
2 tablespoons water
¼ cup dark brown sugar
1 tablespoon honey
1 tablespoon unsalted butter
1 teaspoon grated orange zest
Salt and freshly ground pepper
4 ounces salted roasted cashews, coarsely chopped (¾ cup)

1. MAKE THE PASSION FRUIT CURD: In a medium stainless steel bowl, whisk the egg yolks and whole eggs with the sugar and passion fruit puree until smooth. Set the bowl over a medium saucepan of simmering water and whisk the mixture over moderate heat until very thick and an instant-read thermometer dipped in the mixture registers 165°, about 8 minutes. Remove the bowl from the pan and whisk in the butter. Scrape the curd into a shallow bowl, press plastic directly on the curd and refrigerate until chilled, 2 hours.

2. MAKE THE COCONUT CREAM: In a medium saucepan, combine the coconut milk, sugar, butter and vanilla bean and seeds and bring to a simmer. In a small bowl, dissolve the cornstarch in the water; whisk into the coconut milk and cook over moderate heat, whisking constantly, until thickened, 5 minutes. Discard the vanilla bean. Pour the coconut cream into a shallow bowl, press plastic directly on top of the cream and refrigerate until chilled, 2 hours.

3. MAKE THE POACHED PINEAPPLE: In a saucepan, bring the sugar, water, lemon slices and vanilla bean and seeds to a boil, stirring until the sugar dissolves. Add the pineapple. Cook over moderate heat until the fruit is translucent, 15 minutes. Transfer the pineapple and its cooking liquid to a bowl and refrigerate until chilled, 2 hours.

4. MAKE THE CASHEW PRALINE: Line a large baking sheet with lightly oiled parchment paper. In a medium saucepan, boil the sugar, corn syrup and water until the syrup reaches 300° (hard crack) on a candy thermometer, 6 minutes. Stir in the brown sugar, honey, butter, orange zest and a pinch of salt and pepper. Off the heat, stir in the cashews until coated. Pour the brittle onto the oiled parchment paper. Top with another sheet of oiled parchment paper and roll out the brittle as thinly as possible. Let cool completely, then crack into small pieces.

5. ASSEMBLE THE PARFAITS: Spoon ½ cup of the coconut cream into the bottoms of 6 tall glasses, followed by ½ cup of the passion fruit curd. Using a slotted spoon, add a scant ½ cup of the pineapple to the glasses, followed by a sprinkle of the praline. Repeat the layering with the remaining ingredients. Serve at once. —*Koa Duncan*

NOTE Passion fruit puree is available in the freezer section at specialty markets. One brand worth seeking out is Vergers Boiron, available at lepicerie.com.

PASSION FRUIT AND COCONUT CREAM PARFAIT

pies & fruit desserts

Coconut Pudding with Raspberry Sauce

TOTAL: 30 MIN PLUS 6 HR CHILLING

12 SERVINGS ●

- ¾ cup sifted cornstarch
- ½ teaspoon salt
- 3 cups cold milk
- 3 cups unsweetened coconut milk
- 2 cups plus 2 teaspoons sugar
- 6 ounces raspberries
- 1 teaspoon raspberry liqueur
- ½ teaspoon fresh lemon juice

1. In a bowl, whisk the cornstarch and salt. Whisk in 1 cup of milk until smooth. In a saucepan, mix the remaining milk with the coconut milk and 2 cups of the sugar and bring to a simmer, whisking until dissolved. Whisk in the cornstarch mixture. Cook over moderate heat, whisking constantly, until very thick, 6 minutes. Off the heat, whisk the custard for 1 minute. Let cool. Spoon into twelve ¾-cup ramekins. Refrigerate until chilled and firm, at least 6 hours

2. In a blender, puree the berries, liqueur, lemon juice and remaining sugar; strain. Serve the pudding with the sauce on top.
—*Carolina Buia and Isabel González*

Grapefruit Granité with Mangoes and White Rum Mojito

TOTAL: 35 MIN PLUS 3 HR FREEZING

4 SERVINGS ●

- 2¼ cups fresh pink grapefruit juice (from 2 large grapefruit)
- 3 tablespoons honey
- 1 tablespoon grenadine
- ½ cup mint leaves, plus 4 mint sprigs for garnish
- 3 tablespoons sugar
- ¼ cup white rum
- 3 tablespoons fresh lime juice
- 2 ripe mangoes, peeled and cut into 4 halves

1. In an 8-inch square glass dish, combine the grapefruit juice with the honey and grenadine. Freeze the *granité* until solid, at least 3 hours.

2. In a food processor, puree the mint leaves, sugar, rum and lime juice. Refrigerate.

3. About 30 minutes before serving, transfer the *granité* to the refrigerator to soften. Cut each mango half lengthwise into thin slices. Pour the mojito into shallow bowls. Fan the mango slices in the bowls. Top with large scoops of the *granité*. Garnish with the mint sprigs; serve.—*Jacques Pépin*

Hibiscus and Grapefruit Sorbet

ACTIVE: 15 MIN; TOTAL: 1 HR

4 SERVINGS ● ●

- ¼ cup sugar
- 4 Red Zinger tea bags or plain hibiscus tea bags
- 1 cup fresh pink grapefruit juice

Stir the sugar into 2 cups of boiling water, add the tea bags and steep for 10 minutes. Discard the tea bags. Stir in the grapefruit juice, then chill the liquid in an ice water bath; transfer to an ice cream machine. Freeze according to the manufacturer's instructions. —*Shawn McClain*

Lemon-Thyme Sorbet with Summer Berries

ACTIVE: 20 MIN; TOTAL: 3 HR 30 MIN

4 SERVINGS ● ● ●

Flavored syrups can be used with pureed fruit, fruit juice or fresh herbs to make sorbet in an ice cream machine.

Lemon-Thyme Syrup (recipe follows)

- 6 ounces strawberries, halved,
- 6 ounces raspberries
- 6 ounces blueberries
- 6 ounces sweet cherries, halved

Thyme sprigs, for garnish

---

taste test

3 great raspberry sorbets

SHARON'S SORBET
Owner Phillip Kermanshachi started making his silky-smooth sorbets after being inspired by ones he tasted in a Parisian patisserie.
Details sharons-sorbet.com.

CIAO BELLA
Made with Oregon raspberries according to a traditional recipe from Turin, Italy, this sorbet is tart and intensely fruity.
Details ciaobellagelato.com.

CRÈME CRÉMAILLÈRE
From La Crémaillère in Bedford, New York, these sorbets, prepared in small batches, are sold in 2½- and 5-quart containers.
Details frenchicecream.com.

LEMON-THYME SORBET WITH SUMMER BERRIES

MELON GRANITA TRIO

1. Pour the syrup into an ice cream maker and freeze according to the manufacturer's instructions. Transfer the sorbet to a plastic container, cover and freeze.

2. Shortly before serving, in a bowl, toss the berries with the cherries. Scoop the sorbet into bowls. Spoon the berries on top, garnish with the thyme sprigs and serve.
—*Jean-Georges Vongerichten*

LEMON-THYME SYRUP

ACTIVE: 10 MIN; TOTAL: 2 HR 10 MIN
MAKES ABOUT 2¼ CUPS

- 1 cup plus 2 tablespoons sugar
- ¾ ounce lemon thyme sprigs
- ¾ cup fresh lemon juice

In a saucepan, combine 1½ cups of water with the sugar and bring to a boil, stirring to dissolve the sugar. Add the thyme, cover and let stand for at least 2 hours or overnight. Add the lemon juice and strain.
—*J.G.V.*

Melon Granita Trio

ACTIVE: 45 MIN; TOTAL: 2 HR 30 MIN
6 SERVINGS ● ●

- 2½ cups watermelon chunks, seeded
- ¾ cup sugar
- 1 tablespoon fresh lime juice
- ¼ teaspoon cayenne (optional)
- 1¼ cups water
- 2½ cups honeydew chunks
- 2½ tablespoons fresh lemon juice
- ¼ teaspoon cinnamon (optional)
- 2½ cups cantaloupe chunks

1. MAKE THE WATERMELON GRANITA: In a blender, puree the watermelon with ¼ cup of sugar, the lime juice and cayenne. Pour into a shallow plastic container and freeze until frozen around the edges and slushy in the center, about 30 minutes.

2. MAKE THE HONEYDEW GRANITA: In a small saucepan, stir ¼ cup of sugar with ½ cup plus 2 tablespoons of water over low heat until melted. Let cool; transfer to a blender. Add the honeydew, 1½ tablespoons of lemon juice and the cinnamon and puree. Transfer to a shallow plastic container. Freeze until frozen around the edges and slushy, about 30 minutes.

3. MAKE THE CANTALOUPE GRANITA: In a saucepan, stir the remaining ½ cup plus 2 tablespoons of water with the remaining ¼ cup of sugar over low heat until melted. Let cool; transfer to a blender. Add the cantaloupe and the remaining tablespoon of lemon juice and puree until smooth. Transfer to a shallow plastic container. Freeze until frozen around the edges and slushy in the center, about 30 minutes.

4. Using a fork, stir the granitas every 20 minutes or so, until completely frozen into a mass of fluffy icy shards, 1½ hours. Just before serving, fluff each granita. Scoop into bowls and serve. If the granitas become solid, chop into chunks and puree until fluffy. —*Michel Algazi and Roni Goldbert*

DEVIL'S FOOD CUPCAKES WITH
ESPRESSO MERINGUE (P. 345)

cakes, cookies & more

"Baking cookies is my Achilles' heel [when I'm trying not to overindulge]. They're too easy to grab off the tray."

–Melissa Clark, cookbook author

MINI BLACK-BOTTOM CHEESECAKES

CHOCOLATE TRUFFLE LAYER CAKE

Mini Black-Bottom Cheesecakes

ACTIVE: 20 MIN; TOTAL: 45 MIN

MAKES 12 MINI

CHEESECAKES ● ● ●

This cheesecake is made with creamy fromage blanc. You can also use *lebneh*, a fresh cheese from Lebanon that's thick and tangy, or quark, a mild, soft, faintly tangy cheese.

Vegetable oil spray

24 **plain chocolate wafer cookies, preferably Nabisco**

3 **tablespoons unsalted butter, melted**

8 **ounces cream cheese, softened**

¼ **cup sugar**

6 **ounces *fromage blanc* (⅔ cup), at room temperature**

2 **large eggs**

2 **teaspoons pure vanilla extract**

¼ **cup seedless raspberry preserves, warmed**

1. Preheat the oven to 350°. Line a standard 12-cup muffin pan with foil baking cups and coat with vegetable oil spray. In a food processor, crush the chocolate wafer cookies. Add the butter and process until fine crumbs form. Spoon the chocolate cookie crumbs into the prepared baking cups and press with the bottom of a glass to compact. Bake for 5 minutes, or until almost set. Leave the oven on.

2. In a medium bowl, beat the cream cheese and sugar at medium speed until smooth. Beat in the *fromage blanc*. Add the eggs and vanilla; beat until smooth.

3. Pour the prepared batter into the baking cups, filling them three-quarters full.

4. Bake the cakes for 15 minutes, or until slightly jiggly in the center. Remove from the oven. Spread 1 teaspoon of the raspberry preserves on top of each cake. Transfer the muffin tin to the freezer. Chill the cheesecakes until set, 15 minutes.

5. Remove the cheesecakes from the pan and peel off the foil baking cups. Transfer the cheesecakes to a platter and serve.
—*Grace Parisi*

MAKE AHEAD The cheesecakes can be refrigerated for up to 4 days.

Chocolate Truffle Layer Cake

ACTIVE: 1 HR 30 MIN; TOTAL: 3 HR

PLUS OVERNIGHT CHILLING

16 SERVINGS ● ●

CAKE

10 **ounces bittersweet chocolate, finely chopped**

1 **stick unsalted butter**

1 **tablespoon pure vanilla extract**

⅓ **cup unsweetened cocoa powder**

1 **cup water**

6 **ounces crème fraîche (⅔ cup)**

3 **large eggs**

3 **large egg yolks**

1½ cups granulated sugar
½ cup light brown sugar
1¼ cups all-purpose flour
1 tablespoon baking soda
2 teaspoons baking powder
1 teaspoon salt

WHITE CHOCOLATE GANACHE
1 pound white chocolate, chopped
¾ cup plus 2 tablespoons heavy cream
2 tablespoons unsalted butter

DARK CHOCOLATE GANACHE
1⅓ cups plus 2 tablespoons heavy cream
10 ounces bittersweet chocolate, chopped

CHOCOLATE FROSTING
4 ounces bittersweet chocolate, chopped
3 tablespoons granulated sugar
¼ cup corn syrup
6 tablespoons unsweetened cocoa powder
¼ cup plus 2 tablespoons water
1 tablespoon brandy
1 pound unsalted butter, softened
¾ cup confectioners' sugar, sifted
Bittersweet and white chocolate shavings, for garnish

1. MAKE THE CAKE: Preheat the oven to 350°. Butter two 15-by-12-inch jelly roll pans and line the bottoms of the pans with parchment paper. In a medium saucepan, melt 6 ounces of the finely chopped chocolate with the butter and vanilla over very low heat, stirring gently. Remove the melted chocolate mixture from the heat and let it cool slightly.

2. In a small saucepan, combine the unsweetened cocoa powder with the water and bring to a boil, whisking constantly. Let the cocoa mixture cool slightly, then whisk the mixture into the melted chocolate. Whisk the crème fraîche into the chocolate mixture.

3. In a large bowl, using an electric mixer, beat the whole eggs, egg yolks and both sugars at medium speed until pale and fluffy, 5 minutes. Beat in the chocolate mixture. In a medium bowl, whisk the flour, baking soda, baking powder and salt; transfer to a sifter or a sieve. Sift the dry ingredients and fold into the batter with a large spatula until fully incorporated.

4. Spread the batter evenly between the prepared pans and sprinkle with the remaining 4 ounces of chopped chocolate. Bake the cakes in the lower and middle third of the oven for 25 to 30 minutes, until the centers spring back when lightly pressed; shift the pans halfway through baking. Let the cakes cool completely in the pans.

5. MEANWHILE, MAKE THE WHITE CHOCOLATE GANACHE: In a medium bowl set over a medium saucepan of simmering water, melt the white chocolate. Remove from the heat. Pour off the water in the saucepan and wipe it out. Add the heavy cream and butter to the saucepan and heat until the butter is melted and small bubbles appear around the edges. Whisk the hot cream mixture into the white chocolate. Set the bowl in a cool place until the ganache is firm enough to hold its shape, at least 1 hour.

6. MAKE THE DARK CHOCOLATE GANACHE: In a medium saucepan, heat the cream until small bubbles appear around the edges. Put the chopped chocolate in a heatproof bowl and pour the cream on top. Let stand for 2 to 3 minutes, until the chocolate has melted, then whisk until smooth. Set the bowl in a cool place until the ganache is firm enough to hold its shape, at least 1 hour.

7. MAKE THE CHOCOLATE FROSTING: In a medium saucepan, melt the chocolate over very low heat, stirring frequently. In a small saucepan, whisk together the granulated sugar, corn syrup, cocoa and water and bring to a boil, whisking constantly. Remove from the heat and whisk in the brandy and melted chocolate. Let cool completely, about 30 minutes.

8. In the bowl of a standing electric mixer fitted with a wire whisk, beat the butter at medium speed until light and fluffy. Add the cooled chocolate mixture. At low speed, beat in the confectioners' sugar.

9. ASSEMBLE THE CAKE: Cut out an 11-by-5-inch cardboard rectangle. Place a sheet of parchment or wax paper over each cake and top with a flat cookie sheet or cutting board. Invert the cakes and remove the pans. With the paper attached, trim each cake to an even 15-by-11-inch rectangle, then cut each into three 11-by-5-inch rectangles so there are 6.

10. Spoon a small dollop of the chocolate frosting onto the cardboard rectangle and transfer one cake rectangle to it; peel off the paper. This will be the base. Spread half of the white chocolate ganache on the base and top with another cake rectangle; peel off the paper. Spread half of the dark chocolate ganache on the cake and top with another layer, peeling off the parchment. Spread with 1¼ cups of the chocolate frosting. Repeat with 2 more layers, peeling the parchment off the cake rectangles and spreading them with the remaining white and dark chocolate ganache. Keep the sides even as you build the cake by smoothing them out with a metal cake spatula. Top with the final cake rectangle and peel off the parchment. Coat the sides and top of the cake with a smooth layer of chocolate frosting; refrigerate briefly to set the frosting. Spread the remaining frosting over the cake. Carefully transfer the cake (on its cardboard base) to a platter and refrigerate until firm. Using a hot knife, cut the cake into slices while cold. Let come to room temperature before serving. —Kimberly Sklar

MAKE AHEAD The truffle layer cake can be refrigerated for 3 days or frozen for up to 2 weeks.

cakes, cookies & more

Chocolate-Pecan Cake

TOTAL: 30 MIN

2 SERVINGS ● ●

This quick cake was inspired by New Orleans praline candies, which are made with pecans and caramelized brown sugar. It's small, so it's meant to be shared by two people.

- ½ cup all-purpose flour
- ¼ teaspoon baking powder
- ¼ teaspoon salt
- ⅔ cup sugar
- ¼ cup salted roasted pecans, finely chopped
- ¼ cup semisweet or bittersweet chocolate chips
- 1 large egg, beaten
- 3 tablespoons coconut milk
- 4 tablespoons unsalted butter, 3 tablespoons melted
- 3 tablespoons heavy cream

1. Preheat the oven to 375°. Butter an 8-inch round cake pan. In a medium bowl, whisk the flour with the baking powder and salt. Stir in ⅓ cup of the sugar, the chopped pecans and the chocolate chips. In another bowl, beat the egg with the coconut milk and the 3 tablespoons of melted butter. Whisk in the dry ingredients until combined. Pour the batter into the prepared cake pan and bake for about 22 minutes, or until the cake is springy to the touch. Let the cake cool on a wire rack for 5 minutes before inverting and cutting it into wedges.

2. Meanwhile, in a small saucepan, combine the remaining ⅓ cup of sugar with 2 tablespoons of water and cook over moderately high heat, stirring with a wooden spoon until the sugar is dissolved. Wash down the sides of the pan with a moistened pastry brush. Cook the sugar until it becomes a medium amber, about 4 minutes. Off the heat, carefully stir in the remaining 1 tablespoon of butter and the heavy cream. Drizzle the caramel sauce over the cake wedges and serve right away. —*Nicole Krasinski*

MAKE AHEAD The cake can be wrapped in plastic and refrigerated overnight; bring to room temperature before serving. The caramel can be kept at room temperature overnight.

Double-Chocolate Bundt Cake with Ganache Glaze

ACTIVE: 30 MIN; TOTAL: 1 HR 30 MIN PLUS COOLING

10 TO 12 SERVINGS ● ●

Many Bundt cakes are heavy and buttery, but this one is surprisingly light and incredibly moist under its silky chocolate glaze. Strong-brewed coffee in the batter intensifies the chocolate flavor while cutting the sweetness.

- Vegetable oil spray
- 5 ounces bittersweet chocolate, chopped
- ¾ cup canola oil
- 1 cup sugar
- 1 large egg
- 2 cups all-purpose flour
- ½ cup Dutch-process cocoa powder
- 1 tablespoon baking soda
- ¾ teaspoon salt
- 1 cup strong-brewed coffee
- 1 cup buttermilk
- ⅓ cup heavy cream
- ½ tablespoon corn syrup
- ½ tablespoon unsalted butter

1. Preheat the oven to 350°. Spray a 12-cup Bundt pan with vegetable oil spray. In a small saucepan, melt 2 ounces of the chopped chocolate over low heat, stirring constantly. Scrape the melted chocolate into a medium bowl and let cool slightly. Whisk the canola oil and sugar into the chocolate until smooth, then whisk the egg into the chocolate mixture.

2. In a small bowl, whisk together the flour, cocoa powder, baking soda and salt. Add half of the dry ingredients to the chocolate mixture along with ½ cup of the brewed coffee and ½ cup of the buttermilk; whisk the batter until smooth. Add the remaining dry ingredients, coffee and buttermilk and whisk again until smooth.

3. Pour the batter into the prepared Bundt pan and bake in the lower third of the oven for about 45 minutes, or until a toothpick inserted in the center of the cake comes out with a few moist crumbs attached. Let the chocolate cake cool on a rack for at least 10 minutes, then turn it out and let it cool completely.

4. In a small saucepan, bring the heavy cream to a boil. In a heatproof bowl, combine the remaining 3 ounces of chopped chocolate with the corn syrup and the butter. Pour the hot cream over the chocolate and let stand until melted, about 5 minutes. Whisk until smooth. Let the ganache glaze cool until thick but still pourable, about 5 minutes.

5. Pour the chocolate ganache over the cooled cake. Let the cake stand until the glaze is set, at least 30 minutes, before serving. —*Kate Neumann*

MAKE AHEAD The glazed chocolate cake can be stored in an airtight container for up to 3 days.

---

ingredient

baking chocolate

"I've experimented with other chocolates to break my **Valrhona** habit, but I keep coming back." —*Nicole Krasinski*, pastry chef, Rubicon in San Francisco

**DOUBLE-CHOCOLATE BUNDT CAKE
WITH GANACHE GLAZE**

cakes, cookies & more

Mini Cheesecakes with Wine Gelées

ACTIVE: 30 MIN; TOTAL: 1 HR PLUS CHILLING

MAKES FOUR 3-INCH CAKES ●

CHEESECAKES

- 3 tablespoons unsalted butter, melted, plus more for brushing
- 7 whole graham crackers
- ½ cup plus 1 tablespoon sugar
- 1 large egg
- 1 large egg yolk

Pinch of salt

One 10½-ounce log of fresh goat cheese, softened

5½ ounces plus 2 tablespoons crème fraîche (½ cup)

WINE GELÉES

- 1 envelope unflavored gelatin
- 2½ tablespoons cold water
- 3 tablespoons each of Orange Muscat, rosé, Pinot Noir and tawny port
- 4 teaspoons sugar

1. MAKE THE CHEESECAKES: Preheat the oven to 325°. Line a baking sheet with parchment paper. Cut out four 3-inch rounds of cardboard. Brush the inside of four individual ring molds that are 3 inches across and 2½ inches deep with butter. In a food processor, grind the graham crackers with the melted butter and 1 tablespoon of the sugar. Set the molds on the baking sheet and line the bottoms with the cardboard rounds, trimming to fit. Pack the crumbs into the molds; press to compact. Bake for 10 minutes. Let cool.

2. In a bowl, using an electric mixer, beat the egg, egg yolk, salt and remaining sugar at medium speed until pale and fluffy, about 2 minutes. Add the goat cheese and beat until smooth. Fold in the crème fraîche. Spoon the mixture into the molds and smooth the tops. Bake for about 30 minutes, or until the cheesecakes are just set but not browned. Let cool, then refrigerate the cheesecakes until they are chilled, at least 1 hour.

3. Heat a sharp, thin-bladed knife under hot water; dry the knife. Carefully run the blade around the edge of each cheesecake. Pressing up on the cardboard, ease the cheesecakes out of the molds; return to the baking sheet. Cut four 11-by-2½-inch strips of parchment paper. Wrap the paper around the perimeter of each cheesecake to form a collar that extends 1 inch above the surface; secure with tape.

4. MAKE THE WINE GELÉES: In a bowl, sprinkle the gelatin over the cold water; let soften. Microwave at high power for about 15 seconds, just until the gelatin is melted. Put the 4 wines in separate ramekins. Add 2 teaspoons of sugar to the rosé and 2 to the Pinot Noir and microwave for 20 seconds; stir to dissolve the sugar. Stir 1 teaspoon of the melted gelatin into each of the 4 wines. Let the wines stand until cooled, 10 minutes. Pour one of the wine gelées over each cheesecake and refrigerate until chilled and set, 20 minutes.

5. Remove the parchment-paper collar from each cheesecake. Carefully remove the cardboard bottoms and serve.
—*Kate Zuckerman*

Cocoa Crème Fraîche Cupcakes

TOTAL: 30 MIN

MAKES 16 CUPCAKES ● ●

This wonderfully rich cocoa crème fraîche batter fills a 12-cup muffin pan, with some batter left over. For additional cupcakes, you'll need to set 4 foil cups on a baking sheet.

- 1 cup plus 3 tablespoons all-purpose flour
- ⅔ cup unsweetened cocoa powder
- 1 teaspoon baking powder
- 1 teaspoon salt
- ¼ teaspoon baking soda
- 1 stick plus 6 tablespoons unsalted butter, softened
- 1 cup sugar
- 3 large eggs
- 1 teaspoon pure vanilla extract
- ¾ cup crème fraîche, at room temperature, stirred until runny, plus more for serving

1. Preheat the oven to 350°. Line a 12-cup muffin pan with foil baking cups. Put 4 additional foil cups on a small baking sheet.

2. Sift together the flour, cocoa powder, baking powder, salt and baking soda. In a large bowl, beat the butter with the sugar until light and fluffy. At medium speed, add the eggs one at a time to the butter mixture, beating until each one is fully incorporated before adding the next. Add the vanilla. At low speed, alternately beat in the dry ingredients and the ¾ cup of crème fraîche in 2 batches.

3. Spoon the batter into the foil cups, filling each one two-thirds full. Bake the cupcakes for 15 minutes, or until they are springy when gently pressed and when a cake tester inserted in the center of one comes out clean. Let the cupcakes cool slightly, then remove them from the pan. Place a dollop of crème fraîche on each cupcake and serve immediately.
—*Meg Ray and Caitlan Alissa Williams*

tools

nesting cups

Zyliss Measuring Cups stack neatly for compact storage. **Details** $20 per set; zyliss.com.

Devil's Food Cupcakes with Espresso Meringue

ACTIVE: 30 MIN; TOTAL: 1 HR

MAKES 2 DOZEN CUPCAKES ●

CUPCAKES

Vegetable oil spray

4 ounces unsweetened chocolate, finely chopped

¼ cup Dutch-process cocoa powder, plus more for sprinkling

1¼ cups boiling water

1½ cups all-purpose flour

1 teaspoon baking soda

¼ teaspoon salt

2 sticks unsalted butter, softened

1½ cups packed dark brown sugar

3 large eggs

½ cup buttermilk

1 teaspoon pure vanilla extract

ESPRESSO MERINGUE

3 large egg whites

1½ cups confectioners' sugar

1 teaspoon instant espresso, plus more for sprinkling

1. MAKE THE CUPCAKES: Preheat the oven to 325°. Line 24 muffin cups with paper liners. Lightly spray the paper liners with vegetable oil spray. In a small bowl, mix the chocolate and ¼ cup of cocoa. Add the boiling water and let melt, then whisk until smooth. In a medium bowl, whisk the flour with the baking soda and salt. In a large bowl, using an electric mixer, beat the butter and brown sugar until fluffy. Beat in the eggs, buttermilk and vanilla, then slowly beat in the dry ingredients and the chocolate mixture in 3 alternating batches.

2. Fill the muffin cups three-fourths full with the batter. Bake for 22 to 25 minutes, shifting the pans halfway through, until the cupcakes are springy and a toothpick inserted in the center comes out with a few moist crumbs attached. Let the cupcakes cool in the pans for 15 minutes, then unmold them and transfer to a rack to cool completely.

3. MEANWHILE, MAKE THE ESPRESSO MERINGUE: Mix the egg whites, confectioners' sugar and 1 teaspoon of espresso in a medium stainless steel bowl. Set the bowl over a saucepan of simmering water and heat the whites, whisking constantly, until they are hot to the touch (165°). Transfer the whipped egg whites to the bowl of a standing electric mixer fitted with a whisk and beat at high speed until stiff and glossy, 5 minutes; if using a handheld mixer, beat for 8 minutes.

4. Scoop half of the meringue into a pastry bag fitted with a large (¾-inch) plain tip and pipe the meringue onto half of the cupcakes. Repeat with the remaining espresso meringue and cupcakes. Lightly sprinkle the meringue with cocoa and espresso powder and serve the cupcakes. —*Karen Hatfield*

MAKE AHEAD The frosted devil's food cupcakes can be kept in an airtight container overnight.

Grilled Pound Cake with Mexican Chocolate Sauce and Tropical Fruit

TOTAL: 45 MIN

6 SERVINGS ●

WHIPPED CREAM

1 cup heavy cream

3 tablespoons confectioners' sugar

1 tablespoon dark rum

½ teaspoon pure vanilla extract

MEXICAN CHOCOLATE SAUCE

¾ cup heavy cream

½ teaspoon ground cinnamon

½ teaspoon pure ancho chile powder

1 cup semisweet chocolate chips

½ teaspoon pure vanilla extract

FRUIT SALAD

1 large mango, peeled and cut into ⅓-inch wedges

1 medium papaya—halved, seeded, peeled and cut into ⅓-inch wedges

1 tablespoon coarsely chopped fresh basil

1 teaspoon pure vanilla extract

POUND CAKE

2 tablespoons unsalted butter, softened

Six 1¼-inch slices of homemade or fresh bakery pound cake (about 10 ounces)

3 tablespoons toasted sliced almonds, for garnish

1. MAKE THE WHIPPED CREAM: In a medium bowl, using an electric mixer, softly whip the heavy cream. Add the confectioners' sugar, rum and vanilla and whip the cream until firm peaks form. Refrigerate the whipped cream.

2. MAKE THE CHOCOLATE SAUCE: In a medium saucepan, bring the heavy cream to a simmer over moderately high heat with the cinnamon and chile powder. Add the chocolate chips and vanilla. Remove the chocolate sauce from the heat and let it stand for 1 minute, then whisk to blend the sauce; keep warm.

3. MAKE THE FRUIT SALAD: In a medium bowl, toss the mango and papaya with the basil and vanilla.

4. PREPARE THE POUND CAKE: Light a grill or preheat a grill pan. Butter both sides of the pound cake slices. Grill the cake slices over moderate heat, turning once, until golden, about 2 minutes per side. Set a slice of grilled pound cake on each of 6 plates and top each one with 3 tablespoons of the warm chocolate sauce and the fruit salad. Top each serving with a dollop of the rum whipped cream and sprinkle with the toasted almonds. Pass the remaining chocolate sauce at the table. —*Michelle Bernstein*

MAKE AHEAD The whipped cream and fruit salad can be refrigerated for up to 4 hours; whip the cream gently before serving. The chocolate sauce can be refrigerated for up to 2 days; rewarm before serving.

cakes, cookies & more

Chocolate-Raspberry Whipped Cream Swiss Roll

TOTAL: 1 HR PLUS 8 HR CHILLING

12 SERVINGS ● ●

This delicious cake (see photo, p. 361) is an homage to the classic European princess cake substituting whipped cream for pastry cream and a luscious chocolate glaze for marzipan.

CAKE

- 5 large eggs, separated
- ½ cup plus granulated sugar
- ½ teaspoon pure vanilla extract
- ½ cup cake flour
- ½ teaspoon salt
- 4 tablespoons unsalted butter, melted
- 2 tablespoons confectioners' sugar

FILLING

- 1½ cups heavy cream
- 2 teaspoons sugar
- ½ teaspoon pure vanilla extract
- Pinch of salt
- ¼ cup plus 2 tablespoons seedless raspberry jam

CHOCOLATE GLAZE

- ½ pound bittersweet chocolate, chopped
- ¾ cup heavy cream
- ¼ cup milk
- ¼ cup sugar
- 4 tablespoons unsalted butter, at room temperature

Raspberries, for garnish

1. MAKE THE CAKE: Preheat the oven to 350°. Butter a 15-by-10-inch jelly roll pan, line the pan with parchment paper and butter the paper. In the bowl of a standing electric mixer fitted with a whisk, beat the egg yolks with ¼ cup of the granulated sugar and the vanilla until fluffy, about 3 minutes. Scrape the mixture into a large bowl and fold in the flour.

2. In a clean bowl using a clean whisk, beat the egg whites with the salt at medium speed until soft peaks form. Gradually add the remaining ¼ cup of granulated sugar and beat until the whites are glossy. Using a rubber spatula, fold the whites into the yolk mixture until no streaks remain. Quickly fold in the melted butter. Spread the batter in the pan. Bake in the lower third of the oven for 20 minutes, or until golden and puffy. Let cool in the pan on a rack.

3. Run the blade of a knife around the edge of the jelly roll pan. Dust the cake with the confectioners' sugar and cover with a sheet of plastic wrap and a clean kitchen towel. Top with a cutting board and, holding both the board and the pan, invert the cake. Rap the board firmly against the table, then remove the pan and carefully peel off the parchment paper.

4. MAKE THE FILLING: In a large bowl, whip the cream with the sugar, vanilla and salt to stiff peaks. Using an offset metal spatula, spread the raspberry jam on the cake. Spread the whipped cream evenly over the jam. Begin rolling up the cake from the long side, as tightly as possible, using the kitchen towel and plastic wrap to help shape the roll. Wrap the roll tightly in the plastic and transfer to a baking sheet. Refrigerate for at least 6 hours or, preferably, overnight.

5. MAKE THE CHOCOLATE GLAZE: Put the chocolate in a bowl. In a saucepan, stir the cream, milk and sugar over moderate heat just until the sugar is dissolved. Pour the hot cream over the chocolate; let stand until the chocolate is melted, 3 minutes. Whisk until smooth, then whisk in the butter and let cool slightly.

6. Discard the plastic wrap and transfer the cake to a rack. Pour half of the chocolate glaze all over the top and sides and spread it evenly with an offset spatula. Spread the remaining glaze all over the cake and refrigerate until set, at least 2 hours. Garnish the top with raspberries. Transfer the cake to a platter, cut into slices and serve.
—*Maria Helm Sinskey*

MAKE AHEAD The glazed roll can be refrigerated for up to 2 days before slicing.

Pineapple Upside-Down Cake

ACTIVE: 30 MIN; TOTAL: 1 HR 30 MIN

MAKES ONE 8-INCH CAKE ●

- ¾ cup plus 2 tablespoons light brown sugar
- 1½ sticks unsalted butter, softened
- 1 vanilla bean, split, seeds scraped
- ½ large pineapple—peeled, quartered, cored and sliced ⅓ inch thick
- ½ cup sour cream
- 2 large eggs
- 1 teaspoon pure vanilla extract
- 1¼ cups all-purpose flour
- ¾ cup granulated sugar
- ½ teaspoon baking powder
- ¼ teaspoon baking soda
- ½ teaspoon salt

1. Preheat the oven to 350°. Butter an 8-inch round cake pan. Sprinkle the bottom with 2 tablespoons of brown sugar.

2. In a large skillet, combine the remaining brown sugar, ½ stick of butter and the vanilla bean and seeds. Cook over moderately low heat until the butter is melted. Add the pineapple and cook over moderately low heat, stirring occasionally, until tender, 20 minutes. Using a slotted spoon, arrange the slices in the pan, overlapping if necessary. Remove the vanilla bean and pour the pan juices over the pineapple.

3. In a bowl, whisk ¼ cup of sour cream, the eggs and vanilla. In another bowl, beat the flour, granulated sugar, baking powder, baking soda and salt. Add the remaining butter and sour cream; beat at low speed until smooth, then beat at medium speed until fluffy. Add the sour cream mixture and beat until fluffy, 2 minutes.

4. Spoon the batter over the pineapple and spread evenly. Bake for 40 minutes, or until the cake is deep golden. Let cool for 5 minutes on a rack. Run a knife around the edge of the cake, invert onto a plate and remove the pan. Replace any pineapple that may have stuck to the pan. Serve warm or at room temperature. —*Kristin Ferguson*

PINEAPPLE UPSIDE-DOWN CAKE

LEMONY SEMOLINA-JAM CAKE

Lemony Semolina-Jam Cake

ACTIVE: 30 MIN; TOTAL: 1 HR 45 MIN

MAKES ONE 8-INCH CAKE ●

PASTRY CREAM

- ⅔ cup half-and-half
- 2 large egg yolks
- 2 tablespoons sugar
- 1 teaspoon all-purpose flour
- 4 teaspoons cornstarch

Pinch of salt

- 2 teaspoons unsalted butter, softened
- ½ teaspoon pure vanilla extract

CAKE

- 6 tablespoons unsalted butter, softened
- 1 teaspoon finely grated lemon zest
- 1½ tablespoons fresh lemon juice
- ¾ cup plus 2 tablespoons sugar
- ¾ cup cake flour
- ¼ cup semolina
- 1½ teaspoons baking powder
- ¼ teaspoon salt
- 4 large egg whites (½ cup)
- ¼ cup seedless raspberry preserves

Confectioners' sugar and fresh raspberries, for serving

1. **MAKE THE PASTRY CREAM:** In a small saucepan, bring the half-and-half to a simmer. In a medium bowl, whisk the yolks, sugar, flour, cornstarch and salt. Whisk in the hot half-and-half. Return the mixture to the saucepan and cook over moderate heat, whisking constantly, until very thick, about 3 minutes. Whisk in the butter and vanilla. Scrape the pastry cream onto a large plate and let cool to room temperature, about 10 minutes.

2. **MAKE THE CAKE:** Preheat the oven to 375°. Butter an 8-inch springform pan. In a bowl, whisk the pastry cream with the butter until smooth. Whisk in the lemon zest and juice. Add ¼ cup plus 2 tablespoons of the sugar, the cake flour, semolina, baking powder and salt and whisk the batter until it is smooth.

3. In a clean bowl, using an electric mixer, beat the egg whites at medium speed until soft peaks form. Gradually beat in the remaining sugar at high speed until glossy and stiff. At low speed, beat one-fourth of the beaten whites into the batter, then fold in the rest with a rubber spatula until no streaks of white remain.

4. Scrape the batter into the prepared pan. Bake in the lower third of the oven for 40 minutes, or until golden and a skewer inserted in the center comes out with a few moist crumbs attached. Let cool in the pan for 20 minutes, then remove the ring and base; cool completely on a rack.

5. Using a serrated knife, split the cake in half horizontally. Spread the preserves on the bottom layer and replace the top. Dust with confectioners' sugar and serve with raspberries. —*Michelle Vernier*

cakes, cookies & more

Madrina's Famous Orange Cake

ACTIVE: 1 HR; TOTAL: 3 HR

12 SERVINGS ●

Madrina is spanish for "godmother." Whenever cookbook author Isabel González's mother's *madrina* made this stunning cake, all the neighborhood kids would beg for slices.

CAKE LAYERS

Vegetable oil spray

2¼ cups all-purpose flour

1½ cups sugar

1 tablespoon baking powder

½ teaspoon salt

1 tablespoon finely grated orange zest

3 large eggs

¾ cup fresh orange juice

1 stick unsalted butter, melted and cooled

¼ cup water

FILLING

1 cup fresh orange juice

⅓ cup sugar

3 tablespoons all-purpose flour

2 teaspoons finely grated orange zest

¼ teaspoon salt

2 teaspoons unsalted butter

1 teaspoon fresh lemon juice

ICING

1 cup sugar

⅓ cup water

3 large egg whites

⅛ teaspoon cream of tartar

1. MAKE THE CAKE LAYERS: Preheat the oven to 350°. Spray two 8-inch round cake pans with vegetable oil spray and line the bottoms of the cake pans with parchment paper. Spray the parchment paper.

2. In a large bowl, mix the flour with the sugar, baking powder, salt and orange zest. Using an electric mixer at medium-low speed, beat in the eggs, orange juice, butter and water until blended, about 2 minutes. Divide the batter between the 2 prepared pans and bake for about 35 minutes, or until a toothpick inserted in the center of each cake comes out clean. Let the cake layers cool in the pans for 10 minutes, then invert them onto a rack to cool completely. Peel the parchment paper off the cake layers.

3. MAKE THE FILLING: In a medium saucepan, combine the orange juice, sugar, flour, orange zest and salt and cook over moderate heat, whisking constantly, until the filling is very thick and just beginning to boil, about 8 minutes. Off the heat, whisk the butter and lemon juice into the filling, then transfer it to a bowl. Place a sheet of plastic wrap directly on the surface of the filling and refrigerate it for 30 minutes, or until the filling is chilled.

4. MAKE THE ICING: In a small saucepan, combine the sugar and water and cook over moderate heat until the syrup reaches 240° on a candy thermometer; this can take up to 12 minutes. Meanwhile, in the bowl of a standing electric mixer, beat the egg whites with the cream of tartar until soft peaks form. With the machine on medium-low speed, slowly pour in the hot sugar syrup against the side of the bowl. Once all of the sugar syrup has been added, increase the speed to medium high and beat until the meringue icing is fluffy, glossy and at room temperature, about 8 minutes longer.

5. Using a serrated knife, split each cake layer in half horizontally. Place one of the cake layers, cut side up, on a plate. Spread one-third of the orange filling on the cake layer and cover the filling with the top half of the cake. Spread another third of the orange filling on top of the cake. Repeat with the remaining cake layers and orange filling, ending with a cake layer. Spread the meringue icing all over the top and down the side of the cake. Let the orange cake stand for 1 hour before serving.

—*Isabel González*

MAKE AHEAD The orange cake can be refrigerated, uncovered, overnight.

Angel Food Cake with Three-Berry Compote

ACTIVE: 30 MIN; TOTAL: 1 HR PLUS COOLING

10 SERVINGS ● ●

10 large egg whites, at room temperature (1½ cups)

1½ teaspoons cream of tartar

1¼ cups granulated sugar

¼ teaspoon pure vanilla extract

1 cup cake flour

¾ cup confectioners' sugar

¼ teaspoon salt

2 pints strawberries, sliced

2 pints raspberries

1 pint blackberries

3 tablespoons fresh lemon juice

1. Preheat the oven to 350°. In the bowl of a standing electric mixer, beat the egg whites at medium-high speed until frothy. Add the cream of tartar and beat until firm peaks form. Add ¾ cup of the granulated sugar, 2 tablespoons at a time, beating for 10 seconds before adding more. Beat in the vanilla. Once the ¾ cup of sugar has been added, beat the whites at high speed until stiff, about 4 minutes.

2. In a medium bowl, whisk the cake flour with the confectioners' sugar and salt. Sift the dry ingredients over the beaten whites in 3 batches, folding gently with a large spatula until incorporated. Spoon the batter into an ungreased 10-inch angel food cake pan (do not use nonstick). Bake for 40 minutes, until the cake is risen and golden. Invert the cake in the pan onto a bottle neck and let cool.

3. In a large saucepan, simmer the berries with the remaining ½ cup of granulated sugar and the lemon juice until the juices are released, 10 minutes. Cool slightly.

4. Using a knife, loosen the cake from the pan and remove the side of the pan. Loosen the cake from the pan bottom and the tube. Transfer the cake to a plate. Slice the cake and serve with the warm compote.

—*Hugo Matheson and Kimbal Musk*

ANGEL FOOD CAKE WITH
THREE-BERRY COMPOTE

cakes, cookies & more

Bittersweet Mocha-Pecan Roll
ACTIVE: 45 MIN; TOTAL: 4 HR 30 MIN
10 TO 12 SERVINGS ● ●

This amazing jelly roll cake is not only rich and chocolaty but also ethereal and soufflélike. The recipe is by Alice Medrich, a chocolate expert and award-winning author of *Bittersweet: Recipes and Tales from a Life in Chocolate.*

- 6 ounces milk chocolate, chopped
- 2 teaspoons instant espresso
- 1½ cups heavy cream
- Vegetable oil spray
- ⅓ cup pecan halves
- 2 tablespoons all-purpose flour
- 6 ounces bittersweet chocolate, preferably 70 percent cocoa, chopped
- 1 stick unsalted butter, cut into tablespoons
- 4 large eggs, separated
- ⅔ cup sugar
- ⅛ teaspoon salt
- ⅛ teaspoon cream of tartar
- Unsweetened cocoa powder and confectioners' sugar, for dusting

taste test
best pecans

1. In a large bowl, combine the milk chocolate and instant espresso. In a saucepan, heat the cream. Pour the cream over the chocolate; let stand until melted, then whisk until blended. Refrigerate the mocha cream until cold, about 2 hours.

2. Preheat the oven to 350°. Spray a 16-by-12-inch jelly roll pan with vegetable oil spray. Line the bottom with parchment paper and spray the paper. Spread the pecans on a pie plate and bake for 7 minutes, or until golden. Let cool completely. In a food processor, pulse the pecans with the flour until finely ground.

3. Put the bittersweet chocolate and butter in a heatproof bowl; set the bowl over a saucepan of barely simmering water and stir until melted. Off the heat, whisk in the yolks, ⅓ cup of the sugar and the salt.

4. In a large bowl, beat the egg whites and cream of tartar until frothy. Beat at high speed until soft peaks form. Slowly beat in the remaining ⅓ cup sugar until the whites are firm and glossy. Fold one-fourth of the whites into the chocolate; fold the chocolate and the pecans into the remaining whites until no streaks remain.

5. Spread the batter in the prepared pan and bake for 9 minutes, or until springy. Let the cake cool in the pan on a rack.

6. Run a knife around the edge of the pan. Heavily dust the cake with cocoa powder and cover with a sheet of foil. Place a cutting board over the cake and invert it; remove the pan and parchment paper.

7. Beat the chilled mocha cream at high speed until it is firm and holds its shape. Spread the cream evenly over the cake. Starting at a long side, roll up the cake as tightly as possible, using the foil as a guide. Tightly wrap the cake roll in the foil and slide it onto a cutting board. Refrigerate until firm, about 2 hours. Unwrap the cake and dust with more cocoa. Carefully slide it onto a long platter and dust with confectioners' sugar. Cut into slices and serve.
—*Alice Medrich*

Apple Crumble Cakes with Chestnuts
ACTIVE: 25 MIN; TOTAL: 55 MIN
8 SERVINGS ● ●

This Chinese riff on an American-style streusel-topped coffee cake was created by Shanghai-based fashion designer Han Feng.

- 1½ cups coarsely chopped walnuts
- ⅔ cup light brown sugar
- 1 teaspoon cinnamon
- 2 cups all-purpose flour
- 1 teaspoon baking powder
- 1 teaspoon baking soda
- 1 stick unsalted butter, softened
- 1 cup turbinado sugar
- ½ cup dark brown sugar
- 2 large eggs, beaten
- 1 cup buttermilk
- 2 large Granny Smith apples— peeled and cut into ½-inch dice
- 1 cup roasted chestnuts, quartered
- Sesame or vanilla ice cream, for serving

1. Preheat the oven to 350°. Place eight 8-ounce ramekins on a large rimmed baking sheet. In a bowl, toss the walnuts with the light brown sugar and the cinnamon.

2. In another medium bowl, whisk together the flour, baking powder and baking soda. In a large bowl, blend the butter with the turbinado sugar, the dark brown sugar and the eggs. Gently stir the flour mixture and the buttermilk into the butter-and-sugar mixture until the batter is smooth and blended, then fold the diced apples and quartered chestnuts into the batter.

3. Spoon the cake batter into the ramekins and sprinkle the walnut streusel mixture on top. Bake the crumble cakes for about 40 minutes, or until the topping is browned and a cake tester inserted in the center of the cakes comes out clean. Let the cakes cool for 5 to 10 minutes. Serve the cakes slightly warm with a scoop of ice cream.
—*Han Feng*

Nutty Toffee-Date Cake

ACTIVE: 40 MIN; TOTAL: 1 HR 30 MIN PLUS COOLING

8 SERVINGS ● ●

Though this cake resembles sticky toffee pudding, Kate Neumann, the pastry chef of MK The Restaurant in Chicago, says it's "a dried fruit or two away from my grandmother's plum pudding." It is subtly spiced with both cinnamon and ginger and gets a topping made with toasted nuts and a caramelly toffee sauce.

DATE CAKE

- 10 Medjool dates (7 ounces), pitted
- ¾ cup water
- 1 tablespoon unsulfured molasses
- 1 cup all-purpose flour
- 1 teaspoon baking powder
- ¼ teaspoon baking soda
- ¼ teaspoon cinnamon
- ¼ teaspoon ground ginger
- Salt
- 1 stick unsalted butter, softened
- ½ cup plus 2 tablespoons dark brown sugar
- 1 large egg
- ½ teaspoon pure vanilla extract
- ½ cup walnut halves
- ½ cup pecan halves
- 2 tablespoons corn syrup

TOFFEE SAUCE

- 1 stick unsalted butter
- 1 cup dark brown sugar
- 1 cup heavy cream
- ¼ teaspoon salt

1. MAKE THE DATE CAKE: Preheat the oven to 350°. Butter a 9-inch round cake pan. Cut a 9-inch round out of parchment paper and line the bottom of the cake pan with the round; butter the paper.

2. In a small saucepan, simmer the Medjool dates and the water over moderately low heat until the liquid in the pan is reduced by half and the dates are very soft, about 10 minutes. Scrape the dates and liquid into a food processor. Add the molasses and puree. Let the puree cool.

3. In a medium bowl, whisk the flour with the baking powder, baking soda, cinnamon, ginger and ¼ teaspoon of salt. In another medium bowl, using an electric mixer, beat the butter with ½ cup of the brown sugar until the mixture is fluffy. Beat the egg and vanilla into the butter and sugar mixture, then beat in the dry ingredients. Beat in the date puree.

4. Scrape the batter into the prepared pan and bake for about 30 minutes, or until the cake is springy to the touch. Let the cake cool for 10 minutes in the pan, then turn it out onto a rack. Peel the parchment off the cake and return the parchment paper to the pan.

5. Meanwhile, spread the walnut and pecan halves in a pie plate and bake them for about 9 minutes, or until they are fragrant and golden. Let the nuts cool slightly, then chop them very coarsely. In a small bowl, stir the corn syrup together with the remaining 2 tablespoons of brown sugar and ¼ teaspoon of salt.

6. Scatter the toasted walnuts and pecans over the parchment in the cake pan and drizzle the corn syrup mixture on top. Carefully return the cake to the pan (the same way it came out) and bake the cake for 15 minutes. Let cool slightly, then invert the cake onto a plate, replacing any nuts stuck in the pan.

7. MAKE THE TOFFEE SAUCE: In a medium saucepan, combine the butter with the sugar and bring to a boil over moderate heat, stirring. Off the heat, add the cream to the butter and sugar. Return the sauce to a boil and cook until it is slightly reduced, about 5 minutes. Stir the salt into the sauce and let it cool slightly.

8. Drizzle some of the toffee sauce over the cake and serve right away, passing the rest of the toffee sauce on the side.
—*Kate Neumann*

MAKE AHEAD The drizzled cake can be kept at room temperature in an airtight container for up to 3 days.

Graham Cracker Pound Cake

ACTIVE: 20 MIN; TOTAL: 1 HR 30 MIN

MAKES ONE 8-BY-4-INCH LOAF ●

This easy-to-make pound cake has crushed graham crackers in the batter.

- ½ sleeve of graham crackers, for the crumbs
- Vegetable oil spray
- 1½ sticks unsalted butter, softened
- ½ cup granulated sugar
- ¼ cup dark brown sugar
- 1½ cups cake flour
- ¾ teaspoon baking powder
- ¼ teaspoon salt
- 3 tablespoons whole milk
- 2 tablespoons heavy cream
- 3 large eggs
- 1 tablespoon pure vanilla extract

1. Preheat the oven to 325°. Break up the graham crackers and grind them in a food processor until they are finely ground. Spray an 8-by-4-inch glass loaf pan with vegetable oil spray. In a large bowl, using an electric mixer, cream the softened butter with the granulated sugar and dark brown sugar. In a medium bowl, whisk the cake flour with the graham cracker crumbs, the baking powder and salt. In a small bowl, whisk together the whole milk, heavy cream, eggs and vanilla. With the beater set at medium speed, add the dry and the liquid ingredients to the butter mixture in 3 alternating batches and beat until the batter is smooth.

2. Scrape the cake batter into the prepared loaf pan and bake it in the lower third of the oven for about 55 minutes, or until a toothpick inserted in the center of the pound cake comes out with a few moist crumbs attached. Let the pound cake cool in the pan for 15 minutes, then turn it out onto a rack to cool completely.
—*Megan Garrelts*

MAKE AHEAD The graham cracker pound cake can be kept in an airtight container for up to 3 days or frozen for 2 weeks.

cakes, cookies & more

Pistachio Financiers

ACTIVE: 15 MIN; TOTAL: 40 MIN

MAKES 16 BARQUETTES OR

30 MINI CAKES ● ●

- 1 cup whole blanched almonds, coarsely chopped (see Note)
- ½ cup sugar
- 2 large eggs, beaten
- 5 tablespoons unsalted butter, melted
- 3 tablespoons all-purpose flour

24 to 30 shelled pistachios

1. Preheat the oven to 400°. Butter and flour sixteen 3½-inch-long barquette molds or 30 mini muffin pan cups.

2. In a food processor, grind the almonds to a fine powder. In a bowl, mix the almond powder and sugar. Whisk in the eggs until incorporated, then whisk in the melted butter, followed by the flour. Spoon the batter into the prepared molds or muffin cups and decorate with the pistachios. Bake the cakes until golden brown, about 12 minutes for barquettes and 16 minutes for mini muffins. Let cool slightly, then run a knife around each cake and transfer them to a rack to cool. —*Jing Tio*

NOTE If you want to skip grinding the almonds, use 1 cup of almond flour.

MAKE AHEAD The pistachio financiers can be stored overnight in an airtight container at room temperature.

Harvest Mousse with Spiced Almond Tuiles

ACTIVE: 50 MIN; TOTAL: 2 HR PLUS

4 HR CHILLING

10 SERVINGS ●

MOUSSE

- 2 medium butternut squash (3 pounds), halved lengthwise and seeded
- ½ cup superfine sugar
- 2 tablespoons pure maple syrup
- ¼ teaspoon each of ground cloves, ginger, cardamom, nutmeg and allspice
- 1 envelope unflavored powdered gelatin
- 2 tablespoons cold water
- 3 large egg whites
- 1 cup heavy cream

CANDIED SQUASH

- ½ cup sugar
- ½ cup water
- ½ vanilla bean, split, seeds scraped
- ½ teaspoon freshly ground pepper
- 1 cup diced peeled butternut squash (½-inch cubes)

Lightly sweetened whipped cream and Spiced Almond Tuiles (recipe follows), for serving

1. MAKE THE MOUSSE: Preheat the oven to 350°. Place the squash, cut side down, on a lightly oiled baking sheet. Bake for about 1 hour, until very tender. Let cool slightly, then scoop out the flesh.

2. In a food processor, puree 3 cups of squash with 5 tablespoons of the superfine sugar and the maple syrup until smooth. In a small bowl, stir together the spices; add to the squash and pulse to blend.

3. In a small microwave-safe bowl, sprinkle the gelatin over the cold water. Let stand until softened, 2 to 3 minutes. Warm the gelatin in a microwave oven at high power until just melted, 10 seconds. Add to the squash and pulse to combine. Scrape the squash puree into a large bowl.

4. In a medium bowl, using a handheld electric mixer, beat the whites at medium speed until soft peaks form. With the mixer on, add the remaining superfine sugar and beat until the egg whites are stiff and glossy. Fold the egg whites into the squash puree. Pour the heavy cream into the bowl the whites were in; beat at medium speed until firm. Fold the whipped cream into the squash mousse. Spoon the mousse into 10 parfait glasses and refrigerate until firm, at least 4 hours.

5. MEANWHILE, MAKE THE CANDIED SQUASH: In a small saucepan, combine the sugar, water, vanilla bean and seeds and the pepper and bring to a boil, stirring until the sugar is dissolved. Add the squash cubes and simmer over moderate heat until they're tender and glossy, about 15 minutes. Let the candied squash cubes cool in the syrup.

6. Just before serving, drain the squash cubes. Garnish each mousse with whipped cream and the squash and serve with Spiced Almond Tuiles. —*Barbara Lynch*

SPICED ALMOND TUILES

TOTAL: 1 HR

MAKES ABOUT 40 TUILES ●

- 1 tablespoon unsalted butter
- ½ cup plus 2 tablespoons sugar
- 3 large egg whites
- 1 cup unsalted roasted almonds, ground in a food processor
- 2 tablespoons all-purpose flour
- ¼ teaspoon each of ground cloves, ginger, cardamom, nutmeg and allspice

1. Preheat the oven to 350°. In a medium bowl, using a handheld electric mixer, cream the butter and sugar until combined. Beat in the egg whites, one at a time. Add the ground almonds, flour and the ground spices and beat at low speed until a soft batter forms.

2. Line 2 baking sheets with parchment paper. Spoon level teaspoons of the tuile batter onto the prepared baking sheets, about 4 inches apart. Using an offset spatula, spread the batter into 3-inch rounds. Bake until golden, about 10 minutes. Cool for 1 minute on the baking sheet, then transfer the tuiles to a rack with a spatula. Cool the baking sheets between batches by running the undersides under cold water and drying thoroughly before replacing the parchment paper. Repeat with the remaining batter. —*B.L.*

MAKE AHEAD The tuiles can be stored at room temperature in an airtight container for up to 3 days.

DEEP, DARK CHOCOLATE PUDDING

Deep, Dark Chocolate Pudding

TOTAL: 30 MIN PLUS 4 HR CHILLING

MAKES 3½ CUPS (6 SERVINGS) ● ●

This pudding is just one component of a seven-part dessert at Café Gray in New York City, where executive pastry chef Chris Broberg serves it in a chocolate-coffee tuile alongside figs in port and candied orange peel. This intensely chocolaty, easy-to-make pudding is delicious on its own with whipped cream.

- 5 ounces bittersweet chocolate, chopped
- 2 tablespoons unsalted butter
- 2⅓ cups whole milk
- ½ cup sugar
- Pinch of salt
- 2 tablespoons Dutch-process cocoa powder
- 1 tablespoon cornstarch
- 2 large egg yolks, plus 1 large egg
- 2 teaspoons pure vanilla extract
- 1½ teaspoons instant espresso
- Lightly sweetened whipped cream, for serving

1. Set a fine strainer in a bowl over a larger bowl of ice water. Microwave the chocolate and butter until melted. Let cool slightly. **2.** In a saucepan, simmer 2 cups of the milk, ¼ cup of the sugar and the salt. In a small bowl, whisk the cocoa and cornstarch with the remaining milk. Whisk the cocoa paste into the hot milk. In the same bowl, whisk the yolks and whole egg with the remaining sugar. Gradually whisk some of the hot milk mixture into the eggs to warm them, then whisk the egg mixture into the pan and cook over moderately high heat, whisking, until very thick, about 5 minutes. Remove from the heat and whisk in the chocolate-butter, vanilla and espresso. Strain the pudding into the bowl set in the ice bath and stir until cooled. Place a sheet of plastic wrap directly on the surface of the pudding; refrigerate until chilled, at least 4 hours or overnight. Serve with whipped cream. —*Chris Broberg*

Fennel Cake with Anise Syrup

ACTIVE: 40 MIN; TOTAL: 1 HR 20 MIN

8 TO 10 SERVINGS ●

- 1 tablespoon plus 1 teaspoon fennel seeds
- 2 tablespoons unsalted butter
- 1 large fennel bulb (8 ounces) for the cake—halved, cored and thinly sliced, and 1 small fennel bulb for the syrup—halved, cored and thinly sliced
- 1 cup whole blanched almonds, coarsely chopped
- 1 cup shelled unsalted pistachios
- 6 large eggs, separated
- 1½ cups sugar
- 4 star anise pods
- ½ teaspoon anise seeds
- 1 cup water
- Unsweetened whipped cream, for serving

1. Preheat the oven to 350°. Butter a 10½-inch springform pan; line the bottom with parchment; butter the paper. In a skillet, toast 1 tablespoon of fennel seeds until fragrant, 3 minutes. Transfer to a plate to cool. Melt the butter in the skillet. Add the large fennel bulb and cook over moderate heat until tender 10 minutes. Let cool. **2.** In a food processor, pulse the almonds until finely ground. Transfer to a small bowl. Repeat with the pistachios, adding them to the almonds. In a large bowl, using a handheld mixer, beat the egg yolks with 1 cup of sugar at high speed until light in color, about 2 minutes. At low speed, blend in the toasted fennel seeds and the ground nuts. Stir in the cooked fennel. **3.** In a large, stainless steel bowl, beat the egg whites to firm peaks. Fold one-third of the beaten whites into the cake batter to lighten it, then fold in the remaining whites until no streaks of whites remain. Scrape the batter into the prepared pan, and bake for about 40 minutes, or until the cake is just set. Transfer the fennel cake to a rack and let cool for 20 minutes.

4. In a small skillet, toast the star anise, remaining teaspoon of fennel seeds and the anise seeds over moderate heat until fragrant, about 3 minutes. Add the water and ½ cup sugar and bring to a boil. Add the remaining fennel, cover and simmer over low heat until translucent, 20 minutes. Let cool until warm. **5.** Remove the sides of the springform pan. Transfer the cake to a platter and cut into wedges. Place a slice of cake on each plate, drizzle some syrup on the side and dollop whipped cream on top. —*Dennis Leary*

Brownie Bites

ACTIVE: 15 MIN; TOTAL: 30 MIN

MAKES 2 DOZEN 2-BITE

BROWNIES ● ● ●

These wheat-free, butterless brownies are decadent and dense.

- Vegetable oil spray
- ½ cup plus 2 tablespoons Bob's Red Mill gluten-free, all-purpose baking flour
- ½ cup sugar
- ¼ cup unsweetened cocoa powder
- 1¼ teaspoons baking powder
- ⅛ teaspoon baking soda
- ½ teaspoon salt
- ¼ teaspoon xanthan gum
- ½ cup applesauce
- ¼ cup canola oil
- 1 tablespoon pure vanilla extract
- ½ cup dairy-free mini chocolate chips

Preheat the oven to 325°. Spray 2 mini muffin pans with oil. In a bowl, whisk the flour, sugar, cocoa, baking powder, baking soda, salt and xanthan gum. In another bowl, whisk the applesauce, oil and vanilla; stir into the dry ingredients. Stir in the chocolate chips. Spoon the batter into the muffin pans, filling them three-quarters full. Bake for 15 minutes, or until set. Let the brownies cool in the pans for 15 minutes, then turn out onto a rack to cool completely. —*Erin McKenna*

cakes, cookies & more

Minty Lime Baked Alaska

ACTIVE: 20 MIN; TOTAL: 3 HR

4 SERVINGS ● ●

Instead of making this dessert with the traditional butter cake, F&W's Grace Parisi substitutes nonfat angel food cake. She tops the cake with lime sorbet mixed with finely chopped mint and light rum.

- 6 ounces angel food cake, sliced 1 inch thick
- 1 pint lime sorbet, softened
- 1 tablespoon finely chopped mint
- 1 tablespoon light rum
- ½ teaspoon finely grated lime zest
- 4 large egg whites, at room temperature
- ½ cup superfine sugar

1. Line the bottoms of four ¾-cup ramekins with the angel food cake; cut the cake as necessary to cover the bottoms evenly. Patch any empty spots with cake.

2. Spoon the lime sorbet into a small chilled bowl. Stir in the finely chopped mint, light rum and lime zest. Scoop the sorbet into the ramekins and smooth the surfaces. Freeze until the sorbet is firm, about 1½ hours.

3. In a large bowl, using a handheld electric mixer, beat the egg whites at medium speed until stiff peaks form. Gradually beat in the sugar, then increase the speed to high and beat until the whites are glossy. Run a knife around the rims of the ramekins and turn the sorbet cakes out onto a work surface. Using a spatula, transfer them to a baking sheet, cake side down, at least 4 inches apart. Spread a generous amount of the meringue all over the sorbet cakes. Freeze the baked Alaskas until they are firm, about 1 hour.

4. Preheat the broiler and position an oven rack 6 inches from the heat. Broil the baked Alaskas for about 2 minutes, shifting the pan constantly for even browning. Carefully transfer the baked Alaskas to plates and serve immediately.
—*Grace Parisi*

Chocolate Cookies 'n' Cream Towers

ACTIVE: 1 HR; TOTAL: 2 HR 30 MIN
PLUS 6 HR CHILLING

6 SERVINGS ● ●

CHOCOLATE COOKIES

- 1½ sticks unsalted butter, softened
- ¾ cup confectioners' sugar
- 1 large egg
- 1 teaspoon pure vanilla extract
- ¾ cup unsweetened Dutch-process cocoa powder
- ¼ teaspoon salt
- 1¼ cups all-purpose flour

CHOCOLATE PASTRY CREAM

- 1 cup half-and-half
- 3 large egg yolks
- ¼ cup sugar
- 1½ tablespoons all-purpose flour
- ⅛ teaspoon salt
- 3 ounces bittersweet chocolate, melted
- 1 teaspoon pure vanilla extract

WHIPPED CREAM

- 1 cup heavy cream
- 1 teaspoon confectioners' sugar
- 1 teaspoon pure vanilla extract

1. MAKE THE CHOCOLATE COOKIES: In a medium bowl, using an electric mixer, beat the butter with the confectioners' sugar at low speed until the mixture is smooth. Beat in the egg and vanilla, then beat in the cocoa powder and salt. Add the flour and beat just until combined. Form the cookie dough into 2 disks, wrap them in plastic wrap and refrigerate for about 1 hour, or until the disks are firm.

2. Preheat the oven to 325°. On a lightly floured board, roll each disk of chilled cookie dough to a 10½-inch round, a scant ¼ inch thick. Using a 2½-inch round biscuit cutter, stamp out as many rounds as you can; transfer to a large rimmed baking sheet. Gather the dough scraps, chill briefly and reroll. (You should have 32 to 34 rounds.) Bake the cookies for 10 to 12 minutes, until they are just set. Let cool

for 10 minutes, then transfer the cookies to a wire rack to cool completely.

3. MAKE THE CHOCOLATE PASTRY CREAM: Set a fine sieve over a medium bowl. In a medium saucepan, bring the half-and-half to a simmer; keep warm. In another medium bowl, whisk the egg yolks, sugar, flour and salt until pale, 1 minute. Whisk half of the warm half-and-half into the yolks, then pour the mixture into the pan and cook over moderate heat, whisking constantly, until thickened, 6 minutes. Remove the pan from the heat and whisk in the melted bittersweet chocolate and vanilla. Strain the pastry cream through the sieve and press a piece of plastic wrap directly onto the surface of the cream. Refrigerate the chocolate pastry cream for about 1 hour, or until chilled.

4. MAKE THE WHIPPED CREAM: In a medium bowl, using an electric mixer, beat the cream with confectioners' sugar and the vanilla until firm.

5. Transfer ¾ cup of the whipped cream to a small bowl. Beat in 3 tablespoons of the chocolate pastry cream until a light-chocolate cream forms.

6. ASSEMBLE THE COOKIE TOWERS: Arrange 30 cookies on a work surface. Fill 3 pastry bags fitted with large plain tips with the chocolate pastry cream, light-chocolate cream and whipped cream. Pipe the chocolate pastry cream onto 12 cookies. Pipe the light-chocolate cream onto 6 cookies. Pipe the whipped cream onto the remaining 12 cookies. Stack the towers: Start with a chocolate pastry cream–topped cookie, then a light-chocolate cream–topped cookie, followed by a whipped cream–topped cookie, another chocolate pastry cream–topped cookie and ending with a whipped cream–topped cookie. Pipe a small dollop of any remaining chocolate pastry cream onto the top of each tower. Transfer the cookie towers to a serving platter; refrigerate for at least 6 hours before serving. —*Matt Lewis*

CHOCOLATE COOKIES 'N' CREAM TOWER

cakes, cookies & more

Fluffy, Buttery Cinnamon Rolls

ACTIVE: 1 HR; TOTAL: 4 HR

8 TO 10 SERVINGS ● ●

To serve these to a group, present them in the pan still shaped in a ring, and let everyone pull off his or her own roll.

- 1 cup whole milk
- 2 envelopes active dry yeast
- ½ cup plus 1 pinch of granulated sugar
- 2 sticks unsalted butter, softened
- 1 teaspoon salt, plus more for seasoning
- 2 large eggs
- 4¼ cups sifted all-purpose flour
- ½ cup packed dark brown sugar
- 1 tablespoon plus ⅛ teaspoon ground cinnamon
- 1 cup confectioners' sugar
- 2 tablespoons half-and-half

1. In a small microwave-safe bowl, microwave the milk at high power in 30-second bursts until it's warm but not hot. Stir in the yeast and the pinch of sugar. Let the milk stand until foamy, about 5 minutes.

2. In the bowl of a standing electric mixer fitted with the paddle, beat 1 stick of the butter with the ½ cup of granulated sugar and the teaspoon of salt at medium speed until light and fluffy. Beat in the eggs, 1 at a time, until blended. Add 2 cups of the flour and beat at low speed until incorporated. Beat in the warm milk mixture, scraping in any yeast that has settled in the bottom of the bowl.

3. Switch to a dough hook. Gradually add the remaining 2¼ cups of flour and beat at medium speed until a soft, sticky dough forms, about 5 minutes. Scrape the dough into a large, lightly oiled bowl and cover with plastic wrap. Let the dough stand in a warm place until it is doubled in bulk, about 1 hour.

4. Cut four 15-inch-long sheets of wax paper. Turn the dough out onto a well-floured work surface and divide it into quarters. Working with 1 piece at a time, roll the dough to a 14-by-7-inch rectangle, about ¼ inch thick. Roll the dough rectangle around the rolling pin and unroll it onto a sheet of wax paper. Repeat with the remaining 3 pieces of dough. Transfer 2 sheets of dough to each of 2 baking sheets

and freeze for about 15 minutes, until the dough is well chilled but still pliable.

5. Meanwhile, in a medium bowl, blend the remaining 1 stick of butter with the brown sugar, 1 tablespoon of the cinnamon and a pinch of salt to make the cinnamon-butter filling for the rolls.

6. Evenly spread 1 sheet of dough with one-fourth of the cinnamon butter. Trim the edges to form a neat 12-by-6-inch rectangle. Working from a long side, tightly roll up the dough. Return the dough to the freezer and chill until very cold, about 20 minutes. Repeat with the remaining sheets of dough and cinnamon butter.

7. Butter a 10-inch springform pan. Cut the rolls 1 inch thick (you should have about 48). Arrange the cinnamon rolls, cut side up, in concentric circles in the pan, starting from the edge and working into the center. Cover the rolls with plastic wrap and let them rise in a warm place for about 1 hour, until puffy.

8. Preheat the oven to 350°. In a small bowl, mix the confectioners' sugar with the half-and-half and the remaining ⅛ teaspoon of cinnamon.

9. Remove the plastic from the rolls and bake them for about 40 minutes, until golden and risen and an instant-read thermometer inserted in the center registers 180°. Let stand for 5 minutes, then run a knife around the inside of the pan to loosen the ring from the rolls. Remove the ring. Slide the rolls onto a plate, drizzle with the glaze and serve right away.

—Deborah Racicot

NOTE You can add ¼ cup of chopped pecans or walnuts and ¼ cup of chopped raisins to the buttery filling, if desired.

MAKE AHEAD The unbaked rolls can be covered in plastic wrap and allowed to rise overnight in the refrigerator; let warm to room temperature before baking. The baked cinnamon rolls can be covered in plastic wrap and stored overnight at room temperature. Reheat before serving.

gifts

nostalgic candies

Jacques Torres Chocolate Malt Balls are a terrific take on Whoppers. **Details** $10 for 8 oz; jacquestorres.com.

Sweet Botanicals Organic Animal Shaped Jellies taste like pâtes de fruit. **Details** $6 for 5.3 oz; foragersmarket.com.

Garrison Confections Mint Patty is a big, refined version of the York Peppermint Pattie. **Details** $2 each; garrisonconfections.com.

Baby Boston Cream Cakes

ACTIVE: 1 HR; TOTAL: 2 HR

6 SERVINGS ●

Some historians say the original version of this dessert was invented in 1855 at Boston's Parker House hotel.

CAKES

Vegetable oil–and–flour spray

- 3 large egg yolks
- ¼ cup plus 2 tablespoons milk
- 1 teaspoon pure vanilla extract
- 6 tablespoons unsalted butter, softened
- 1 cup plus 2 tablespoons all-purpose flour
- ¾ cup sugar
- 2 teaspoons baking powder

Pinch of salt

- 2 tablespoons heavy cream

PASTRY CREAM

- ¾ cup milk
- ½ vanilla bean, split, seeds scraped
- 1 large egg
- 3 tablespoons sugar
- 1 tablespoon all-purpose flour
- 1½ teaspoons cornstarch

Pinch of salt

- 1½ tablespoons unsalted butter
- ½ teaspoon pure vanilla extract

CHOCOLATE GLAZE

- ¼ cup heavy cream
- 2 tablespoons light corn syrup
- 3 ounces bittersweet chocolate, chopped
- ½ teaspoon pure vanilla extract

Pinch of salt

1. MAKE THE CAKES: Preheat the oven to 350°. Spray six 6-ounce ramekins with vegetable oil–flour baking spray; line the bottoms with parchment or wax paper and spray the paper.

2. In a small bowl, whisk the egg yolks with 2 tablespoons of the milk and the vanilla. In a medium bowl, beat the butter, flour, sugar, baking powder and salt at low speed until smooth. Beat in the remaining ¼ cup of milk and the heavy cream, then beat at medium speed until fluffy, about 2 minutes. Slowly beat in the egg yolk mixture. Scrape the batter into the ramekins and bake for 25 minutes, or until the cakes are puffy and golden. Let cool for 15 minutes, then invert the cakes onto a rack to cool completely. Discard the paper.

3. MEANWHILE, MAKE THE PASTRY CREAM: In a saucepan, heat the milk with the vanilla bean and seeds. In a small bowl, whisk the egg, sugar, flour, cornstarch and salt. Whisk in half of the hot milk, then scrape the mixture into the saucepan and whisk over moderate heat, until thick, about 3 minutes. Off the heat, whisk in the butter and vanilla. Strain the pastry cream into a bowl; discard the vanilla bean. Press plastic wrap onto the surface of the pastry cream and refrigerate for 1 hour.

4. MAKE THE CHOCOLATE GLAZE: In a small saucepan, heat the heavy cream and corn syrup. Off the heat, whisk in the chocolate, vanilla and salt until smooth. Transfer to a bowl and let cool slightly.

5. Split each cake horizontally. Spoon the pastry cream between the layers. Spoon the glaze on top of the cakes, letting it drip down the sides. Transfer the cakes to plates and serve. —*Natasha MacAller*

Coconut Pudding with Pineapple and Candied Cashews

ACTIVE: 30 MIN; TOTAL: 2 HR 30 MIN

6 SERVINGS ●

This rich, creamy pudding has deep tropical flavors and a sweet, nutty garnish. Here it's molded in an 8-inch square pan, but it can also be prepared in individual custard cups or ramekins. Cooking the pineapple mixture is key because raw pineapple contains an enzyme that prevents a pudding from setting.

- 2 cups fresh pineapple, cut into ½-inch pieces
- ¼ cup granulated sugar
- 1 envelope unflavored powdered gelatin
- ¼ cup water

One 14-ounce can sweetened condensed milk

One 14-ounce can unsweetened coconut milk

- 1 tablespoon plus 1 teaspoon fresh lime juice
- ⅛ teaspoon pure vanilla extract
- 1 large egg white
- 2 tablespoons light brown sugar
- ½ cup salted roasted cashews, split lengthwise

1. In a small skillet, cook the pineapple with the granulated sugar over moderate heat, stirring occasionally, until the sugar is dissolved and the pineapple is just tender, about 5 minutes. Transfer the cooked pineapple to an 8-inch square glass or ceramic baking dish.

2. In a small saucepan, sprinkle the gelatin over the water and let stand until softened, about 5 minutes.

3. Meanwhile, in a large bowl, whisk the sweetened condensed milk with the coconut milk, 1 tablespoon of the lime juice and the vanilla.

4. Warm the gelatin over moderate heat, swirling the pan, until dissolved. Pour the gelatin mixture into the condensed milk mixture and stir gently until blended.

5. In a stainless steel bowl, beat the egg white until firm peaks form; fold into the condensed-milk mixture, then pour the mixture over the pineapple. Cover and refrigerate until set, at least 2 hours.

6. Meanwhile, in a small skillet, combine the brown sugar with the remaining 1 teaspoon of lime juice and cook over moderately high heat until just melted. Add the cashews and stir to coat. Transfer to a plate to cool and harden.

7. Carefully cut the coconut pudding into squares and transfer to plates with a spatula. Sprinkle each square with candied cashews and serve. —*Aniamma Philips*

MAKE AHEAD The pudding can be refrigerated overnight.

cakes, cookies & more

Chocolate Shortbread Cookies
ACTIVE: 30 MIN; TOTAL: 1 HR 30 MIN
MAKES 2½ DOZEN COOKIES ●

This recipe is easiest to make using a plain three-inch round cookie cutter. For Christmas, you can use a reindeer-shaped cutter (as pictured on opposite page).

- 2 sticks unsalted butter, softened
- 1 cup confectioners' sugar
- 1 teaspoon pure vanilla extract
- ⅔ cup Dutch-process cocoa
- 1½ cups all-purpose flour, plus more for rolling
- 1 teaspoon kosher salt

1. In the bowl of a standing electric mixer fitted with a paddle, beat the butter until creamy. Add the sugar and beat until fluffy. Add the vanilla, then beat in the cocoa on low speed. Beat in the flour and salt; the dough will be very soft.

2. Divide the dough in half and place each half between 2 large sheets of parchment paper or plastic wrap. Roll out the dough to ¼ inch thick and transfer to 2 baking sheets. Refrigerate until firm, at least 30 minutes.

3. Preheat the oven to 350°. Working with one piece of dough at a time, remove the top sheet of parchment and invert the dough onto a lightly floured work surface; remove the second sheet of parchment. Using a floured 3-inch cookie cutter (or a decorative cutter), stamp out cookies as close together as possible. Transfer the cookies to parchment paper–lined baking sheets and bake for about 14 minutes, or until fragrant and firm. Let cool on the baking sheets for 10 minutes, then, using a metal spatula, transfer the cookies to a rack to cool completely. Reroll the scraps, and stamp out more cookies, chilling the scraps between batches.
—Maria Helm Sinskey

MAKE AHEAD The following three cookie doughs can be refrigerated for up to three days. The cookies can be stored in an airtight container at room temperature for up to 1 week.

Gingerbread Cookies
ACTIVE: 40 MIN; TOTAL: 1 HR 30 MIN
MAKES 2½ DOZEN COOKIES ●

- 1¾ cups all-purpose flour
- ½ teaspoon baking soda
- ½ teaspoon salt
- 1 teaspoon ground ginger
- ½ teaspoon ground cinnamon
- ¼ teaspoon ground cloves
- 6 tablespoons unsalted butter, softened
- ½ cup dark brown sugar
- 2 tablespoons molasses
- 1 large egg
- ½ teaspoon pure vanilla extract
- **Royal Icing (recipe follows)**

1. In a bowl, whisk the flour, baking soda, salt, ginger, cinnamon and cloves. In the bowl of a standing mixer fitted with a paddle, beat the butter, sugar and molasses at medium speed until fluffy. Add the egg and vanilla; beat until blended. Beat in the dry ingredients until combined.

2. Divide the dough in half. Place each half between 2 large sheets of parchment paper or plastic. Roll out the dough ¼ inch thick and transfer to 2 baking sheets. Refrigerate until firm, at least 30 minutes.

3. Preheat the oven to 375°. Working with one piece of dough at a time, remove the top sheet of parchment and invert the dough onto a lightly floured work surface; remove the second sheet of parchment. Roll the dough to ⅛ inch thick. With a floured 3-inch cookie cutter, stamp out cookies as close together as possible. Transfer to parchment paper–lined baking sheets. Bake for 15 minutes, or until puffed and firm. Let cool slightly on the baking sheets, then, using a metal spatula, transfer to a rack to cool completely. Reroll the scraps to stamp out more cookies, chilling the scraps between batches.

4. Using a small paint brush or a pastry bag fitted with a small, plain tip, decorate the cookies with the Royal Icing. Let dry before serving. *—Maria Helm Sinskey*

Royal Icing
TOTAL: 10 MIN
MAKES 1½ CUPS ●

- 2 large egg whites
- ¼ teaspoon cream of tartar
- **Pinch of salt**
- ½ teaspoon pure vanilla extract
- 2¾ cups confectioners' sugar

In a bowl, using a handheld electric mixer, beat the whites with the cream of tartar, salt and vanilla at low speed until foamy. Increase the speed to medium; gradually beat in the sugar. Continue beating until the icing is stiff. Use at once.
—Maria Helm Sinskey

Lemon-Scented Sugar Cookies
ACTIVE: 30 MIN; TOTAL: 1 HR 30 MIN
MAKES 2½ DOZEN COOKIES ●

- 2 sticks unsalted butter, softened
- 1 cup turbinado sugar, plus more for sprinkling
- 1 tablespoon finely grated lemon zest
- 1 large egg yolk
- 2 cups all-purpose flour, plus more for rolling
- ½ teaspoon salt
- ¼ teaspoon baking powder

1. In the bowl of a standing electric mixer fitted with a paddle, beat the butter until creamy. Add the 1 cup of turbinado sugar and the lemon zest and beat at medium speed until fluffy. Add the egg yolk and beat until smooth. In a medium bowl, whisk the flour with the salt and baking powder. Beat the dry ingredients into the butter at medium-low speed; the dough will be very soft.

2. Divide the dough in half and place each half between 2 large sheets of parchment paper or plastic wrap. Roll out the dough to ¼ inch thick; transfer to 2 baking sheets. Refrigerate until firm, at least 30 minutes.

3. Preheat the oven to 375°. Working with one piece of dough at a time, remove the top sheet of parchment and invert the dough onto a lightly floured surface;

360

CHOCOLATE-RASPBERRY WHIPPED
CREAM SWISS ROLL (P. 346)

CHOCOLATE SHORTBREAD,
GINGERBREAD AND LEMON-
SCENTED SUGAR COOKIES

CHOCOLATE-ALMOND SALTINE TOFFEE

NO-BAKE CHOCOLATE CUSTARD

remove the second sheet of parchment. Using a floured 3-inch cookie cutter, stamp out cookies as close together as possible. Transfer the cookies to parchment paper–lined baking sheets and sprinkle with turbinado sugar. Bake for 12 to 14 minutes, or until golden. Let cool on the baking sheet for 10 minutes, then, using a metal spatula, transfer to a rack to cool completely. Reroll the scraps, and stamp out more cookies, chilling between batches. —*Maria Helm Sinskey*

Chocolate-Almond Saltine Toffee
TOTAL: 30 MIN
MAKES 2 ½ POUNDS ● ● ○

 6 ounces sliced almonds (1½ cups)
Approximately 60 saltine crackers (not low-sodium)
1½ cups sugar
 3 sticks unsalted butter
 2 tablespoons light corn syrup
 ½ pound bittersweet chocolate, chopped into ½-inch pieces

1. Preheat the oven to 350°. Spread the almonds on a baking sheet and toast for about 6 minutes, until golden.

2. Line a 17-by-12-inch rimmed baking sheet with a silicone mat or lightly buttered parchment paper. Arrange the saltine crackers on the baking sheet in a single layer, patching any holes with cracker bits; slight gaps are okay.

3. In a medium saucepan, combine the sugar, butter and corn syrup and cook over low heat until the sugar is melted. Brush the side of the pan with a moistened pastry brush to wash down any sugar crystals. Cook the syrup over moderate heat without stirring until it starts to brown around the edge, about 5 minutes. Insert a candy thermometer into the syrup and simmer, stirring with a wooden spoon, until a honey-colored caramel forms and the temperature reaches 300°, about 6 minutes longer.

4. Slowly and carefully pour the caramel

over the crackers, being sure to cover most of them evenly. Using an offset spatula, spread the caramel to cover any gaps. Let cool for 3 minutes, then sprinkle the chopped chocolate evenly on top. Let stand until the chocolate is melted, about 3 minutes, then spread the chocolate evenly over the toffee. Spread the almonds evenly over the chocolate. Freeze the toffee until set, about 15 minutes.

5. Invert the toffee onto a work surface and peel off the mat. Invert again, break into large shards. Serve. —*Nicole Plue*

MAKE AHEAD The chocolate-almond saltine toffee can be refrigerated for up to 2 weeks in an airtight container.

No-Bake Chocolate Custard
TOTAL: 20 MIN
2 SERVINGS ● ●
This silky chocolate custard appears regularly on the dessert menu at Rubicon in San Francisco. Pastry chef Nicole Krasinski suggests serving it slightly chilled.

- ¼ cup milk
- 3 tablespoons sugar
- 1 large egg yolk
- 3 ounces bittersweet chocolate, finely chopped, plus shaved chocolate, for serving

Pinch of salt
- 2 tablespoons unsalted butter, softened
- ½ cup heavy cream

Pinch of ground cinnamon

1. In a small saucepan, combine the milk with 2 tablespoons of the sugar and heat until the milk is steaming and the sugar is dissolved. Put the egg yolk in a small bowl and gradually whisk the hot milk into the bowl. Return the mixture to the saucepan and cook over moderate heat, whisking constantly, until the custard is slightly thickened, for about 2 minutes.

2. Off the heat, add the chopped chocolate and the salt to the pudding and whisk until smooth. Whisk in the butter. Pour the cus-

tard into 2 shallow bowls and refrigerate briefly, about 5 minutes.

3. Meanwhile, in a medium bowl, beat the heavy cream with the cinnamon and the remaining 1 tablespoon of sugar until softly whipped. Dollop the whipped cream on the custards, sprinkle the chocolate shavings on the cream and serve at once. —*Nicole Krasinski*

MAKE AHEAD The chocolate custards can be prepared through Step 2 and refrigerated overnight. Serve the custards chilled or at room temperature.

Lime-Scented Poppy-Seed Rice Pudding with Mango
ACTIVE: 30 MIN; TOTAL: 2 HR PLUS COOLING TIME
12 SERVINGS ●
- 2½ quarts whole milk
- 14 ounces short-grain rice (2 cups)
One 14-ounce can unsweetened coconut milk
- 1 vanilla bean, split and seeds scraped
- 2 tablespoons poppy seeds
- 1¼ cups sugar
- ½ cup heavy cream
Finely grated zest of 1 lime
- 6 ripe mangoes—peeled and cut into 1-inch dice

1. In a medium enameled cast-iron casserole, bring the milk, rice, coconut milk, vanilla bean and seeds and poppy seeds to a simmer over moderately high heat, stirring. Reduce the heat to low and simmer, stirring often, until the rice is tender, about 1 hour and 20 minutes.

2. Stir the sugar, cream and lime zest into the rice and simmer, stirring occasionally, until it is sweet and fragrant, about 10 minutes. Let cool to room temperature, then cover tightly and refrigerate until chilled, about 2 hours. Served topped with the mango.

—*Marcus Samuelsson*

Large and Luscious Two-Chip Oatmeal Cookies
ACTIVE: 1 HR; TOTAL: 2 HR
MAKES TWENTY 4-INCH COOKIES ● ●
These irresistible chocolate-chip oatmeal cookies are filled with shredded coconut to make them extra chewy.

- 1 cup plus 2 tablespoons all-purpose flour
- ½ teaspoon baking soda
- ⅛ teaspoon baking powder
- ¼ teaspoon salt
- 1½ sticks unsalted butter, at room temperature
- ½ cup plus 2 tablespoons packed light brown sugar
- ½ cup granulated sugar
- 1 large egg
- 1 large egg white
- 1½ teaspoons pure vanilla extract
- 1½ cups quick-cooking rolled oats
- 1 cup semisweet chocolate chips
- ½ cup white-chocolate chips
- ¾ cup sweetened shredded coconut

1. In a medium bowl, whisk the flour with the baking soda, baking powder and salt. In a large bowl, using an electric mixer, beat the butter with the brown sugar at medium speed until blended. Beat in the granulated sugar until light and fluffy, about 2 minutes. Beat in the whole egg, egg white and vanilla. At low speed, beat in the dry ingredients, in 2 additions. With a large wooden spoon, mix in the oats, semisweet and white-chocolate chips and the coconut. Cover the cookie dough and refrigerate for 1 hour, until chilled.

2. Preheat the oven to 375°. Line 3 large baking sheets with parchment paper. Using a rounded tablespoon, spoon mounds of dough onto the baking sheets, at least 3 inches apart. Bake the cookies for 14 minutes, or until golden and just set. Let cool on the baking sheets for 5 minutes, then transfer the cookies to a rack to cool completely. —*Lisa Yockelson*

cakes, cookies & more

Chocolate Chip Cookie Ice Cream Bars

ACTIVE: 30 MIN; TOTAL: 4 HR

16 SERVINGS ●

Store-bought break-and-bake cookies, which come packaged in eight-inch squares, are the secret to these easy ice cream sandwich bars. Simply roll out all the dough to create one giant cookie, then bake, slice and layer it with store-bought ice cream and hot fudge sauce. The best part: dipping the bars into crushed chocolate toffee candy to form a super-crunchy shell.

- 1 package prescored break-and-bake chocolate chip cookie dough, at room temperature
- 2 pints vanilla ice cream, softened slightly
- ¼ cup hot fudge sauce, warmed
- ¼ cup salted roasted almonds, coarsely chopped
- ¼ cup chocolate-coated toffee bits or one 1½-ounce chocolate-coated toffee bar, coarsely chopped

1. Preheat the oven to 350°. Set the cookie dough in a 13-by-9-inch baking pan. Place a sheet of plastic wrap on top and evenly press or roll the dough to fill the baking pan. Remove the plastic wrap from the dough and bake for 14 minutes, or until lightly browned. Leave the cookie until it is completely cool in the baking pan

2. Invert the cookie onto a work surface and slide it back into the baking pan, bottom side up. Trim the edges if necessary. Scoop the vanilla ice cream over the cookie in large dollops. Place a sheet of plastic wrap on top and press or roll the ice cream into an even layer. Freeze for 1 hour, until the ice cream is just firm.

3. Remove the plastic wrap. Drizzle the warm fudge sauce all over the ice cream. Cover again with plastic wrap and freeze for 1 hour longer, until firm.

4. Invert the baking pan onto a cutting board and tap gently to release the cookie bar. Flip the cookie bar over so it is ice cream side up. Using a sharp, heavy knife, cut the bar in half crosswise, forming two 9-by-6½-inch rectangles. Sandwich the cookie bar rectangles together and press hard to seal. Wrap in plastic and freeze for at least 1 hour, until firm.

5. In a bowl, combine the almonds with the toffee pieces. Using a sharp, heavy knife, cut the ice cream cookie into 16 bars. Press one side of each bar into the almond and toffee mixture. Return the bars to the freezer or serve immediately.

—*Grace Parisi*

MAKE AHEAD The ice cream bars can be stacked and frozen in an airtight container for up to 2 weeks.

Rice Pudding with Dried Apricots

ACTIVE: 15 MIN; TOTAL: 2 HR 30 MIN

10 SERVINGS ● ●

Bits of dried fruit, such as apricots, cherries or golden raisins, add a bit of chewiness to this creamy Mexican rice pudding.

- 10 ounces long-grain white rice (1¼ cups), rinsed
- 2½ cups water
- 1 teaspoon kosher salt
- One 3-inch cinnamon stick
- 2½ cups milk
- 1 cup sugar
- Finely grated zest of 1 lime
- 1 teaspoon pure vanilla extract
- ⅓ cup diced dried apricots, dried cherries or golden raisins
- ½ cup heavy cream or half-and-half

1. In a large saucepan, combine the rice with the water, salt and cinnamon stick and bring to a boil. Cover and cook over moderately low heat until the liquid is absorbed but the rice is not quite tender, about 15 minutes. Add the milk, sugar and lime zest and bring to a boil over high heat. Reduce the heat to moderate and cook, stirring frequently, until the rice is tender but firm and suspended in thick, creamy liquid, about 10 minutes. Remove the rice pudding from the heat and discard the cinnamon stick.

2. Stir the vanilla and the dried apricots into the rice pudding. Transfer to a shallow bowl, cover with plastic wrap and refrigerate the rice pudding until it is chilled, about 2 hours. Just before serving the pudding, stir in the heavy cream.

—*Mateo Granados*

Lemon-Poppy Polenta Cookie and Huckleberry Sorbet Sandwiches

ACTIVE: 25 MIN; TOTAL: 2 HR 45 MIN

MAKES 16 SANDWICHES ●

If huckleberry sorbet is unavailable, any tart sorbet (like raspberry, lemon or boysenberry) would be a delicious substitute.

- 1 cup instant polenta
- ¾ cup all-purpose flour, plus more for dusting
- ⅔ cup confectioners' sugar
- ⅛ teaspoon baking powder
- Pinch of salt
- 5 tablespoons unsalted butter, at room temperature
- 3 tablespoons solid vegetable shortening, at room temperature
- Finely grated zest of 1 lemon
- 1 large egg, at room temperature
- 1 tablespoon poppy seeds
- About 2 pints huckleberry sorbet, softened slightly

1. In a food processor, combine the polenta with the ¾ cup of flour, confectioners' sugar, baking powder and salt and pulse to blend. Add the butter, shortening and lemon zest and pulse until the mixture resembles coarse sand. Add the egg and poppy seeds and pulse just until the dough forms a ball. Pat the dough into a disk and wrap in plastic; refrigerate the disk for at least 1 hour, or until firm.

2. Preheat the oven to 350°. Generously flour a work surface and a rolling pin. Roll out the dough to ⅛ inch thick. Using a

LEMON-POPPY POLENTA COOKIE AND SORBET SANDWICHES

MANHATTAN ICE CREAM FLOAT

floured 2¼-inch round biscuit cutter, stamp out 28 cookies as close together as possible. Gather the dough scraps together and gently reroll the dough, then stamp out 4 more cookies. Carefully transfer to 2 ungreased baking sheets.

3. Bake the cookies on the upper and lower racks of the oven for 18 minutes, or until they are golden; shift the baking sheets from top to bottom and front to back halfway through baking to ensure even browning. Let the cookies cool on the sheets.

4. To form sandwiches, scoop about ¼ cup of the sorbet onto 16 cookies. Top with the remaining cookies, pressing lightly to help evenly spread the sorbet. Set the sandwiches on a baking sheet. Freeze for about 1 hour, or until firm.
—*Mary Ellen Carroll and Donna Wingate*
MAKE AHEAD The cookies can be made up to 3 days ahead. Let cool completely, then store in an airtight container.

Manhattan Ice Cream Float
TOTAL: 30 MIN
4 SERVINGS ● ●
Chef Gabriel Frasca creates dishes that are classically inspired and whimsical, such as an ice cream float that is a clever riff on the Manhattan. For this superquick version of his dessert, vanilla ice cream is blended with bourbon and a high-quality black cherry soda like Stewart's or IBC.

 2 **pints vanilla ice cream, slightly softened**
 ¼ **cup plus 2 tablespoons bourbon**
 ½ **pint heavy cream**
1½ **tablespoons sweet vermouth**
 1 **tablespoon sugar**
Dash of Angostura bitters
 1 **liter cherry soda, or three 12-ounce bottles, chilled**
Maraschino cherries, for garnish

1. Put the vanilla ice cream in a food processor. With the machine running and working quickly, add the bourbon and process it with the ice cream just until they are combined. Spread the softened vanilla ice cream in a large, shallow plastic container and freeze until the ice cream is firm enough to scoop, about 20 minutes.

2. Meanwhile, whip the heavy cream with the sweet vermouth, the sugar and the Angostura bitters until the heavy cream forms soft peaks. Refrigerate the flavored whipped cream until it is chilled.

3. Divide the cherry soda among 4 tall glasses, filling them each two-thirds full. Scoop a quarter of the vanilla ice cream into each of the glasses and top them each with a dollop of the flavored whipped cream. Garnish the Manhattan ice cream floats with the maraschino cherries and serve the floats immediately.
—*Gabriel Frasca*

● FAST ● HEALTHY ● MAKE AHEAD ● STAFF FAVORITE

cakes, cookies & more

Little Chocolate Pots

ACTIVE: 15 MIN; TOTAL: 2 HR 15 MIN
6 SERVINGS ●

Sensuous and not too sweet, these chocolate pot de crèmes use only four ingredients, so it's essential they are top quality. Look for the best chocolate and ultrarich Devonshire (or clotted) cream.

- ½ cup Devonshire cream, plus more for serving
- ½ cup whole milk
- 1 large egg
- 6 ounces bittersweet chocolate, preferably 65 percent cocoa, finely chopped (1¼ cups)

1. In a small saucepan, bring the cream and milk to a simmer over moderate heat. In a small bowl, beat the egg. Slowly whisk ½ cup of the simmering cream into the beaten egg, then whisk the mixture into the cream in the saucepan. Cook for 30 seconds, whisking constantly.

2. Put the bittersweet chocolate in a blender. Pour in the hot cream mixture and let stand for 3 minutes. Blend until smooth, about 30 seconds. Set 6 espresso cups on a baking sheet and fill them with the chocolate cream. Cover and refrigerate until chilled and firm, about 2 hours. Top each chocolate pot with a dollop of Devonshire cream. Serve. —*Nick Nairn*

MAKE AHEAD The pots can be refrigerated for up to 2 days.

superfast

desserts

MINT ICE CREAM BROWNIE CAKE

Line a springform pan with crumbled chocolate brownies. Top with softened vanilla ice cream mixed with crushed mint candies, sprinkle with chopped chocolate and freeze. Serve with chocolate sauce.

HOLIDAY RUM-AND-CHOCOLATE TRIFLE

Brush sliced pound cake with raspberry jam. Layer with whipped cream flavored with rum and drizzle with chocolate sauce.
—*Maria Helm Sinskey*

Espresso Gelées with Candied Pistachios

ACTIVE: 20 MIN; TOTAL: 35 MIN PLUS
6 HR SETTING
4 SERVINGS ● ●

CANDIED PISTACHIOS
- 1½ teaspoons granulated sugar
- 1½ teaspoons hot water
- ¼ cup shelled pistachios
- 1 tablespoon turbinado sugar

GELÉES
- 1 teaspoon unflavored powdered gelatin
- 1 tablespoon cold water
- ¼ cup sugar
- 1 cup freshly brewed espresso

TOPPING
- ¼ cup 2 percent Greek yogurt
- ½ tablespoon confectioners' sugar

1. **MAKE THE CANDIED PISTACHIOS:** Preheat the oven to 350°. Line a cookie sheet with parchment paper. In a bowl, stir the granulated sugar with the hot water. Add the pistachios and turbinado sugar; stir to coat. Spread the pistachios on the cookie sheet and bake until crisp, about 8 minutes. Let cool, then break into pieces.

2. **MAKE THE GELÉES:** In a small glass bowl, sprinkle the gelatin over the cold water and let stand until softened, 5 minutes. Stir the sugar into the espresso until dissolved. Stir in the gelatin until dissolved and pour into 4 espresso cups. Refrigerate the gelées until set on top, 2 hours. Cover with plastic wrap and chill until thoroughly set, at least 4 hours longer.

3. **MAKE THE TOPPING:** In a bowl, stir the yogurt with the confectioners' sugar. Top each gelée with a dollop of yogurt, sprinkle with the candied pistachios and serve.
—*Melissa Clark*

Pots de Crème with Chocolate, Chile and Espresso

ACTIVE: 30 MIN; TOTAL: 2 HR PLUS
3 HR CHILLING
6 SERVINGS ● ●

Some chefs will do anything to get customers to try something they believe in. Chef Alison Barshak, of Alison at Blue Bell in Blue Bell, Pennsylvania, will send out her chocolate pot de crème to any diner who doubts that the combination of spicy chiles and chocolate is delicious. Invariably, this turns the skeptic into a believer.

- 2¼ cups light cream or half-and-half
- 2 dried ancho chiles—stemmed, seeded and coarsely chopped
- 4½ ounces bittersweet chocolate, finely chopped
- 2 tablespoons sugar
- Pinch of salt
- 6 large egg yolks
- 1½ teaspoons pure vanilla extract
- 1 teaspoon instant espresso powder
- Boiling water
- Lightly sweetened whipped cream and dulce de leche, for serving

1. Preheat the oven to 325°. In a small saucepan, bring the cream to a simmer. Add the chiles, cover and set aside to steep for 45 minutes. Strain the cream into a bowl and discard the chiles.

2. In a medium saucepan, combine the chocolate and ½ cup of the strained cream and cook over low heat, stirring, until the chocolate is melted. Whisk in the sugar and salt. Stir the remaining strained cream into the saucepan. Gently warm the chocolate cream over low heat.

3. In a medium bowl, using an electric mixer, beat the egg yolks until slightly thickened. At low speed, beat in one-fourth of the warm chocolate cream along with the vanilla and espresso powder. Return the mixture to the chocolate cream in the saucepan and cook over low heat for 3 minutes, stirring constantly.

cakes, cookies & more

4. Set six 4-ounce ramekins in a baking pan; divide the custard among them. Fill the pan with boiling water to reach halfway up the sides of the ramekins. Cover the pan with foil and poke several holes in the top. Bake for 25 minutes, or until the custards are just set and a dark rim has formed around the edge. Remove the foil. Let the custards cool in the water, 20 minutes. Refrigerate until cold, at least 3 hours. Serve with whipped cream and warmed dulce de leche. —*Alison Barshak*

MAKE AHEAD The pots de crème can be refrigerated for up to 2 days.

Vanilla and Cranberry Panna Cotta Parfaits

ACTIVE: 1 HR; TOTAL: 8 HR

20 SERVINGS ●

Food stylist Alison Attenborough uses fragrant orange-flavor water in her tart cranberry jelly to give the dessert a lovely citrus scent.

CRANBERRY JELLY

- 3 tablespoons unflavored powdered gelatin
- 2 quarts cranberry juice
- ¼ cup honey
- 1 teaspoon orange-flower water (Optional)

PANNA COTTA

- 1 tablespoon plus 2 teaspoons unflavored powdered gelatin
- 2 tablespoons cold water
- 6 cups heavy cream
- 3¾ cups plain whole milk yogurt
- 1½ cups sugar
- 2 vanilla beans, split lengthwise, seeds scraped

Red currants and mint leaves, for garnish

1. MAKE THE CRANBERRY JELLY: In a small bowl, sprinkle the unflavored powdered gelatin evenly over 2 cups of the cranberry juice. Let the mixture stand until the gelatin has softened, about 5 minutes.

2. In a medium saucepan, bring the remaining 6 cups of cranberry juice to a simmer. Remove from the heat and stir in the honey and orange-flower water. Whisk in the gelatin mixture. Cool for about 1 hour, stirring occasionally.

3. MEANWHILE, MAKE THE PANNA COTTA: In a small bowl, sprinkle the gelatin evenly over the water and let stand until softened, about 5 minutes. In a large heatproof bowl, whisk 3 cups of the heavy cream with the yogurt.

4. In a medium saucepan, combine the remaining 3 cups of heavy cream with the sugar and the vanilla beans and seeds and bring to a simmer over moderately high heat, stirring often to dissolve the sugar. Remove the saucepan from the heat and whisk the gelatin mixture into the hot vanilla cream. Strain the cream through a fine-mesh sieve set over the yogurt mixture and whisk thoroughly to blend. Let yogurt panna cotta cool for about 45 minutes, stirring occasionally.

5. Set 20 small and sturdy plastic glasses on a tray. Ladle ¼ cup of the yogurt panna cotta mixture into each glass (see Note) and refrigerate until set, about 3 hours.

6. Carefully ladle about 6½ tablespoons of the cranberry jelly over the panna cotta layer and refrigerate until set, about 2 hours.

7. About 30 minutes before adding the last layer, gently warm the remaining panna cotta just until melted. Ladle ¼ cup into each glass. Cover the glasses with plastic wrap and refrigerate until firm, about 2 hours longer. Serve chilled, garnished with small clusters of red currants and mint leaves.

—*Alison Attenborough*

NOTE Tilt the glasses in muffin pans or egg cartons, if desired. While assembling the dessert, if the panna cotta or jelly becomes too firm to pour into the glasses, warm gently just until melted.

MAKE AHEAD The panna cottas can be refrigerated for up to 3 days.

Green Tea Panna Cotta

ACTIVE: 15 MIN; TOTAL: 15 MIN PLUS 6 HR CHILLING

4 SERVINGS ● ●

Green tea powder, which is full of antioxidants, is used in green tea ice cream and pastry cream. This recipe transforms it into another dessert—a cool custard with a topping made of buttermilk and whole milk (lighter than heavy cream). The bright green powder is sold in small tins at tea shops and Japanese markets. Be sure to ask for *matcha,* which has a cleaner, clearer flavor than *sencha.*

- 1¾ teaspoons powdered gelatin
- 2 tablespoons cold water
- 1½ cups whole milk
- ¼ cup plus 3 tablespoons sugar

Pinch of salt

- 1½ cups low-fat buttermilk
- 2 teaspoons powdered *matcha* green tea

1. In a small bowl, sprinkle the gelatin over the water. Let stand for 5 minutes, until the gelatin softens.

2. In a medium saucepan, combine the milk, sugar and salt and warm over moderate heat for about 3 minutes, stirring frequently to dissolve the sugar. Remove from the heat and whisk in the gelatin until completely dissolved, then whisk in the buttermilk. Pour 1 cup of this mixture into a measuring cup; cover and refrigerate until ready to use.

3. In a small bowl, whisk the green tea powder with ¼ cup of the remaining buttermilk mixture until dissolved. Pour the dissolved green tea into the buttermilk mixture in the saucepan and whisk well.

4. Pour the tea mixture into four 8-ounce glasses; refrigerate until just set, about 3 hours. Melt the 1 cup of refrigerated buttermilk mixture in a microwave oven until pourable but still cold, about 15 seconds. Top each panna cotta with the buttermilk mixture. Cover and refrigerate until firm, at least 3 hours. —*Susan Spungen*

cakes, cookies & more

Raspberry Jam Bomboloni

ACTIVE: 45 MIN; TOTAL: 1 HR 45 MIN
PLUS OVERNIGHT CHILLING
MAKES ABOUT 32 BOMBOLONI ●

Pastry chef Kate Neumann of Chicago's MK The Restaurant reports that whenever she offers *bomboloni* (Italian doughnut holes) on the dessert menu, they inevitably sell out. She sometimes makes the *bomboloni* at home, too: "They are easy to prepare in advance and then fry at the last moment," she explains, "and they are also quite easy to dress up." Neumann fills the *bomboloni* with fruit jams or with chocolate ganache, then rolls them in sugar and in spices like anise and cardamom as soon as they come out of the frying pan. She serves them immediately: "The key to greatness, for me," she adds, "is serving the doughnuts fresh and warm."

- ½ cup plus 1 tablespoon lukewarm water
- 1½ envelopes active dry yeast (3¼ teaspoons)
- 1½ tablespoons honey
- 3 cups all-purpose flour, plus more for dusting
- 3 tablespoons milk
- 6 large egg yolks
- ⅓ cup granulated sugar, plus more for rolling
- 2 teaspoons kosher salt
- 3 tablespoons unsalted butter, softened
- 3 cups canola oil, for frying
- ¾ cup seedless raspberry preserves

Confectioners' sugar, for dusting

1. In the bowl of a standing electric mixer, combine the lukewarm water with the active dry yeast, the honey and 1 cup plus 2 tablespoons of the flour. (Alternatively, whisk the ingredients together by hand.) Cover the yeast mixture with plastic wrap and set it aside to stand at room temperature until it is foamy, about 1 hour.

2. Return the bowl to the mixer, fitted with a dough hook. Add the remaining 1¾ cups plus 2 tablespoons of flour, along with the milk, egg yolks, ⅓ cup of granulated sugar and the salt. Mix at low speed until blended, then add the butter and knead at medium speed until silky but sticky, about 5 minutes; the dough will not pull away from the side of the bowl. Using an oiled spatula, scrape the dough into an oiled bowl and cover with plastic wrap. Refrigerate overnight. The dough will not rise.

3. In a large saucepan, heat the canola oil to 360°. Line a rack with paper towels. Fill a shallow bowl with ½ inch of granulated sugar. On a lightly floured surface, roll out the dough to a scant ½ inch thick. Using a 1¾-inch round biscuit cutter, stamp out 32 rounds; do not reroll the dough. Fry the rounds, 8 at a time, until browned, about 4 minutes. Be sure to keep the oil between 360° and 375°. Drain the *bomboloni* on paper towels, then roll them in the granulated sugar. Continue frying and rolling the remaining *bomboloni*.

4. Fit a pastry bag with a plain doughnut (or a ¼-inch) tip and fill with the preserves (you can also use a squeeze bottle). Poke the tip three-fourths of the way into the *bomboloni* and squeeze in the preserves, pulling the tip out slightly as you squeeze to fill them as much as possible. Dust the *bomboloni* with confectioners' sugar and serve warm. —*Kate Neumann*

Greek Yogurt Panna Cotta with Honey-Glazed Apricots

TOTAL: 30 MIN PLUS 3 HR CHILLING
6 SERVINGS ●

Pastry chef Kate Neumann describes this cool, delicate dessert as "just fruit and cream, barely sweetened. It has the qualities of custard without the egginess. The Greek yogurt makes it wonderfully tangy." She tops the panna cotta with dried apricots plumped in wine and honey.

- 1 envelope unflavored gelatin (2¼ teaspoons)
- 2 tablespoons cold water
- 1 cup heavy cream
- ⅓ cup sugar
- 1 vanilla bean, split and seeds scraped out and reserved
- One 17.6-ounce tub of Greek yogurt, such as Fage Total brand (2 cups)
- 1 cup dried apricots
- 1 cup semidry white wine, such as Vouvray
- ¼ cup honey

1. In a small bowl, sprinkle the unflavored gelatin over the cold water and let the mixture stand until the gelatin is softened, about 5 minutes. In a small saucepan, combine the heavy cream with the sugar and vanilla bean and seeds and bring the vanilla cream to a simmer. Remove the saucepan from the heat and stir the softened gelatin into the vanilla cream until it is melted. In a medium bowl, whisk the yogurt until it is smooth. Gradually whisk the vanilla cream into the yogurt; remove the vanilla bean. Pour the panna cotta mixture into six ½-cup ramekins and refrigerate until set, at least 3 hours.

2. Meanwhile, in a small saucepan, simmer the dried apricots in the white wine over moderately low heat until the apricots are plump and the wine has reduced by half, about 20 minutes. Stir the honey into the apricots and their sauce and simmer the syrup until thickened, about 5 minutes. Set the apricots aside and let cool.

3. Run a knife around the inside of each ramekin. Set a plate on top of each ramekin and invert each panna cotta onto the plate; you may have to tap and shake the ramekins to loosen the panna cottas. Slice the honey-glazed apricots and spoon them on top of the panna cottas. Drizzle the panna cottas with some of the honey syrup and serve immediately.
—*Kate Neumann*

GREEK YOGURT PANNA COTTA
WITH HONEY-GLAZED APRICOTS

Cookbook authors Isabel González, left, and Carolina Buia ladle out highballs of their Puerto Rican Rum Punch (p. 374).

drinks

"I feel like you have to have at least one cocktail on your menu that is controversial. It gives people a sense of discovery."

–Duggan McDonnell, mixologist, San Francisco

THE DUKE OF BEDFORD

BLONDIE MARYS

The Duke of Bedford

TOTAL: 5 MIN

MAKES 1 DRINK ● ●

Gabriel Stulman, co-owner of the Little Owl, a Mediterranean restaurant in Manhattan's West Village, uses a hand-cranked machine to crush the ice for cocktails like this one.

Crushed ice

- 3 ounces manzanilla sherry
- 6 mint leaves, crushed, plus 1 mint sprig
- 1 ounce Aranciata (orange soda)
- 1 teaspoon sugar
- 3 dashes of Angostura bitters

Cucumber slice, for garnish

Fill a julep glass with crushed ice. In a cocktail shaker, combine the sherry, mint leaves, Aranciata, sugar and bitters; shake well. Strain over the ice and garnish with the mint sprig and cucumber slice. —Gabriel Stulman

Blondie Marys

ACTIVE: 15 MIN; TOTAL: 2 HR 15 MIN

MAKES 12 DRINKS ●

- 4½ pounds yellow tomatoes, cut into chunks
- 1 cup vodka
- 2 tablespoons fresh lemon juice
- 1½ tablespoons prepared horseradish
- 1 tablespoon Worcestershire sauce
- 1 tablespoon Tabasco

Kosher salt and freshly ground pepper

Ice

- 12 celery sticks, for garnish

Working in batches, puree the tomatoes in a blender or food processor until smooth. Strain the puree through a fine sieve set over a bowl. Add the vodka, lemon juice, horseradish, Worcestershire sauce and Tabasco and season with salt and pepper. Pour into a pitcher and refrigerate until chilled, 2 hours. Serve over ice, garnished with celery sticks. —Amy Giaquinta

Apple-Brandy Hot Toddies

TOTAL: 10 MIN

MAKES 8 DRINKS ●

A hot toddy is basically a shot or two of any potent spirit added to a cup of hot water. At Paley's Place in Portland, Oregon, bartender Suzanne Bozarth puts a French spin on this warming drink with a slug of apple brandy such as Calvados.

- 1½ cups water
- 2 tablespoons plus 2 teaspoons honey
- ½ cup fresh lemon juice
- 2 cups apple brandy, preferably Calvados

Eight 3-inch cinnamon sticks

In small saucepan, boil the water. Remove from the heat. Stir in the honey until dissolved, then the lemon juice and apple brandy. Set a cinnamon stick in each of 8 mugs or heatproof glasses, pour in the hot liquid and serve. —Suzanne Bozarth

drinks

Jalapeño Margaritas

ACTIVE: 20 MIN; TOTAL: 3 DAYS
6 SERVINGS ●

- 1 jalapeño, poked with a knife
- 1⅓ cups tequila
- 1 cup orange liqueur
- 1 cup fresh lime juice (10 limes)
- 3 tablespoons superfine sugar
- Kosher salt and ice

1. In a jar, steep the jalapeño and tequila at room temperature for 3 days.
2. Strain into a large pitcher and discard the jalapeño. Stir in the orange liqueur, lime juice and sugar.
3. Pour some salt and a small amount of margarita mixture onto 2 rimmed plates. Dip the rims of 6 glasses into the margarita, then the salt. Fill each glass with ice, pour in the margarita and serve.
—*Carolina Buia and Isabel González*

Ginger Margarita

ACTIVE: 5 MIN; TOTAL: 45 MIN
MAKES 1 DRINK ●

This cocktail is a standout at Jean-Georges Vongerichten's Spice Market restaurant in New York City, where bartenders mix tequila and other margarita ingredients with potent ginger-lime syrup. Vongerichten also rims the glass with ground ginger and salt instead of the usual plain salt.

- 1 teaspoon ground ginger
- 2 teaspoons kosher salt
- Ice
- 3 tablespoons añejo tequila
- 1½ tablespoons Ginger-Lime Syrup (recipe follows)
- 1 tablespoon Cointreau
- 1 teaspoon fresh lime juice
- 1 lime wedge, for garnish

On a plate, mix the ginger and salt. Moisten the rim of a margarita glass with water; dip the rim in the ginger salt. Fill a shaker with ice. Add the tequila, syrup, Cointreau and lime juice and shake well. Strain into the glass, garnish with the lime wedge and serve. —*Jean-Georges Vongerichten*

GINGER-LIME SYRUP

ACTIVE: 25 MIN; TOTAL: 40 MIN
MAKES 1 CUP ● ●

- 4 ounces fresh ginger, peeled and thinly sliced (1 cup)
- 1 cup fresh lime juice
- 1 cup sugar

In a saucepan, boil the ginger, lime juice and sugar for 2 minutes. Let cool to warm, then puree in a blender. Pour into a fine strainer. Press on the ginger to extract as much syrup as you can. —*J.G.V.*

Mango-Ginger Margarita

TOTAL: 10 MIN
MAKES 1 DRINK ●

- 2 thin slices fresh ginger, peeled
- 1 teaspoon sugar
- 3 tablespoons tequila
- 3 tablespoons mango nectar
- 1 tablespoon fresh lime juice
- ½ tablespoon triple sec
- Ice
- 1 thin mango slice, for garnish

In a cocktail shaker, muddle the ginger with the sugar. Add the tequila, mango nectar, lime juice, triple sec and ice. Shake well and strain into a chilled martini glass. Garnish with the mango slice and serve. —*E. Michael Reidt*

Trader Vic's Mai Tai

TOTAL: 15 MIN
MAKES 1 DRINK ●

- Ice
- 1½ ounces aged Jamaican rum
- ½ ounce orange curaçao
- 1 ounce fresh lime juice
- ½ ounce almond syrup
- ¼ ounce Simple Syrup (p. 378)
- Mint sprig, for garnish
- Maraschino cherry, for garnish

In a cocktail shaker filled with crushed ice, shake the rum, curaçao, lime juice and almond and simple syrups well and strain over crushed ice. Garnish with the mint sprig and cherry. —*Vincenzo Marianella*

Hibiscus-Tequila Cocktails

ACTIVE: 15 MIN; TOTAL: 30 MIN
MAKES 4 DRINKS ●

- ½ cup dried hibiscus flowers (see Note)
- 2½ cups water
- ¼ cup plus 1 tablespoon sugar
- ½ cup tequila
- ¼ cup fresh lime juice
- 4 dashes of habanero hot sauce

1. Boil the hibiscus flowers in water for 1 minute. Cover, remove from the heat and let steep for 15 minutes. Strain the tea into a bowl and stir in the sugar until dissolved. Refrigerate until well chilled.
2. Stir the tequila, lime juice and hot sauce into the tea. Pour into ice-filled highball glasses and serve. —*Jacques Pépin*
NOTE Dried hibiscus flowers are sold in Latin and Caribbean markets and health food stores. Red Zinger tea bags can be substituted.

Ultimate Mojito

ACTIVE: 5 MIN; TOTAL: 25 MIN
MAKES 1 DRINK ●

- ½ cup water
- ½ cup sugar
- 1 cup packed mint leaves, plus 1 sprig
- 1 tablespoon fresh lime juice
- Ice
- ¼ cup plus 1 tablespoon light rum
- 2 tablespoons chilled club soda

1. In a saucepan, stir the water and sugar over moderate heat just until dissolved. Reserve 15 mint leaves. Add the remaining leaves to the syrup. Let steep until cool. Strain and refrigerate for up to 1 week.
2. In a cocktail shaker, muddle the 15 reserved mint leaves with the lime juice and 1 tablespoon of the mint syrup. Add ice, the rum and club soda and shake well.
3. Fill a highball glass with ice. Pour the drink through a fine strainer. Garnish with the mint sprig. —*Ryan McGrale*

drinks

Passion Fruit Caipiroskas

TOTAL: 10 MIN

MAKES 6 DRINKS ● ●

Brazil is famous for the caipirinha, but less well known for the classic *caipiroska* cocktail that combines vodka, lime juice and sugar.

- ¾ cup frozen pure passion fruit puree, thawed (see Note)
- ¾ cup sugar
- ¾ cup fresh lime juice (from 5 limes), plus 6 thin lime wheels
- 1 cup plus 2 tablespoons vodka (9 ounces)
- 6 cups crushed ice

1. In a pitcher, stir together the passion fruit puree, sugar and lime juice until the sugar is dissolved.
2. Stir in the vodka. Fill 6 tumblers with the ice and pour the drink over the ice. Garnish with the lime wheels and serve.
—*Michelle Bernstein*

NOTE Frozen passion fruit puree is available at specialty food shops. Vergers Boiron is a terrific brand. In a pinch, substitute passion fruit sorbet and reduce the sugar in the recipe.

technique
mix drinks like a pro

Vincenzo Marianella creates some of L.A.'s most sensational cocktails at Sidebar. Here he shares his secrets on how anyone can mix a cocktail like a bar chef:

1. Always use fresh citrus juices Before you start using gelées or foams, go back to the best-quality ingredients. All you need is fresh citrus, simple syrup (p. 378) and top-quality spirits and you are assured a great cocktail.

Puerto Rican Rum Punch

ACTIVE: 10 MIN; TOTAL: 1 HR 10 MIN

MAKES 6 DRINKS ● ●

Many Caribbean cocktails use light rum but the dark rum here adds sweetness and depth.

- ⅔ cup fresh lime juice
- ⅓ cup superfine sugar
- 1 cup gold rum (8 ounces)
- ¼ cup orange liqueur (2 ounces)
- ¼ cup grenadine (2 ounces)
- One 750-milliliter bottle sparkling wine, such as Spanish cava, chilled
- Fresh pineapple chunks, for garnish

In a large pitcher, combine the lime juice and sugar and stir briskly until the sugar is dissolved. Add the rum, orange liqueur and grenadine and chill the rum mixture for about 1 hour. Just before serving, add the sparkling wine and pineapple chunks and serve in punch glasses.
—*Carolina Buia and Isabel González*

NOTE The punch can be doubled.

MAKE AHEAD The rum mixture can be refrigerated overnight. Stir in the sparkling wine and pineapple chunks just before serving.

2. Be able to free pour Practice pouring 2 ounces, 1½ ounces, 1 ounce, ½ ounce and ¼ ounce. "When I was working in London they tested us every day and recorded the results in a book," Marianella says.

3. Know a recipe's basic proportions A margarita is 2 shots of tequila, 1 shot of Cointreau and ¾ shot of lime juice. "Even if I riff on the recipe, the proportions won't change much," Marianella says.

4. Have the right tools All you need is a Boston shaker, a hand juicer for citrus (all great cocktails have citrus) and a jigger for measuring.

Pineapple Planter's Punch

TOTAL: 10 MIN

MAKES 8 DRINKS ●

- ½ cup canned chopped pineapple in heavy syrup, plus ¼ syrup from the can
- 2 ounces dark rum
- 6 ounces white rum
- 6 ounces spiced rum
- 6 ounces aged rum
- 3 ounces fresh lime juice
- 8 ounces chilled fresh orange juice
- Ice
- About 16 ounces club soda
- 8 orange slices and 8 mint sprigs, for garnish

In a cocktail shaker, muddle the chopped pineapple with the syrup and the dark rum. Strain the mixture through a fine sieve into a pitcher and add the white, spiced and aged rums as well as the lime juice and orange juice. Pour into ice-filled collins glasses and top with club soda. Garnish with the orange slices and mint sprigs and serve. —*Vincenzo Marianella*

La Floridita

TOTAL: 5 MIN

MAKES 1 DRINK ●

This drink was inspired by a cocktail at a famous Hemingway haunt in Havana.

- Ice
- ¼ cup plus 2 tablespoons light rum (3 ounces)
- 3 tablespoons sweet vermouth (1½ ounces)
- 1 tablespoon white crème de cacao (½ ounce)
- 1 tablespoon fresh lime juice (½ ounce)
- 1½ teaspoons grenadine (¼ ounce)

Fill a cocktail shaker with ice. Add all of the ingredients and shake vigorously for 15 seconds. Strain into a chilled martini glass and serve immediately.
—*Carolina Buia and Isabel González*

The Columbus

TOTAL: 5 MIN

MAKES 1 DRINK ●

This apricot-orange cocktail may have been named The Columbus because apricots were brought to the New World by the Spaniards. Cookbook author Isabel González discovered it in an old drink book that belonged to her grandfather. The original recipe calls for golden rum; she prefers the fruitiness of orange rum.

Ice

¼ cup orange rum (2 ounces)

3 tablespoons apricot brandy (1½ ounces)

1 tablespoon fresh lime juice (½ ounce)

Orange twist, for garnish

Fill a cocktail shaker with ice. Add the rum, brandy and lime juice and shake for 15 seconds. Strain into a chilled martini glass, garnish with the orange twist and serve.
—*Carolina Buia and Isabel González*

Hot Buttered Rum

TOTAL: 15 MIN

MAKES 4 DRINKS ●

Spiking this hot toddy with a dark rum like Gosling's gives it an especially rich flavor.

2 tablespoons unsalted butter, softened

1 tablespoon light brown sugar

½ teaspoon pure vanilla extract

1 cup water

1 cup unsweetened apple juice

Four 6-inch cinnamon sticks

1 cup dark rum

In a small bowl, blend the butter with the brown sugar and vanilla. In a medium saucepan, bring the water and apple juice to a boil. Place a cinnamon stick in each of 4 mugs or heatproof glasses. Add ¼ cup of the rum, ½ cup of the boiling liquid and a heaping half tablespoon of the vanilla butter to each mug. Stir with the cinnamon stick and serve at once. —*Grace Parisi*

Coconut Martini

TOTAL: 5 MIN

MAKES 1 DRINK ●

This sweet, creamy tropical martini is like a sophisticated piña colada, with vodka as well as rum for extra kick.

Ice

¼ cup cream of coconut (2 ounces), such as Coco López

¼ cup vodka (2 ounces)

¼ cup coconut rum (2 ounces)

Ground cinnamon and

1 cinnamon stick, for garnish

Fill a cocktail shaker with ice. Add the cream of coconut, vodka and coconut rum and shake vigorously for 15 seconds. Strain into a chilled martini glass, garnish with a pinch of ground cinnamon and the cinnamon stick and serve right away.
—*Carolina Buia and Isabel González*

Vodka-Thyme Lemonade

ACTIVE: 5 MIN; TOTAL: 2 HR 15 MIN

MAKES 1 DRINK

1 tablespoon sugar

Ice

3 lemon wedges

¼ cup Lemon-Thyme Syrup (p. 337)

¼ cup vodka

Splash of club soda

1 thyme sprig, for garnish

1. Spread the sugar in a shallow dish. Moisten the rim of a highball glass with water and dip the rim in the sugar to coat. Fill the highball glass with ice.

2. In a cocktail shaker, muddle the lemon wedges with the Lemon-Thyme Syrup. Add 1 cup of ice and the vodka and shake well. Strain the vodka mixture into the highball glass and top with club soda. Garnish the vodka lemonade with the thyme sprig and serve right away.
—*Jean-Georges Vongerichten*

MAKE AHEAD The Lemon-Thyme Syrup can be refrigerated for up to 5 days.

The Mission

TOTAL: 5 MIN

MAKES 1 DRINK ●

Bartender Lucy Brennan of Mint/820 in Portland, Oregon, has been inspiring local bartenders with improbably delicious drinks—avocado daiquiries and beet martinis—that have helped make Portland one of the country's most dynamic cocktail cities.

½ tablespoon sugar

½ tablespoon warm water

Ice

¼ cup vanilla vodka

2 tablespoons fig puree (see Note)

1 tablespoon ruby port

1 tablespoon fresh lemon juice

1 edible flower, for garnish

In a cocktail shaker, stir the sugar in the water until dissolved. Fill the shaker with ice. Add the vodka, fig puree, port and lemon juice. Shake well and strain into a chilled martini glass. Garnish with the flower. —*Lucy Brennan*

NOTE Frozen fig puree is available from boironfreres.com.

Don't Give Up the Ship

TOTAL: 5 MIN

MAKES 1 DRINK ●

Ben Dougherty of Seattle's Zig Zag Cafe and his partner Kacy Fitch pore over old cocktail guides in search of quirky forgotten recipes—like this nicely bitter gin drink that calls for the unlikely pairing of Dubonnet, a sweet French aperitif, and Fernet Branca, a bitter Italian digestif.

Ice

3 tablespoons gin

1 tablespoon Dubonnet Rouge

½ tablespoon Grand Marnier

½ tablespoon Fernet Branca

Fill a pint glass two-thirds full with ice. Add the rest of the ingredients and stir briskly in one direction for 30 seconds. Strain into a chilled martini glass.
—*Ben Dougherty*

drinks

Sour Red

TOTAL: 5 MIN

MAKES 1 DRINK ●

At Seattle's Crush, which serves modern American food in a century-old Tudor house, mixologist Ryan Magarian adds a dose of red wine syrup for a sweet-tart twist on the classic New York Sour.

Ice

2 ounces gin

1 ounce Red Wine Syrup (recipe follows)

½ ounce fresh lemon juice

One 3-inch strip of orange zest and 1 red grape, for garnish

Half fill a cocktail shaker with ice. Add the gin, Red Wine Syrup and lemon juice; shake well. Strain into a rocks glass. Garnish with a an orange zest and red grape threaded on a bamboo skewer.
—*Ryan Magarian*

RED WINE SYRUP

TOTAL: 10 MIN PLUS CHILLING

MAKES ⅔ CUP ● ●

½ cup dry red wine

½ cup sugar

In a small saucepan, simmer the wine and sugar over moderate heat, stirring, until the sugar has dissolved. Remove from the heat and let cool. —*R.M.*

MAKE AHEAD The syrup can be refrigerated for up to 2 weeks.

Jerezano

TOTAL: 10 MIN

MAKES 1 DRINK ●

Sherry, which originated in the Jerez region of Spain, is the soul of this warm drink, which is best served after dinner.

¼ cup hot brewed espresso (2 ounces)

2 tablespoons cream sherry (1 ounce)

In a heatproof glass, combine the espresso and sherry and serve immediately.
—*Isabel González*

Silver Lining

TOTAL: 5 MIN

MAKES 1 DRINK ● ●

To get this foamy drink, Joseph Schwartz of Manhattan's Little Branch tinkered with a classic silver rye fizz, which gets its head from a shaken egg white.

Ice

3 tablespoons rye whiskey

1½ tablespoons fresh lemon juice

1½ tablespoons Licor 43

1 medium egg white

¼ cup chilled club soda

Fill a cocktail shaker with ice. Add the rye, lemon juice, Licor 43 and egg white and shake vigorously for 15 seconds. Fill a highball glass with ice, preferably 1 or 2 large chunks. Strain the drink into the glass. Top with half of the club soda. Wait a moment for the head to form, then add the remaining club soda. Serve right away.
—*Joseph Schwartz*

Cranberry Caipirinha

TOTAL: 5 MIN

MAKES 1 DRINK ●

Chef Marcus Samuelsson was born in Africa but raised in Sweden. He gives his version of the caipirinha a Swedish flavor by muddling cranberries along with the usual lime and replacing the Brazilian cachaça (made from sugarcane juice) with Scandinavian aquavit (a spirit infused with either dill or caraway).

Ice

10 fresh cranberries, chopped

1 tablespoon sugar

1 tablespoon water

2 lime wedges

⅓ cup aquavit

Fill a rocks glass with ice. In a cocktail shaker, muddle the cranberries with the sugar, water and 1 of the lime wedges. Add the aquavit and a handful of ice and shake well. Strain into the glass. Garnish with the remaining lime wedge and serve immediately. —*Marcus Samuelsson*

Citrus-Cinnamon Punch

TOTAL: 25 MIN PLUS CHILLING

MAKES ABOUT 2 QUARTS

Cinnamon flavors lots of holiday drinks, from eggnog to mulled wine. Here it appears in a punch that's delicious spiked with Grand Marnier.

ORANGE REDUCTION

2¼ cups fresh orange juice

Strips of zest from 2 navel oranges

Three 3-inch-long cinnamon sticks, broken into pieces

PUNCH

3 cups fresh orange juice

2 cups fresh red grapefruit juice

1 tablespoon grenadine syrup

2½ cups cold grapefruit soda (20 ounces)

Orange slices and ground cinnamon, for garnish

1. MAKE THE ORANGE REDUCTION: In a saucepan, boil the orange juice, zest and cinnamon sticks over moderately high heat until reduced to 1 cup. Strain and let cool.

2. MAKE THE PUNCH: In a large glass pitcher, combine the orange reduction with the orange and grapefruit juices and the grenadine. Stir well and refrigerate until chilled, about 1 hour. Just before serving, pour in the grapefruit soda. Dust the orange slices with cinnamon and serve in the punch. —*Marcia Kiesel*

Virgin Mojito

TOTAL: 5 MIN

MAKES 1 DRINK ●

15 mint leaves

1 teaspoon raw sugar

1 ounce fresh lime juice

½ ounce Simple Syrup (p. 378)

Ice

4 ounces chilled ginger ale

In a cocktail shaker, muddle the mint, sugar, lime juice and Simple Syrup. Add ice, shake well and pour into a highball glass. Top with ginger ale.
—*Charles Hardwick*

CITRUS-CINNAMON PUNCH

drinks

Fresco

TOTAL: 15 MIN
MAKES 1 DRINK ●

Ice
- 4 ounces club soda
- 1½ ounces peach nectar
- 1 ounce cranberry juice
- ¾ ounce fresh grapefruit juice
- ½ ounce fresh lime juice
- ½ ounce Simple Syrup (recipe follows)
- 2 dashes of Angostura bitters
- 2 thyme sprigs

Fill a cocktail shaker with ice. Add all of the remaining ingredients except 1 thyme sprig and shake well. Strain into an ice-filled highball glass and garnish it with the remaining thyme sprig. —*Kathy Casey*

SIMPLE SYRUP

TOTAL: 10 MIN
MAKES ABOUT 1½ CUPS ● ●
- 1 cup sugar
- 1 cup water

Bring the sugar and water to a boil; simmer until the sugar is dissolved. —*K.C.*
MAKE AHEAD The simple syrup can be refrigerated for up to 3 weeks.

tools
designer ice

Fred's "Cool Jewels" ice tray gives "on the rocks" glamorous appeal: It makes ice in six classic gem cuts. **Details** $9.50; spoonsisters.com.

Ice Breaker

TOTAL: 5 MIN
MAKES 1 DRINK ●

A magazine photograph of frozen grapes inspired A.J. Gilbert, who owns the playful Luna Park restaurants in Los Angeles and San Francisco, to make this drink. It utilizes grapes in three forms: an ice wine, a frozen grape garnish and a vodka made from distilled grapes, such as Cîroc or Roth.

Ice
- 1½ ounces late-harvest or ice wine
- 1½ ounces vodka, preferably Cîroc
- 2 red grapes and 2 green grapes, frozen, for garnish

Fill half of a cocktail shaker with ice. Add the wine and vodka and shake well. Strain into a martini glass, garnish with the frozen grapes and serve.—*A.J. Gilbert*

Rosé Sangria

TOTAL: 5 MIN
MAKES 1 DRINK ●

At Café Gray in New York City, sommelier Matthew Conway adds pear balsamic vinegar and fresh quince syrup to this fruity cocktail.

- 5 ounces sparkling Italian demi-sec rosé or Lambrusco, chilled
- 1 ounce unsweetened apple juice
- ¾ ounce Grand Marnier
- 1 slice red apple, for garnish

In a wineglass, combine the rosé, apple juice and Grand Marnier and stir gently. Garnish with the apple slice.
—*Matthew Conway*

Caribbean Lemonade

ACTIVE: 5 MIN; TOTAL: 1 HR 5 MIN
MAKES 6 DRINKS ●

Instead of making sangria (which is usually a mix of red wine, fruit juice, club soda and sometimes liqueur), Isabel González, co-author of *Latin Chic,* mixes this deliciously tart punch for parties using red wine, fresh lemon juice and sugar.

- 2 cups fresh lemon juice
- ⅔ cup superfine sugar
- 4 cups dry red wine, such as Malbec
- 1 lemon, thinly sliced into rounds and seeded

In a large pitcher, stir the lemon juice and sugar until the sugar is dissolved. Add the wine and chill for 1 hour. Add the lemon. Serve in punch glasses.—*Isabel González*
NOTE The punch can be doubled.
MAKE AHEAD The punch can be refrigerated overnight.

XXX Martini

TOTAL: 5 MIN
MAKES 1 DRINK ●

Squid ink
Ice
- ¼ cup plus 2 tablespoons vodka
- 1 teaspoon olive juice from a jar of cocktail olives
- 3 pitted green olives, for garnish

In a cocktail shaker, stir together a dash of squid ink with ½ teaspoon of water. Add the ice, vodka and olive juice. Shake well. Strain into a chilled martini glass. Garnish with the olives. —*Duggan McDonnell*

The Adige

TOTAL: 5 MIN
MAKES 1 DRINK ●

Scott Lawrence, beverage director at the Italian-inspired Jovia restaurant in New York City, loves using Italian ingredients in his cocktails. He pairs Italian Sauvignon Blanc and *amaro* (a digestivo) for this slightly bitter concoction.

Ice
Dash of Angostura bitters
- ½ ounce Amaro Nonino
- 2 ounces Sauvignon Blanc

Club soda
- 1 orange wheel

Fill a large wineglass one-third full of ice. Add the bitters, *amaro* and wine and top with a splash of club soda. Float the orange wheel on top.—*Scott Lawrence*

Sangrita

ACTIVE: 5 MIN; TOTAL: 2 HOURS 5 MIN
MAKES 15 TO 20 DRINKS

- 2 cups tomato juice
- ¼ cup fresh orange juice
- 1 tablespoon sugar
- 4 dashes of hot sauce

Dash of Worcestershire sauce
Dash of olive brine from a jar
    of green olives
Pinch of freshly ground black
    pepper

In a pitcher, combine all of the ingredients and refrigerate until chilled, at least 2 hours. Stir the sangrita well, pour into chilled shot glasses and serve immediately.
—Greg Morris

Sparkling Pomegranate Punch

TOTAL: 20 MIN
12 SERVINGS ●

- 1 quart pomegranate juice
- 2 cups fresh orange juice, strained
- 2 cups chilled limeade

One 750-milliliter bottle Prosecco
Lime and orange slices, for garnish
Ice

- 1 cup pomegranate seeds

In a punch bowl, combine the pomegranate juice, orange juice and limeade. Pour in the Prosecco and float lime and orange slices on top. Fill 12 glasses with ice and sprinkle in the pomegranate seeds. Ladle the punch into the glasses and serve.
—Maria Helm Sinskey

Cava and Pomegranate Cocktails

TOTAL: 20 MIN
MAKES 12 DRINKS ●

Two 750-milliliter bottles cava or other
    sparkling dry white wine, chilled
- ¼ cup pomegranate juice
Seeds from 1 pomegranate

Fill 12 flutes with cava. Add 1 teaspoon of the pomegranate juice to each flute, garnish with pomegranate seeds and serve.
—José Andrés

Rio-Style Ginger Beer Floats

TOTAL: 20 MIN
4 SERVINGS ●

This sweet, fizzy drink, made with orange juice, passion fruit and mango sorbet, is a Brazilian take on a typical American root beer float.

- 1 pint mango sorbet
- 2 cups chilled fresh orange juice
- 2 bottles chilled ginger beer
- 4 ripe passion fruits, halved

Scoop ½ cup of mango sorbet into each of 4 tall glasses and then add ½ cup of the orange juice to each glass. Pour in the ginger beer, scoop the seeds from the passion fruits on top and serve immediately with long straws. —Eric Ripert

VARIATION To make an all-pineapple version of this gingery float, use pineapple sorbet, pineapple juice and crushed chunks of fresh pineapple.

Sparkling Lime-Mint Coolers

TOTAL: 35 MIN
MAKES 12 DRINKS ● ● ● ◦

- 13 limes
- 2 cups water
- 1½ cups sugar
- 2 bunches of mint (2 ounces),
    12 small sprigs reserved,
    the rest coarsely chopped
    (with stems)
- 8 cups chilled sparkling water
Ice

1. Using a vegetable peeler, remove the zest from 8 of the limes, leaving behind as much of the bitter white pith as possible. Juice all 13 limes.
2. In a medium saucepan, combine the water with the sugar, chopped mint and lime zest strips and bring to a simmer. Cook over moderate heat for 5 minutes. Remove from the heat and let cool for 30 minutes. Strain the syrup into a large pitcher. Stir in the lime juice and sparkling water. Serve in ice-filled glasses, garnished with the mint sprigs. —Christophe Emé

Cucumber Cooler

TOTAL: 20 MIN
MAKES 1 DRINK ●

- ½ small seedless cucumber,
    grated, plus 4 thin cucumber
    slices
- ½ cup fresh pineapple chunks
- 2 ounces pineapple juice
- ¼ ounce Simple Syrup
    (p. 378)
Ice
- 1 ounce chilled club soda

1. Put the grated cucumber in a cheesecloth-lined strainer set over a small bowl. Twist and squeeze the cheesecloth to extract as much of the liquid as possible; you should have 2 ounces of cucumber water.
2. In a cocktail shaker, muddle the pineapple chunks and pineapple juice with the Simple Syrup. Add the cucumber water and ice to the shaker; shake well. Pour the cooler into a highball glass, top with the soda and cucumber slices and serve immediately. —Gillian Ballance

Doncellita

TOTAL: 5 MIN
MAKES 1 DRINK ●

In Cuba, doncellita is slang for nipple, which explains the name of this milky coffee liqueur drink with its nipplelike maraschino cherry garnish.

- 2 tablespoons coffee liqueur
    (1 ounce), chilled
- 1 tablespoon evaporated milk
    (½ ounce), chilled
- 1 maraschino cherry, for
    garnish

Pour the chilled coffee liqueur into a clear shot glass. Very slowly and carefully add the chilled evaporated milk in a thin stream, keeping it as much as possible on top of the coffee liqueur. The drink should have 2 separate layers, with the milk on top. Gently add the maraschino cherry and serve the Doncellita immediately.
—Carolina Buia and Isabel González

Wine service at The Modern
at New York City's Museum of
Modern Art

wine pairings

"Wine is much more than a beverage. It's a romance, a story, a drama—all those things that are basically putting on a show."

–Francis Ford Coppola, filmmaker and vintner

champagne & sparkling wines

Champagne, which is produced only in the Champagne region of France, is the greatest sparkling wine in the world—it's effervescent and lively, at the same time offering tremendous complexity and finesse. Champagnes are usually a blend of grapes, typically Pinot Noir and Chardonnay, often with a touch of Pinot Meunier as well. They range from dry (brut) to mildly sweet (demi-sec) to very sweet (doux). Different producers, or "houses," have different styles, too, ranging from light and delicate to rich and full-flavored. Many other countries also make sparkling wines. Those from North America tend to be more fruit-forward than most Champagnes. Cava, an inexpensive sparkler from Spain, often has an earthy character. Italy's Prosecco is also affordable, and popular for its engaging foaminess and hint of sweetness on the finish. Sparkling wines make great aperitifs, but they're also good throughout the meal, especially with shellfish and salty or spicy dishes.

DRY, LIGHT CHAMPAGNE
Perrier Jouët Grand Brut (France)
Guy Charlemagne Blanc de Blancs Champagne (France)
Taittinger Brut La Française (France)
PAIRINGS
- Crispy Monkfish with Capers, p. 203
- Pan-Fried Oysters with Creamy Radish and Cucumber Salad, p. 223

DRY, RICH CHAMPAGNE
Pol Roger Brut NV (France)
Gosset Brut Excellence (France)
Bollinger Brut Special Cuvée (France)
PAIRINGS
- Roasted Chicken with Garlic-Thyme Butter, p. 92
- Roasted Turkey with Lemon-Garlic Gravy, p. 110
- Crunchy Almond-Crusted Duck Breasts with Chanterelle Salad, p. 116
- Seared Scallops and Corn Cakes with Bacon Vinaigrette, p. 224

DRY, FRUITY SPARKLING WINE
Zardetto Prosecco Brut (Italy)
Mionetto Prosecco (Italy)
Domaine Carneros Brut (California)
Mumm Napa Brut Prestige (California)
PAIRINGS
- Spaghetti Carbonara with Green Peas, p. 73
- Pasta Shells with Peas and Ham, p. 81
- Lemon-and-Pickled-Pepper-Glazed Ham, p. 164
- Prosecco-Battered Cod with Mint Aioli, p. 190

DRY, EARTHY SPARKLING WINE
Freixenet Cordon Negro Brut Cava (Spain)
Gramona Gran Cuvée (Spain)
Mont Marçal Brut Reserva Cava (Spain)
PAIRINGS
- Chicken with Potatoes and Fried Eggs, p. 89
- White Anchovy and Crisp Pita Bread Salad, p. 208

whites

ALBARIÑO & VINHO VERDE
The Albariño grape produces Spain's best white wines, fresh, lively bottlings that pair especially well with seafood—no surprise, as Albariño is grown in Galicia, where the fishing industry drives the economy. Mostly made in stainless steel tanks without oak, Albariño has crisp flavors that suggest grapefruit and other citrus fruits, with a light mineral edge. Vinho Verde, or "green wine," from northern Portugal, often blends the Albariño grape (called Alvarinho there) with local varieties Loureiro and Trajadura. Bottled so young that it often has a lightly spritzy quality, Vinho Verde has a razor-sharp acidity and ocean freshness; it too is an ideal match for raw shellfish.

ZESTY, FRESH ALBARIÑO/VINHO VERDE
Condes de Albarei Albariño (Spain)
Martín Códax Albariño (Spain)
Quinta da Aveleda Vinho Verde (Portugal)
PAIRINGS
- Vietnamese Chicken Meatballs in Lettuce Wraps, p. 102
- Cod with Cockles and White Wine, p. 188
- Tuna and Potato Salad, p. 193
- Jumbo Shrimp Salad, p. 219
- Steamed Cockles in Scallion Broth, p. 223
- Pride of Baltimore Crab Cakes, p. 225
- Pickled Vegetable-Seafood Salad, p. 230

wine pairings

CHARDONNAY & WHITE BURGUNDY

Chardonnay is grown in almost every wine-producing country in the world, and it's used to create wines in a wide range of styles. It is originally from France's Burgundy region, where the best white Burgundies are powerful and rich, with complex fruit flavors and notes of earth and minerals. More affordable Chardonnays from Burgundy—for instance, those simply labeled Bourgogne Blanc—are crisp and lively, with apple and lemon flavors. Chardonnays from America, Australia and Chile tend to be ripe and full-bodied, even buttery, with higher alcohol levels and vanilla notes from oak aging. Recently, however, more and more wine regions have been experimenting with fruity, fresh Chardonnays produced with very little or even no oak aging. Pair Chardonnays in the leaner Burgundian style with roasted chicken or seafood; the more voluptuous New World Chardonnays pair well with pasta dishes made with cream or cheese, with lobster or other rich seafood and with Asian dishes that include coconut milk.

RICH, COMPLEX WHITE BURGUNDY

Olivier Leflaive Meursault-Charmes 1er Cru
  (France)
Leroy Bourgogne Blanc (France)
Deux Montille Meursault (France)

PAIRINGS
• Pasta with Salmon Caviar, p. 79
• Classic Roasted Turkey, p. 110
• Poached Salmon with Caper-Butter Sauce, p. 199
• Lobster with Udon Noodles, Bok Choy and Citrus,
  p. 231
• Lobster Fideos, p. 232

LIGHT, CRISP WHITE BURGUNDY

Oliver Merlin Mâcon La Roche Vineuse (France)
Dominique Cornin Domaine de Lalande
  Mâcon Chaintré (France)
Domaine William Fèvre Chablis (France)

PAIRINGS
• Cauliflower and Crab Ravioli, p. 78
• Blanquette de Veau, p. 175
• Halibut with Mixed Beans and Lemon-Butter Sauce,
  p. 178
• Grilled Sea Bass with Parsley-Anchovy Sauce, p. 182
• Crispy Shrimp in Kataifi Crust, p. 215
• Bay Scallop Pan Roast, p. 229

RIPE, LUXURIOUS CHARDONNAY

Ramey Carneros (California)
Penfolds Thomas Hyland (Australia)
Shingleback (Australia)
Kumeu River Maté's Vineyard (New Zealand)

PAIRINGS
• Roasted Stuffed Turkey with Giblet Gravy, p. 109
• Boudin Blanc with Leeks and Mustard Sauce, p. 173
• Stuffed Whole Wild Salmon, p. 193
• Cedar-Planked Salmon with Grainy Mustard Glaze,
  p. 196
• Shrimp-Stuffed Triple-Baked Potatoes, p. 216
• Lobster Pappardelle with Chive Butter, p. 233

FRUITY, LOW-OAK CHARDONNAY

Nozzole Le Bruniche (Italy)
Yalumba Y Series Unwooded (Australia)

PAIRINGS
• Whole Wheat Spaghetti with Pancetta, Chestnuts
  and Vin Santo, p. 76
• Grant's Mac and Cheese, p. 82
• Wine-Baked Chicken Legs with Marjoram, p. 96
• Roasted Chicken with Herb Jus, p. 97
• Braised Pork with Pearl Onions and Grapes, p. 163
• Pan-Fried River Trout with Corn Cakes and Red
  Pepper Coulis, p. 180
• Pan-Fried Snapper with Buttery Parsnip Puree, p. 186
• Pan-Fried Flounder with Poblano-Corn Relish, p. 187
• Chive Salmon with Remoulade, p. 194
• Crab Salad with Caesar Vinaigrette, p. 226
• Scallops with Summer Squash, p. 227

CHENIN BLANC

Chenin Blanc is the star of France's Loire region, where it's used for complex Vouvrays and Savennières. Chenin has also proved to be at home in parts of California (particularly the little-known Clarksburg region), in Washington State and in South Africa, which produces some of the best-value white wines around—tart, medium-bodied whites with flavors of apple and peach. The more affordable South African, Californian and Washington versions are good with light fish or simple poultry dishes.

FRUITY, SOFT CHENIN BLANC

Hogue (Washington State)
Vinum Cellars CNW (California)
Pecan Stream (South Africa)

PAIRINGS
- Chicken Curry with Potatoes and Squash, p. 90
- Goat Cheese-Stuffed Chicken, p. 99
- Pulled Capon and Watercress Salad with Citrus Dressing, p. 119
- Shrimp Masala, p. 230

COMPLEX, AROMATIC CHENIN BLANC

Domaine des Baumard Savennières (France)
Domaine Huet Le Haut-Lieu Sec Vouvray
  (France)

PAIRINGS
- Herb-Roasted Pheasants with Endives and Horseradish Puree, p. 119
- Poached Red Snapper with Papaya and Mango Sauce Vierge, p. 185
- Seared Tuna with Kimchi and Scallion Pancakes, p. 190
- Soft-Shell Crabs with Lemon Aioli and Sweet Onion, p. 225

GEWÜRZTRAMINER

One of the most easily identifiable grapes—the flamboyant aroma recalls roses, lychee nuts and spices such as clove and allspice—Gewürztraminer reaches its peak in France's Alsace region, producing luxuriant, full-bodied wines ranging from dry to quite sweet, with flavors of apricot, apple and baking spices. Gewürztraminer pairs well with classic Alsace cuisine—a rich tarte flambée made with ham and Gruyère, for instance. American Gewürztraminers tend to be less dense and unctuous, though they typically have a touch of sweetness on the finish and a delicate spiciness. Pair them with Asian food of all kinds.

RICH ALSACE GEWÜRZTRAMINER

Hugel & Fils (France)
Domaine Bott-Geyl (France)

PAIRINGS
- Pierogi Choucroute, p. 84
- Red Fish Curry, p. 202
- Vietnamese-Style Jumbo Shrimp on Sugarcane, p. 214

SPICY AMERICAN GEWÜRZTRAMINER

Navarro Vineyards (California)
Thomas Fogarty (California)

PAIRINGS
- Jasmine Rice, Chicken and Almond Stir-Fry, p. 100
- Balsamic-Glazed Duck Legs with Figs, p. 113
- Crab Salad with Ginger and Dried Orange Peel, p. 225
- Thai Red Curry Mussels with Fried Potatoes, p. 229
- Bahian Seafood Stew with Coconut and Tomato, p. 231

GRÜNER VELTLINER

Grüner Veltliner, from Austria, has recently become a darling of top American sommeliers, after decades of near obscurity in the United States. A refreshing, medium-bodied, peppery white wine with stone fruit flavors, it goes with everything from green salads to cold poached salmon to roasted chicken. The best Grüners can be quite expensive and have enormous aging potential.

PEPPERY, REFRESHING GRÜNER VELTLINER

Hirsch Veltliner #1 (Austria)
Domäne Wachau Terrassen Federspiel (Austria)

PAIRINGS
- Bacon-Wrapped Chicken Breasts, p. 93
- Mustard-and-Herb Chicken, p. 106
- Grilled Pork Tenderloin Salad, p. 163
- Cornmeal-Crusted Flounder, p. 188
- Scallops with Brussels Sprouts, p. 226

PINOT BLANC & PINOT BIANCO

These are two names for the same grape; the first one is French and the second Italian. The French versions, from Alsace, are musky and creamy-textured; those from Italy have zippier acidity, with pear or even soft citrus flavors. American Pinot Blancs are usually made in the French style, as the name suggests. Pour Pinot Blancs with cheese-based dishes; Pinot Biancos go nicely with light foods like chicken breasts or flaky white fish in a simple sauce.

ZIPPY, FRESH PINOT BIANCO

J. Hofstätter (Italy)
Alois Lageder (Italy)

PAIRINGS
- Lemony Broccoli and Chickpea Rigatoni, p. 76
- Chicken with Zucchini Salad, p. 100
- Grilled Swordfish Steaks with Basil-Caper Butter, p. 202
- Grilled Soft-Shell Crabs with Lemon Mayonnaise and Apple-Fennel Salad, p. 224

wine pairings

CREAMY, SUPPLE PINOT BLANC
Domaines Schlumberger Les Princes Abbés (France)
Chalone Vineyard (California)
PAIRINGS
- Thai-Style Chicken Legs, p. 102
- Baked Rice and Beans with White Veal Sausage, p. 174
- Potato-Crusted Salmon with Herb Salad, p. 193
- Creole Grilled Shrimp Rolls, p. 212

PINOT GRIS & PINOT GRIGIO
Pinot Gris (from France's Alsace) and Pinot Grigio (from Italy) are the same grape variety. Italian Pinots (and others modeled on them) tend to be light, simple wines with suggestions of peach and melon. These crisp, fresh whites are ideal as an aperitif or with light seafood or chicken breast dishes. Bottlings from Alsace are richer, with strong notes of almonds, spice and sometimes honey. American versions, mainly from Oregon, often tend more toward the Alsace style, and thus are mostly labeled Pinot Gris. They go well with creamy pastas or smoked foods.

LIGHT, FRESH PINOT GRIGIO
Elena Walch (Italy)
Kris (Italy)
PAIRINGS
- Spaghetti with Lemon, Chile and Creamy Spinach, p. 77
- Orzo Risotto with Buttery Shrimp, p. 81
- Tea-Steamed Cod Baked in Paper, p. 188
- Grilled Squid Salad with Celery Leaf Pesto, p. 226

FULL-BODIED, RICH PINOT GRIS
Domaine Marcel Deiss Beblenheim (France)
Trimbach Réserve (France)
Elk Cove (Oregon)
A to Z Wineworks (Oregon)
PAIRINGS
- Crispy Quails with Chile Jam and Three-Bean Salad, p. 118
- Spicy Ginger Pork in Lettuce Leaves, p. 163
- Seared Hamachi with Carrot Salad and Yuzu Dressing, p. 179
- Guinness-Glazed Halibut, p. 181
- Gingery Panko-Crusted Salmon with Asian Vegetables, p. 194
- Tasmanian-Pepper Poached Salmon, p. 196
- Shrimp Salad with Croutons, p. 214

RIESLING
Riesling is one of the great white grapes, and the style of the wines it produces varies dramatically by region. German Rieslings balance impressive acidity with apple and citrus fruit flavors, and range from dry and refreshing to sweet and unctuous. Alsace and Austrian Rieslings are higher in alcohol, which makes them more full-bodied, but they are quite dry, full of mineral notes. Australia's Rieslings (the best are from the Clare Valley) are zippy and full of lime and other citrus flavors. Those from Washington State tend to split the difference, offering juicy, appley fruit and lively acidity, with a hint of sweetness. Rieslings are extraordinarily versatile with food. In general, pair lighter, crisper Rieslings with delicate (or raw) fish; more substantial Rieslings are good with Asian food, chicken, salmon and tuna.

TART, CITRUSY RIESLING
Annie's Lane (Australia)
Mr. Riggs (Australia)
PAIRINGS
- Fresh Cheese Spaetzle, p. 82
- Sesame Chicken Salad with Ginger-Lime Dressing, p. 102
- Lemongrass-Barbecued Pork with Rice-Vermicelli Salad, p. 154
- Shrimp and Papaya Salad, p. 216
- Spicy Shrimp and Cellophane-Noodle Salad, p. 220

VIVID, LIGHTLY SWEET RIESLING
Dr. Loosen Dr. L (Germany)
S. A. Prüm Essence (Germany)
Covey Run (Washington State)
PAIRINGS
- Cider-Braised Ham with Apple-Onion Compote, p. 166
- Stuffed Pork Tenderloins with Bacon and Apple Riesling Sauce, p. 155
- Pork Chops with Sticky Rice and Thai Green-Chile Sauce, p. 168
- Spicy Butter-Steamed Bass, p. 178
- Red Snapper with Citrus and Fennel Salad, p. 186
- Fried Spanish Mackerel with Cilantro Sauce, p. 201
- Fish Tacos with Crispy Pickled Jalapeños, p. 209
- Grilled Citrus Shrimp with Vegetable Slaw, p. 213
- Moo Shu Shrimp, p. 213
- Peel-and-Eat Shrimp with Barbecue Spices, p. 216
- Shrimp Salad with Sweet Chile Dressing, p. 219

FULL-BODIED, MINERALLY RIESLING

Domaines Schlumberger Les Princes Abbés (France)
Weingut Bründlmayer (Austria)

PAIRINGS

- Grilled Chinese Chicken Salad, p. 88
- Buckshot Gumbo, p. 116
- Braised Rabbit with Mustard and Summer Savory, p. 150
- Sautéed Pork Cutlets with Prosciutto, Sage and Lemon, p. 159
- Choucroute Garnie, p. 164
- Olive Oil-Poached Salmon with Fresh Horseradish, p. 195

SAUVIGNON BLANC

Sauvignon's herbal scent and tart, citrus-driven flavors make it instantly identifiable. The best regions for Sauvignon are the Loire Valley in France, where it takes on a firm, minerally depth; New Zealand, where it recalls the tartness of gooseberries and, sometimes, an almost green, jalapeño-like note; California, where it pairs crisp grassiness and a melon-like flavor; and South Africa, particularly the Cape region, where it combines the minerality of France with the rounder fruit of California. Sauvignon Blanc teams well with light fish, shellfish, salads and green vegetables, and it's a perfect aperitif, too.

LIVELY, TART SAUVIGNON BLANC

Geyser Peak Winery (California)
Voss Vineyards (California)

PAIRINGS

- Halibut with Soy-Ginger Dressing, p. 182
- Crispy Sea Bass with Noodles, p. 183
- Snapper and Spiced Crab with Lime-Coriander Broth, p. 185
- Sautéed Spanish Mackerel with Black-Eyed Pea Salad, p. 200
- California Spot Prawns with Thai Seasoning, p. 218
- Shrimp with Fresh Citrus Sauce, p. 220

MINERALLY, COMPLEX SAUVIGNON BLANC

Concha y Toro Terrunyo (Chile)
Didier Dagueneau Pouilly-Fumé Cuvée Silex (France)

PAIRINGS

- Veal Scallopine with Paprika Sauce and Grapefruit Watercress Salad, p. 173

- Sautéed Bass with Lemongrass, p. 183
- Smoky Tuna and Bacon Burgers with Lemongrass Aioli, p. 192
- Grouper with Jicama and Black Bean Sauce, p. 202
- Smoky Citrus Shrimp with Parsley, p. 213
- Shrimp and Avocado Salad, p. 219

SOAVE, VERDICCHIO & GAVI

These three light, usually inexpensive wines from Italy all match well with a wide range of foods. Soave, mostly made from the Garganega grape, is a fruity white that often has an almond note. Verdicchio, made from the grape of the same name, has a lemony zestiness. Gavi, made from a grape called Cortese, is typically tart, with an aroma that suggests fresh limes. All pair well with herby pasta sauces like pesto, white fish or vegetable dishes.

FRESH, LIVELY SOAVE OR SIMILAR ITALIAN WHITE

Anselmi San Vincenzo (Italy)
Pieropan Soave Classico (Italy)
Ceretto Arneis (Italy)
Fazi Battaglia Verdicchio dei Castelli di Jesi Classico (Italy)

PAIRINGS

- Sage Fettucine, p. 72
- Pappardelle with Zucchini and Mint-Parsley Pesto, p. 74
- Pork and Leeks with Avgolemono Sauce, p. 160
- Fresh Tuna Salad with Avocado, p. 191

VERMENTINO

An up-and-coming white grape from the coastal regions of Italy, Vermentino marries vivacious acidity with stony minerality. The best Vermentinos come from very different parts of Italy—from Liguria in the north and from the island of Sardinia, off the central west coast. Drink Vermentino with seafood dishes of all kinds.

FRESH, MINERALLY VERMENTINO

Antinori (Italy)
Argiolas Costamolino (Italy)

PAIRINGS

- Crab and Artichoke Orzo Salad, p. 81
- Grilled Sardines with Eggplant Puree and Tarragon Dressing, p. 207
- Ligurian Seafood Stew, p. 207

- Grilled Oysters with Spicy Tarragon Butter, p. 220
- Manila Clams with Hot Soppressata and Sweet Vermouth, p. 221

VIOGNIER

Viogniers are seductive white wines, lush with peach and honeysuckle scents, a round, mouth-filling texture and little acidity. The Condrieu region in France's Rhône Valley produces the world's greatest Viogniers, and they can often be quite expensive; California and occasionally Australia have also had success with this grape. Viognier pairs well with grilled seafood; it's also a good match for most foods flavored with fruit salsas.

LUSH, FRAGRANT VIOGNIER
Heggies Vineyard (Australia)
Jean-Luc Colombo La Violette (France)
Calera (California)
PAIRINGS
- Malaysian Glazed Chicken Wings, p. 95
- Chicken with Red Curry–Peanut Glaze, p. 101
- Roasted Turkey with Muscat and Dried Fruit Gravy, p. 110
- Grilled Striped Bass with Plums and Potato Mushroom Papillotes, p. 182
- Vinegar-Poached Sturgeon with Thyme-Butter Sauce, p. 208
- Spicy Fish Cakes with Nuoc Cham Sauce and Fried Garlic Chips, p. 209
- Crunchy Shrimp Cakes, p. 218
- Viognier-Steamed Clams with Bacon and Parsnips, p. 223

rosés

Rosé—that is, dry rosé—may be the world's most underrated wine. Combining the light, lively freshness of white wines with the fruit and depth of reds, good rosés pair well with a remarkable range of foods, from delicate fish like sole to meats such as pork and veal. They also complement a range of ethnic cuisines—Chinese, Thai, Mexican and Greek. The best rosés, from southern France, are typically blends of grapes such as Syrah, Grenache, Cinsaut and Mourvèdre. Italy, Greece and Spain also produce terrific, refreshing rosés. American and Australian rosés, which tend to be fruitier and heavier, can also be very good.

FRESH, FRUITY ROSÉ
Castello di Ama (Italy)
Les Domaniers de Puits Mouret (France)
Château Pesquié Les Terrasses (France)
Wölffer Estate (New York)
PAIRINGS
- Spaghetti with Cauliflower, p. 76
- Turkey Kibbe Kebabs with Two Sauces, p. 107
- Spicy Turkey Posole, p. 110
- Duck Confit Quesadillas, p. 114
- Minty Lamb and Sausage Orzo with Grilled Artichokes, p. 141
- Marinated Pork Chops with Herb Salsa, p. 170
- Patio Pig Pickin', p. 167
- Pan-Seared Halibut with Tomato Vinaigrette, p. 180
- Grilled Tuna with Fried Manchego, p. 192
- Grilled Wild Salmon Skewers with Orange Tomato Jam, p. 200
- Indian Swordfish Packets, p. 201
- Bouillabaisse, p. 204
- Sardinian-Style Paella, p. 204
- Tunisian Prawns with Kerkennaise Sauce, p. 220

reds

BARBERA

Barbera, which grows primarily in Italy's Piedmont region, mostly produces medium-bodied wines with firm acidity and flavors suggesting red cherries with a touch of spice. (Barrel-aged versions tend to be more full-bodied, as well as more expensive.) A great wine for pastas with meat- or tomato-based sauces, Barbera is also good with game and hard cheeses.

BRIGHT, TART BARBERA
Coppo Camp du Rouss (Italy)
Michele Chiarlo Barbera d'Asti (Italy)
Prunotto Barbera d'Asti Fiulot (Italy)
PAIRINGS
- Pappardelle with Lamb Ragù, p. 73
- Orecchiette Bolognese with Chestnuts, p. 84
- Braised Chicken with Peppers, p. 93
- Lentils with Chicken Sausage, p. 104
- Roasted Pork with Sticky Mango Glaze, p. 157

wine pairings

BEAUJOLAIS & GAMAY

Gamay, the grape of France's Beaujolais region, makes wines that embody everything that region is known for: light, fruity, easy-to-drink reds, ideal for a party or a picnic. Typically they are not aged in oak barrels and are released early (Beaujolais Nouveau, which appears on shelves little more than a month after the grapes are harvested, is the extreme example). Little Gamay is grown outside of Beaujolais, but what has been planted pairs well with the same foods as Beaujolais: light chicken dishes, salads, cheeses and charcuterie.

FRUITY, LIGHT-BODIED BEAUJOLAIS/GAMAY

Brunet Domaine de Robert Fleurie (France)
Georges Duboeuf Jean Descombes Morgon
  (France)
Brick House Gamay (Oregon)

PAIRINGS
- Chicken with Mulato Chile Sauce, p. 92
- Chicken in Red Wine Vinegar, p. 99
- Chicken–Black Bean Quesadillas, p. 101
- Green-Chile Burgers with Fried Eggs, p. 135
- Smoky Meat Loaf with Prune Ketchup, p. 138
- Pork Meat Loaf with Chickpeas, p. 170
- Pork with Gingersnap Sauce, p. 174
- Chorizo-Crusted Cod, p. 188

CABERNET SAUVIGNON

Arguably the most significant red wine grape, Cabernet Sauvignon has traveled far beyond its origins in France's Bordeaux—it's now widely planted in almost every wine-producing country. Depending on climate, Cabernet can make either firm, tannic wines that recall red currants with a touch of tobacco or green bell pepper (colder climates) or softer wines that recall ripe black currants or black cherries (warmer climates). It almost always has substantial tannins, which help great Cabernets age for many years. The classic pairing with Cabernet is lamb, but it goes well with almost any meat—beef, pork, venison, even rabbit.

FIRM, COMPLEX CABERNET SAUVIGNON

D'Arenberg The High Trellis (Australia)
Château d'Issan Margaux (France)
Robert Craig Mt. Veeder (California)

PAIRINGS
- Strip Steak with Arugula Pesto, p. 123

- Scottish Beef Stew, p. 130
- Braised Lamb with Peppers and Oregano, p. 141
- Braised Pork Shanks, p. 159

RICH, RIPE CABERNET SAUVIGNON

Beringer Napa Valley (California)
Penfolds Bin 407 (Australia)
Bodega Catena Zapata Catena (Argentina)

PAIRINGS
- Seared Tri-Tip Steak with Asian Black-Bean Rice Cakes, p. 126
- Strip Steak and Vegetables with Garlicky Olivada, p. 128
- Garlic-Rubbed Leg of Lamb with Leeks, p. 145
- Braised Lamb Shanks with Roasted Broccoli and Squash, p. 147

DOLCETTO

Though Dolcetto means "little sweet one," wines from this Italian grape are dry, grapey, tart, simple reds distinguished by their vibrant purple color and ebullient berry juiciness. Dolcettos should be drunk young, with antipasti, pastas with meat sauces or roasted poultry of any kind.

JUICY, FRESH DOLCETTO

Einaudi (Italy)
Giacosa (Italy)
Prunotto (Italy)
Marcarini (Italy)

PAIRINGS
- Vegetable-and-Ravioli Lasagna, p. 85
- Beer-Braised Chicken Stew with Fava Beans, p. 104
- Beef Tenderloin "Dogs" with Corn Relish, p. 125
- Ground Lamb and Shallot Kebabs with Pomegranate Molasses, p. 148
- Lamb Salad with Arugula and Raspberry Vinaigrette, p. 150
- Spicy Stewed Sausages with Three Peppers, p. 174

GRENACHE

When made well, Grenache produces full-bodied, high-alcohol red wines that tend to be low in acidity and full of black cherry and raspberry flavors. Grenache is often blended with other grapes to make dark, powerful reds in regions such as France's Châteauneuf-du-Pape or Spain's Rioja and Priorato. On its own in Australia and the United States, it can produce deeply fruity, juicy wines that go perfectly with grilled meats, sausages and highly spiced dishes.

JUICY, SPICY GRENACHE
Domaine Les Pallières Gigondas (France)
Domaine du Cayron Gigondas (France)
Bodegas Nekeas El Chaparral deVega Sindoa
 Grenache (Spain)
Beckmen Vineyards (California)
D'Arenberg The Custodian (Australia)
PAIRINGS
- Chicken and Okra Fricassee, p. 95
- Garam Masala-Crusted Chicken with Fig Jus, p. 98
- Skirt Steak with Moroccan Spice Rub and Yogurt Sauce, p. 122
- Chile-Rubbed Flank Steak with White Polenta, p. 126
- Lamb Cutlets with Romesco, p. 141
- Lamb Chops with Pomegranate-Pistachio Couscous, p. 146

MALBEC
Originally used as a blending grape in France's Bordeaux region, Malbec has found its true home in Argentina's Mendoza region. There, it produces darkly fruity wines with hints of black pepper and leather—like a traditional rustic country red, but with riper, fuller fruit. Malbecs are often very affordable, too, and go wonderfully with steaks and roasts, hearty stews and grilled sausages.

RUSTIC, PEPPERY MALBEC
Terrazas de los Andes (Argentina)
Bodega Catena Zapata Catena (Argentina)
Altos Los Hormigas (Argentina)
PAIRINGS
- Spicy Steak Salad with Blue Cheese Dressing, p. 130
- Beef-Stuffed Poblano Chiles, p. 137
- Mixed Grill with Chimichurri Sauces and Roasted Peppers, p. 169
- Feijoada, p. 170

MERLOT
The most widely planted grape in France's Bordeaux region isn't Cabernet Sauvignon; it's Merlot. That's because Merlot blends so well with other grapes, and also because Merlot's gentle succulence and plummy flavors have gained favor as worldwide tastes have shifted toward fruitier, easier-drinking wines. Good Merlots are made in France, Italy, Chile, the United States and Australia, and all of them tend to share supple, velvety tannins and round black cherry or plum flavors. Merlot pairs beautifully with many foods—try it with pâtés or other charcuterie, pork or veal roasts, rich, cheesy gratins and even hamburgers.

LIVELY, FRUITY MERLOT
Falesco (Italy)
Columbia Crest Grand Estates (Washington State)
Blackstone Winery (California)
PAIRINGS
- Grilled Beef with Sesame Dressing, p. 122
- Caesar Salad with Meatballs, p. 130
- Hamburgers with Chowchow, p. 134

DEEP, VELVETY MERLOT
Paloma Vineyard (California)
Geyser Peak Winery Shorenstein Vineyard
 (California)
Pepper Bridge Winery (Washington State)
Shafer (California)
PAIRINGS
- Tenderloin with Sake-Mirin Butter, p. 129
- Scallion-and-Brie-Stuffed Burgers, p. 132
- Grilled Pork Chops with Orange Barbecue Sauce, p. 166

NEBBIOLO, BAROLO & BARBARESCO
Nebbiolo is the greatest grape of Italy's Piedmont. And if you ask a farmer, it is unquestionably one of the most difficult to grow. Certainly it is formidable, with fierce tannins and acidity, but it is also gloriously scented—"tar and roses" is the classic description—and has a supple, evocative flavor that lingers on the tongue. Those flavors are more substantial and emphatic in Barolos and more delicate and filigreed in Barbarescos, the two primary wines from Piedmont. Pour good Nebbiolo with foods such as braised short ribs, beef roasts, bollito misto and anything that involves truffles.

COMPLEX, AROMATIC NEBBIOLO
Paolo Scavino Barolo (Italy)
Produttori del Barbaresco Barbaresco(Italy)

PAIRINGS
- Pasta with Robiola and Truffles, p. 74
- Garlicky Grilled Beef Tenderloin with Herbs, p. 126
- Salt-Crusted Prime Rib Roast, p. 135

PINOT NOIR & RED BURGUNDY

Pinot Noir probably inspires more rhapsodies—and disappointments—among wine lovers than any other grape. When it's good, it's ethereally aromatic, with flavors ranging from ripe red berries to sweet black cherries, and tannins that are firm but never obtrusive. (When bad, unfortunately, it's acidic, raspy and bland.) The greatest Pinot Noirs come from France's Burgundy region, age-worthy wines that are usually quite expensive. More affordable and typically more fruit-forward Pinots can be found from California and Oregon as well as New Zealand, Chile and Australia. Pinot Noir pairs well with a wide range of foods—fruitier versions make a great match with salmon or other fatty fish, roasted chicken or pasta dishes; bigger, more tannic Pinots are ideal with duck and other game birds, casseroles or, of course, stews such as beef bourguignon.

COMPLEX, ELEGANT PINOT NOIR
Louis Jadot Gevrey-Chambertin (France)
Felton Road (New Zealand)
Domaine Drouhin Laurène (Oregon)
PAIRINGS
- Chicken with Morels and Tarragon Cream Sauce, p. 89
- Roasted Blue Foot Chickens with Glazed Parsnips and Carrots, p. 98
- Spiced Squabs with Onion Compote, p. 118
- Pork Roast with Sausage, Fruit and Nut Stuffing, p. 160
- Salmon with Mushroom Sauce, p. 199
- Grilled Salmon with Teriyaki Shiitake, p. 200

RIPE, JUICY PINOT NOIR
Goldeneye Anderson Valley (California)
Rodney Strong Russian River Valley (California)
La Crema Sonoma Coast (California)
PAIRINGS
- Chicken Breasts with Rosemary and Thyme, p. 88
- Pancetta-Wrapped Roasted Turkey, p. 106
- Duck Breast, Lentil and Parsnip Salad, p. 112
- Keralan Duck Curry, p. 113

- Fennel-Scented Duck Breasts with Pinot Noir Sauce, p. 116
- Grilled Skirt Steak and Peaches, p. 124
- Beef Tenderloin with Ancho and Fennel Seeds, p. 129
- Lamb Stew with Root Vegetables, p. 144
- Salmon with Roasted Shiitakes and Mushroom Sauce, p. 196
- Grilled Salmon with Sweet Onions and Red Bell Peppers, p. 199

RIOJA & TEMPRANILLO

Tempranillo, the top red grape of Spain, is best known as the main component in red Rioja, where it contributes earthy cherry flavors and firm structure. It is also used in almost every other region of Spain, and generally produces medium-bodied, firm reds suitable for meat dishes of all kinds, particularly lamb.

EARTHY, MEDIUM-BODIED TEMPRANILLO
Ramón Bilbao Rioja Mirto (Spain)
Pesquera Ribera del Duero (Spain)
Montecillo Rioja Crianza (Spain)
PAIRINGS
- Braised Chicken Legs with Green Olives, p. 95
- Chorizo-Stuffed Capon with Sorrel Brown Butter, p. 114
- Hanger Steak with Shallots and Mushrooms, p. 123
- Parmesan and Herb-Crusted Beef Tenderloin, p. 129
- Grilled Spiced Lamb Chops with Vegetable Ragout, p. 142

SANGIOVESE

Sangiovese is primarily known for the principal role it plays in Tuscan wines such as Chianti, Brunello and Carmignano, though these days more and more of it is also being grown in the United States and Australia. Italian Sangioveses have vibrant acidity and substantial tannins, along with fresh cherry fruit and herbal scents. New World versions tend toward softer acidity and fleshier fruit. Pair Sangioveses with rare steaks, roasted game birds (or wild boar), rich chicken or mushroom dishes or anything with tomato sauce.

CHERRY-INFLECTED, EARTHY SANGIOVESE
Fattoria del Fèlsina Chianti (Italy)
Antinori Pèppoli Chianti Classico (Italy)
Ruffino Chianti (Italy)

SYRAH & SHIRAZ

Probably no other grape scores higher on the intensity meter than Syrah. It's the marquee grape of France's Rhône Valley, where it makes smoky, powerful reds with hints of black pepper. It has also become the signature grape of Australia, where it's known as Shiraz, and typically produces fruitier, less tannic wines marked by sweet blackberry flavors. American Syrahs lean more toward the Australian mold, thanks to California's similarly moderate weather; there are a few very good, earthy Syrahs coming from South Africa, too. Barbecued foods with a smoky char pair nicely with Syrah, as do lamb, venison and game birds.

INTENSE, SPICY SYRAH

Jaboulet Crozes-Hermitage (France)
Copain Eaglepoint Ranch (California)
Fairview (South Africa)

ROUND, DEEP-FLAVORED SYRAH

Qupé Central Coast (California)
Paraiso Santa Lucia Highlands (California)
Red Bicyclette (France)

FRUITY, LUSCIOUS SHIRAZ

3 Rings Barossa Valley (Australia)
Tintara McLaren Vale (Australia)
Rosemount Hunter Valley (Australia)

ZINFANDEL

Though Zinfandel is descended from the Croatian grape Crljenak, the wine it produces is entirely Californian in character. The California wine country's warm, easygoing weather gives Zinfandel a jammy, juicy fruitiness (except when it's made into dull, lightly sweet white Zinfandel). Typically high in both alcohol and flavor—boysenberries with a touch of brambly spiciness—Zinfandel is the perfect cookout wine, great with grilled burgers, sausages or chicken, or even chips and dip.

INTENSE, FRUITY ZINFANDEL

Seghesio Sonoma (California)
Rancho Zabaco Sonoma Heritage Vines (California)
St. Francis Old Vines (California)
Green & Red Vineyard Chiles Canyon (California)

a

recipe index

d

recipe index

i

j

k

l

recipe index

recipe index

recipe index

Elia Aboumrad, a contestant on the Bravo reality show *Top Chef*, helped to open L'Atelier de Joël Robuchon in Paris and Las Vegas.

Grant Achatz, an F&W Best New Chef 2002, is the chef and co-owner of Alinea Restaurant in Chicago.

Michel Algazi is the cofounder of Palapa Azúl, a company that sells fruit bars, sorbet and ice cream.

David Alhadeff is the owner and founder of The Future Perfect boutique in Brooklyn, New York.

José Andrés owns seven restaurants in Washington DC and hosts his own television cooking show in Spain. He is the author of *Tapas: A Taste of Spain in America*.

Cathal Armstrong, an F&W Best New Chef 2006, is the chef and owner of Restaurant Eve and the fish-and-chips house Eamonn's A Dublin Chipper, both in Old Town Alexandria, Virginia.

Andy Arndt is the executive chef at the Ojai Valley Inn & Spa, in Ojai, California.

Alison Attenborough is a food stylist and regular contributor to F&W.

Ludovic Augendre is the executive pastry chef at Fauchon in New York City.

Marc Aumont is the pastry chef at Terrace 5 at the Museum of Modern Art in New York City.

Andy Ayers is the chef and owner of Riddle's Penultimate Café & Wine Bar in St. Louis, Missouri.

Gillian Ballance is the wine director for the PlumpJack Group, a business management company that owns Jack Falstaff and a number of other businesses in California.

Alison Barshak is the chef and owner of Alison at Blue Bell in Blue Bell, Pennsylvania.

Mario Batali is the chef and owner of seven New York City restaurants, as well as Italian Wine Merchants. He is the host of Food Network shows *Molto Mario* and *Ciao America* and has appeared on *Iron Chef America*. He has authored several cookbooks; his most recent is *Mario Tailgates Nascar Style*.

Kay Baumhefner is the executive chef at Della Fattoria in Petaluma, California.

Rick Bayless, an F&W Best New Chef 1988, is the chef and owner of Frontera Grill and Topolobampo in Chicago, the host of the PBS series *Mexico One Plate at a Time* and the author of numerous cookbooks, including *Mexican Everyday*.

Octavio Becerra was the *chef de cuisine* at Patina in Los Angeles.

Zoe Behrens is the pastry chef at 1789 Restaurant in Washington DC.

Jonathan Benno, an F&W Best New Chef 2006, is the *chef de cuisine* at Per Se in New York City.

Michelle Bernstein is the chef and co-owner of Michy's Latin Miami in Miami.

Brian Bistrong is the executive chef at The Harrison in New York City.

Daniel Boulud, an F&W Best New Chef 1988, is the chef and owner of Daniel, Café Boulud and db Bistro Moderne in New York City and spin-offs in Las Vegas and Palm Beach, Florida. He is the host of *After Hours with Daniel* and has authored six cookbooks; his most recent is *Braise*.

Suzanne Bozarth is the bartender at Paley's Place in Portland, Oregon.

Philippe Braun is the executive chef at L'Atelier de Joël Robuchon in Paris.

Lucy Brennan is a bartender at Mint/820 in Portland, Oregon.

Stuart Brioza, an F&W Best New Chef 2003, is the executive chef at Rubicon in San Francisco.

Chris Broberg is the executive pastry chef at Café Gray in New York City.

Michael Brock is the pastry chef at Boule in Los Angeles.

Celia Brooks Brown is a food writer, TV chef, caterer and the author of three vegetarian cookbooks, including *World Vegetarian Classics*. She currently leads gastrotours through London.

Morgan Brownlow is the chef and co-owner of Clarklewis in Portland, Oregon.

Spencer Budros is the pastry chef and co-owner of Pistachio, a pastry shop in Columbus, Ohio.

Carolina Buia is a television reporter and the co-author of *Latin Chic: Entertaining with Style and Sass*.

David Burke is the chef and owner of David Burke's Primehouse in Chicago, David Burke Fromagerie in New Jersey, David Burke at Bloomingdale's and davidburke & donatella in New York City.

Burham Cagda is the chef and owner of Imam in Gaziantep, Turkey.

Kenny Callaghan is the executive chef at Blue Smoke in New York City.

Floyd Cardoz is the executive chef and co-owner of Tabla in New York City and the co-author of *One Spice, Two Spice*.

Michael Carlson, an F&W Best New Chef 2006, is the executive chef and co-owner of Schwa in Chicago.

Andrew Carmellini, an F&W Best New Chef 2000, is the executive chef at A Voce in New York City.

Mary Ellen Carroll, artist and filmmaker, is the co-creator of Itinerant Gastronomy, an avant-garde food project.

Kathy Casey is a consultant for Volterra Restaurant in Seattle, Washington.

Bryan Caswell is the *chef de cuisine* at Bank by Jean-Georges in Houston, Texas.

David Chang, an F&W Best New Chef 2006, is the chef and owner of Momofuku and Momofuku Ssäm Bar in New York City.

Melissa Clark is a freelance food writer who contributes regularly to F&W. She has written and co-authored 18 cookbooks; her most recent is *The Skinny: How to Fit into Your Little Black Dress Forever*.

Jim Clendenen founded Au Bon Climat winery in Santa Barbara County, California, and earned an F&W American Wine Award as 2001's Winemaker of the Year.

Matthew Conway is the sommelier at Café Gray in New York City.

Rebecca Courchesne is the pastry chef at Frog Hollow Farm in Brentwood, CA.

Terry Crandall is the chef at The Peninsula Hotel in Chicago.

Cliff Crooks, a contestant on the Bravo reality show *Top Chef*, is the chef at Salute! in New York City.

Mike Davis is the executive chef and co-owner of 26brix in Walla Walla, Washington.

Traci Des Jardins, an F&W Best New Chef 1995, is the co-owner and chef of Jardinière and Mijita restaurants in San Francisco.

Colin Devlin is the owner of Dressler in Brooklyn, New York.

Mary Ellen Diaz is the founder and executive chef at First Slice, a Chicago soup kitchen.

Harold Dieterle, formerly of The Harrison in New York City, was Bravo's season one *Top Chef* winner. He plans to open his own restaurant, Perilla, in Manhattan.

Bruce Dillon is the *chef de cuisine* at Suba in New York City.

Ben Dougherty is the owner and bartender at Zig Zag Café in Seattle.

Mary Dumont, an F&W Best New Chef 2006, is the chef at the Dunaway Restaurant in Portsmouth, New Hampshire.

Koa Duncan was the pastry chef at Water Grill in Los Angeles.

Christophe Emé, an F&W Best New Chef 2005, is the chef and co-owner of Ortolan in Los Angeles.

Ola Fendert is the chef and owner of Oola in San Francisco.

Han Feng is a Shanghai-based fashion designer who created the costumes for the Metropolitan Opera's production of *Madama Butterfly* in New York City.

Kristin Ferguson is the pastry consultant at Firefly Bistro in South Pasadena, California.

Bobby Flay is the chef and owner of Bolo, Bar Americain and Mesa Grill in New York City, Bobby Flay Steak in Atlantic City, Mesa Grill in Las Vegas and the soon-to-open Mesa Grill at the Atlantis resort in the Bahamas. He also stars in several shows on Food Network, including *BBQ with Bobby Flay*, *FoodNation*, *Boy Meets Grill*, *Throwdown* and *Iron Chef America*. He is the resident chef on CBS's *Early Show* and has several cookbooks; his most recent is *Grilling for Life*.

Gabriel Frasca is the co-executive chef at Straight Wharf in Nantucket.

Betty Fraser, a contestant on the Bravo reality show *Top Chef*, is the co-owner of Grub in Hollywood.

Jose Garces is the chef and owner of Amada and Tinto restaurants in Philadelphia.

Megan Garrelts is the pastry chef and co-owner of Bluestem in Kansas City, Missouri.

Ian Garrone is the son of John and Toby Garrone, owners of Far West Fungi in San Francisco.

Gerald Gass is a personal chef at McEvoy Ranch in Petaluma, California, and the author of *The Olive Harvest Cookbook*.

Evangelos Gerovassiliou is a winemaker and the owner of Domaine Gerovassiliou, a winery in Greece.

Amy Giaquinta grows tomatoes for select clients in Napa Valley, California.

A.J. Gilbert is the owner of the Luna Park restaurants in Los Angeles and San Francisco.

Andrew Goetz is the co-owner of Malin+Goetz, which sells botanical beauty products In New York City.

Roni Goldbert is the cofounder of Palapa Azúl, a company that sells fruit bars, sorbet and ice cream.

Will Goldfarb is the chef and owner of Room 4 Dessert in New York City.

Isabel González is the editor in chief of *Tu Vida-Latin Life* and the co-author of *Latin Chic*.

Tim Goodell, an F&W Best New Chef 2000, is the owner of Domaine Restaurants in southern California, which includes 25 Degrees, Tropicana, Dakota, Village Bakery and Red Pearl Kitchen.

Mateo Granados was the executive chef at Healdsburg's Dry Creek Kitchen in California. He owns his own catering company, Mateo Granados Catering.

Tommy Habetz was the chef at the Gotham BLDG Tavern in Portland, Oregon.

Matthew Hamilton was the chef and owner of Uovo in New York City.

Abderrazak Haouari is the chef and owner of Chez Haouari on the Tunisian island of Djerba.

contributors

Charles Hardwick is the bar manager at Blue Owl in New York City.

Amy Hase is the business partner and wife of furniture designer Todd Hase.

Karen Hatfield is the pastry chef and co-owner of Hatfield's in Los Angeles.

Naomi Hebberoy is the co-owner of Clarklewis in Portland, Oregon.

John Hennigan is the executive chef at Restaurant LuLu in San Francisco.

Daniel Humm, an F&W Best New Chef 2005, is the executive chef at Eleven Madison Park in New York City.

Peter Ireland is the chef and owner of Carpenter & Main in Norwich, Vermont.

Kozo Iwata is the owner of Delica RF-1 in San Francisco.

Jennifer Jasinski is the executive chef and co-owner of Rioja and Bistro Vendôme restaurants in Denver.

Jennifer Joyce is the author of *Diva Cooking: Unashamedly Glamorous Party Food, The Well-Dressed Salad, Small Bites, Lunchboxes* and *Diner.*

Paul Kahan, an F&W Best New Chef 1999, is the executive chef and co-owner of Blackbird and Avec in Chicago.

Douglas Keane, an F&W Best New Chef 2006, is the chef and co-owner of Cyrus in Healdsburg, California, and co-owner of Market in Napa Valley.

Melissa Kelly is the executive chef and co-owner of Primo in Rockland, Maine, Orlando, Florida, and Tucson.

Marcia Kiesel is the F&W test kitchen supervisor and co-author of *The Simple Art of Vietnamese Cooking.*

Jamie Kimm is a personal chef who has worked for photographer Annie Leibovitz.

Nicole Krasinski is the pastry chef at Rubicon in San Francisco.

Gabriel Kreuther, an F&W Best New Chef 2003, is the executive chef at The Modern, located in New York City's Museum of Modern Art.

Allen Kuehn is the chef at San Francisco Fish Company in San Francisco.

Michael Laiskonis is the pastry chef at Le Bernardin in New York City.

Tara Lane was the pastry chef at Blackbird in Chicago.

Annabel Langbein is the author of 12 cookbooks, including *Assemble: Sensational Food Made Simple.*

Scott Lawrence is the beverage director at Jovia in New York City.

Dennis Leary is the executive chef and owner of Canteen in San Francisco.

Christopher Lee, an F&W Best New Chef 2006, is the executive chef at Gilt in New York City.

Edward Lee is the head chef and owner of 610 Magnolia in Louisville, Kentucky.

Ludovic Lefebvre is the executive chef at Bastide in Los Angeles.

David LeFevre is the executive chef at Water Grill in Los Angeles.

Jonnatan Leiva is the executive chef at Jack Falstaff in San Francisco.

David Lentz is the chef and owner of The Hungry Cat in Hollywood, California.

Matt Lewis is the co-owner of Baked in Brooklyn, New York City.

Tim Love is the executive chef and owner of Lonesome Dove Western Bistro, Duce and White Elephant Saloon in Fort Worth, Texas, and Lonesome Dove Western Bistro in New York City.

Barbara Lynch, an F&W Best New Chef 1996, is the chef and owner of No. 9 Park, B&G Oysters and The Butcher Shop in Boston.

Natasha MacAller is a pastry chef and consultant.

Troy MacLarty is the chef at Lovely Hula Hands in Portland, Oregon.

Pino Maffeo, an F&W Best New Chef 2006, is the executive chef at Restaurant L in Boston.

Ryan Magarian is the mixologist at Crush in Seattle, Washington.

Matthew Malin is the co-owner of Malin+Goetz, which sells botanical beauty products in New York City.

Vincenzo Marianella is the mixologist at Providence in Los Angeles.

Daniel Martinez is the chef at Thirst, a wine bar in Portland, Oregon.

Hugo Matheson is the co-chef and co-owner of The Kitchen in Boulder, Colorado.

Sarah Matthews is a personal chef and the caterer for Talley Vineyards in California's Arroyo Grande Valley.

Dean Maupin is the executive chef at Clifton Inn in Charlottesville, Virginia.

Shawn McClain is the executive chef and co-owner of Spring, Custom House and Green Zebra restaurants in Chicago.

Sue McCown is the chef and owner of Coco La Ti Da, a dessert restaurant in Seattle.

Duggan McDonnell was the bartender at Frisson in San Francisco.

Nan McEvoy is the owner of McEvoy Ranch in Petaluma, California, and The McEvoy Ranch shop in San Francisco's Ferry Building.

Ryan McGrale is the bartender at No. 9 Park in Boston.

Erin McKenna is the chef and owner of BabyCakes NYC, a vegan bakery in New York City.

Alice Medrich is a chocolate expert and the author of seven cookbooks, including *Bittersweet: Recipes* and *Tales from a Life in Chocolate*.

Marc Meyers is the chef and owner of Five Points and Cookshop in New York City and the author of *Brunch*.

Sue Moore is co-owner of Let's Be Frank, an all-natural hot dog cart company in San Francisco.

Greg Morris is the owner of The Spanish Kitchen, The Belmont Restaurant and Stone Fire Pizza in California.

Angie Mosier is the baker and owner of Blue-Eyed Daisy Bakeshop in Palmetto, Georgia.

Kimbal Musk is co-chef and co-owner of The Kitchen in Boulder, Colorado.

David Myers, an F&W Best New Chef 2003, is the chef and owner of Sona, Boule and soon-to-open Comme Ça in West Hollywood, California.

Nick Nairn is a chef, television personality and the owner of Nick Nairn Cook School in Scotland.

Kate Neumann is the pastry chef at MK The Restaurant in Chicago.

Andy Nusser is the executive chef and co-owner of Casa Mono in New York City.

Pichet Ong is the chef and owner of P*ONG in New York City.

Vitaly Paley is the executive chef and owner of Paley's Place in Portland, Oregon.

Dionisis Papanikolauo is the chef at 7 Seas in Thessaloníki, Greece.

Grace Parisi is the F&W test kitchen senior associate and the author of *Get Saucy: Make Dinner a New Way Every Day with Simple Sauces, Marinades, Dressings, Glazes, Pestos, Pasta Sauces, Salsas, and More*.

Marco Pasanella is the owner of Pasanella and Son, a wineshop in New York City.

Daniel Patterson, an F&W Best New Chef 1997, is the chef and owner of Coi Restaurant in San Francisco and the co-author of *Aroma*.

Zak Pelaccio is the executive chef and owner of Fatty Crab and 5 Ninth and the consulting executive chef at 230 Fifth in New York City.

Claudine Pépin is the co-host, with her father, Jacques Pépin, of three Public Television series. She currently works as a cooking instructor at A Cook's Kitchen in Denver, Colorado.

Jacques Pépin is an F&W contributing editor, master chef, television personality and cooking teacher. He is the author of the memoir *The Apprentice: My Life in the Kitchen* and 23 cookbooks, including *Jacques Pépin: Fast Food My Way,* the companion volume to the Public Television series. Personal chef to three French heads of state, including Charles de Gaulle, before moving to the United States in 1959, Pépin is a 2004 recipient of the French Legion of Honor.

Aniamma Philip is the co-owner of Philipkutty's Farm on the southwest coast of India, where she is also a chef and cooking teacher.

Nina Planck is the founder of farmers' markets in London and two "Real Food" outdoor markets in Manhattan. She is the author of *Real Food: What to Eat and Why*.

Nicole Plue is the pastry chef at Julia's Kitchen at COPIA in Napa Valley.

Ryan Poli is the executive chef at Butter in Chicago.

Michael Psilakis is the executive chef and owner of Onera and Dona restaurants in New York City.

Deborah Racicot is the pastry chef at Gotham Bar & Grill in New York City.

Steven Raichlen is an award-winning author of 27 books. His PBS series, *Barbecue University with Steven Raichlen*, is based on his popular cooking school at The Greenbrier resort in White Sulfur Springs, West Virginia. He is also the creator of the Best of Barbecue line of grilling accessories.

Meg Ray is the co-chef and co-owner of Miette bakery in San Francisco.

E. Michael Reidt, an F&W Best New Chef 2001, is the executive chef and co-owner of Sevilla in Santa Barbara, California.

Nicki Reiss is a French-trained personal chef for numerous Hollywood celebrities and a consultant for the Dole Wellness Center.

Cyril Renaud is the executive chef and owner of Fleur de Sel in New York City.

Eric Ripert is executive chef and co-owner of Le Bernardin in New York City and co-author of *Le Bernardin Cookbook: Four Star Simplicity* and *A Return to Cooking*.

Joël Robuchon is the chef and owner of Joël Robuchon in Las Vegas, L'Atelier de Joël Robuchon in Paris, Las Vegas, New York, London, Monte Carlo and Tokyo, A Table in Paris, and A Galera in Macau.

Michael Romano, an F&W Best New Chef 1991, is the executive chef at Union Square Cafe in New York City.

Melissa Rubel is the F&W test kitchen associate.

Jeri Ryan is the co-owner of Ortolan in Los Angeles.

Marcus Samuelsson is the chef and co-owner of Aquavit and Scandinavia House AQ Café in New York City, as well as the author of numerous cookbooks; his most recent is *The Soul of a New Cuisine*.

contributors

Suvir Saran is the co-executive chef and owner of Devi in New York and Veda in Delhi's Connaught Place. He is also the co-author of *Indian Home Cooking: A Fresh Introduction to Indian Food.*

John Schaefer was the executive chef at Gramercy Tavern in New York City.

Michael Schlow, an F&W Best New Chef 1996, is the executive chef and co-owner of Radius and Via Matta restaurants in Boston and the author of *It's About Time.*

Joseph Schwartz is the co-owner and bartender at Little Branch in New York City.

Ron Siegel, an F&W Best New Chef 1999, is the executive chef at The Dining Room at the Ritz-Carlton in San Francisco.

Maria Helm Sinskey, an F&W Best New Chef 1996, is the culinary director of Robert Sinskey Vineyards in Napa Valley and the author of *The Vineyard Kitchen.*

Foteini Sioni is the chef at Restaurant Náoussaiiko in Náoussa, Greece.

Kimberly Sklar is the pastry chef at Literati II in Los Angeles.

Constance Snow is the author of *The Rustic Table* and the IACP award-winning *Gulf Coast Kitchens,* among other books.

Deborah Snyder is the pastry chef at Lever House in New York City.

Susan Spungen was the founding food editor and editorial director for food at Martha Stewart Living Omnimedia. She is the co-author of *Martha Stewart's Hors d'Oeuvres Handbook* and the author of *Recipes: A Collection for the Modern Cook.*

Doug Stonebreaker is the founder and owner of Prather Ranch Meat Co. in San Francisco.

Gabriel Stulman is the co-owner of The Little Owl in New York City.

Jean-Claude Szurdak, best friend of Jacques Pépin, has cooked for three French heads of state. He was a pastry chef and the owner of Jean-Claude catering company in New York City.

Sam Talbot, a contestant on the Bravo reality show *Top Chef,* was the chef at Williamsburgh Café in Brooklyn, New York.

Brian Talley is the owner of Talley Vineyards in California's Arroyo Grande Valley.

Bryant Terry is a chef, food activist and co-author of *Grub.*

Jake Tilson is a writer and photographer whose most recent work, *A Tale of Two Kitchens,* is a food memoir, photojournal and cookbook.

Jing Tio is the owner of Le Sanctuaire culinary boutique in Los Angeles.

Amy Tornquist is the chef at the Museum Café at Duke University and the owner of Sage & Swift Gourmet Catering in Durham, North Carolina.

Jeff Tunks is the executive chef and owner of Acadiana, DC Coast, TenPenh and Ceiba restaurants in Washington DC.

Michelle Vernier is the pastry chef at Wildwood in Portland, Oregon.

Sai Viswanath is the executive chef at DeWolf Tavern in Bristol, Rhode Island.

Joe Vitale is the executive chef of Napa-based Melissa Teaff Catering.

Jean-Georges Vongerichten, an F&W contributing editor, is the chef and co-owner of numerous restaurants around the world, including Jean Georges, Spice Market and Perry St. in New York City. He has co-authored *Simple Cuisine: The Easy, New Approach to Four-Star Cooking, Jean-Georges: Cooking at Home with a Four-Star Chef* and *Simple to Spectacular.*

Annie Wayte is the chef at Nicole Farhi and 202 restaurants in New York City and the author of *Keep It Seasonal.*

Kathleen Webber is the baker and co-owner of Della Fattoria in Petaluma, California.

Andrew Weil is a holistic doctor and author of 10 books; his most recent is *Healthy Aging.*

Rollie Wesen was the chef at Rivers in Portland, Oregon.

Debra Whiting is the executive chef and co-owner of Red Newt Winery Bistro in Hector, New York.

Felicia Willett is the executive chef and owner of Felicia Suzanne's Downtown Memphis in Memphis, Tennessee.

Caitlin Alissa Williams is the co-chef and co-owner of Miette bakery in San Francisco.

Jason Wilson, an F&W Best New Chef 2006, is the chef and owner of Crush in Seattle.

Donna Wingate is an artist and co-creator of Itinerant Gastronomy, an avant-garde food project.

Paula Wolfert, an F&W contributing editor, is the author of many award-winning cookbooks, including *Mediterranean Cooking, Couscous and Other Good Food from Morocco* and the recently updated *Cooking of Southwest France.*

Stewart Woodman, an F&W Best New Chef 2006, was the chef and owner of Five in Minneapolis.

Lisa Yockelson is a journalist and the author of *Chocolate Chocolate.*

Kate Zuckerman is the pastry chef at Chanterelle in New York City and author of *The Sweet Life.*

photographs